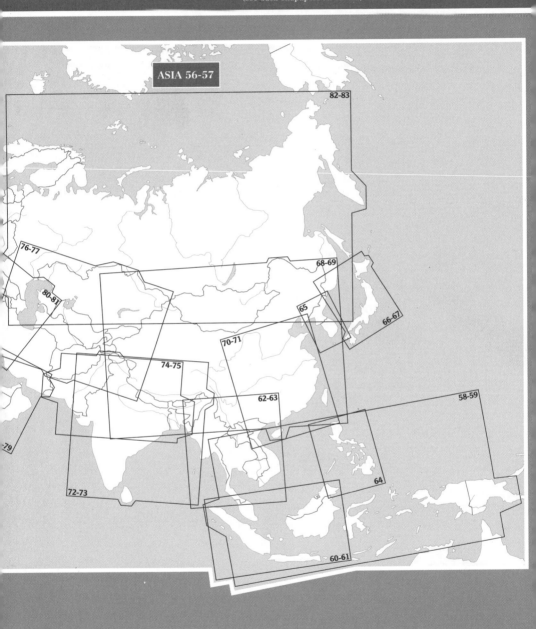

ASIA 56-57

82-83

76-77

80-81

68-69

65

66-67

70-71

74-75

62-63

58-59

-79

64

72-73

60-61

THE TIMES

ATLAS
OF THE
WORLD
COMPACT EDITION

Times Books, 77-85 Fulham Palace Road,
London W6 8JB

First published 1991
First published as The Times Atlas
of the World Compact Edition 1994
Second Edition 2000

Printed and bound in the UK

ISBN 0 7230 1083 8

NH10484

www.fireandwater.com
visit the book lover's website

THE  TIMES
ATLAS
OF THE
WORLD
COMPACT EDITION

TIMES BOOKS
London

4

Contents

The World Today

Pages	Title	Scale
8-31	STATES AND TERRITORIES OF THE WORLD	
32	CITIES	
33	CONTINENTS, OCEANS AND SEAS	
34-35	ISLANDS, MOUNTAINS, LAKES AND RIVERS	
36-37	CLIMATE	
38-39	LAND COVER	
40-41	POPULATION	
42-43	TRAVEL	

Atlas of the World

Pages	Title	Scale
44	INTRODUCTION TO THE ATLAS	
45	MAP SYMBOLS	
46-47	**WORLD** COUNTRIES	1:120 000 000
48-49	**OCEANIA**	1:50 000 000
50-51	**AUSTRALIA**	1:20 000 000
52-53	**AUSTRALIA** SOUTHEAST	1:7 500 000
54	**NEW ZEALAND**	1:7 500 000
55	**ANTARCTICA**	1:45 000 000

Contents

Pages	Title	Scale
56-57	**ASIA**	1:55 000 000
58-59	**SOUTHEAST ASIA**	1:25 000 000
60-61	**MALAYSIA** and **INDONESIA** West	1:12 000 000
62-63	**CONTINENTAL SOUTHEAST ASIA**	1:12 000 000
64	**PHILIPPINES**	1:12 000 000
65	**NORTH KOREA** and **SOUTH KOREA**	1:6 500 000
66-67	**JAPAN**	1:7 500 000
68-69	**CHINA** and **MONGOLIA**	1:25 000 000
70-71	**CHINA** Central	1:12 000 000
72-73	**SOUTH ASIA**	1:15 000 000
74-75	**PAKISTAN, INDIA** North and **BANGLADESH**	1:12 000 000
76-77	**CENTRAL ASIA**	1:15 000 000
78-79	**ARABIAN PENINSULA**	1:12 000 000
80-81	**EAST MEDITERRANEAN**	1:12 000 000
82-83	**RUSSIAN FEDERATION**	1:30 000 000
84-85	**EUROPE**	1:25 000 000
86-87	**EUROPEAN RUSSIAN FEDERATION**	1:15 000 000
88-89	**NORTHEAST EUROPE**	1:6 000 000
90-91	**UKRAINE** and **MOLDOVA**	1:6 000 000

CONTENTS

Pages	Title	Scale

EUROPE (continued)

Pages	Title	Scale
92-93	**SCANDINAVIA AND ICELAND**	1:7 500 000
94-95	**BRITISH ISLES**	1:6 000 000
96	**SCOTLAND**	1:3 000 000
97	**IRELAND**	1:3 000 000
98-99	**ENGLAND AND WALES**	1:3 000 000
100-101	**NORTHWEST EUROPE**	1:3 000 000
102-103	**CENTRAL EUROPE**	1:6 000 000
104-105	**FRANCE AND SWITZERLAND**	1:6 000 000
106-107	**SPAIN AND PORTUGAL**	1:6 000 000
108-109	**ITALY AND THE BALKANS**	1:6 000 000
110-111	**GREECE, ROMANIA AND BULGARIA**	1:6 000 000
112-113	**AFRICA**	1:45 000 000
114-115	**NORTHWEST AFRICA**	1:20 000 000
116-117	**NORTHEAST AFRICA**	1:20 000 000
118-119	**CENTRAL AFRICA**	1:15 000 000
120-121	**SOUTHERN AFRICA**	1:15 000 000
122-123	**REPUBLIC OF SOUTH AFRICA**	1:7 500 000
124-125	**NORTH AMERICA**	1:40 000 000
126-127	**CANADA**	1:25 000 000
128-129	**CANADA WEST**	1:12 000 000

Contents

Pages	Title	Scale

NORTH AMERICA (continued)

Pages	Title	Scale
130-131	**CANADA** EAST	1:12 000 000
132-133	**UNITED STATES OF AMERICA**	1:20 000 000
134-135	**USA** WEST	1:8 000 000
136-137	**USA** NORTH CENTRAL	1:8 000 000
138-139	**USA** SOUTH CENTRAL	1:8 000 000
140-141	**USA** NORTHEAST	1:8 000 000
142-143	**USA** SOUTHEAST	1:8 000 000
144-145	**MEXICO**	1:12 000 000
146-147	**CENTRAL AMERICA** AND THE **CARIBBEAN**	1:15 000 000

SOUTH AMERICA

Pages	Title	Scale
148-149	**SOUTH AMERICA**	1:35 000 000
150-151	**SOUTH AMERICA** NORTH	1:20 000 000
152-153	**SOUTH AMERICA** SOUTH	1:20 000 000
154-155	**BRAZIL** SOUTHEAST	1:7 500 000

OCEANS

Pages	Title	Scale
156-157	**PACIFIC OCEAN**	1:90 000 000
158	**ATLANTIC OCEAN**	1:90 000 000
159	**INDIAN OCEAN**	1:90 000 000
160	**ARCTIC OCEAN**	1:45 000 000

| 161-240 | **INDEX** | |

STATES AND TERRITORIES OF THE WORLD

All independent countries and major territories are included in this list of the states and territories of the world; the list is arranged in alphabetical order by the conventional name form. For independent states, the full country name is given below the conventional name, if this is different; for territories, the status is given. The capital city name is given in the conventional form with the local name or alternate name in brackets.

The statistics used for the area and population are the latest available and include estimates. The information on languages and religions is based on the latest information on 'de facto' speakers of the language or 'de facto' adherents of the religion. The information available on languages and religions varies greatly from country to country, some countries include questions in censuses others do not, in which case best estimates are used. The order of the languages and religions reflect their relative importance within the country; generally, languages or religions are included when more than one per cent of the population are estimated to be speakers or adherents.

Membership of the following international organizations is shown by the abbreviations below, territories are not shown as having separate memberships of these organizations.

APEC	Asia-Pacific Economic Cooperation
ASEAN	Association of Southeast Asian Nations
CARICOM	Caribbean Community
CIS	Commonwealth of Independent States
Comm.	The Commonwealth
EU	European Union
OECD	Organization for Economic Co-operation and Development
OPEC	Organization of Petroleum Exporting Countries
SADC	Southern African Development Community
UN	United Nations

AFGHANISTAN
Islamic Emirate of Afghanistan

Area Sq Km	652 225	Religions	Sunni Muslim, Shi'a
Area Sq Miles	251 825		Muslim
Population	21 354 000	Currency	Afghani
Capital	Kābul	Organizations	UN
Languages	Dari, Pushtu, Uzbek,Turkmen	Map page	76–77

ALBANIA
Republic of Albania

Area Sq Km	28 748	Religions	Sunni Muslim,
Area Sq Miles	11 100		Albanian Orthodox,
Population	3 119 000		Roman Catholic
Capital	Tirana (Tiranë)	Currency	Lek
Languages	Albanian, Greek	Organizations	UN
		Map page	109

ALGERIA
Democratic and Popular Republic of Algeria

Area Sq Km	2 381 741	Religions	Sunni Muslim
Area Sq Miles	919 595	Currency	Dinar
Population	30 081 000	Organizations	OPEC, UN
Capital	Algiers (Alger)	Map page	114–115
Languages	Arabic, French, Berber		

American Samoa
United States Unincorporated Territory

Area Sq Km	197	Religions	Protestant, Roman
Area Sq Miles	76		Catholic
Population	63 000	Currency	US dollar
Capital	Fagatogo	Map page	49
Languages	Samoan, English		

ANDORRA
Principality of Andorra

Area Sq Km	465	Religions	Roman Catholic
Area Sq Miles	180	Currency	French franc,
Population	72 000		Spanish peseta
Capital	Andorra la Vella	Organizations	UN
Languages	Spanish, Catalan, French	Map page	104

ANGOLA
Republic of Angola

Area Sq Km	1 246 700	Religions	Roman Catholic,
Area Sq Miles	481 354		Protestant, traditional
Population	12 092 000		beliefs
Capital	Luanda	Currency	Kwanza
Languages	Portuguese, Bantu, local languages	Organizations	SADC, UN
		Map page	120

Anguilla
United Kingdom Overseas Territory

Area Sq Km	155	Religions	Protestant, Roman
Area Sq Miles	60		Catholic
Population	8 000	Currency	E. Carib. dollar
Capital	The Valley	Map page	147
Languages	English		

ANTIGUA AND BARBUDA

Area Sq Km	442	Religions	Protestant, Roman
Area Sq Miles	171		Catholic
Population	67 000	Currency	E. Carib. dollar
Capital	St John's	Organizations	CARICOM,
Languages	English, creole		Comm., UN
		Map page	147

ARGENTINA
Argentine Republic

Area Sq Km	2 766 889	Religions	Roman Catholic,
Area Sq Miles	1 068 302		Protestant
Population	36 123 000	Currency	Peso
Capital	Buenos Aires	Organizations	UN
Languages	Spanish, Italian,	Map page	152-153
	Amerindian		
	languages		

ARMENIA
Republic of Armenia

Area Sq Km	29 800	Religions	Armenian Orthodox
Area Sq Miles	11 506	Currency	Dram
Population	3 536 000	Organizations	CIS, UN
Capital	Yerevan (Erevan)	Map page	81
Languages	Armenian, Azeri		

Aruba
Self-governing Netherlands Territory

Area Sq Km	193	Religions	Roman Catholic,
Area Sq Miles	75		Protestant
Population	94 000	Currency	Florin
Capital	Oranjestad	Map page	147
Languages	Papiamento, Dutch,		
	English		

Ascension
Dependency of St Helena

Area Sq Km	88	Religions	Protestant, Roman
Area Sq Miles	34		Catholic
Population	1 100	Currency	Pound sterling
Capital	Georgetown	Map page	113
Languages	English		

AUSTRALIA
Commonwealth of Australia

Area Sq Km	7 682 395	Religions	Protestant, Roman
Area Sq Miles	2 966 189		Catholic, Orthodox
Population	18 520 000	Currency	Dollar
Capital	Canberra	Organizations	APEC, Comm.,
Languages	English, Italian,		OECD, UN
	Greek	Map page	50-51

Australian Capital Territory (Federal Territory)

Area Sq Km	2 400	Population	299 243
Area Sq Miles	927	Capital	Canberra

Jervis Bay Territory

Area Sq Km	73
Area Sq Miles	28

New South Wales (State)

Area Sq Km	801 600	Population	6 038 696
Area Sq Miles	309 499	Capital	Sydney

Northern Territory

Area Sq Km	1 346 200	Population	195 101
Area Sq Miles	519 771	Capital	Darwin

Queensland (State)

Area Sq Km	1 727 200	Population	3 368 850
Area Sq Miles	666 876	Capital	Brisbane

South Australia (State)

Area Sq Km	984 000	Population	1 427 936
Area Sq Miles	379 925	Capital	Adelaide

Tasmania (State)

Area Sq Km	67 800	Population	459 659
Area Sq Miles	26 178	Capital	Hobart

Victoria (State)

Area Sq Km	227 600	Population	4 373 520
Area Sq Miles	87 877	Capital	Melbourne

Western Australia (State)

Area Sq Km	2 525 500	Population	1 726 095
Area Sq Miles	975 101	Capital	Perth

AUSTRIA
Republic of Austria

Area Sq Km	83 855	Religions	Roman Catholic,
Area Sq Miles	32 377		Protestant
Population	8 140 000	Currency	Schilling, Euro
Capital	Vienna (Wien)	Organizations	EU, OECD, UN
Languages	German, Croatian,	Map page	102-103
	Turkish		

AZERBAIJAN
Azerbaijani Republic

Area Sq Km	86 600	Religions	Shi'a Muslim, Sunni
Area Sq Miles	33 436		Muslim, Russian and
Population	7 669 000		Armenian Orthodox
Capital	Baku (Bakı)	Currency	Manat
Languages	Azeri, Armenian,	Organizations	CIS, UN
	Russian, Lezgian	Map page	81

Azores (Arquipélago dos Açores)
Autonomous Region of Portugal

Area Sq Km	2 300	Religions	Roman Catholic,
Area Sq Miles	888		Protestant
Population	243 600	Currency	Portuguese escudo
Capital	Ponta Delgada	Map page	112
Languages	Portuguese		

THE BAHAMAS
Commonwealth of the Bahamas

Area Sq Km	13 939	Religions	Protestant, Roman
Area Sq Miles	5 382		Catholic
Population	296 000	Currency	Dollar
Capital	Nassau	Organizations	CARICOM, Comm.,
Languages	English, creole		UN
		Map page	146-147

BAHRAIN
State of Bahrain

Area Sq Km	691	Religions	Shi'a Muslim, Sunni
Area Sq Miles	267		Muslim, Christian
Population	595 000	Currency	Dinar
Capital	Manama	Organizations	UN
	(Al Manāmah)	Map page	79
Languages	Arabic, English		

BANGLADESH
People's Republic of Bangladesh

Area Sq Km	143 998	Religions	Sunni Muslim, Hindu
Area Sq Miles	55 598	Currency	Taka
Population	124 774 000	Organizations	Comm.,UN
Capital	Dhaka (Dacca)	Map page	75
Languages	Bengali, English		

BARBADOS

Area Sq Km	430	Religions	Protestant, Roman
Area Sq Miles	166		Catholic
Population	268 000	Currency	Dollar
Capital	Bridgetown	Organizations	CARICOM,
Languages	English, creole		Comm.,UN
		Map page	147

BELARUS
Republic of Belarus

Area Sq Km	207 600	Religions	Belorussian Orthodox,
Area Sq Miles	80 155		Roman Catholic
Population	10 315 000	Currency	Rouble
Capital	Minsk	Organizations	CIS, UN
Languages	Belorussian, Russian	Map page	88-89

BELGIUM
Kingdom of Belgium

Area Sq Km	30 520	Religions	Roman Catholic,
Area Sq Miles	11 784		Protestant
Population	10 141 000	Currency	Franc, Euro
Capital	Brussels (Bruxelles)	Organizations	EU, OECD, UN
Languages	Dutch (Flemish),	Map page	100
	French (Walloon),		
	German		

BELIZE

Area Sq Km	22 965	Religions	Roman Catholic,
Area Sq Miles	8 867		Protestant
Population	230 000	Currency	Dollar
Capital	Belmopan	Organizations	CARICOM, Comm.,
Languages	English, Spanish,		UN
	Mayan, creole	Map page	147

BENIN
Republic of Benin

Area Sq Km	112 620	Religions	Traditional beliefs,
Area Sq Miles	43 483		Roman Catholic, Sunni
Population	5 781 000		Muslim
Capital	Porto-Novo	Currency	CFA franc
Languages	French, Fon,	Organizations	UN
	Yoruba, Adja,	Map page	114
	local languages		

Bermuda
United Kingdom Overseas Territory

Area Sq Km	54	Religions	Protestant, Roman
Area Sq Miles	21		Catholic
Population	64 000	Currency	Dollar
Capital	Hamilton	Map page	125
Languages	English		

BHUTAN
Kingdom of Bhutan

Area Sq Km	46 620	Religions	Buddhist, Hindu
Area Sq Miles	18 000	Currency	Ngultrum
Population	2 004 000	Organizations	UN
Capital	Thimphu	Map page	75
Languages	Dzongkha,		
	Nepali, Assamese		

BOLIVIA
Republic of Bolivia

Area Sq Km	1 098 581	Religions	Roman Catholic,
Area Sq Miles	424 164		Protestant, Baha'i
Population	7 957 000	Currency	Boliviano
Capital	La Paz/Sucre	Organizations	UN
Languages	Spanish, Quechua,	Map page	152
	Aymara		

Bonaire
part of Netherlands Antilles

Area Sq Km	288	Religions	Roman Catholic,
Area Sq Miles	111		Protestant
Population	14 218	Currency	NA guilder
Capital	Kralendijk	Map page	147
Languages	Dutch, Papiamento		

Bonin Islands (Ogasawara-shotō)
part of Japan

Area Sq Km	104	Map page	69
Area Sq Miles	40		
Population	2 300		
Capital	Omura		

BOSNIA-HERZEGOVINA
Republic of Bosnia and Herzegovina

Area Sq Km	51 130	Religions	Sunni Muslim, Serbian
Area Sq Miles	19 741		Orthodox, Roman
Population	3 675 000		Catholic, Protestant
Capital	Sarajevo	Currency	Marka
Languages	Bosnian, Serbian,	Organizations	UN
	Croatian	Map page	109

BURUNDI
Republic of Burundi

Area Sq Km	27 835	Religions	Roman Catholic,
Area Sq Miles	10 747		traditional beliefs,
Population	6 457 000		Protestant
Capital	Bujumbura	Currency	Franc
Languages	Kirundi (Hutu,	Organizations	UN
	Tutsi), French	Map page	119

BOTSWANA
Republic of Botswana

Area Sq Km	581 370	Religions	Traditional beliefs,
Area Sq Miles	224 468		Protestant, Roman
Population	1 570 000		Catholic
Capital	Gaborone	Currency	Pula
Languages	English,Setswana,	Organizations	Comm., SADC, UN
	Shona, local	Map page	120
	languages		

CAMBODIA
Kingdom of Cambodia

Area Sq Km	181 000	Religions	Buddhist, Roman
Area Sq Miles	69 884		Catholic, Sunni Muslim
Population	10 716 000	Currency	Riel
Capital	Phnom Pénh (Phnom	Organizations	ASEAN, UN
	Penh)	Map page	63
Languages	Khmer, Vietnamese		

BRAZIL
Federative Republic of Brazil

Area Sq Km	8 547 379	Religions	Roman Catholic,
Area Sq Miles	3 300 161		Protestant
Population	165 851 000	Currency	Real
Capital	Brasília	Organizations	UN
Languages	Portuguese	Map page	150-151

CAMEROON
Republic of Cameroon

Area Sq Km	475 442	Religions	Roman Catholic,
Area Sq Miles	183 569		traditional beliefs,
Population	14 305 000		Sunni Muslim,
Capital	Yaoundé		Protestant
Languages	French, English,	Currency	CFA franc
	Fang, Bamileke, local	Organizations	Comm., UN
	languages	Map page	118

BRUNEI
State of Brunei Darussalam

Area Sq Km	5 765	Religions	Sunni Muslim, Buddhist,
Area Sq Miles	2 226		Christian
Population	315 000	Currency	Dollar
Capital	Bandar Seri Begawan	Organizations	APEC, ASEAN,
Languages	Malay, English,		Comm., UN
	Chinese	Map page	61

CANADA
Federation

Area Sq Km	9 970 610	Religions	Roman Catholic,
Area Sq Miles	3 849 674		Protestant, Eastern
Population	30 563 000		Orthodox, Jewish
Capital	Ottawa	Currency	Dollar
Languages	English, French,	Organizations	APEC, Comm.,
	Inuktitut		OECD, UN
		Map page	126-127

BULGARIA
Republic of Bulgaria

Area Sq Km	110 994	Religions	Bulgarian Orthodox,
Area Sq Miles	42 855		Sunni Muslim
Population	8 336 000	Currency	Lev
Capital	Sofia (Sofiya)	Organizations	UN
Languages	Bulgarian, Turkish,	Map page	110
	Romany,		
	Macedonian		

Alberta (Province)

Area Sq Km	661 190	Population	2 914 900
Area Sq Miles	255 287	Capital	Edmonton

British Columbia (Province)

Area Sq Km	947 800	Population	4 009 900
Area Sq Miles	365 948	Capital	Victoria

Manitoba (Province)

Area Sq Km	649 950	Population	1 138 000
Area Sq Miles	250 947	Capital	Winnipeg

BURKINA
Democratic Republic of Burkina Faso

Area Sq Km	274 200	Religions	Sunni Muslim,
Area Sq Miles	105 869		traditional beliefs,
Population	11 305 000		Roman Catholic
Capital	Ouagadougou	Currency	CFA franc
Languages	French, Moore	Organizations	UN
	(Mossi), Fulani, local	Map page	114
	languages		

New Brunswick (Province)

Area Sq Km	73 440	Population	753 000
Area Sq Miles	28 355	Capital	Fredericton

Newfoundland (Province)

Area Sq Km	405 720	Population	544 400
Area Sq Miles	156 649	Capital	St John's

Northwest Territories (Territory)

Area Sq Km	1 432 320	Population	45 500
Area Sq Miles	553 022	Capital	Yellowknife

CANADA
Federation

Nova Scotia (Province)
Area Sq Km 55 490	Population 934 000
Area Sq Miles 21 425	Capital Halifax

Nunavut (Territory)
Area Sq Km 1 994 000	Population 22 000
Area Sq Miles 769 888	Capital Iqaluit

Ontario (Province)
Area Sq Km 1 068 580	Population 11 411 500
Area Sq Miles 412 581	Capital Toronto

Prince Edward Island (Province)
Area Sq Km 5 660	Population 136 400
Area Sq Miles 2 185	Capital Charlottetown

Québec (Province)
Area Sq Km 1 540 680	Population 7 333 300
Area Sq Miles 594 860	Capital Québec

Saskatchewan (Province)
Area Sq Km 652 330	Population 1 024 400
Area Sq Miles 251 866	Capital Regina

Yukon Territory (Territory)
Area Sq Km 483 450	Population 31 700
Area Sq Miles 186 661	Capital Whitehorse

Canary Islands (Islas Canarias)
Autonomous Community of Spain

Area Sq Km 7 447	Religions Roman Catholic
Area Sq Miles 2 875	Currency Peseta
Population 1 606 522	Map page 114
Capital Santa Cruz de Tenerife	
Languages Spanish	

CAPE VERDE
Republic of Cape Verde

Area Sq Km 4 033	Religions Roman Catholic,
Area Sq Miles 1 557	Protestant
Population 408 000	Currency Escudo
Capital Praia	Organizations UN
Languages Portuguese, creole	Map page 46

 # Cayman Islands
United Kingdom Overseas Territory

Area Sq Km 259	Religions Protestant, Roman
Area Sq Miles 100	Catholic
Population 36 000	Currency Dollar
Capital George Town	Map page 146
Languages English	

CENTRAL AFRICAN REPUBLIC

Area Sq Km 622 436	Religions Protestant, Roman
Area Sq Miles 240 324	Catholic, traditional
Population 3 485 000	beliefs, Sunni Muslim
Capital Bangui	Currency CFA franc
Languages French, Sango,	Organizations UN
Banda, Baya, local	Map page 118
languages	

Ceuta
Spanish Territory

Area Sq Km 19	Religions Roman Catholic,
Area Sq Miles 7	Muslim
Population 68 796	Currency Peseta
Capital Ceuta	Map page 106
Languages Spanish, Arabic	

CHAD
Republic of Chad

Area Sq Km 1 284 000	Religions Sunni Muslim, Roman
Area Sq Miles 495 755	Catholic, Protestant,
Population 7 270 000	traditional beliefs
Capital Ndjamena	Currency CFA franc
Languages Arabic, French, Sara,	Organizations UN
local languages	Map page 115

Chatham Islands
part of New Zealand

Area Sq Km 963	Religions Protestant
Area Sq Miles 372	Currency Dollar
Population 732	Map page 49
Capital Waitangi	
Languages English	

CHILE
Republic of Chile

Area Sq Km 756 945	Religions Roman Catholic,
Area Sq Miles 292 258	Protestant
Population 14 824 000	Currency Peso
Capital Santiago	Organizations APEC, UN
Languages Spanish, Amerindian	Map page 152-153
languages	

CHINA
People's Republic of China

Area Sq Km 9 584 492	Religions Confucian, Taoist,
Area Sq Miles 3 700 593	Buddhist, Christian,
Population 1 262 817 000	Sunni Muslim
Capital Beijing (Peking)	Currency Yuan
Languages Mandarin, Wu,	Organizations APEC, UN
Cantonese, Hsiang,	Map page 68-69
regional languages	

Anhui (Province)
Area Sq Km 139 000	Population 60 130 000
Area Sq Miles 53 668	Capital Hefei

Bejing (Municipality)
Area Sq Km 16 800	Population 12 510 000
Area Sq Miles 6 487	Capital Beijing (Peking)

Chongqing (Municipality)
Area Sq Km 23 000	Population 14 600 000
Area Sq Miles 8 880	Capital Chongqing

Fujian (Province)
Area Sq Km 121 400	Population 32 370 000
Area Sq Miles 46 873	Capital Fuzhou

Gansu (Province)

| Area Sq Km 453 700 | Population 24 380 000 |
| Area Sq Miles 175 175 | Capital Lanzhou |

Guangdong (Province)

| Area Sq Km 178 000 | Population 68 680 000 |
| Area Sq Miles 68 726 | Capital Guangzhou |

Guangxi Zhuangzu Zizhiqu (Autonomous Region)

| Area Sq Km 236 000 | Population 45 430 000 |
| Area Sq Miles 91 120 | Capital Nanning |

Guizhou (Province)

| Area Sq Km 176 000 | Population 35 080 000 |
| Area Sq Miles 67 954 | Capital Guiyang |

Hainan (Province)

| Area Sq Km 34 000 | Population 7 240 000 |
| Area Sq Miles 13 127 | Capital Haikou |

Hebei (Province)

| Area Sq Km 187 700 | Population 64 370 000 |
| Area Sq Miles 72 471 | Capital Shijiazhuang |

Heilongjiang (Province)

| Area Sq Km 454 600 | Population 37 010 000 |
| Area Sq Miles 175 522 | Capital Harbin |

Henan (Province)

| Area Sq Km 167 000 | Population 91 000 000 |
| Area Sq Miles 64 479 | Capital Zhengzhou |

Hong Kong (Special Administrative Region)

Area Sq Km 1 075	Population 6 706 965
Area Sq Miles 415	Capital Hong Kong
	Currency Hong Kong dollar
	Organizations ASEAN

Hubei (Province)

| Area Sq Km 185 900 | Population 57 720 000 |
| Area Sq Miles 71 776 | Capital Wuhan |

Hunan (Province)

| Area Sq Km 210 000 | Population 63 920 000 |
| Area Sq Miles 81 081 | Capital Changsha |

Jiangsu (Province)

| Area Sq Km 102 600 | Population 70 660 000 |
| Area Sq Miles 39 614 | Capital Nanjing |

Jiangxi (Province)

| Area Sq Km 166 900 | Population 40 630 000 |
| Area Sq Miles 64 440 | Capital Nanchang |

Jilin (Province)

| Area Sq Km 187 000 | Population 25 920 000 |
| Area Sq Miles 72 201 | Capital Changchun |

Liaoning (Province)

| Area Sq Km 147 400 | Population 40 920 000 |
| Area Sq Miles 56 911 | Capital Shenyang |

Macau (Special Administrative Region)

Area Sq Km 17	Population 459 000
Area Sq Miles 7	Capital Macau
	Currency Pataca

Nei Mongol Zizhiqu (Inner Mongolia) (Autonomous Region)

| Area Sq Km 1 183 000 | Population 22 840 000 |
| Area Sq Miles 456 759 | Capital Huhhot |

Ningxia Huizu Zizhiqu (Autonomous Region)

| Area Sq Km 66 400 | Population 5 130 000 |
| Area Sq Miles 25 637 | Capital Yinchuan |

Qinghai (Province)

| Area Sq Km 721 000 | Population 4 810 000 |
| Area Sq Miles 278 380 | Capital Xining |

Shaanxi (Province)

| Area Sq Km 205 600 | Population 35 140 000 |
| Area Sq Miles 79 383 | Capital Xi'an |

Shandong (Province)

| Area Sq Km 153 300 | Population 87 050 000 |
| Area Sq Miles 59 189 | Capital Jinan |

Shanghai (Municipality)

| Area Sq Km 6 300 | Population 14 150 000 |
| Area Sq Miles 2 432 | Capital Shanghai |

Shanxi (Province)

| Area Sq Km 156 300 | Population 30 770 000 |
| Area Sq Miles 60 348 | Capital Taiyuan |

Sichuan (Province)

| Area Sq Km 569 000 | Population 98 650 000 |
| Area Sq Miles 219 692 | Capital Chengdu |

Tianjin (Municipality)

| Area Sq Km 11 300 | Population 9 420 000 |
| Area Sq Miles 4 363 | Capital Tianjin |

Xinjiang Uygur Zizhiqu (Sinkiang) (Autonomous Region)

| Area Sq Km 1 600 000 | Population 16 610 000 |
| Area Sq Miles 617 763 | Capital Ürümqi |

Xizang Zizhiqu (Tibet) (Autonomous Region)

| Area Sq Km 1 228 400 | Population 2 400 000 |
| Area Sq Miles 474 288 | Capital Lhasa |

Yunnan (Province)

| Area Sq Km 394 000 | Population 39 900 000 |
| Area Sq Miles 152 124 | Capital Kunming |

Zhejiang (Province)

| Area Sq Km 101 800 | Population 43 190 000 |
| Area Sq Miles 39 305 | Capital Hangzhou |

Christmas Island
Australian External Territory

Area Sq Km	135	Religions	Buddhist, Sunni
Area Sq Miles	52		Muslim, Protestant,
Population	2 195		Roman Catholic
Capital	The Settlement	Currency	Australian dollar
Languages	English	Map page	58

Cook Islands
Self-governing New Zealand Territory

Area Sq Km	293	Religions	Protestant, Roman
Area Sq Miles	113		Catholic
Population	19 000	Currency	Dollar
Capital	Avarua	Map page	49
Languages	English, Maori		

Cocos Islands (Keeling Islands)
Australian External Territory

Area Sq Km	14	Religions	Sunni Muslim,
Area Sq Miles	5		Christian
Population	637	Currency	Australian dollar
Capital	West Island	Map page	58
Languages	English		

COSTA RICA
Republic of Costa Rica

Area Sq Km	51 100	Religions	Roman Catholic,
Area Sq Miles	19 730		Protestant
Population	3 841 000	Currency	Colón
Capital	San José	Organizations	UN
Languages	Spanish	Map page	146

COLOMBIA
Republic of Colombia

Area Sq Km	1 141 748	Religions	Roman Catholic,
Area Sq Miles	440 831		Protestant
Population	40 803 000	Currency	Peso
Capital	Bogotá	Organizations	APEC, UN
Languages	Spanish, Amerindian	Map page	150
	languages		

CÔTE D'IVOIRE
Republic of Côte d'Ivoire

Area Sq Km	322 463	Religions	Sunni Muslim, Roman
Area Sq Miles	124 504		Catholic, traditonal
Population	14 292 000		beliefs, Protestant
Capital	Yamoussoukro	Currency	CFA franc
Languages	French, creole, Akan,	Organizations	UN
	local languages	Map page	114

COMOROS
Federal Islamic Republic of the Comoros

Area Sq Km	1 862	Religions	Sunni Muslim, Roman
Area Sq Miles	719		Catholic
Population	658 000	Currency	Franc
Capital	Moroni	Organizations	UN
Languages	Comorian, French,	Map page	121
	Arabic		

CROATIA
Republic of Croatia

Area Sq Km	56 538	Religions	Roman Catholic,
Area Sq Miles	21 829		Serbian Orthodox,
Population	4 481 000		Sunni Muslim
Capital	Zagreb	Currency	Kuna
Languages	Croatian, Serbian	Organizations	UN
		Map page	109

CONGO
Republic of Congo

Area Sq Km	342 000	Religions	Roman Catholic,
Area Sq Miles	132 047		Protestant, traditional
Population	2 785 000		beliefs, Sunni Muslim
Capital	Brazzaville	Currency	CFA franc
Languages	French, Kongo,	Organizations	UN
	Monokutuba, local	Map page	118
	languages		

CUBA
Republic of Cuba

Area Sq Km	110 860	Religions	Roman Catholic,
Area Sq Miles	42 803		Protestant
Population	11 116 000	Currency	Peso
Capital	Havana (La Habana)	Organizations	UN
Languages	Spanish	Map page	146

CONGO, DEMOCRATIC REPUBLIC OF

Area Sq Km	2 345 410	Religions	Christian, Sunni
Area Sq Miles	905 568		Muslim
Population	49 139 000	Currency	Franc
Capital	Kinshasa	Organizations	SADC, UN
Languages	French, Lingala,	Map page	118-119
	Swahili, Kongo, local		
	languages		

Curaçao
part of Netherlands Antilles

Area Sq Km	444	Religions	Roman Catholic,
Area Sq Miles	171		Protestant
Population	115 448	Currency	NA guilder
Capital	Willemstad	Map page	147
Languages	Dutch, Papiamento		

CYPRUS
Republic of Cyprus

Area Sq Km	9 251	Religions	Greek Orthodox, Sunni
Area Sq Miles	3 572		Muslim
Population	771 000	Currency	Pound
Capital	Nicosia (Lefkosia)	Organizations	Comm., UN
Languages	Greek, Turkish,	Map page	80
	English		

CZECH REPUBLIC

Area Sq Km	78 864	Religions	Roman Catholic,
Area Sq Miles	30 450		Protestant
Population	10 282 000	Currency	Koruna
Capital	Prague (Praha)	Organizations	UN
Languages	Czech, Moravian,	Map page	102-103
	Slovak		

DENMARK
Kingdom of Denmark

Area Sq Km	43 075	Religions	Protestant
Area Sq Miles	16 631	Currency	Krone
Population	5 270 000	Organizations	EU, OECD, UN
Capital	Copenhagen	Map page	93
	(København)		
Languages	Danish		

DJIBOUTI
Republic of Djibouti

Area Sq Km	23 200	Religions	Sunni Muslim,
Area Sq Miles	8 958		Christian
Population	623 000	Currency	Franc
Capital	Djibouti	Organizations	UN
Languages	Somali, Afar, French,	Map page	117
	Arabic		

DOMINICA
Commonwealth of Dominica

Area Sq Km	750	Religions	Roman Catholic,
Area Sq Miles	290		Protestant
Population	71 000	Currency	E. Carib. dollar
Capital	Roseau	Organizations	CARICOM, Comm.,
Languages	English, creole		UN
		Map page	147

DOMINICAN REPUBLIC

Area Sq Km	48 442	Religions	Roman Catholic,
Area Sq Miles	18 704		Protestant
Population	8 232 000	Currency	Peso
Capital	Santo Domingo	Organizations	UN
Languages	Spanish, creole	Map page	147

Easter Island (Isla de Pascua)
part of Chile

Area Sq Km	171	Religions	Roman Catholic
Area Sq Miles	66	Currency	Peso
Population	2 764	Map page	157
Capital	Hanga Roa		
Languages	Spanish		

East Timor
under UN Transitional Administration

Area Sq Km	14 874	Religions	Roman Catholic
Area Sq Miles	5 743	Currency	Rupiah
Population	857 000	Map page	59
Capital	Dili		
Languages	Portuguese, Tetun,		
	English		

ECUADOR
Republic of Ecuador

Area Sq Km	272 045	Religions	Roman Catholic
Area Sq Miles	105 037	Currency	Sucre
Population	12 175 000	Organizations	APEC, UN
Capital	Quito	Map page	150
Languages	Spanish, Quechua,		
	Amerindian languages		

EGYPT
Arab Republic of Egypt

Area Sq Km	1 000 250	Religions	Sunni Muslim, Coptic
Area Sq Miles	386 199		Christian
Population	65 978 000	Currency	Pound
Capital	Cairo (El Qâhira)	Organizations	UN
Languages	Arabic	Map page	116

EL SALVADOR
Republic of El Salvador

Area Sq Km	21 041	Religions	Roman Catholic,
Area Sq Miles	8 124		Protestant
Population	6 032 000	Currency	Colón
Capital	San Salvador	Organizations	UN
Languages	Spanish	Map page	146

EQUATORIAL GUINEA
Republic of Equatorial Guinea

Area Sq Km	28 051	Religions	Roman Catholic,
Area Sq Miles	10 831		traditional beliefs
Population	431 000	Currency	CFA franc
Capital	Malabo	Organizations	UN
Languages	Spanish, French, Fang	Map page	118

ERITREA
State of Eritrea

Area Sq Km	117 400	Religions	Sunni Muslim, Coptic
Area Sq Miles	45 328		Christian
Population	3 577 000	Currency	Nakfa
Capital	Asmara	Organizations	UN
Languages	Tigrinya, Tigre	Map page	116

ESTONIA
Republic of Estonia

Area Sq Km	45 200	Religions	Protestant, Estonian
Area Sq Miles	17 452		and Russian Orthodox
Population	1 429 000	Currency	Kroon
Capital	Tallinn	Organizations	UN
Languages	Estonian, Russian	Map page	88

ETHIOPIA
Federal Democratic Republic of Ethiopia

Area Sq Km	1 133 880	Religions	Ethiopian Orthodox,
Area Sq Miles	437 794		Sunni Muslim,
Population	59 649 000		traditional beliefs
Capital	Addis Ababa	Currency	Birr
	(Ãdis Ābeba)	Organizations	UN
Languages	Oromo, Amharic,	Map page	117
	Tigrinya, local		
	languages		

Falkland Islands
United Kingdom Overseas Territory

Area Sq Km	12 170	Religions	Protestant, Roman
Area Sq Miles	4 699		Catholic
Population	2 000	Currency	Pound
Capital	Stanley	Map page	153
Languages	English		

GABON
Gabonese Republic

Area Sq Km	267 667	Religions	Roman Catholic,
Area Sq Miles	103 347		Protestant, traditonal
Population	1 167 000		beliefs
Capital	Libreville	Currency	CFA franc
Languages	French, Fang, local	Map page	118
	languages		

Faroe Islands
Self-governing Danish Territory

Area Sq Km	1 399	Religions	Protestant
Area Sq Miles	540	Currency	Danish krone
Population	43 000	Map page	94
Capital	Tórshavn		
	(Thorshavn)		
Languages	Faroese, Danish		

Galapagos Islands (Islas Galápagos)
part of Ecuador

Area Sq Km	8 010	Religions	Roman Catholic
Area Sq Miles	3 093	Currency	Sucre
Population	10 207	Map page	125
Capital	Puerto Baquerizo		
	Moreno		
Languages	Spanish		

FIJI
Sovereign Democratic Republic of Fiji

Area Sq Km	18 330	Religions	Christian, Hindu, Sunni
Area Sq Miles	7 077		Muslim
Population	796 000	Currency	Dollar
Capital	Suva	Organizations	UN, Comm.
Languages	English, Fijian,	Map page	49
	Hindi		

THE GAMBIA
Republic of The Gambia

Area Sq Km	11 295	Religions	Sunni Muslim,
Area Sq Miles	4 361		Protestant
Population	1 229 000	Currency	Dalasi
Capital	Banjul	Organizations	Comm., UN
Languages	English, Malinke,	Map page	114
	Fulani, Wolof		

FINLAND
Republic of Finland

Area Sq Km	338 145	Religions	Protestant, Greek
Area Sq Miles	130 559		Orthodox
Population	5 154 000	Currency	Markka, Euro
Capital	Helsinki (Helsingfors)	Organizations	EU, OECD, UN
Languages	Finnish, Swedish	Map page	92-93

Gaza
semi-autonomous region

Area Sq Km	363	Religions	Sunni Muslim, Shi'a
Area Sq Miles	140		Muslim
Population	1 036 000	Currency	Israeli shekel
Capital	Gaza	Map page	80
Languages	Arabic		

FRANCE
French Republic

Area Sq Km	543 965	Religions	Roman Catholic,
Area Sq Miles	210 026		Protestant, Sunni
Population	58 683 000		Muslim
Capital	Paris	Currency	Franc, Euro
Languages	French, Arabic	Organizations	EU, OECD, UN
		Map page	104-105

GEORGIA
Republic of Georgia

Area Sq Km	69 700	Religions	Georgian Orthodox,
Area Sq Miles	26 911		Russian Orthodox,
Population	5 059 000		Sunni Muslim
Capital	T'bilisi	Currency	Lari
Languages	Georgian, Russian,	Organizations	CIS, UN
	Armenian, Azeri,	Map page	81
	Ossetian, Abkhaz		

French Guiana
French Overseas Department

Area Sq Km	90 000	Religions	Roman Catholic
Area Sq Miles	34 749	Currency	French franc
Population	167 000	Map page	151
Capital	Cayenne		
Languages	French, creole		

GERMANY
Federal Republic of Germany

Area Sq Km	357 028	Religions	Protestant, Roman
Area Sq Miles	137 849		Catholic
Population	82 133 000	Currency	Mark, Euro
Capital	Berlin	Organizations	EU, OECD, UN
Languages	German, Turkish	Map page	102

French Polynesia
French Overseas Territory

Area Sq Km	3 265	Religions	Protestant, Roman
Area Sq Miles	1 261		Catholic
Population	227 000	Currency	Pacific franc
Capital	Papeete	Map page	49
Languages	French, Tahitian,		
	Polynesian languages		

GHANA
Republic of Ghana

Area Sq Km	238 537	Religions	Christian, Sunni
Area Sq Miles	92 100		Muslim, traditional
Population	19 162 000		beliefs
Capital	Accra	Currency	Cedi
Languages	English, Hausa,	Organizations	Comm., UN
	Akan, local languages	Map page	114

Gibraltar

United Kingdom Overseas Territory

Area Sq Km	7	Religions	Roman Catholic,
Area Sq Miles	3		Protestant, Sunni
Population	25 000		Muslim
Capital	Gibraltar	Currency	Pound
Languages	English, Spanish	Map page	106

GREECE

Hellenic Republic

Area Sq Km	131 957	Religions	Greek Orthodox, Sunni
Area Sq Miles	50 949		Muslim
Population	10 600 000	Currency	Drachma
Capital	Athens (Athina)	Organizations	EU, OECD, UN
Languages	Greek	Map page	111

Greenland

Self-governing Danish Territory

Area Sq Km	2 175 600	Religions	Protestant
Area Sq Miles	840 004	Currency	Danish krone
Population	56 000	Map page	127
Capital	Nuuk (Godthåb)		
Languages	Greenlandic, Danish		

GRENADA

Area Sq Km	378	Religions	Roman Catholic,
Area Sq Miles	146		Protestant
Population	93 000	Currency	E. Carib. dollar
Capital	St George's	Organizations	CARICOM, Comm.,
Languages	English, creole		UN
		Map page	147

Guadeloupe
French Overseas Department

Area Sq Km	1 780	Religions	Roman Catholic
Area Sq Miles	687	Currency	French franc
Population	443 000	Map page	147
Capital	Basse-Terre		
Languages	French, creole		

Guam

United States Unincorporated Territory

Area Sq Km	541	Religions	Roman Catholic
Area Sq Miles	209	Currency	US dollar
Population	161 000	Map page	59
Capital	Hagåtña		
Languages	Chamorro, English,		
	Tagalog		

GUATEMALA

Republic of Guatemala

Area Sq Km	108 890	Religions	Roman Catholic,
Area Sq Miles	42 043		Protestant
Population	10 801 000	Currency	Quetzal
Capital	Guatemala	Organizations	UN
	(Guatemala City)	Map page	146
Languages	Spanish, Mayan		
	languages		

Guernsey

United Kingdom Crown Dependency

Area Sq Km	78	Religions	Protestant, Roman
Area Sq Miles	30		Catholic
Population	64 555	Currency	Pound
Capital	St Peter Port	Map page	95
Languages	English, French		

GUINEA

Republic of Guinea

Area Sq Km	245 857	Religions	Sunni Muslim,
Area Sq Miles	94 926		traditional beliefs,
Population	7 337 000		Christian
Capital	Conakry	Currency	Franc
Languages	French, Fulani,	Organizations	UN
	Malinke, local	Map page	114
	languages		

GUINEA-BISSAU

Republic of Guinea-Bissau

Area Sq Km	36 125	Religions	Traditional beliefs,
Area Sq Miles	13 948		Sunni Muslim,
Population	1 161 000		Christian
Capital	Bissau	Currency	CFA franc
Languages	Portuguese, crioulo,	Organizations	UN
	local languages	Map page	114

GUYANA

Co-operative Republic of Guyana

Area Sq Km	214 969	Religions	Protestant, Hindu,
Area Sq Miles	83 000		Roman Catholic, Sunni
Population	850 000		Muslim
Capital	Georgetown	Currency	Dollar
Languages	English, creole,	Organizations	CARICOM, Comm.,
	Amerindian		UN
	languages	Map page	150

HAITI

Republic of Haiti

Area Sq Km	27 750	Religions	Roman Catholic,
Area Sq Miles	10 714		Protestant, Voodoo
Population	7 952 000	Currency	Gourde
Capital	Port-au-Prince	Organizations	UN
Languages	French, creole	Map page	147

HONDURAS

Republic of Honduras

Area Sq Km	112 088	Religions	Roman Catholic,
Area Sq Miles	43 277		Protestant
Population	6 147 000	Currency	Lempira
Capital	Tegucigalpa	Organizations	UN
Languages	Spanish, Amerindian	Map page	147
	languages		

HUNGARY

Republic of Hungary

Area Sq Km	93 030	Religions	Roman Catholic,
Area Sq Miles	35 919		Protestant
Population	10 116 000	Currency	Forint
Capital	Budapest	Organizations	OECD, UN
Languages	Hungarian	Map page	103

ICELAND
Republic of Iceland

Area Sq Km	102 820	Religions	Protestant
Area Sq Miles	39 699	Currency	Króna
Population	276 000	Organizations	OECD, UN
Capital	Reykjavík	Map page	92
Languages	Icelandic		

 ## INDIA
Republic of India

Area Sq Km	3 065 027	Religions	Hindu, Sunni Muslim,
Area Sq Miles	1 183 414		Shi'a Muslim, Sikh,
Population	982 223 000		Christian
Capital	New Delhi	Currency	Rupee
Languages	Hindi, English, many	Organizations	Comm., UN
	regional languages	Map page	72-73

 ## INDONESIA
Republic of Indonesia

Area Sq Km	1 919 445	Religions	Sunni Muslim,
Area Sq Miles	741 102		Protestant, Roman
Population	206 338 000		Catholic, Hindu,
Capital	Jakarta		Buddhist
Languages	Indonesian, local	Currency	Rupiah
	languages	Organizations	APEC, ASEAN,
			OPEC, UN
		Map page	58-59

 ## IRAN
Islamic Republic of Iran

Area Sq Km	1 648 000	Religions	Shi'a Muslim, Sunni
Area Sq Miles	636 296		Muslim
Population	65 758 000	Currency	Rial
Capital	Tehrān	Organizations	OPEC, UN
Languages	Farsi, Azeri, Kurdish,	Map page	81
	regional languages		

 ## IRAQ
Republic of Iraq

Area Sq Km	438 317	Religions	Shi'a Muslim, Sunni
Area Sq Miles	169 235		Muslim, Christian
Population	21 800 000	Currency	Dinar
Capital	Baghdād	Organizations	OPEC, UN
Languages	Arabic, Kurdish,	Map page	81
	Turkmen		

 ## IRELAND, REPUBLIC OF

Area Sq Km	70 282	Religions	Roman Catholic,
Area Sq Miles	27 136		Protestant,
Population	3 681 000	Currency	Punt, Euro
Capital	Dublin	Organizations	EU, OECD, UN
	(Baile Átha Cliath)	Map page	97
Languages	English, Irish		

 ## Isle of Man
United Kingdom Crown Dependency

Area Sq Km	572	Religions	Protestant, Roman
Area Sq Miles	221		Catholic
Population	77 000	Currency	Pound
Capital	Douglas	Map page	98
Languages	English		

 ## ISRAEL
State of Israel

Area Sq Km	20 770	Religions	Jewish, Sunni Muslim,
Area Sq Miles	8 019		Christian, Druze
Population	5 984 000	Currency	Shekel
Capital	Jerusalem	Organizations	UN
	(Yerushalayim)	Map page	80
	(El Quds)		
Languages	Hebrew, Arabic		

 ## ITALY
Italian Republic

Area Sq Km	301 245	Religions	Roman Catholic
Area Sq Miles	116 311	Currency	Lira, Euro
Population	57 369 000	Organizations	EU, OECD, UN
Capital	Rome (Roma)	Map page	108-109
Languages	Italian		

 ## JAMAICA

Area Sq Km	10 991	Religions	Protestant, Roman
Area Sq Miles	4 244		Catholic
Population	2 538 000	Currency	Dollar
Capital	Kingston	Organizations	CARICOM, Comm.,
Languages	English, creole		UN
		Map page	146

Jammu and Kashmir
Disputed territory (India/Pakistan)

Area Sq Km	222 236	Map page	74-75
Area Sq Miles	85 806		
Population	13 000 000		
Capital	Srinagar		

 ## JAPAN

Area Sq Km	377 727	Religions	Shintoist, Buddhist,
Area Sq Miles	145 841		Christian
Population	126 281 000	Currency	Yen
Capital	Tōkyō	Organizations	APEC, OECD, UN
Languages	Japanese	Map page	66-67

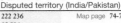 ## Jersey
United Kingdom Crown Dependency

Area Sq Km	116	Religions	Protestant, Roman
Area Sq Miles	45		Catholic
Population	89 136	Currency	Pound
Capital	St Helier	Map page	95
Languages	English, French		

 ## JORDAN
Hashemite Kingdom of Jordan

Area Sq Km	89 206	Religions	Sunni Muslim,
Area Sq Miles	34 443		Christian
Population	6 304 000	Currency	Dinar
Capital	'Ammān	Organizations	UN
Languages	Arabic	Map page	80

Juan Fernández Islands
part of Chile

Area Sq Km	179	Religions	Roman Catholic
Area Sq Miles	69	Map page	157
Population	516		
Capital	San Juan Bautista		
Languages	Spanish		

KAZAKHSTAN
Republic of Kazakhstan

Area Sq Km	2 717 300	Religions	Sunni Muslim, Russian
Area Sq Miles	1 049 155		Orthodox, Protestant
Population	16 319 000	Currency	Tenge
Capital	Astana (Akmola)	Organizations	CIS, UN
Languages	Kazakh, Russian,	Map page	76-77
	Ukrainian, German,		
	Uzbek, Tatar		

KENYA
Republic of Kenya

Area Sq Km	582 646	Religions	Christian, traditional
Area Sq Miles	224 961		beliefs
Population	29 008 000	Currency	Shilling
Capital	Nairobi	Organizations	Comm., UN
Languages	Swahili, English, local	Map page	119
	languages		

KIRIBATI
Republic of Kiribati

Area Sq Km	717	Religions	Roman Catholic,
Area Sq Miles	277		Protestant
Population	81 000	Currency	Australian dollar
Capital	Bairiki	Organizations	Comm., UN
Languages	Gilbertese, English	Map page	49

KUWAIT
State of Kuwait

Area Sq Km	17 818	Religions	Sunni Muslim, Shi'a
Area Sq Miles	6 880		Muslim, Christian,
Population	1 811 000		Hindu
Capital	Kuwait (Al Kuwayt)	Currency	Dinar
Languages	Arabic	Organizations	OPEC, UN
		Map page	78

KYRGYZSTAN
Kyrgyz Republic

Area Sq Km	198 500	Religions	Sunni Muslim, Russian
Area Sq Miles	76 641		Orthodox
Population	4 643 000	Currency	Som
Capital	Bishkek (Frunze)	Organizations	CIS, UN
Languages	Kyrgyz, Russian,	Map page	77
	Uzbek		

LAOS
Lao People's Democratic Republic

Area Sq Km	236 800	Religions	Buddhist, traditional
Area Sq Miles	91 429		beliefs
Population	5 163 000	Currency	Kip
Capital	Vientiane	Organizations	ASEAN, UN
	(Viangchan)	Map page	62-63
Languages	Lao, local languages		

LATVIA
Republic of Latvia

Area Sq Km	63 700	Religions	Protestant, Roman
Area Sq Miles	24 595		Catholic, Russian
Population	2 424 000		Orthodox
Capital	Rīga	Currency	Lat
Languages	Latvian, Russian	Organizations	UN
		Map page	88

LEBANON
Republic of Lebanon

Area Sq Km	10 452	Religions	Shi'a Muslim, Sunni
Area Sq Miles	4 036		Muslim, Christian
Population	3 191 000	Currency	Pound
Capital	Beirut (Beyrouth)	Organizations	UN
Languages	Arabic, Armenian,	Map page	80
	French		

LESOTHO
Kingdom of Lesotho

Area Sq Km	30 355	Religions	Christian, traditional
Area Sq Miles	11 720		beliefs
Population	2 062 000	Currency	Loti
Capital	Maseru	Organizations	Comm., SADC, UN
Languages	Sesotho, English,	Map page	123
	Zulu		

LIBERIA
Republic of Liberia

Area Sq Km	111 369	Religions	Traditional beliefs,
Area Sq Miles	43 000		Christian, Sunni
Population	2 666 000		Muslim
Capital	Monrovia	Currency	Dollar
Languages	English, creole, local	Organizations	UN
	languages	Map page	114

LIBYA
Socialist People's Libyan Arab Jamahiriya

Area Sq Km	1 759 540	Religions	Sunni Muslim
Area Sq Miles	679 362	Currency	Dinar
Population	5 339 000	Organizations	OPEC, UN
Capital	Tripoli (Ṭarābulus)	Map page	115
Languages	Arabic, Berber		

LIECHTENSTEIN
Principality of Liechtenstein

Area Sq Km	160	Religions	Roman Catholic,
Area Sq Miles	62		Protestant
Population	32 000	Currency	Swiss franc
Capital	Vaduz	Organizations	UN
Languages	German	Map page	105

LITHUANIA
Republic of Lithuania

Area Sq Km	65 200	Religions	Roman Catholic,
Area Sq Miles	25 174		Protestant, Russian
Population	3 694 000		Orthodox
Capital	Vilnius	Currency	Litas
Languages	Lithuanian, Russian,	Organizations	UN
	Polish	Map page	88

Lord Howe Islands
part of Australia

Area Sq Km	17	Population	371
Area Sq Miles	6	Map page	51

 ## LUXEMBOURG
Grand Duchy of Luxembourg

Area Sq Km	2 586	Religions	Roman Catholic
Area Sq Miles	998	Currency	Franc, Euro
Population	422 000	Organizations	EU, OECD, UN
Capital	Luxembourg	Map page	100
Languages	Letzeburgish,		
	German, French		

 ## MACEDONIA (F.Y.R.O.M.)
Republic of Macedonia

Area Sq Km	25 713	Religions	Macedonian Orthodox,
Area Sq Miles	9 928		Sunni Muslim
Population	1 999 000	Currency	Denar
Capital	Skopje	Organizations	UN
Languages	Macedonian,	Map page	111
	Albainian, Turkish		

 ## MADAGASCAR
Republic of Madagascar

Area Sq Km	587 041	Religions	Traditional beliefs,
Area Sq Miles	226 658		Christian, Sunni
Population	15 057 000		Muslim
Capital	Antananarivo	Currency	Franc
Languages	Malagasy, French	Organizations	UN
		Map page	121

Madeira
Autonomous Region of Portugal

Area Sq Km	779	Religions	Roman Catholic,
Area Sq Miles	301		Protestant
Population	259 000	Currency	Portuguese escudo
Capital	Funchal	Map page	114
Languages	Portuguese		

 ## MALAWI
Republic of Malawi

Area Sq Km	118 484	Religions	Christian, traditional
Area Sq Miles	45 747		beliefs, Sunni Muslim
Population	10 346 000	Currency	Kwacha
Capital	Lilongwe	Organizations	Comm.,SADC, UN
Languages	Chichewa, English,	Map page	121
	local languages		

 ## MALAYSIA
Federation of Malaysia

Area Sq Km	332 965	Religions	Sunni Muslim, Buddhist,
Area Sq Miles	128 559		Hindu, Christian,
Population	21 410 000		traditional beliefs
Capital	Kuala Lumpur	Currency	Ringgit
Languages	Malay, English,	Organizations	APEC, ASEAN,
	Chinese, Tamil, local		Comm., UN
	languages	Map page	60-61

 ## MALDIVES
Republic of the Maldives

Area Sq Km	298	Religions	Sunni Muslim
Area Sq Miles	115	Currency	Rufiyaa
Population	271 000	Organizations	Comm., UN
Capital	Male	Map page	56
Languages	Divehi (Maldivian)		

 ## MALI
Republic of Mali

Area Sq Km	1 240 140	Religions	Sunni Muslim,
Area Sq Miles	478 821		traditional beliefs,
Population	10 694 000		Christian
Capital	Bamako	Currency	CFA franc
Languages	French, Bambara,	Organizations	UN
	local languages	Map page	114

 ## MALTA
Republic of Malta

Area Sq Km	316	Religions	Roman Catholic
Area Sq Miles	122	Currency	Lira
Population	384 000	Organizations	Comm.,UN
Capital	Valletta	Map page	84
Languages	Maltese, English		

 ## MARSHALL ISLANDS
Republic of Marshall Islands

Area Sq Km	181	Religions	Protestant, Roman
Area Sq Miles	70		Catholic
Population	60 000	Currency	US dollar
Capital	Dalap-Uliga-Darrit	Organizations	UN
Languages	English, Marshallese	Map page	48

Martinique
French Overseas Department

Area Sq Km	1 079	Religions	Roman Catholic,
Area Sq Miles	417		traditional beliefs
Population	389 000	Currency	French franc
Capital	Fort-de-France	Map page	147
Languages	French, creole		

MAURITANIA
Islamic Arab and African Republic of Mauritania

Area Sq Km	1 030 700	Religions	Sunni Muslim
Area Sq Miles	397 955	Currency	Ouguiya
Population	2 529 000	Organizations	UN
Capital	Nouakchott	Map page	114
Languages	Arabic, French, local		
	languages		

MAURITIUS
Republic of Mauritius

Area Sq Km	2 040	Religions	Hindu, Roman
Area Sq Miles	788		Catholic, Sunni Muslim
Population	1 141 000	Currency	Rupee
Capital	Port Louis	Organizations	Comm., SADC, UN
Languages	English, creole,	Map page	113
	Hindi, Bhojpuri,		
	French		

Mayotte
French Territorial Collectivity

Area Sq Km	373	Religions	Sunni Muslim,
Area Sq Miles	144		Christian
Population	144 944	Currency	French franc
Capital	Dzaoudzi	Map page	121
Languages	French, Mahorian		

Melilla
Spanish Territory

Area Sq Km	13	Religions	Roman Catholic,
Area Sq Miles	5		Muslim
Population	59 576	Currency	Peseta
Capital	Melilla	Map page	114
Languages	Spanish, Arabic		

MEXICO
United Mexican States

Area Sq Km	1 972 545	Religions	Roman Catholic,
Area Sq Miles	761 604		Protestant
Population	95 831 000	Currency	Peso
Capital	México (Mexico	Organizations	APEC, OECD, UN
	City)	Map page	144-145
Languages	Spanish, Amerindian		
	languages		

MICRONESIA, FEDERATED STATES OF

Area Sq Km	701	Religions	Roman Catholic,
Area Sq Miles	271		Protestant
Population	114 000	Currency	US dollar
Capital	Palikir	Organizations	UN
Languages	English, Chuukese,	Map page	48
	Pohnpeian, local		
	languages		

MOLDOVA
Republic of Moldova

Area Sq Km	33 700	Religions	Romanian Orthodox,
Area Sq Miles	13 012		Russian Orthodox
Population	4 378 000	Currency	Leu
Capital	Chişinău (Kishinev)	Organizations	CIS, UN
Languages	Romanian,	Map page	90
	Ukrainian, Gagauz,		
	Russian		

MONACO
Principality of Monaco

Area Sq Km	2	Religions	Roman Catholic
Area Sq Miles	1	Currency	French franc
Population	33 000	Organizations	UN
Capital	Monaco-Ville	Map page	105
Languages	French, Monegasque,		
	Italian		

MONGOLIA

Area Sq Km	1 565 000	Religions	Buddhist, Sunni Muslim
Area Sq Miles	604 250	Currency	Tugrik
Population	2 579 000	Organizations	UN
Capital	Ulaanbaatar	Map page	68-69
	(Ulan Bator)		
Languages	Khalka (Mongolian),		
	Kazakh, local languages		

Montserrat
United Kingdom Overseas Territory

Area Sq Km	100	Religions	Protestant, Roman
Area Sq Miles	39		Catholic
Population	11 000	Currency	E. Carib. dollar
Capital	Plymouth	Organizations	CARICOM
Languages	English	Map page	147

MOROCCO
Kingdom of Morocco

Area Sq Km	446 550	Religions	Sunni Muslim
Area Sq Miles	172 414	Currency	Dirham
Population	27 377 000	Organizations	UN
Capital	Rabat	Map page	114
Languages	Arabic, Berber,		
	French		

MOZAMBIQUE
Republic of Mozambique

Area Sq Km	799 380	Religions	Traditional beliefs,
Area Sq Miles	308 642		Roman Catholic, Sunni
Population	18 880 000		Muslim
Capital	Maputo	Currency	Metical
Languages	Portuguese, Makua,	Organizations	Comm., SADC, UN
	Tsonga, local	Map page	121
	languages		

MYANMAR
Union of Myanmar

Area Sq Km	676 577	Religions	Buddhist, Christian,
Area Sq Miles	261 228		Sunni Muslim
Population	44 497 000	Currency	Kyat
Capital	Yangôn (Rangoon)	Organizations	ASEAN, UN
Languages	Burmese, Shan,	Map page	62-63
	Karen, local languages		

NAMIBIA
Republic of Namibia

Area Sq Km	824 292	Religions	Protestant, Roman
Area Sq Miles	318 261		Catholic
Population	1 660 000	Currency	Dollar
Capital	Windhoek	Organizations	Comm., SADC, UN
Languages	English, Afrikaans,	Map page	121
	German, Ovambo,		
	local languages		

NAURU
Republic of Nauru

Area Sq Km	21	Religions	Protestant, Roman
Area Sq Miles	8		Catholic
Population	11 000	Currency	Australian dollar
Capital	Yaren	Organizations	Comm., UN
Languages	Nauruan, English	Map page	48

NEPAL
Kingdom of Nepal

Area Sq Km	147 181	Religions	Hindu, Buddhist, Sunni
Area Sq Miles	56 827		Muslim
Population	22 847 000	Currency	Rupee
Capital	Kathmandu	Organizations	UN
Languages	Nepali, Maithili,	Map page	75
	Bhojpuri, English,		
	local languages		

NETHERLANDS
Kingdom of the Netherlands

Area Sq Km	41 526	Religions	Roman Catholic,
Area Sq Miles	16 033		Protestant, Sunni
Population	15 678 000		Muslim
Capital	Amsterdam/The	Currency	Guilder, Euro
	Hague	Organizations	EU, OECD, UN
	('s-Gravenhage)	Map page	100
Languages	Dutch, Frisian		

Netherlands Antilles
Self-governing Netherlands Territory

Area Sq Km	800	Religions	Roman Catholic,
Area Sq Miles	309		Protestant
Population	213 000	Currency	NA guilder
Capital	Willemstad	Map page	147
Languages	Dutch, Papiamento,		
	English		

New Caledonia
French Overseas Territory

Area Sq Km	19 058	Religions	Roman Catholic,
Area Sq Miles	7 358		Protestant, Sunni
Population	206 000		Muslim
Capital	Nouméa	Currency	Pacific franc
Languages	French, local	Map page	48
	languages		

NEW ZEALAND

Area Sq Km	270 534	Religions	Protestant, Roman
Area Sq Miles	104 454		Catholic
Population	3 796 000	Currency	Dollar
Capital	Wellington	Organizations	APEC, Comm.,
Languages	English, Maori		OECD, UN
		Map page	54

NICARAGUA
Republic of Nicaragua

Area Sq Km	130 000	Religions	Roman Catholic,
Area Sq Miles	50 193		Protestant
Population	4 807 000	Currency	Córdoba
Capital	Managua	Organizations	UN
Languages	Spanish, Amerindian	Map page	146
	languages		

NIGER
Republic of Niger

Area Sq Km	1 267 000	Religions	Sunni Muslim,
Area Sq Miles	489 191		traditional beliefs
Population	10 078 000	Currency	CFA franc
Capital	Niamey	Organizations	UN
Languages	French, Hausa,	Map page	115
	Fulani, local		
	languages		

NIGERIA
Federal Republic of Nigeria

Area Sq Km	923 768	Religions	Sunni Muslim,
Area Sq Miles	356 669		Christian, traditional
Population	106 409 000		beliefs
Capital	Abuja	Currency	Naira
Languages	English, Hausa,	Organizations	Comm., OPEC, UN
	Yoruba, Ibo, Fulani,	Map page	115
	local languages		

Niue
Self-governing New Zealand Overseas Territory

Area Sq Km	258	Religions	Christian
Area Sq Miles	100	Currency	NZ dollar
Population	2 000	Map page	48
Capital	Alofi		
Languages	English, Polynesian		

Norfolk Island
Australian External Territory

Area Sq Km	35	Religions	Protestant, Roman
Area Sq Miles	14		Catholic
Population	2 000	Currency	Australian dollar
Capital	Kingston	Map page	48
Languages	English		

Northern Mariana Islands
United States Commonwealth

Area Sq Km	477	Religions	Roman Catholic
Area Sq Miles	184	Currency	US dollar
Population	70 000	Map page	59
Capital	Saipan		
Languages	English, Chamorro,		
	local languages		

NORTH KOREA
People's Democratic Republic of North Korea

Area Sq Km	120 538	Religions	Traditional beliefs,
Area Sq Miles	46 540		Chondoist, Buddhist
Population	23 348 000	Currency	Won
Capital	P'yŏngyang	Organizations	UN
Languages	Korean	Map page	65

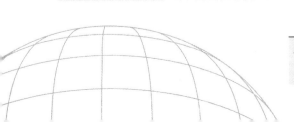

NORWAY
Kingdom of Norway

Area Sq Km	323 878	Religions	Protestant, Roman
Area Sq Miles	125 050		Catholic
Population	4 419 000	Currency	Krone
Capital	Oslo	Organizations	OECD, UN
Languages	Norwegian	Map page	92-93

OMAN
Sultanate of Oman

Area Sq Km	309 500	Religions	Ibadhi Muslim, Sunni
Area Sq Miles	119 499		Muslim
Population	2 382 000	Currency	Rial
Capital	Muscat (Masqat)	Organizations	UN
Languages	Arabic, Baluchi,	Map page	79
	Indian languages		

PAKISTAN
Islamic Republic of Pakistan

Area Sq Km	803 940	Religions	Sunni Muslim, Shi'a
Area Sq Miles	310 403		Muslim, Christian,
Population	148 166 000		Hindu
Capital	Islamabad	Currency	Rupee
Languages	Urdu, Punjabi,	Organizations	Comm., UN
	Sindhi, Pushtu,	Map page	74
	English		

PALAU
Republic of Palau

Area Sq Km	497	Religions	Roman Catholic,
Area Sq Miles	192		Protestant, traditional
Population	19 000		beliefs
Capital	Koror	Currency	US dollar
Languages	Palauan, English	Organizations	UN
		Map page	59

PANAMA
Republic of Panama

Area Sq Km	77 082	Religions	Roman Catholic,
Area Sq Miles	29 762		Protestant, Sunni
Population	2 767 000		Muslim
Capital	Panamá	Currency	Balboa
	(Panama City)	Organizations	UN
Languages	Spanish, English,	Map page	146
	Amerindian languages		

PAPUA NEW GUINEA
Independent State of Papua New Guinea

Area Sq Km	462 840	Religions	Protestant, Roman
Area Sq Miles	178 704		Catholic, traditional
Population	4 600 000		beliefs
Capital	Port Moresby	Currency	Kina
Languages	English, Tok Pisin	Organizations	Comm., UN
	(creole), local	Map page	59
	languages		

PARAGUAY
Republic of Paraguay

Area Sq Km	406 752	Religions	Roman Catholic,
Area Sq Miles	157 048		Protestant
Population	5 222 000	Currency	Guaraní
Capital	Asunción	Organizations	UN
Languages	Spanish, Guaraní	Map page	152

PERU
Republic of Peru

Area Sq Km	1 285 216	Religions	Roman Catholic,
Area Sq Miles	496 225		Protestant
Population	24 797 000	Currency	Sol
Capital	Lima	Organizations	APEC, UN
Languages	Spanish, Quechua,	Map page	150
	Aymara		

PHILIPPINES
Republic of the Philippines

Area Sq Km	300 000	Religions	Roman Catholic,
Area Sq Miles	115 831		Protestant, Sunni
Population	72 944 000		Muslim, Aglipayan
Capital	Manila	Currency	Peso
Languages	English, Pilipino,	Organizations	APEC, ASEAN, UN
	Cebuano, local	Map page	64
	languages		

Pitcairn Islands
United Kingdom Overseas Territory

Area Sq Km	45	Religions	Protestant
Area Sq Miles	17	Currency	NZ dollar
Population	46	Map page	49
Capital	Adamstown		
Languages	English		

POLAND
Polish Republic

Area Sq Km	312 683	Religions	Roman Catholic, Polish
Area Sq Miles	120 728		Orthodox
Population	38 718 000	Currency	Złoty
Capital	Warsaw (Warszawa)	Organizations	OECD, UN
Languages	Polish, German	Map page	103

PORTUGAL
Portuguese Republic

Area Sq Km	88 940	Religions	Roman Catholic,
Area Sq Miles	34 340		Protestant
Population	9 869 000	Currency	Escudo, Euro
Capital	Lisbon (Lisboa)	Organizations	EU, OECD, UN
Languages	Portuguese	Map page	106

Puerto Rico
United States Commonwealth

Area Sq Km	9 104	Religions	Roman Catholic,
Area Sq Miles	3 515		Protestant
Population	3 810 000	Currency	US dollar
Capital	San Juan	Map page	147
Languages	Spanish, English		

QATAR
State of Qatar

Area Sq Km	11 437	Religions	Sunni Muslim
Area Sq Miles	4 416	Currency	Riyal
Population	579 000	Organizations	OPEC, UN
Capital	Doha (Ad Dawḥah)	Map page	79
Languages	Arabic		

Réunion
French Overseas Department

Area Sq Km	2 551	Religions	Roman Catholic
Area Sq Miles	985	Currency	French franc
Population	682 000	Map page	113
Capital	St-Denis		
Languages	French, creole		

St Eustatius
part of Netherlands Antilles

Area Sq Km	21	Religions	Protestant, Roman
Area Sq Miles	8		Catholic
Population	1 900	Currency	NA guilder
Capital	Oranjestad	Map page	147
Languages	Dutch, English		

Rodrigues Island
part of Mauritius

Area Sq Km	104	Religions	Christian
Area Sq Miles	40	Currency	Rupee
Population	35 221	Map page	159
Capital	Port Mathurin		
Languages	English, creole		

St Helena
United Kingdom Overseas Territory

Area Sq Km	121	Religions	Protestant, Roman
Area Sq Miles	47		Catholic,
Population	5 644	Currency	Pound sterling
Capital	Jamestown	Map page	113
Languages	English		

 ## ROMANIA

Area Sq Km	237 500	Religions	Romanian Orthodox,
Area Sq Miles	91 699		Protestant, Roman
Population	22 474 000		Catholic
Capital	Bucharest (Bucureşti)	Currency	Leu
Languages	Romanian, Hungarian	Organizations	UN
		Map page	110

ST KITTS AND NEVIS
Federation of St Kitts and Nevis

Area Sq Km	261	Religions	Protestant, Roman
Area Sq Miles	101		Catholic
Population	39 000	Currency	E. Carib. dollar
Capital	Basseterre	Organizations	CARICOM, Comm.,
Languages	English, creole		UN
		Map page	147

 ## RUSSIAN FEDERATION

Area Sq Km	17 075 400	Religions	Russian Orthodox,
Area Sq Miles	6 592 849		Sunni Muslim,
Population	147 434 000		Protestant
Capital	Moscow (Moskva)	Currency	Rouble
Languages	Russian, Tatar,	Organizations	APEC, CIS, UN
	Ukrainian, local	Map page	82-83
	languages		

ST LUCIA

Area Sq Km	616	Religions	Roman Catholic,
Area Sq Miles	238		Protestant
Population	150 000	Currency	E. Carib. dollar
Capital	Castries	Organizations	CARICOM, Comm.,
Languages	English, creole		UN
		Map page	147

RWANDA
Republic of Rwanda

Area Sq Km	26 338	Religions	Roman Catholic,
Area Sq Miles	10 169		traditional beliefs,
Population	6 604 000		Protestant
Capital	Kigali	Currency	Franc
Languages	Kinyarwanda,	Organizations	UN
	French, English	Map page	119

St Maarten
part of Netherlands Antilles

Area Sq Km	34	Religions	Protestant, Roman
Area Sq Miles	13		Catholic
Population	38 567	Currency	NA guilder
Capital	Philipsburg	Map page	147
Languages	Dutch, English		

Saba
part of Netherlands Antilles

Area Sq Km	13	Religions	Roman Catholic,
Area Sq Miles	5		Protestant
Population	1 200	Currency	NA guilder
Capital	Bottom	Map page	147
Languages	Dutch, English		

Saint Martin
Dependency of Guadeloupe

Area Sq Km	54	Religions	Roman Catholic
Area Sq Miles	21	Currency	French franc
Population	28 518	Map page	147
Capital	Marigot		
Languages	French, creole		

St Barthélémy
Dependency of Guadeloupe

Area Sq Km	21	Languages	French, creole
Area Sq Miles	8	Religions	Roman Catholic
Population	5 038	Currency	French franc
Capital	Gustavia	Map page	147

St Pierre and Miquelon
French Territorial Collectivity

Area Sq Km	242	Religions	Roman Catholic
Area Sq Miles	93	Currency	French franc
Population	7 000	Map page	131
Capital	St-Pierre		
Languages	French		

ST VINCENT AND THE GRENADINES

Area Sq Km	389	Religions	Protestant, Roman
Area Sq Miles	150		Catholic
Population	112 000	Currency	E. Carib. dollar
Capital	Kingstown	Organizations	CARICOM, Comm.,
Languages	English, creole		UN
		Map page	147

SAMOA
Independent State of Samoa

Area Sq Km	2 831	Religions	Protestant, Roman
Area Sq Miles	1 093		Catholic
Population	174 000	Currency	Tala
Capital	Apia	Organizations	Comm., UN
Languages	Samoan, English	Map page	49

SAN MARINO
Republic of San Marino

Area Sq Km	61	Religions	Roman Catholic
Area Sq Miles	24	Currency	Italian lira
Population	26 000	Organizations	UN
Capital	San Marino	Map page	108
Languages	Italian		

SÃO TOMÉ AND PRÍNCIPE
Democratic Republic of São Tomé and Príncipe

Area Sq Km	964	Religions	Roman Catholic,
Area Sq Miles	372		Protestant
Population	141 000	Currency	Dobra
Capital	São Tomé	Organizations	UN
Languages	Portuguese, creole	Map page	113

SAUDI ARABIA
Kingdom of Saudi Arabia

Area Sq Km	2 200 000	Religions	Sunni Muslim, Shi'a
Area Sq Miles	849 425		Muslim
Population	20 181 000	Currency	Riyal
Capital	Riyadh (Ar Riyāḍ)	Organizations	OPEC, UN
Languages	Arabic	Map page	78-79

SENEGAL
Republic of Senegal

Area Sq Km	196 720	Religions	Sunni Muslim, Roman
Area Sq Miles	75 954		Catholic, traditional
Population	9 003 000		beliefs
Capital	Dakar	Currency	CFA franc
Languages	French, Wolof, Fulani,	Organizations	UN
	local languages	Map page	114

SEYCHELLES
Republic of the Seychelles

Area Sq Km	455	Religions	Roman Catholic,
Area Sq Miles	176		Protestant
Population	76 000	Currency	Rupee
Capital	Victoria	Organizations	Comm., SADC, UN
Languages	English, French,	Map page	113
	creole		

SIERRA LEONE
Republic of Sierra Leone

Area Sq Km	71 740	Religions	Sunni Muslim,
Area Sq Miles	27 699		traditional beliefs
Population	4 568 000	Currency	Leone
Capital	Freetown	Organizations	Comm., UN
Languages	English, creole,	Map page	114
	Mende, Tèmne, local		
	languages		

SINGAPORE
Republic of Singapore

Area Sq Km	639	Religions	Buddhist, Taoist, Sunni
Area Sq Miles	247		Muslim, Christian,
Population	3 476 000		Hindu
Capital	Singapore	Currency	Dollar
Languages	Chinese, English,	Organizations	APEC, ASEAN,
	Malay, Tamil		Comm., UN
		Map page	60

SLOVAKIA
Slovak Republic

Area Sq Km	49 035	Religions	Roman Catholic,
Area Sq Miles	18 933		Protestant, Orthodox
Population	5 377 000	Currency	Koruna
Capital	Bratislava	Organizations	UN
Languages	Slovak, Hungarian,	Map page	103
	Czech		

SLOVENIA
Republic of Slovenia

Area Sq Km	20 251	Religions	Roman Catholic,
Area Sq Miles	7 819		Protestant
Population	1 993 000	Currency	Tólar
Capital	Ljubljana	Organizations	UN
Languages	Slovene, Croatian,	Map page	108-109
	Serbian		

SOLOMON ISLANDS

Area Sq Km	28 370	Religions	Protestant, Roman
Area Sq Miles	10 954		Catholic
Population	417 000	Currency	Dollar
Capital	Honiara	Organizations	Comm., UN
Languages	English, creole, local	Map page	48
	languages		

SOMALIA
Somali Democratic Republic

Area Sq Km	637 657	Religions	Sunni Muslim
Area Sq Miles	246 201	Currency	Shilling
Population	9 237 000	Organizations	UN
Capital	Muqdisho	Map page	117
	(Mogadishu)		
Languages	Somali, Arabic		

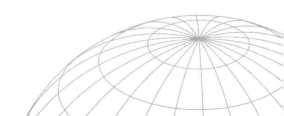

SOUTH AFRICA, REPUBLIC OF

Area Sq Km	1 219 090	Religions	Protestant, Roman
Area Sq Miles	470 693		Catholic, Sunni
Population	39 357 000		Muslim, Hindu
Capital	Pretoria/Cape Town	Currency	Rand
Languages	Afrikaans, English,	Organizations	Comm., SADC, UN
	nine official local	Map page	122-123
	languages		

 ### SOUTH KOREA
Republic of South Korea

Area Sq Km	99 274	Religions	Buddhist, Protestant,
Area Sq Miles	38 330		Roman Catholic
Population	46 109 000	Currency	Won
Capital	Seoul (Sŏul)	Organizations	APEC, UN
Languages	Korean	Map page	65

SPAIN
Kingdom of Spain

Area Sq Km	504 782	Religions	Roman Catholic
Area Sq Miles	194 897	Currency	Peseta, Euro
Population	39 628 000	Organizations	EU, OECD, UN
Capital	Madrid	Map page	106-107
Languages	Castilian, Catalan,		
	Galician, Basque		

SRI LANKA
Democratic Socialist Republic of Sri Lanka

Area Sq Km	65 610	Religions	Buddhist, Hindu,
Area Sq Miles	25 332		Sunni Muslim, Roman
Population	18 455 000		Catholic
Capital	Sri Jayewardenepura	Currency	Rupee
	Kotte	Organizations	Comm., UN
Languages	Sinhalese, Tamil,	Map page	73
	English		

SUDAN
Republic of the Sudan

Area Sq Km	2 505 813	Religions	Sunni Muslim,
Area Sq Miles	967 500		traditional beliefs,
Population	28 292 000		Christian
Capital	Khartoum	Currency	Dinar
Languages	Arabic, Dinka,	Organizations	UN
	Nubian, Beja, Nuer,	Map page	116-117
	local languages		

 ### SURINAME
Republic of Suriname

Area Sq Km	163 820	Religions	Hindu, Roman Catholic,
Area Sq Miles	63 251		Protestant,
Population	414 000		Sunni Muslim
Capital	Paramaribo	Currency	Guilder
Languages	Dutch,	Organizations	CARICOM, UN
	Surinamese,	Map page	151
	English, Hindi		

Svalbard
part of Norway

Area Sq Km	61 229	Religions	Protestant
Area Sq Miles	23 641	Currency	Krone
Population	2 591	Map page	82
Capital	Longyearbyen		
Languages	Norwegian		

SWAZILAND
Kingdom of Swaziland

Area Sq Km	17 364	Religions	Christian, traditional
Area Sq Miles	6 704		beliefs
Population	952 000	Currency	Lilangeni
Capital	Mbabane	Organizations	Comm., SADC, UN
Languages	Swazi, English	Map page	123

SWEDEN
Kingdom of Sweden

Area Sq Km	449 964	Religions	Protestant,
Area Sq Miles	173 732		Roman Catholic
Population	8 875 000	Currency	Krona
Capital	Stockholm	Organizations	EU, OECD, UN
Languages	Swedish	Map page	92-93

SWITZERLAND
Swiss Confederation

Area Sq Km	41 293	Religions	Roman Catholic,
Area Sq Miles	15 943		Protestant,
Population	7 299 000	Currency	Franc
Capital	Bern (Berne)	Organizations	OECD
Languages	German, French,	Map page	105
	Italian, Romansch		

SYRIA
Syrian Arab Republic

Area Sq Km	185 180	Religions	Sunni Muslim, Shi'a
Area Sq Miles	71 498		Muslim, Christian
Population	15 333 000	Currency	Pound
Capital	Damascus (Dimashq)	Organizations	UN
Languages	Arabic, Kurdish,	Map page	80
	Armenian		

TAIWAN
Republic of China

Area Sq Km	36 179	Religions	Buddhist, Taoist,
Area Sq Miles	13 969		Confucian, Christian
Population	21 908 135	Currency	Dollar
Capital	T'aipei	Organizations	APEC
Languages	Mandarin, Min,	Map page	71
	Hakka, local		
	languages		

TAJIKISTAN
Republic of Tajikistan

Area Sq Km	143 100	Religions	Sunni Muslim
Area Sq Miles	55 251	Currency	Rouble
Population	6 015 000	Organizations	CIS, UN
Capital	Dushanbe	Map page	77
Languages	Tajik, Uzbek, Russian		

TANZANIA
United Republic of Tanzania

Area Sq Km	945 087	Religions	Shi'a Muslim, Sunni
Area Sq Miles	364 900		Muslim, traditional
Population	32 102 000		beliefs, Christian
Capital	Dodoma	Currency	Shilling
Languages	Swahili, English,	Organizations	Comm., SADC, UN
	Nyamwezi, local	Map page	119
	languages		

THAILAND
Kingdom of Thailand

Area Sq Km	513 115	Religions	Buddhist, Sunni
Area Sq Miles	198 115		Muslim
Population	60 300 000	Currency	Baht
Capital	Bangkok (Krung	Organizations	APEC, ASEAN, UN
	Thep)	Map page	62-63
Languages	Thai, Lao, Chinese,		
	Malay, Mon-Khmer		
	languages		

TOGO
Republic of Togo

Area Sq Km	56 785	Religions	Traditional beliefs,
Area Sq Miles	21 925		Christian, Sunni
Population	4 397 000		Muslim
Capital	Lomé	Currency	CFA franc
Languages	French, Ewe, Kabre,	Organizations	UN
	local languages	Map page	114

Tokelau
New Zealand Overseas Territory

Area Sq Km	10	Religions	Christian
Area Sq Miles	4	Currency	NZ dollar
Population	1 000	Map page	49
Capital	none		
Languages	English, Tokelauan		

TONGA
Kingdom of Tonga

Area Sq Km	748	Religions	Protestant, Roman
Area Sq Miles	289		Catholic
Population	98 000	Currency	Pa'anga
Capital	Nuku'alofa	Organizations	Comm., UN
Languages	Tongan, English	Map page	49

TRINIDAD AND TOBAGO
Republic of Trinidad and Tobago

Area Sq Km	5 130	Religions	Roman Catholic,
Area Sq Miles	1 981		Hindu, Protestant,
Population	1 283 000		Sunni Muslim
Capital	Port of Spain	Currency	Dollar
Languages	English, creole,	Organizations	CARICOM, Comm.,
	Hindi		UN
		Map page	147

Tristan da Cunha
Dependency of St Helena

Area Sq Km	98	Religions	Protestant, Roman
Area Sq Miles	38		Catholic
Population	300	Currency	Pound sterling
Capital	Settlement of	Map page	113
	Edinburgh		
Languages	English		

TUNISIA
Republic of Tunisia

Area Sq Km	164 150	Religions	Sunni Muslim
Area Sq Miles	63 379	Currency	Dinar
Population	9 335 000	Organizations	UN
Capital	Tunis	Map page	115
Languages	Arabic, French		

TURKEY
Republic of Turkey

Area Sq Km	779 452	Religions	Sunni Muslim, Shi'a
Area Sq Miles	300 948		Muslim
Population	64 479 000	Currency	Lira
Capital	Ankara	Organizations	OECD, UN
Languages	Turkish, Kurdish	Map page	80

TURKMENISTAN
Republic of Turkmenistan

Area Sq Km	488 100	Religions	Sunni Muslim, Russian
Area Sq Miles	188 456		Orthodox
Population	4 309 000	Currency	Manat
Capital	Ashgabat (Ashkhabad)	Organizations	CIS, UN
Languages	Turkmen, Uzbek,	Map page	76
	Russian		

Turks and Caicos Islands
United Kingdom Overseas Territory

Area Sq Km	430	Religions	Protestant
Area Sq Miles	166	Currency	US dollar
Population	16 000	Map page	147
Capital	Grand Turk		
	(Cockburn Town)		
Languages	English		

TUVALU
Monarchy

Area Sq Km	25	Religions	Protestant
Area Sq Miles	10	Currency	Dollar
Population	11 000	Organizations	Comm.
Capital	Vaiaku	Map page	49
Languages	Tuvaluan, English		

UGANDA
Republic of Uganda

Area Sq Km	241 038	Religions	Roman Catholic,
Area Sq Miles	93 065		Protestant, Sunni
Population	20 554 000		Muslim, traditional
Capital	Kampala		beliefs
Languages	English, Swahili,	Currency	Shilling
	Luganda, local	Organizations	Comm., UN
	languages	Map page	119

 **UKRAINE**
Republic of Ukraine

Area Sq Km	603 700	Religions	Ukrainian Orthodox,
Area Sq Miles	233 090		Ukrainian Catholic,
Population	50 861 000		Roman Catholic
Capital	Kiev (Kyiv)	Currency	Hryvnia
Languages	Ukrainian, Russian	Organizations	CIS, UN
		Map page	90-91

 **UNITED ARAB EMIRATES**
Federation of Emirates

Area Sq Km	83 600	Religions	Sunni Muslim, Shi'a
Area Sq Miles	32 278		Muslim
Population	2 377 453	Currency	Dirham
Capital	Abu Dhabi	Organizations	OPEC, UN
	(Abū Ẓabī)	Map page	79
Languages	Arabic, English		

Abu Dhabi (Abū Ẓabī) (Emirate)

Area Sq Km	73 060	Population	928 360
Area Sq Miles	28 209	Capital	Abu Dhabi (Abū Ẓabī)

Ajman (Emirate)

Area Sq Km	260	Population	118 812
Area Sq Miles	100	Capital	Ajman

Dubai (Emirate)

Area Sq Km	3 900	Population	674 101
Area Sq Miles	1 506	Capital	Dubai

Fujairah (Emirate)

Area Sq Km	1 300	Population	76 254
Area Sq Miles	502	Capital	Fujairah

Ras al Khaimah (Emirate)

Area Sq Km	1 700	Population	144 430
Area Sq Miles	656	Capital	Ras al Khaimah

Sharjah (Emirate)

Area Sq Km	2 600	Population	400 339
Area Sq Miles	1 004	Capital	Sharjah

Umm al Qaiwain (Emirate)

Area Sq Km	780	Population	35 157
Area Sq Miles	301	Capital	Umm al Qaiwain

UNITED KINGDOM
of Great Britain and Northern Ireland

Area Sq Km	244 082	Religions	Protestant, Roman
Area Sq Miles	94 241		Catholic, Muslim
Population	58 649 000	Currency	Pound
Capital	London	Organizations	Comm., EU, OECD,
Languages	English, Welsh,		UN
	Gaelic	Map page	94-95

England (Constituent country)

Area Sq Km	130 423	Population	49 284 200
Area Sq Miles	50 357	Capital	London

Northern Ireland (Province)

Area Sq Km	14 121	Population	1 675 000
Area Sq Miles	5 452	Capital	Belfast

Scotland (Constituent country)

Area Sq Km	78 772	Population	5 122 500
Area Sq Miles	30 414	Capital	Edinburgh

Wales (Principality)

Area Sq Km	20 766	Population	2 926 900
Area Sq Miles	8 018	Capital	Cardiff

UNITED STATES OF AMERICA

Area Sq Km	9 809 378	Religions	Protestant, Roman
Area Sq Miles	3 787 422		Catholic, Sunni Muslim,
Population	274 028 000		Jewish
Capital	Washington D.C.	Currency	Dollar
Languages	English, Spanish	Organizations	APEC, OECD, UN
		Map page	132-133

Alabama (State)

Area Sq Km	135 775	Population	4 351 999
Area Sq Miles	52 423	Capital	Montgomery

Alaska (State)

Area Sq Km	1 700 130	Population	614 010
Area Sq Miles	656 424	Capital	Juneau

Arizona (State)

Area Sq Km	295 274	Population	4 668 631
Area Sq Miles	114 006	Capital	Phoenix

Arkansas (State)

Area Sq Km	137 741	Population	2 538 303
Area Sq Miles	53 182	Capital	Little Rock

California (State)

Area Sq Km	423 999	Population	32 666 550
Area Sq Miles	163 707	Capital	Sacramento

Colorado (State)

Area Sq Km	269 618	Population	3 970 971
Area Sq Miles	104 100	Capital	Denver

Connecticut (State)

Area Sq Km	14 359	Population	3 274 069
Area Sq Miles	5 544	Capital	Hartford

Delaware (State)

Area Sq Km 6 446	Population 743 603
Area Sq Miles 2 489	Capital Dover

District of Columbia (District)

Area Sq Km 176	Population 523 124
Area Sq Miles 68	Capital Washington

Florida (State)

Area Sq Km 170 312	Population 14 915 980
Area Sq Miles 65 758	Capital Tallahassee

Georgia (State)

Area Sq Km 153 951	Population 7 642 207
Area Sq Miles 59 441	Capital Atlanta

Hawaii (State)

Area Sq Km 28 314	Population 1 193 001
Area Sq Miles 10 932	Capital Honolulu

Idaho (State)

Area Sq Km 216 456	Population 1 228 684
Area Sq Miles 83 574	Capital Boise

Illinois (State)

Area Sq Km 150 007	Population 13 045 326
Area Sq Miles 57 918	Capital Springfield

Indiana (State)

Area Sq Km 94 327	Population 5 899 195
Area Sq Miles 36 420	Capital Indianapolis

Iowa (State)

Area Sq Km 145 754	Population 2 862 447
Area Sq Miles 56 276	Capital Des Moines

Kansas (State)

Area Sq Km 213 109	Population 2 629 067
Area Sq Miles 82 282	Capital Topeka

Kentucky (State)

Area Sq Km 104 664	Population 3 936 499
Area Sq Miles 40 411	Capital Frankfort

Louisiana (State)

Area Sq Km 134 273	Population 4 368 967
Area Sq Miles 51 843	Capital Baton Rouge

Maine (State)

Area Sq Km 91 652	Population 1 244 250
Area Sq Miles 35 387	Capital Augusta

Maryland (State)

Area Sq Km 32 134	Population 5 134 808
Area Sq Miles 12 407	Capital Annapolis

Massachusetts (State)

Area Sq Km 27 337	Population 6 147 132
Area Sq Miles 10 555	Capital Boston

Michigan (State)

Area Sq Km 250 737	Population 9 817 242
Area Sq Miles 96 810	Capital Lansing

Minnesota (State)

Area Sq Km 225 181	Population 4 725 419
Area Sq Miles 86 943	Capital St Paul

Mississippi (State)

Area Sq Km 125 443	Population 2 752 092
Area Sq Miles 48 434	Capital Jackson

Missouri (State)

Area Sq Km 180 545	Population 5 438 559
Area Sq Miles 69 709	Capital Jefferson City

Montana (State)

Area Sq Km 380 847	Population 880 453
Area Sq Miles 147 046	Capital Helena

Nebraska (State)

Area Sq Km 200 356	Population 1 662 719
Area Sq Miles 77 358	Capital Lincoln

Nevada (State)

Area Sq Km 286 367	Population 1 746 898
Area Sq Miles 110 567	Capital Carson City

New Hampshire (State)

Area Sq Km 24 219	Population 1 185 048
Area Sq Miles 9 351	Capital Concord

New Jersey (State)

Area Sq Km 22 590	Population 8 115 011
Area Sq Miles 8 722	Capital Trenton

New Mexico (State)

Area Sq Km 314 937	Population 1 736 931
Area Sq Miles 121 598	Capital Santa Fe

New York (State)

Area Sq Km 141 090	Population 18 175 301
Area Sq Miles 54 475	Capital Albany

UNITED STATES OF AMERICA

North Carolina (State)
Area Sq Km 139 396	Population 7 546 493
Area Sq Miles 53 821	Capital Raleigh

North Dakota (State)
Area Sq Km 183 123	Population 638 244
Area Sq Miles 70 704	Capital Bismarck

Ohio (State)
Area Sq Km 116 104	Population 11 209 493
Area Sq Miles 44 828	Capital Columbus

Oklahoma (State)
Area Sq Km 181 048	Population 3 346 713
Area Sq Miles 69 903	Capital Oklahoma City

Oregon (State)
Area Sq Km 254 819	Population 3 281 974
Area Sq Miles 98 386	Capital Salem

Pennsylvania (State)
Area Sq Km 119 290	Population 12 001 451
Area Sq Miles 46 058	Capital Harrisburg

Rhode Island (State)
Area Sq Km 4 002	Population 988 480
Area Sq Miles 1 545	Capital Providence

South Carolina (State)
Area Sq Km 82 898	Population 3 835 962
Area Sq Miles 32 007	Capital Columbia

South Dakota (State)
Area Sq Km 199 742	Population 738 171
Area Sq Miles 77 121	Capital Pierre

Tennessee (State)
Area Sq Km 109 158	Population 5 430 621
Area Sq Miles 42 146	Capital Nashville

Texas (State)
Area Sq Km 695 673	Population 19 759 614
Area Sq Miles 268 601	Capital Austin

Utah (State)
Area Sq Km 219 900	Population 2 099 758
Area Sq Miles 84 904	Capital Salt Lake City

Vermont (State)
Area Sq Km 24 903	Population 590 883
Area Sq Miles 9 615	Capital Montpelier

Virginia (State)
Area Sq Km 110 771	Population 6 791 345
Area Sq Miles 42 769	Capital Richmond

Washington (State)
Area Sq Km 184 674	Population 5 689 263
Area Sq Miles 71 303	Capital Olympia

West Virginia (State)
Area Sq Km 62 758	Population 1 811 156
Area Sq Miles 24 231	Capital Charleston

Wisconsin (State)
Area Sq Km 169 652	Population 5 223 500
Area Sq Miles 65 503	Capital Madison

Wyoming (State)
Area Sq Km 253 347	Population 480 907
Area Sq Miles 97 818	Capital Cheyenne

URUGUAY
Oriental Republic of Uruguay
Area Sq Km 176 215	Religions Roman Catholic,
Area Sq Miles 68 037	Protestant, Jewish
Population 3 289 000	Currency Peso
Capital Montevideo	Organizations UN
Languages Spanish	Map page 153

UZBEKISTAN
Republic of Uzbekistan
Area Sq Km 447 400	Religions Sunni Muslim, Russian
Area Sq Miles 172 742	Orthodox
Population 23 574 000	Currency Sum
Capital Tashkent	Organizations CIS, UN
Languages Uzbek, Russian,	Map page 76-77
Tajik, Kazakh	

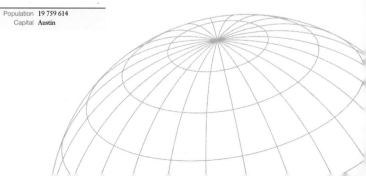

VANUATU
Republic of Vanuatu

Area Sq Km	12 190	Religions	Protestant, Roman
Area Sq Miles	4 707		Catholic, traditional
Population	182 000		beliefs
Capital	Port Vila	Currency	Vatu
Languages	English, Bislama	Organizations	Comm., UN
	(creole),French	Map page	48

Wallis and Futuna Islands
French Overseas Territory

Area Sq Km	274	Religions	Roman Catholic
Area Sq Miles	106	Currency	Pacific franc
Population	14 000	Map page	49
Capital	Matā'utu		
Languages	French, Wallisian,		
	Futunian		

VATICAN CITY
Vatican City State

Area Sq Km	0.5	Religions	Roman Catholic
Area Sq Miles	0.2	Currency	Italian lira
Population	480	Map page	108
Capital	Vatican City		
Languages	Italian		

West Bank
Territory occupied by Israel

Area Sq Km	5 860	Religions	Sunni Muslim, Jewish,
Area Sq Miles	2 263		Shi'a Muslim, Christian
Capital	none	Map page	80
Languages	Arabic, Hebrew		

VENEZUELA
Republic of Venezuela

Area Sq Km	912 050	Religions	Roman Catholic,
Area Sq Miles	352 144		Protestant
Population	23 242 000	Currency	Bolívar
Capital	Caracas	Organizations	OPEC, UN
Languages	Spanish, Amerindian	Map page	150
	languages		

Western Sahara
Disputed territory (Morocco)

Area Sq Km	266 000	Religions	Sunni Muslim
Area Sq Miles	102 703	Currency	Moroccan dirham
Population	275 000	Map page	114
Capital	Laâyoune		
Languages	Arabic		

VIETNAM
Socialist Republic of Vietnam

Area Sq Km	329 565	Religions	Buddhist, Taoist,
Area Sq Miles	127 246		Roman Catholic,
Population	77 562 000		Cao Dai, Hoa Hoa
Capital	Ha Nôi (Hanoi)	Currency	Dong
Languages	Vietnamese, Thai,	Organizations	APEC, ASEAN, UN
	Khmer, Chinese,	Map page	62-63
	local languages		

YEMEN
Republic of Yemen

Area Sq Km	527 968	Religions	Sunni Muslim, Shi'a
Area Sq Miles	203 850		Muslim
Population	16 887 000	Currency	Rial
Capital	San'a'	Organizations	UN
Languages	Arabic	Map page	78-79

Virgin Islands (U.K.)
United Kingdom Overseas Territory

Area Sq Km	153	Religions	Protestant, Roman
Area Sq Miles	59		Catholic
Population	20 000	Currency	US dollar
Capital	Road Town	Map page	147
Languages	English		

YUGOSLAVIA
Federal Republic of Yugoslavia

Area Sq Km	102 173	Religions	Serbian Orthodox,
Area Sq Miles	39 449		Montenegrin Orthodox,
Population	10 635 000		Sunni Muslim
Capital	Belgrade (Beograd)	Currency	Dinar
Languages	Serbian, Albanian,	Organizations	UN
	Hungarian	Map page	109

Virgin Islands (U.S.)
United States Unincorporated Territory

Area Sq Km	352	Religions	Protestant,
Area Sq Miles	136		Roman Catholic
Population	94 000	Currency	US dollar
Capital	Charlotte Amalie	Map page	147
Languages	English, Spanish		

ZAMBIA
Republic of Zambia

Area Sq Km	752 614	Religions	Christian, traditional
Area Sq Miles	290 586		beliefs
Population	8 781 000	Currency	Kwacha
Capital	Lusaka	Organizations	Comm., SADC, UN
Languages	English, Bemba,	Map page	120-121
	Nyanja, Tonga, local		
	languages		

ZIMBABWE
Republic of Zimbabwe

Area Sq Km	390 759	Religions	Christian, traditional
Area Sq Miles	150 873		beliefs
Population	11 377 000	Currency	Dollar
Capital	Harare	Organizations	Comm., SADC, UN
Languages	English, Shona,	Map page	121
	Ndebele		

CITIES

THE WORLD'S LARGEST CITIES

Figures are for the urban agglomeration, defined as the population contained within the contours of a contiguous territory inhabited at urban levels without regard to administrative boundaries. They incorporate the population within a city plus the suburban fringe lying outside of, but adjacent to, the city boundaries.

City	Population	Continent
Tōkyō Japan	28 025 000	Asia
México Mexico	18 131 000	North America
Mumbai India	18 042 000	Asia
São Paulo Brazil	17 711 000	South America
New York USA	16 626 000	North America
Shanghai China	14 173 000	Asia
Lagos Nigeria	13 488 000	Africa
Los Angeles USA	13 129 000	North America
Calcutta India	12 900 000	Asia
Buenos Aires Argentina	12 431 000	South America
Seoul South Korea	12 215 000	Asia
Beijing China	12 033 000	Asia
Karachi Pakistan	11 774 000	Asia
Delhi India	11 680 000	Asia
Dhaka Bangladesh	10 979 000	Asia
Manila Philippines	10 818 000	Asia
Cairo Egypt	10 772 000	Africa
Ōsaka Japan	10 609 000	Asia
Rio de Janeiro Brazil	10 556 000	South America
Tianjin China	10 239 000	Asia
Jakarta Indonesia	9 815 000	Asia
Paris France	9 638 000	Europe
İstanbul Turkey	9 413 000	Asia
Moscow Russian Federation	9 299 000	Europe
London United Kingdom	7 640 000	Europe
Lima Peru	7 443 000	South America
Tehrān Iran	7 380 000	Asia
Bangkok Thailand	7 221 000	Asia
Chicago USA	6 945 000	North America
Bogotá Colombia	6 834 000	South America
Hyderabad India	6 833 000	Asia
Chennai India	6 639 000	Asia
Essen Germany	6 559 000	Europe
Hangzhou China	6 389 000	Asia
Hong Kong China	6 097 000	Asia
Lahore Pakistan	6 030 000	Asia
Shenyang China	5 681 000	Asia
Changchun China	5 566 000	Asia
Bangalore India	5 544 000	Asia
Harbin China	5 475 000	Asia
Chengdu China	5 293 000	Asia
Santiago Chile	5 261 000	South America
Guangzhou China	5 162 000	Asia
St Petersburg Russian Federation	5 132 000	Europe
Kinshasa Dem. Rep. Congo	5 068 000	Africa
Baghdād Iraq	4 796 000	Asia
Jinan China	4 789 000	Asia
Wuhan China	4 750 000	Asia
Toronto Canada	4 657 000	North America
Yangôn Myanmar	4 458 000	Asia
Algiers Algeria	4 447 000	Africa
Philadelphia USA	4 398 000	North America
Qingdao China	4 376 000	Asia
Milan Italy	4 251 000	Europe
Pusan South Korea	4 239 000	Asia
Belo Horizonte Brazil	4 160 000	South America
Ahmadabad India	4 154 000	Asia
Madrid Spain	4 072 000	Europe
San Francisco USA	4 051 000	North America
Alexandria Egypt	3 995 000	Africa
Washington D.C. USA	3 927 000	North America
Dallas USA	3 912 000	North America
Guadalajara Mexico	3 908 000	North America
Chongqing China	3 896 000	Asia
Medellín Colombia	3 831 000	South America
Detroit USA	3 785 000	North America
Handan China	3 763 000	Asia
Frankfurt Germany	3 700 000	Europe
Porto Alegre Brazil	3 699 000	South America
Ha Nôi Vietnam	3 678 000	Asia
Sydney Australia	3 665 000	Oceania
Santo Domingo Dominican Republic	3 601 000	North America
Singapore Singapore	3 587 000	Asia
Casablanca Morocco	3 535 000	Africa
Katowice Poland	3 488 000	Europe
Pune India	3 485 000	Asia
Bandung Indonesia	3 420 000	Asia
Monterrey Mexico	3 416 000	North America
Montréal Canada	3 401 000	North America
Nagoya Japan	3 377 000	Asia
Nanjing China	3 375 000	Asia
Houston USA	3 365 000	North America
Abidjan Côte d'Ivoire	3 359 000	Africa
Xi'an China	3 352 000	Asia
Berlin Germany	3 337 000	Europe
Riyadh Saudi Arabia	3 328 000	Asia
Recife Brazil	3 307 000	South America
Düsseldorf Germany	3 251 000	Europe
Ankara Turkey	3 190 000	Asia
Melbourne Australia	3 188 000	Oceania
Salvador Brazil	3 180 000	South America
Dalian China	3 153 000	Asia
Caracas Venezuela	3 153 000	South America
Addis Ababa Ethiopia	3 112 000	Africa
Athens Greece	3 103 000	Europe
Cape Town South Africa	3 092 000	Africa
Cologne Germany	3 067 000	Europe
Maputo Mozambique	3 017 000	Africa
Naples Italy	3 012 000	Europe
Fortaleza Brazil	3 007 000	South America
San Diego USA	2 983 000	North America
Boston USA	2 915 000	North America
Chittagong Bangladesh	2 906 000	Asia
Kita-Kyūshū Japan	2 898 000	Asia
Kiev Ukraine	2 897 000	Europe
T'aipei Taiwan	2 880 000	Asia
Inch'ŏn South Korea	2 837 000	Asia
Barcelona Spain	2 819 000	Europe
Khartoum Sudan	2 748 000	Africa
P'yŏngyang North Korea	2 726 000	Asia
Kābul Afghanistan	2 716 000	Asia
Guatemala Guatemala	2 697 000	North America
Atlanta USA	2 689 000	North America
Stuttgart Germany	2 688 000	Europe
Rome Italy	2 688 000	Europe
Hamburg Germany	2 680 000	Europe
Luanda Angola	2 665 000	Africa
Eşfahān Iran	2 644 000	Asia
Phoenix USA	2 607 000	North America
Lucknow India	2 565 000	Asia
Taegu South Korea	2 559 000	Asia
Curitiba Brazil	2 519 000	South America
Surabaya Indonesia	2 507 000	Asia
Tashkent Uzbekistan	2 495 000	Asia
Kanpur India	2 447 000	Asia
Johannesburg South Africa	2 412 000	Africa
İzmir Turkey	2 399 000	Asia
Mashhad Iran	2 378 000	Asia
Arbīl Iraq	2 368 000	Asia
Minneapolis USA	2 363 000	North America
Surat India	2 341 000	Asia
Damascus Syria	2 335 000	Asia
Nairobi Kenya	2 320 000	Africa
Munich Germany	2 306 000	Europe
Havana Cuba	2 302 000	North America
Taiyuan China	2 280 000	Asia
Zhengzhou China	2 275 000	Asia
Birmingham United Kingdom	2 271 000	Europe
Warsaw Poland	2 269 000	Europe
Manchester United Kingdom	2 252 000	Europe
Guiyang China	2 230 000	Asia
Faisalabad Pakistan	2 228 000	Asia
Miami USA	2 210 000	North America
Aleppo Syria	2 173 000	Asia
Tel Aviv-Yafo Israel	2 170 000	Asia
Jaipur India	2 143 000	Asia
Bucharest Romania	2 130 000	Europe
Guayaquil Ecuador	2 127 000	South America
Peshawar Pakistan	2 094 000	Asia
Seattle USA	2 084 000	North America
Cali Colombia	2 082 000	South America
Dakar Senegal	2 077 000	Africa
Vienna Austria	2 072 000	Europe
St Louis USA	2 071 000	North America
Nagpur India	2 060 000	Asia
Beirut Lebanon	2 058 000	Asia
Dar es Salaam Tanzania	2 051 000	Africa
Tampa USA	2 051 000	North America
Gujranwala Pakistan	2 048 000	Asia
Tripoli Libya	2 041 000	Africa
Baltimore USA	2 040 000	North America
Lanzhou China	2 021 000	Asia
Budapest Hungary	2 017 000	Europe
Accra Ghana	2 010 000	Africa

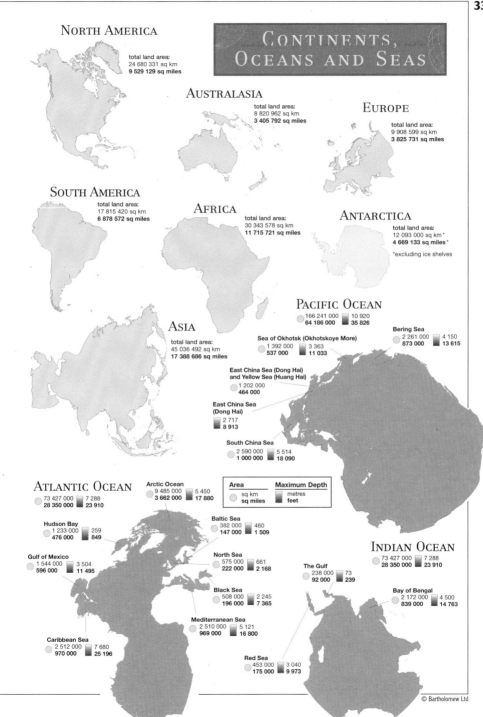

NORTH AMERICA

total land area:
24 680 331 sq km
9 529 129 sq miles

CONTINENTS, OCEANS AND SEAS

AUSTRALASIA

total land area:
8 820 962 sq km
3 405 792 sq miles

EUROPE

total land area:
9 908 599 sq km
3 825 731 sq miles

SOUTH AMERICA

total land area:
17 815 420 sq km
6 878 572 sq miles

AFRICA

total land area:
30 343 578 sq km
11 715 721 sq miles

ANTARCTICA

total land area:
12 093 000 sq km *
4 669 133 sq miles *

*excluding ice shelves

PACIFIC OCEAN

166 241 000 | 10 920
64 186 000 | **35 826**

ASIA

total land area:
45 036 492 sq km
17 388 686 sq miles

Sea of Okhotsk (Okhotskoye More)
1 392 000 | 3 363
537 000 | **11 033**

Bering Sea
2 261 000 | 4 150
873 000 | **13 615**

**East China Sea (Dong Hai)
and Yellow Sea (Huang Hai)**
1 202 000
464 000

**East China Sea
(Dong Hai)**
2 717
8 913

South China Sea
2 590 000 | 5 514
1 000 000 | **18 090**

ATLANTIC OCEAN

73 427 000 | 7 288
28 350 000 | **23 910**

Arctic Ocean
9 485 000 | 5 450
3 662 000 | **17 880**

Area	Maximum Depth
sq km	metres
sq miles	**feet**

Hudson Bay
1 233 000 | 259
476 000 | **849**

Baltic Sea
382 000 | 460
147 000 | **1 509**

INDIAN OCEAN

73 427 000 | 7 288
28 350 000 | **23 910**

Gulf of Mexico
1 544 000 | 3 504
596 000 | **11 495**

North Sea
575 000 | 661
222 000 | **2 168**

The Gulf
238 000 | 73
92 000 | **239**

Black Sea
508 000 | 2 245
196 000 | **7 365**

Bay of Bengal
2 172 000 | 4 500
839 000 | **14 763**

Mediterranean Sea
2 510 000 | 5 121
969 000 | **16 800**

Caribbean Sea
2 512 000 | 7 680
970 000 | **25 196**

Red Sea
453 000 | 3 040
175 000 | **9 973**

© Bartholomew Ltd

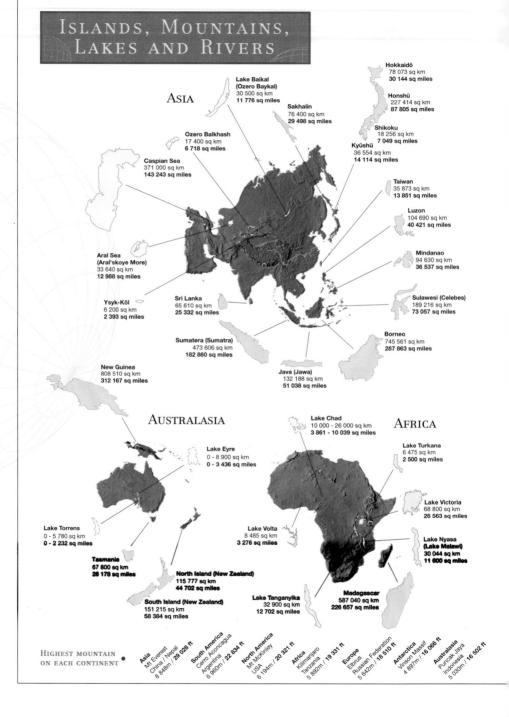

ISLANDS, MOUNTAINS, LAKES AND RIVERS

ASIA

Lake Baikal (Ozero Baykal)
30 500 sq km
11 776 sq miles

Sakhalin
76 400 sq km
29 498 sq miles

Hokkaidō
78 073 sq km
30 144 sq miles

Honshū
227 414 sq km
87 805 sq miles

Shikoku
18 256 sq km
7 049 sq miles

Kyūshū
36 554 sq km
14 114 sq miles

Ozero Balkhash
17 400 sq km
6 718 sq miles

Caspian Sea
371 000 sq km
143 243 sq miles

Taiwan
35 873 sq km
13 851 sq miles

Luzon
104 690 sq km
40 421 sq miles

Mindanao
94 630 sq km
36 537 sq miles

Aral Sea (Aral'skoye More)
33 640 sq km
12 988 sq miles

Ysyk-Köl
6 200 sq km
2 393 sq miles

Sri Lanka
65 610 sq km
25 332 sq miles

Sulawesi (Celebes)
189 216 sq km
73 057 sq miles

Sumatera (Sumatra)
473 606 sq km
182 860 sq miles

Borneo
745 561 sq km
287 863 sq miles

New Guinea
808 510 sq km
312 167 sq miles

Java (Jawa)
132 188 sq km
51 038 sq miles

AUSTRALASIA

Lake Chad
10 000 - 26 000 sq km
3 861 - 10 039 sq miles

AFRICA

Lake Eyre
0 - 8 900 sq km
0 - 3 436 sq miles

Lake Turkana
6 475 sq km
2 500 sq miles

Lake Victoria
68 800 sq km
26 563 sq miles

Lake Torrens
0 - 5 780 sq km
0 - 2 232 sq miles

Lake Volta
8 485 sq km
3 276 sq miles

Lake Nyasa (Lake Malawi)
30 044 sq km
11 600 sq miles

Tasmania
67 800 sq km
26 178 sq miles

North Island (New Zealand)
115 777 sq km
44 702 sq miles

South Island (New Zealand)
151 215 sq km
58 384 sq miles

Lake Tanganyika
32 900 sq km
12 702 sq miles

Madagascar
587 040 sq km
226 657 sq miles

HIGHEST MOUNTAIN ON EACH CONTINENT ●

Asia
Mt Everest
China / Nepal
8 848m / **29 028 ft**

South America
Cerro Aconcagua
Argentina
6 960m / **22 834 ft**

North America
Mt McKinley
USA
6 194m / **20 321 ft**

Africa
Kilimanjaro
Tanzania
5 892m / **19 331 ft**

Europe
Elbrus
Russian Federation
5 642m / **18 510 ft**

Antarctica
Vinson Massif
4 897m / **16 066 ft**

Australasia
Puncak Jaya
Indonesia
5 030m / **16 502 ft**

EUROPE

Vänern
6 686 sq km
2 156 sq miles

Iceland
102 820 sq km
39 699 sq miles

Spitsbergen
37 814 sq km
14 600 sq miles

Great Britain
218 476 sq km
84 354 sq miles

Novaya Zemlya
90 650 sq km
35 000 sq miles

Lake Onega
(Onezhskoye Ozero)
9 600 sq km
3 706 sq miles

Ireland
83 045 sq km
32 064 sq miles

Rybinskoye
Vodokhranilishche
5 180 sq km
2 000 sq miles

Sardinia
(Sardegna)
24 090 sq km
9 301 sq miles

Sicily
(Sicilia)
25 426 sq km
9 817 sq miles

Lake Ladoga
(Ladozhskoye Ozero)
18 390 sq km
7 100 sq miles

SOUTH AMERICA

Lago Titicaca
8 340 sq km
3 220 sq miles

Isla de Chiloé
8 394 sq km
3 240 sq miles

West Falkland
5 413 sq km
2 090 sq miles

East Falkland
6 760 sq km
2 610 sq miles

Isla Grande de
Tierra del Fuego
47 000 sq km
18 147 sq miles

ANTARCTICA

NORTH AMERICA

Greenland
2 175 600 sq km
840 004 sq miles

Ellesmere Island
196 236 sq km
75 767 sq miles

Victoria Island
217 291 sq km
83 897 sq miles

Great Bear Lake
31 328 sq km
12 095 sq miles

Great Slave Lake
28 568 sq km
11 030 sq miles

Baffin Island
507 451 sq km
195 927 sq miles

Lake Winnipeg
24 387 sq km
9 415 sq miles

Newfoundland
108 860 sq km
42 031 sq miles

Lake Superior
82 100 sq km
31 698 sq miles

Lake Huron
59 600 sq km
23 011 sq miles

Lake Ontario
18 960 sq km
7 320 sq miles

Hispaniola
76 192 sq km
29 418 sq miles

Lake Michigan
57 800 sq km
22 316 sq miles

Lake Erie
25 700 sq km
9 922 sq miles

Cuba
110 860 sq km
42 803 sq miles

HIGHEST MOUNTAINS IN THE WORLD

Mt Everest China/Nepal	Asia	8 848m / 29 028ft
K2 China/Jammu and Kashmir	Asia	8 611m / 28 251ft
Kangchenjunga India/Nepal	Asia	8 586m / 28 169ft
Lhotse China/Nepal	Asia	8 516m / 27 939ft
Makalu China/Nepal	Asia	8 463m / 27 765ft
Cho Oyu China/Nepal	Asia	8 201m / 26 906ft
Dhaulagiri Nepal	Asia	8 167m / 26 794ft
Manaslu Nepal	Asia	8 163m / 26 781ft
Nanga Parbat Jammu and Kashmir	Asia	8 126m / 26 660ft
Annapurna I Nepal	Asia	8 091m / 26 545ft
Gasherbrum I China/Jammu and Kashmir	Asia	8 068m / 26 469ft
Broad Peak China/Jammu and Kashmir	Asia	8 047m / 26 401ft
Gasherbrum II China/Jammu and Kashmir	Asia	8 035m / 26 361ft
Xixabangma Feng China	Asia	8 012m / 26 286ft
Annapurna II Nepal	Asia	7 937m / 26 040ft
Nuptse Nepal	Asia	7 885m / 25 869ft
Himalchul Nepal	Asia	7 864m / 25 800ft
Masherbrum Jammu and Kashmir	Asia	7 821m / 25 659ft
Nanda Devi India	Asia	7 816m / 25 643ft
Rakaposhi Jammu and Kashmir	Asia	7 788m / 25 551ft
Namjagbarwa Feng China	Asia	7 756m / 25 446ft
Kamet China	Asia	7 756m / 25 446ft

LONGEST RIVERS IN THE WORLD

Nile	Africa	6 695 km / 4 160 mls
Amazon (Amazonas)	South America	6 516 km / 4 049 mls
Yangtze (Chang Jiang)	Asia	6 380 km / 3 964 mls
Mississippi-Missouri	North America	5 969 km / 3 709 mls
Ob'-Irtysh	Asia	5 568 km / 3 459 mls
Yenisey-Angara-Selenga	Asia	5 550 km / 3 448 mls
Huang He (Yellow River)	Asia	5 464 km / 3 395 mls
Congo	Africa	4 667 km / 2 900 mls
Río de la Plata-Paraná	South America	4 500 km / 2 796 mls
Irtysh	Asia	4 440 km / 2 759 mls
Mekong	Asia	4 425 km / 2 749 mls
Heilong Jiang (Amur-Argun'	Asia	4 416 km / 2 744 mls
Lena-Kirenga	Asia	4 400 km / 2 734 mls
Mackenzie-Peace-Finlay	North America	4 241 km / 2 635 mls
Niger	Africa	4 184 km / 2 599 mls
Yenisey	Asia	4 090 km / 2 541 mls
Missouri	North America	4 086 km / 2 539 mls
Mississippi	North America	3 765 km / 2 339 mls
Murray-Darling	Australasia	3 750 km / 2 330 mls
Ob'	Asia	3 701 km / 2 300 mls
Volga	Europe	3 688 km / 2 291 mls
Purus	South America	3 218 km / 2 000 mls

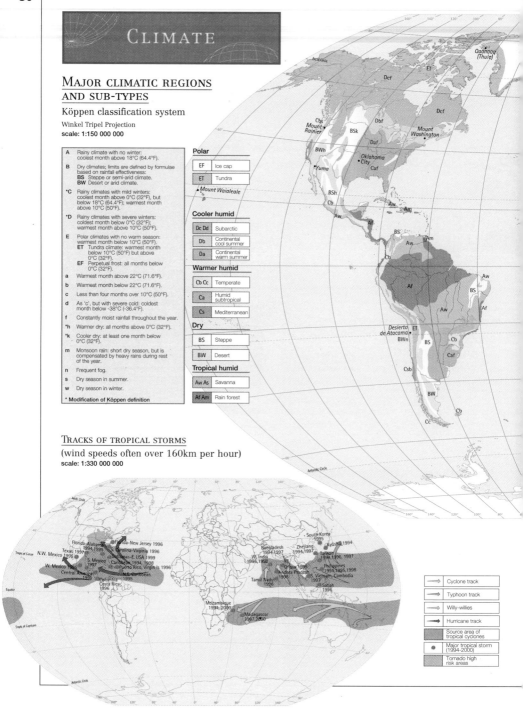

CLIMATE

MAJOR CLIMATIC REGIONS AND SUB-TYPES

Köppen classification system

Winkel Tripel Projection
scale: 1:150 000 000

A Rainy climate with no winter: coolest month above 18°C (64.4°F).

B Dry climates; limits are defined by formulae based on rainfall effectiveness:
BS Steppe or semi-arid climate.
BW Desert or arid climate.

°C Rainy climates with mild winters: coolest month above 0°C (32°F), but below 18°C (64.4°F); warmest month above 10°C (50°F).

°D Rainy climates with severe winters: coldest month below 0°C (32°F); warmest month above 10°C (50°F).

E Polar climates with no warm season: warmest month below 10°C (50°F).
ET Tundra climate: warmest month below 10°C (50°F) but above 0°C (32°F).
EF Perpetual frost: all months below 0°C (32°F).

a Warmest month above 22°C (71.6°F).

b Warmest month below 22°C (71.6°F).

c Less than four months over 10°C (50°F).

d As 'c', but with severe cold: coldest month below -38°C (-36.4°F).

f Constantly moist rainfall throughout the year.

°h Warmer dry: all months above 0°C (32°F).

°k Cooler dry: at least one month below 0°C (32°F).

m Monsoon rain: short dry season, but is compensated by heavy rains during rest of the year.

n Frequent fog.

s Dry season in summer.

w Dry season in winter.

* Modification of Köppen definition

Polar

| EF | Ice cap |
| ET | Tundra |

Cooler humid

Dc Dd	Subarctic
Db	Continental cool summer
Da	Continental warm summer

Warmer humid

Cb Cc	Temperate
Ca	Humid subtropical
Cs	Mediterranean

Dry

| BS | Steppe |
| BW | Desert |

Tropical humid

| Aw As | Savanna |
| Af Am | Rain forest |

TRACKS OF TROPICAL STORMS

(wind speeds often over 160km per hour)
scale: 1:330 000 000

	Cyclone track
	Typhoon track
	Willy-willies
	Hurricane track
	Source area of tropical cyclones
•	Major tropical storm (1994-2000)
	Tornado high risk areas

WORLD WEATHER EXTREMES

Highest shade temperature	57.8°C/136°F Al 'Azīzīyah, Libya (13th September 1922)
Hottest place — Annual mean	34.4°C/93.9°F Dalol, Ethiopia
Driest place — Annual mean	0.1 mm/0.004 inches Desierto de Atacama, Chile
Most sunshine — Annual mean	90% Yuma, Arizona, USA (over 4 000 hours)
Least sunshine	Nil for 182 days each year, South Pole
Lowest screen temperature	-89.2°C/-128.6°F Vostok Station, Antarctica (21st July 1983)
Coldest place — Annual mean	-56.6°C/-69.9°F Plateau Station, Antarctica
Wettest place — Annual mean	11 873 mm/467.4 inches Meghalaya, India
Most rainy days	Up to 350 per year Mount Waialeale, Hawaii, USA
Windiest place	322 km per hour/200 miles per hour in gales, Commonwealth Bay, Antarctica

Highest surface wind speed		
	High altitude	372 km per hour/231 miles per hour Mount Washington, New Hampshire, USA, (12th April 1934)
	Low altitude	333 km per hour/207 miles per hour Qaanaaq (Thule), Greenland (8th March 1972)
	Tornado	512 km per hour/318 miles per hour Oklahoma City, Oklahoma, USA (3rd May 1999)
Greatest snowfall		31 102 mm/1 224.5 inches Mount Rainier, Washington, USA (19th February 1971 — 18th February 1972)
Heaviest hailstones		1 kg/2.21 lb Gopalganj, Bangladesh (14th April 1986)
Thunder-days Average		251 days per year Tororo, Uganda
Highest barometric pressure		1 083.8 mb Agata, Siberia, Rus. Fed. (31st December 1968)
Lowest barometric pressure		870 mb 483 km/300 miles west of Guam, Pacific Ocean (12th October 1979)

LAND COVER

WORLD LAND COVER

Goode Interrupted Homolosine Projection
scale: 1: 125 000 000
DISCover map courtesy of IGBP, JRC and USGS

	1. Evergreen needleleaf forest
	2. Evergreen broadleaf forest
	3. Deciduous needleleaf forest
	4. Deciduous broadleaf forest
	5. Mixed forest
	6. Closed shrublands
	7. Open shrublands
	8. Woody savannas
	9. Savannas
	10. Grasslands
	11. Permanent wetlands
	12. Croplands
	13. Urban and built-up
	14. Cropland/Natural vegetation mosaic
	15. Snow and Ice
	16. Barren or sparsely vegetated
	17. Water bodies

CONTINENTAL LAND COVER COMPOSITION

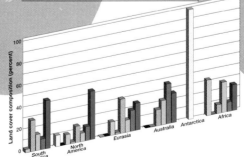

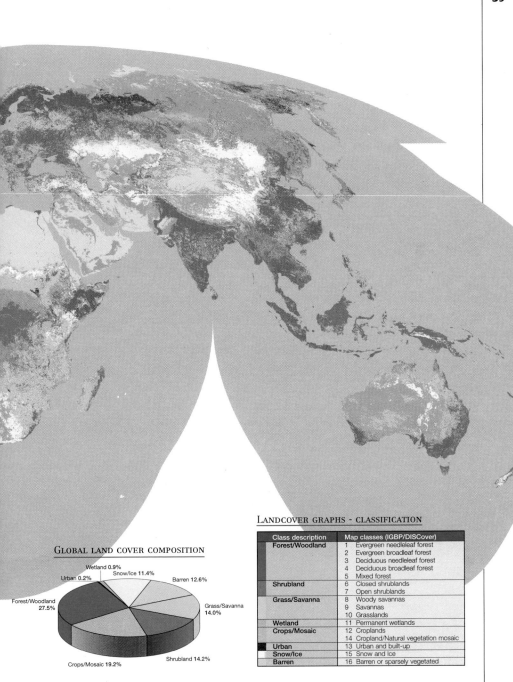

GLOBAL LAND COVER COMPOSITION

- Wetland 0.9%
- Urban 0.2%
- Snow/Ice 11.4%
- Barren 12.6%
- Grass/Savanna 14.0%
- Shrubland 14.2%
- Crops/Mosaic 19.2%
- Forest/Woodland 27.5%

LANDCOVER GRAPHS - CLASSIFICATION

Class description	Map classes (IGBP/DISCover)	
Forest/Woodland	1	Evergreen needleleaf forest
	2	Evergreen broadleaf forest
	3	Deciduous needleleaf forest
	4	Deciduous broadleaf forest
	5	Mixed forest
Shrubland	6	Closed shrublands
	7	Open shrublands
Grass/Savanna	8	Woody savannas
	9	Savannas
	10	Grasslands
Wetland	11	Permanent wetlands
Crops/Mosaic	12	Croplands
	14	Cropland/Natural vegetation mosaic
Urban	13	Urban and built-up
Snow/Ice	15	Snow and Ice
Barren	16	Barren or sparsely vegetated

POPULATION

WORLD POPULATION DISTRIBUTION AND THE WORLD'S MAJOR CITIES

Winkel Tripel Projection
scale : 1:145 000 000

POPULATION DENSITY

per sq mile
500 100 25 5 0

Inhabitants   Uninhabited

200 40 10 2 0
per sq km

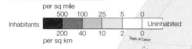

URBAN AGGLOMERATIONS WITH OVER 5 MILLION INHABITANTS

- 5 million - 10 million
- 10 million - 20 million
- over 20 million

TOP TEN COUNTRIES BY POPULATION AND POPULATION DENSITY 1998

TOTAL POPULATION 1998	COUNTRY	RANK	COUNTRY	POPULATION DENSITY 1998 (countries with populations over 10 million)	
				per sq mile	per sq km
1 262 817 000	China	1	Bangladesh	2 244	866
982 223 000	India	2	Taiwan	1 568	606
274 028 000	USA	3	South Korea	1 203	465
206 338 000	Indonesia	4	Netherlands	978	378
165 851 000	Brazil	5	Japan	866	334
148 166 000	Pakistan	6	Belgium	861	332
147 434 000	Russian Federation	7	India	830	320
126 281 000	Japan	8	Sri Lanka	729	281
124 774 000	Bangladesh	9	Philippines	630	243
106 409 000	Nigeria	10	UK	622	240

KEY POPULATION STATISTICS FOR MAJOR REGIONS

	Population 1998 (millions)	Growth (per cent)	Infant mortality rate	Total fertility rate (years)	Life expectancy
World	5 901	1.33	57	2.7	65
More developed regions	1 182	0.28	9	1.6	75
Less developed regions	4 719	1.59	63	3.0	63
Africa	749	2.37	87	5.1	51
Asia	3 585	1.38	57	2.6	66
Europe	729	0.03	12	1.4	73
Latin America and the Caribbean	504	1.57	36	2.7	69
North America	305	0.85	7	1.9	77
Oceania	30	1.30	24	2.4	74

Except for population (1998), the data are annual averages projected for the period 1995-2000. Regional and continental areas follow United Nations definitions.

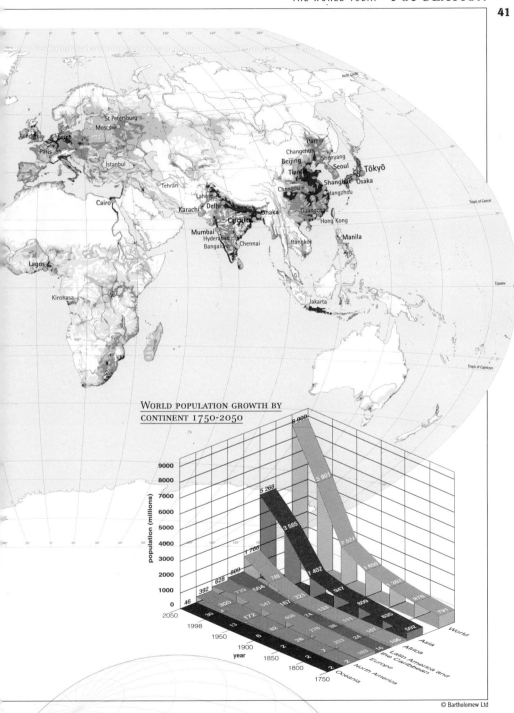

WORLD POPULATION GROWTH BY
CONTINENT 1750-2050

© Bartholomew Ltd

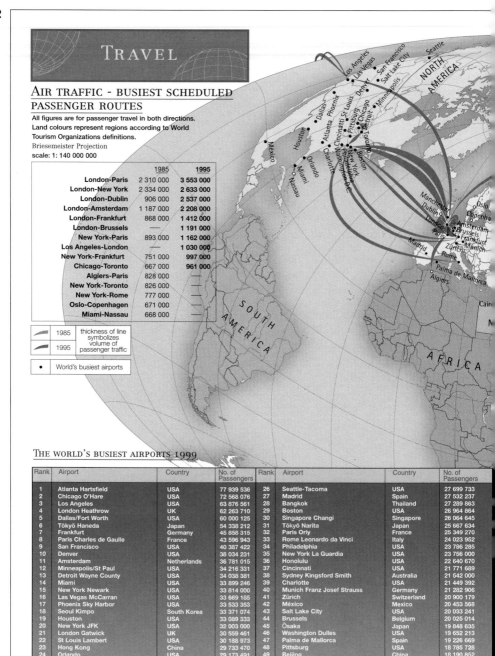

TRAVEL

AIR TRAFFIC - BUSIEST SCHEDULED PASSENGER ROUTES

All figures are for passenger travel in both directions.
Land colours represent regions according to World
Tourism Organizations definitions.
Briesemeister Projection
scale: 1: 140 000 000

	1985	1995
London-Paris	2 310 000	3 553 000
London-New York	2 334 000	2 633 000
London-Dublin	906 000	2 537 000
London-Amsterdam	1 187 000	2 208 000
London-Frankfurt	868 000	1 412 000
London-Brussels	—	1 191 000
New York-Paris	893 000	1 162 000
Los Angeles-London	—	1 030 000
New York-Frankfurt	751 000	997 000
Chicago-Toronto	667 000	961 000
Algiers-Paris	828 000	—
New York-Toronto	826 000	—
New York-Rome	777 000	—
Oslo-Copenhagen	671 000	—
Miami-Nassau	668 000	—

1985	thickness of line symbolizes volume of passenger traffic
1995	

• World's busiest airports

THE WORLD'S BUSIEST AIRPORTS 1999

Rank	Airport	Country	No. of Passengers	Rank	Airport	Country	No. of Passengers
1	Atlanta Hartsfield	USA	77 939 536	26	Seattle-Tacoma	USA	27 699 733
2	Chicago O'Hare	USA	72 568 076	27	Madrid	Spain	27 532 237
3	Los Angeles	USA	63 876 561	28	Bangkok	Thailand	27 289 863
4	London Heathrow	UK	62 263 710	29	Boston	USA	26 964 864
5	Dallas/Fort Worth	USA	60 000 125	30	Singapore Changi	Singapore	26 064 645
6	Tōkyō Haneda	Japan	54 338 212	31	Tōkyō Narita	Japan	25 667 634
7	Frankfurt	Germany	45 858 315	32	Paris Orly	France	25 349 270
8	Paris Charles de Gaulle	France	43 596 943	33	Rome Leonardo da Vinci	Italy	24 023 952
9	San Francisco	USA	40 387 422	34	Philadelphia	USA	23 786 285
10	Denver	USA	38 034 231	35	New York La Guardia	USA	23 756 000
11	Amsterdam	Netherlands	36 781 015	36	Honolulu	USA	22 640 670
12	Minneapolis/St Paul	USA	34 216 331	37	Cincinnati	USA	21 771 689
13	Detroit Wayne County	USA	34 038 381	38	Sydney Kingsford Smith	Australia	21 542 000
14	Miami	USA	33 899 246	39	Charlotte	USA	21 449 392
15	New York Newark	USA	33 814 000	40	Munich Franz Josef Strauss	Germany	21 282 906
16	Las Vegas McCarran	USA	33 669 185	41	Zürich	Switzerland	20 900 179
17	Phoenix Sky Harbor	USA	33 533 353	42	México	Mexico	20 453 568
18	Seoul Kimpo	South Korea	33 371 074	43	Salt Lake City	USA	20 033 241
19	Houston	USA	33 089 333	44	Brussels	Belgium	20 025 014
20	New York JFK	USA	32 003 000	45	Ōsaka	Japan	19 848 635
21	London Gatwick	UK	30 559 461	46	Washington Dulles	USA	19 652 213
22	St Louis Lambert	USA	30 188 973	47	Palma de Mallorca	Spain	19 226 669
23	Hong Kong	China	29 733 470	48	Pittsburg	USA	18 785 728
24	Orlando	USA	29 173 491	49	Beijing	China	18 190 652
25	Toronto Lester B. Pearson	Canada	27 771 473	50	Manchester	UK	17 760 065

For airport locations see map

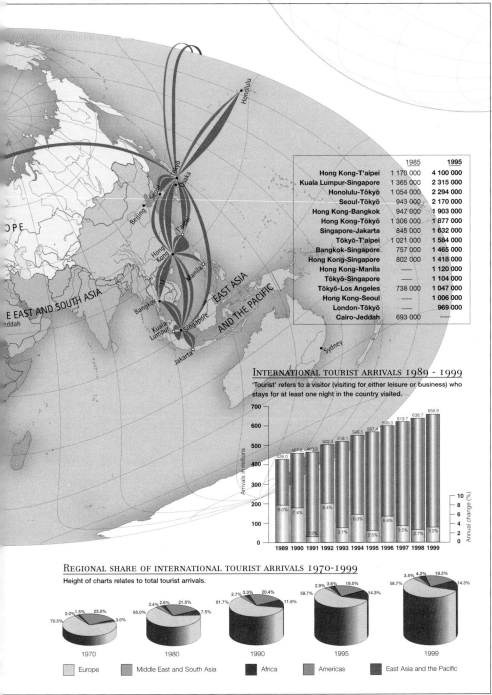

	1985	1995
Hong Kong-T'aipei	1 170 000	4 100 000
Kuala Lumpur-Singapore	1 365 000	2 315 000
Honolulu-Tōkyō	1 054 000	2 294 000
Seoul-Tōkyō	943 000	2 170 000
Hong Kong-Bangkok	947 000	1 903 000
Hong Kong-Tōkyō	1 306 000	1 877 000
Singapore-Jakarta	845 000	1 632 000
Tōkyō-T'aipei	1 021 000	1 584 000
Bangkok-Singapore	757 000	1 465 000
Hong Kong-Singapore	802 000	1 418 000
Hong Kong-Manila	—	1 120 000
Tōkyō-Singapore	—	1 104 000
Tōkyō-Los Angeles	738 000	1 047 000
Hong Kong-Seoul	—	1 006 000
London-Tōkyō	—	969 000
Cairo-Jeddah	693 000	—

INTERNATIONAL TOURIST ARRIVALS 1989 - 1999

'Tourist' refers to a visitor (visiting for either leisure or business) who stays for at least one night in the country visited.

Arrivals in millions: 426.0, 457.6, 463.3, 502.3, 518.1, 549.5, 567.4, 599.0, 619.7, 636.7, 656.9

Annual change (%): 8.0%, 7.4%, 1.2%, 8.4%, 3.1%, 6.0%, 7.5%, 6.6%, 3.5%, 2.7%, 3.2%

REGIONAL SHARE OF INTERNATIONAL TOURIST ARRIVALS 1970-1999

Height of charts relates to total tourist arrivals.

1970 — 70.5%, 2.0%, 1.5%, 23.0%, 3.0%

1980 — 65.0%, 3.4%, 2.6%, 21.5%, 7.5%

1990 — 61.7%, 2.7%, 3.3%, 20.4%, 11.9%

1995 — 59.7%, 2.9%, 3.6%, 19.5%, 14.3%

1999 — 58.7%, 3.5%, 4.2%, 19.3%, 14.3%

Europe | Middle East and South Asia | Africa | Americas | East Asia and the Pacific

© Bartholomew Ltd

INTRODUCTION TO THE ATLAS

PLACE NAMES

The spelling of place names on maps has always been a matter of great complexity, because of the variety of the world's languages and the systems used to write them down. There is no standard way of spelling names or of converting them from one alphabet, or symbol set, to another. Instead, conventional ways of spelling have evolved in each of the world's major languages, and the results often differ significantly from the name as it is spelled in the original language.
Familiar examples of English conventional names include Munich (München), Florence (Firenze) and Moscow (from the transliterated form, Moskva).

In this atlas, local name forms are used where these are in the Roman alphabet, though for major cities, and main physical features, conventional English names are given first. The local forms are those which are officially recognized by the government of the country concerned, usually as represented by its official mapping agency. This is a basic principle laid down by the United Kingdom government's Permanent Committee on Geographical Names (PCGN) and the equivalent United States Board on Geographic Names, (BGN). Prominent English-language and historic names are not neglected, however. These, and significant superseded names and alternate spellings, are included in brackets on the maps where space permits, and are cross-referenced in the index.

Country names are shown in conventional English form and include any recent changes promulgated by national governments and adopted by the United Nations. The names of continents, oceans, seas and under-water features in international waters also appear in English throughout the atlas, as do those of other international features where such an English form exists and is in common use. International features are defined as features crossing one or more international boundary.

BOUNDARIES

The status of nations, their names and their boundaries, are shown in this atlas as they are at the time of going to press, as far as can be ascertained. Where an international boundary symbol appears in the sea or ocean it does not necessarily infer a legal maritime boundary, but shows which off-shore islands belong to which country. The extent of island nations is shown by a short boundary symbol at the extreme limits of the area of sea or ocean within which all land is part of that nation.

Where international boundaries are the subject of dispute it may be that no portrayal of them will meet with the approval of any of the countries involved, but it is not seen as the function of this atlas to try to adjudicate between the rights and wrongs of political issues. Although reference mapping at atlas scales is not the ideal medium for indicating the claims of many

separatist and irredentist movements, every reasonable attempt is made to show where an active territorial dispute exists, and where there is an important difference between 'de facto' (existing in fact, on the ground) and 'de jure' (according to law) boundaries. This is done by the use of a different symbol where international boundaries are disputed, or where the alignment is unconfirmed, to that used for settled international boundaries. Cease-fire lines are also shown by a separate symbol. For clarity, disputed boundaries and areas are annotated where this is considered necessary. The atlas aims to take a strictly neutral viewpoint of all such cases, based on advice from expert consultants.

PROJECTIONS

Map projections have been selected specifically for the area and scale of each map, or suite of maps. As the only way to show the Earth with absolute accuracy is on a globe, all map projections are compromises. Some projections seek to maintain correct area relationships (equal area projections), true distances and bearings from a point (equidistant projections) or correct angles and shapes (conformal projections); others attempt to achieve a balance between these properties. The choice of projections used in this atlas has been made on an individual continental and regional basis. Projections used, and their individual parameters, have been defined to minimize distortion and to reduce scale errors as much as possible. The projection used is indicated at the bottom left of each map page.

ABBREVIATIONS

Arch.	Archipelago		
B.	Bay		
	Bahía, Baia	Portuguese	bay
	Bahía	Spanish	bay
	Baie	French	bay
C.	Cape		
	Cabo	Portuguese, Spanish	cape, headland
	Cap	French	cape, headland
Co	Cerro	Spanish	hill, peak, summit
E.	East, Eastern		
Est.	Estrecho	Spanish	strait
G.	Gebel	Arabic	hill, mountain
Gt	Great		
I.	Island, Isle		
	Ilha	Portuguese	island
	Islas	Spanish	island
Is	Islands, Isles		
	Islas	Spanish	islands
Khr.	Khrebet	Russian	mountain range
L.	Lake		
	Loch	(Scotland)	lake
	Lough	(Ireland)	lake
	Lac	French	lake
	Lago	Portuguese, Spanish	lake
M.	Mys	Russian	cape, point
Mt	Mount		
	Mont	French	hill, mountain
Mt.	Mountain		

Mte	Monte	Portuguese, Spanish	hill, mountain
Mts	Mountains		
	Monts	French	hills, mountains
N.	North, Northern		
O.	Ostrov	Russian	island
Pt	Point		
Pta	Punta	Italian, Spanish	cape, point
R.	River		
	Rio	Portuguese	river
	Río	Spanish	river
	Rivière	French	river
Ra.	Range		
S.	South, Southern		
	Salar, Salina, Salinas	Spanish	salt pan, salt pans
Sa	Serra	Portuguese	mountain range
	Sierra	Spanish	mountain range
Sd	Sound		
S.E.	Southeast, Southeastern		
St	Saint		
	Sankt	German	
	Sint	Dutch	saint
Sta	Santa	Italian, Portuguese, Spanish	saint
Ste	Sainte	French	saint
Str.	Strait		
W.	West, Western		
	Wadi, Wâdi, Wādī	Arabic	watercourse

SCALE

In order to directly compare like with like throughout the world it would be necessary to maintain a single scale throughout the atlas. However, the desirability of mapping the more densely populated areas of the world at larger scales, and other geographical considerations, such as the need to fit a homogeneous physical region within a uniform rectangular page format, mean that a range of scales have been used. Scales for continental maps range between 1:25 000 000 and 1:55 000 000, depending on the size of the continental land mass being covered. Scales for regional maps are typically in the range 1:15 000 000 to 1:25 000 000. Mapping for most countries is at scales between 1:6 000 000 and 1:12 000 000, although for the more densely populated areas of Europe the scale increases to 1:3 000 000.

TRANSPORT

=== Motorway

— Main road

- - - Track

— Main railway

⊥⊥⊥⊥ Canal

✈ Main airport

BOUNDARIES

▦▦ International boundary

· ▪ ◆ Disputed international boundary or alignment unconfirmed

Undefined international boundary in the sea.
All land within this boundary is part of state or territory named.

▬▬ Administrative boundary
Shown for selected countries only.

●●●● Ceasefire line or other boundary described on the map

MAP SYMBOLS

LAND AND WATER FEATURES

Lake

Impermanent lake

Salt lake or lagoon

Impermanent salt lake

Dry salt lake or salt pan

— River

- - - - Impermanent river

Ice cap / Glacier

)123(Pass
Height in metres

∴ Site of special interest

⌣ Oasis

nnnn Wall

RELIEF

Contour intervals used in layer-colouring, for land height and sea depth

METRES FEET

METRES FEET	
5000	16404
3000	9843
2000	6562
1000	3281
500	1640
200	656
0	0

LAND B.S.L.

200	656
4000	13124
6000	19686

1234 Summit
△ Height in metres

Ocean pages

METRES FEET

METRES	FEET
0	0
200	656
2000	6562
3000	9843
4000	13124
5000	16404
6000	19686
7000	22967
9000	29529

123 Ocean deep
In metres.

STYLES OF LETTERING

Cities and towns are explained separately

		Physical features	
Country	**FRANCE**	Island	*Gran Canaria*
Overseas Territory/Dependency	**Guadeloupe**	Lake	*Lake Erie*
Disputed Territory	AKSAI CHIN	Mountain	*Mt Blanc*
Administrative name Shown for selected countries only.	**SCOTLAND**	River	*Thames*
Area name	PATAGONIA	Region	*LAPPLAND*

CITIES AND TOWNS

Population	National Capital	Administrative Capital Shown for selected countries only	Other City or Town
over 1 million	**BEIJING** □	Sydney ○	New York ○
500 000 to 1 million	**BANGUI** □	Edmonton ○	Jeddah ○
100 000 to 500 000	WELLINGTON □	Edinburgh ○	Apucarana ○
50 000 to 100 000	PORT OF SPAIN □	Bismarck ○	Invercargill ○
under 50 000	MALABO □	Charlottetown ○	Ceres ○

Built-up area
Scale 1:3 000 000 only

CONTINENTAL MAPS

BOUNDARIES

— International boundary   - - - - - - Disputed international boundary   ········ Ceasefire line

CITIES AND TOWNS

National Capital   **Beijing** □   Other City or Town   **New York** ○

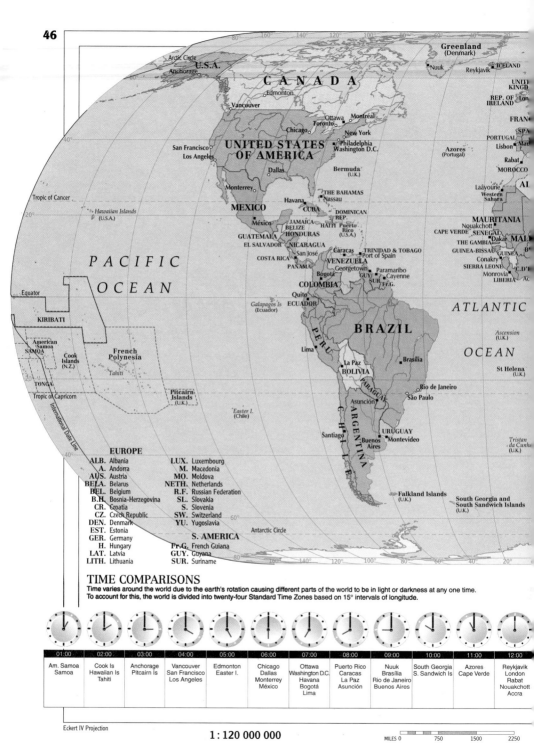

Greenland
(Denmark)

• Nuuk   Reykjavik • ICELAND

Arctic Circle
Anchorage **U.S.A.**

C A N A D A

○ Edmonton

Vancouver

Ottawa Montréal
Toronto
Chicago □   • New York

UNITED STATES • Philadelphia
OF AMERICA   Washington D.C.

San Francisco
Los Angeles

Dallas

Bermuda
(U.K.)

UNITED
KINGD■

REP. OF Lon
IRELAND

FRAN■

SPA■
PORTUGAL
Lisbon   Mad■
Azores   Rabat
(Portugal)   **MOROCCO**

Tropic of Cancer

Monterrey•

Havana ■ THE BAHAMAS
■ Nassau

Laâyoune
Western
Sahara

AL■

Hawaiian Islands
(U.S.A.)

MEXICO
México ■

CUBA   DOMINICAN
REP.
JAMAICA HAITI Puerto
BELIZE   Rico
GUATEMALA HONDURAS (U.S.A.)
EL SALVADOR NICARAGUA
COSTA RICA San José TRINIDAD & TOBAGO
PANAMA Caracas■ Port of Spain
Bogotá **VENEZUELA**
Georgetown Paramaribo
COLOMBIA GUY. ● Cayenne
SUR. ■F.G.

MAURITANIA
Nouakchott ■
CAPE VERDE SENEGAL
THE GAMBIA Dakar **MALI**
GUINEA-BISSAU GUINEA B■
Conakry■
SIERRA LEONE C.D'I■
Monrovia LIBERIA Ac■

P A C I F I C

O C E A N

Equator

KIRIBATI

American
Samoa
SAMOA   Cook
Islands
(N.Z.) French
Polynesia

Tahiti

TONGA

Tropic of Capricorn

Pitcairn
Islands
(U.K.)

International Date Line

Easter I.
(Chile)

Quito●
Galapagos Is **ECUADOR**
(Ecuador)

Lima●

B R A Z I L

Brasília●

La Paz
BOLIVIA

Rio de Janeiro
São Paulo

A T L A N T I C

Ascension
(U.K.)

O C E A N

St Helena
(U.K.)

Asunción●

Santiago●

ARGENTINA

Montevideo
Buenos **URUGUAY**
Aires

Tristan
da Cunha
(U.K.)

EUROPE
ALB. Albania
A. Andorra
AUS. Austria
BELA. Belarus
BEL. Belgium
B.H. Bosnia-Herzegovina
CR. Croatia
CZ. Czech Republic
DEN. Denmark
EST. Estonia
GER. Germany
H. Hungary
LAT. Latvia
LITH. Lithuania

LUX. Luxembourg
M. Macedonia
MO. Moldova
NETH. Netherlands
R.F. Russian Federation
SL. Slovakia
S. Slovenia
SW. Switzerland
YU. Yugoslavia

S. AMERICA
Fr.G. French Guiana
GUY. Guyana
SUR. Suriname

Falkland Islands
(U.K.)

South Georgia and
South Sandwich Islands
(U.K.)

Antarctic Circle

TIME COMPARISONS

Time varies around the world due to the earth's rotation causing different parts of the world to be in light or darkness at any one time.
To account for this, the world is divided into twenty-four Standard Time Zones based on 15° intervals of longitude.

01:00	02:00	03:00	04:00	05:00	06:00	07:00	08:00	09:00	10:00	11:00	12:00
Am. Samoa Samoa	Cook Is Hawaiian Is Tahiti	Anchorage Pitcairn Is	Vancouver San Francisco Los Angeles	Edmonton Easter I.	Chicago Dallas Monterrey México	Ottawa Washington D.C. Havana Bogotá Lima	Puerto Rico Caracas La Paz Asunción	Nuuk Brasília Rio de Janeiro Buenos Aires	South Georgia S. Sandwich Is	Azores Cape Verde	Reykjavik London Rabat Nouakchott Accra

Eckert IV Projection

1 : 120 000 000

MILES 0   750   1500   2250

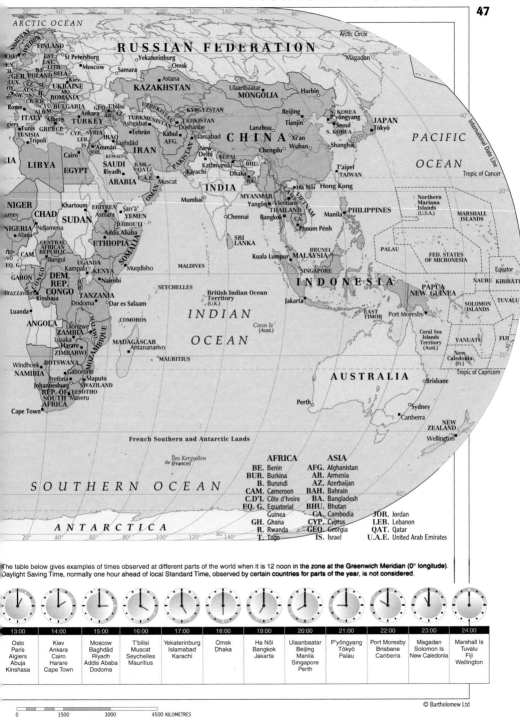

The table below gives examples of times observed at different parts of the world when it is 12 noon in the zone at the Greenwich Meridian (0° longitude). Daylight Saving Time, normally one hour ahead of local Standard Time, observed by certain countries for parts of the year, is not considered.

AFRICA		ASIA	
BE.	Benin	AFG.	Afghanistan
BUR.	Burkina	AR.	Armenia
B.	Burundi	AZ.	Azerbaijan
CAM.	Cameroon	BAH.	Bahrain
C.D'I.	Côte d'Ivoire	BA.	Bangladesh
EQ. G.	Equatorial	BHU.	Bhutan
	Guinea	CA.	Cambodia	JOR.	Jordan
GH.	Ghana	CYP.	Cyprus	LEB.	Lebanon
R.	Rwanda	GEO.	Georgia	QAT.	Qatar
T.	Togo	IS.	Israel	U.A.E.	United Arab Emirates

13:00	14:00	15:00	16:00	17:00	18:00	19:00	20:00	21:00	22:00	23:00	24:00
Oslo	Kiev	Moscow	T'bilisi	Yekaterinburg	Omsk	Ha Nôi	Ulaanbaatar	P'yŏngyang	Port Moresby	Magadan	Marshall Is
Paris	Ankara	Baghdād	Muscat	Islamabad	Dhaka	Bangkok	Beijing	Tōkyō	Brisbane	Solomon Is	Tuvalu
Algiers	Cairo	Riyadh	Seychelles	Karachi		Jakarta	Manila	Palau	Canberra	New Caledonia	Fiji
Abuja	Harare	Addis Ababa	Mauritius				Singapore				Wellington
Kinshasa	Cape Town	Dodoma					Perth				

© Bartholomew Ltd

0   1500   3000   4500 KILOMETRES

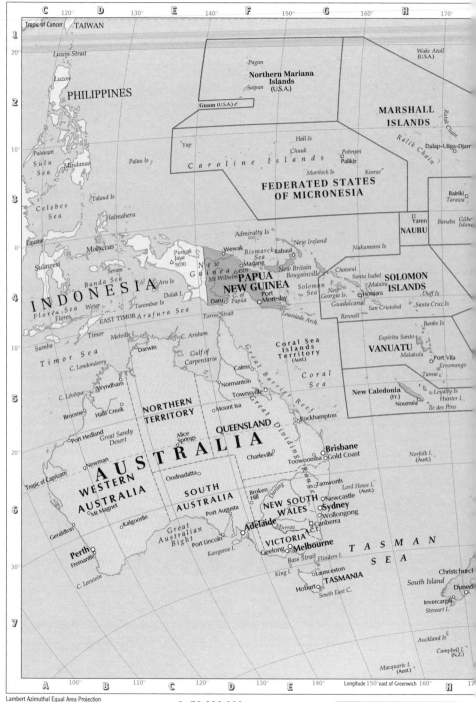

Lambert Azimuthal Equal Area Projection

1 : 50 000 000

MILES 0   500   1000

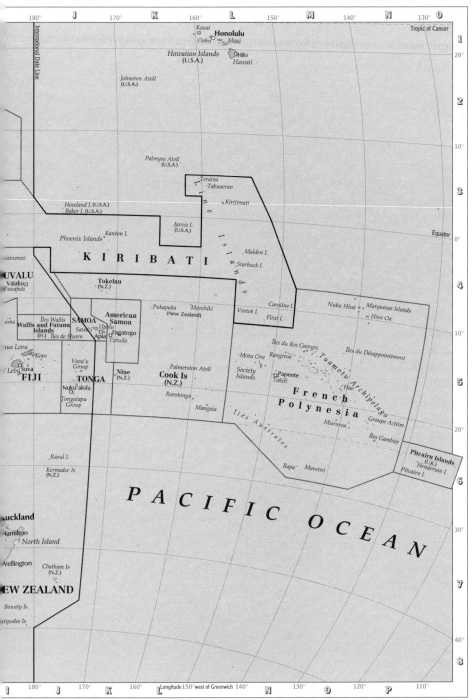

International Date Line

180° · 170° · 160° · 150° · 140° · 130°

Tropic of Cancer

Kauai
Honolulu
Oahu · Maui

Hawaiian Islands
(U.S.A.)

Hilo
Hawaii

20°

Johnston Atoll
(U.S.A.)

10°

Palmyra Atoll
(U.S.A.)

Teraina
Tabuaeran

Kiritimati

Howland I. (U.S.A.)
Baker I. (U.S.A.)

Jarvis I.
(U.S.A.)

Kanton I.

Phoenix Islands

Equator 0°

K I R I B A T I

Malden I.

Starbuck I.

Janumea

UVALU
Vaiaku
Funafuti

Tokelau
(N.Z.)

Pukapuka *Manihiki*
(New Zealand)

Vostok I.

Caroline I.

Nuku Hiva *Marquesas Islands*

Hiva Oa

Flint I.

10°

Iles Wallis
Wallis and Futuna
Islands
(Fr.) *Iles de Hoorn*

uma

SAMOA
Savaii
Upolu
Apia

American
Samoa
Fagatogo
Tutuila

Iles du Roi Georges

Motu One *Rangiroa*

Iles du Désappointement

Tuamotu Archipelago

ua Levu
Koro
Lefu Suva

FIJI

Vava'u
Group

TONGA

Nuku'alofa

Tongatapu
Group

Niue
(N.Z.)

Cook Is
(N.Z.)

Rarotonga

Palmerston Atoll

Society
Islands

Papeete
Tahiti

Hao

F r e n c h
P o l y n e s i a

Mururoa

Groupe Actéon

Iles Gambier

20°

Mangaia

Iles Australes

Pitcairn Islands
(U.K.)
Henderson I.
Pitcairn I.

Raoul I.

Kermadec Is
(N.Z.)

Rapa *Marotiri*

P A C I F I C   O C E A N

30°

Auckland

Hamilton
North Island

Wellington

Chatham Is
(N.Z.)

EW ZEALAND

Bounty Is

tipodes Is

40°

180° · 170° · 160° · Longitude 150° west of Greenwich 140° · 130° · 120° · 110°

0   500   1000   1500 KILOMETRES

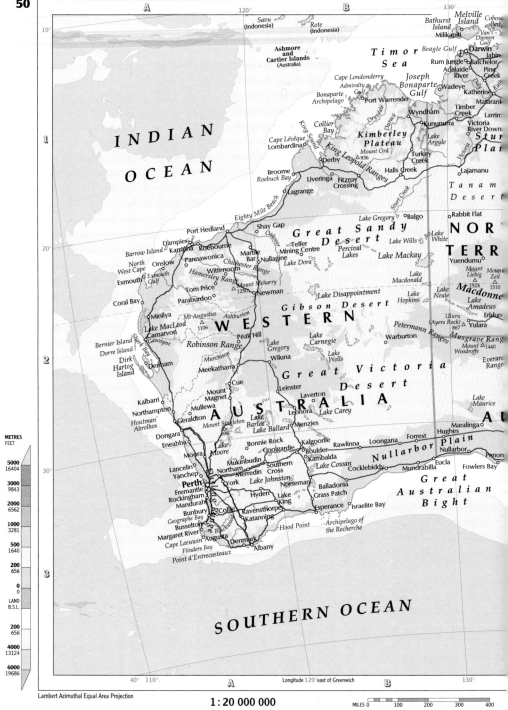

A 120° B 130°

Savu (Indonesia)   Rote (Indonesia)

Melville Island   Cobour Peni
Bathurst Island

Ashmore and Cartier Islands (Australia)

Van Diemen Gulf
Milikapiti

Beagle Gulf   Darwin   Jabi
Rum Jungle   Batchelor

T i m o r S e a

Adelaide   Ping
River   Creek

Cape Londonderry   Joseph Bonaparte Gulf   Wadeye   Katherine   Matarank

Admiralty Gulf

Bonaparte Archipelago   Port Warrender

Wyndham   Kunnunurra   Timber Creek   Larrim

Victoria River Down   Stur Plai

Collier Bay

Cape Lévêque   Kimberley Plateau   Lake Argyle   Turkey Creek

Lombardina   Mount Ord 936   King Leopold Ranges

I N D I A N

O C E A N

Broome   Derby   Halls Creek   Lajamanu

Roebuck Bay   Liveringa   Fitzroy Crossing   T a n a m   D e s e r

Lagrange

Eighty Mile Beach

Lake Gregory   Balgo   Rabbit Flat

Port Hedland   Shay Gap   G r e a t S a n d y D e s e r t   N O R

Dampier   Roebourne   Oakover   Lake Wills   Lake White   T E R R

Barrow Island   Karratha   Pannawonica   Marble Bar   Telfer Mining Centre   Percival Lakes   Lake Mackay   Yuendumu

North West Cape   Onslow   Wittenoom   Chichester Range   Nullagine   Lake Dora   Mount Liebig   Moun Zeil 1510

Exmouth   Hamersley Range   Mount Myharry   Newman   Lake Disappointment   Lake Macdonald   Macdonne

Exmouth Gulf   Tom Price   1250   Lake Hopkins   Lake Neale   Lake Amadeus   Erldun

Coral Bay   Paraburdoo   G i b s o n D e s e r t   Uluru (Ayers Rock) 867   Yulara

Minilya   Mt Augustus 1106   Ashburton   W E S T E R N   Petermann Ranges   Musgrave Rang

Lake MacLeod   Lake Carnegie   Warburton   Mount 1440 Woodroffe

Bernier Island   Carnarvon   Gascoyne   Peak Hill   Lake Gregory   Everar Range

Dorre Island   Robinson Range   Wiluna   Lake Wells

Dirk Hartog Island   Denham   Murchison   G r e a t V i c t o r i a

Meekatharra   D e s e r t

Cue   A U S T R A L I A   Lake Maurice

Kalbarri   Mount Magnet   Leinster   Laverton   Lake Carey   Maralinga   AU

Northampton   Mullewa   Leonora   Menzies   Hughes

Houtman Abrolhos   Geraldton   Mount Singleton   Lake Barlee   Forrest   Nullarbor

Dongara   Lake Ballard   Loongana   N u l l a r b o r P l a i n   Penon

Eneabba   Bonnie Rock   Kalgoorlie   Rawlinna   Fowlers Bay

Moora   Lake Moore   Coolgardie   Boulder   Cocklebiddy   Mundrabilla   Eucla   G r e a t

Lancelin   Mukinbudin   Kambalda   Lake Cowan   A u s t r a l i a n

Yanchep   Northam   Merredin   Southern Cross   Norseman   B i g h t

Perth   York   Lake Johnston   Balladonia

Fremantle   Hyden   Lake King   Grass Patch

Rockingham   Collie   Esperance   Israelite Bay

Mandurah   Geographe Bay   Ravensthorpe

Bunbury   Busselton   Katanning   Hood Point   Archipelago of the Recherche

Margaret River   Augusta   Denmark

Cape Leeuwin   Flinders Bay   Albany

Point d'Entrecasteaux

S O U T H E R N O C E A N

METRES FEET
5000 16404
3000 9843
2000 6562
1000 3281
500 1640
200 656
0 0
LAND B.S.L.
200 656
4000 13124
6000 19686

A 40° 110°   Longitude 120° east of Greenwich   B 130°

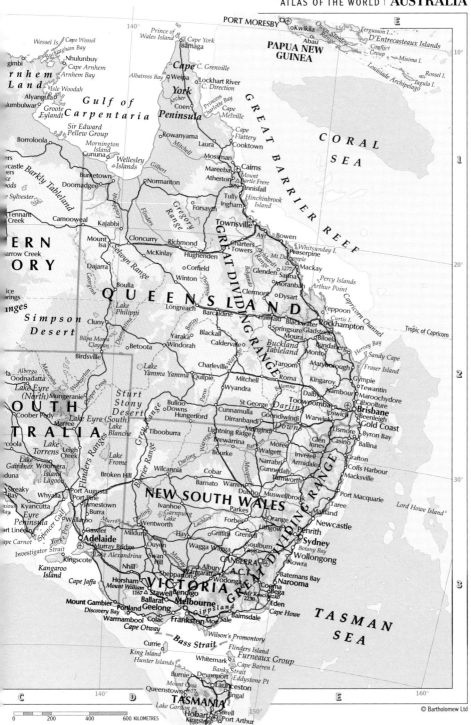

PORT MORESBY

PAPUA NEW GUINEA

Kwikila
Abau
D'Entrecasteaux Islands
Fergusson I.
Owen Stanley Range
Conflict Group
Misima I.
Louisiade Archipelago
Rossel I.
Tagula I.

Prince of Wales Island
Cape York
Bamaga
Cape Grenville
C. Direction
Lockhart River

Cape York Peninsula

Albatross Bay
Weipa
Archer
Princess Charlotte Bay
Coen
Cape Melville

GREAT BARRIER REEF

CORAL SEA

Cape Flattery
Kowanyama
Cooktown
Laura
Mossman

Wessel Is
Cape Wessel
Buckingham Bay
Nhulunbuy
Cape Arnhem
Arnhem Bay

Arnhem Land
Isle Woodah
Alyangula
Groote Eylandt
Umbulwar
Sir Edward Pellew Group
Borroloola

Gulf of Carpentaria

Mornington Island
Gununa
Wellesley Islands
Gilbert

Mareeba
Cairns
Atherton
Mount Bartle Frere
Innisfail
Tully
Ingham
Hinchinbrook Island

Normanton

Burketown
Doomadgee

Barkly Tableland

Forsayth

Gregory Range

Townsville
Ayr
Bowen
Whitsunday I.
Charters Towers
Proserpine
Mt Dalrymple
1277
Mackay

QUEENSLAND

GREAT DIVIDING RANGE

Camooweal
Kajabbi
Cloncurry
Richmond
Hughenden
Corfield
Glenden
Sarina
Moranbah

Mount Isa
McKinlay
Winton
Clermont
Dysart

Dajarra
Boulia
Longreach
Barcaldine
Emerald
Blackwater
Springsure
Moura
Biloela
Rockhampton
Curtis I.
Capricorn Channel

Simpson Desert

Lake Philippi
Cluny
Yaraka
Blackall
Caldervale
Gladstone

Tropic of Capricorn

Bilpa Morea Claypan
Betoota
Windorah
Buckland Tableland
Taroom
Monto
Bundaberg
Hervey Bay
Sandy Cape

Birdsville
Charleville
Maryborough
Fraser Island
Sandy Cape

OUTH TRALIA

Sturt Stony Desert

Lake Yamma Yamma
Quilpie
Mitchell
Roma
Kingaroy
Gympie
Tewantin
Maroochydore

Oodnadatta
Coober Pedy

Wyandra
Bollon
Toowoomba
Nambour
Caboolture

Marree

Great Range

Bulloo Downs
Hungerford
St George
Goondiwindi
Warwick
Ipswich
Brisbane
Beenleigh
Gold Coast
Byron Bay

Lake Eyre (North)
Mungeranie
Tibooburra
Cunnamulla
Dirranbandi
Moonie
Lismore
Ballina

Lake Eyre (South)
Leigh Creek
Lake Blanche
Lightning Ridge
Mungindi
Casino

Lake Torrens
Lake Frome
Brewarrina
Moree
Glen Innes
Grafton

Woomera
Marla
Olympic Dam
Broken Hill
Wilcannia
Bourke
Walgett
Narrabri
Inverell
Coffs Harbour

Leigh Creek

NEW SOUTH WALES

Cobar
Barton
Gunnedah
Armidale
Macksville

Whyalla
Port Augusta
Port Pirie
Barnato
Warren
Dubbo
Muswellbrook
Tamworth
Port Macquarie

Eyre Peninsula
Spencer Gulf
Jamestown
Burra
Ivanhoe
Garnpung Lake
Parkes
Taree
Lord Howe Island

Kyancutta

Wilpena
Gawler
Mildura
Wentworth
Hay
Forbes
Orange
Maitland

Adelaide
Murray Bridge
Ouyen
Wagga Wagga
Griffith
Grenfell
Goulburn
Yass
Newcastle

Kingscote
Lake Alexandrina
Swan Hill
Nhill
CANBERRA
A.C.T.
Sydney
Botany Bay
Wollongong

Kangaroo Island
Cape Jaffa
Horsham
Shepparton
Wangaratta
Albury
Wodonga
Cooma
Mt Kosciusko
2230
Batemans Bay
Narooma
Bega

VICTORIA
Stawell
Bendigo
Mt William
1167
Ballarat
Melbourne
Eden
Cape Howe

Mount Gambier
Portland
Geelong
Gippsland
Frankston
Moe
Sale
Bairnsdale

TASMAN SEA

Warrnambool
Colac
Cape Otway
Wilson's Promontory

Discovery Bay

Bass Strait
Currie
King Island
Hunter Islands
Whitemark
Flinders Island
Furneaux Group
Cape Barren I.
Banks Strait
Eddystone Pt

Burnie
Devonport
Bingal
Queenstown
Mount Ossa
1617
Launceston

Lake Gordon

TASMANIA
Hobart
Sorell
Port Arthur
Kingston

0   200   400   600 KILOMETRES

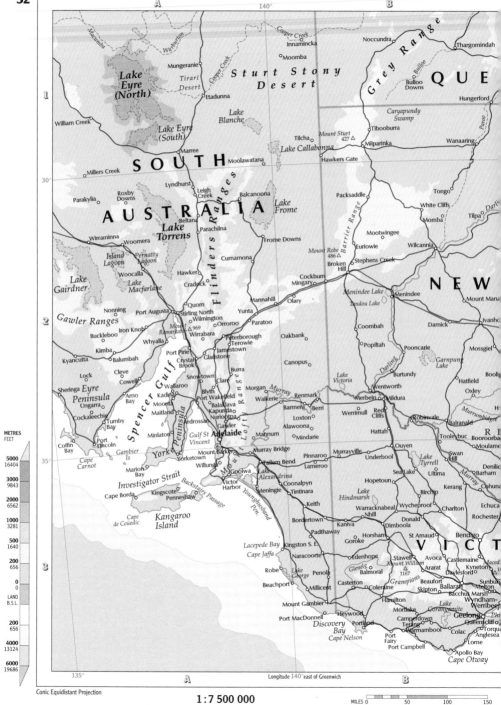

METRES
FEET

5000 16404
3000 9843
2000 6562
1000 3281
500 1640
200 656
0 0
LAND B.S.L.
200 656
4000 13124
6000 19686

Conic Equidistant Projection

1 : 7 500 000

MILES 0   50   100   150

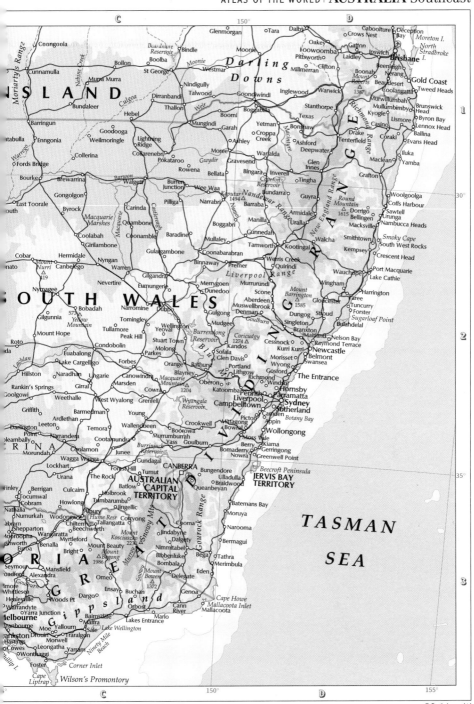

0   100   200 KILOMETRES

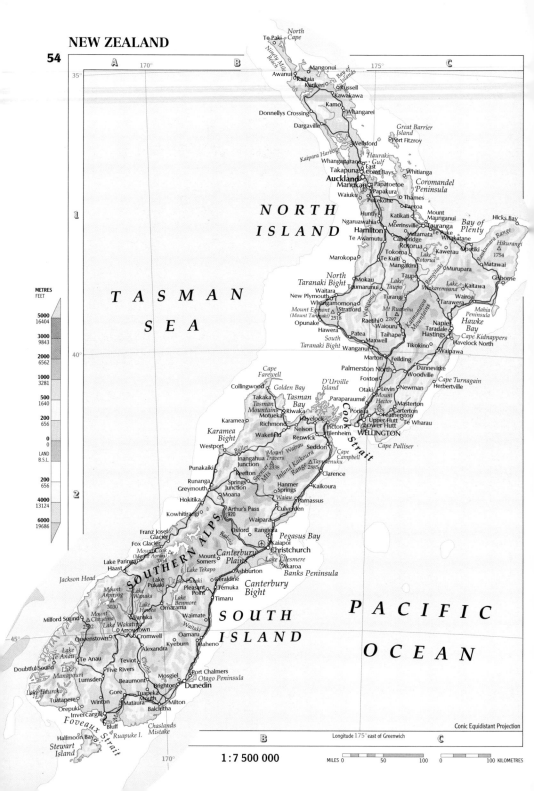

NORTH
ISLAND

SOUTH
ISLAND

TASMAN
SEA

PACIFIC
OCEAN

North Cape
Te Paki
Ninety Mile Beach
Mangonui
Awanui
Kaitaia
Bay of Islands
Kerikeri
Russell
Kawakawa
Kamo
Donnellys Crossing
Whangarei
Dargaville
Great Barrier Island
Wellsford
Port Fitzroy
Kaipara Harbour
Whangaparaoa
Hauraki Gulf
Whitianga
Takapuna
East Coast Bays
Auckland
Coromandel Peninsula
Manukau
Papatoetoe
Waiuku
Papakura
Thames
Pukekohe
Paeroa
Huntly
Katikati
Mount Maunganui
Hicks Bay
Ngaruawahia
Morrinsville
Tauranga
Bay of Plenty
Hamilton
Cambridge
Te Puke
Whakatane
Te Awamutu
Matamata
Rotorua
Opotiki
Hikurangi 1754
Marokopa
Tokoroa
Waiouru
Kawerau
Matawai
Te Kuiti
Lake Rotorua
Murupara
Mangakino
Taupo
Gisborne
North Taranaki Bight
Mokau
Taumarunui
Lake Taupo
Lake Waikaremoana
Kaitawa
Waitara
New Plymouth
Whangamomona
Stratford
Mt Ruapehu
Wairoa
Mount Egmont (Mount Taranaki) 2518
Raetihi 2297
Tarawera
Mahia Peninsula
Opunake
Napier
Hawke Bay
Hawera
Taradale
Patea
Taihape
Hastings
Maxwell
Tikokino
Havelock North
Wanganui
Cape Kidnappers
Marton
Waipawa
Feilding
Dannevirke
Palmerston North
Woodville
Cape Farewell
Foxton
Cape Turnagain
D'Urville Island
Otaki
Newman
Herbertville
Collingwood
Golden Bay
Levin
Mount Hector 1529
Masterton
Takaka
Tasman Bay
Paraparaumu
Carterton
Tasman Mountains
Riwaka
Porirua
Featherston
Motueka
Upper Hutt
Te Wharau
Karamea
Mapua
Lower Hutt
Richmond
Nelson
Picton
WELLINGTON
Karamea Bight
Wakefield
Blenheim
Westport
Renwick
Cape Palliser
Buller
Mount Wairau
Seddon
Inangahua Junction
Travers 2338
Spenser Mts
Inland Kaikoura Range
Cape Campbell
Punakaiki
Reefton
Tapuaenuku 2885
Runanga
Springs Junction
Hanmer Springs
Clarence
Greymouth
Moana
Kaikoura
Hokitika
Waiau
Amberley
Arthur's Pass (920)
Culverden
Kowhitirangi
Waipara
Franz Josef Glacier
Oxford
Rangiora
Pegasus Bay
Fox Glacier
Kaiapoi
Mount Cook (Mount Aoraki) 3754
Mount Somers
Canterbury Plains
Christchurch
Lake Paringa
Lake Tekapo
Ashburton
Lake Ellesmere
Akaroa
Haast
Banks Peninsula
Jackson Head
Lake Pukaki
Geraldine
Mount Aspiring 3030
Pleasant Point
Temuka
Canterbury Bight
Lake Wanaka
Lake Hawea
Timaru
Milford Sound
Mount Christina 2502
Omarama
Lake Wakatipu
Waimate
Queenstown
Arrowtown
Waitaki
Oamaru
Lake Te Anau
Cromwell
Kyeburn
Maheno
Te Anau
Alexandra
Doubtful Sound
Teviot
Lake Manapouri
Five Rivers
Clutha
Mosgiel
Otago Peninsula
Lake Hauroko
Lumsden
Beaumont
Brighton
Dunedin
Tuatapere
Winton
Gore
Tuapeka Mouth
Milton
Orepuki
Mataura
Balclutha
Invercargill
Chaslands Mistake
Foveaux Strait
Bluff
Ruapuke I.
Halfmoon Bay
Stewart Island

SOUTHERN ALPS

Conic Equidistant Projection

Longitude 175° east of Greenwich

1 : 7 500 000

MILES 0   50   100   0   100 KILOMETRES

METRES FEET

5000	16404
3000	9843
2000	6562
1000	3281
500	1640
200	656
0	0
LAND B.S.L.	
200	656
4000	13124
6000	19686

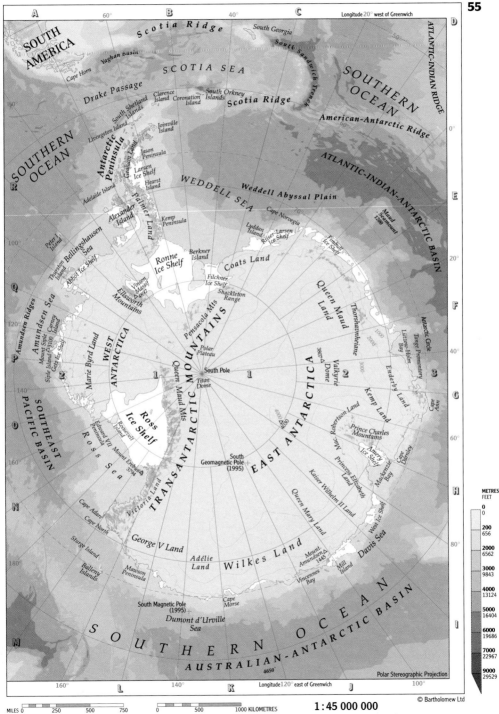

METRES
FEET

0	0
200	656
2000	6562
3000	9843
4000	13124
5000	16404
6000	19686
7000	22967
9000	29529

© Bartholomew Ltd

MILES 0   250   500   750

0   500   1000 KILOMETRES

1 : 45 000 000

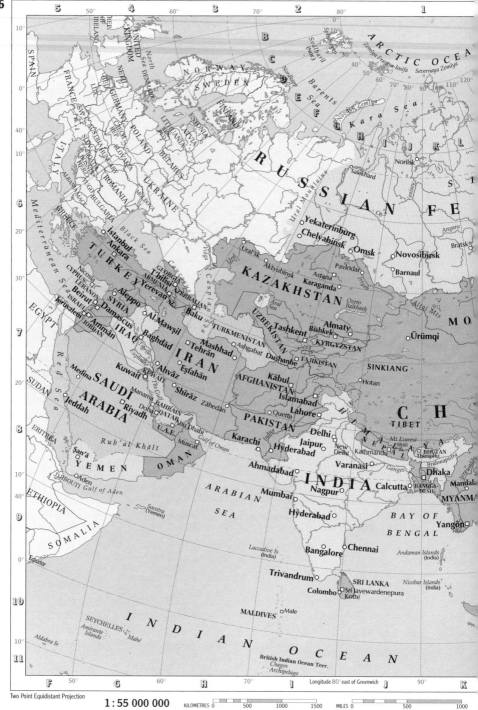

Two Point Equidistant Projection

1 : 55 000 000

KILOMETRES 0   500   1000   1500   MILES 0   500   1000

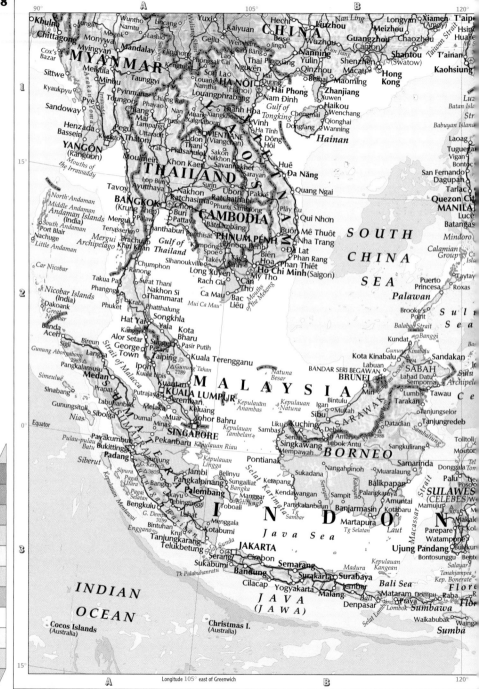

METRES
FEET

5000
16404

3000
9843

2000
6562

1000
3281

500
1640

200
656

0
0

LAND
B.S.L.

200
656

4000
13124

6000
19686

Albers Equal Area Conic Projection

Longitude 105° east of Greenwich

1 : 25 000 000

MILES 0   250   500

135° D 150° E

Tropic of Cancer

Nansei-shotō
(Japan)

WAN

Philippine
Sea

arri

gan

uzon

illo
inds

PHILIPPINES

PACIFIC
OCEAN

Pagan

Northern
Mariana
Islands
(U.S.A.)

Saipan
Tinian

15°

Daet
Catanduanes
Legaspi
Sorsogon
nblon
Irosin Catarman
Masbate *Samar*
Roxas Catbalogan
ilay Taclaban
Bacolod Cebu
lo
egros *Bohol*
gbiliaran *Bohol Sea*
Butuan
Surigao
oquieta Iligan Cagayan de Oro
gadian Cotabato *Mindanao*
Zamboanga Davao
abela Mati
Moro
Gulf General Santos

Hagåtña
(Agana)
Guam
(U.S.A.)

Rota

Mariana Trench

Ulithi Fais

Yap
Colonia

Ngulu

Sorol

Faraulep

FEDERATED STATES
OF MICRONESIA

C a r o l i n e
Islands

2

Eauripik

East Caroline
Basin

0°

b e s

a

Kepulauan
Talaud
Sangir

Morotai
Daruba
Tobelo

St Matthias
Group Mussau I.

Kepulauan
Sangire

menanjung Manado
Minahasa Tondano Ternate **Halmahera**
Kwandang Sao-Siu
Gorontalo
Kepulauan
Togian
Luwuk Peleng Todeli
taba Banggai *Mangole* Obi
Kepulauan Kepulauan Sula
Manui
Kendari Namlea Piru
Raha Wowoni Buru Ambon
Buton
Baubau *Kepulauan*
Tukangbesi

Waigeo

Pelleluhu Is
Hermit Is Admiralty
Islands Lorengau New Hanover
Manus I. Umbukul Kavieng
Wuvulu New
Island Ireland
Aitape Schouten Islands
Maprik Wewak Bogia Manam I.
Sepik Madang Long
Island

Bismarck Archipelago
Bismarck Sea Rabaul
Ulamona 2438
Kimbe *New Britain*
Umboi Lau

Kwoka
Selat Dampir 3000 Jazirah Manokwari Biak
Salawati Sorong Doberai Numfoor Selat Yapen
Labuna Bacan Misool Inanwatan Ransiki Yapen Serui Sarmi
Tifore Waigeo Teluk Wandammen Tg d'Urville
Tidore (Moluccas) Afanlap Babo Nabire Vanimo
Kofiau Fakfak cenderawasih
Seram Sea Seram Teluk Berau **IRIAN JAYA** Jayapura
S I A Piru Bula Babo Taritatu
Ambon Saparua Kaimana Pk Jaya Pk
Seram Adi Enarotali Pegunungan Van Rees
Kepulauan Amamapare Lorentz Trikora
Banda Watubela Maoke
Kai Besar Kepulauan 5030 4730
Kepulauan Kai Kecil Tual Dobo Wokam 4700
Banda Benjina Kobroör
Banda Sea Larat Aru Sia Trangan
Kepulauan Tanimbar Tg Deyong
Kepulauan Damar Wuliaru Saumlakki P. Dolak Murray
Alor Kepulauan Roma Kaiwatu Babar Digul
Kalabahi Wetar Leti Tg Vals
Larantuka Alor Huaki Selaru Merauke
Dili Maliana Kepulauan Sermata
deh Kefamenanu Manatuto
a w u 2960 **EAST**
Sea Kupang **TIMOR**
vu Rote

Pegunungan

Central Ra. Wilhelm 4509
Mendi Mount Goroka Huon
PAPUA Hagen Peninsula Gasmata
NEW GUINEA Wau Morobe
Kiunga Kikori Kerema Lae
NEW Balimo Gulf Mt
GUINEA Morehead of Papua Victoria
Daru Kwikila
Bereina Abau
PORT
MORESBY Alotau
Thursday Samarai
Island C. York
Prince of Wales Bamaga
Island

Schouten Islands

Kikori

Trobriand
Islands
Losuia
D'Entrecasteaux Is
Bolubolu
Goschen Strait

150°

Arafura Sea

AUSTRALIA

C. Wessel
Wessel Is

Nhulunbuy
C. Arnhem

Gulf
of
Carpentaria

Weipa
C. Grenville
Lockhart River

C. Melville
Timor Sea
Melville
Island

Bathurst Island
Beagle Gulf
Batchelor
Adelaide River Pine Creek

Milikapiti Van Diemen
Croker I.
Jabiru

Milingimbi
Alyangula

Coen
Cape York
Peninsula

C. Flattery
Cooktown
Laura

Darwin
Arnhem
Land

15°

135° D

© Bartholomew Ltd

0 250 500 750 KILOMETRES

A 100°   B   110°

Phangnga
Ban Khok Kloi
Thalang Thung Nakhon Si Thammarat   Mui Ca Mau   Năm Căn   Côn Son
Phuket Krabi Song Khao Chum Thong
   Thung   **VIETNAM**
THAILAND Trang Phatthalung
       Thale Luang
    Satun Hat Songkhla
    Yai Pattani
 Langkawi Sadao Yala Narathiwat
   Kangar Rangae Kota
 Alor Setar   Bharu
 Sungei Petani   Pasir
   Butterworth Kuala Kerai Putih
 George Kuala Terengganu
 Town **MALAYSIA**
  Kuala Gunung
  Kangsar Tahan Dungun
 Taiping   △2189 Kenyir
  Ipoh **PENINSULAR** Cukai
  Kampar **MALAYSIA**
   Kuala Lipis
  Bagan Teluk Anson Kuantan
  Datuk **KUALA**
   LUMPUR Temerloh Pekan
 Tebingtinggi Kisaran Kelang   Bahau
 Pematangsiantar Tanjungbalai Putrajaya Seremban Endau
 Sidikalang Prapat Danau Labuhanbilik Melaka Segamat Mersing
  Singkil Toba Balige   Muar Keluang
   Rantauprapat Bagansiapiapi Batu Pahat
 Sibolga   Dumai Bengkalis
 Gunungsitoli Gunungtua Duri Johor Bahru
 Padangsidimpuan   Bintan
   Daludalu   Tanjungpinang
 Telukdalam Natal Hutanopan Minas
 Airbangis Talu   Pekanbaru Kepulauan Riau
 Telo Bangkinang
 Tanahmasa Payakumbuh Kampar
 Tanahbala Pulau- Tembilahan Lingga Daik
  pulau Batu Padangpanjang   Rengat Singkep Kepulauan
 Kagologolo Bukittinggi   Lingga
  Solok Sijunjung Kualatungal
 Padang Painan   Simpang
 Muarasiberut Gunung Batanghari Jambi
 Kaliet Kerinci Muaratembesi
  △3805 Muarabungo
 Sungaipenuh Bangko
   Sarolangun
  Mukomuko Surulangun
 Pagai Burai Sekayu **Palembang**
 Utara   Lubuklinggau Musi Plaju
 Pagai Cuup Tebingtinggi Kayuagung
 Selatan Bengkulu Lahat Prabumulih
  Gunung Martapura
  Dempo△ Menggala
  3159 Muaradua
 Bintuhan Gunung Resag Kotabumi
  △2232 Metro
 Enggano Krui Kotaagung Tanjungkarang-
    Telukbetung
 Tanjung Cina Sumangka Selesi
  Krakatau△ Serang **JAKARTA**
  Selat Sunda Rangkasbitung Karawang
 Panaitan Bogor Cirebon
 Deli Sukabumi Garut
 Tk Palabuhanratu **Bandung** Gunung
    Slamet△
 Sindangbarang Ciamis 3428
  Cilacap Kebumen

 SOUTH CHI

 Natuna Besar
  Panarik
 Kepulauan
 Anambas Subi Besar
 Jemaja Kubu Sambas
 Kepulauan   Liku Kuching
 Tambelan Pemangkat Siluas
   Singkawang Bengkayang
  Mempawah Ngabang
   Pontianak Balaiberku
    Kubu
  Telukbatang
 Pulau-pulau
 Karimata Sukadana
   Ketapang
 Rajik Belangi
 Koba Kendawanga
 Tanjungpandan Manggar
 Toboali Dendang Tanju
 Belitung   Samb

 IND
 JAV

 Tanjung
 Indramayu
 Pekalong
 Tegal
 Temanggung

 Andaman
 Sea
 Pulau
 We Sabang
 Banda Aceh
 Sigli
 Bireun Lhokseumawe
 Calang Takengon Peureula
 Gunung Abongabong Langsa
  △2985
 Blangkejeren Pangkalansusu
 Gunung Leuser Belawan
  △3145
 Tapaktuan Binjai
  Medan
 Simeuluë
 Sinabang

 Nias
 Sirombu

 Pulau-pulau
 Banyak

 Strait of Malacca

 SUMATERA

 Pegunungan Barisan

 Kepulauan Mentawai

 Siberut
 Sipura
 Pagai

 INDIAN

 OCEAN

 J A V A
 (J A W A)

 METRES
 FEET
 5000 16404
 3000 9843
 2000 6562
 1000 3281
 500 1640
 200 656
 0 0
 LAND
 B.S.L.
 200 656
 4000 13124
 6000 19686

 Equator 0°

 2

 10°

 A Longitude 100° east of Greenwich B 110°

 Albers Equal Area Conic Projection

 1:12 000 000

 MILES 0   100   200   300

© Bartholomew Ltd

0   200   400 KILOMETRES

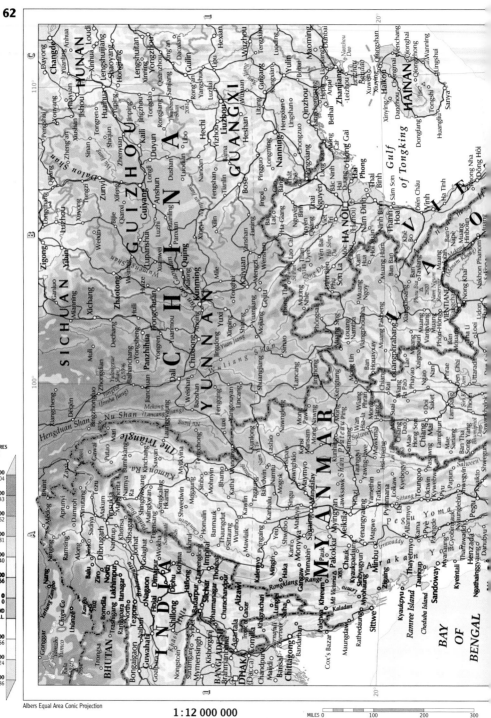

METRES
FEET

5000
16404

3000
9843

2000
6562

1000
3281

500
1640

200
656

0
0

LAND
B.S.L.

200
656

4000
13124

6000
19686

MILES 0   100   200   300

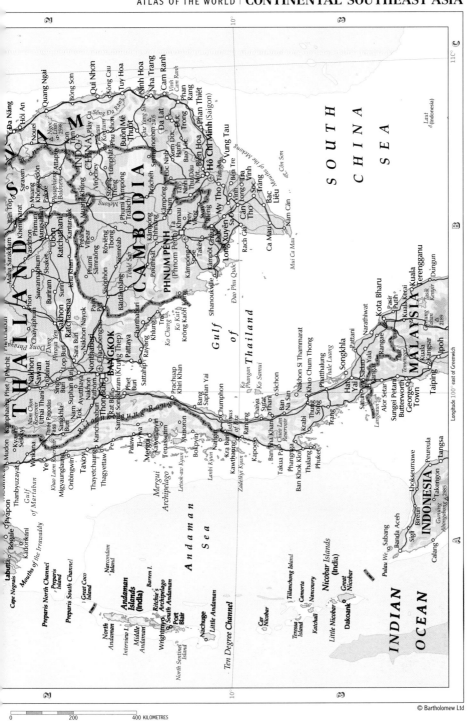

S O U T H   C H I N A   S E A

INDIAN OCEAN

ANDAMAN SEA

Gulf of Thailand

Gulf of Martaban

THAILAND

CAMBODIA

PHNUM PENH (Phnom Penh)

BANGKOK

MALAYSIA

INDONESIA

Ho Chi Minh (Saigon)

0   200   400 KILOMETRES

© Bartholomew Ltd

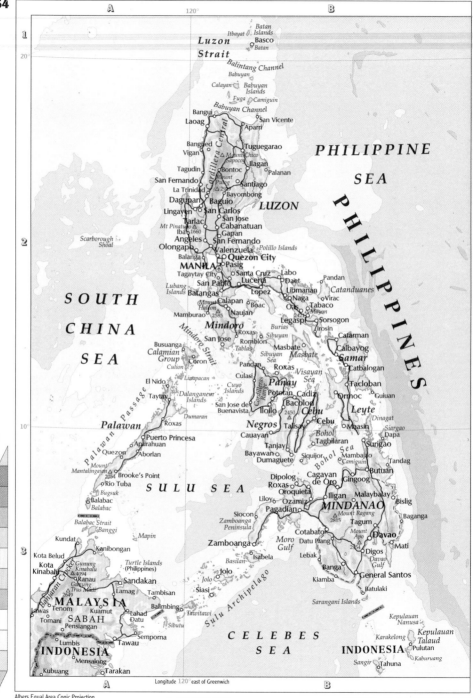

PHILIPPINE
SEA

PHILIPPINES

SOUTH
CHINA
SEA

LUZON

Luzon
Strait

Batan
Islands
Itbayat Basco
Batan

Balintang Channel
Babuyan
Calayan *Babuyan*
Islands
Fuga *Camiguin*
Babuyan Channel
Bangui
Laoag San Vicente
Aparri

Banguled Tuguegarao
Vigan Ilagan
Mount *Chico*
Sapocoy
Tagudin Bontoc Palanan
San Fernando *Mount*
Pulag Santiago
La Trinidad △29
Dagupan Bayombong
Baguio
Lingayen San Carlos
Tarlac San Jose
Mt Pinatubo Cabanatuan
Iba 1660 Gapan
Angeles San Fernando
Olongapo Valenzuela *Polillo Islands*
Balanga Quezon City
MANILA Pasig
Tagaytay City Santa Cruz Labo Pandan
San Pablo Lucena Daet
Lubang Batangas Libmanan *Catanduanes*
Islands Lopez Naga Virac
Mount Calapan Boac Oas Tabaco
Halcon Naujan *Minan*
2585 *Burias* Legaspi Sorsogon
Mamburao *Mindoro* Roxas *Sibuyan* Irosin
San Jose Romblon Catarman
Busuanga *Tablas* Masbate Calbayog
Calamian Coron Pandan **Masbate** *Samar*
Group *Culion* *Sibuyan* Roxas Catbalogan
Sea *Visayan*
Culasi *Sea* Tacloban
El Nido *Cuyo* *Panay* Ormoc Guiuan
Islands Pototan Cadiz
Taytay *Dalanganem* San Jose de Iloilo Bacolod *Leyte*
Islands Buenavista 2450 **Cebu** *Dinagat*
Dumaran Roxas **Negros** Talisay Cebu *Siargao*
Maasin Dapa
Palawan Cauayan *Bohol*
Puerto Princesa Tanjay Tagbilaran Surigao
Apurahuan Bayawan Siquijor *Camiguin*
Quezon Dumaguete Tandag
Aborlan Butuan
Mount Dipolog Cagayan Gingoog
Mantalingaiam △ Roxas de Oro
2054 Brooke's Point Oroquieta Iligan Malaybalay
Rio Tuba Liloy Ozamiz **MINDANAO** Bislig
Bugsuk Siocon Pagadian *Mount Ragang*
Balabac *Zamboanga* 2815 Baganga
Balabac *Peninsula* Cotabato Tagum
Mount
Balabac Strait Zamboanga *Moro* Datu Piang *Apo* **Davao**
Banggi *Mapin* *Gulf* Lebak *Davao* Mati
Kundat Isabela Banga *Gulf*
Kota Belud Kanibongan *Turtle Islands* Kiamba General Santos
Kota (Philippines) *Basilan* Batulaki
Kinabalu Ranau Sandakan *Jolo* *Sarangani Islands*
Gunung Jolo
Kinabalu *Trus Madi* Lamag Siasi
4094 Tambisan *Kepulauan*
Gunung *Nanusa*
2649 Balimbing
MALAYSIA Kuamut Lahad *Sibutu* **CELEBES** *Kepulauan*
Tenom Datu *Tawitawi* *Talaud*
SABAH *Karakelong* *Pulutan*
Tomani Pensiangan Semporna **SEA**
Lumbis Tawau
INDONESIA **INDONESIA** *Sangir* *Kaburuang*
Mensalong Tarakan *Tahuna*
Kubuang

Banguled Central
Cordillera Central
Mindoro Strait
Palawan Passage
Cordillera Range
Sulu Sea **SULU SEA**
Sulu Archipelago
Banjaran Crocker

METRES
FEET

5000 16404
3000 9843
2000 6562
1000 3281
500 1640
200 656
0 0
LAND
B.S.L.
200 656
4000 13124
6000 19686

Scarborough
Shoal

Longitude 120° east of Greenwich

Albers Equal Area Conic Projection

1 : 12 000 000

KILOMETRES 0   200   400
MILES 0   100   200   300

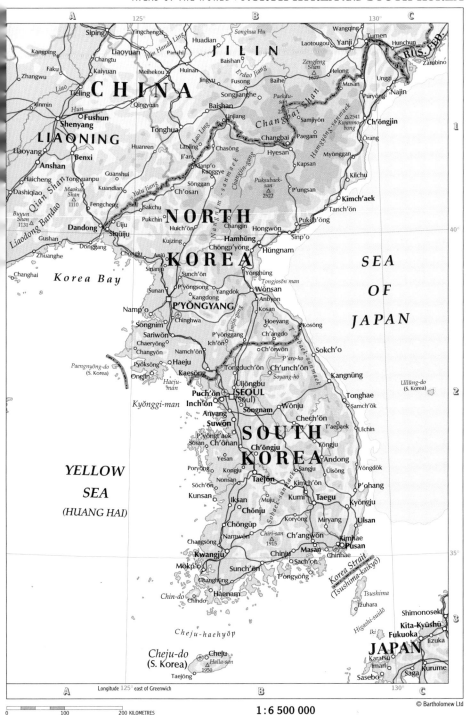

A   125°   B   130°   C

Siping   Yingchengzi   Huadian   *Songhua Hu*   Wangqing   Tumen   Hunchun   RUS. FED.

Kangping   Liaoyuan   *Jin Handa Ling*   Panshi   **J I L I N**   Laotougou   Yanji   Zarubino

Faku   Changtu   Kaiyuan   Meihekou   Huinan   Baishan   *Zengfeng Shan*   Helong   Unggi

Zhangwu   *Liao*   Tieling   Qingyuan   Fusong   Jingyu   *Erdao Jiang*   Baihe   Musan   Najin

Xinmin   *Hun*   **Fushun**   Songjianghe   *Paektu-san*   Puryong

C H I N A   Baishan   *Changbai Shan*   Ch'ŏngjin

Shenyang   Tonghua   Linjiang   Samjiyŏn   △2541 *Kwanmo-bong*

L I A O N I N G   Huanren   Laoling   *Lao Ling*   Chasŏng   Changbai   Paegam   Ŏrang

Liaoyang   **Benxi**   Ji'an   Manp'o   Hyesan   Kapsan   Myŏnggan

Anshan   Guanshui   Kanggye   *Changjin-gang*   *Puksubaek-san* △2522   P'ungsan   Kilchu

Haicheng   Tongyuanpu   Kuandian   Söngan   **Kimch'aek**

Dashiqiao   *Maokui Shan* △1110   *Yalu Jiang*   Ch'osan   Tanch'ŏn

Buyun Shan △1131   Fengcheng   Sakchu   Pukchin   **N O R T H**   Pukch'ŏng

Dandong   **Sinŭiju**   Huich'ŏn   Changjin   Hongwŏn

Liaodong Bandao   Gushan   Kujizing   **Hamhŭng**   Sinp'o

Zhuanghe   Donggang   Chŏngju   **K O R E A**   **Chŏngp'yŏng**   **Hŭngnam**   40°

Changhai   Anju   Sinanju   Sunch'ŏn   Yŏnghŭng   **S E A**

Korea Bay   *Tongjosŏn man*   **O F**

Sunan   P'yŏngsong   Yangdok   **Wŏnsan**   **J A P A N**

Namp'o   Kangdong   **P'YŎNGYANG**   Anbyŏn

Chinghwa   Kosan   Hoeyang   Kosŏng

Songnim   P'yŏnggang   Ch'angdo

Sariwŏn   Ich'ŏn   Ch'ŏrwŏn

Chaeryŏng   Namch'ŏn   *P'aro-ho*   Sokch'o

Changyŏn   **Haeju**   Tongduch'ŏn   Ch'unch'ŏn   *Soyang-ho*

Paengnyŏng-do (S. Korea)   Pyŏksŏng   Kaesŏng   Kangnŭng   *Ullŭng-do (S. Korea)*

Ongjin   *Haeju-man*   **Ŭijŏngbu**

Puch'ŏn   **SEOUL**   Tonghae

Kyŏnggi-man   **Inch'ŏn**   Sŏul   **Wŏnju**   Samch'ŏk

Anyang   Songnam   Chech'ŏn

Suwŏn   P'yŏngt'aek   T'aebaek   Ulchin

Sosan   Ch'ŏnan   **Ch'ŏngju**   Yŏngju

S O U T H

Yesan   Ch'ŏngju   Sangju   Ŭisŏng   Yŏngdŏk

Poryŏng   Kongju   **K O R E A**   Andong

Taejŏn   Kimch'ŏn   P'ohang

Söch'ŏn   Nonsan   Kumi   **Taegu**

Kunsan   Iksan   Muju   Kyŏngju

Chŏnju   Koryŏng   Miryang   **Ulsan**

Chŏngŭp   Ch'angwŏn

Changsŏng   Namwŏn   *Chiri-san* △1915   **Kimhae**   Masan   **Pusan**

Kwangju   Chinju   Chinhae

Mokp'o   Sunch'ŏn   Sach'ŏn   T'ongyŏng

Changhŭng   *Korea Strait (Tsushima-kaikyō)*

Chin-do   Chindo   Haenam   *Tsushima*   Izuhara

YELLOW

SEA   Shimonoseki

(HUANG HAI)   *Higashi-suidō*   **Kita-Kyūshū**

Iki   **Fukuoka**   Iizuka

Cheju-haehyŏp   Karatsu   **J A P A N**

Cheju-do (S. Korea)   Cheju   *Halla-san* △1950   Imari   Kurume

Taejŏng   Saga   Sasebo

A   Longitude 125° east of Greenwich   B   130°   C

0   100   200 KILOMETRES

0   50   100   150 MILES

1 : 6 500 000

© Bartholomew Ltd

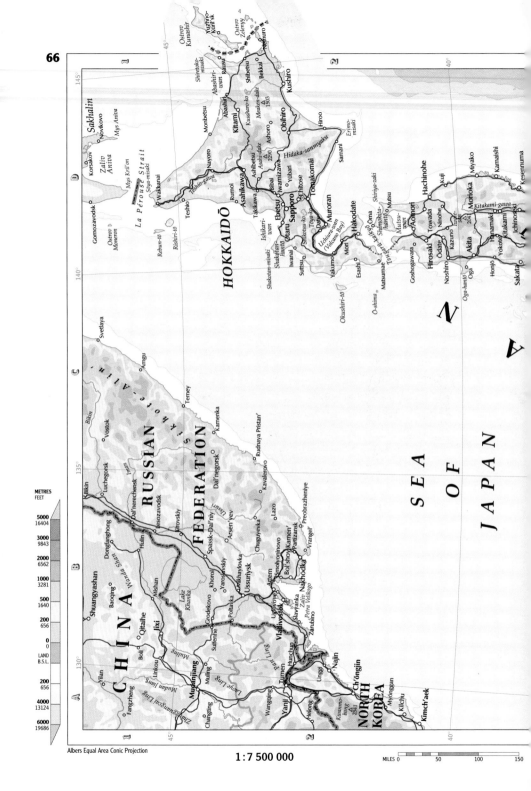

Map Labels

Sakhalin

Korsakov
Gornozavodsk
Novikovo
Mys Aniva
Zaliv Aniva
Ostrov Moneron
Mys Kril'on

La Pérouse Strait

Ostrov Kunashir
Ostrov Zelenyy
Yuzhno-Kuril'sk
Nemuro
Shiretoko-misaki
Rausu
Shibetsu
Bekkai
Kushiro
Abashiri-wan
Abashiri
Meakan-dake 1503
Ashoro
Obihiro
Hiroo
Erimo-misaki
Shiretoko-misaki

HOKKAIDŌ

Wakkanai
Sōya-misaki
Teshio-gawa
Nayoro
Monbetsu
Rumoi
Teshio
Reton-tō
Rishiri-tō
Asahikawa
Kitami
Kussharo-ko
Asahi-dake 2290
Ashibetsu
Takkawa
Bibai
Iwamizawa
Hidaka-sammyaku
Samani
Ishikari-wan
Ishikari-gawa
Otaru
Ebetsu
Sapporo
Yubari
Chitose
Iwanai
Tomakomai
Muroran
Date
Tōya-ko
Uchiura-wan
(Volcano Bay)
Hakodate
Shakotan-misaki
Shakotan-hantō
Suttsu
Yakumo
Mori
Oshamambe
Esashi
Okushiri-tō
O-shima
Matsumae
Shiroma
Shiriya-zaki
Shimokita-hantō
Mutsu
Ōma
Mutsu-wan
Tsugaru-kaikyō

N

Hachinohe
Kuji
Towada
Ninohe
Hirosaki
Aomori
Kazuno
Towada
Odate
Noshiro
Oga-hantō
Oga
Hondō
Sakata
Akita
Yokote
Honjō
Morioka
Miyako
Yamada
Kamaishi
Kitakami-gawa
Kitakami
Hanamaki
Ichinoseki
Kesennuma

A

Goshogawara

RUSSIAN FEDERATION

Sikhote-Alin'

Svetlaya
Amgu
Terney
Kamenka
Bikin
Vostok
Luchegorsk
Iman
Dal'nerechensk
Rudnaya Pristan'
Dal'negorsk
Kavalerovo
Kirovskiy
Spassk-Dal'niy
Arsen'yev
Yakovlevka
Lazo
Chuguyevka
Preobrazheniye
Khorol
Mikhaylovka
Ussuriysk
Partizansk
Smolyaninovo
Bol'shoy Kamen'
Nakhodka
Vrangel'
Artem
Ugolovoye
Nadezhdino
Petra Velikogo
Vladivostok
Slavyanka
Zalin
Zarubino

CHINA

Shuangyashan
Baoqing
Dongfanghong
Qitaihe
Jixi
Wanda Shan
Mishan
Lake Khanka
Grodekovo
Poltavka
Suifenhe
Mudanjiang
Muling
Bol
Linkou
Yilan
Fangzheng
Zhangguangcai Ling
Changting
Wangqing
Yanji
Helong
Laoye Ling
Tumen
Hunchun
Kraskino
Kovanino-bong

NORTH KOREA

Najin
Unggi
Ch'ŏngjin
Myŏnggan
Kimch'aek
Kilchu

SEA OF JAPAN

Scale

METRES	FEET
5000	16404
3000	9843
2000	6562
1000	3281
500	1640
200	656
0	0
LAND B.S.L.	
200	656
4000	13124
6000	19686

Albers Equal Area Conic Projection

1 : 7 500 000

MILES 0   50   100   150

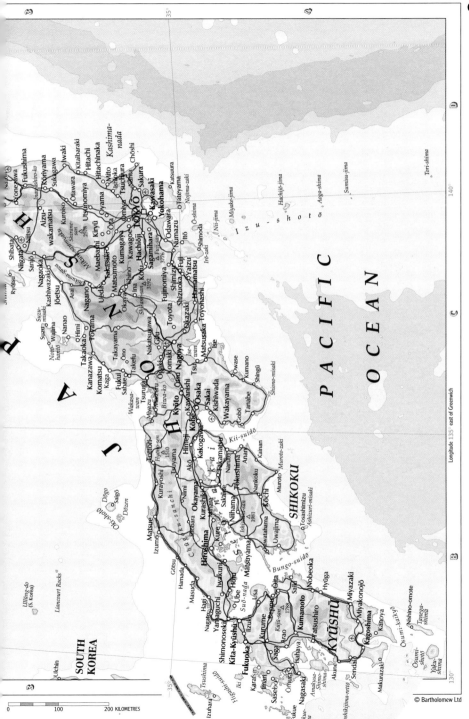

SOUTH
KOREA

P A C I F I C

O C E A N

Izu-shotō

SHIKOKU

KYŪSHŪ

© Bartholomew Ltd

0   100   200 KILOMETRES

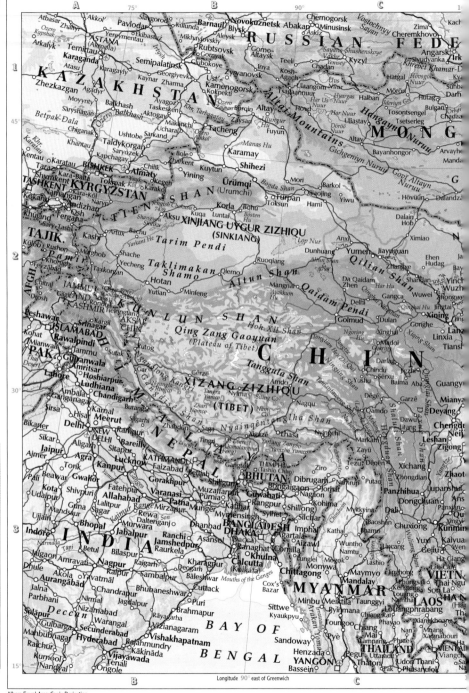

0   250   500   750 KILOMETRES

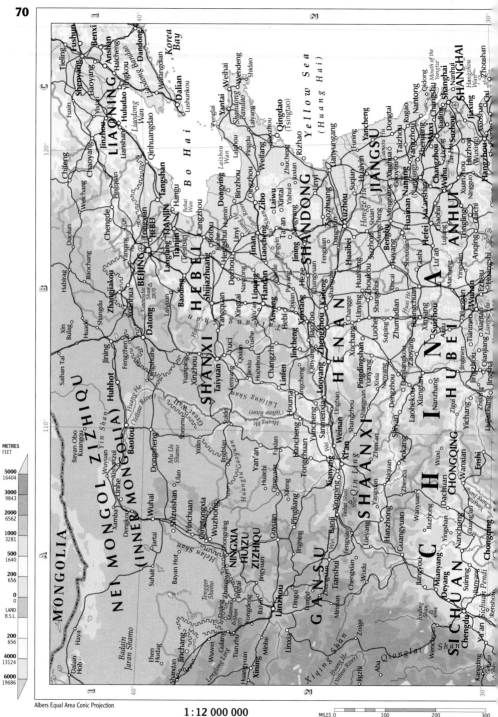

Albers Equal Area Conic Projection

1:12 000 000

MILES 0   100   200   300

METRES
FEET

5000
16404

3000
9843

2000
6562

1000
3281

500
1640

200
656

0
0

LAND
B.S.L.

200
656

4000
13124

6000
19686

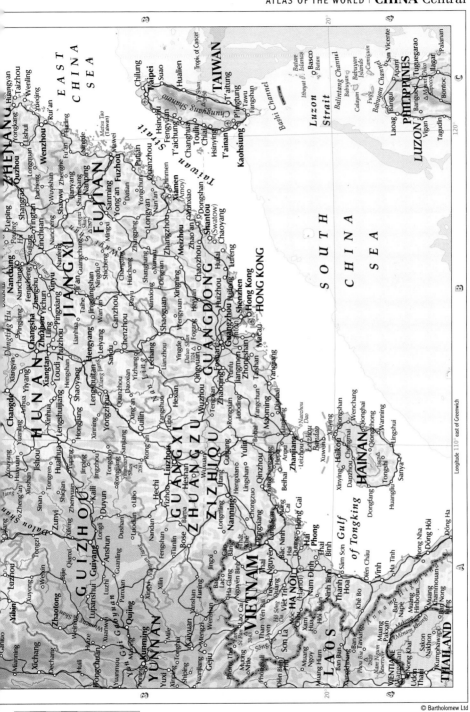

© Bartholomew Ltd

0   200   400 KILOMETRES

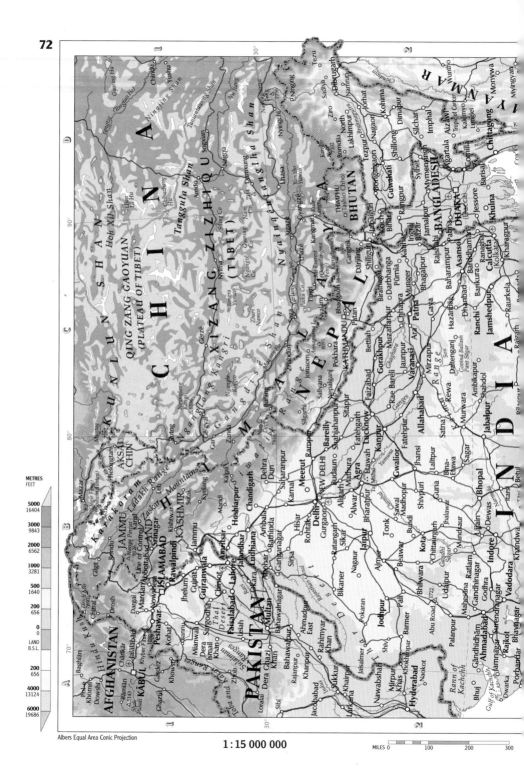

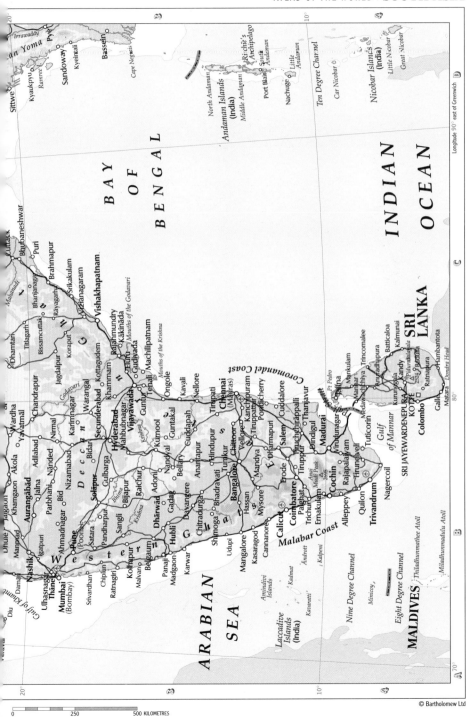

20°

10°

Irrawaddy

an Yoma

Sittwe

Kyaukpyu

Ramree I.

Sandoway

Kyeintali

Bassein

Cape Negrais

Pye

North Andaman

Andaman Islands
(India)

Ritchie's
Archipelago

Middle Andaman

South
Andaman

Port Blair

Nachug

Little
Andaman

Ten Degree Channel

Car Nicobar

Nicobar Islands
(India)

Little Nicobar

Great Nicobar

B A Y

O F

B E N G A L

I N D I A N

O C E A N

Longitude 90° east of Greenwich

Cuttack

Bhubaneshwar

Puri

Brahmapur

Mahanadi

Dhantari

Titlagarh

Bissamcuttak

Jagdalpur

Bhanjanagar

Rayagarth

Srikakulam

Vizianagaram

Vishakhapatnam

Koraput

Bastar

Mouths of the Godavari

Rajahmundry

Kakinada

Eluru

Gudivada

Machilipatnam

Mouths of the Krishna

**SRI
LANKA**

Trincomalee

Batticaloa

Kalmunai

Mankulam

Medawachchiya

Anuradhapura

Kurunegala

Kandy

Pidurutalagala
2524

Badulla

Ratnapura

Galle

Hambantota

Matara

Dondra Head

Corrmandel Coast

Chennai
(Madras)

Tirupati

Kanchipuram

Tiruppattur

Pondicherry

Cuddalore

Pt. Pedro

Jaffna

Palk Bay

Mannar

Gulf
of Mannar

**SRI JAYEWARDENEPURA
KOTTE**

Colombo

80°

Madgaon

Karwar

Panaji

Belgaum

Hubli

Gadag

Davangere

Chitradurga

Bhadravati

Shimoga

Hassan

Mandya

Bangalore

Mysore

Coimbatore

Palghat

Trichur

Ernakulam

Cochin

Alleppey

Quilon

Trivandrum

Nagercoil

Tuticorin

Tirunelveli

Rajapalaiyam

Virudunagar

Madurai

Dindigul

Karur

Salem

Erode

Tiruppur

Dharmapuri

Krishnagiri

Vellore

Chittoor

Anantapur

Hindupur

Tumkur

Kolar

Bellary

Adoni

Kurnool

Nandyal

Cuddapah

Tirupati

Ongole

Nellore

Kavali

Guntur

Vijayawada

Tenali

Khammam

Warangal

Hyderabad

Secunderabad

Mahbubnagar

Gulbarga

Bidar

Nizamabad

Karimnagar

Kottagudem

Bijapur

Raichur

Bhima

Krishna

Sangli

Kolhapur

Satara

Ratnagiri

Chiplun

Srivardhan

Pune
(Poona)

Mumbai
(Bombay)

Thane

Ulhasnagar

Nashik

Ahmadnagar

Bid

Parbhani

Nanded

Latur

Osmanabad

Solapur

Pandharpur

Bijapur

Dharwad

Belgaum

Goa

Deccan

Wardha

Yavatmal

Akola

Aurangabad

Jalna

Adilabad

Nirmal

Nizamabad

Khamgaon

Akot

Talgaon

Jalgaon

Dhule

Manpad

Igatpuri

Godavari

Diu

Damah

Gulf of Khambat

20°

M A L D I V E S

Miladhunmadhulu Atoll

Thiladhunmathee Atoll

North Maalhosmadulu Atoll

Eight Degree Channel

Nine Degree Channel

Minicoy

Kalpeni

Andrott

Kadmat

Amindivi
Islands

Karavatti

**Laccadive
Islands
(India)**

A R A B I A N

S E A

70°

10°

© Bartholomew Ltd

0   250   500 KILOMETRES

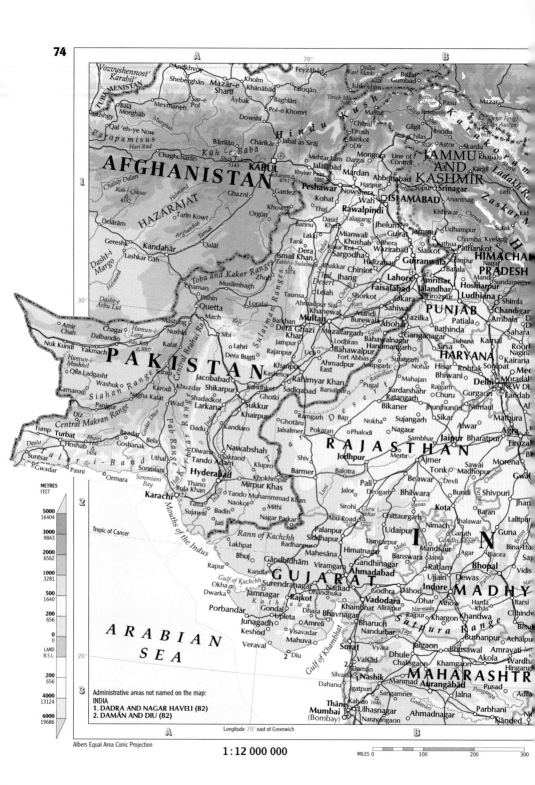

1 : 12 000 000

Albers Equal Area Conic Projection

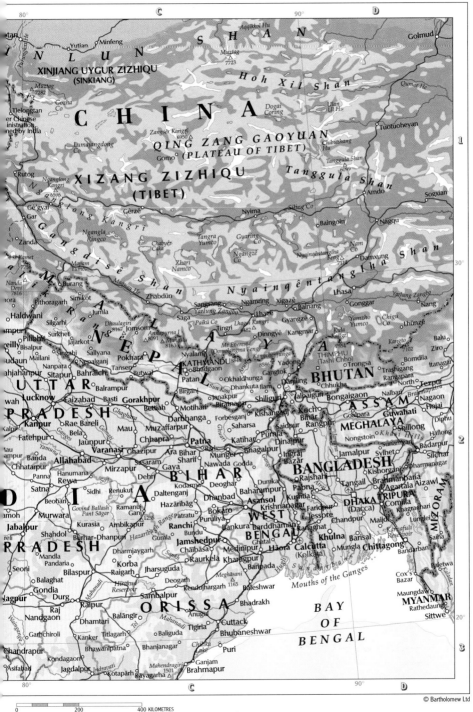

BAY

OF

BENGAL

0   200   400 KILOMETRES

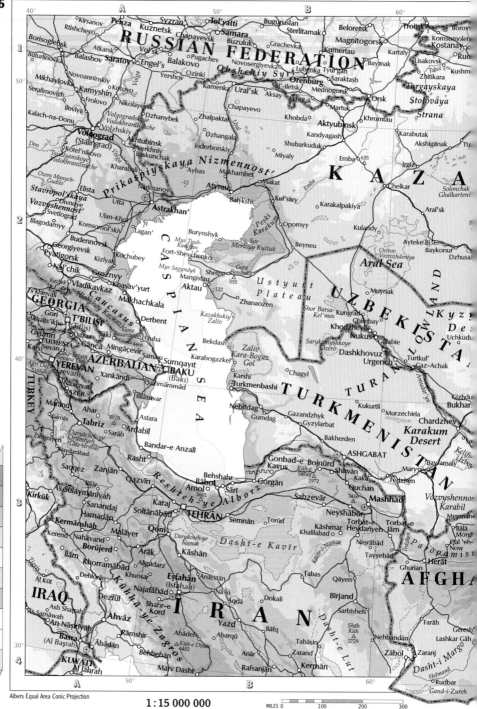

1 : 15 000 000

MILES 0   100   200   300

Petropavlovsk

Ishim

Tayynsha Kishkenekol'
Saumalkol' Kokshetau
Ruzayevka Makinsk
Balkashino Akkol'
esil' Atbasar Yereymentau
Zhaltyr **ASTANA**
Derzhavinsk (Akmola)
Ozero Osakarovka
Tengiz
angel'dy Kyshak Arkalyk **Temirtau**

K a z a k h s k i y **Karaganda**
M e l k o s o p o c h n i k
Atasu Sarysu
Katpayev Zhayrem Agadyr'
hezkazgan **Zhezkazgan**

Gora Ayeat
464
Betpak-Dala
Moyynty
Saryshagan
Balkhash

Ozero
Kyzylorda Akzhaykyn
Chiganak
Chilli

Khr. Karatau
Kentau Moyynkum
Turkestan Shu 1520

Syrdar'ya Karatau Kara-Balta **Tokmak**
Taraz **BISHKEK**
Shymkent Tura-
Ryskulova Chaek

Kara-Kol
Kara-Kol
TASHKENT Chirchik
Ayakkuduk Chinaz Angren Namangan
ydarkul' Gora Andizhan Jalal-Abad
Khayatbashi Almalyk Kokand Osh
2169 Gulistan Fergana
avoi Dzhizak Khujand
Kattakurgan Sary-Tash

Samarkand Qullai
Chimtarga Lenin
Guzar 5487 Garmo Peak
Karshi Shahrisabz **TAJIKISTAN** 7134
Guzar **DUSHANBE** **P a m i r**
Denau Norak
Kerki Shurchi Rushon Murghob
Qurghonteppa Kulob Alichur
Termez Vakhsh Feyzabad Khorugh

80°
Karasuk
Slavgorod
Ozero
Kulundinskoye
Kulunda
Aleysk
Mikhaylovskiy **Biysk**
RUSSIAN
Pavlodar
Ekibastuz Gornyak **FEDERATION**
Irtysh Glubokoye Leninogorsk Altai Mountains
Semipalatinsk Ust'-Kamenogorsk Gora Belukha
4506 Youyi
Zyryanovsk Feng
Georgiyevka Kurchum
Kokpekti Ozero Burqin Altay
Kaynar Zharma Zaysan
1559 Zaysan Ulungur
Ayagoz Taskesken Khrebet Tarbagatay Hu
Aktogay Makanchi **Tacheng**
Konyrat Ebinur
Ozero Sarkand Ucharal Alakol Karamay Manas
Lepsy Hu Hu
Ushtobe Khr. Dzhungarskiy Alatau Shihezi
Taldykorgan Balpyk Bi Bole
Saryozek Kuytun
Khantau Zharkent **Yining** Borohoro Shan
Kapchagayskoye Xinyuan
Kapchagay Chilik
Otar **Almaty** Kegen
Kunges Alatau Kegen **T I E N** Luntai
Ysyk- Karakol Tengish Chokusu Kuqa Korla
KYRGYZSTAN Kol 7439 **S H A N**
Balykchy Aksu Bohu
Chaek 3390 Tarim He
Naryn Akqi Shayyou
Shuohu
Turugart Toxkan He **XINJIANG UYGUR ZIZHIQU**
Pass Artux Bachu Tarim Pendi
3752 Kashi **(SINKIANG)**
Kaxgar He Shache Qiemo
Kongur Taklimakan Shamo
Shan Yecheng Misalay
719 Kaqung **C H I N A**
Zangguy Hotan Yutian Minfeng
Mazar Muztag
Taxkorgan **K U N L U N S H A N**

40°

50°

1

2

Altay

3

Port Said
(Bûr Sa'îd)
GAZA
Suez Canal
Ismâ'iliya
Suez
(El Suweis)
Z'afarâna
Ras
G. Gharib
Gemsa
Hurghada
Bûr Safâga
Quseir
Marsa Alam

GULF OF SUEZ

Dead Sea
El 'Arîsh
Be'er Sheva
ISRAEL
Petra
Elat
JORDAN
Al Karak
Tafilah
Ma'an
Al 'Isâwîya

Turayf
40°

An Najaf
Ad Dîwânîyah
Al Hayy
Amârah
Ash Shatrah
As Samâwah
Euphrates
An Nâsirîyah
Sûq ash Shuyûkh

IRAQ

Hawr al Hammâr
Basra
(Al Basrah)
Raudhatain
KU
Hawa
Al Jahra
As Subayhi

Sinai
Nuweiba el Muzeina
Haql
Jabal Lawz
2579
Al Mudawwarah
Hâlat 'Ammâr
Al Bi'r
Tabûk

An Nafûd

Ash Shabakah
An Nâsirîyah
'Ar'ar
Rafha'
Ash Shu'bah
Hafar al Bâtin
Jabal al Kâ'
325
Qaryat al Ulyâ
Ash Shum

Gebel Katherina 2637
Jabal ad Dubbagh 2350
El Tûr
Sharm el Sheikh
Al Muwaylih
Dubâ

Qakat al Mu'azzam
Taymâ'
Jubbah
Mawqaq
Hâ'il
Ash Shu'aybah

Jabal Gharib 1751

EGYPT

Marsa Alam
Berenice
Bir Shalatein

Gebel Hamâta 1977

Ad Dâr al Hamrâ'
Al'Ula
Al Badâ'i'
Khaybar
Hanak
Umm Lajj

Ghazzâlah
Tâbah
Samîrah
As Sulaymî
Hulayfah
Hujr
Nuqrah
SÂHUQ

Jabal az Zalma 1258
Al Kahfâ
Al Quwârah
Buraydah

HILLÎZ

Jabal Radwâ 1814
Sûq Suwayq
Yanbu' al Bahr
Badr Hunayn
Rayyis

Jabal Tim
'Uqlat as Suqûr
Ar Rass
'Unayzah
Az Zilfi
Al Artâwîyah
Al Majma'ah
Asharat
Ruma

SAUDI

Al Hanâkîyah
Ash Shubaykhîyah
Nafy
'Ariah
Ad Di'îyah
RIYADH
(Ar Riyad)
Al Jubaylah
As Salâmîyah
Ad Dilam

Medina
(Al Madînah)
Al Musayjid

Jabal Shi'b

'Ad Dawâdimî
'Ad Quwayyah
Al Ruwaydah

Mahd adh Dhahab
'Afif

Halabân

Khashm Mâwân 1025

Al Hillah

HIJAZ

Mastûrah
Umm al Birak
Rabigh
Jabal Umm Mukhhar

Ad Dafînah

AD DAHNÂ

Al Hârith

Tuwwal
Khulays

Madrakah
As Sûq
As Sûq
Al Hawîyah
Turabah
Wâdi Ranyah
'Amâ'ir

Jabal Hasan
Zalim
Jabal Kursh

ARABIA

Layla
Al Badi

JABAL TUWAYQ

Jeddah
(Jiddah)
Mecca
(Makkah)
At Tâ'if

Mastâbah

Jabal Sadî
Al 'Aqîq
Al Junaynah
Al Mindak

Al Khamâsîn
As Sulayyil
Kumdah

HALAIB TRIANGLE
UNDER SUDANESE ADMINISTRATION
Jebel Asoteriba 2215
Halaib
Marsa Delwein

Wadi Oko

Salâla
Dungunab

Muhammad Qol

SUDAN

Nubian Desert

Jebel Oda 2259

Port Sudan

Al Lith
Baljurshi
Dawqah
Qam Hadil
Al Qunfidhah
An Nimâs
Dirs
Al Birk

Qal'at Bîshah
Al 'Alayyah
Tathlîth
Hamdah

Wâdi Tathlîth

Banî Ma'arid

'Urûq al Awârik

RUB'

Kamob Sanha
Sinkat
Musmar
Erheib
Haiya
Derudeb

Al Birk
Abha
Harajâ
Ash Shuqayq
Ad Darb

Khamis Mushayt
Zahrân
Najrân
Ash Sharawrah
Husn Âl 'Abr

ASIR

2780
Karora
Algena
Hagar Nish Plateau
Mount Shara 2603
Nakfa
Afabet

Sabyâ
Jîzân
Abu 'Arish
Mîdi
Jazâ'ir Farasân
Kamarân
Az Zaydîyah

'Âd Darb
Sa'dah
Râmlat Dahm

Khamir
Hajjah
Al Mahwît
Manâkhah
Bâjil

Al Hazm al-Jawf
Raydah
'Amrân
3760
SAN'A'
Ma'rib
Ma'bar

YEME

ERITREA

Aroma
Kassala
New Halfa
Teseney
Akordat
Keren
Barentu
Mendefera
ASMARA
Dekhemhare
Adi Keyih

Massawa
Dahlak Atchipelago
Mersa Fatma

RED SEA

As Sahif
Al Hudaydah
Bayt al Faqih
Zabid
Al Khawkhah

Dhamâr
Yarîm
Ibb
Ta'izz
Qattabah
Hays
Al Mukhâ

Radâ'
Al Bayda'
Ataq
Lawdar
Habban

Kolulu
Kêmêse
Om Hajer
Gedaref

Aksum
Adîgrat
Adwa
Mek'elê

DENAKIL

Jabal Thamar 2512
Mûsaymir
Zhijibâr
Ash Shaykh Uthman

ETHIOPIA

Adi Ark'ay
Silasê
Simîen Mountains 4533
Gallabat

2131
Assab

Ed Az Zuqur

Mawza
Dhubâb
Lahij
Am Nâbiyah
At Turbah
Bâb al Mandab
Aden
('Adan)

METRES
FEET

5000
16404

3000
9843

2000
6562

1000
3281

500
1640

200
656

0
0

LAND
B.S.L.

200
656

4000
13124

6000
19686

MILES 0   100   200   300   0   200   400 KILOMETRES

A

30°

B

CHIŞINĂU

Târgu Mureş
Miercurea-Ciuc
Bacău
Tighina
Tiraspol
Berezivka
Mykolayiv
Nova Kakhovka
Tokmak
Mariupol'
Taganrog

Ighişoara
Sebeş
Vaslui
Odesa
Kherson
Armyans'k
Berdyans'k
Melitopol'
Gulf of Taganrog
Bataysk

Sibiu
Deva
Fagăraş
Sfântu Gheorghe
Vylkove
Artsyz
Bilhorod-Dnistrovs'kyy
Novooleksiyivka
Krasnoperekops'k
Staromynskaya
Akhtarsk

Lugoj
Caransebeş
Reşiţa
Braşov
Focşani
Iecuci
Bolhrad
Karkinits'ka Zatoka
Nyzhn'ohirs'ky
Dzhankoy
Timashevsk
Primorsko-Akhtarsk
Pavlovska

Drobeta
Piteşti
Galaţi
Buzău
Brăila
Izmayil
Chornomors'ke
Kerch
Temryuk
Slavyans'ka-na-Kubari

Turnu Severin
ROMANIA
Ploieşti
Babadag
Yevpatoriya
Crimea
Feodosiya
Krymsk
Krasnoda

Craiova
Slatina
Roşiori de Vede
BUCHAREST
(Bucureşti)
Danube
(Dunărea)
Constanţa
Simferopol'
Roman Kosh
Sudak
Novorossiysk
Khadyzhensk

Calafat
Caracal
Corabia
Ruse
Călăraşi
Mangalia
Sevastopol'
Novorossiysk
Tuapse

Montana
Vraţa
Pleven
Dobrich
Razgrad
Kavarna
Soch

Botevgrad
Lovech
Shumen
Varna

Pernik
SOFIYA
Kazanlŭk
Stara Zagora
Sliven
Burgas

B L A C K   S E A

Kyustendil
Plovdiv
Dimitrovgrad

Blagoevgrad
Khaskovo

BULGARIA

Kočani
Sandanski
Smolyan
Kŭrdzhali
Kirklareli
Saray

Strumica
Drama
Xanthi
Edirne
Çorlu
Silivri

Serres
Kavala
Komotini
Keşan
Tekirdağ
İstanbul
Cide
İnebolu
İnce Burun
Sinop

Thessaloniki
Thasos
Gökçeada
Gelibolu
Marmara Denizi
Şarköy
Kadıköy
Körfez
Zonguldak
Ereğli
Karabük
Boyabat
Bafra
Samsun

Polygyros
Limnos
İmroz
Çanakkale
Can
Bursa
Gemlik
Sakarya
Düzce
Bolu
Gerede
Tosya
Vezirköprü
Merzifon
Terme
Ordu
Trabzo

Volos
Aegean Sea
Lesbos
Ezine
Edremit
Susurluk
İnegöl
Uludağ 2543
Bilecik
Göynük
Çankırı
Osmancık
Amasya
Çorum
Kızılırmak
Tokat
Şebinkarahisar
Giresun

GREECE
Mytilini
Bergama
Demirci
Simav
Eskişehir
Bozüyük
Beypazarı
Kalecik
Sungurlu
Turhal
Yıldızeli
Sivas
Suşehri
Erzinc

Evvoia
Chalkida
Chios
Bornova
Akhisar
Manisa
Gediz
Banaz
Afyon
ANKARA
Polatlı
Kırıkkale
Yozgat
Akdağmadeni
Zara
Divriği

ATHENS
(Athina)
Chios
Alaşehir
Uşak
Sandıklı
Aksehir
Tuz Gölü
Kırşehir
Kaman
Kayseri
Erciyes Dağı 3917
Pınarbaşı
Elazığ

Peiraias
Andros
İzmir
Aydın
Civril
Isparta
Egirdir Gölü
Aksaray
Hasan Dağı 3268
Niğde
Elbistan
Ergani
Siverek

Ermoupoli
Tinos
Syros
Kuşadası
Samos
Büyükmenderes
Denizli
Burdur
Beyşehir Gölü
Karapınar
Konya
Ereğli
Karaman
Kahramanmaraş
Adıyaman
Malatya

Paros
Naxos
İos
Bodrum
Milas
Muğla
Yatağan
Bucak
Korkuteli
Karaman
Tarsus
Adana
Gaziantep
Viranşehir
Akçaka

Milos
Santorini
Krytiko Pelagos
Marmaris
Dalaman
Elmalı
Serik
Manavgat
Ermenek
Silifke
İçel
Erdemli
Kilis
Birecik
Euphrates (Fırat)

Chania
Irakleio
Agios Nikolaos
Karpathos (Scarpanto)
Fethiye
Antalya
Alanya
Anamur
Antakya (Antioch) (Hatay)
İskenderun (Alexandretta)
Aleppo (Halab)
SYRIA

Rethymno
Lindos
Rhodes (Rodos)
Kaş Megisti
Antalya Körfezi
Cape Apostolos Andreas
İdlib
Ma'arrat an Nu'mān
Ar Raqqah
Al Furā

CRETE (KRITI)
Siteia
Ierapetra
NICOSIA (Lefkosia)
Kyrenia
Al Lādhiqiyah
Hamāh
Hims

Cape Arnaoutis
Polis
Evrychou
Famagusta
Baniyās
Tadmur

MEDITERRANEAN SEA
CYPRUS
Pafos
Lemesos
Larnaka
Tartūs
Trâblous (Tripoli)

BEIRUT (Beyrouth)
Sidon
Zahlé
An Nabk
Sab' Ābār

LEBANON
Soûr
Sea of Galilee (L. Tiberias)
As Suwaydā'

Al Bardi
Umm Sa'ad
Marsa Matrûh
DAMASCUS (Dimashq)

Alexandria (El Iskandarîya)
El 'Amîriya
Baltîm
Dumyât
Hefa
Nazareth
Irbid
Al Mafraq
Syrian Desert
(Bādiyat ash Sham)

LIBYA
Libyan Plateau
El Hammam
Damanhûr
El Mansûra
Benha
Zagazig
ISRAEL
Tel Aviv-Yafo
Rehovot
Nablus
WEST BANK
Az Zarqā'
AMMAN

Marsa Matrûh
Kafr el Sheikh
Tanta
Port Said (Bûr Sa'îd)
Ismâ'îlya
JERUSALEM
GAZA
Be'er Sheva'
Al Karak
Turayf

Qattâra Depression
Shubrâ el Kheima
CAIRO (El Qâhira)
Suez (El Suweis)
El 'Arish
At Tafilah
Ma'an
JORDAN

Siwa Oasis
Qara
El Gîza
Giza Pyramid
Memphis
Suez
Dead Sea
Petra

EGYPT
Siwa
El Faiyûm
Beni Suef
Z'afarâna
Sinai
Al 'Aqabah
Al Mudawwarah
Hālat 'Ammâr
SAUDI
Al Jawf

Bawiti
Beni Mazâr
Maghâgha
Nuweiba el Muzeina
Haql
G. Katherina 2637
G. el Lawz 2579
Al Bi'r

METRES / FEET

5000 / 16404
3000 / 9843
2000 / 6562
1000 / 3281
500 / 1640
200 / 656
0 / 0
LAND B.S.L.
200 / 656
4000 / 13124
6000 / 19686

Albers Equal Area Conic Projection

Longitude 30° east of Greenwich

1 : 12 000 000

MILES 0   100   200   300

1
2
3

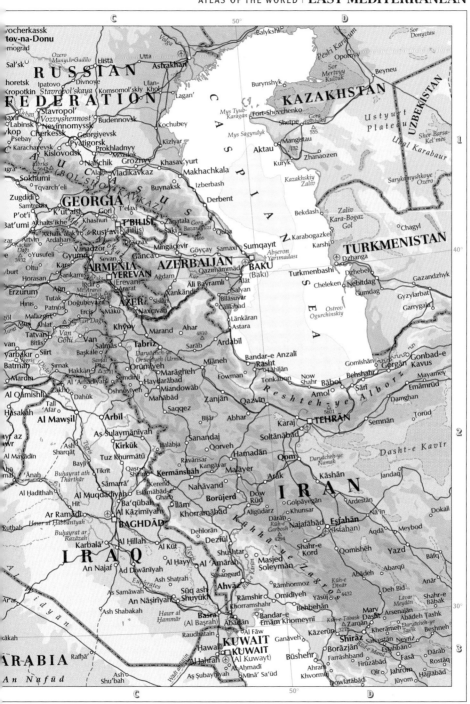

0   200   400 KILOMETRES

Conic Equidistant Projection

1 : 30 000 000

Longitude 75° east of Greenwich

MILES 0   200   400   600

METRES
FEET

5000	16404
3000	9843
2000	6562
1000	3281
500	1640
200	656
0	0
LAND	B.S.L.
200	656
4000	13124
6000	19686

© Bartholomew Ltd

0   500   1000 KILOMETRES

LIE. LIECHTENSTEIN
MACE. MACEDONIA
SLOV. SLOVENIA

Chamberlin Trimetric Projection

1 : 25 000 000

MILES 0   250   500

H 40° I 50° J 60° K 70° L 80° M

B A R E N T S
S E A

Novaya
Zemlya

kapp

Ostrov Kolguyev

Ob'

Vorkuta

2

RUSSIAN FEDERATION

kapp

Murmansk

White Sea

Archangel

Syktyvkar

U r a l   M o u n t a i n s

3

50°

NLAND

Lake
Onega

Lake
Ladoga

Helsinki

St Petersburg

Perm'

Tallinn

ONIA

Yaroslavl'

Volga

Nizhniy
Novgorod

Kazan

iga
VIA

Moscow

Ryazan'

Samara

Orenburg

NIA
ius

Minsk

Saratov

KAZAKHSTAN

4

40°

BELARUS

Homyel'

Voronezh

Aral Sea

Kiev

Kharkiv

Don

Volgograd

Volga

UZBEKISTAN

U K R A I N E

Dnipropetrovs'k

Donets'k

Rostov
na-Donu

Astrakhan

Caspian Sea

MOLDOVA

Chisinău

Dniepr

Sea
of Azov

Krasnodar

Grozny

TURKMENISTAN

Odesa

OMANIA

Bucharest

Black Sea

C a u c a s u s

GEORGIA

AZERBAIJAN

40°

Sofia

BULGARIA

ARMENIA

Istanbul

5

Thessaloniki

Aegean
Sea

T U R K E Y

I R A N

ECE

Athens

Crete

CYPRUS

SYRIA

Euphrates

I R A Q

Tigris

30°

LEBANON

G 30° H 40° I 50° J

© Bartholomew Ltd

0 250 500 750 KILOMETRES

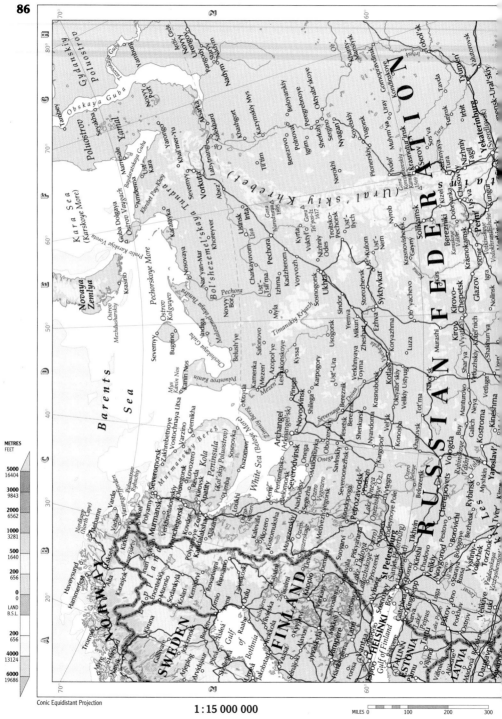

RUSSIAN FEDERATION

Gydanskiy Poluostrov
Poluostrov Yamal
Kara Sea (Karskoye More)
Novaya Zemlya
Ostrov Kolguyev
Barents Sea
Pechorskoye More
Bol'shezemel'skaya Tundra
Ural'skiy Khrebet
Obskaya Guba
Timanskiy Kryazh
Poluostrov Kamin
White Sea (Beloye More)
Kola Peninsula (Kol'skiy Poluostrov)
Murmansk
Arkhangel'sk (Archangel)
Severodvinsk
Yekaterinburg
Perm
Syktyvkar
Vorkuta
Vologda
Kotlas
Yaroslavl'
Kostroma
St Petersburg (Sankt-Peterburg)
Petrozavodsk
Lake Ladoga
Lake Onega
Novgorod

NORWAY
SWEDEN
FINLAND
HELSINKI
ESTONIA
TALLINN
LATVIA

Gulf of Bothnia
Gulf of Finland

Tromsø
Hammerfest
Narvik
Kiruna
Luleå
Oulu
Tampere

Conic Equidistant Projection

1 : 15 000 000

METRES FEET
5000 / 16404
3000 / 9843
2000 / 6562
1000 / 3281
500 / 1640
200 / 656
0 / 0
LAND B.S.L.
200 / 656
4000 / 13124
6000 / 19686

MILES 0   100   200   300

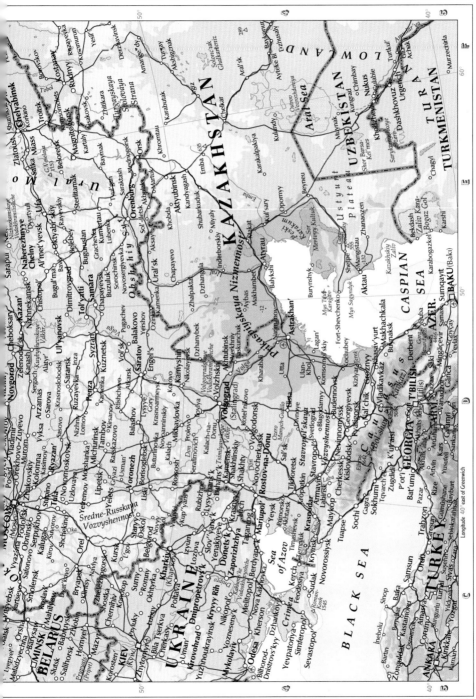

0   250   500 KILOMETRES

FINLAND

Kouvola
Anjalankoski
Hamina
Vyborg

Mäntsälä
Järvenpää
Tuusula Porvoo Loviisa Kotka Vyborgskiy Zaliv
Espoo Oylsi
Kirkkonummi Vantaa Zelenogorsk
HELSINKI
(Helsingfors) Ostrov Ostrov
Hanko Ekenäs Gogland Moshchnyy Lomonoso
Sosnovyy Bor Petrodvore

SWEDEN
Uppsala
Norrtälje Åland Mariehamn
Märsta Kökar Korpo
Sollentuna Åkersberga
Täby
STOCKHOLM
Västerhaninge
Nynäshamn

60° 20° A B C

Gulf of Finland

TALLINN Maardu
Keila Kehra Kohtla- Narva Ust- Gatcl
Paldiski Aman Vaida Järve Sillamäe Bay Kingisepp Voloso
Rakvere Jõhvi Narva Sivers
Kalana Kärdla Vormsi Tapa Kiviõli Slantsy Os'mino Mshinsk
Hiiumaa Kaina Rapla Vaide Narvskoye Vdkhr. Luga
Emmaste Mustjala Orissaare Mahu **ESTONIA** Rakke Vasknarva Luga
Haapsalu Emumägi Raja Gdov
△166 Lake
Kuressaare Pärnu Virtsu Vändra Põltsamaa Jõgeva Peipus Plyussa
Saaremaa Viljandi Tartu Yamm
Sääre Vörtsjärv Ülenurme 200 Strugi-
Mazirbe Kihnu Mõisaküla Elva Krasnyye
Irbe Strait Ruhnu Põlva Lake
Kolkasrags Salacgrīva Valka Valga Võru Pskov
Ventspils Dundaga Roja Limbaži Valmiera Pechory Porkhov
Ovišrags Akmeņrags Talsi Saulkrasti Cēsis Smiltene Rauna Alūksne Palkino Slavkovic'
Gulf of Rauna Gulbene Ostrov Dedovici
Pāvilosta Kuldīga Riga Jūrmala Garkalne Sigulda Balvi Chikhachevo
Liepāja Aizpute Tukums **RĪGA** Madona Kārsava Rēzekne Bezhanitsy
Skrunda Saldus Dobele Jelgava Iecava Kokneae Barkava Mežvidi Pustoshka
Nīca **LATVIA** Aizkraukle Jēkabpils Viļāni Ludza Opochka
Mažeikiai Bauska Līvāni Preiļi Malta Sebezh Neve
Skuodas Naujoji Krāslava
Kretinga Venta Akmenė Pasvalys Biržai Daugava Dagda Yezyaryshch
Plungė Kuršėnai Pakruojis Rokiškis Viški
Klaipėda Telšiai **Šiauliai** Radviliškis Dokšycy Visaginas Kupiškis Kraslava Rasony
Medvėgalio Kelmė Panevėžys **Daugavpils** Zarasai Druya Vyerkhnyadzvinsk Harado
Courland △235 Silalė Raseiniai **LITHUANIA** Utena Braslaw Myory Navapolatsk Obal'
Lagoon Gargždai Ukmergė Ignalina Sharkawshchyna Polatsk Ushachy Shumilina
Nida Šilutė Kedainiai Dökštas Negilio Varapayeva Hlybokaye Byeshankovich'
Svetlogorsk Pagėgiai Jonava Molėtai △kalnis Pastavy Myadzyel Narach
Zelenogradsk Sovetsk Taurage Jurbarkas Švenčionys Abrade
Gulf of Svetly Neman Šakiai Širvintos Dokshytsy Byahoml' Syann
Gdańsk **RUS. FED.** Kaunas Neris Pastavy Chashniki
Mamonovo Baltiysk **Kaliningrad** Norelkiškės **VILNIUS** Astravyets Vilyeyka Plyeshchanitsy Kokhanav
Frombork Gvardeysk Chernyakhovsk Vilkaviškis Grigiškės Smarhon' Talachyn
Branievo Bagrationovsk Gusev Kybartai Prienai Trakai Maladzyechna Barysaw Krupki
Elbląg Bartoszyce Korsze Goldap Marijampolė Alytus Šalčininkai Varéna Ašmyany Valozhyn Zaslawye Smalyavichy Zhodzina Byerazino
Malbork Pasłęk Dobre Gižycko Olecko Lazdijai Sejny Druskininkai Merkinė Voranava Zaslawye Smilavichy Chervyen'
Kwidzyn Miasto Suwałki Ivye Lida Ivatsevichy **MINSK** Uskhodni
Iława Ostróda Olsztyn Węgorzewo Augustów Shchuchyn Byaroawka △345 Byalynichy
△Góra Pojezierze Mazurskie Ełk Grajewo Karelichy Dzyarzhynsk Smilavichy Byerazino
Nidzica Jeziero Navahrudak Stowbtsy Mar''ina Horka Klichaw
Brodnica Działdowo Śniardwy Mońki Masty Zel'va Baranavichy Nyasvizh Kapyl Asipovichy Babruysk
Mława Łomża Narew Nyoman Słonim Staraya Darohi Rahachow
Ciechanów Ostrołęka Zambrów Białystok Vawkavysk Lyakhavichy Klyetsk Slutsk Hlusk Dubrovna Zhlobin
POLAND Nizina Ostrów Svislach **BELARUS** Salihorsk Lyuban' Zhytkavichy Svyetlahorsk
Płock Legionowo Wyszków Bug Hajnówka Ivatsevichy Hantsavichy Mal'kavichy Aktsyabrski
Kutno Pruszków Mińsk Siedlce Pruzhany Byaroza Dzyatlavichy Vasilyevichy
WARSAW Mazowiecki Zhabinka Kamyanyets Tsyelyakhany Luninyets Kalinkavichy
Żyrardów (Warszawa) Kobryn Drahichyn Pinsk Marshes Pyetrykaw Khoyniki
Zgierz Skierniewice Łuków Biała Brest Ivanava Mazyr
Łódź Wisła Podlaska Malaryta Zarichne Pripyats (Pripet) Yel'sk
Tomaszów Parczew Lioboml' Kamin'-Kashyrs'kyy Lyubeshiv Stolin Lyel'chytsy Narowlya
Mazowiecki Dęblin Pina Dubrovytsya
Pionki Puławy Lubartów Kovel' Kuznetsovs'k Volodymyrets' Klesiv Ovruch
Piotrków Radom Lublin Ratne Manevychi △220 Olevs'k Polis'ke
Trybunalski Koriskó Chełm Turiys'k **UKRA** Narodychi
Skarżysko- Ostrowiec Liuboml' Styr Rokytne Luhyny
Kamienna Starachowice Świętokrzyski Krasnystaw Sarny
Kielce △Łysica Polis'ke
611

Longitude 25° east of Greenwich

1 : 6 000 000

METRES
FEET

5000 16404
3000 9843
2000 6562
1000 3281
500 1640
200 656
0 0
LAND B.S.L.
200 656
4000 13124
6000 19686

MILES 0 50 100 150

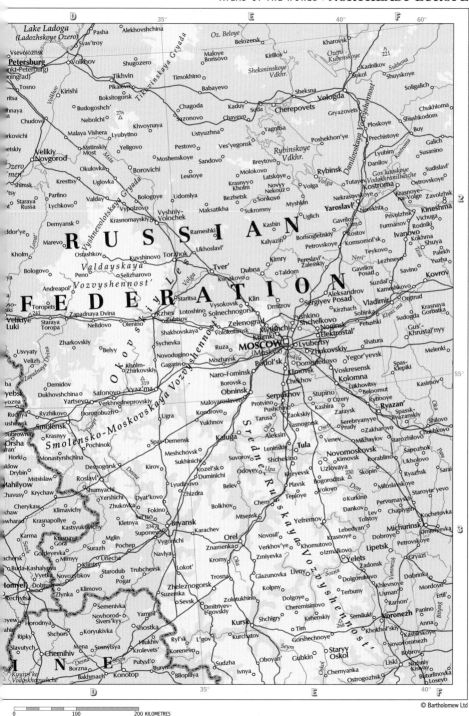

Lake Ladoga
(Ladozhskoye Ozero)
Pasha   Alekhovshchina
Vsevolozsk   Syas'troy
Petersburg   Volkhov   Shugozero
(nkt-Peterburg)   Tikhvin
ningrad)   Pikalevo
Tosno   Kirishi   Boksitogorsk   Babayevo
ritsa   Budogoshch'   Chagoda   Kaduy   Suda
Chudovo   Nebolchi   Sazonovo   Chayevo
Khvoynaya   Ustyuzhna
rkovichi   Malaya Vishera   Lyubytino   Yagnitsa
etskiy   Velikiy   Mstinskiy   Yeligovo   Pestovo   Ves'yegonsk
Novgorod   Most   Moshenskoye   Sandovo
Ozero   Okulovka   Borovichi   Lesnoye   Molokovo
men   Kresttsy   Uglovka   Bologoye   Udomlya   Bezhetsk   Sonkovo
tsy   Parfino   Valday   Vypolzovo   Maksatikha   Sukromny
Staraya   Lychkovo   Vyshniy-   Rameshki   Kashin
Russa   Krasnomayskiy   Volochek
ddor'ye   Demyansk   Likhoslavl'   Kalyazin
Marevo   Ostashkov   Kuvshinovo   Torzhok
Kholm   Valdayskaya   Peno   Selizharovo   Tver'   Dubna
Bologoye   Vozvyshennost'   Staritsa   Konakovo   Taldom
ya   Andreapol   Toropets   Zapadnaya Dvina   Rzhev   Lotoshino   Solnechnogorsk
so-   Velikiye   Staraya   Nelidovo   Olenino   Shakhovskaya   Volokolamsk
Luki   Toropa   Zharkovskiy   Belyy   Sychevka   Ruza
Usvyaty   Kholm-   Novodugino   Mozhaysk
Velizh   Zhirkovskiy   Gagarin   Naro-Fominsk
ba   Demidov   Vyaz'ma   Borovsk
yebsk   Dukhovshchina   Safonovo   Verkhnedneprovskiy
yozna   Yartsevo   Obninsk
Rudnya   Ryzhikovo   Dorogobuzh   Ugra   Maloyaroslavets
ushevsk   Smolensk   Krasnyy   Pochinok   Yukhnov
Orsha   Monastyrshchina   Spas-Demensk   Kaluga
ran'   Horki   Desnogorsk   Meshchovsk
klow   Drybin   Mstsislav'   Shumyachi   Sukhinichi
Mahilyow   Roslavl'   Kirov   Kozel'sk   Odoyevo
Chavusy   Krychaw   Yershichi   Dyat'kovo   Lyudinovo   Zhizdra   Belev
Cherykaw   Klimavichy   Zhukovka   Fokino   Bolkhov
khaw   Krasnapollye   Sel'tso   Mtsensk
wharad'   Kastsyukovichy   Kletnya   Bryansk   Karachev
Karma   Krasnaya   Mglin   Suponevo   Vygonichi   Orel   Novosil'
Gora   Surazh   Pochep   Znamenka   Verkhov'ye
achersk   Gordeyevka   Unecha   Navlya   Kromy
Buda-Kashalyova   Mirnyy   Klintsy   Lokot'   Trosna
Vyetka   Novozybkov   Starodub   Trubchevsk   Zheleznogorsk
omyel   Dobrush   Pogar   Zolotukhino
Rechytsa   Zlynka   Klimovo   Suzemka   Sevsk   Dmitriyev-
L'govskiy
oyew   Semenivka   Novhorod-   Yampil'   Shostka   Kursk
Horodnya   Sivers'kyy   Shchigry
ahin   Ripky   Shchors   Koryukivka   Hlukhiv   Ryl'sk   L'gov   Kurchatov   Tim
Slavutych   Mena   Sosnytsya   Krolevets'   Korenevo   Oboyan'
Chernihiv   Borzna   Putyvl'   Sudzha   Gubkin
INE   Bakhmach   Konotop   Bilopillya   Ivnya   Chernyanka
Kyivs'ke   Vdskhvshche

Oz. Beloye
Belozersk   Kharovsk
Maloye   Kirillov   Ozero
Borisovo   Kadnikov   Kubenskoye   Sukhona   221
Sheksninskoye   Sokol   Shuyskoye
Vdkhr.   Soligalich
Timokhino   Sheksna   Vologda   Gryazovets   Chukhloma
Cherepovets   Ploskoye   Shushkodom
Poshekhon'ye   Prechistoye   Buy
Rybinskoye   Lyubim   Galich
Vdkhr.   Danilov   Susanino
Breytovo   Gor'kovskoye   Sudislavl'
Latskoye   Rybinsk   Tutayev   Vdokhranilishche   Ostrovskoye
Krasnyy   Nekouz   Volga   Kostroma   Nerekhta   Na-Volge   Zavolzhsk   Kineshma
Kholm   Myshkin   Yaroslavl'   Privolzhsk   Vichuga   Rodniki
Uglich   Gavrilov-   Furmanov   Ivanovo   Kokhma   Shuya
Borisoglebskiy   Yam   Komsomol'sk   Teykovo   Palekh
Petrovskoye   Rostov   Nerl   Lezhnevo   Yuzha
Pereslavl'-   Gavrilov   Savino   Kovrov
Zalesskiy   Posad   Suzdal'   Kameshkovo
Aleksandrov   Kirzhach   Sobinka   Vladimir   Orgtrud   Krasnaya
Sergiyev Posad   Petushki   Sudogda   Gorbatka
Pushkino   Shchelkovo   Noginsk   Gus'-
Mytishchi   Elektrostal'   Khrustal'nyy
MOSCOW   Lyubertsy   Shatura   Melenki
(Moskva)   Zhukovskiy   Yegor'yevsk   Spas-
Podol'sk   Domodedovo   Voskresensk   Klepiki   Kasimov
Chekhov   Klimovsk   Kolomna   Lukhovitsy
Serpukhov   Stupino   Ozery   Rybnoye
Protvino   Kashira   Zaraysk   Ryazan'   Spassk-
Pushchino   Zaokskiy   Yasnogorsk   Serebryanyye   Zakharovo   Ryazanskiy   Shilovo
Tarusa   Prudy   Starozhilovo
Aleksin   Venev   Mikhaylov   Sarai
Leninskiy   Tula   Novomoskovsk   Ko:oblino   Ryazhsk
Shchekino   Kimovsk   Uzlovaya   Skopin   Miloslavskoye
Plavsk   Bogoroditsk   Don   Kurkino   Pervomayskiy   Staroyur'yevo
Teploye   Volovo   Dankov   Lev   Chaplygin   Kochetovka
Chern   Tolstoy   Lebedyan'   Michurinsk   Dmitriyevka
Yefremov   Krasnoye   Dobroye   Petrovskoye
Khomutovo   Izmalkovo   Lipetsk   Gryazi
Zmiyevka   Dolgorukovo   Yelets   Zadonsk   Dobrinka
Glazunovka   Livny   Sosna   Terbuny   Usman'   Mordovo
Kolpny   Dolgoye   Khlevnoye   Ertil'
Cheremisinovo   Semiluki   Ramon'   Panino
Kshenskiy   268   Khokhol'skiy   Anna
Gorshechnoye   Voronezh   Bifurg
Staryy   Kashirskoye
Gorshechnoye   Oskol   Novovoronezh
Gubkin   Liski   Nizhniy   Bobrov
Chernyanka   Kisyay   Buturlinovka
Ostrogozhsk   Loseyo

© Bartholomew Ltd

0   100   200 KILOMETRES

Ciechanów
Zambrów
Ostrów
Mazowiecka
Wyszków
Legionowo
WARSAW
(Warszawa)
Pruszków
Minsk
Mazowiecki
Siedlce
Łuków
Radom
Pionki
Puławy
Skarzysko-
Kamienna
Starachowice
Ostrowiec
Świętokrzyski
Łysica
611
Sandomierz
Staszów
Tarnobrzeg
Stalowa
Wola
Mielec
Bilgoraj
Dębica
Tarnów
Rzeszów
Jasło
Gorlice
Krosno
Sanok
SLOVAKIA
Košice
Michalovce
Uzhhorod
HUNGARY
Debrecen
Oradea
ROMANIA

Nizina
POLAND
Lublin
Chełm
Zamość

Vawkavysk Zel'va
Białystok Svislach Slonim
Hajnówka
Pruzhany
Kamyanets
Zhabinka
Brest
Biała
Podlaska
Parczew
Lubartów
Lubaczów
Przeworsk
Jarosław
Zhovkva
Yavoriv
Horodok
Przemyśl
Drohobych
Boryslav
Turka
Uzhhorod
Svalyava

BELARUS

Baranavichy Nyasvizh Asipovichy Babruysk
Lyakhavichy Klyetsk Kapyl' Starrya Darohi Ramachow
Ivatsevichy Hantsavichy Salihorsk Slutsk Lyuban' Hlusk Zhlobin
Byaroza Tsyelyakhany Mal'kavichy Zhytkavichy Kapatskyevichy Homy
Drahichyn Ivanava Pinsk Luninyets Dzyatlavichy Lyel'chytsy Narowlya Brahin

UKRAINE

Rivne
Ternopil'
Chernivtsi

MOLDOVA
CHIŞINĂU
(Kishinev)
Tighina
Tiraspol

BULGARIA
BUCHAREST
(Bucureşti)

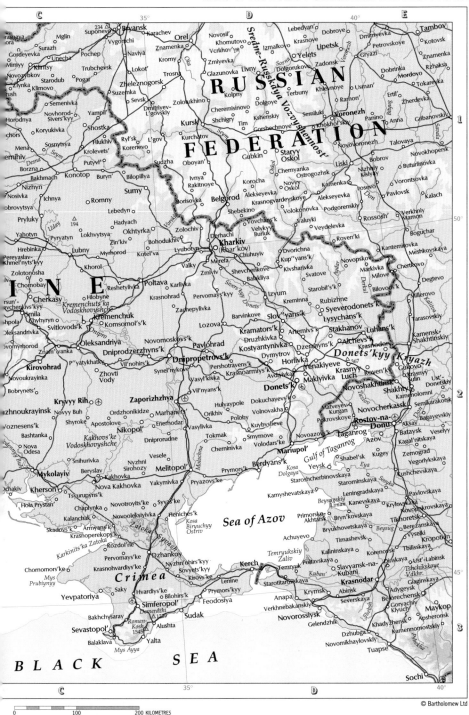

0   100   200 KILOMETRES

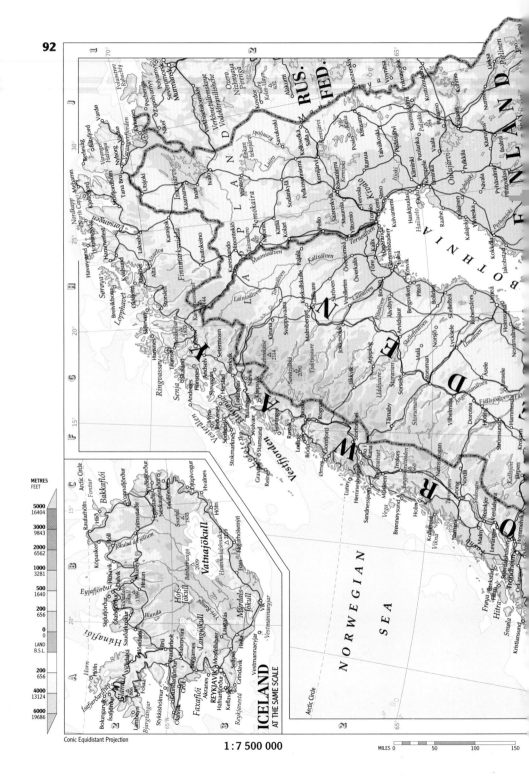

RUS. FED.

FINLAND

BOTHNIA

NORWEGIAN SEA

Arctic Circle

METRES	FEET
5000	16404
3000	9843
2000	6562
1000	3281
500	1640
200	656
0	0
LAND	B.S.L.
200	656
4000	13124
6000	19686

Vatnajökull

ICELAND
AT THE SAME SCALE

Conic Equidistant Projection

1 : 7 500 000

MILES 0   50   100   150

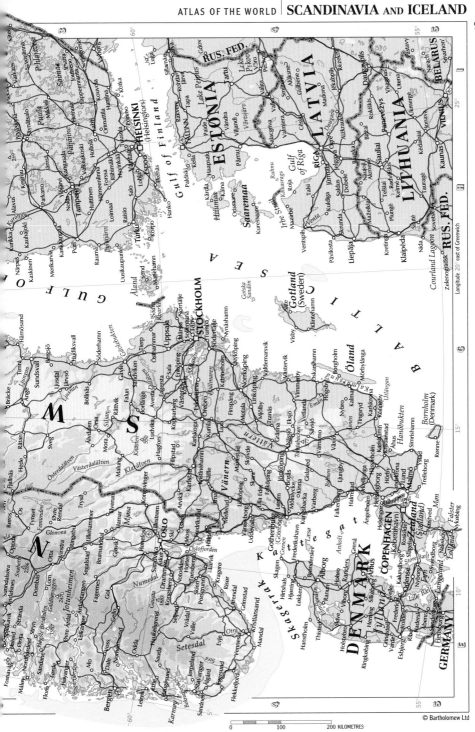

0   100   200 KILOMETRES

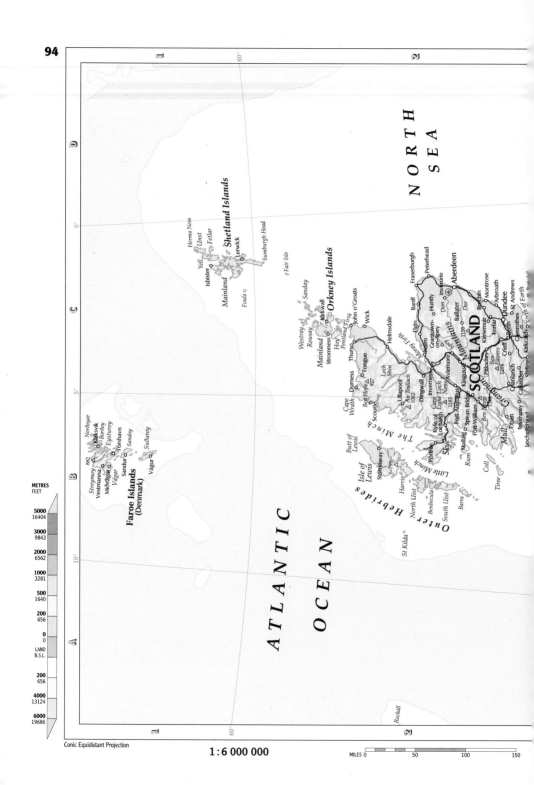

NORTH SEA

ATLANTIC OCEAN

SCOTLAND

Shetland Islands

Herma Ness
Yell
Unst
Fetlar
Isbister
Mainland
Lerwick
Sumburgh Head
Foula ○
○ Fair Isle

Orkney Islands

Westray
Rousay
Sanday
Mainland
Stronness
Hoy
Kirkwall
John o'Groats
Pentland Firth
Wick
Helmsdale
Thurso
Tongue
Durness
Loch Shin
Cape Wrath
Ben Hope △ 927
Scourie
Ullapool
Dingwall
An Teallach △ 1062
Loch Maree
Loch Ness
Ben Nevis △ 1183
Inverness
Aviemore
Nairn
Elgin
Grantown-on-Spey
Ben Macdui △ 1309
1135 △
Ballater
Dee
Banff
Huntly
Fraserburgh
Peterhead
Aberdeen
Inverurie
Don
Brechin
Montrose
Arbroath
Forfar
Kirriemuir
St Andrews
Dundee
Loch
Firth of Forth
Perth
Crieff
Pitlochry
Blair Atholl
Ben Lawers △ 1214
Callander
Stirling
Kirkcaldy
Inveraray
Oban
Lochgilphead
Grampian Mountains
Fort William
Spean Bridge
Fort Augustus
Kyle of Lochalsh
Mallaig
Portree
Skye
Rum
Eigg
Coll
Tiree
Mull
Barra

Outer Hebrides

Butt of Lewis
Isle of Lewis
Stornoway
Harris
North Uist
Benbecula
South Uist
St Kilda
The Minch
Little Minch

Rockall ○

Faroe Islands (Denmark)

Norðoyar
Nólsoy
Bordoy
882 △
Streymoy
Kalsoy
Eysturoy
Vestmanna
Tórshavn
Miðvágur
Vágur
Sandur
Sandoy
Suðuroy
Vágur

METRES	FEET
5000	16404
3000	9843
2000	6562
1000	3281
500	1640
200	656
0	0
LAND B.S.L.	
200	656
4000	13124
6000	19686

Conic Equidistant Projection

1 : 6 000 000

MILES 0   50   100   150

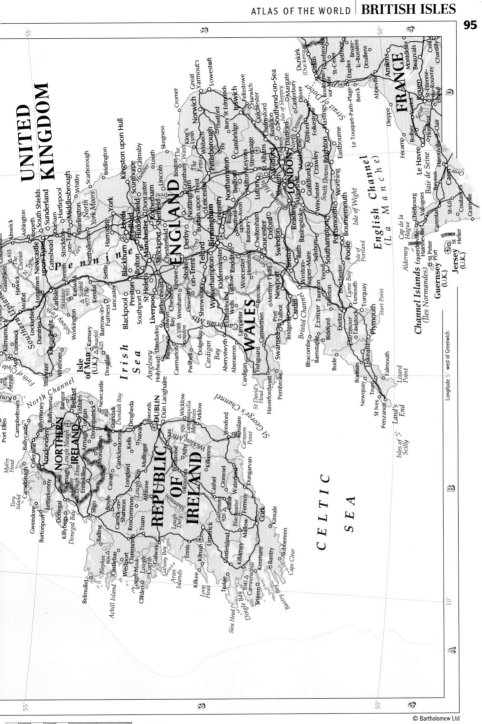

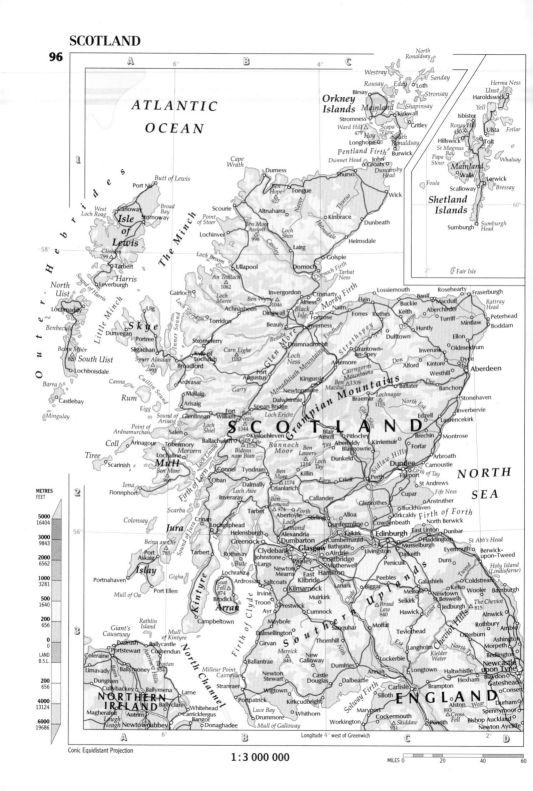

ATLANTIC
OCEAN

North Ronaldsay
Westray
Rousay *Eday* *Loth* *Sanday*
Birsay *Stronsay*
Orkney Mainland
Islands Stromness Kirkwall *Shapinsay*
Ward Hill △ *Scapa* Gritley
479 *Hoy* South
Longhope *Ronaldsay* Burwick
Pentland Firth
Dunnet Head John
Cape *Duncansby* O'Groats
Wrath Durness *Head*
Ben Thurso Wick
Hope Tongue
927 Dunbeath
Altnaharra
Scourie *Loch*
Point *Shin*
of Stoer Ben More Kinbrace
Assynt Helmsdale
Lochinver 998 *Loch*
Shin
Lairg Golspie
An Teallach Ullapool Dornoch
1062 *Dornoch Firth*
Loch Invergordon *Tarbat*
Gairloch *Maree* Cromarty *Ness*
Loch Ben Wyvis Alness *Moray Firth* Lossiemouth Rosehearty
Torridon △1046 *Black* Nairn Elgin Buckie Banff Macduff Fraserburgh
Achnasheen Dingwall *Isle* Fortrose Forres Rothes Keith *Rattray*
Beauly Inverness Dufftown Huntly Turriff Aberchirder Peterhead
Stromeferry *Beauly* Drumnadrochit Huntly Inverurie Mintlaw Boddam
Kyle of Carn Eighe Strathspey Ellon Oldmeldrum
Lochalsh 1183 Loch Grantown- Don Dyce
Broadford Ness on-Spey Westhill Kintore Aberdeen
Fort *Cairngorm* Alford
Augustus *Mountains* Banchory
Garry *Monadhliath Mountains* Ben △1309 Ballater Stonehaven
Macdui *North Esk* Inverbervie
Newtonmore Braemar Lochnagar
Kingussie 1155 Edzell Laurencekirk
Dalwhinnie Brechin
Spean *Grampian Mountains* Montrose
Bridge Loch Ericht Blair △1344 *Sidlaw Hills*
Fort Glen Atholl Forfar
William Nevis Kinlochleven Pitlochry Kirriemuir
Ballachulish △1150 *Rannoch* Aberfeldy Blairgowrie Arbroath
Bidean *Moor* Ben Tay Carnoustie
nam Bian Lawers Dunkeld Dundee
1214 *Loch* Tayport *Firth of Tay*
Connel Tyndrum Ben *Tay* Perth St Andrews
Oban More Killin *Earn* Crieff *Fife Ness*
1174 Cupar
Dalmally Crianlarich Callander Glenrothes Anstruther
Inveraray Ben Buckhaven
Loch Awe Lomond Kirkcaldy *Firth of Forth*
△974 Stirling North Berwick
Crinan Tarbet Aberfoyle Alloa Cowdenbeath Dunbar
Lochgilphead *Loch* Falkirk East Linton
Helensburgh *Lomond* Dumbarton Cumbernauld Edinburgh Haddington *St Abb's Head*
Greenock Alexandria Bathgate Musselburgh
Clydebank **Glasgow** Airdrie Livingston Dalkeith Eyemouth Berwick-
Johnstone Coatbridge Peebles Duns upon-Tweed
Rothesay Paisley Penicuik *Holy Island*
Newton Motherwell *(Lindisfarne)*
Largs Mearns East Hamilton Galashiels Coldstream
Lochranza Goat Kilbride Lanark Biggar Melrose Kelso
Fell Ardrossan Newton Selkirk St Boswells Wooler *The Cheviot*
874 Saltcoats Kilmarnock Muirkirk Jedburgh △815 Alnwick
Brodick Irvine Hawick Rothbury
Arran Troon Prestwick Cumnock *Broad Amble*
Campbeltown Ayr Sanquhar Moffat *Law* Teviothead Ashington
Maybole 840 Cheviot Hills Otterburn Morpeth
Dalmellington Thornhill Langholm *North Tyne* Bedlington
Merrick Girvan New Dumfries Kielder Haltwhistle Newcastle
△843 Galloway Lockerbie Water Longtown upon Tyne
Ballantrae Newton Castle Annan Blaydon Gateshead
Stewart Douglas Dalbeattie Carlisle Brampton Hexham Consett
Wigtown Kirkcudbright Silloth *Solway Firth* Alston 893△ *Wear* Durham
Stranraer Whithorn Maryport Cockermouth *Cross Bishop Auckland*
Portpatrick Mull of Galloway Workington △Skiddaw *Fell* Penrith Newton Aycliffe
951

NORTH
SEA

SCOTLAND

Southern Uplands

ENGLAND

The Minch
Little Minch
Inner Sound
Sound of Harris
Sound of
Arisaig
Sound of Jura
Firth of Lorn
Firth of Clyde
North Channel

Butt of Lewis
Port Nis
West Carloway
Broad
Bay
Stornoway
Loch Roag
Isle
of
Lewis
Clisham
799 △
Tarbert
Harris
Leverburgh
North
Uist
Lochmaddy
Benbecula
Benn Mhòr
620 △ **South Uist**
Lochboisdale
Barra
Castlebay
Mingulay

Outer Hebrides

Uig
Dunvegan
Portree
Skye
Sligachan
Sgurr Alasdair
993 △
Cuillin Sound

Mallaig
Arisaig
Glenfinnan
Salen
Point of
Ardnamurchan
Tobermory
Morvern
Lochaline
Mull
Ben More
966 △
Iona
Fionnphort

Coll
Arinagour
Tiree
Scarinish

Colonsay

Jura
Beinn an Òir
△785
Port
Askaig
Tarbert
Islay
Portnahaven
Gigha
Port Ellen
Mull of Oa

Kintyre

Rathlin
Island
Giant's
Causeway
Portrush
Portstewart Cushendun
Coleraine
Limavady Ballymoney
Dungiven
Cullybackey Ballymena
Magherafelt Antrim
Lough
Neagh Newtownabbey
NORTHERN
IRELAND
Ballycastle
Ballyclare
Carrickfergus
Bangor
Donaghadee
Glenarm
△554
Trostan
Mull
of Kintyre
Larne
Whitehead

Milleur Point
Cairnryan

Loch Broom
Loch Torridon
Loch Maree
Glen More
Strathspey
Loch Ness
Loch Garry
Loch Shiel
Glen Coe
Loch Linnhe
Loch Leven
Loch Lomond
Loch Tay
Loch Earn
Loch Fyne
Sound of Mull

Shetland Islands inset:
Herma Ness
Unst
Haroldswick
Yell
Isbister
Ronas Hill *Ulsta* *Fetlar*
450 △
Hillswick Toft
St Magnus Whalsay
Bay Walls
Papa **Mainland**
Stour Lerwick
Foula Scalloway *Bressay*
Sumburgh *Sumburgh*
Head

Shetland
Islands

Fair Isle

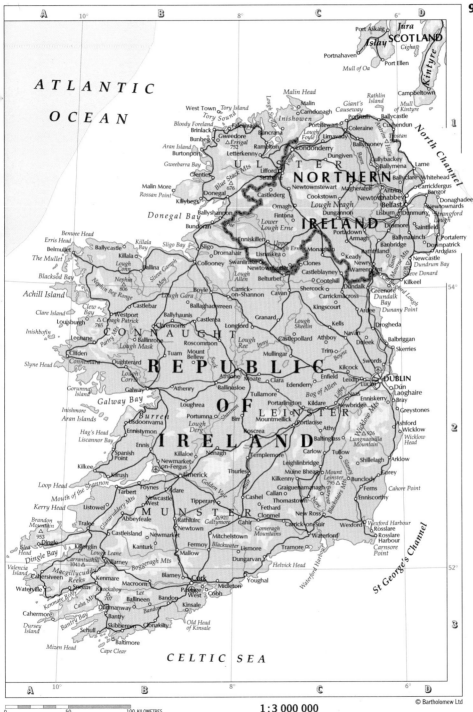

1 : 3 000 000

0   50   100 KILOMETRES

© Bartholomew Ltd

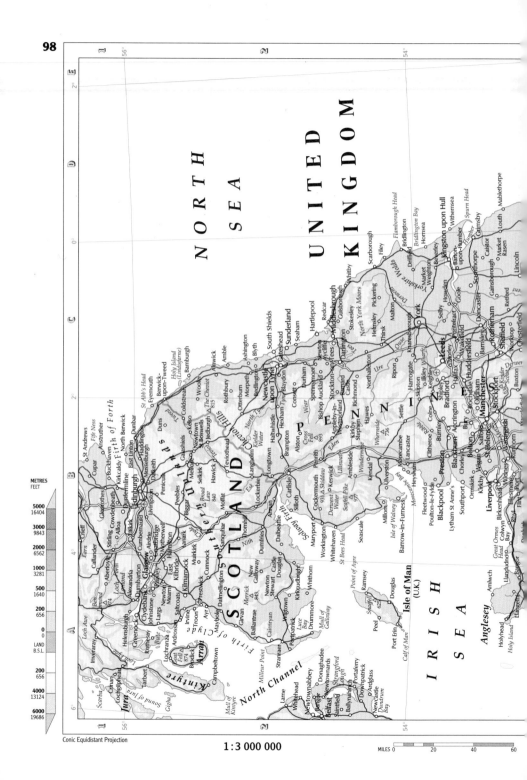

NORTH SEA

UNITED KINGDOM

SCOTLAND

Southern Uplands

Cheviot Hills

PENNINES

IRISH SEA

Isle of Man
(U.K.)

North Channel

Anglesey

Firth of Forth

Firth of Clyde

Kintyre

METRES
FEET

5000	16404
3000	9843
2000	6562
1000	3281
500	1640
200	656
0	0
LAND	B.S.L.
200	656
4000	13124
6000	19686

Conic Equidistant Projection

1:3 000 000

MILES 0   20   40   60

0   50   100 KILOMETRES

A 4° B 6° C

NORTH

SEA

West Frisian Islands

East Frisian Islands
Spiekeroog
Langeoog
Norderney
Juist
Norderney
Lange
Borkum
Wittr
Westerholt
OSTFRIESLA
Norden
Borkum

Schiermonnikoog
Ameland
Terschelling
West-
Terschelling
Hollum
Oost-
Vlieland
Lauwersmeer Eenrum
Uithuizen
Hinte
Aurich
Wies
Delfzijl
Emden
Ferwerd
Dokkum
Bedum
Appingedam
Leer
Weste
Oenkerk
Kollum
Groningen
Winschoten
Brücklingen
(Saterland)
Vlieland
Harlingen
Franeker
Leeuwarden
Hoogezand-
Sappemeer
Veendam
Papenbu
Texel
Witmarsum
Roordahuizum
Drachten
Assen
Stadskanaal
Frieso
Walchum
Sustrum
Den Helder
Bolsward
Sneek
Heerenveen
Beilen
Emmen
Haren (Ems)
Löningen
Meppen
Schagen
Wolvega
Steenwijk
Hoogeveen
Coevorden
Lingen
(Ems)
Nieuwe-Niedorp
Enkhuizen
Creil
Meppel
Hardenberg
Groß-Hesepe
Fürste
Heerhugowaard
Bergen
Urk
Emmeloord
Hardenberg
Kloosterhaar
Vriezenveen
Nordhorn
Alkmaar
Castricum
Hoorn
Lelystad
Dronten
Kampen
Zwolle
Ommen
Almelo
Oldenzaal
Gronau
(Westfalen)
Ibben
Beverwijk
IJmuiden
Zaandam
Purmerend
Heerde
Raalte
Hengelo
Enschede
Emsdetten
Teny
Zandvoort
Haarlem
AMSTERDAM
Bussum
Harderwijk
Nijverdal
Borne
Gronau
Steinfurt
Greven
Hillegom
Amstelveen
Naarden
Apeldoorn
Deventer
Noordwijk-Binnen
Torenberg 107△
Eibergen
Ahaus
Havixbeck
Katwijk aan Zee
Leiden
Alphen aan den Rijn
Hilversum
Amersfoort
Ede
Zutphen
Winterswijk
Coesfeld
Mür
THE HAGUE ('s-Gravenhage)
(Den Haag)
Waddinxveen
Utrecht
Veenendaal
Barneveld
Hoog-Keppel
Dülmen
Hoek van Holland
(Hook of Holland)
Delft
Gouda
Nieuwegein
Wageningen
Doesburg
Doetinchem
Borken
MÜNSTERLAND
Rotterdam
Schoonhoven
Arnhem
Velen
Vlaardingen
Capelle aan de IJssel
Tiel
Nijmegen
Zevenaar
Bocholt
Dorsten
Recklinghausen
Hellevoetsluis
Spijkenisse
Culemborg
Oss
Wijchen
Kleve
Wesel
Marl
Haml
Scharendijke
Dordrecht
Gorinchem
's-Hertogenbosch
Uden
Goch
Dinslaken
Gelsenkirchen
Herne
Dortm
Burgh-
Haamstede
Zierikzee
Oosterhout
Waalwijk
Erp
Keveler
Duisburg
Bottrop
Essen
Bochum
Westkapelle
Middelburg
Roosendaal
Breda
Tilburg
Boxtel
St Anthonis
Venray
Mülheim an der Ruhr
Ratingen
Hagen
Iserl
Koudekerke
Halsteren
Bergen op Zoom
Helmond
Deurne
Kessel
Krefeld
Solingen
Wuppertal
Vlissingen
Hoogerheide
Eindhoven
Venlo
Mönchengladbach
Neuss
Remscheid
Zeebrugge Heist
Knokke
Zandvliet
Brecht
Turnhout
Weert
Roermond
Viersen
Düsseldorf
Lüdenscheid
Ostend
(Oostende)
Blankenberge
Sluis
Maldegem
St-Laureins
Kapellen
Westmalle
Arendonk
Lommel
Bocholt
Herkenbosch
Wegberg
Grevenbroich
Leverkusen
Attend
Nieuwpoort
Meetkerke
Philippine
Schilde
Lille
Luyksgestel
Kessel
Sittard
Hückelhoven
Dormagen
Gummersb
Furne
Zedelgem
Bruges
(Brugge)
Eeklo
Antwerpen
(Anvers)
Geel
Bocholt
Weert
Maaseik
Heinsberg
Bergisch Gladbach
Ol
Diksmuide
Torhout
Wingene
Lier
Willebroek
Beringen
Hechtel
Heerlen
Kerkrade
Köln (Cologne)
Wiehl
Roeselare
Deinze
Gent
(Gand)
Mechelen
Aarschot
Diest
Genk
Borgheim
Erft
Overath
Ieper
Kortrijk
Leie
Wichelen
Aalst
Vilvoorde
Leuven
Tienen
Hasselt
Maastricht
Heerlen
Eschweiler
Frechen
Menen
Oudenaarde
Anderlecht
BRUSSELS
(Bruxelles)
Schaerbeek
Mechelen
Eupen
Kerpen
Düren
Bergheim
Bonn
Königswinter
Roubaix
Mouscron
Ronse
Uccle
Halle
Waterloo
Borgloon
Tongeren
Aachen
Stolberg
(Rheinland)
Bad Münstereifel
St Augustin
Betz
Lille
Villeneuve
d'Ascq
Ath
Nivelles
Fleurus
Eghezée
Braives
Liège
Verviers
Mechernich
Kreuzau
Zülpich
BELGIUM
Lens
Soignies
Andenne
Spa
Malmédy
Kallo
Bad Neuenahr-
Ahrweiler
Meckenheim
Altenkir
Wester
Douai
Mons
Charleroi
Namur
Assesse
Durbuy
Vielsalm
St-Vith
Dahlem
Adenau
Neuwied
Montal
Valenciennes
Châtelet
Montignies-
le-Château
Ciney
Marche-
en-Famenne
Hillesheim
Koblenz
Lahnste
Cambrai
Maubeuge
Beaumont
Dinant
La Roche-
en-Ardenne
Houffalize
Gerolstein
Mayen
Bopp
Aulnoye-
Aymeries
Philippeville
Rochefort
Arzfeld
Manderscheid
Blankenrath
Simmer
(Hunsrü
Caudry
Avesnes-
sur-Helpe
Couvin
Beauraing
St-Hubert
Bastogne
Clervaux
Neuerburg
Bitburg
Wittlich
Bernkastel-Kues
Birk
am Rh
Péronne
Guise
Hirson
Rocroi
Montherme
Bièvre
Libramont
Wiltz
LUXEMBOURG
Etelbrück
Prüm
Daun
Cochem
Emmelsha
St-Quentin
Vervins
Bogny-sur-Meuse
Vresse
Paliseul
Bouillon
Neufchâteau
Arlon
Redange
Mersch
Echternach
Morbach
Bad Kreuznach
Sobernheim
Chauny
Marle
Rozoy-
sur-Serre
Charleville-
Mézières
316△
Sedan
Carignan
Virton
LUXEMBOURG
Pétange
Remich
Konz
Saarburg
Idar-Oberstein
Nohfelden
Donners
Noyon
Laon
Rethel
Omont
Mouzon
Stenay
Arlon
Alzette
Mettlach
St Wendel
Wolfstein
Attichy
La Capelle
Guise
Hayange
Orange
Rombas
Saarlouis
Homburg
Neunkirchen
Kaiserslau
FRANCE
Soissons
Guignicourt
Aisne
Vouziers
Dun-sur-
Meuse
Longuyon
Thionville
Merzig
Courmelles
Fismes
Béthény
Consenvoye
Spincourt
Homburg
Villers-
Cotterêts
Tinqueux
Reims

Longitude 6° east of Greenwich

METRES
FEET

5000 16404
3000 9843
2000 6562
1000 3281
500 1640
200 656
0 0
LAND
B.S.L.
200 656
4000 13124
6000 19686

Conic Equidistant Projection

1:3 000 000

MILES 0   20   40   60

0   50   100 KILOMETRES

Conic Equidistant Projection

1 : 6 000 000

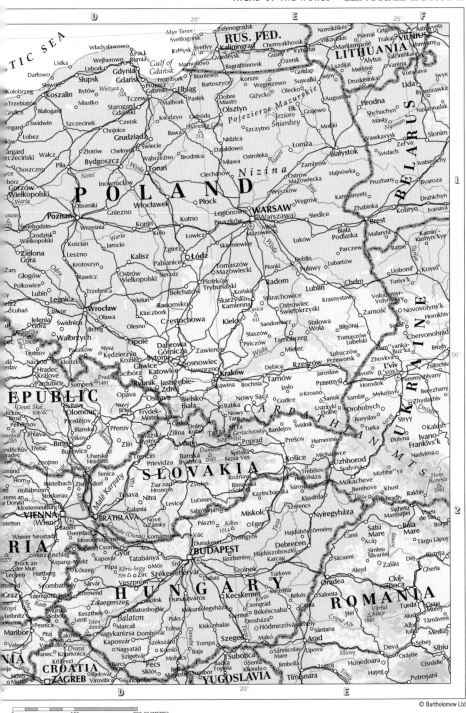

0   100   200 KILOMETRES

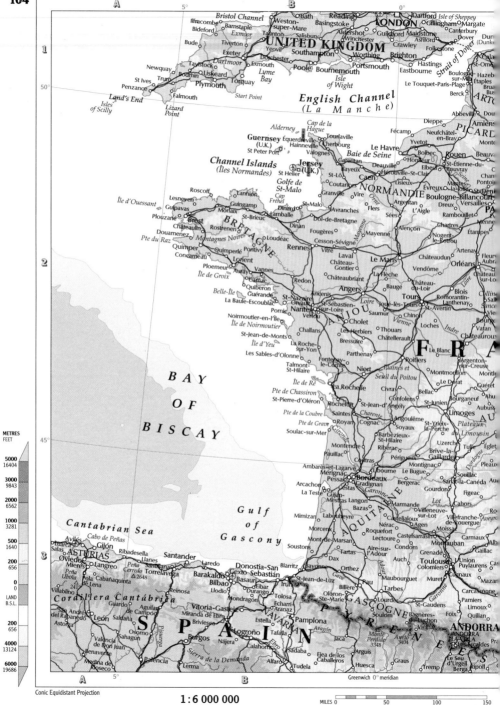

Bristol Channel
Weston-super-Mare
Ilfracombe
Barnstaple
Bideford
Exmoor
Bude
Tiverton
Newquay
Tavistock
Dartmoor
Exmouth
Liskeard
St Ives
Truro
Bodmin
Penzance
Plymouth
Torquay
Falmouth
Land's End
Isles of Scilly
Lizard Point
Start Point

Bath Reading
Basingstoke
LONDON
Gillingham Margate
Aldershot Guildford Maidstone Canterbury
Salisbury Winchester Crawley Ashford Dover
Yeovil Southampton Worthing Brighton Folkestone
Dorchester Poole Bournemouth Portsmouth Hastings
Lyme Bay Isle of Wight Eastbourne
Le Touquet-Paris-Plage
Berck

UNITED KINGDOM

English Channel
(La Manche)

Cap de la Hague
Alderney
Guernsey (U.K.)
St Peter Port
Cherbourg
Valognes
Jersey (U.K.)
St Helier
Golfe de St-Malo
Cap Fréhel

Channel Islands
(Îles Normandes)

Dieppe
Fécamp
Le Havre
Baie de Seine
Deauville
Honfleur
Caen
St-Lô
Coutances
Avranches
Vire
Flers
Argentan

NORMANDIE

Rouen
Beauvais
St-Étienne-du-Rouvray
Elbeuf
Évreux
Lisieux
L'Aigle
Dreux
Sées
Alençon
Mayenne

BAY
OF
BISCAY

Île d'Ouessant
Lesneven
Guipavas
Plouzane
Brest
Châteaulin
Douarnenez
Pte du Raz
Quimper
Concarneau
Ploemeur
Auray
Belle-Île
La Baule-Escoublac
Pornic
Noirmoutier-en-l'Île
Île de Noirmoutier
St-Jean-de-Monts
Île d'Yeu
Les Sables-d'Olonne

Roscoff
Lannion
Morlaix
Guingamp
St-Brieuc
Montagnes Noires
Quimperlé
Lorient
Vannes
Île de Groix
Quiberon
Guérande
St-Nazaire

BRETAGNE
Rostrenen
Pontivy
Lamballe
Dinan
Loudéac
Cesson-Sévigné
Rennes
Vitré
Laval
Château-Gontier
Redon
Châteaubriant
Ancenis
Orvault
Nantes
Vertou
Challans
La Roche-sur-Yon

St-Malo
Dinard
Dol-de-Bretagne
Fougères

Mayenne
Le Mans
La Flèche
Baugé
Saumur
Cholet
Les Herbiers
Bressuire

Chartres
Nogent-le-Rotrou
Vendôme
Château-du-Loir
Tours
Joué-lès-Tours
St-Avertin
Chinon
Loches
Thouars
Châtellerault

Étampes
Orléans
Blois
Romorantin-Lanthenay

FRA

Cantabrian Sea
Gulf of Gascony

Noirmoutier
Fontenay-le-Comte
Talmont-St-Hilaire
Île de Ré
Pte de Chassiron
St-Pierre-d'Oléron
Pte de la Coubre
Pte de Grave
Soulac-sur-Mer

La Rochelle
Niort
Parthenay
Civray
Confolens
Rochefort
St-Jean-d'Angély
Saintes
Royan
Cognac
Charente

Poitiers
Bellac
St-Junien
Limoges
Angoulême
St-Yrieix-la-Perche
Soyaux
Barbezieux-St-Hilaire
Uzerche
Périgueux
Brive-la-Gaillarde

Montendre
Pauillac
Riberac
Ambarès-et-Lagrave
Mérignac
Pessac
Bordeaux
Gradignan
Arcachon
La Teste
Mimizan
Labouheyre
Morcenx
Soustons
Biarritz
Donostia-San Sebastián

AQUITAINE

Coutras
Libourne
Le Bugue
Montignac
Bergerac
Gourdon
Figeac
Langon
Bazas
Marmande
Villeneuve-sur-Lot
Agen
Castelsarrasin
Moissac
Montauban
Toulouse

GASCOGNE

Cantabrian Sea
Cabo de Peñas
Avilés
Gijón
Ribadesella
Llanes
Santander
Laredo
Dax
Bayonne
Orthez
Pau
ASTURIAS
Oviedo
Mieres
Langreo
Torrelavega
Barakaldo
Bilbao
Basauri
Irún
St-Jean-de-Luz
Tarbes
Muret

SPAIN

Cordillera Cantábrica
León
Astorga
Sahagún
Palencia
Burgos
Osorno
Vitoria-Gasteiz
Miranda de Ebro
Logroño
Estella
Pamplona
NAVARRA
Jaca
Huesca

PYRÉNÉES
ANDORRA

METRES
FEET

5000	16404
3000	9843
2000	6562
1000	3281
500	1640
200	656
0	0
LAND	B.S.L.
200	656
4000	13124
6000	19686

Conic Equidistant Projection

1 : 6 000 000

MILES 0   50   100   150

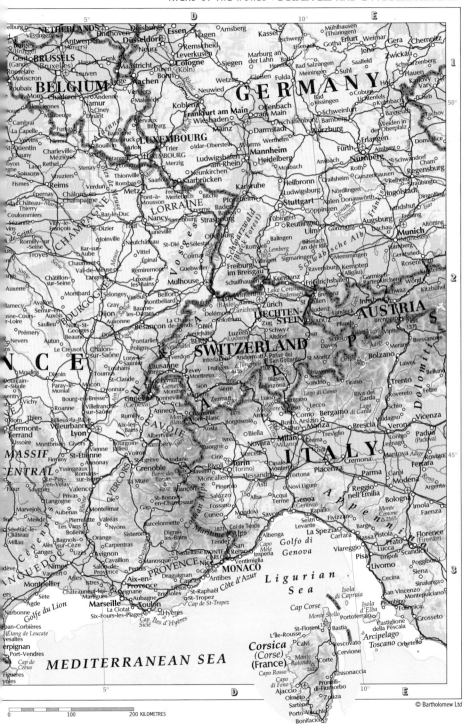

0   100   200 KILOMETRES

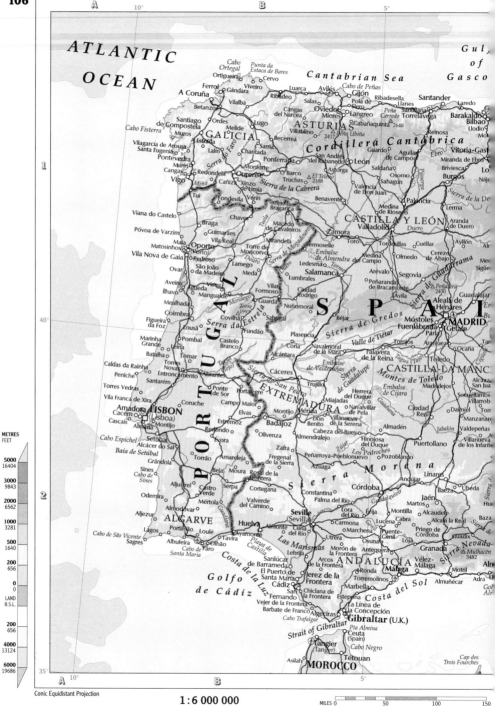

ATLANTIC

OCEAN

Cabo
Ortegal   Punta da
Ortigueira   Estaca de Bares
Cervo   **Cantabrian Sea**

Ferrol   Viveiro   Avilés   Cabo de Peñas
Gándara   Luarca   Gijón   Ribadesella   Santander   Laredo
A Coruña   Ribadeo   Salas   Pola de   Llanes   Barakaldo
Betanzos   Vilalba   Cangas   Oviedo   Siero   Santillana   Torrelavega   Bilbao
          del Narcea   Mieres   Langreo   Peña   Reinosa   Llodio   Mo
Santiago   Ordes   Melide   Lugo   **ASTURIAS**   Cabañaquinta   Cerredo   2648   Vitoria-Gast
Cabo Fisterra   de Compostela   Villablino   2417   Peña Ubiña   Osorno   Miranda de Ebro
Muros   **GALICIA**   Becerreá   *Cordillera Cantábrica*   Guardo   Aguilar   Briviesca   Burgos

ATLANTIC OCEAN

Gulf
of
Gasco

1

Vilagarcía de Arousa   Estrada   Sarria   del Rabanedo   León   de Campóo   Vitoria-Gast
Santa Eugenia   Lalín   Chantada   San Andrés   Saldaña   Osorno   Lo
Pontevedra   Ponferrada   Astorga   Sahagún   Burgos   Nájé
Marín   Redondela   O Barco   Sierra de la Cabrera   Truchas   El Teleno   Palencia   Lerma   Sierra de la De
Cangas   Ourense   2188   Valencia   Medina
Vigo   Xinzo   Benavente   de Don Juan   de Rioseco
Tui   de Limia   Zamora   Toro   **CASTILLA Y LEÓN**   Aranda
          Fondevila   Verín   Valladolid   *Duero*   de Duero
Viana do Castelo   Bragança   Macedo   Tordesillas   Cuéllar   Ayllón   Alr

40°

Conic Equidistant Projection

1 : 6 000 000

METRES
FEET

5000
16404

3000
9843

2000
6562

1000
3281

500
1640

200
656

0
0

LAND
B.S.L.

200
656

4000
13124

6000
19686

2

MILES 0   50   100   150

© Bartholomew Ltd

METRES
FEET

5000
16404

3000
9843

2000
6562

1000
3281

500
1640

200
656

0
0

LAND
B.S.L.

200
656

4000
13124

6000
19686

Conic Equidistant Projection

1:6 000 000

Longitude 10° east of Greenwich

MILES 0   50   100   150

0   100   200 KILOMETRES

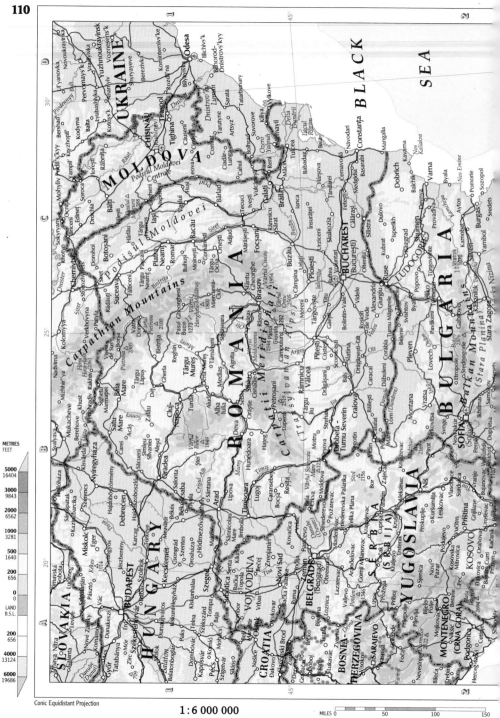

METRES
FEET

5000
16404

3000
9843

2000
6562

1000
3281

500
1640

200
656

0
0

LAND
B.S.L.

200
656

4000
13124

6000
19686

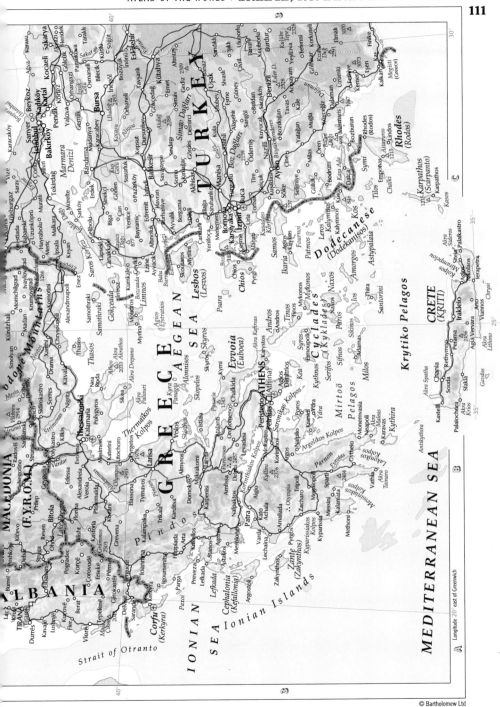

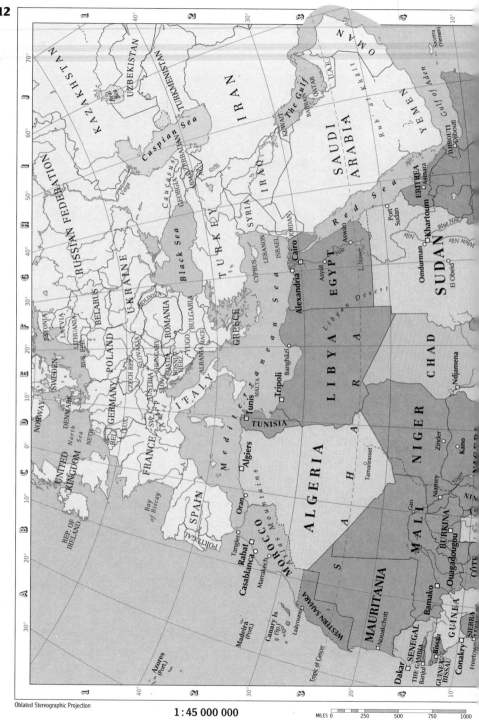

70°

40°

30°

20°

10°

KAZAKHSTAN

UZBEKISTAN

TURKMENISTAN

Aral Sea

RUSSIAN FEDERATION

UKRAINE

BELARUS

ESTONIA

LATVIA

LITHUANIA

RUS. FED.

POLAND

SWEDEN

NORWAY

DENMARK

North Sea

NETH.

UNITED KINGDOM

REP. OF IRELAND

Bay of Biscay

GERMANY

BEL.

FRANCE

SPAIN

PORTUGAL

Azores (Port.)

Madeira (Port.)

Canary Is (Sp.)

CZECH REP.

SVK.

AUSTRIA

SLOVENIA

CROATIA

HUNGARY

BOSNIA HERZ.

YUGO.

ALBANIA

MACE.

ROMANIA

MOLDOVA

BULGARIA

ITALY

GREECE

MALTA

TUNIS

TUNISIA

Tripoli

Banghāzī

Algiers

Oran

Tangier

Rabat

Casablanca

Marrakech

MOROCCO

Atlas Mountains

WESTERN SAHARA

Laâyoune

Nouakchott

MAURITANIA

Dakar

SENEGAL

THE GAMBIA

Banjul

GUINEA BISSAU

Bissau

Conakry

GUINEA

Freetown

SIERRA

Ouagadougou

BURKINA

CÔTE

Bamako

MALI

Gao

NIGER

Niamey

Zinder

Kano

NIG.

NDjamena

CHAD

Tamanrasset

ALGERIA

SAHARA

S A H A R A

LIBYA

S A H A R A

Libyan Desert

EGYPT

Alexandria

Cairo

Asyūt

L. Nasser

Aswān

Nile

Nile

SUDAN

Omdurman

Khartoum

El Obeid

White Nile

Blue Nile

Port Sudan

ERITREA

Asmara

DJIBOUTI

Djibouti

Mediterranean Sea

Black Sea

TURKEY

CYPRUS

LEBANON

ISRAEL

SYRIA

IRAQ

JORDAN

KUWAIT

BAHRAIN

QATAR

U.A.E.

The Gulf

SAUDI ARABIA

Rub' al Khali

YEMEN

OMAN

Socotra (Yemen)

Gulf of Aden

Red Sea

IRAN

Caspian Sea

Caucasus

GEORGIA

ARMENIA

AZERBAIJAN

Volga

Oblated Stereographic Projection

1 : 45 000 000

MILES 0   250   500   750   1000

Tropic of Cancer

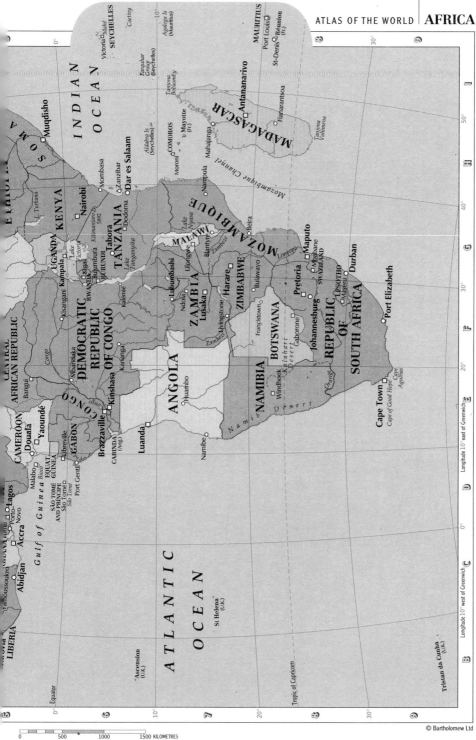

SEYCHELLES

Victoria Mahé

Coetivy

MAURITIUS

Port Louis

St-Denis Réunion (Fr.)

Farquhar Group (Seychelles)

Agalega Is (Mauritius)

INDIAN OCEAN

Muqdisho

Antananarivo

Tanjona Bobaomby

MADAGASCAR

Antsiranana

Fianarantsoa

Toamasina

Mahajanga

COMOROS

Moroni

Mayotte (Fr.)

Aldabra Is (Seychelles)

Tanjona Volimena

Mombasa

Zanzibar

Dar es Salaam

Mozambique Channel

S O M A L I A

E Q U A T

L. Turkana

KENYA

Nairobi

UGANDA

Kampala

Kisangani

Lake Victoria

RWANDA

Kigali

Bujumbura

BURUNDI

Lake Tanganyika

TANZANIA

Tabora

Dodoma

Kilimanjaro 5892

Lake Nyasa

MALAWI

Lilongwe

Blantyre

Nampula

MOZAMBIQUE

Beira

Maputo

Limpopo

Mbabane

SWAZILAND

Durban

CENTRAL AFRICAN REPUBLIC

Bangui

DEMOCRATIC REPUBLIC OF CONGO

Mbandaka

Congo

Kinshasa

Kananga

Kalemie

Lubumbashi

Ndola

ZAMBIA

Lusaka

Livingstone

Zambezi

ZIMBABWE

Harare

Bulawayo

Francistown

Pretoria

Johannesburg

LESOTHO

Maseru

Port Elizabeth

CAMEROON

Douala

Yaoundé

EQUAT. GUINEA

Malabo

Bioco

SÃO TOMÉ AND PRÍNCIPE

São Tomé

São Tomé

CONGO

Libreville

GABON

Brazzaville

Port Gentil

CABINDA (Ang.)

Luanda

ANGOLA

Huambo

Namibe

NAMIBIA

Windhoek

Kalahari Desert

BOTSWANA

Gaborone

Namib Desert

Cape Town

Cape of Good Hope

Cape Agulhas

REPUBLIC OF SOUTH AFRICA

Orange

LIBERIA

Yamoussoukro

Abidjan

Accra

Porto-Novo

Lagos

Gulf of Guinea

ATLANTIC OCEAN

St Helena (U.K.)

Ascension (U.K.)

Tristan da Cunha (U.K.)

Tropic of Capricorn

Equator

0   500   1000   1500 KILOMETRES

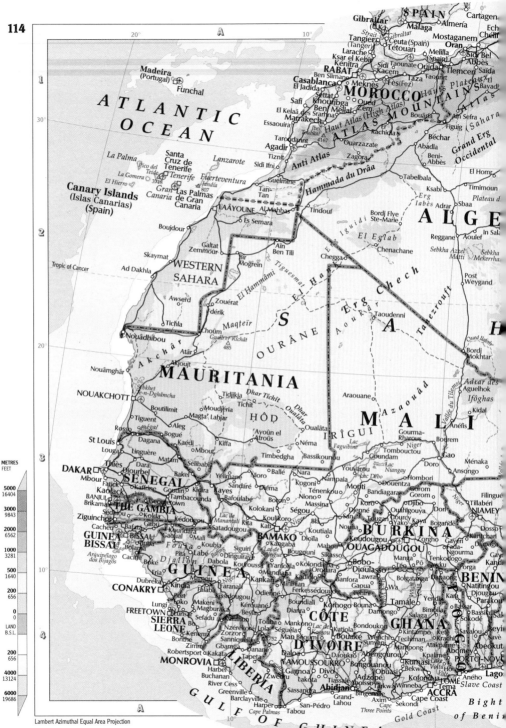

METRES
FEET

5000
16404

3000
9843

2000
6562

1000
3281

500
1640

200
656

0
0

LAND
B.S.L.

200
656

4000
13124

6000
19686

Lambert Azimuthal Equal Area Projection

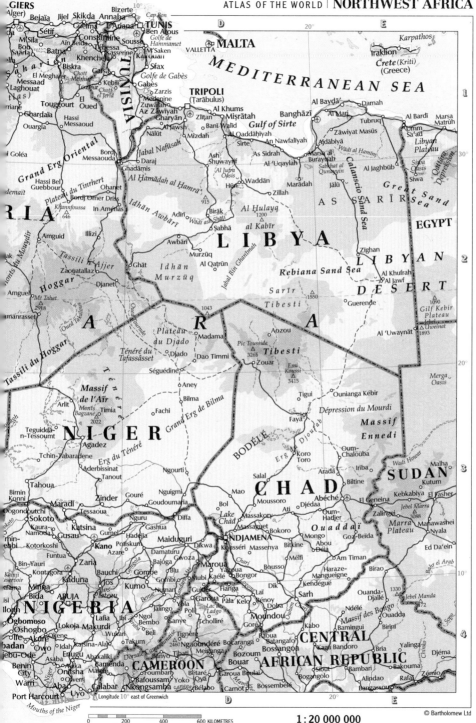

1 : 20 000 000

```
0        200      400        600 KILOMETRES

0      100     200      300      400 MILES
```

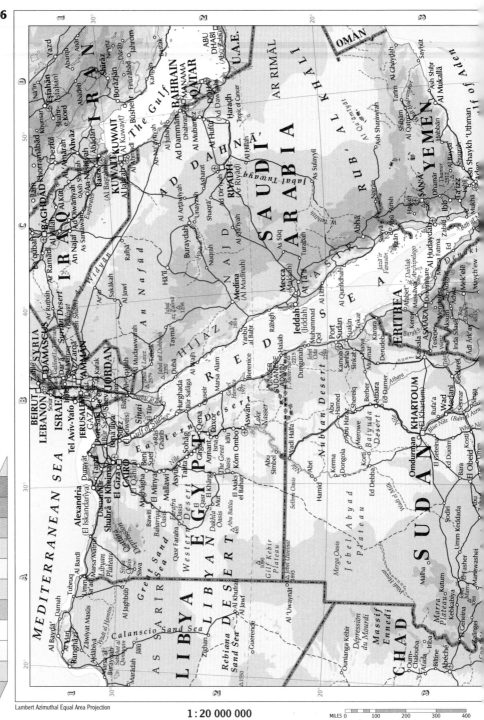

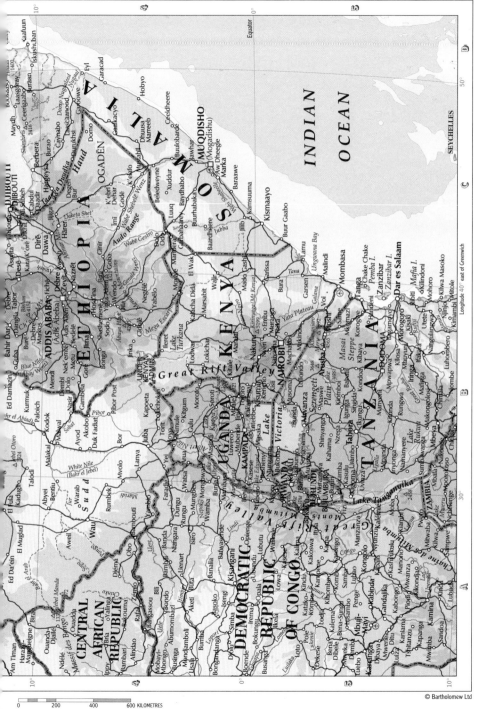

0   200   400   600 KILOMETRES

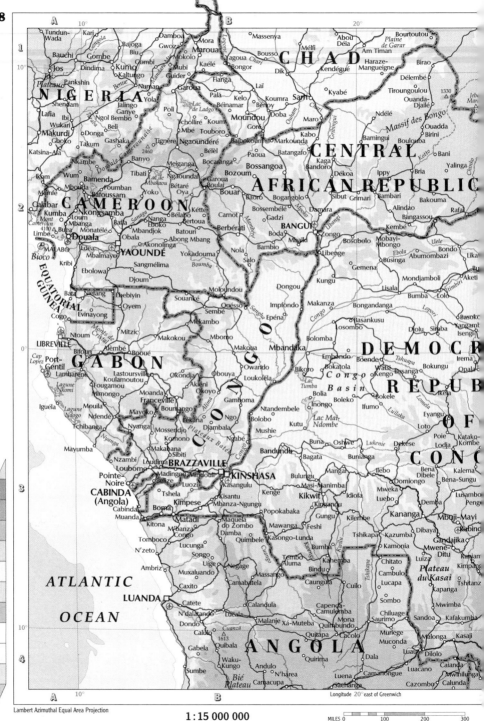

Lambert Azimuthal Equal Area Projection

1:15 000 000

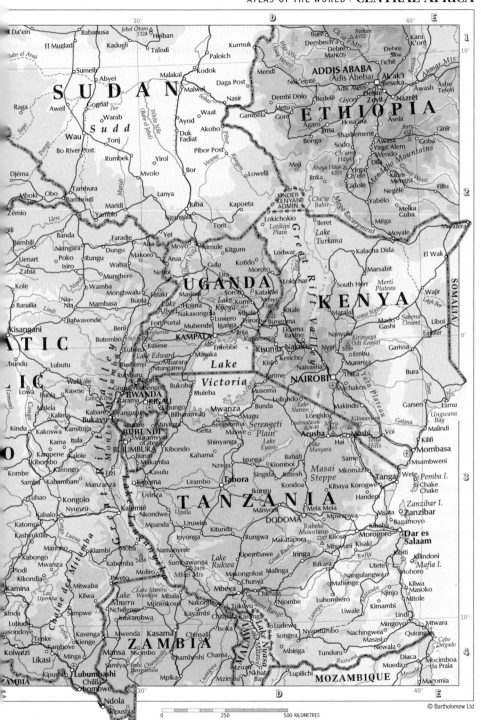

Da'ein
Babanusa
Jebel Otoro 1324
Heiban
Kurmuk
Bure
Dembech'a △4152
Birhan Mts
Kara K'orē
10° 1

El Muglad
Kadugli
Talodi
Paloich
Debre Markos
Debre Sina
Fiche
Nazrēt

Sumeih
Abyei
Malakal
Kodok
Mendi
Nek'emtē
ADDIS ABABA (Ādis Ābeba)
Ak'ak'ī Beseka
Awash

Raga
Aweil
Gogrial
Jur
Malwal
Daga Post
Dembi Dolo
Bedelē
Adis Alem
Debre Zeyit
Giyon
Awash Teferī

Warab
Nasir
Metu
Gorē
Hosaïna
Ch'amo
Āsela

Wau
Tonj
Waat
Gambēla
Agaro
Jima
Shashemenē
Awasa
Goba
Ginir

S u d d
Ayod
Akobo
Bonga
Sodo
Yirga Alem
Wendo
Batu △4321

Bo River Post
Duk Fadiat
Maji
Jinka
Abaya Hayk' 4203
Negēlē
Kibre Mengist
Filtu

Djéma
Rumbek
Yirol
Pibor Post
Ch'et'e
Gidolē

Tambura
Mvolo
Bor
Loweli
UNDER KENYAN ADMIN
Che'w Bahir
Yabēlo
Melka Guba

Mboki
Obo
Bamb'uti
Maridi
Juba
Kapoeta
Lokichokio
Lotikipi Plain
Īleret
Lake Turkana
Moyale

Zémio
Yambio
Ngangala
Torit
Kalacha Dida
SOMALIA
Mandera

Bili
Banda
Yei
Moyo
Nimule
Kitgum
Lodwar
El Wak

Bambili
Niangara
Dungu
Aba
Makoro
Arua
Gulu
Kotido
Moroto
Lokichar
Marsabit

Lienart
Poko
Rungu
Watsa
Nebbi
Lira
Soroti
Katakwi
Mt Elgon
South Horr
Merti Plateau
Wajir

Kole
Wamba
Mungbere
Mongbwalu
Bunia
Fataki
Hoima
Lake Kyoga
Kumi
4321
Kitale
Maralal
Mado Gashi
Sabena Desert
Liboi

Banalia
Nia-Nia
Mambasa
Lake Albert
Nakasongola
Mbale
Ororo
Eldama Ravine
Nanyuki
Kirinyaga △(Mt Kenya) 5199
Garissa
Equator 0°

Kisangani
Bafwasende
Beni
Butembo
Fort Portal
Mubende
Iganga
Jinja
Kakamega
Kisumu
Nakuru
Nyeri
Embu

TIC
Lubutu
Margherita 5110 Pk
Kasese
KAMPALA
Entebbe
Masaka
Kericho
Naivasha
Muranga
Thika
Bura

IC
Ubundu
Lutubu
Lubero
Lake Edward
Bushenyi
Mbarara
Ntungamo
Lake
Kisii
Jarime
NAIROBI
Machakos
Tana
Lamu

Lowa
Walikale
Goma Rutshuru
Katarama
Bukoba
Muleba
Victoria
Musoma
Lollondo
Makindu
Garsen
Ungwana Bay

Kindu
Kasese
Lake Kivu
RWANDA
KIGALI
Kibondo
Bilharamulo
Mwanza
Magu
Bunda
Lake Natron
Longido
Kilimanjaro △5892
Galana
Malindi

Kakoswa
Bukavu
Cyangugu
Butare
Muyinga
Geita
Maswe
Sengerema
Serengeti Plain
Arusha
Doolmalasin △3648
Meru △4565
Voi
Kilifi

Kama
Itula
Kamituga
BURUNDI
Muramvya
Kibondo
Shinyanga
Lake Eyasi
Moshi
Teita Hills
Mombasa

Kampene
Kalole
BUJUMBURA
Citega
Kahama
Igunga
Babati
Same
Msambweni

Kibombo
Kasongo
Bururi
Makamba
Nzega
Kiomboi
Babati
Mkomazi
Tanga
Wete
Pemba I.

Kombe
Samba
Kabambare
Manzanza
Kasulu
Urambo
Tabora
Kondoa
Kibaya
Korogwe
Handeni
Chake Chake

Lubao
Kongolo
Uvinza
Kigoma
Manyoni
Mela Mela
Mpwapwa
Msata
Bagamoyo
Zanzibar I.

Katompi
Nyunzu
Kalemié
Nkondwe
Ugalla
TANZANIA
DODOMA
Kilosa
Morogoro
Zanzibar

Kashyukulu
Manono
Mpanda
Uruwira
Kitunda
Rubeho Mountains 2287
Mbuyuni
Kisaki
Kibaha
Dar es Salaam

Kabongo
Klambi
Moba
Inyonga
Namanyere
Rungwa
Makatapora
Iringa
Rufiji
Kibiti
Klindoni
Mafia I.

Piodi
Mwanza
Kabemba △2438
Sumbawanga △2418
Kipembawe
Ifakara
Utete
Mohoro

Kikondja
Mitwaba
Moliro
Mbizi Mts
Makongolosi
Chunya
Mafinga
Mahenge
Nangulangwa
Kilwa Masoko

Kamina
Kilwa
Lake Mweru Wantipa
Mbala
Nakonde
Tukuyu
Njombe
Luhombero
Njinjo
Mitole

Kinda
Sampwe
Nchelenge
Mporokoso
Kayambi
Chitipa
Karonga
Ludewa
Kimambi

Lubudi
Kasenga
Mwenda
Kasama
Chinsali
Isoka
Songea
Nyamtumbo
Liwale
Lindi
Mingoyo
Mtwara

Jasondoye
Tenke
Kienge
Kambove
Minga
Mansa
Nsombo
Chambeshi
Chama
Mbinga
Tunduru
Newala
Quionga
Cabo Delgado

Kolwezi
Likasi
Kipushi
Samfya
Lake Bangweulu
Mpika
Mzimba
Nkhata Bay
Lupilichi
Masasi
Diaca
Mocimboa da Praia

ZAMBIA
Lubumbashi
Chilila
Dombwe
Ndola
Kipushia
Mzuzu
MOZAMBIQUE
Macomia

ZAMBIA

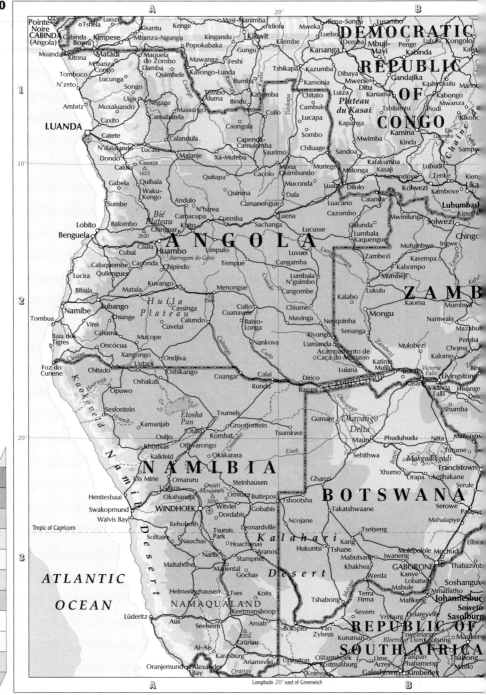

Pointe
Noire
CABINDA
(Angola)

Luozi
Tshela
Cabinda
Kimpese
Kenge
Masi-Manimba
Idiofa
Mweka
Luebo
Bena-Sungi
Lusambo

DEMOCRATIC

Kisantu
Kingandu
Kikwit
Kilembe
Kananga
Demba
Mbuji-
Mayi
Penge
Lubao
Kongolo
Kaba

Boma
Mbanza-Ngungu
Popokabaka
Gungu
Tshikapa
Kazumba
Dibaya
Mwene-
Ditu
Gandajika
Kabinda
Kabongo
Kikondi
Manok

REPUBLIC

Muanda
Kitona
Matadi
Maquela
do Zombo
Mawanga
Feshi
Kasongo-Lunda
Bumba
Kamonia
Mwanza

Mbanza
Congo
Damba
Quimbele
Luiza
Kaniama
Ishitanzu
Piodi

OF

Tomboco
Lucunga
Songo
Uíge
Negage
Kahemba
Chitato
Cambulo
Kapanga
Kamina
Kikonk

N'zeto
Muxaluando
Massango
Bindu
Cuilo
Lucapa
Mwimba
Kinda
Sampy

CONGO

Ambriz
Caxito
Carnabatela
Caungula
Sombo
Sandoa
Lubudi

LUANDA
Catete
Calandula
Capenda-
Camulemba
Saurimo
Chiluage
Mona
Quimbundo
Kafakumba
Kasaji
Lubudi
Lika

N'dalatando
Tucala
Malanje
Xá-Muteba
Cacolo
Muriege
Malonga
Nasondoy
Tenke
Kien

Dondo
Calulo
Cuanza
1613
Quitapa
Muconda
Luau
Dilolo
Kolwezi
Kambove

Gabela
Quibala
Quirima
Dala
Luacano
Caianda
Solwezi
Chingc

Sumbe
Waku-
Kungo
Andulo
Camanongue
Luena
Cazombo
Calunda
Mwinilunga

Lobito
Balombo
Bié
Plateau
Khito
Cuemba
Sachanga
Lucusse
Lumbala
Kaquengue
Mufumbwe
Kasempa
Ingwe

Benguela
Chinguar
2620
ANGOLA
Luvuei
Cangamba
Zambezi
Kabompo
Mumbeji

Cubal
Huambo
Umpulo
Tempué
Lumbala
N'guimbo
Lukulu
ZAMB

Caluquembe
Cagonda
Chipindo
Menongue
Cangombe
Kalabo
Kaoma
Mumbwa

Lucira
Quilengues
Kuvango
Cuito
Cuanavale
Chiume
Mongu
Namwala
Mazabu

Bibala
Matala
Huíla
Plateau
Cassinga
Caiundo
Baixo-
Longa
Mavinga
Neriquinha
Senanga
Mulobezi
Choma
Kalomo

Namibe
Lubango
Chiange
Cuvelai
Nankova
Rivungo
Uamanda
Acampamento de
Caça do Mucusso
Katima
Mulilo
Pemba

Tombua
Virei
Cahama
Mucope
Cuito
Luiana
Livingstone

Baía dos
Tigres
Oncócua
Xangongo
Ondjiva
Calai
Dirico
Bagani
CAPRIVI STRIP
Victoria
Falls
Hwange

Foz do
Cunene
Chitado
Uutapi
Oshikango
Cuangar
Rundu
Victoria
Falls
Shumba

Opuwo
Oshakati
Tsumeb
Gumare
Okavango
Delta
Maun
Phuduhudu
Nata
Maitengw

Sesfontein
Kamanjab
Etosha
Pan
Grootfontein
Tsumkwe
Sehithwa
Orapa
Letlhakane
Francistown

Khorixas
Outjo
Otavi
Kombat
Xhumo
Makgadikgadi
Tutume

Kalkfeld
Otjiwarongo
Okakarara
Ghanzi
BOTSWANA
Serowe

Uis Mine
Omaruru
NAMIBIA
Steinhausen
Tshootsha
Takatshwaane
Serule

Hentiesbaai
Okahandja
Witvlei
Gobabis
Ncojane
Mahalapye

Swakopmund
WINDHOEK
Dordabis
Tsetseng

Walvis Bay
Rehoboth
Leonardville
Kang
Molepolole
Mochudi

Tropic of Capricorn
Solitaire
Tsumis
Park
Hoachanas
Kalahari
Hukuntsi
Tshane
Mabutsane
Jwaneng
GABORONE
Thabazim

Nauchas
Narib
Stampriet
Khakhea
Kanye
Lobatse
Soshanguv

ATLANTIC
Maltahöhe
Mariental
Gochas
Desert
Werda
Mabule
Mmabatho
Johannesbur

OCEAN
Helmeringhausen
Tses
Koës
Tshabong
Terra
Firma
Mafikeng
Soweto

Lüderitz
Aus
Keetmanshoop
Severn
Vryburg
Delareyville
Sasolburg

NAMAQUALAND
Seeheim
Aroab
Bokspits
Van
Zylsrus
Kuruman
REPUBLIC OF

Ai-Ais
Grünau
Upington
Olifantshoek
Postmasburg
SOUTH AFRICA

Oranjemund
Alexander
Bay
Orange
Keimoe
Galeshewe
Kimberley

Lambert Azimuthal Equal Area Projection

1 : 15 000 000

MILES 0   100   200   300

METRES
FEET

5000
16404

3000
9843

2000
6562

1000
3281

500
1640

200
656

0
0

LAND
B.S.L.

200
656

4000
13124

6000
19686

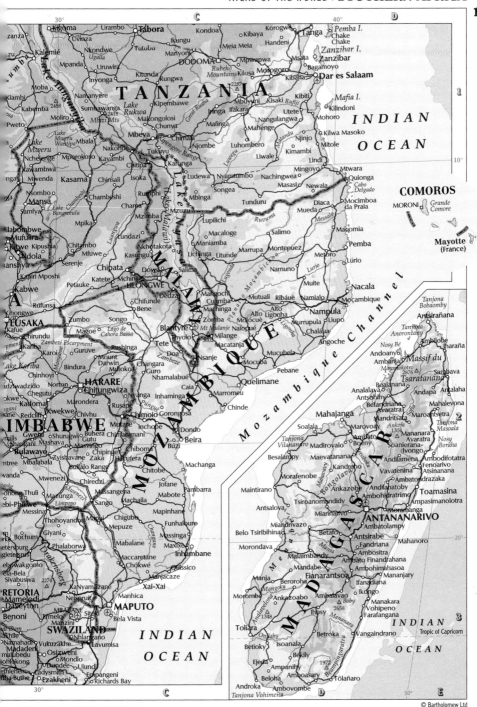

0   250   500 KILOMETRES

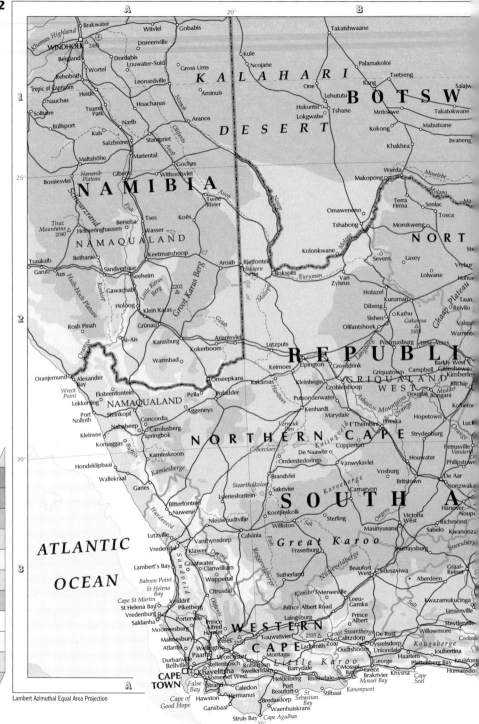

NAMIBIA

KALAHARI DESERT

BOTSW

NORT

REPUBLI

GRIQUALAND WEST

NORTHERN CAPE

SOUTH A

ATLANTIC

OCEAN

WESTERN CAPE

CAPE TOWN

Great Karoo

Little Karoo

METRES / FEET scale:

METRES	FEET
5000	16404
3000	9843
2000	6562
1000	3281
500	1640
200	656
0	0
LAND	B.S.L.
200	656
4000	13124
6000	19686

Lambert Azimuthal Equal Area Projection

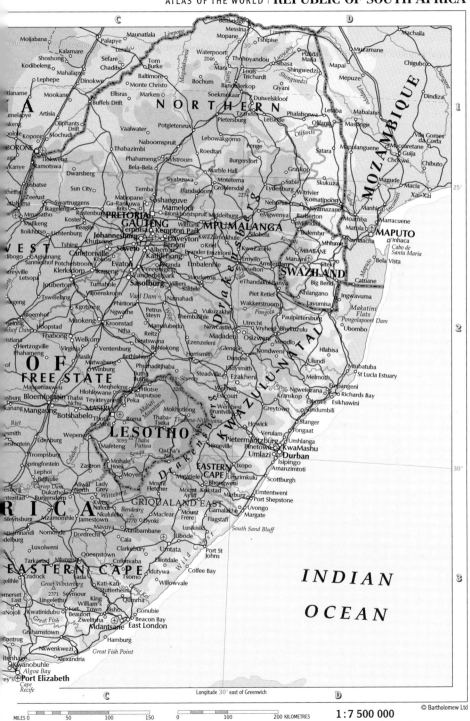

Longitude 30° east of Greenwich

INDIAN

OCEAN

MILES 0   50   100   150   0   100   200 KILOMETRES   1 : 7 500 000

1 : 40 000 000

MILES 0   200   400   600   800

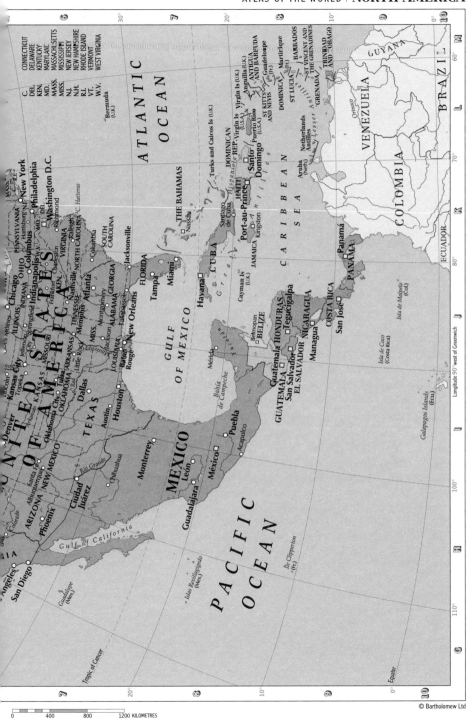

ATLANTIC OCEAN

PACIFIC OCEAN

UNITED STATES OF AMERICA

MÉXICO

GULF OF MEXICO

CARIBBEAN SEA

THE BAHAMAS

CUBA

VENEZUELA

COLOMBIA

BRAZIL

GUYANA

New York
Philadelphia
Washington D.C.
Richmond
Columbus
Chicago
Indianapolis
Columbia
Charleston
Raleigh
Nashville
Atlanta
Jacksonville
Tampa
Miami
New Orleans
Memphis
Montgomery
Tallahassee
Jackson
Baton Rouge
Little Rock
Dallas
Houston
Austin
San Antonio
Oklahoma City
Tulsa
Kansas City
Topeka
Denver
Santa Fe
Albuquerque
Phoenix
San Diego
Los Angeles
Lincoln
Des Moines
Jefferson City

Havana
Nassau
Santiago de Cuba
Port-au-Prince
Santo Domingo
Kingston
San Juan

Monterrey
León
Guadalajara
México
Puebla
Acapulco
Ciudad Juárez
Chihuahua

TEXAS
NEW MEXICO
ARIZONA
OKLAHOMA
KANSAS
MISSOURI
ARKANSAS
LOUISIANA
MISS.
ALABAMA
GEORGIA
FLORIDA
SOUTH CAROLINA
NORTH CAROLINA
VIRGINIA
TENNESSEE
ILLINOIS
INDIANA
OHIO
PENNSYLVANIA
KENTUCKY

CONNECTICUT
DELAWARE
KENTUCKY
MARYLAND
MASSACHUSETTS
MISSISSIPPI
NEW JERSEY
NEW HAMPSHIRE
RHODE ISLAND
VERMONT
WEST VIRGINIA

C.
DEL.
KEN.
MD.
MASS.
MISS.
N.J.
N.H.
R.I.
VT.
W.V.

Bermuda (U.K.)
Turks and Caicos Is (U.K.)
Virgin Is (U.K.)
Virgin Is (U.S.A.)
Puerto Rico (U.S.A.)
Cayman Is (U.K.)
Netherlands Antilles
Aruba (Neth.)
Guadeloupe (Fr.)
Martinique (Fr.)
Anguilla (U.K.)
ANTIGUA AND BARBUDA
ST KITTS AND NEVIS
DOMINICA
ST LUCIA
BARBADOS
ST VINCENT AND THE GRENADINES
GRENADA
TRINIDAD AND TOBAGO

HAITI
DOMINICAN REP.
JAMAICA

GUATEMALA
BELIZE
HONDURAS
EL SALVADOR
NICARAGUA
COSTA RICA
PANAMA

Belmopan
Tegucigalpa
San Salvador
Managua
San José
Panamá

GULF OF CALIFORNIA

Rio Grande

Tropic of Cancer

Equator

Galápagos Islands (Ecu.)

Isla del Coco (Costa Rica)

Isla de Malpelo (Col.)

Île Clipperton (Fr.)

Islas Revillagigedo (Mex.)

Orinoco

ECUADOR

Longitude 90° west of Greenwich

© Bartholomew Ltd

| 0 | 400 | 800 | 1200 KILOMETRES |

ARCTIC OCEAN

BEAUFORT SEA

Queen Elizabeth Islands

Parry Islands

Victoria Island

NUN

CANADA

ALASKA

U.S.A.

Brooks Range

Kuskokwim Mountains

Alaska Peninsula

Gulf of Alaska

PACIFIC OCEAN

YUKON TERRITORY

NORTHWEST TERRITORIES

BRITISH COLUMBIA

ALBERTA

SASKATCHEWAN

MANITOBA

Lake Winnipeg

Vancouver Island

WASHINGTON

OREGON

IDAHO

MONTANA

WYOMING

N. DAKOTA

S. DAKOTA

NEBRASKA

MINNESOTA

CALIFORNIA

NEVADA

U.S.A.

Edmonton

Calgary

Seattle

Portland

Sacramento

Reno

Boise

Salt Lake

Winnipeg

Minneapolis

Fargo

Bismarck

METRES FEET

5000	16404
3000	9843
2000	6562
1000	3281
500	1640
200	656
0	0
LAND B.S.L.	
200	656
4000	13124
6000	19686

Lambert Azimuthal Equal Area Projection

Longitude 105° west of Greenwich

1 : 25 000 000

MILES 0   250   500

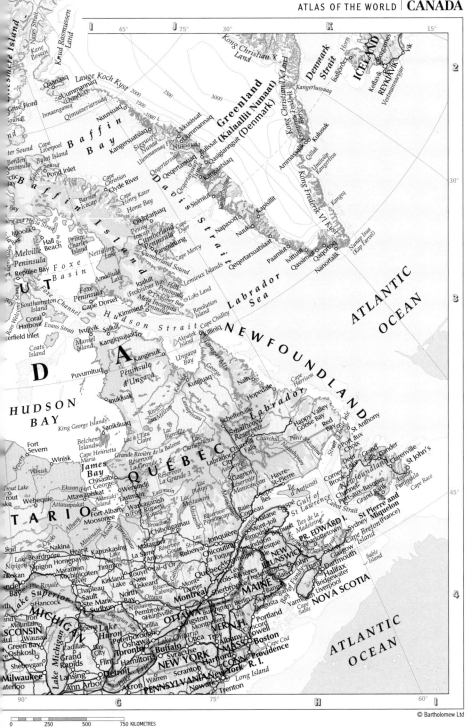

© Bartholomew Ltd

0   250   500   750 KILOMETRES

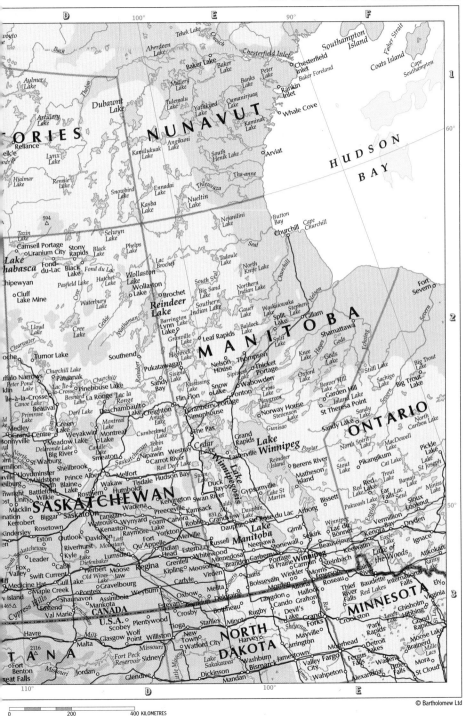

© Bartholomew Ltd

0   200   400 KILOMETRES

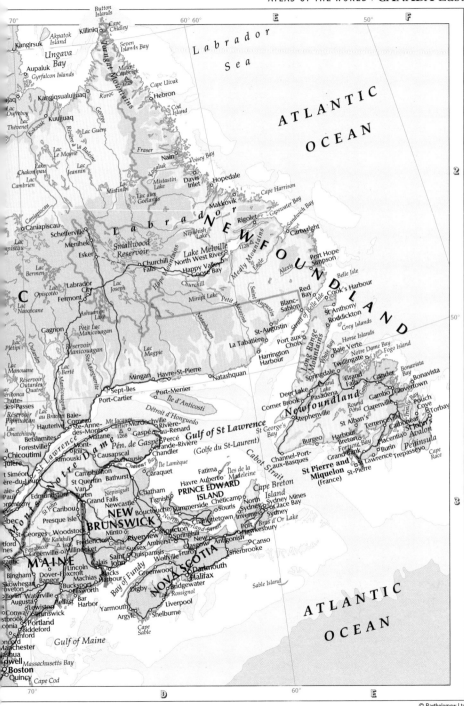

Button Islands
70°
Killiniq
Cape Chidley
60° 60°
E
50°
F

Akpatok Island
Seven Islands Bay
Labrador

Kangirsuk
Mount Caubvick 1268

Sea

Aupaluk
Gyrfalcon Islands

Ungava Bay

Koroc
Cape Uivak

ATLANTIC

Kangiqsualujjuaq
Hebron

jaq
Lac Dufreboy
Kuujjuaq
Cod Island

OCEAN

Lac Thévenet
Koksoak
George
Lac Guers

Rivière à la Baleine
Fraser
Nain

Lac Le Moyne
Voisey Bay

Lac Chakonipau
Lac Jeannin
Kogaluk

Lac Cambrien
Mistinibi
Mistastin Lake
Davis Inlet
Hopedale

Lac aux Goélands
Makkovik
Cape Harrison

Caniapiscau
Gooswater Bay

Caniapiscau
Schefferville
L a b r a d o r
Nipishish Lake
Rigolet
Goose water Bay
Sandwich Bay

Lac apiscau

Menihek
Smallwood Reservoir
Lake Melville
1128
Cartwright

Lac Bermen
Esker
Churchill Falls
North West River
Medly Mountains
Port Hope Simpson

Lac au Brach
Labrador City
Happy Valley
Eagle
Alexis

C
Lac Opiscotéo
Fermont
Lac Joseph
Churchill
Red Bay
Cook's Harbour
Belle Isle

Lac Naococane
Ashuanipi Lake
Minipi Lake
Petit Mecatina
Blanc-Sablon
St Anthony
Roddickton

Gagnon
Petit Lac Manicouagan
Nataskhuan
St-Augustin
Strait of Belle Isle
Grey Islands

Lac Plétipi
Réservoir Manicouagan
Lac Magpie
La Tabatière
Port aux Choix
Horse Islands
Baie Verte

Lac Manouane
Ste Marguerite
Harrington Harbour
White Bay
Notre Dame Bay
Fogo Island

Réservoir Outardes Quatre
Lac Berté
Mingan
Havre-St-Pierre
Natashquan
Springdale
Twillingate
Bonavista Bay
Bonavista

éribouca
chute-des-Passes
Manicouagan
Sept-îles
Port-Menier
île d'Anticosti
Deer Lake
Grand Lake
Gander
Gambo
Cloverton

Réservoir Pipmuacan
Lac Onatchiway
Hauterive
Ste-Anne-des-Monts
Détroit d'Honguedo
Corner Brook
Pasadena
Grand Falls
Pond
Clarenville
Trinity Bay
Pouch Cove

a
Chicoutimi
Forestville
Baie-Comeau
Mt Jacques Cartier 1268
Murdochville
Rivière-au-Renard
Gulf of St Lawrence
Stephenville
St Alban's
Round Pond
Terrenceville
Carbonear
Torbay

jutere
Betsiamites
Matane
Gaspé
Grande-Rivière
George's
St John's

St Siméon
Jolin
Rimouski
Percé
Chandler
(Golfe du St-Laurent)
Burgeo
Bretor
Fortune Bay
Placentia
St John's
Avalon

ère-du-Loup
Causapscal
Pén. de Gaspé
île Lamèque
Bay
Channel-Port-aux-Basques
Grand Bank
Burin
Trepassey
Cape Race

aie-
Paul
Campbellton
Chaleur Bay
Caraquet
Fatima
îles de la Madeleine
St Pierre and Miquelon (France)
St-Pierre
St Lawrence

ontmagny
Edmundston
St Quentin
Bathurst
Nepisiguit
Havre Auberto
Cabot
Strait

bec
Caribou
Van Buren
Grand Falls
Chatham
PRINCE EDWARD
Cape Breton

Presque Isle
Woodstock
Newcastle
Tignish
ISLAND
North
Island

ford
Mt Katahdin 1606
Minto
Bouctouche
Summerside
Chéticamp
Sydney Mines
Glace Bay

nes
Greenville
Millinocket
NEW
BRUNSWICK
Riverview
Moncton
Charlottetown
Inverness
Sydney
Port
Bras d'Or Lake

Bingham
Fredericton
Grand Lake
Sussex
Springhill
New
Antigonish
Canso

MAINE
Lincoln
Saint John
Quispamsis
Amherst
Truro
Sherbrooke

Dover-Foxcroft
Calais
Wolfville
NOVA SCOTIA

Bangor
Machias
Blacks Harbour
Greenwood
Dartmouth
Sable Island

Skowhegan
Waterville
Buckspost
Digby
Bridgewater
Halifax

oveton
Belfast
Bar Harbor
Bay of Fundy
Lake Rossignol

Conway
Brunswick
Liverpool

stbrook
Portland
Yarmouth
Shelburne

conia
Biddeford
Argyle

Sanford
Cape Sable

anchester
Gulf of Maine

shua
owell
Massachusetts Bay

Boston
Quincy
Cape Cod

ATLANTIC

OCEAN

70°
D
60°
E

© Bartholomew Ltd

0   200   400 KILOMETRES

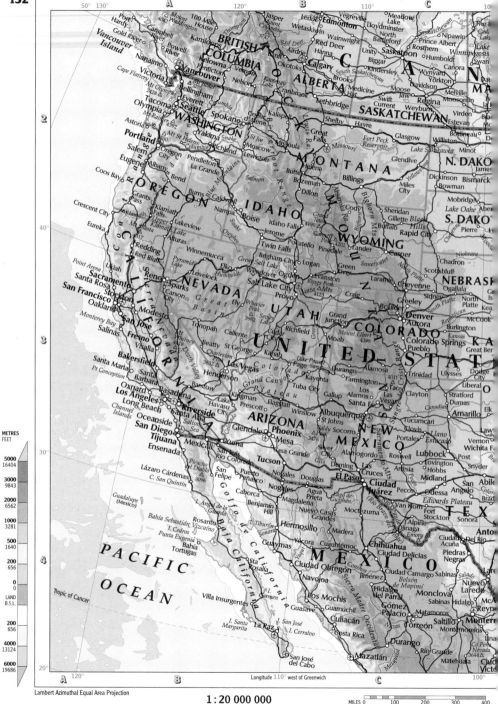

METRES
FEET

5000
16404

3000
9843

2000
6562

1000
3281

500
1640

200
656

0
0

LAND
B.S.L.

200
656

4000
13124

6000
19686

Lambert Azimuthal Equal Area Projection

1 : 20 000 000

MILES 0   100   200   300   400

Longitude 110° west of Greenwich

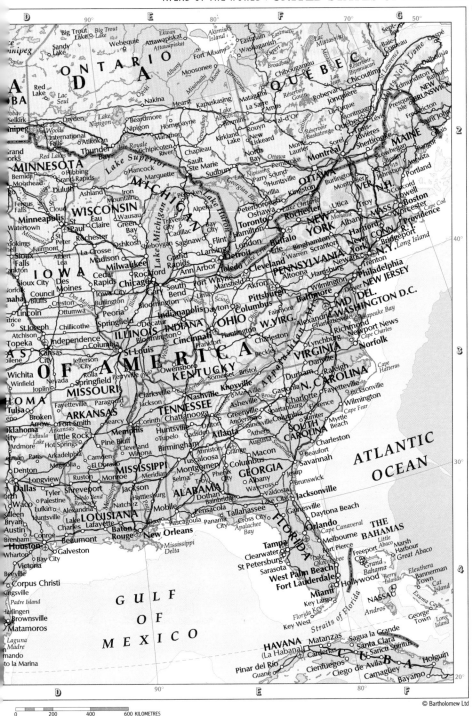

© Bartholomew Ltd

0   200   400   600 KILOMETRES

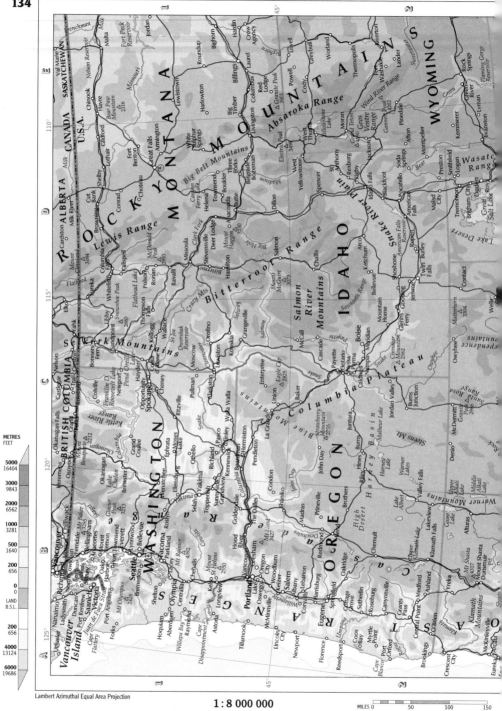

Lambert Azimuthal Equal Area Projection

1 : 8 000 000

MILES 0   50   100   150

METRES
FEET

5000	16404
3000	9843
2000	6562
1000	3281
500	1640
200	656
0	0
LAND	B.S.L.
200	656
4000	13124
6000	19686

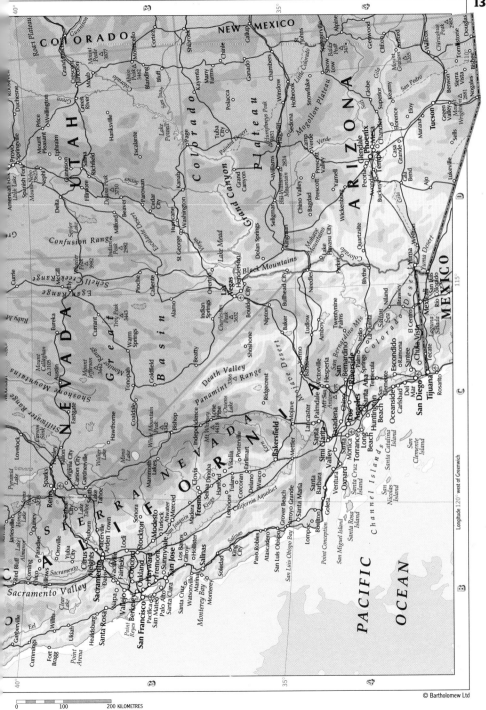

PACIFIC OCEAN

MEXICO

NEW MEXICO

COLORADO

UTAH

NEVADA

ARIZONA

CALIFORNIA

Grand Canyon

Colorado Plateau

Mogollon Plateau

Death Valley

Great Basin

Sierra Nevada

Sacramento Valley

Mojave Desert

Yuma Desert

Confusion Range

Panamint Range

Channel Islands

Phoenix

Tucson

Las Vegas

Sacramento

San Francisco

San Jose

Los Angeles

San Diego

Tijuana

Mexicali

Longitude 120° west of Greenwich

© Bartholomew Ltd

0   100   200 KILOMETRES

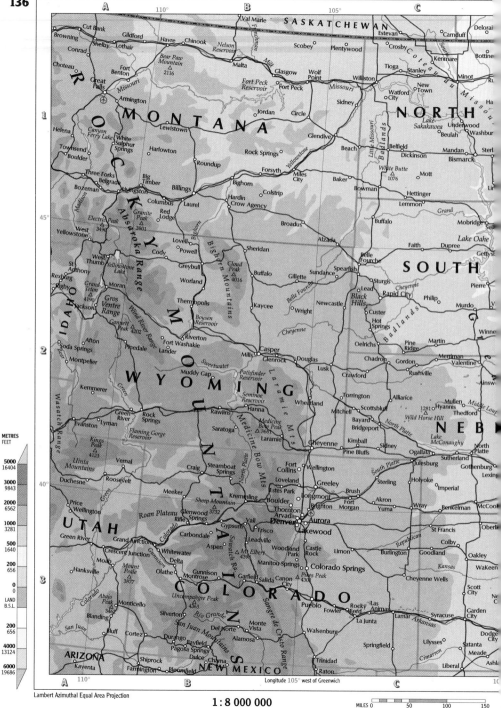

A 110° B 105° C

SASKATCHEWAN

Val Marie
Browning Cut Bank
Gildford Havre Chinook Nelson Scobey Plentywood Crosby Estevan Carduff Delorai
Conrad Shelby Lothair Reservoir Coteau Kenmare Bottine
Choteau Fort Bear Paw Malta Glasgow Wolf Tioga Stanley New Minot Ru
Great Benton Mountain Fort Peck Point Williston Watford Town Ha
Falls Missouri △ 2116 Reservoir Fort Peck Missouri City New Misso
Armington Jordan Circle Sidney NORTH
R O MONTANA Lake
Helena Lewistown Glendive Sakakawea Underwood
Canyon White Beach Belfield Beulah Washbur
Townsend Ferry Lake Sulphur Harlowton Rock Springs Little Missouri Badlands Dickinson Mandan Sterl
Boulder Springs Roundup Forsyth Miles Bowman Hettinger Bismarck Lir
Three Forks Big Billings Bighorn City Baker White Butte Lemmon Grand Mobridge Sell
Belgrade Timber Hardin Colstrip △ 1076 Mott
Bozeman Livingston Laurel Crow Agency Bowman Buffalo Faith Dupree Gettys
45° Columbus Red Broadus Alzada Belle S O U T H
Electric Granite Lodge Fourche Lead Sturgis Philip Pierre
West Peak Peak Lovell Sheridan Cheyenne Rapid City Murdo V
Yellowstone △ 3490 △ 3901 Cody Cloud Buffalo Sundance Black Custer Winne
West Yellowstone Powell Peak Gillette Hills Hot Pine
St Thumb Lake Greybull △ 4016 Newcastle Springs Martin Ridge
Anthony Worland Belle Fourche Oelrichs Badlands Merriman
Rexburg Grand Moran Thermopolis Kaycee Wright Chadron Gordon Valentine Ainsw
Rigby Teton Boysen Cheyenne
△ 4190 Gros Reservoir Riverton Casper Lusk Crawford Rushville
Jackson Ventre Fort Washakie Mills Glenrock Douglas
Soda Springs Range Gannett Lander Sweetwater Pathfinder Torrington Alliarice Mullen
Afton Peak Muddy Gap Reservoir Wheatland Scottsbluff 1281 Hyannis Thedford
Montpelier △ 4202 Seminoe Mitchell △ Wild Horse Hill
Kemmerer W Y O M I N G Reservoir Bayard North Platte N E B
Green Rawlins Medicine Bridgeport Lake
Evanston River Rock Saratoga Bow Peak Cheyenne Kimball McConaughy North
Lyman Springs Hanna △ 3661 Laramie Sidney Ogallala Platte
Flaming Gorge Laramie Pine Bluffs Sutherland
Kings Reservoir Medicine Bow Mts Cheyenne Julesburg Gothenburg
Peak Fort Wellington Holyoke Lexing
△ 4123 Craig Steamboat Collins Greeley Sterling Imperial
Uinta Springs Estes Park Loveland Brush
Mountains Roosevelt Kremmling Longmont Fort Akron Wray Benkelman McCool
Duchesne Meeker Boulder Brighton Morgan Yuma
Sheep Mountain Thornton Denver Aurora St Francis Oberli
Price Roan Plateau △ 3732 Vail Frisco Arvada Lakewood Colby
Wellington Glenwood Republican
Green River Rifle Springs Gypsum Leadville Woodland Castle Limon Burlington Goodland Oakley
Grand Junction Carbondale Aspen △ Mt Elbert Park Rock Kansas WaKeen
U T A H Crescent Junction Whitewater △ 4399 Manitou Springs Colorado Springs Cheyenne Wells Scott
Moab Delta Gunnison Salida Canon Pikes Peak City Ne
Hanksville Mount Olathe Montrose City △ 4301 Garden
Peale Garfield Pueblo Rocky Las City
△ 3877 C O L O R A D O Fowler Ford Animas Oakley
Abajo Uncompahgre Peak Lamar Arkansas Syracuse
Colorado Peak △ 4363 Walsenburg La Junta Dodge
Monticello △ 3461 Silverton Monte Springfield City
Blanding Rio Grande Vista Ulysses Satanta
San Juan Del Norte Alamosa Meade
Bluff Cortez Durango San Juan Mountains Trinidad Liberal Ashla
ARIZONA Bayfield Sangre de Cristo Range Raton
Kayenta Shiprock Pagosa Springs
Farmington Bloomfield NEW MEXICO
A 110° B Longitude 105° west of Greenwich C 10

Lambert Azimuthal Equal Area Projection

1 : 8 000 000

METRES FEET

5000 16404
3000 9843
2000 6562
1000 3281
500 1640
200 656
0 0
LAND B.S.L.
200 656
4000 13124
6000 19686

MILES 0 50 100 150

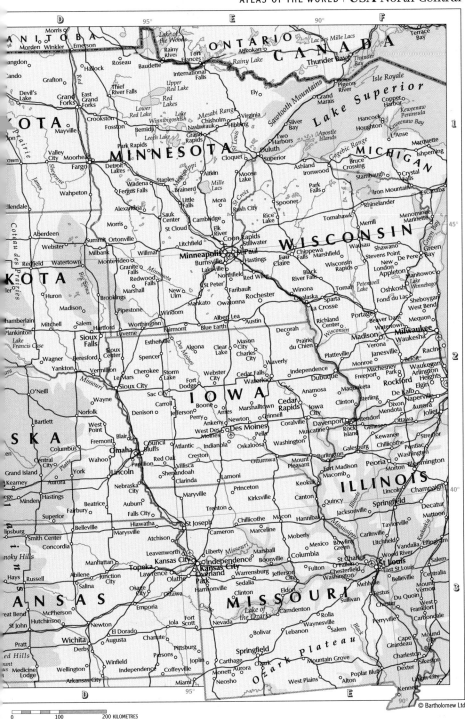

0   100   200 KILOMETRES

© Bartholomew Ltd

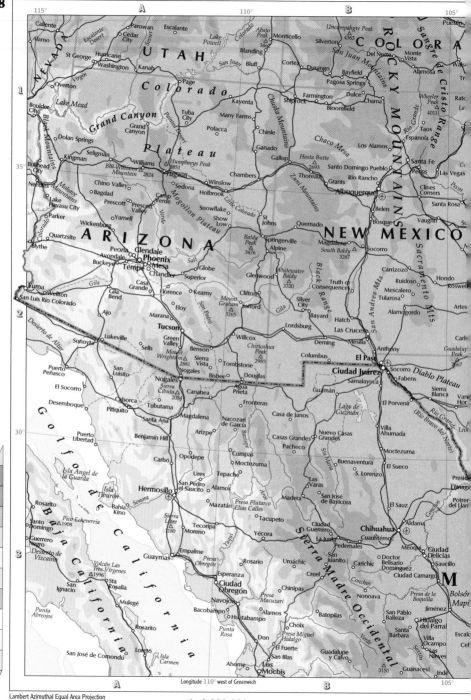

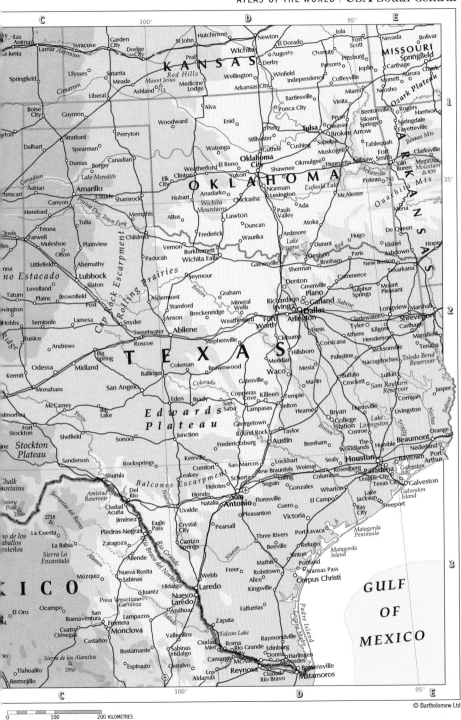

0   100   200 KILOMETRES

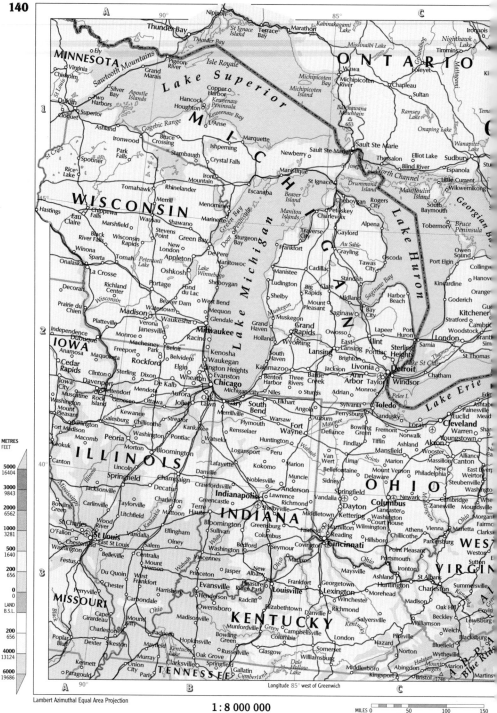

METRES
FEET

5000
16404

3000
9843

2000
6562

1000
3281

500
1640

200
656

0
0

LAND
B.S.L.

200
656

4000
13124

6000
19686

Lambert Azimuthal Equal Area Projection

Longitude 85° west of Greenwich

1 : 8 000 000

MILES 0   50   100   150

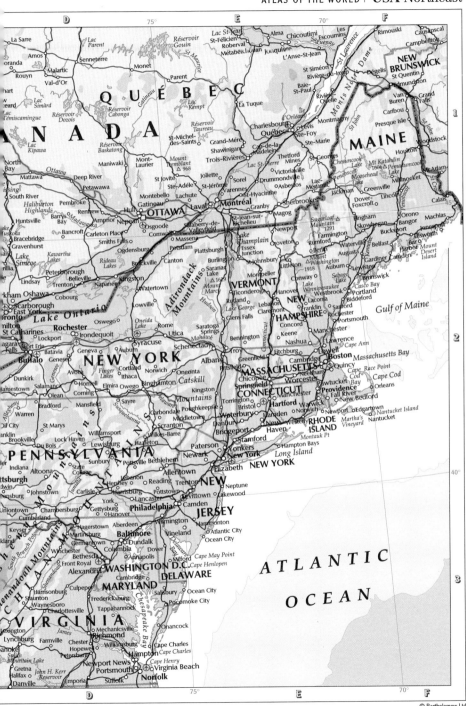

© Bartholomew Ltd

0   100   200 KILOMETRES

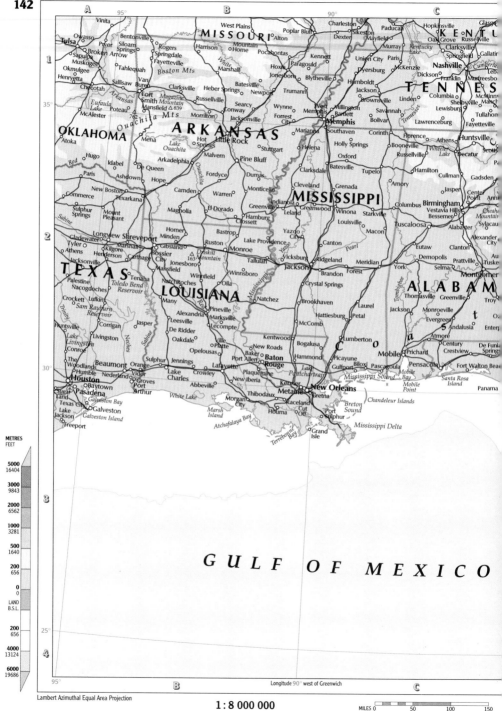

1 : 8 000 000

MILES 0   50   100   150

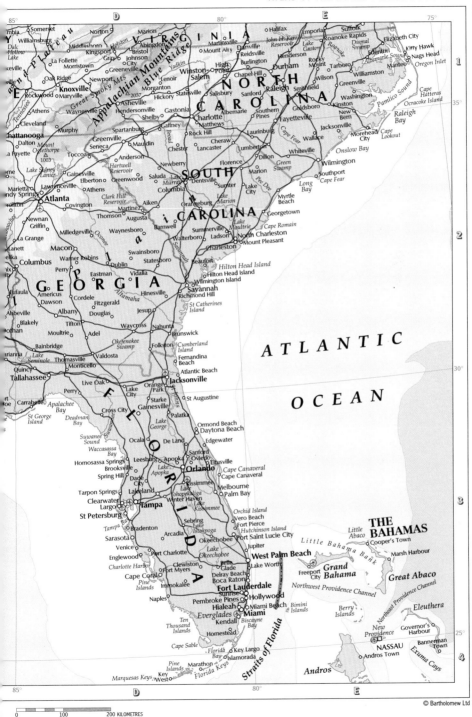

© Bartholomew Ltd

0   100   200 KILOMETRES

A 110° B

ARIZONA

NEW MEXICO

UNITE

M E X I

BAJA CALIFORNIA

G o l f o   d e   C a l i f o r n i a

SIERRA MADRE OCCIDENTAL

Islas Revillagigedo
(Mexico)

P A C I F I C

O C E A N

METRES
FEET

5000	16404
3000	9843
2000	6562
1000	3281
500	1640
200	656
0	0
LAND	B.S.L.
200	656
4000	13124
6000	19686

20°

A

Longitude 110° west of Greenwich

B

Lambert Azimuthal Equal Area Projection

1 : 12 000 000

MILES 0   100   200   300

0   200   400 KILOMETRES

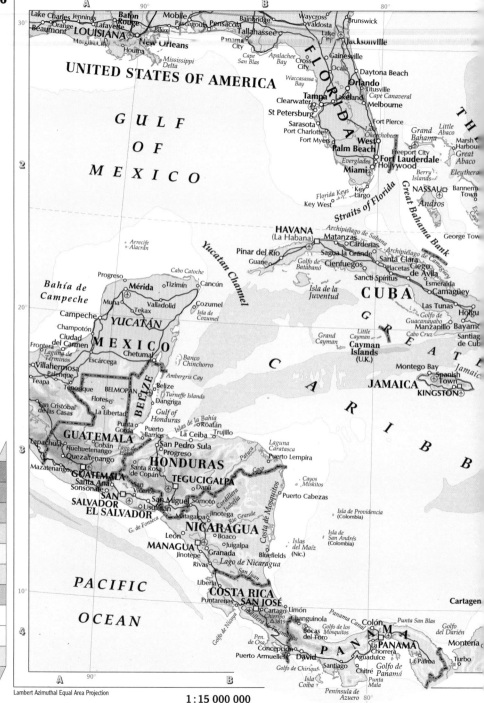

GULF

OF

MEXICO

UNITED STATES OF AMERICA

Lake Charles Jennings
Beaumont Orange Lafayette
LOUISIANA
Morgan City
New Orleans
Houma
Mississippi Delta

Baton Rouge
Biloxi
Pascagoula
Mobile
Pensacola
Bainbridge
Tallahassee
Panama City
Cape San Blas
Apalachee Bay
Cross City
Waccasassa Bay

Waycross
Valdosta
Lake City
Gainesville
Ocala

Brunswick
Jacksonville
Daytona Beach

FLORIDA

Orlando
Titusville
Cape Canaveral
Melbourne
Fort Pierce

Tampa
Clearwater
St Petersburg
Sarasota
Port Charlotte
Fort Myers
Lakeland

West Palm Beach
Fort Lauderdale
Hollywood
Miami
Everglades

Lake Okeechobee

Grand Bahama
Freeport City

Little Abaco
Marsh Harbour
Great Abaco
Eleuthera

Berry Islands

Florida Keys
Key West
Key Largo

NASSAU
Andros

Bannerm Town

George Tow

Straits of Florida

Great Bahama Bank

Arrecife Alacrán

Yucatan Channel

HAVANA (La Habana)
Pinar del Río
Guane
Golfo de Batabanó

Matanzas
Cárdenas
Sagua la Grande
Cienfuegos

Archipiélago de Sabana

Santa Clara
Placetas
Sancti Spíritus

Ciego de Ávila
Esmeralda

Archipiélago de Camagüey

Camagüey

CUBA

Las Tunas
Holguín

Bahía de Campeche

Progreso
Mérida
Muna
Tekax
Valladolid
Tizimín
Cancún
Cozumel
Isla de Cozumel

Campeche
Champotón
Ciudad del Carmen
Frontera
Laguna de Términos
Villahermosa
Palenque
Teapa
Tenosique
Escárcega

YUCATAN

MEXICO

Chetumal
Banco Chinchorro

Isla de la Juventud

Golfo de Guacanayabo
Cabo Cruz
Manzanillo
Bayamo
Santiago de Cub

GREAT

Grand Cayman
Little Cayman
Cayman Islands (U.K.)

Montego Bay
Spanish Town
JAMAICA
KINGSTON

Jamaic

San Cristóbal de las Casas
La Libertad
Flores

BELMOPAN
Belize
Dangriga
Turneffe Islands

BELIZE

Ambergris Cay

Gulf of Honduras

Islas de la Bahía
Roatán
La Ceiba
Trujillo

Punta Gorda
Puerto Barrios
Lago de Izabal
San Pedro Sula
Progreso

Laguna Caratasca
Puerto Lempira

CARIBB

B

GUATEMALA
Tapachula
Cobán
Huehuetenango
Quezaltenango
Mazatenango
Santa Rosa de Copán
GUATEMALA
Santa Ana
Sonsonate
SAN SALVADOR
EL SALVADOR
San Vicente
San Miguel
Usulatán

HONDURAS

TEGUCIGALPA
Danlí
Somoto

Cayos Miskitos

Puerto Cabezas

Patuca
Coco
Cordillera Isabelia

Jinotega
Matagalpa
Río Grande

G. de Fonseca

Costa de Mosquitos

Isla de Providencia (Colombia)

NICARAGUA
León
Boaco
MANAGUA
Jinotepe
Granada
Rivas
Juigalpa
Bluefields

Lago de Nicaragua
San Juan

Islas del Maíz (Nic.)

Isla de San Andrés (Colombia)

PACIFIC

OCEAN

Liberia
COSTA RICA
Puntarenas
SAN JOSÉ
Chirripó △3819
Cartago
Limón

Cartagen

Bocas del Toro
Changuinola
Golfo de los Mosquitos
Colón
Panama Canal
Punta San Blas
Golfo del Darién
Turbo

Pen. de Osa
Golfo de Nicoya
Puerto Armuelles
Concepción
David
Santiago
Bocas del Toro
Aguadulce
La Chorrera
PANAMA
PANAMA
Chitré
Golfo de Panamá
La Palma

Montería

Golfo de Chiriquí
Punta Mala
Isla Coiba
Península de Azuero

Lambert Azimuthal Equal Area Projection

1 : 15 000 000

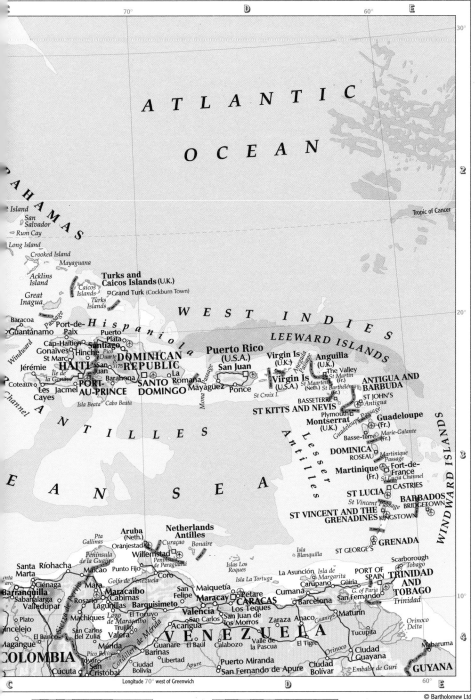

A T L A N T I C

O C E A N

Tropic of Cancer

B A H A M A S

Island
San Salvador
Rum Cay

Long Island

Crooked Island
Mayaguana

Acklins Island
Great Inagua

Turks and Caicos Islands (U.K.)
Caicos Islands
Turks Islands
Grand Turk (Cockburn Town)

W E S T   I N D I E S

LEEWARD ISLANDS

Baracoa
Guantánamo
Cap-Haïtien
St Marc
Gonaïves
Hinche
Port-de-Paix
Puerto Plata
Pico Duarte 3175
Santiago
Jérémie
Île de la Gonâve
HAITI San Juan
Coteaux
Les Cayes
Jacmel
PORT-AU-PRINCE
Barahona
DOMINICAN REPUBLIC
La Romana
SANTO DOMINGO
Isla Beata Cabo Beata

Hispaniola

Puerto Rico (U.S.A.)
San Juan
Mayagüez Ponce

St Croix I.

Mona Passage

Virgin Is (U.K.)
Virgin Is (U.S.A.)
St Maarten (Neth.) St Martin (Fr.)
St Barthélémy (Fr.)

Anguilla (U.K.)
The Valley

Anegada Passage

ANTIGUA AND BARBUDA
ST JOHN'S
Antigua

BASSETERRE
ST KITTS AND NEVIS
Montserrat (U.K.)
Plymouth

Guadeloupe (Fr.)
Basse-terre (Fr.)
Marie-Galante

Guadeloupe Passage

DOMINICA
ROSEAU
Martinique Passage

Martinique (Fr.)
Fort-de-France
St Lucia Channel
CASTRIES
ST LUCIA

St Vincent Passage
BARBADOS
BRIDGETOWN

ST VINCENT AND THE GRENADINES
KINGSTOWN

W I N D W A R D   I S L A N D S

Windward Passage

A N T I L L E S

Lesser Antilles

E A N   S E A

Channel

Pta Gallinas
Aruba (Neth.)
Oranjestad
Netherlands Antilles
Curaçao Bonaire
Willemstad
ST GEORGE'S **GRENADA**

Isla Blanquilla

Scarborough
Tobago
PORT OF SPAIN
TRINIDAD AND TOBAGO

Santa Ríohacha
Marta
Ciénaga
Maicao Punto Fijo
Coro
Peninsula de la Guajira
Punto Fijo
Península de Paraguaná

Islas Los Roques
La Asunción Isla de Margarita
Isla La Tortuga
Carúpano
G. of Paria
Güiria
Trinidad

Barranquilla
Sabanalarga
Valledupar
Plato
El Banco
Magangué
Sincelejo

Maracaibo
Cabimas
Machiques
San Carlos del Zulia
Lagunillas
El Toruyo
Trujillo
Rosario
Mara
Golfo de Venezuela
Lago de Maracaibo

Barquisimeto
San Felipe
Maracay
Valencia
Acarigua
San Carlos
Los Teques
Los Morros
CARACAS
Maiquetía
Petare

Cumana
Barcelona
San Fernando
Maturín
Orinoco Delta
Tucupita
Mabaruma

COLOMBIA
Cúcuta
San Cristóbal
Pico Bolívar
Mérida
Barinas
Ciudad Bolivia
Libertad
Valera
Guanare
El Baúl
Apure
VENEZUELA
Calabozo
Valle de la Pascua
Zaraza
Aragua
Guanipa
El Tigre
Ciudad Guayana
Ciudad Bolívar
Orinoco
Embalse de Guri
GUYANA
Puerto Miranda
San Fernando de Apure
Cordillera de Mérida

Longitude 70° west of Greenwich

© Bartholomew Ltd

MILES 0   100   200   300

0   250   500 KILOMETRES

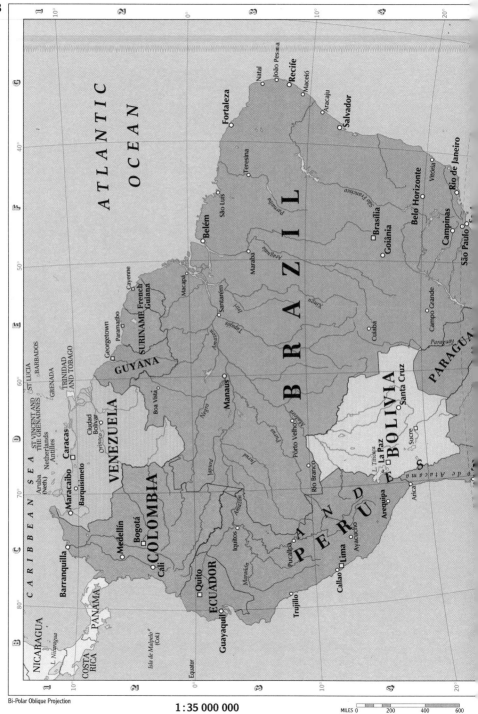

Bi-Polar Oblique Projection

1 : 35 000 000

MILES 0   200   400   600

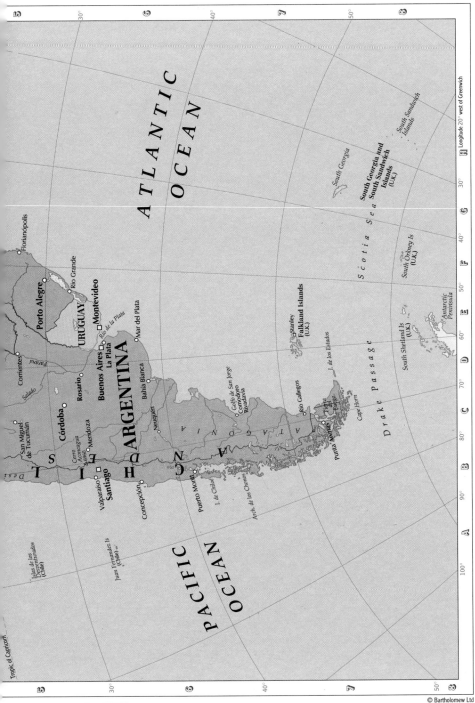

Longitude 20° west of Greenwich

ATLANTIC OCEAN

PACIFIC OCEAN

Tropic of Capricorn

South Sandwich Islands

South Georgia

South Georgia and South Sandwich Islands (U.K.)

Scotia Sea

South Orkney Is (U.K.)

Antarctic Peninsula

South Shetland Is (U.K.)

Falkland Islands (U.K.)

Stanley

Drake Passage

Cape Horn

I. de los Estados

Tierra del Fuego

Punta Arenas

Río Gallegos

Golfo de San Jorge

Comodoro Rivadavia

Florianópolis

Porto Alegre

Río Grande

URUGUAY

Montevideo

La Plata

Río de la Plata

Mar del Plata

Buenos Aires

ARGENTINA

Bahía Blanca

Corrientes

Paraná

Salado

Rosario

Córdoba

San Miguel de Tucumán

Cerro Aconcagua 6960

Mendoza

Neuquén

PATAGONIA

Santiago

Valparaíso

CHILE

ANDES

Concepción

Puerto Montt

I. de Chiloé

Arch. de los Chonos

Islas de los Desventurados (Chile)

Juan Fernández Is (Chile)

Desventuradas

PACIFIC OCEAN

0   500   1000 KILOMETRES

© Bartholomew Ltd

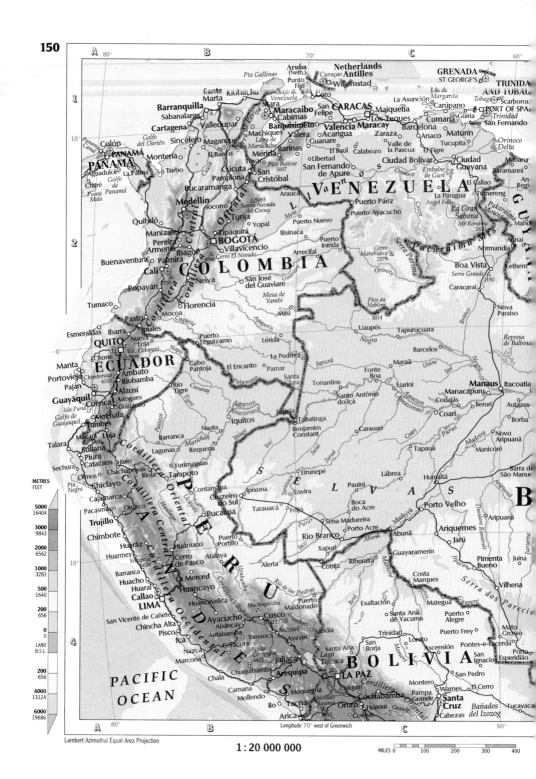

A 80° B 70° C 60°

Netherlands
Aruba (Neth.) Curaçao **Antilles** **GRENADA**
Pta Gallinas Willemstad ST GEORGE'S **TRINIDA**
Punto Fijo Margarita Tobago Scarborou
Barranquilla Venezuela Oro La Asunción **AND TOBAG**
Sabanalarga Mara **CARACAS** Maiquetía Carúpano **PORT OF SPA**
Maracaibo Felipe Trinidad
Cabimas Los Teques Cumaná San Fernando
Cartagena Valledupar **Barquisimeto** **Valencia Maracay** Barcelona Maturín
Machiques **Valera** Acarigua Anaco Tucupita
Golfo Lago de Tovar Guanare Zaraza Orinoco
Montería del Darién Sincelejo Magangué Maracaibo El Baúl Calabozo Valle de Delta
Colón El Banco **Mérida** Barinas la Pascua El Tigre
PANAMÁ Turbo Libertad Ciudad Bolívar **Ciudad** Mabarur
PANAMÁ Pico Bolívar San Fernando Embalse **Guayana** An
Aguadulce La Palma Cúcuta 5007 de Apure Orinoco de Guri El Callao Regi
Chitré Golfo Pamplona San La Páragua Tumereng
Funta Panama Bucaramanga Cristóbal Arauca **VeNEZUELA** Angel Falls
Mala **Medellín** Socorro 5493 El La Gran
Sierra Nevada Meta Puerto Páez Sabana Mt Roraima
Quibdó **Tunja** del Cocuy Puerto Ayacucho 287
Manizales Yopal Ahnai
Pereira Zipaquirá Bisinaca Puerto Normandia
Armenia Villavicencio Inírida Cerro Boa Vista
Buenaventura Ibagué Cerro El Nevado Marahuaca Serra Grande
Cali 6750 Arrecifal 2579 1150
Popayán Neiva **COLOMBIA** Orinoco Caracaraí
San José
Tumaco Florencia del Guaviare Mesa de Pico da Nova
Yambí Neblina Paraíso
Pasto Mocoa Mitú 3014
Esmeraldas Ibarra Ipiales Caquetá Uaupés Tapurucuara Represa
QUITO Nueva Puerto Lérida Negro Barcelos de Balbina
Loja Leguízamo
Chone Vol. Cotopaxi Napo Maraã Unini
ECUADOR Cabo La Pedrera **Manaus** Itacoatia
Manta Pantoja El Encanto Pamar Santa Manacapuru
Portoviejo Ambato Clara Fonte Codajás Beruri Autazes
Riobamba Río Tonantins Boa Iarini Coari
Paján Alausí Tigre Curaray Putumayo Santo Antônio Borba
Guayaquil Azogues do Içá Amazon Coari Novo
Isla Puná Cuenca Gualaceo Amazonas Amazon Purus Aripuanã
Golfo de Iquitos Leticia Carauari Manicoré
Guayaquil Machala Tabatinga Barra de
Tumbes Nauta Benjamim Tapauá São Manue
Macará Loja Constant Juruá
Talara Sullana Barranca Marañón Humaitá B
Piura Lagunas Requena Eirunepé Novo
Catacaos Jaén Yurimaguas Juruá Lábrea Aripuanã
Sechura Chachapoyas Rioja S E L V A S Theodoro Roosevelt
Olmos Tarapoto Ipixuna Pauini
Pta Chiclayo Contamana Porto Velho Ariquemes
Negra Cajamarca Envira Janú
Cruzeiro Boca Jamari
Pacasmayo Otuzco do Sul Tarauacá do Acre Sena Madureira Abunã Juína
Trujillo Pucallpa Feijó Porto Acre Pimenta
Chimbote Puerto Río Branco Purus Bueno Vilhena
Portillo Xapuri Guayaramerín Costa
Huaraz Huánuco Alerta Cobija Marques Mategua
Huarmey Cerro Atalaya P E R U Riberalta Santa Ana Puerto
Barranca de Pasco Serra dos Parecis
Huacho La Merced Río de las Piedras de Yacuma Alegre
Huaral Huancayo Exaltación Mato
Callao Huancavelica Machupicchu Puerto Santa Ana Grosso
LIMA Ayacucho **Cusco** Maldonado de Yacuma Puerto Frey Porto
San Vicente de Cañete Abancay (CUZCO) Loreto Esperidião
Chincha Alta Antabamba Sicuani Sandia San Ascensión Pontes-e-Lacerda
Pisco Yanaoca Ayaviri Borja Trinidad Porto
Ica Corococo Santa Ana San Loreto
Nazca 6425 Juliaca de Yacuma Ignacio
Marcona Chuquibamba Lago **BOLIVIA** San Pedro
Chala **Arequipa** **LA PAZ** Titicaca El Cerro
Camana Colquiri Montero Pampa Warnes Tucavaca
PACIFIC Moquegua Cochabamba Grande **Santa** Bañados
Mollendo Oruro Huanuni **Cruz** del Izozog
OCEAN Ilo Tacna Sajama Grande Corque Cabezas
Arica

METRES
FEET
5000 16404
3000 9843
2000 6562
1000 3281
500 1640
200 656
0 0
LAND B.S.L.
200 656
4000 13124
6000 19686

Longitude 70° west of Greenwich

A 80° B C 60°

Lambert Azimuthal Equal Area Projection

1 : 20 000 000

MILES 0 100 200 300 400

ATLANTIC

OCEAN

GEORGETOWN
Paradise
New Amsterdam
Totness
PARAMARIBO
Albina St-Laurent-du-Maroni
Sinnamary
Brokopondo
Kourou Cayenne
Professor van
Blommestein Meer Guisanbourg
SURINAME French
Juliana Top Guiana
1230 Ini Oiapoque
Pontoetoe

Lourenço Calçoene
Ilha de Maracá
Amapá

Serra Tumucumaque
Mouths of the
Amazon

Macapá
Porto Santana Ilha
Caviana
Arere Mazagão Cabo
Paru Chaves Maguarinho
Baia de Marajó
Serra Almeirim Salinópolis
Oriximiná Parauaquara 359 Ilha de Bragança
Óbidos Marajó Belém Viseu
Juruti Monte Breves Castanhal
Alegre Portel Muana Acará Curuparu Ilha de São Marcos
Parintins Santarém Cametá Pinheiro São Luís
Altamira Tucuruí Viana Parnaíba Camocim
Itaituba Itapicuru Luzilândia Caucaia Fortaleza
Represa Mirim Santa Codó Tianguá Cascavel
Tucuruí Luzia Bacabal Piripiri Sobral Aracati
Jacunda Pedreiras Caxias Timon Campo Maior Canindé Quixadá Macau
Maraba Pres. Dutra Teresina Crateús Boa Mossoró Touros
Jacareacanga Araras Imperatriz Grajaú Barra do Buriti Bravo Palmeirais Taua Viagem Natal
Manuelzinho São Tocantinópolis Corda Açude Boa Floriano Iguatu Icó
Felix Xinguara Porto Franco Esperança Picos Crato Mamanguape
Araguaína Jerumenha Oeiras Juazeiro João
B R A Z I L Conceição Balsas Uruçuí Paulistana do Norte Grande Pessoa
do Araguaia Carolina Canto do Buriti São Raimundo Salgueiro Jaboatão Olinda
Santa Maria Pedro Caracol Nonato Floresta Caruaru Recife
das Barreiras Afonso Gilbués Nova Petrolina Garanhuns Cabo
Peixoto de Porto Remanso Juazeiro Paulo Rio Largo
Azevedo Nacional Corrente Xique Senhor do Bonfim Monte Santo Afonso Maceió
Ilha do Dianópolis Xique Irecê Lagarto Arapiraca
Porto Bananal Natividade Barreiras Ibotirama Jacobina Estância
dos Gaúchos Óbidos São Serrinha Aracaju
Porto Artur Felix Gurupi Santana Bom Jesus Itaberaba Feira Alagoinhas
Diamantino da Lapa de Santana Camaçari
Rosário Oeste Porangatu Correntina Jequié Sto. Antônio de Jesus Salvador
Barra do Bugres Uruaçu Niquelândia Posse Brumado Ipiaú Ubaitaba
Cuiabá Cavalcante Guanámbi Itabuna Ilhéus
Cáceres Rondonópolis Barra do Formosa Januária Espinosa Vitória da Una
Garças Goiás Anápolis Arinos Conquista Itapetinga Porto Seguro
Alto Iporá Trindade Luziânia Unaí Montes Janaúba Salinas Almenara
Garças BRASÍLIA Vianópolis Claros Teófilo Alcobaça
Itiquira Goiânia Paraúna Paracatu Otôni
Puerto Coxim Jataí Itumbiara Araguari Patos
Isabel Corumbá Rio Verde de Mato Grosso Uberlândia de Minas

Equator

© Bartholomew Ltd

0   200   400   600 KILOMETRES

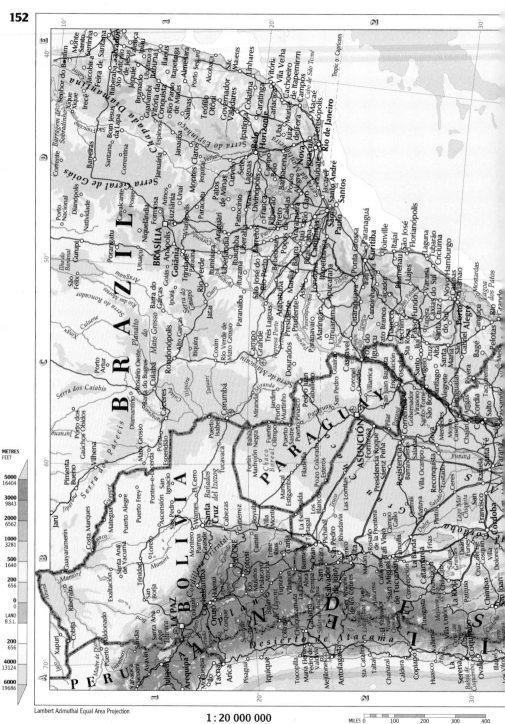

METRES
FEET

5000
16404

3000
9843

2000
6562

1000
3281

500
1640

200
656

0

LAND
B.S.L.

200
656

4000
13124

6000
19686

Lambert Azimuthal Equal Area Projection

1 : 20 000 000

MILES 0   100   200   300   400

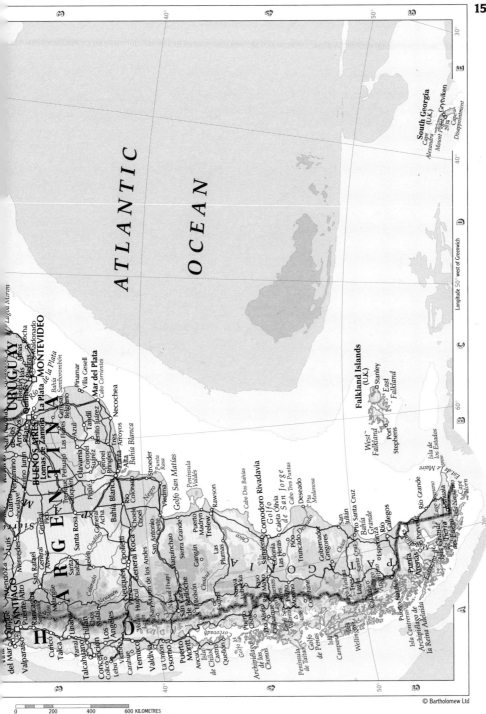

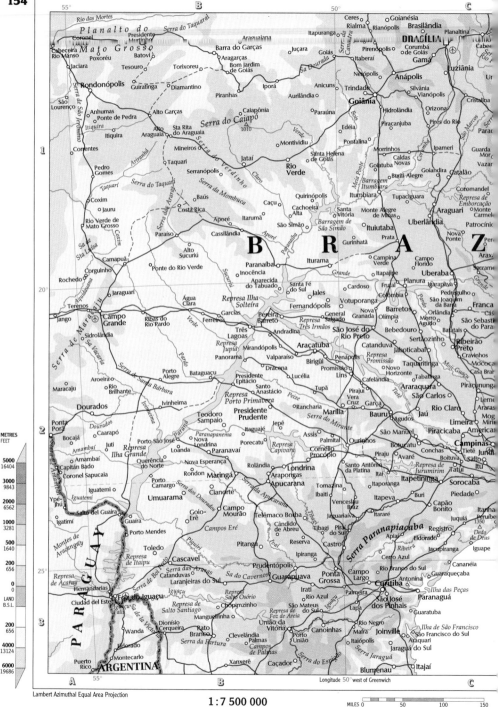

1 : 7 500 000

MILES 0   50   100   150

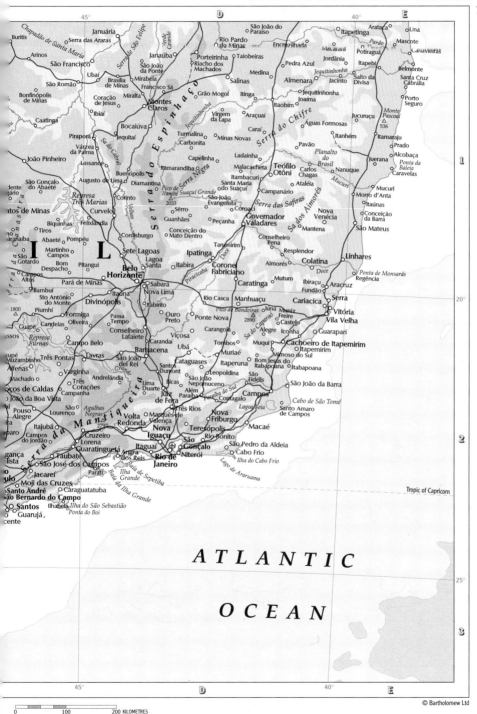

ATLANTIC

OCEAN

Tropic of Capricorn

0   100   200 KILOMETRES

© Bartholomew Ltd

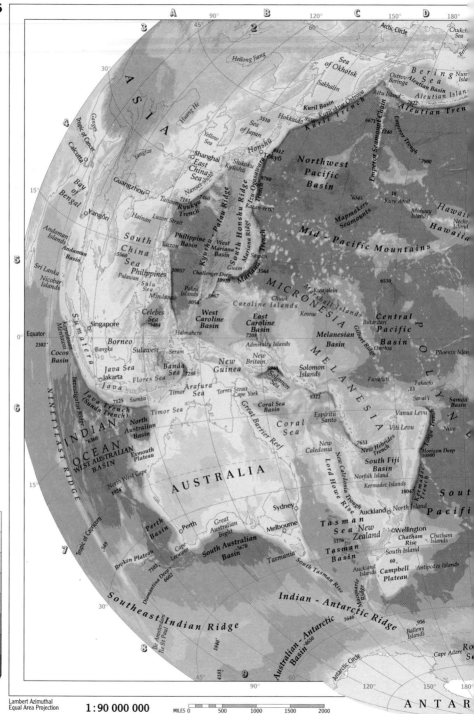

A   90°   B   120°   C   150°   D   180°

Arctic Circle

Chukchi
Sea

Bering
Sea

Sea
of Okhotsk

Heilong Jiang

Sakhalin

Ostrov Aleutian Nun
Beringa Isla

A S I A

Aleutian Basin

Kuril Basin

Aleutian Islan

Hokkaido Kuril'skiye Ostrova

Aleutian Tren

Attu Island

Huang He

Kuril Trench 7822

Ganges

Emperor Trough 1240

Tropic of Cancer

Yellow
Sea

Honshū

3510

Sea
of Japan

Northwest
Pacific
Basin

Emperor Seamount Chain

7900

Calcutta

Yangtze

Shanghai

Tōkyō

East
China
Sea

Shikoku

6412

Kyūshū

15°

Guangzhou

Nansei-shotō

Izu-Ogasawara Trench

Bay
of
Bengal

Taitung

7181

7460

Ryukyu
Trench

Katan-rettō

6345

Kure Atoll

18

Hawaii

Yangon

Hainan

Luzon Strait

West
Mariana
Basin

Midway
Islands

Mid - Pacific Mountains

Necker
Island

Hawaiia

Andaman
Islands

South

Luzon

Philippine
Basin

South Honshu Ridge

9780

Mariana Ridge

Mapmakers
Seamounts

Andaman
Basin

China

5560

Saipan

Mariana Trench

Sri Lanka

Philippines

10057

Challenger Deep
10920

Guam

6530

Nicobar
Islands

Palawan

Sulu
Sea

Mindanao

1564

MICRONESIA

Kwajalein

Kermadec
Menicout

2302

Cocos
Basin

Singapore

Celebes
Sea

5484

West
Caroline
Basin

East
Caroline
Basin

Caroline Islands

Chuuk

Marshall Islands

Kosrae

Central
Pacific
Basin

Butaritari

Gilbert Ridge

POLYNE

Equator

Borneo

Halmahera

7208

Melanesian
Basin

Onotoa

Phoenix Islan

Bangka

Sulawesi

Seram

Admiralty Islands

Java Sea

Banda
Sea

New
Guinea

New
Britain

Solomon
Islands

Funafuti

Fakaofo

Jakarta

7288

8940

Samoa
Basin

Java

Flores Sea

Solomon
Sea

8322

Savai'i

13

NINETYEAST RIDGE

INDIAN

Arafura
Sea

Torres Strait
Cape York

Coral Sea
Basin

Espíritu
Santo

Vanua Levu

Niue

Timor

7125 Sumba

7633

Viti Levu

Timor Sea

OCEAN

7360

North
Australian
Basin

Great Barrier Reef

Coral
Sea

New
Caledonia

New Hebrides
Trench

South Fiji
Basin

Horizon Deep
10800

WEST AUSTRALIAN
BASIN

Exmouth
Plateau

New Caledonia Trough

Norfolk Island

Lord Howe Rise

Kermadec Islands

North West Cape

1924

10047

Sout

15°

AUSTRALIA

Sydney

Tasman
Sea

Auckland

North Island

Pacifi

Perth
Basin

Perth

Great
Australian
Bight

Melbourne

New
Zealand

5176

Wellington

Chatham
Rise

Chatham
Islands

Tropic of Capricorn

590

Broken Plateau

7102

Cape
Leeuwin

South Australian
Basin

5670

Tasman
Basin

South Island

60

Diamantina Deep 6602

Tasmania

South Tasman Rise

Auckland
Islands

Campbell
Plateau

Antipodes Islands

Macquarie Ridge

Indian - Antarctic Ridge

Southeast Indian Ridge

1646

956

Balleny
Islands

Ro
S

The Amsterdam
Île St Paul

1580

Australian - Antarctic
Basin

4650

Cape Adare

4181

Antarctic Circle

45°

90°

60°

120°

150° 180°

ANTAR

METRES
FEET

0	0
200	656
2000	6562
3000	9843
4000	13124
5000	16404
6000	19686
7000	22967
9000	29529

Lambert Azimuthal
Equal Area Projection

1 : 90 000 000

MILES 0   500   1000   1500   2000

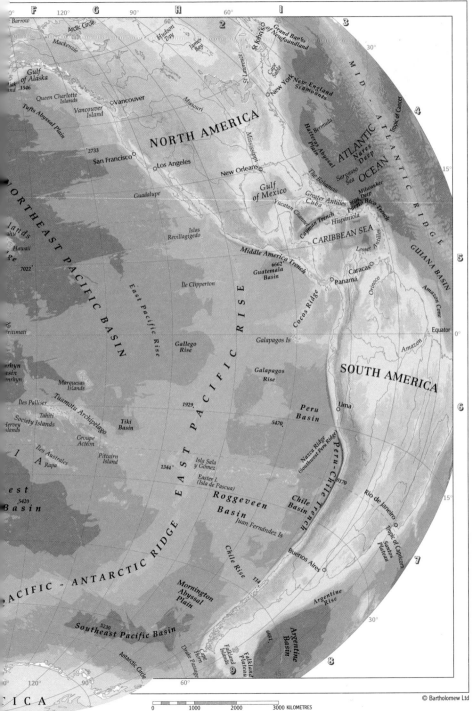

F 120° G 90° H 60° I

Barrow
Arctic Circle
Mackenzie
Hudson Bay
James Bay
St John's
Grand Banks of Newfoundland
Tshazars Is
Cape Sable
Cape
New York
New England Seamounts
MID-ATLANTIC RIDGE
Tropic of Cancer
30°

Gulf of Alaska
1546
Queen Charlotte Islands
Vancouver Island
Vancouver
Missouri
Bermuda
Hatteras Abyssal Plain
ATLANTIC
Nares Deep
4
15°

Tufts Abyssal Plain
2733
San Francisco
Los Angeles
NORTH AMERICA
Mississippi
New Orleans
Gulf of Mexico
The Bahamas
Sargasso Sea
OCEAN
RIDGE

NORTHEAST PACIFIC BASIN
Guadalupe
Islas Revillagigedo
Yucatan
Greater Antilles
Cuba
Milwaukee Deep
3605 Deep
Puerto Rico Trench
GUIANA BASIN

Hawaii
7022
Middle America Trench
Cayman Trench
Hispaniola
CARIBBEAN SEA
Lesser Antilles
5

Kiritimati
East Pacific Rise
Ile Clipperton
6662
Guatemala Basin
Caracas
Panama
Orinoco
Amazon Cone

Penrhyn Basin
Gallego Rise
Cocos Ridge
Galapagos Is
Equator 0°

Marquesas Islands
Galapagos Rise
SOUTH AMERICA
Amazon

Iles Palliser
Tahiti
Society Islands
Hervey Islands
Tuamotu Archipelago
Tiki Basin
1929
Lima
Peru Basin
6

Groupe Acteon
Pitcairn Island
5470

Iles Australes
Rapa
1344
Isla Sala y Gómez
Easter I. (Isla de Pascua)
Peru-Chile Trench
Nazca Ridge (Southeast Peru Ridge)
8170
Rio de Janeiro
15°

West Basin
5420
Roggeveen Basin
Juan Fernández Is
Chile Basin
Buenos Aires
Tropic of Capricorn
Santos Plateau
7

PACIFIC-ANTARCTIC RIDGE
EAST PACIFIC RISE
Chile Rise
114
Argentine Rise
30°

Mornington Abyssal Plain
5230
Southeast Pacific Basin
6687
Argentine Basin

Antarctic Circle
Cape Horn
Drake Passage
Falkland Islands
Falkland Plateau
8

CICA
120° 90° 60°

0 1000 2000 3000 KILOMETRES

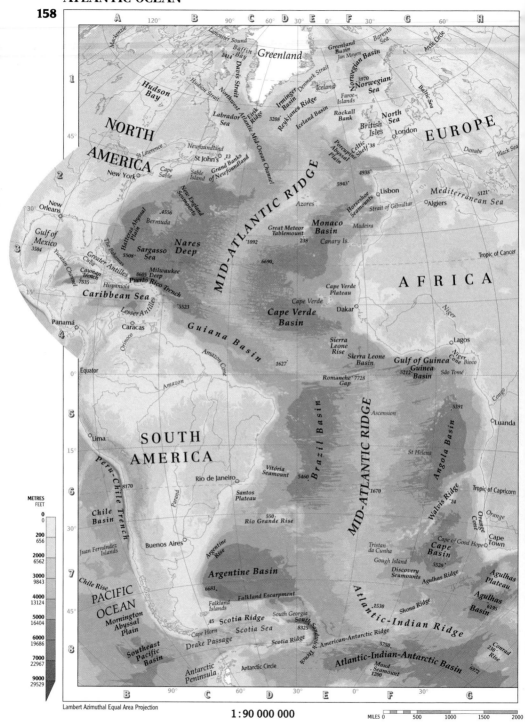

ATLANTIC OCEAN

A 120° **B** 90° **C** 60° **D** 30° **E** **F** 30° **G** 60° **H**

Mackenzie

Lancaster Sound

Baffin Bay 2414

Greenland

Greenland Basin

Barents Sea

Arctic Circle

Davis Strait

Jan Mayen

Norwegian Basin 3970

Norwegian Sea

Baltic Sea

1

Hudson Bay

Hudson Strait

Northwest Atlantic Mid-Ocean Channel

Irminger Basin

Denmark Strait

Iceland

Faroe Islands

Rockall Bank

North Sea

NORTH

Labrador Sea

Eirik Ridge

Reykjanes Ridge 3208

Iceland Basin

Porcupine Abyssal Plain

Celtic Shelf 38

British Isles

London

EUROPE

Danube

Black Sea

AMERICA

St Lawrence

Newfoundland

St John's 13

Grand Banks of Newfoundland

4938

2

Cape Sable

Sable Island

5943

Azores

Lisbon

Mediterranean Sea 5121

New York

New England Seamounts

Great Meteor Tablemount

Monaco Basin 238

Horseshoe Seamounts

Strait of Gibraltar

Algiers

New Orleans

4556

Bermuda

Hatteras Abyssal Plain

MID-ATLANTIC RIDGE

1092

Madeira

Canary Is.

3

30°

Gulf of Mexico 3504

The Bahamas

Nares Deep

Sargasso Sea

5508

6690

Tropic of Cancer

15°

Greater Antilles

Cuba

Cayman Trench 7535

Milwaukee Deep 8605

Puerto Rico Trench

Cape Verde Plateau

AFRICA

Yucatán Channel

Hispaniola

Caribbean Sea

Lesser Antilles

5523

Cape Verde

Dakar

Cape Verde Basin

Niger

4

Panamá

Caracas

Guiana Basin

Sierra Leone Rise

Lagos

Niger Cone Bioco

Orinoco

Amazon Cone

1627

Sierra Leone Basin

Gulf of Guinea

Guinea Basin

5212

São Tomé

0°

Equator

Amazon

Romanche 7728 Gap

Congo

5

Lima

SOUTH

Brazil Basin

Ascension

5391

Luanda

Angola Basin

15°

AMERICA

St Helena

MID-ATLANTIC RIDGE

Peru-Chile Trench

Vitória Seamount

6

8170

Rio de Janeiro

Paraná

Santos Plateau

5460

1670

Walvis Ridge 24

Tropic of Capricorn

Orange Cone

Orange

METRES FEET

0	0
200	656
2000	6562
3000	9843
4000	13124
5000	16404
6000	19686
7000	22967
9000	29529

30°

Chile Basin

550

Río Grande Rise

Tristan da Cunha

Cape Basin

Cape of Good Hope

Cape Town

7

Juan Fernández Islands

Buenos Aires

Argentine Rise

Gough Island

5520

Discovery Seamounts

Agulhas Ridge

Agulhas Plateau

Chile Rise

PACIFIC

Argentine Basin

6681

1530

Shona Ridge

Agulhas Basin 5195

45°

OCEAN

Mornington Abyssal Plain

Falkland Islands

Falkland Escarpment

45

Scotia Ridge

South Georgia

8325

South Sandwich Trench

Atlantic-Indian Ridge

5750

Conrad Rise 230

Cape Horn

Drake Passage

Scotia Sea

Scotia Ridge

American-Antarctic Ridge

Atlantic-Indian-Antarctic Basin

6972

8

Southeast Pacific Basin

Antarctic Peninsula

Antarctic Circle

Maud Seamount 1200

B 90° **C** 60° **D** 30° **E** 0° **F** 30° **G**

Lambert Azimuthal Equal Area Projection

1 : 90 000 000

MILES 0 · 500 · 1000 · 1500 · 2000

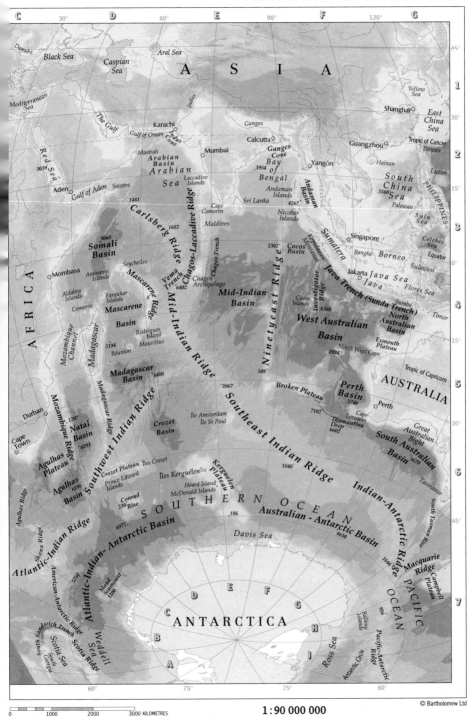

C 30° D 60° E 90° F 120° G

Danube
Black Sea
Caspian Sea
Aral Sea
Mediterranean Sea
The Gulf
Red Sea
3039
Aden
Gulf of Aden
Socotra

A S I A
Karachi
Indus Cone
Gulf of Oman
Masirah
Arabian Basin
Mumbai
Ganges
Arabian Sea
Calcutta
Ganges Cone
3954
Bay of Bengal
Yangon
Shanghai
Yellow Sea
East China Sea
Tropic of Cancer
Taiwan
Guangzhou
Hainan
Luzon
South China Sea
5560

Mombasa
Laccadive Islands
Andaman Islands
Sri Lanka
4267
Andaman Basin
Cape Comorin
1481
Carlsberg Ridge
1682
Maldives
Nicobar Islands
Singapore
Palawan
Sulu Sea
Celebes Sea
Equator

Somali Basin
Seychelles
Amirante Islands
2302
Cocos Basin
Sumatera
Bangka
Borneo
Sulawesi
Jakarta
Java Sea
Flores Sea
Java
5605
Java Trench (Sunda Trench)
Sumba
North Australian Basin
Timor
Comoros
Aldabra Islands
Farquhar Islands
Mascarene Basin
6402
Chagos Archipelago
Mid-Indian Basin
6360
Cocos Islands
Investigator Ridge
West Australian Basin
North West Cape
Exmouth Plateau
1924

Durban
Cape Town
Madagascar
5194
Rodrigues Island
Mauritius
Réunion
6400
Madagascar Basin
2067
549
Ninetyeast Ridge
Broken Plateau
7102
Perth Basin
5746
Perth
Cape Leeuwin
Diamantina Deep 6602
Great Australian Bight
South Australian Basin
5670
Tasmania

Agulhas Plateau
1207
Natal Basin
6291
Mozambique Ridge
Madagascar Ridge
Crozet Basin
Île Amsterdam
Île St Paul
1840
Southeast Indian Ridge
Indian-Antarctic Ridge
Macquarie Ridge
Campbell Plateau

Agulhas
6195
Agulhas Basin
Crozet Plateau
Îles Crozet
Prince Edward Islands
Îles Kerguélen
Kerguelen Plateau
Heard Island
McDonald Islands
Conrad Rise 230
Southwest Indian Ridge
S O U T H E R N   O C E A N
186
Australian-Antarctic Basin
4630
P A C I F I C   O C E A N

Agulhas Ridge
Shona Ridge
American-Antarctic Ridge
3791
Mond Seamount 1200
6972
Atlantic-Indian Ridge
Atlantic-Indian Basin
Davis Sea
Antarctic Circle
Balleny Islands
956
Pacific-Antarctic Ridge

South Sandwich Trench
South Georgia
Scotia Sea
Scotia Ridge
Weddell Sea
A N T A R C T I C A

60° 75° 75° 60°

1 : 90 000 000

0 1000 2000 3000 KILOMETRES

© Bartholomew Ltd

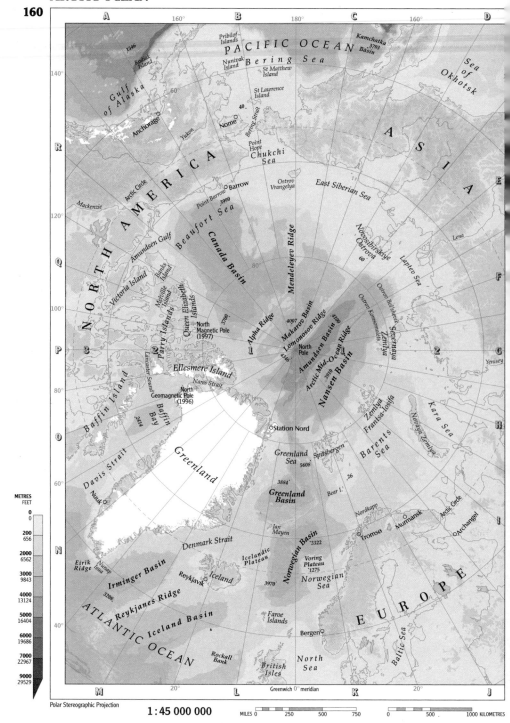

ARCTIC OCEAN

160

A 160° B 180° C 160° D

PACIFIC OCEAN

140°

Pribilof
Islands

Kamchatka
3703
Basin

Kodiak
Island
1546

Bering Sea

Nunivak
Island

Sea
of
Okhotsk

St Matthew
Island

60°

Gulf
of
Alaska

St Lawrence
Island

A S I A

Anchorage

Nome

Bering Strait

40.

Yukon

Point
Hope

E

Chukchi
Sea

Ostrov
Vrangelya

East Siberian Sea

Arctic Circle

70°

Barrow

Mackenzie

Point Barrow

120°

Novosibirskiye
Ostrova
60

Lena

Laptev Sea

Beaufort Sea

3990

Amundsen Gulf

80°

Mendeleyev Ridge

Canada Basin

Banks
Island

Ostrov Bol'shevik

F

Victoria Island

Melville
Island

Ostrov Komsomolets

Severnaya
Zemlya

Q

100°

Makarov
Basin

3700

Queen Elizabeth
Islands

Alpha Ridge

4097

North
Magnetic Pole
(1997)

Lomonosov Ridge

3900

Kara
Sea

2

North
Pole

Amundsen Basin

4156

4100

Zemlya

Yenisey

Parry Islands

Ellesmere Island

Lancaster Sound

Arctic Mid-Ocean Ridge

Nansen Basin

Zemlya
Frantsa-Iosifa

Novaya Zemlya

P

80°

Baffin
Island

Nares Strait

North
Geomagnetic Pole
(1996)

2414

H

Davis Strait

Baffin
Bay

Station Nord

Greenland

Greenland
Sea

5608

Spitsbergen

Barents
Sea

O

60°

Nuuk

Greenland
Basin

3884

Bear I.

.26

Nordkapp

Mumansk

Arkhangel

Arctic Circle

Jan
Mayen

Tromsø

Denmark Strait

Icelandic
Plateau

Voring
Plateau
1275

Norwegian Basin

Bergen

EUROPE

N

Eirik
Ridge

Nanok
Islar

3208.

Reykjanes Ridge

Reykjavik

Iceland

3970

3322

Norwegian
Sea

Baltic Sea

40°

ATLANTIC OCEAN

Iceland Basin

Faroe
Islands

Bergen

Rockall
Bank

British
Isles

North
Sea

M 20° L Greenwich 0° meridian K 20° J

METRES
FEET

0
0

200
656

2000
6562

3000
9843

4000
13124

5000
16404

6000
19686

7000
22967

9000
29529

Polar Stereographic Projection

1 : 45 000 000

MILES 0   250   500   750

0   500 .   1000 KILOMETRES

INTRODUCTION TO THE INDEX

The index includes all names shown on the maps in the Atlas of the World. Names are referenced by page number and by a grid reference. The grid reference correlates to the alphanumeric values which appear within each map frame. Each entry also includes the country or geographical area in which the feature is located. Entries relating to names appearing on insets are indicated by a small box symbol: □, followed by a grid reference if the inset has its own alphanumeric values.

Name forms are as they appear on the maps, with additional alternative names or name forms included as cross-references which refer the user to the entry for the map form of the name. Names beginning with Mc or Mac are alphabetized exactly as they appear. The terms Saint, Sainte, etc, are abbreviated to St, Ste, etc, but alphabetized as if in the full form.

Names of physical features beginning with generic geographical terms are permuted – the descriptive term is placed after the main part of the name. For example, Lake Superior is indexed as Superior, Lake; Mount Everest as Everest, Mount. This policy is applied to all languages.

Entries, other than those for towns and cities, include a descriptor indicating the type of geographical feature. Descriptors are not included where the type of feature is implicit in the name itself.

Administrative divisions are included to differentiate entries of the same name and feature type within the one country. In such cases, duplicate names are alphabetized in order of administrative division. Additional qualifiers are also included for names within selected geographical areas.

INDEX ABBREVIATIONS

admin. div.	administrative division	g.	gulf	Port.	Portugal
aut. comm.	autonomous community	Ger.	Germany	prov.	province
Afgh.	Afghanistan	Guat.	Guatemala	pt	point
Alg.	Algeria	hd	headland	r.	river
Arg.	Argentina	Hond.	Honduras	r. mouth	river mouth
Austr.	Australia	i.	island	reg.	region
aut. reg.	autonomous region	imp. l.	impermanent lake	resr	reservoir
aut. rep.	autonomous republic	Indon.	Indonesia	rf	reef
Azer.	Azerbaijan	is.	islands	Rus. Fed.	Russian Federation
b.	bay	isth.	isthmus	S.	South
B.I.O.T.	British Indian Ocean Territory	Kazakh.	Kazakhstan	salt l.	salt lake
		Kyrg.	Kyrgyzstan	sea chan.	sea channel
Bangl.	Bangladesh	l.	lake	special admin. reg.	special administrative region
Bol.	Bolivia	lag.	lagoon		
Bos.-Herz.	Bosnia Herzegovina	Lith.	Lithuania	str.	strait
Bulg.	Bulgaria	Lux.	Luxembourg	Switz.	Switzerland
c.	cape	Madag.	Madagascar	Tajik.	Tajikistan
Can.	Canada	Maur.	Mauritania	Tanz.	Tanzania
C.A.R.	Central African Republic	Mex.	Mexico	terr.	territory
Col.	Colombia	Moz.	Mozambique	Thai.	Thailand
Czech Rep.	Czech Republic	mt.	mountain	Trin. and Tob.	Trinidad and Tobago
Dem. Rep. Congo	Democratic Republic of Congo	mts	mountains	Turkm.	Turkmenistan
		mun.	municipality	U.A.E.	United Arab Emirates
depr.	depression	N.	North	U.K.	United Kingdom
des.	desert	Neth.	Netherlands	Ukr.	Ukraine
Dom. Rep.	Dominican Republic	Neth. Antilles	Netherland Antilles	union terr.	union territory
E.	east	Nic.	Nicaragua	Uru.	Uruguay
esc.	escarpment	N.Z.	New Zealand	U.S.A.	United States of America
est.	estuary	Pak.	Pakistan	Uzbek.	Uzbekistan
Eth.	Ethiopia	Para.	Paraguay	val.	valley
Equat. Guinea	Equatorial Guinea	pen.	peninsula	Venez.	Venezuela
Fin.	Finland	Phil.	Philippines	vol.	volcano
for.	forest	plat.	plateau	vol. crater	volcanic crater
Fr. Guiana	French Guiana	P.N.G.	Papua New Guinea	W.	west
Fr. Polynesia	French Polynesia	Pol.	Poland	Yugo.	Yugoslavia

A

100 C2 Aachen Ger.
102 C2 Aalen Ger.
100 B2 Aalst Belgium
93 I3 Äänekoski Fin.
100 DE Aarau Switz.
100 B2 Aarschot Belgium
70 A2 Aba China
119 D2 Aba Dem. Rep. Congo
115 C4 Aba Nigeria
81 C2 Ābādān Iran
81 D2 Abādeh Iran
81 D3 Ābādeh Ţashk Iran
114 B1 Abadla Alg.
155 C1 Abaeté Brazil
　Abagnar Qi China see
　Xilinhot
135 E3 Abajo Peak U.S.A.
115 C4 Abakaliki Nigeria
83 H3 Abakan Rus. Fed.
150 B4 Abancay Peru
81 D2 Abarqū Iran
66 D2 Abashiri Japan
66 D2 Abashiri-wan b. Japan
59 D3 Abau P.N.G.
　Abaya, Lake Eth. see
　Ābaya Hāyk'
117 B4 Ābaya Hāyk' l. Eth.
　Blue Nile
83 H3 Abaza Rus. Fed.
108 A2 Abbasanta Sardinia Italy
104 C1 Abbeville France
143 C2 Abbeville AL U.S.A.
142 B3 Abbeville LA U.S.A.
97 B2 Abbeyfeale Rep. of Ireland
74 B1 Abbottabad Pak.
55 R2 Abbott Ice Shelf
　Antarctica
115 E3 Abéché Chad
114 B4 Abengourou Côte d'Ivoire
93 E4 Åbenrå Denmark
114 C4 Abeokuta Nigeria
99 A3 Aberaeron U.K.
96 C2 Aberchirder U.K.
　Abercorn Zambia see
　Mbala
99 B4 Aberdare U.K.
99 A3 Aberdaron U.K.
53 D2 Aberdeen Austr.
122 B3 Aberdeen S. Africa
96 C2 Aberdeen U.K.
141 D3 Aberdeen MD U.S.A.
137 D1 Aberdeen SD U.S.A.
134 B1 Aberdeen WA U.S.A.
129 E1 Aberdeen Lake Can.
96 C2 Aberfeldy U.K.
96 B2 Aberfoyle U.K.
99 B4 Abergavenny U.K.
　Abergwaun U.K. see
　Fishguard
　Aberhonddu U.K. see
　Brecon
139 C2 Abernathy U.S.A.
134 B2 Abert, Lake U.S.A.
　Abertawe U.K. see
　Swansea
　Aberteifi U.K. see
　Cardigan
99 B4 Abertillery U.K.
99 A3 Aberystwyth U.K.
86 F2 Abez' Rus. Fed.
78 B3 Abhā Saudi Arabia
81 C2 Abhar Iran
　Abiad, Bahr el r.
　Sudan/Uganda see
　White Nile
114 B4 Abidjan Côte d'Ivoire
137 D3 Abilene KS U.S.A.
139 D2 Abilene TX U.S.A.
99 C4 Abingdon U.K.
140 C3 Abingdon U.S.A.
91 D3 Abinsk Rus. Fed.
130 B3 Abitibi, Lake Can.
　Åbo Fin. see Turku
74 B1 Abohar India
114 B4 Aboisso Côte d'Ivoire
114 C4 Abomey Benin
60 A1 Abongabong, Gunung mt. Indon.
118 B2 Abong Mbang Cameroon
64 A3 Aborlan Phil.
115 D3 Abou Déia Chad
106 B2 Abrantes Port.
152 B2 Abra Pampa Arg.
138 A3 Abreojos, Punta pt Mex.
116 B2 'Abri Sudan
136 A2 Absaroka Range mts U.S.A.

81 C1 Abşeron Yarımadası pen. Azer.
78 B3 Abū 'Arīsh Saudi Arabia
116 A2 Abu Ballûs hill Egypt
79 C2 Abu Dhabi U.A.E.
116 B3 Abu Hamed Sudan
116 B3 Abu Haraz Sudan
118 01 Abuja Nigeria
81 C2 Abū Kamāl Syria
118 C2 Abumombazi Dem. Rep. Congo
152 B1 Abunã r. Bol.
150 C3 Abunã Brazil
74 B2 Abu Road India
78 B2 Abū Şādi, Jabal hill Saudi Arabia
116 B2 Abu Simbel Egypt
116 A3 Abu Zabad Sudan
　Abū Zabī U.A.E. see
　Abu Dhabi
117 A4 Abyei Sudan
145 B2 Acambaro Mex.
120 B2 Acampamento de Caça do Mucusso Angola
106 B1 A Cañiza Spain
144 B2 Acaponeta Mex.
145 C3 Acapulco Mex.
151 E3 Acará Brazil
154 A3 Acaray, Represa de resr Para.
150 C2 Acarigua Venez.
110 B1 Acâş Romania
145 C3 Acatlán Mex.
145 C3 Acayucán Mex.
114 B4 Accra Ghana
98 B3 Accrington U.K.
74 B2 Achalpur India
97 A2 Achill Island Rep. of Ireland
101 D1 Achim Ger.
96 B2 Achnasheen U.K.
91 D2 Achuyevo Rus. Fed.
111 C3 Acıpayam Turkey
109 C3 Acireale Sicily Italy
147 C2 Acklins Island Bahamas
153 A3 Aconcagua, Cerro mt. Arg.
104 C3 A Coruña Spain
108 A2 Acqui Terme Italy
103 D2 Ács Hungary
49 N6 Actéon, Groupe is Fr. Polynesia
145 C2 Actopán Mex.
139 D2 Ada U.S.A.
　Adabazar Turkey see
　Sakarya
79 C2 Adam Oman
111 B3 Adamas Greece
135 B3 Adams Peak U.S.A.
　'Adan Yemen see Aden
80 B2 Adana Turkey
　Adapazarı Turkey see
　Sakarya
97 B2 Adare Rep. of Ireland
55 M2 Adare, Cape Antarctica
78 B2 Ad Dafīnah Saudi Arabia
78 B2 Ad Dahnā' des. Saudi Arabia
79 B2 Ad Dahnā' des. Saudi Arabia
114 A2 Ad Dakhla Western Sahara
79 C2 Ad Dammām Saudi Arabia
78 A2 Ad Dār al Ḥamrā' Saudi Arabia
78 B3 Ad Darb Saudi Arabia
78 B2 Ad Dawādimī Saudi Arabia
　Ad Dawḩah Qatar see
　Doha
78 B2 Ad Dilam Saudi Arabia
78 B2 Ad Dir'īyah Saudi Arabia
117 B4 Addis Ababa Eth.
81 C2 Ad Dīwānīyah Iraq
143 D2 Adel U.S.A.
52 A2 Adelaide Austr.
55 A3 Adelaide Island Antarctica
50 C1 Adelaide River Austr.
101 D2 Adelebsen Ger.
55 K2 Adélie Land Antarctica
78 B3 Aden Yemen
116 C3 Aden, Gulf of Somalia/Yemen
115 C3 Aderbissinat Niger
79 C2 Adh Dhayd U.A.E.
59 C3 Adi i. Indon.
78 A2 Adī Ark'ay Eth.
108 B1 Adige r. Italy
116 B3 Adīgrat Eth.
78 A3 Adi Keyih Eritrea
74 B3 Adilabad India

115 D2 Adīrī Libya
141 E2 Adirondack Mountains U.S.A.
　Ādīs Ābeba Eth. see
　Addis Ababa
117 B4 Ādīs Alem Eth.
80 B2 Adıyaman Turkey
118 01 Adjud Romania
50 B1 Admiralty Gulf Austr.
128 A2 Admiralty Island U.S.A.
59 D3 Admiralty Islands P.N.G.
73 B3 Adoni India
104 B3 Adour r. France
106 C2 Adra Spain
114 B2 Adrar Alg.
140 C2 Adrian MI U.S.A.
139 C1 Adrian TX U.S.A.
108 B2 Adriatic Sea Europe
　Adua Eth. see Ādwa
116 B3 Ādwa Eth.
83 K2 Adycha r. Rus. Fed.
91 D3 Adygeysk Rus. Fed.
114 B4 Adzopé Côte d'Ivoire
111 B3 Aegean Sea Greece/Turkey
101 D1 Aerzen Ger.
106 B1 A Estrada Spain
116 B3 Afabet Eritrea
　Affreville Alg. see
　Khemis Miliana
76 C3 Afghanistan country Asia
78 B2 'Afīf Saudi Arabia
80 B2 Afyon Turkey
115 C3 Agadez Niger
114 B1 Agadir Morocco
77 D2 Agadyr' Kazakh.
113 I7 Agalega Islands Mauritius
　Agana Guam see Hagåtña
74 B2 Agar India
119 D2 Āgaro Eth.
75 D2 Agartala India
81 C2 Ağdam Azer.
105 C3 Agde France
105 C3 Agen France
122 A2 Aggeneys S. Africa
111 B3 Agia Vervara Greece
111 B3 Agios Dimitrios Greece
111 C3 Agios Efstratios i. Greece
111 C3 Agios Kirykos Greece
111 C3 Agios Nikolaos Greece
78 A3 Agirwat Hills Sudan
123 C2 Agisanang S. Africa
110 B1 Agnita Romania
74 B2 Agra India
81 C2 Ağrı Turkey
　Ağrı Dağı mt. Turkey see
　Ararat, Mount
108 B3 Agrigento Sicily Italy
111 B3 Agrinio Greece
109 B2 Agropoli Italy
87 E3 Agryz Rus. Fed.
144 B2 Agua Brava, Laguna lag. Mex.
154 B3 Água Clara Brazil
145 C3 Aguada Mex.
146 B4 Aguadulce Panama
144 B2 Aguanaval r. Mex.
144 B1 Agua Prieta Mex.
144 B2 Aguascalientes Mex.
155 D1 Águas Formosas Brazil
154 C2 Agudos Brazil
106 B1 Águeda Port.
114 C3 Aguelhok Mali
106 C1 Aguilar de Campóo Spain
107 C2 Águilas Spain
144 B3 Aguililla Mex.
122 B3 Agulhas, Cape S. Africa
158 F7 Agulhas Basin sea feature Southern Ocean
155 D2 Agulhas Negras mt. Brazil
158 F7 Agulhas Plateau sea feature Southern Ocean
158 F7 Agulhas Ridge sea feature S. Atlantic Ocean
111 C2 Ağva Turkey
81 C2 Ahar Iran
100 C1 Ahaus Ger.
81 C2 Ahlat Turkey
100 C2 Ahlen Ger.
74 B2 Ahmadabad India
74 B3 Ahmadnagar India
74 B2 Ahmadpur East Pak.
74 B1 Ahmadpur Sial Pak.
117 C4 Ahmar Mountains Eth.
　Ahmedabad India see
　Ahmadabad

　Ahmednagar India see
　Ahmadnagar
144 B2 Ahome Mex.
81 D3 Ahram Iran
101 E1 Ahrensburg Ger.
104 C2 Ahun France
93 F4 Åhus Sweden
81 C2 Āīn Dār Iran
　Ahvenanmaa is Fin. see
　Åland
122 A2 Ai-Ais Namibia
80 B2 Aigialousa Cyprus
111 B3 Aigio Greece
　Aihui China see Heihe
　Aijal India see Aizawl
143 D2 Aiken U.S.A.
155 D1 Aimorés Brazil
155 D1 Aimorés, Serra dos hills Brazil
105 D2 Ain r. France
107 E2 Aïn Azel Alg.
115 C1 Aïn Beïda Alg.
114 B2 'Aïn Ben Tili Maur.
107 D2 Aïn Defla Alg.
114 B1 Aïn Sefra Alg.
136 D2 Ainsworth U.S.A.
　Aintab Turkey see
　Gaziantep
107 D2 Aïn Taya Alg.
107 D2 Aïn Tédélès Alg.
107 C2 Aïn Temouchent Alg.
60 A1 Airbangis Indon.
128 C2 Airdrie Can.
96 C3 Airdrie U.K.
104 B3 Aire-sur-l'Adour France
101 E3 Aisch r. Ger.
128 A1 Aishihik Lake Can.
100 A3 Aisne r. France
59 D3 Aitape P.N.G.
137 E1 Aitkin U.S.A.
110 B1 Aiud Romania
105 D3 Aix-en-Provence France
　Aix-la-Chapelle Ger. see
　Aachen
105 D2 Aix-les-Bains France
75 D2 Aizawl India
88 C2 Aizkraukle Latvia
88 B2 Aizpute Latvia
67 C3 Aizu-wakamatsu Japan
105 D3 Ajaccio Corsica France
　Ajayameru India see Ajmer
115 E1 Ajdābiyā Libya
79 C2 'Ajman U.A.E.
74 B2 Ajmer India
　Ajmer-Merwara India see
　Ajmer
138 A2 Ajo U.S.A.
119 D2 Ak'ak'ī Beseka Eth.
　Akamagaseki Japan see
　Shimonoseki
54 B2 Akaroa N.Z.
87 E3 Akbulak Rus. Fed.
80 B2 Akçakale Turkey
114 A3 Akchâr reg. Maur.
111 C3 Akdağ mt. Turkey
80 B2 Akdağmadeni Turkey
88 A2 Åkersberga Sweden
118 C2 Aketi Dem. Rep. Congo
81 C1 Akhalk'alak'i Georgia
81 C1 Akhalts'ikhe Georgia
79 C2 Akhḍar, Jabal mts Oman
111 C3 Akhisar Turkey
87 D4 Akhtubinsk Rus. Fed.
118 B3 Akiéni Gabon
130 B2 Akimiski Island Can.
66 D3 Akita Japan
114 A3 Akjoujt Maur.
　Akkerman Ukr. see
　Bilhorod-Dnistrovs'kyy
77 D1 Akkol' Kazakh.
　Ak-Mechet Kazakh. see
　Kyzylorda
88 B2 Akmenrags pt Latvia
　Akmola Kazakh. see
　Astana
67 B4 Akō Japan
117 B4 Akobo Sudan
74 B2 Akola India
118 B2 Akonolinga Cameroon
78 A3 Akordat Eritrea
131 D1 Akpatok Island Can.
77 D2 Akqi China
92 □A3 Akranes Iceland
111 B3 Akrathos, Akra pt Greece
136 C2 Akron CO U.S.A.
140 C2 Akron OH U.S.A.
75 B1 Aksai Chin terr. Asia
80 B2 Aksaray Turkey
86 F2 Aksarka Rus. Fed.

76 B1 Aksay Kazakh.
91 D2 Aksay Rus. Fed.
80 B2 Akşehir Turkey
76 C2 Akshiganak Kazakh.
77 E2 Aksu China
116 B3 Aksum Eth.
76 B2 Aktau Kazakh.
77 D2 Aktogay Kazakh.
88 C3 Aktsyabrski Belarus
76 B1 Aktyubinsk Kazakh.
67 B4 Akune Japan
115 C4 Akure Nigeria
92 □B2 Akureyri Iceland
Akyab Myanmar see Sittwe
111 D2 Akyazı Turkey
77 C2 Akzhaykyn, Ozero salt l. Kazakh.
142 C2 Alabama r. U.S.A.
142 C2 Alabama state U.S.A.
142 C2 Alabaster U.S.A.
111 C3 Alaçatı Turkey
145 D2 Alacrán, Arrecife rf Mex.
81 C1 Alagir Rus. Fed.
151 F4 Alagoinhas Brazil
107 C1 Alagón Spain
78 B2 Al Aḩmadī Kuwait
77 E2 Alakol', Ozero salt l. Kazakh.
92 J2 Alakurtti Rus. Fed.
78 B3 Al 'Alayyah Saudi Arabia
81 C2 Al 'Amādīyah Iraq
81 C2 Al 'Amārah Iraq
135 C3 Alamo U.S.A.
138 B2 Alamogordo U.S.A.
144 A2 Alamos Mex.
144 B2 Alamos Mex.
144 B2 Alamos r. Mex.
136 B3 Alamosa U.S.A.
93 G3 Åland is Fin.
Åland Islands Fin. see Åland
80 B2 Alanya Turkey
Alappuzha India see Alleppey
80 B3 Al 'Aqabah Jordan
78 B2 Al 'Aqiq Saudi Arabia
107 C2 Alarcón, Embalse de resr Spain
78 B2 Al Arṭāwīyah Saudi Arabia
61 C2 Alas Indon.
111 C3 Alaşehir Turkey
128 A2 Alaska state U.S.A.
124 D4 Alaska, Gulf of U.S.A.
126 B3 Alaska Peninsula U.S.A.
126 C3 Alaska Range mts U.S.A.
81 C2 Alāt Azer.
87 D3 Alatyr' Rus. Fed.
150 B3 Alausí Ecuador
93 H3 Alavus Fin.
52 B2 Alawoona Austr.
79 C2 Al 'Ayn U.A.E.
108 A2 Alba Italy
107 C2 Albacete Spain
78 A2 Al Badā'i' Saudi Arabia
78 B2 Al Badī' Saudi Arabia
110 B1 Alba Iulia Romania
109 C2 Albania country Europe
50 A3 Albany Austr.
130 B2 Albany r. Can.
143 D2 Albany GA U.S.A.
141 E2 Albany NY U.S.A.
134 B2 Albany OR U.S.A.
115 E1 Al Bardī Libya
Al Başrah Iraq see Basra
51 D1 Albatross Bay Austr.
115 E1 Al Baydā' Libya
78 B3 Al Baydā' Yemen
143 D1 Albemarle U.S.A.
143 E1 Albemarle Sound sea chan. U.S.A.
108 A2 Albenga Italy
51 C2 Alberga watercourse Austr.
119 D2 Albert, Lake Dem. Rep. Congo/Uganda
128 C2 Alberta prov. Can.
100 B2 Albert Kanaal canal Belgium
137 E2 Albert Lea U.S.A.
117 B4 Albert Nile r. Sudan/Uganda
123 C2 Alberton S. Africa
Albertville Dem. Rep. Congo see Kalémie
105 D2 Albertville France
104 C3 Albi France
151 D2 Albina Suriname
78 A2 Al Bi'r Saudi Arabia
78 B3 Al Birk Saudi Arabia
78 B2 Al Biyāḍ reg. Saudi Arabia

93 E4 Ålborg Denmark
81 C2 Alborz, Reshteh-ye mts Iran
107 C2 Albox Spain
106 B2 Albufeira Port.
138 B1 Albuquerque U.S.A.
79 C2 Al Buraymī Oman
53 C3 Albury Austr.
106 B2 Alcácer do Sal Port.
106 C1 Alcalá de Henares Spain
106 C2 Alcalá la Real Spain
108 B3 Alcamo Sicily Italy
107 C1 Alcañiz Spain
106 B2 Alcántara Spain
107 C2 Alcantarilla Spain
106 C2 Alcaraz Spain
106 C2 Alcaraz, Sierra de mts Spain
106 C2 Alcaudete Spain
106 C2 Alcázar de San Juan Spain
Alcazarquivir Morocco see Ksar el Kebir
91 D2 Alchevs'k Ukr.
155 E1 Alcobaça Brazil
107 C1 Alcora Spain
107 C2 Alcoy Spain
107 D2 Alcúdia Spain
113 H6 Aldabra Islands Seychelles
138 B3 Aldama Mex.
145 C2 Aldama Mex.
83 J3 Aldan Rus. Fed.
83 J2 Aldan r. Rus. Fed.
99 D3 Aldeburgh U.K.
95 C4 Alderney i. Channel Is
99 C4 Aldershot U.K.
114 A3 Aleg Maur.
155 D2 Alegre Brazil
152 C2 Alegrete Brazil
89 D1 Alekhovshchina Rus. Fed.
89 E2 Aleksandrov Rus. Fed.
Aleksandrovsk Ukr. see Zaporizhzhya
83 K3 Aleksandrovsk-Sakhalinskiy Rus. Fed.
Alekseyevka Kazakh. see Akkol'
91 D1 Alekseyevka Rus. Fed.
91 D1 Alekseyevka Rus. Fed.
89 E3 Aleksin Rus. Fed.
109 D2 Aleksinac Yugo.
118 B3 Alèmbé Gabon
155 D2 Além Paraíba Brazil
93 F3 Ålen Norway
104 C2 Alençon France
80 B2 Aleppo Syria
150 B4 Alerta Peru
105 C3 Alès France
110 B1 Aleşd Romania
Aleşki Ukr. see Tsyurupyns'k
108 A2 Alessandria Italy
Alessio Albania see Lezhë
93 E3 Ålesund Norway
156 D2 Aleutian Basin sea feature Bering Sea
124 A4 Aleutian Islands U.S.A.
83 L3 Alevina, Mys c. Rus. Fed.
128 A2 Alexander Archipelago is U.S.A.
122 A2 Alexander Bay S. Africa
142 C2 Alexander City U.S.A.
55 A2 Alexander Island Antarctica
53 C3 Alexandra Austr.
54 A3 Alexandra N.Z.
153 E5 Alexandra, Cape S. Georgia
Alexandra Land i. Rus. Fed. see Zemlya Aleksandry
111 B2 Alexandreia Greece
116 A1 Alexandria Egypt
110 C2 Alexandria Romania
123 C3 Alexandria S. Africa
96 B3 Alexandria U.K.
142 B2 Alexandria LA U.S.A.
137 D1 Alexandria MN U.S.A.
141 D3 Alexandria VA U.S.A.
52 A3 Alexandrina, Lake Austr.
111 C2 Alexandroupoli Greece
131 E2 Alexis r. Can.
128 B2 Alexis Creek Can.
77 E1 Aleysk Rus. Fed.
107 C1 Alfaro Spain
81 C3 Al Fāw Iraq
101 D2 Alfeld (Leine) Ger.
155 C2 Alfenas Brazil
96 C2 Alford U.K.

Al Fujayrah U.A.E. see Fujairah
Al Furāt r. Iraq/Syria see Euphrates
93 E4 Ålgård Norway
106 B2 Algarve reg. Port.
106 B2 Algeciras Spain
107 C2 Algemesí Spain
78 A3 Algena Eritrea
Alger Alg. see Algiers
114 C1 Algeria country Africa
79 C3 Al Ghaydah Yemen
108 A2 Alghero Sardinia Italy
79 B2 Al Ghwaybiyah Saudi Arabia
115 C1 Algiers Alg.
123 C3 Algoa Bay S. Africa
137 E2 Algona U.S.A.
78 B2 Al Hadīthah Iraq
79 C2 Al Ḩajar al Gharbī mts Oman
115 D2 Al Ḩamādah al Ḩamrā' plat. Libya
107 C2 Alhama de Murcia Spain
78 B2 Al Ḩanākīyah Saudi Arabia
81 C2 Al Ḩasakah Syria
78 B2 Al Ḩawīyah Saudi Arabia
81 C2 Al Ḩayy Iraq
78 B3 Al Ḩazm al-Jawf Yemen
79 C3 Al Ḩibāk des. Saudi Arabia
81 C2 Al Ḩillah Iraq
78 B2 Al Ḩillah Saudi Arabia
79 B2 Al Ḩinnāh Saudi Arabia
78 B3 Al Ḩudaydah Yemen
79 B2 Al Ḩufūf Saudi Arabia
115 D2 Al Ḩulayq al Kabīr hills Libya
79 C2 'Alīābād Iran
111 C3 Aliağa Turkey
111 B2 Aliakmonas r. Greece
81 C2 Äli Bayramlı Azer.
107 C2 Alicante Spain
139 D3 Alice U.S.A.
109 C3 Alice, Punta pt Italy
51 C2 Alice Springs Austr.
77 D3 Alichur Tajik.
74 B2 Aligarh India
81 C2 Alīgūdarz Iran
69 E1 Alihe China
118 B3 Alima r. Congo
118 C2 Alindao C.A.R.
111 C3 Aliova r. Turkey
74 B2 Alīrājpur India
117 C3 Ali Sabieh Djibouti
78 A1 Al 'Isāwīyah Saudi Arabia
123 C3 Aliwal North S. Africa
115 E2 Al Jaghbūb Libya
78 B2 Al Jahrah Kuwait
79 C2 Al Jamalīyah Qatar
115 E2 Al Jawf Libya
78 A2 Al Jawf Saudi Arabia
115 D1 Al Jawsh Libya
106 B2 Aljezur Port.
79 B2 Al Jubayl Saudi Arabia
78 B2 Al Jubaylah Saudi Arabia
115 D2 Al Jufra Oasis Libya
78 B2 Al Junaynah Saudi Arabia
106 B2 Aljustrel Port.
78 B2 Al Kahfah Saudi Arabia
79 C2 Al Kāmil Oman
80 B2 Al Karak Jordan
81 C2 Al Kāẓimīyah Iraq
79 C2 Al Khābūrah Oman
78 B2 Al Khamāsīn Saudi Arabia
79 C2 Al Khaṣab Oman
78 B3 Al Khawkhah Yemen
79 C2 Al Khawr Qatar
115 E2 Al Khufrah Libya
115 D1 Al Khums Libya
79 B2 Al Khunn Saudi Arabia
78 A2 Al Kidan well Saudi Arabia
79 B2 Al Kir'ānah Qatar
100 B1 Alkmaar Neth.
81 C2 Al Kūt Iraq
Al Kuwayt Kuwait see Kuwait
80 B2 Al Lādhiqīyah Syria
75 C2 Allahabad India
83 L2 Allakh-Yun' Rus. Fed.
78 A2 'Allāqi, Wādī el watercourse Egypt
141 D2 Allegheny r. U.S.A.
141 D3 Allegheny Mountains U.S.A.
97 B1 Allen, Lough l. Rep. of Ireland
145 B2 Allende Mex.
145 B2 Allende Mex.

141 D2 Allentown U.S.A.
73 B4 Alleppey India
101 D1 Aller r. Ger.
136 C2 Alliance NE U.S.A.
140 C2 Alliance OH U.S.A.
78 B2 Al Lith Saudi Arabia
96 C2 Alloa U.K.
131 C3 Alma Can.
Alma-Ata Kazakh. see Almaty
106 B2 Almada Port.
106 C2 Almadén Spain
Al Madīnah Saudi Arabia see Medina
80 B2 Al Mafraq Jordan
114 B2 Al Mahbas Western Sahara
78 B3 Al Maḩwīt Yemen
78 B2 Al Majma'ah Saudi Arabia
77 C2 Almalyk Uzbek.
Al Manāmah Bahrain see Manama
135 B2 Almanor, Lake U.S.A.
107 C2 Almansa Spain
79 C2 Al Mariyyah U.A.E.
115 E1 Al Marj Libya
77 D2 Almaty Kazakh.
81 C2 Al Mawşil Iraq
81 C2 Al Mayādīn Syria
106 C1 Almazán Spain
151 D3 Almeirim Brazil
100 C1 Almelo Neth.
155 D1 Almenara Brazil
106 B1 Almendra, Embalse de resr Spain
106 B2 Almendralejo Spain
106 C2 Almería Spain
106 C2 Almería, Golfo de b. Spain
87 E3 Al'met'yevsk Rus. Fed.
78 B2 Al Mindak Saudi Arabia
79 B2 Al Mish'āb Saudi Arabia
106 B2 Almodôvar Port.
106 B2 Almonte Spain
75 B2 Almora India
79 B2 Al Mubarrez Saudi Arabia
79 C2 Al Muḑaibī Oman
80 B3 Al Mudawwarah Jordan
79 B3 Al Mukallā Yemen
78 B3 Al Mukhā Yemen
106 C2 Almuñécar Spain
81 C2 Al Muqdādīyah Iraq
78 A2 Al Musayjid Saudi Arabia
78 A2 Al Muwaylih Saudi Arabia
111 B3 Almyros Greece
96 B2 Alness U.K.
98 C2 Alnwick U.K.
62 A1 Along India
111 B3 Alonnisos i. Greece
59 C3 Alor i. Indon.
59 C3 Alor, Kepulauan is Indon.
60 B1 Alor Setar Malaysia
Alor Star Malaysia see Alor Setar
Alost Belgium see Aalst
59 C3 Alotau P.N.G.
86 C2 Alozero Rus. Fed.
140 C2 Alpena U.S.A.
160 Q1 Alpha Ridge sea feature Arctic Ocean
100 B1 Alphen aan den Rijn Neth.
138 B2 Alpine AZ U.S.A.
139 C2 Alpine TX U.S.A.
84 E4 Alps mts Europe
79 B3 Al Qa'āmīyāt reg. Saudi Arabia
115 D1 Al Qaddāḩīyah Libya
78 B2 Al Qā'īyah Saudi Arabia
81 C2 Al Qāmishlī Syria
80 B2 Al Qaryatayn Syria
79 B2 Al Qaşab Saudi Arabia
79 B3 Al Qaţn Yemen
115 D2 Al Qaţrūn Libya
80 B2 Al Qunayţirah Syria
78 B3 Al Qunfidhah Saudi Arabia
78 B2 Al Quwārah Saudi Arabia
78 B2 Al Quwayīyah Saudi Arabia
101 D2 Alsfeld Ger.
98 B2 Alston U.K.
92 H2 Alta Norway
92 H2 Altaelva r. Norway
68 B1 Altai Mountains Asia
143 D2 Altamaha r. U.S.A.
151 D3 Altamira Brazil
109 C2 Altamura Italy
144 A1 Altar, Desierto de des. Mex.
77 E2 Altay China
68 C1 Altay Mongolia

105 D2 **Altdorf** Switz.
107 C2 **Altea** Spain
92 H1 **Alteidet** Norway
101 F2 **Altenburg** Ger.
100 C2 **Altenkirchen (Westerwald)** Ger.
101 F1 **Altentreptow** Ger.
111 C3 **Altınoluk** Turkey
111 D3 **Altıntaş** Turkey
152 B1 **Altiplano** plain Bol.
96 B1 **Altnaharra** U.K.
154 B1 **Alto Araguaia** Brazil
107 C1 **Alto del Moncayo** mt. Spain
154 B1 **Alto Garças** Brazil
121 C2 **Alto Ligonha** Moz.
121 C2 **Alto Molócuè** Moz.
99 C4 **Alton** U.K.
137 E3 **Alton** U.S.A.
129 E3 **Altona** Can.
141 D2 **Altoona** U.S.A.
154 B1 **Alto Sucuriú** Brazil
102 C2 **Altötting** Ger.
68 C2 **Altun Shan** mt. China
68 B2 **Altun Shan** mts China
134 B2 **Alturas** U.S.A.
139 D2 **Altus** U.S.A.
88 C2 **Alūksne** Latvia
78 A2 **Al 'Ulá** Saudi Arabia
115 D1 **Al 'Uqaylah** Libya
91 C3 **Alushta** Ukr.
115 E2 **Al 'Uwaynāt** Libya
139 D1 **Alva** U.S.A.
145 C3 **Alvarado** Mex.
93 F3 **Älvdalen** Sweden
93 F3 **Älvdalen** val. Sweden
92 H2 **Älvsbyn** Sweden
78 A2 **Al Wajh** Saudi Arabia
79 C2 **Al Wakrah** Qatar
74 B2 **Alwar** India
81 C2 **Al Widyān** plat. Iraq/Saudi Arabia
Alxa Youqi China see Ehen Hudag
Alxa Zuoqi China see Bayan Hot
51 C1 **Alyangula** Austr.
88 B3 **Alytus** Lith.
136 C1 **Alzada** U.S.A.
101 D3 **Alzey** Ger.
50 C2 **Amadeus, Lake** salt flat Austr.
127 H2 **Amadjuak Lake** Can.
106 B2 **Amadora** Port.
78 B2 **Amā'ir** Saudi Arabia
67 B4 **Amakusa-Shimo-shima** i. Japan
93 F4 **Åmal** Sweden
111 B3 **Amaliada** Greece
59 D3 **Amamapare** Indon.
154 A2 **Amambaí** Brazil
154 B2 **Amambaí** r. Brazil
154 A2 **Amambai, Serra de** hills Brazil/Para.
69 E3 **Amami-O-shima** i. Japan
69 E3 **Amami-shotō** is Japan
77 C1 **Amangel'dy** Kazakh.
109 C3 **Amantea** Italy
123 D3 **Amanzimtoti** S. Africa
151 D2 **Amapá** Brazil
106 B2 **Amareleja** Port.
88 B2 **Amari** Estonia
139 C1 **Amarillo** U.S.A.
108 B2 **Amaro, Monte** mt. Italy
80 B1 **Amasya** Turkey
150 D2 **Amazon** r. S. America
151 E2 **Amazon, Mouths of the** Brazil
Amazonas r. S. America see Amazon
157 I5 **Amazon Cone** sea feature S. Atlantic Ocean
74 B1 **Ambala** India
121 □D3 **Ambalavao** Madag.
121 □D2 **Ambanja** Madag.
104 B3 **Ambarès-et-Lagarve** France
150 B3 **Ambato** Ecuador
121 □D2 **Ambato Boeny** Madag.
121 □D3 **Ambato Finandrahana** Madag.
121 □D2 **Ambatolampy** Madag.
121 □D2 **Ambatondrazaka** Madag.
101 E3 **Amberg** Ger.
146 B3 **Ambergris Cay** i. Belize
75 C2 **Ambikapur** India
121 □D2 **Ambilobe** Madag.
98 C2 **Amble** U.K.
98 B2 **Ambleside** U.K.
121 □D3 **Amboasary** Madag.
121 □D2 **Ambodifotatra** Madag.

121 □D2 **Ambohidratrimo** Madag.
121 □D3 **Ambohimahasoa** Madag.
Amboina Indon. see Ambon
59 C3 **Ambon** Indon.
59 C3 **Ambon** i. Indon.
121 □D3 **Ambositra** Madag.
121 □D3 **Ambovombe** Madag.
135 C4 **Amboy** U.S.A.
Ambre, Cap d' c. Madag. see Bobaomby, Tanjona
120 A1 **Ambriz** Angola
Ambrizete Angola see N'zeto
86 F2 **Amderma** Rus. Fed.
75 D1 **Amdo** China
145 B2 **Amealco** Mex.
144 B2 **Ameca** Mex.
100 B1 **Ameland** i. Neth.
154 C2 **Americana** Brazil
55 D4 **American-Antarctic Ridge** sea feature S. Atlantic Ocean
134 D2 **American Falls** U.S.A.
134 D2 **American Falls Reservoir** U.S.A.
135 D2 **American Fork** U.S.A.
49 J5 **American Samoa** terr. S. Pacific Ocean
143 D2 **Americus** U.S.A.
100 B1 **Amersfoort** Neth.
55 H2 **Amery Ice Shelf** Antarctica
137 E2 **Ames** U.S.A.
111 B3 **Amfissa** Greece
83 J2 **Amga** Rus. Fed.
66 C1 **Amgu** Rus. Fed.
115 C2 **Amguid** Alg.
83 K3 **Amgun'** r. Rus. Fed.
131 D3 **Amherst** Can.
104 C2 **Amiens** France
79 C3 **Amilhayt, Wādī al** r. Oman
73 B3 **Amindivi Islands** India
122 A1 **Aminuis** Namibia
74 A2 **Amir Chah** Pak.
129 D2 **Amisk Lake** Can.
139 C3 **Amistad Reservoir** Mex./U.S.A.
98 A3 **Amlwch** U.K.
80 B2 **'Ammān** Jordan
127 J2 **Ammassalik** Greenland
78 B3 **An Nābiyah** Yemen
81 D2 **Amol** Iran
111 C3 **Amorgos** i. Greece
142 C2 **Amory** U.S.A.
130 C3 **Amos** Can.
Amoy China see Xiamen
121 □D3 **Ampanihy** Madag.
155 C2 **Amparo** Brazil
121 □D2 **Ampasimanolotra** Madag.
107 D1 **Amposta** Spain
78 B3 **Amrān** Yemen
74 B2 **Amraoti** India see Amravati
74 B2 **Amravati** India
74 B2 **Amreli** India
74 B1 **Amritsar** India
100 B1 **Amstelveen** Neth.
100 B1 **Amsterdam** Neth.
123 D2 **Amsterdam** S. Africa
156 A8 **Amsterdam, Île** i. Indian Ocean
103 C2 **Amstetten** Austria
115 E3 **Am Timan** Chad
76 B2 **Amudar'ya** r. Asia
126 F1 **Amund Ringnes Island** Can.
55 J3 **Amundsen, Mount** Antarctica
160 H1 **Amundsen Basin** sea feature Arctic Ocean
126 D2 **Amundsen Gulf** Can.
55 P2 **Amundsen Ridge** sea feature Southern Ocean
55 P2 **Amundsen Sea** Antarctica
61 C2 **Amuntai** Indon.
Amur r. China/Rus. Fed. see Heilong Jiang
78 A3 **'Amur, Wadi** watercourse Sudan
61 D2 **Anabanua** Indon.
83 I2 **Anabar** r. Rus. Fed.
83 I2 **Anabarskiy Zaliv** b. Rus. Fed.
150 C2 **Anaco** Venez.
134 D2 **Anaconda** U.S.A.
134 B1 **Anacortes** U.S.A.
139 D1 **Anadarko** U.S.A.
80 B1 **Anadolu Dağları** mts Turkey

83 M2 **Anadyr'** Rus. Fed.
83 M2 **Anadyr'** r. Rus. Fed.
81 C2 **'Ānah** Iraq
145 B2 **Anáhuac** Mex.
73 B3 **Anai Mudi Peak** India
121 □D2 **Analalava** Madag.
121 □D3 **Analavelona** mts Madag.
60 B1 **Anambas, Kepulauan** is Indon.
137 E2 **Anamosa** U.S.A.
80 B2 **Anamur** Turkey
67 B4 **Anan** Japan
73 B3 **Anantapur** India
74 B1 **Anantnag** Jammu and Kashmir
90 B2 **Anan'yiv** Ukr.
91 D3 **Anapa** Rus. Fed.
154 C1 **Anápolis** Brazil
81 D2 **Anār** Iran
152 B2 **Añatuya** Arg.
65 B2 **Anbyon** N. Korea
104 B2 **Ancenis** France
126 C2 **Anchorage** U.S.A.
108 B2 **Ancona** Italy
153 A4 **Ancud** Chile
Anda China see Daqing
93 E3 **Åndalsnes** Norway
106 C2 **Andalucía** aut. comm. Spain
Andalusia aut. comm. Spain see Andalucía
142 C2 **Andalusia** U.S.A.
159 F3 **Andaman Basin** sea feature Indian Ocean
73 D3 **Andaman Islands** India
63 A2 **Andaman Sea** Indian Ocean
121 □D2 **Andapa** Madag.
100 B2 **Andelst** Neth.
92 G2 **Andenes** Norway
100 B2 **Andenne** Belgium
100 B2 **Anderlecht** Belgium
105 D2 **Andermatt** Switz.
126 D2 **Anderson** r. Can.
126 C2 **Anderson** AK U.S.A.
140 B2 **Anderson** IN U.S.A.
143 D2 **Anderson** SC U.S.A.
148 C3 **Andes** mts S. America
121 □D2 **Andilamena** Madag.
121 □D2 **Andilanatoby** Madag.
77 D2 **Andizhan** Uzbek.
74 A1 **Andkhvoy** Afgh.
121 □D2 **Andoany** Madag.
Andong China see Dandong
65 B2 **Andong** S. Korea
104 C3 **Andorra** country Europe
104 C3 **Andorra la Vella** Andorra
99 C4 **Andover** U.K.
89 D2 **Andreapol'** Rus. Fed.
155 D2 **Andrelândia** Brazil
139 C2 **Andrews** U.S.A.
109 C2 **Andria** Italy
121 □D3 **Androka** Madag.
Andropov Rus. Fed. see Rybinsk
146 C2 **Andros** i. Bahamas
111 B3 **Andros** Greece
111 B3 **Andros** i. Greece
143 E4 **Andros Town** Bahamas
73 B3 **Andrott** i. India
90 B1 **Andrushivka** Ukr.
92 G2 **Andselv** Norway
106 C2 **Andújar** Spain
120 A2 **Andulo** Angola
114 C3 **Anéfis** Mali
147 D3 **Anegada Passage** Virgin Is (U.K.)
114 C4 **Aného** Togo
107 D1 **Aneto** mt. Spain
115 D3 **Aney** Niger
83 H3 **Angara** r. Rus. Fed.
68 C1 **Angarsk** Rus. Fed.
93 G3 **Änge** Sweden
Angel, Salto del waterfall Venez. see Angel Falls
144 A2 **Angel de la Guarda, Isla** i. Mex.
64 B2 **Angeles** Phil.
150 C2 **Angel Falls** Venez.
93 F4 **Ängelholm** Sweden
92 G3 **Ångermanälven** r. Sweden
104 B2 **Angers** France
129 E1 **Angikuni Lake** Can.
52 B3 **Anglesea** Austr.
98 A3 **Anglesey** i. U.K.
121 C2 **Angoche** Moz.
79 C2 **Angohrān** Iran
120 A2 **Angola** country Africa
140 C2 **Angola** U.S.A.

158 F6 **Angola Basin** sea feature S. Atlantic Ocean
128 A2 **Angoon** U.S.A.
104 C2 **Angoulême** France
155 D2 **Angra dos Reis** Brazil
77 D2 **Angren** Uzbek.
147 D3 **Anguilla** terr. West Indies
93 F4 **Anholt** i. Denmark
71 B3 **Anhua** China
70 B2 **Anhui** prov. China
154 B1 **Anhumas** Brazil
Anhwei prov. China see Anhui
154 C1 **Anicuns** Brazil
66 D1 **Aniva, Mys** c. Rus. Fed.
66 D1 **Aniva, Zaliv** b. Rus. Fed.
88 C1 **Anjalankoski** Fin.
104 B2 **Anjou** reg. France
65 B2 **Anjū** N. Korea
70 A2 **Ankang** China
80 B2 **Ankara** Turkey
121 □D3 **Ankazoabo** Madag.
121 □D2 **Ankazobe** Madag.
137 E2 **Ankeny** U.S.A.
102 C1 **Anklam** Ger.
121 □D2 **Ankofa** mt. Madag.
70 B2 **Anlu** China
55 G3 **Ann, Cape** Antarctica
141 E2 **Ann, Cape** U.S.A.
89 F3 **Anna** Rus. Fed.
115 C1 **Annaba** Alg.
101 F2 **Annaberg-Buchholtz** Ger.
80 B2 **An Nabk** Syria
78 B2 **An Nafūd** des. Saudi Arabia
150 D2 **Annai** Guyana
81 C2 **An Najaf** Iraq
63 B2 **Annam Highlands** mts Laos/Vietnam
96 C3 **Annan** U.K.
141 D3 **Annapolis** U.S.A.
75 C2 **Annapurna I** mt. Jammu and Kashmir/Nepal
140 C2 **Ann Arbor** U.S.A.
150 D2 **Anna Regina** Guyana
An Nás Rep. of Ireland see Naas
81 C2 **An Nāşiriyah** Iraq
115 D1 **An Nawfaliyah** Libya
105 D2 **Annecy** France
78 B3 **An Nimāş** Saudi Arabia
71 A3 **Anning** China
142 C2 **Anniston** U.S.A.
105 C2 **Annonay** France
79 B2 **An Nu'ayriyah** Saudi Arabia
121 □D2 **Anorontany, Tanjona** hd Madag.
111 C3 **Ano Viannos** Greece
71 B3 **Anpu** China
70 B2 **Anqing** China
101 E3 **Ansbach** Ger.
70 C1 **Anshan** China
71 A3 **Anshun** China
78 A1 **An Sirhān, Wādī** watercourse Saudi Arabia
139 D2 **Anson** U.S.A.
114 C3 **Ansongo** Mali
96 C2 **Anstruther** U.K.
150 B4 **Antabamba** Peru
121 □D2 **Antalaha** Madag.
80 B2 **Antakya** Turkey
80 B2 **Antalya** Turkey
80 B2 **Antalya Körfezi** g. Turkey
121 □D2 **Antananarivo** Madag.
55 A2 **Antarctic Peninsula** Antarctica
96 B2 **An Teallach** mt. U.K.
106 C2 **Antequera** Spain
138 B2 **Anthony** U.S.A.
114 B1 **Anti Atlas** mts Morocco
105 D3 **Antibes** France
131 D3 **Anticosti, Île d'** i. Can.
Anticosti Island Can. see Anticosti, Île d'
131 D3 **Antigonish** Can.
147 D3 **Antigua** i. West Indies
147 D3 **Antigua and Barbuda** country West Indies
145 C2 **Antiguo-Morelos** Mex.
111 B3 **Antikythira** i. Greece
Antioch Turkey see Antakya
49 I8 **Antipodes Islands** N.Z.
An t-Ob U.K. see Leverburgh
152 A2 **Antofagasta** Chile
154 C3 **Antonina** Brazil
António Enes Moz. see Angoche
97 C1 **Antrim** U.K.

97 C1 **Antrim Hills** U.K.
121 D2 **Antsalova** Madag.
Antseranana Madag. *see* Antsirañana
121 D2 **Antsirañana** Madag.
121 D2 **Antsirañana** Madag.
121 D2 **Antsohihy** Madag.
Antwerp Belgium *see* Antwerpen
100 B2 **Antwerpen** Belgium
An Uaimh Rep. of Ireland *see* Navan
75 C2 **Anugul** India
74 B2 **Anupgarh** India
73 C4 **Anuradhapura** Sri Lanka
Anvers Belgium *see* Antwerpen
68 C2 **Anxi** China
51 C3 **Anxious Bay** Austr.
70 B2 **Anyang** China
65 B2 **Anyang** S. Korea
108 B2 **Anzio** Italy
67 C4 **Aoga-shima** *i.* Japan
66 D2 **Aomori** Japan
Aoraki *mt.* N.Z. *see* Cook, Mount
108 A1 **Aosta** Italy
114 B2 **Aoukâr** *reg.* Mali/Maur.
114 C2 **Aoulef** Alg.
115 D2 **Aozou** Chad
143 D3 **Apalachee Bay** U.S.A.
150 C3 **Apaporis** *r.* Col.
154 B2 **Aparecida do Tabuado** Brazil
64 B2 **Aparri** Phil.
86 C2 **Apatity** Rus. Fed.
144 B3 **Apatzingán** Mex.
100 B1 **Apeldoorn** Neth.
100 C1 **Apen** Ger.
Apennines *mts* Italy *see* Appennino
49 J5 **Apia** Samoa
154 C2 **Apiaí** Brazil
64 B3 **Apo, Mount** *vol.* Phil.
101 E2 **Apolda** Ger.
52 B3 **Apollo Bay** Austr.
143 D3 **Apopka** U.S.A.
143 D3 **Apopka, Lake** U.S.A.
154 B1 **Aporé** Brazil
154 B1 **Aporé** *r.* Brazil
140 A1 **Apostle Islands** U.S.A.
80 B2 **Apostolos Andreas, Cape** Cyprus
91 C2 **Apostolove** Ukr.
133 F3 **Appalachian Mountains** U.S.A.
108 A2 **Appennino** *mts* Italy
53 D2 **Appin** Austr.
100 C1 **Appingedam** Neth.
98 B2 **Appleby-in-Westmorland** U.K.
140 B2 **Appleton** U.S.A.
108 B2 **Aprilia** Italy
62 A1 **Aprunyi** India
91 D3 **Apsheronsk** Rus. Fed.
Apsheronskaya Rus. Fed. *see* Apsheronsk
154 B2 **Apucarana** Brazil
154 B2 **Apucarana, Serra da** *hills* Brazil
64 A3 **Apurahuan** Phil.
147 D4 **Apure** *r.* Venez.
78 A2 **Aqaba, Gulf of** Asia
81 D2 **'Aqdā** Iran
75 C1 **Aqqikkol Hu** *salt l.* China
154 A1 **Aquidauana** *r.* Brazil
104 B3 **Aquitaine** *reg.* France
75 C2 **Ara** India
117 A4 **Arab, Bahr el** *watercourse* Sudan
56 B4 **Arabian Sea** Indian Ocean
151 F4 **Aracaju** Brazil
154 A2 **Aracanguy, Montes de** *hills* Para.
151 F3 **Aracati** Brazil
154 B2 **Araçatuba** Brazil
155 D1 **Aracruz** Brazil
155 D1 **Araçuaí** Brazil
110 B1 **Arad** Romania
115 E3 **Arada** Chad
79 C2 **'Arādah** U.A.E.
156 C6 **Arafura Sea** Austr./Indon.
154 B1 **Aragarças** Brazil
107 C1 **Aragón** *aut. comm.* Spain
107 C1 **Aragón** *r.* Spain
151 E3 **Araguaia** *r.* Brazil
151 E3 **Araguaiana** Brazil
151 E3 **Araguaína** Brazil
154 C1 **Araguari** Brazil
67 C3 **Arai** Japan
115 C2 **Arak** Alg.

81 C2 **Arāk** Iran
62 A1 **Arakan Yoma** *mts* Myanmar
81 C1 **Araks** *r.* Armenia/Turkey
76 C2 **Aral Sea** *salt l.* Kazakh./Uzbek.
76 C2 **Aral'sk** Kazakh.
Aral'skoye More *salt l.* Kazakh./Uzbek. *see* Aral Sea
106 C1 **Aranda de Duero** Spain
109 D2 **Arandelovac** Yugo.
97 B1 **Aran Island** Rep. of Ireland
97 B2 **Aran Islands** Rep. of Ireland
106 C1 **Aranjuez** Spain
122 A1 **Aranos** Namibia
139 D3 **Aransas Pass** U.S.A.
67 B4 **Arao** Japan
114 B3 **Araouane** Mali
151 F3 **Arapiraca** Brazil
154 B2 **Arapongas** Brazil
154 C3 **Araquari** Brazil
78 B1 **'Ar'ar** Saudi Arabia
154 C2 **Araraquara** Brazil
151 D3 **Araras** Brazil
154 C2 **Araras** Brazil
154 B1 **Araras, Serra das** *hills* Brazil
154 B3 **Araras, Serra das** *mts* Brazil
81 C2 **Ararat** Armenia
52 B3 **Ararat** Austr.
81 C2 **Ararat, Mount** Turkey
155 D2 **Araruama, Lago de** *lag.*
155 E1 **Arataca** Brazil
Aratürük China *see* Yiwu
150 B2 **Arauca** Col.
154 C1 **Araxá** Brazil
81 C2 **Arbīl** Iraq
129 E2 **Arborg** Can.
96 C2 **Arbroath** U.K.
74 A2 **Arbu Lut, Dasht-e** *des.* Afgh.
104 B3 **Arcachon** France
143 D3 **Arcadia** U.S.A.
134 B2 **Arcata** U.S.A.
145 B3 **Arcelia** Mex.
86 D2 **Archangel** Rus. Fed.
51 D1 **Archer** *r.* Austr.
52 A2 **Arco** U.S.A.
106 B2 **Arcos de la Frontera** Spain
127 G2 **Arctic Bay** Can.
Arctic Institute Islands Rus. Fed. *see* Arkticheskogo Instituta, Ostrova
160 J1 **Arctic Mid-Ocean Ridge** *sea feature* Arctic Ocean
160 **Arctic Ocean**
126 D2 **Arctic Red** *r.* Can.
81 C2 **Ardabīl** Iran
81 C1 **Ardahan** Turkey
93 E3 **Ardalstangen** Norway
97 C2 **Ardee** Rep. of Ireland
100 B3 **Ardennes** *plat.* Belgium
135 B3 **Arden Town** U.S.A.
81 D2 **Ardestān** Iran
97 D1 **Ardglass** U.K.
53 C2 **Ardlethan** Austr.
139 D2 **Ardmore** U.S.A.
96 A2 **Ardnamurchan, Point of** U.K.
52 A2 **Ardrossan** Austr.
96 B3 **Ardrossan** U.K.
96 B2 **Ardvasar** U.K.
135 B3 **Arena, Point** U.S.A.
93 E4 **Arendal** Norway
101 E1 **Arendsee (Altmark)** Ger.
150 B4 **Arequipa** Peru
151 D3 **Arere** Brazil
106 C1 **Arévalo** Spain
108 B2 **Arezzo** Italy
108 B2 **Argenta** Italy
104 B2 **Argentan** France
153 C2 **Argentina** *country* S. America
158 D7 **Argentine Basin** *sea feature* S. Atlantic Ocean
157 I8 **Argentine Rise** *sea feature* S. Atlantic Ocean
153 A5 **Argentino, Lago** *l.* Arg.
104 C2 **Argenton-sur-Creuse** France
110 C2 **Argeş** *r.* Romania
74 A1 **Arghandab** *r.* Afgh.

111 B3 **Argolikos Kolpos** *b.* Greece
111 B3 **Argos** Greece
111 B3 **Argostoli** Greece
107 C1 **Arguis** Spain
69 F1 **Argun'** *r.* China/Rus. Fed.
131 D3 **Argyle** U.S.A.
50 B1 **Argyle, Lake** Austr.
Argyrokastron Albania *see* Gjirokastër
Ar Horqin Qi China *see* Tianshan
93 F4 **Århus** Denmark
122 A2 **Ariamsvlei** Namibia
152 A1 **Arica** Chile
96 A2 **Arinagour** U.K.
155 C1 **Arinos** Brazil
150 D4 **Aripuanã** Brazil
150 C3 **Aripuanã** *r.* Brazil
150 C3 **Ariquemes** Brazil
154 B1 **Ariranhá** *r.* Brazil
96 B2 **Arisaig** U.K.
96 B2 **Arisaig, Sound of** *sea chan.* U.K.
138 A2 **Arizona** *state* U.S.A.
144 A1 **Arizpe** Mex.
78 B2 **'Arjah** Saudi Arabia
61 C2 **Arjasa** Indon.
92 G2 **Arjeplog** Sweden
142 B2 **Arkadelphia** U.S.A.
77 C1 **Arkalyk** Kazakh.
142 B2 **Arkansas** *r.* U.S.A.
142 B1 **Arkansas** *state* U.S.A.
137 D3 **Arkansas City** U.S.A.
Arkhangel'sk Rus. Fed. *see* Archangel
97 C2 **Arklow** Rep. of Ireland
102 C1 **Arkona, Kap** *c.* Ger.
82 G1 **Arkticheskogo Instituta, Ostrova** *is* Rus. Fed.
105 C3 **Arles** France
139 D2 **Arlington** U.S.A.
140 B2 **Arlington Heights** U.S.A.
115 C3 **Arlit** Niger
100 B3 **Arlon** Belgium
97 C1 **Armagh** U.K.
116 B2 **Armant** Egypt
87 D4 **Armavir** Rus. Fed.
81 C1 **Armenia** *country* Asia
150 B2 **Armenia** Col.
Armenopolis Romania *see* Gherla
144 B3 **Armería** Mex.
53 D2 **Armidale** Austr.
134 D1 **Armington** U.S.A.
130 B2 **Armstrong** Can.
91 C2 **Armyans'k** Ukr.
Armyanskaya S.S.R. *country* Asia *see* Armenia
80 B2 **Arnaoutis, Cape** Cyprus
130 D2 **Arnaud** *r.* Can.
Arnauti, Cape Cyprus *see* Arnaoutis, Cape
100 B2 **Arnhem** Neth.
51 C1 **Arnhem, Cape** Austr.
51 C1 **Arnhem Bay** Austr.
51 C1 **Arnhem Land** *reg.* Austr.
108 B2 **Arno** *r.* Italy
52 A2 **Arno Bay** Austr.
130 C3 **Arnprior** Can.
101 D2 **Arnsberg** Ger.
101 E2 **Arnstadt** Ger.
122 A2 **Aroab** Namibia
154 B2 **Aroeira** Brazil
101 D2 **Arolsen** Ger.
78 A3 **Aroma** Sudan
108 A1 **Arona** Italy
144 B2 **Aros** *r.* Mex.
81 C2 **Ar Ramādī** Iraq
96 B3 **Arran** *i.* U.K.
80 B2 **Ar Raqqah** Syria
105 C1 **Arras** France
78 B2 **Ar-Rass** Saudi Arabia
79 C2 **Ar Rayyān** Qatar
150 C2 **Arrecifal** Col.
145 C3 **Arriagá** Mex.
79 C2 **Ar Rimāl** *reg.* Saudi Arabia
Ar Riyāḍ Saudi Arabia *see* Riyadh
54 A2 **Arrowtown** N.Z.
135 B3 **Arroyo Grande** U.S.A.
145 C2 **Arroyo Seco** Mex.
79 C2 **Ar Rustāq** Oman
81 C2 **Ar Ruṭbah** Iraq
78 B2 **Ar Ruwaydah** Saudi Arabia
81 D3 **Arsenaján** Iran

66 B2 **Arsen'yev** Rus. Fed.
111 B3 **Arta** Greece
144 B3 **Arteaga** Mex.
66 B2 **Artem** Rus. Fed.
91 D2 **Artemivs'k** Ukr.
104 C2 **Artenay** France
138 C2 **Artesia** U.S.A.
51 E2 **Arthur Point** Austr.
54 B2 **Arthur's Pass** N.Z.
152 C3 **Artigas** Uru.
129 D1 **Artillery Lake** Can.
123 C1 **Artisia** Botswana
104 C1 **Artois** *reg.* France
90 B2 **Artsyz** Ukr.
Artur de Paiva Angola *see* Kuvango
77 D3 **Artux** China
81 C1 **Artvin** Turkey
59 C3 **Aru, Kepulauan** *is* Indon.
119 D2 **Arua** Uganda
147 D3 **Aruba** *terr.* West Indies
75 C2 **Arun** *r.* Nepal
119 D3 **Arusha** Tanz.
136 B3 **Arvada** U.S.A.
68 C1 **Arvayheer** Mongolia
129 E1 **Arviat** Can.
92 G2 **Arvidsjaur** Sweden
93 F4 **Arvika** Sweden
108 A2 **Arzachena** *Sardinia* Italy
87 D3 **Arzamas** Rus. Fed.
107 C2 **Arzew** Alg.
100 C2 **Arzfeld** Ger.
Arzila Morocco *see* Asilah
101 F2 **Aš** Czech Rep.
115 C4 **Asaba** Nigeria
66 D2 **Asahi-dake** *vol.* Japan
66 D2 **Asahikawa** Japan
78 B3 **Asālé** *l.* Eth.
75 C2 **Asansol** India
117 C3 **Asayita** Eth.
130 C3 **Asbestos** Can.
122 B2 **Asbestos Mountains** S. Africa
119 E2 **Asbe Teferi** Eth.
109 C2 **Ascea** Italy
152 B1 **Ascensión** Bol.
113 B6 **Ascension** *i.* S. Atlantic Ocean
101 D3 **Aschaffenburg** Ger.
100 C2 **Ascheberg** Ger.
101 E2 **Aschersleben** Ger.
108 B2 **Ascoli Piceno** Italy
119 C2 **Asela** Eth.
92 G3 **Åsele** Sweden
111 B3 **Asenovgrad** Bulg.
78 B2 **Asharat** Saudi Arabia
50 A2 **Ashburton** *watercourse* Austr.
54 B2 **Ashburton** N.Z.
142 B2 **Ashdown** U.S.A.
143 D1 **Asheville** U.S.A.
53 D1 **Ashford** Austr.
97 C2 **Ashford** Rep. of Ireland
99 D3 **Ashford** U.K.
76 B3 **Ashgabat** Turkm.
66 D2 **Ashibetsu** Japan
98 C2 **Ashington** U.K.
67 B4 **Ashizuri-misaki** *pt* Japan
Ashkhabad Turkm. *see* Ashgabat
136 D3 **Ashland** *KS* U.S.A.
140 C3 **Ashland** *KY* U.S.A.
140 C2 **Ashland** *OH* U.S.A.
134 B2 **Ashland** *OR* U.S.A.
140 A1 **Ashland** *WI* U.S.A.
53 C1 **Ashley** U.S.A.
88 C3 **Ashmyany** Belarus
66 D2 **Ashoro** Japan
81 C2 **Ash Shabakah** Iraq
78 B3 **Ash Sharawrah** Saudi Arabia
Ash Shāriqah U.A.E. *see* Sharjah
81 C2 **Ash Sharqāṭ** Iraq
81 C2 **Ash Shaṭrah** Iraq
78 B3 **Ash Shaykh 'Uthman** Yemen
79 B3 **Ash Shiḥr** Yemen
79 C2 **Ash Shināṣ** Oman
78 B2 **Ash Shu'aybah** Saudi Arabia
78 B2 **Ash Shu'bah** Saudi Arabia
78 B2 **Ash Shubaykīyah** Saudi Arabia
78 B3 **Ash Shumlūl** Saudi Arabia
78 B3 **Ash Shuqayq** Saudi Arabia
115 D1 **Ash Shuwayrif** Libya
140 C2 **Ashtabula** U.S.A.
131 D2 **Ashuanipi Lake** Can.
75 B3 **Asifabad** India
106 B2 **Asilah** Morocco

108 A2 **Asinara, Golfo dell'** b. Sardinia Italy
108 A2 **Asinara, Isola** i. Sardinia Italy
82 G3 **Asino** Rus. Fed.
88 B2 **Asipovichy** Belarus
78 B2 **'Asir** reg. Saudi Arabia
93 F4 **Asker** Norway
93 F4 **Askim** Norway
68 C1 **Askiz** Rus. Fed.
116 B3 **Asmara** Eritrea
93 F4 **Åsnen** l. Sweden
116 B2 **Asoteriba, Jebel** mt. Sudan
103 D2 **Aspang-Markt** Austria
136 B3 **Aspen** U.S.A.
139 C2 **Aspermont** U.S.A.
54 A2 **Aspiring, Mount** N.Z.
116 C3 **Assab** Eritrea
78 B3 **Aş Şaḩīf** Yemen
78 B2 **As Salamīyah** Saudi Arabia
75 D2 **Assam** state India
81 C2 **As Samāwah** Iraq
79 C2 **Aş Şanām** reg. Saudi Arabia
115 E2 **As Sarīr** reg. Libya
108 A3 **Assemini** Sardinia Italy
100 C1 **Assen** Neth.
100 B2 **Assesse** Belgium
115 D1 **As Sidrah** Libya
129 D3 **Assiniboia** Can.
128 C2 **Assiniboine, Mount** Can.
154 B2 **Assis** Brazil
78 B2 **Aş Şubayḩīyah** Kuwait
81 C2 **As Sulaymānīyah** Iraq
78 B2 **As Sulaymī** Saudi Arabia
78 B2 **As Sulayyil** Saudi Arabia
78 B2 **As Sūq** Saudi Arabia
80 B2 **As Suwaydā'** Syria
79 C2 **As Suwayq** Oman
111 B3 **Astakos** Greece
77 D1 **Astana** Kazakh.
81 C2 **Astara** Iran
100 B2 **Asten** Neth.
108 A2 **Asterabad** Iran see Gorgān
74 B1 **Asti** Italy
106 B1 **Astor** Jammu and Kashmir
134 B1 **Astorga** Spain
Astoria U.S.A.
87 D4 **Astrabad** Iran see Gorgān
Astrakhan' Rus. Fed.
Astrakhan' Bazar Azer. see Cälilabad
88 C3 **Astravyets** Belarus
Astrida Rwanda see Butare
106 B1 **Asturias** aut. comm. Spain
111 C3 **Astypalaia** i. Greece
152 C2 **Asunción** Para.
116 B2 **Aswân** Egypt
116 B2 **Asyût** Egypt
152 B2 **Atacama, Desierto de** des. Chile
152 B2 **Atacama, Salar de** salt flat Chile
114 C4 **Atakpamé** Togo
111 B3 **Atalanti** Greece
150 B4 **Atalaya** Peru
155 D1 **Ataléia** Brazil
78 B3 **'Ataq** Yemen
114 A2 **Atâr** Maur.
135 B3 **Atascadero** U.S.A.
77 D2 **Atasu** Kazakh.
116 B3 **Atbara** Sudan
116 B3 **Atbara** r. Sudan
77 C1 **Atbasar** Kazakh.
142 B3 **Atchafalaya Bay** U.S.A.
137 D3 **Atchison** U.S.A.
Ateransk Kazakh. see Atyrau
108 B2 **Aterno** r. Italy
108 B2 **Atessa** Italy
100 A2 **Ath** Belgium
128 C2 **Athabasca** Can.
129 C2 **Athabasca** r. Can.
129 D2 **Athabasca, Lake** Can.
97 C2 **Athboy** Rep. of Ireland
97 B2 **Athenry** Rep. of Ireland
111 B3 **Athens** Greece
142 C2 **Athens** AL U.S.A.
143 D2 **Athens** GA U.S.A.
140 C3 **Athens** OH U.S.A.
143 D1 **Athens** TN U.S.A.
139 D2 **Athens** TX U.S.A.
51 D1 **Atherton** Austr.
Athina Greece see Athens
97 C2 **Athlone** Rep. of Ireland
111 B3 **Athos** mt. Greece
97 C2 **Athy** Rep. of Ireland

115 D3 **Ati** Chad
130 A3 **Atikokan** Can.
87 D3 **Atkarsk** Rus. Fed.
143 D2 **Atlanta** U.S.A.
137 D2 **Atlantic** U.S.A.
143 D2 **Atlantic Beach** U.S.A.
141 E3 **Atlantic City** U.S.A.
55 D3 **Atlantic-Indian-Antarctic Basin** sea feature S. Atlantic Ocean
158 E8 **Atlantic-Indian Ridge** sea feature Southern Ocean
158 **Atlantic Ocean**
122 A3 **Atlantis** S. Africa
114 B1 **Atlas Mountains** Africa
114 C1 **Atlas Saharien** mts Alg.
128 A2 **Atlin** Can.
128 A2 **Atlin Lake** Can.
142 C2 **Atmore** U.S.A.
152 B2 **Atocha** Bol.
139 D2 **Atoka** U.S.A.
75 C2 **Atrai** r. India
80 B2 **Aţ Ṭafīlah** Jordan
78 B2 **Aţ Ṭā'if** Saudi Arabia
63 B2 **Attapu** Laos
111 C3 **Attavyros** mt. Greece
130 B2 **Attawapiskat** Can.
130 B2 **Attawapiskat** r. Can.
130 B2 **Attawapiskat Lake** Can.
100 C2 **Attendorn** Ger.
100 A3 **Attichy** France
78 B3 **At Turbah** Yemen
135 B3 **Atwater** U.S.A.
76 B2 **Atyrau** Kazakh.
105 D3 **Aubagne** France
105 C3 **Aubenas** France
126 D2 **Aubry Lake** Can.
142 C2 **Auburn** AL U.S.A.
135 B3 **Auburn** CA U.S.A.
140 B2 **Auburn** IN U.S.A.
141 E2 **Auburn** ME U.S.A.
137 D2 **Auburn** NE U.S.A.
141 D2 **Auburn** NY U.S.A.
104 C2 **Aubusson** France
104 C3 **Auch** France
54 B1 **Auckland** N.Z.
48 H9 **Auckland Islands** N.Z.
117 C4 **Audo Range** mts Eth.
101 F2 **Aue** Ger.
101 F2 **Auerbach** Ger.
102 C2 **Augsburg** Ger.
50 A3 **Augusta** Austr.
109 C3 **Augusta** Sicily Italy
143 D2 **Augusta** GA U.S.A.
137 D3 **Augusta** KS U.S.A.
141 F2 **Augusta** ME U.S.A.
155 D1 **Augusto de Lima** Brazil
103 E1 **Augustów** Pol.
50 A2 **Augustus, Mount** Austr.
100 A2 **Aulnoye-Aymeries** France
Aumale Alg. see Sour el Ghozlane
122 B2 **Auob** watercourse Namibia/S. Africa
131 D2 **Aupaluk** Can.
74 B2 **Aurangābād** India
104 B2 **Auray** France
100 C1 **Aurich** Ger.
154 B1 **Aurilândia** Brazil
104 C3 **Aurillac** France
136 C3 **Aurora** CO U.S.A.
140 B2 **Aurora** IL U.S.A.
137 D3 **Aurora** MO U.S.A.
137 D2 **Aurora** NE U.S.A.
122 A2 **Aus** Namibia
140 C2 **Au Sable** r. U.S.A.
137 E2 **Austin** MN U.S.A.
135 C3 **Austin** NV U.S.A.
139 D2 **Austin** TX U.S.A.
49 L6 **Australes, Îles** is Fr. Polynesia
50 B2 **Australia** country Oceania
55 K4 **Australian-Antarctic Basin** sea feature Southern Ocean
53 C3 **Australian Capital Territory** admin. div. Austr.
102 C2 **Austria** country Europe
150 D3 **Autazes** Brazil
144 B3 **Autlán** Mex.
105 C2 **Autun** France
105 C2 **Auvergne** reg. France
105 C2 **Auvergne, Monts d'** mts France
105 C2 **Auxerre** France
105 D2 **Auxonne** France
105 C2 **Avallon** France
131 E3 **Avalon Peninsula** Can.
154 C2 **Avaré** Brazil
91 D2 **Avdiyivka** Ukr.

106 B1 **Aveiro** Port.
109 B2 **Avellino** Italy
108 B2 **Aversa** Italy
100 A2 **Avesnes-sur-Helpe** France
93 G3 **Avesta** Sweden
104 C3 **Aveyron** r. France
108 B2 **Avezzano** Italy
96 C2 **Aviemore** U.K.
109 C2 **Avigliano** Italy
105 C3 **Avignon** France
106 C1 **Ávila** Spain
106 B1 **Avilés** Spain
52 B3 **Avoca** Austr.
141 D2 **Avoca** U.S.A.
109 C3 **Avola** Sicily Italy
99 C4 **Avon** r. England U.K.
99 B3 **Avon** r. England U.K.
99 B4 **Avon** r. England U.K.
138 A2 **Avondale** U.S.A.
104 B2 **Avranches** France
54 B1 **Awanui** N.Z.
119 D2 **Awasa** Eth.
117 C4 **Awash** Eth.
117 C3 **Awash** r. Eth.
115 D2 **Awbārī** Libya
117 C4 **Aw Dheegle** Somalia
96 B2 **Awe, Loch** l. U.K.
117 A4 **Aweil** Sudan
115 C4 **Awka** Nigeria
114 A2 **Awserd** Western Sahara
126 F1 **Axel Heiberg Island** Can.
114 B4 **Axim** Ghana
150 B4 **Ayacucho** Peru
77 E2 **Ayagoz** Kazakh.
77 E2 **Ayagoz** Kazakh. see Ayagoz
77 C2 **Ayakkuduk** Uzbek.
68 B2 **Ayakkum Hu** salt l. China
106 B2 **Ayamonte** Spain
83 K3 **Ayan** Rus. Fed.
150 B4 **Ayaviri** Peru
74 A1 **Āybak** Afgh.
76 A2 **Aýbas** Kazakh.
91 D2 **Aydar** r. Ukr.
77 C2 **Aýdarkul', Ozero** l. Uzbek.
111 C3 **Aydın** Turkey
77 C2 **Ayeat, Gora** hill Kazakh.
Ayers Rock hill Austr. see Uluru
83 I2 **Aykhal** Rus. Fed.
99 C4 **Aylesbury** U.K.
106 C1 **Ayllón** Spain
129 D1 **Aylmer Lake** Can.
117 B4 **Ayod** Sudan
83 M2 **Ayon, Ostrov** i. Rus. Fed.
114 B3 **'Ayoûn el 'Atroûs** Maur.
51 D1 **Ayr** Austr.
96 B3 **Ayr** U.K.
98 A2 **Ayre, Point of** Isle of Man
76 C2 **Ayteke Bi** Kazakh.
110 C2 **Aytos** Bulg.
145 C3 **Ayutla** Mex.
63 B2 **Ayutthaya** Thai.
111 C3 **Ayvacık** Turkey
111 C3 **Ayvalık** Turkey
91 C3 **Ayya, Mys** pt Ukr.
114 B3 **Azaouâd** reg. Mali
114 C3 **Azaouagh, Vallée de** watercourse Mali/Niger
115 D3 **Azare** Nigeria
Azbine mts Niger see L'Aïr, Massif de
81 C1 **Azerbaijan** country Asia
Azerbaydzhanskaya S.S.R. country Asia see Azerbaijan
150 B3 **Azogues** Ecuador
86 D2 **Azopol'ye** Rus. Fed.
112 A2 **Azores** aut. reg. N. Atlantic Ocean
91 D2 **Azov** Rus. Fed.
91 D2 **Azov, Sea of** Rus. Fed./Ukr.
Azraq, Bahr el r. Sudan see Blue Nile
106 B2 **Azuaga** Spain
146 B4 **Azuero, Península de** pen. Panama
153 C3 **Azul** Arg.
108 A3 **Azzaba** Alg.
Aẕ Ẕahrān Saudi Arabia see Dhahran
80 B2 **Az Zarqā'** Jordan
115 D1 **Az Zāwiyah** Libya
78 B3 **Az Zaydīyah** Yemen
114 C2 **Azzel Matti, Sebkha** salt pan Alg.
78 B2 **Az Zilfī** Saudi Arabia
78 B3 **Az Zuqur** i. Yemen
78 B3 **Az Zuqur** i. Yemen

B

117 C4 **Baardheere** Somalia
77 C3 **Bābā, Kūh-e** mts Afgh.
111 C3 **Baba Burnu** pt Turkey
110 C2 **Babadag** Romania
111 C2 **Babaeski** Turkey
116 C3 **Bāb al Mandab** str. Africa/Asia
61 C2 **Babana** Indon.
119 C1 **Babanusa** Sudan
59 C3 **Babar** i. Indon.
119 D3 **Babati** Tanz.
89 E2 **Babayevo** Rus. Fed.
59 C2 **Babeldaob** i. Palau
128 B2 **Babine** r. Can.
128 B2 **Babine Lake** Can.
59 C3 **Babo** Indon.
81 D2 **Bābol** Iran
122 A3 **Baboon Point** S. Africa
88 C3 **Babruysk** Belarus
Babu China see Hexian
64 B2 **Babuyan** i. Phil.
64 B2 **Babuyan Channel** Phil.
64 B2 **Babuyan Islands** Phil.
151 E3 **Bacabal** Brazil
145 D3 **Bacalar** Mex.
59 C3 **Bacan** i. Indon.
110 C1 **Bacău** Romania
52 B3 **Bacchus Marsh** Austr.
77 D3 **Bachu** China
129 E1 **Back** r. Can.
109 C1 **Bačka Palanka** Yugo.
109 C1 **Bačka Topola** Yugo.
52 A3 **Backstairs Passage** Austr.
62 B1 **Bac Lac** Vietnam
63 B3 **Bac Liêu** Vietnam
62 B1 **Băc Ninh** Vietnam
138 B3 **Bacobampo** Mex.
64 B2 **Bacolod** Phil.
130 C2 **Bacqueville, Lac** l. Can.
Bada China see Xilin
70 A1 **Badain Jaran Shamo** des. China
106 B2 **Badajoz** Spain
Badaojiang China see Baishan
75 D2 **Badarpur** India
101 E2 **Bad Berka** Ger.
101 E2 **Bad Berleburg** Ger.
101 E1 **Bad Bevensen** Ger.
100 C2 **Bad Dürkheim** Ger.
100 C2 **Bad Ems** Ger.
103 D2 **Baden** Austria
102 B2 **Baden-Baden** Ger.
101 E2 **Bad Harzburg** Ger.
101 D2 **Bad Hersfeld** Ger.
102 C2 **Bad Hofgastein** Austria
101 D2 **Bad Homburg vor der Höhe** Ger.
101 D1 **Bad Iburg** Ger.
74 A2 **Badin** Pak.
Bādiyat ash Shām des. Asia see Syrian Desert
101 E2 **Bad Kissingen** Ger.
100 C3 **Bad Kreuznach** Ger.
136 C1 **Badlands** reg. ND U.S.A.
136 C2 **Badlands** reg. SD U.S.A.
101 E2 **Bad Lauterberg im Harz** Ger.
101 D2 **Bad Lippspringe** Ger.
101 D2 **Bad Mergentheim** Ger.
101 D2 **Bad Nauheim** Ger.
100 C2 **Bad Neuenahr-Ahrweiler** Ger.
101 E2 **Bad Neustadt an der Saale** Ger.
101 E1 **Bad Oldesloe** Ger.
101 D2 **Bad Pyrmont** Ger.
78 A2 **Badr Ḩunayn** Saudi Arabia
101 D1 **Bad Salzuflen** Ger.
101 E2 **Bad Salzungen** Ger.
101 C1 **Bad Schwartau** Ger.
101 E1 **Bad Segeberg** Ger.
73 C4 **Badulla** Sri Lanka
101 D1 **Bad Zwischenahn** Ger.
106 C2 **Baeza** Spain
114 A3 **Bafatá** Guinea-Bissau
127 H2 **Baffin Bay** sea Can./Greenland
118 B3 **Baffin Island** Can.
118 B2 **Bafia** Cameroon
114 A3 **Bafing** r. Guinea/Mali
118 B2 **Bafoulabé** Mali
118 B2 **Bafoussam** Cameroon
81 D2 **Bāfq** Iran
80 B1 **Bafra** Turkey
79 C2 **Bāft** Iran
119 C2 **Bafwasende** Dem. Rep. Congo

119 D3 Bagamoyo Tanz.
Bagan Datoh Malaysia see Bagan Datuk
60 B1 Bagan Datuk Malaysia
64 B3 Bagariya Phil.
120 B2 Bagani Namibia
60 B1 Bagansiapiapi Indon.
118 B3 Bagata Dem. Rep. Congo
91 E2 Bagayevskiy Rus. Fed.
138 A2 Bagdad U.S.A.
152 C3 Bagé Brazil
81 C2 Baghdād Iraq
79 C1 Bāghīn Iran
77 C3 Baghlān Afgh.
104 C3 Bagnères-de-Luchon France
105 C3 Bagnols-sur-Cèze France
Bago Myanmar see Pegu
88 B3 Bagrationovsk Rus. Fed.
Bagrax China see Bohu
64 B2 Baguio Phil.
115 C3 Bagzane, Monts mts Niger
75 C2 Baharampur India
116 A2 Bahariya Oasis Egypt
60 B1 Bahau Malaysia
74 B2 Bahawalnagar Pak.
74 B2 Bahawalpur Pak.
Bahia Brazil see Salvador
153 B3 Bahía Blanca Arg.
144 A2 Bahía Kino Mex.
152 C2 Bahía Negra Para.
144 A2 Bahía Tortugas Mex.
117 B3 Bahir Dar Eth.
79 C2 Bahlā Oman
75 C2 Bahraich India
79 C2 Bahrain country Asia
79 D2 Bāhū Kālāt Iran
89 D3 Bahushewsk Belarus
110 C2 Baia Romania
120 A2 Baia dos Tigres Angola
110 B1 Baia Mare Romania
118 B2 Baïbokoum Chad
69 E1 Baicheng China
Baidoa Somalia see Baydhabo
Baie-aux-Feuilles Can. see Tasiujaq
131 D3 Baie-Comeau Can.
Baie-du-Poste Can. see Mistissini
131 C3 Baie-St-Paul Can.
131 E3 Baie Verte Can.
62 A1 Baihanchang China
65 B1 Baihe China
69 D1 Baikal, Lake Rus. Fed.
Baile Átha Cliath Rep. of Ireland see Dublin
110 B2 Băileşti Romania
68 C2 Baima China
75 C2 Bainang China
143 D2 Bainbridge U.S.A.
75 D1 Baingoin China
48 I3 Bairiki Kiribati
53 C3 Bairnsdale Austr.
65 B1 Baishan Jilin China
65 B1 Baishan Jilin China
120 A2 Baixo-Longa Angola
70 A2 Baiyin China
116 B3 Baiyuda Desert Sudan
103 D2 Baja Hungary
144 A1 Baja California pen. Mex.
61 D2 Bajawa Indon.
78 B3 Bājil Yemen
115 D3 Bajoga Nigeria
109 D2 Bajram Curri Albania
114 A3 Bakel Senegal
135 C3 Baker CA U.S.A.
142 B2 Baker LA U.S.A.
136 C1 Baker MT U.S.A.
134 C2 Baker OR U.S.A.
134 B1 Baker, Mount vol. U.S.A.
129 E1 Baker Foreland hd Can.
49 J3 Baker Island terr. N. Pacific Ocean
129 E1 Baker Lake Can.
129 E1 Baker Lake l. Can.
135 C3 Bakersfield U.S.A.
Bakharden Turkm. see Bakherden
91 C3 Bakhchysaray Ukr.
76 B3 Bakherden Turkm.
91 C1 Bakhmach Ukr.
Bakhmut Ukr. see Artemivs'k
Bākhtarān Iran see Kermānshāh
Bakı Azer. see Baku
111 C2 Bakırköy Turkey

92 ☐C2 Bakkaflói b. Iceland
118 C2 Bakouma C.A.R.
81 C1 Baku Azer.
99 B3 Bala U.K.
64 A3 Balabac Phil.
64 A3 Balabac i. Phil.
61 C1 Balabac Strait Malaysia/Phil.
75 C2 Balaghat India
60 C2 Balaiberkuak Indon.
52 A2 Balaklava Austr.
91 C3 Balaklava Ukr.
91 D2 Balakliya Ukr.
87 D3 Balakovo Rus. Fed.
76 C3 Bālā Morghāb Afgh.
145 C3 Balancán Mex.
111 C3 Balan Dağı hill Turkey
64 B2 Balanga Phil.
75 C2 Balāngīr India
87 D3 Balashov Rus. Fed.
103 D2 Balaton l. Hungary
Balaton, Lake Hungary see Balaton
103 D2 Balatonboglár Hungary
150 D3 Balbina, Represa de resr Brazil
97 C2 Balbriggan Rep. of Ireland
52 A2 Balcanoona Austr.
110 C2 Balchik Bulg.
54 A3 Balclutha N.Z.
139 C3 Balcones Escarpment U.S.A.
129 E2 Baldock Lake Can.
140 D2 Baldwin U.S.A.
129 D2 Baldy Mountain hill Can.
138 B2 Baldy Peak U.S.A.
Baleares, Islas is Spain see Balearic Islands
107 D3 Balearic Islands is Spain
155 E1 Baleia, Ponta da pt Brazil
75 C2 Bāleshwar India
50 B2 Balgo Austr.
79 B3 Bālhaf Yemen
61 C2 Bali i. Indon.
60 A1 Balige Indon.
75 C2 Baliguda India
111 C3 Balıkesir Turkey
61 C2 Balikpapan Indon.
64 A3 Balimbing Phil.
59 D3 Balimo P.N.G.
102 B2 Balingen Ger.
64 B2 Balintang Channel Phil.
61 C2 Bali Sea Indon.
78 B3 Baljurshī Saudi Arabia
110 B2 Balkan Mountains Bulg./Yugo.
77 C1 Balkashino Kazakh.
77 D2 Balkhash Kazakh.
Balkhash, Lake Kazakh. see Balkhash, Ozero
77 D2 Balkhash, Ozero l. Kazakh.
Balla Balla Zimbabwe see Mbalabala
96 B3 Ballachulish U.K.
50 B3 Balladonia Austr.
97 B2 Ballaghaderreen Rep. of Ireland
92 G2 Ballangen Norway
96 B3 Ballantrae U.K.
52 B3 Ballarat Austr.
50 B2 Ballard, Lake salt flat Austr.
96 C2 Ballater U.K.
114 B3 Ballé Mali
55 M3 Balleny Islands Antarctica
53 D1 Ballina Austr.
97 B1 Ballina Rep. of Ireland
97 B2 Ballinasloe Rep. of Ireland
97 B3 Ballineen Rep. of Ireland
139 D2 Ballinger U.S.A.
97 B2 Ballinrobe Rep. of Ireland
97 C1 Ballycastle U.K.
97 B1 Ballycastle Rep. of Ireland
97 C1 Ballyhaunis Rep. of Ireland
97 C1 Ballymena U.K.
97 C1 Ballymoney U.K.
97 D1 Ballynahinch U.K.
97 B1 Ballyshannon Rep. of Ireland
95 B2 Ballyvoy U.K.
52 B3 Balmoral Austr.
139 C2 Balmorhea U.S.A.
120 A2 Balombo Angola
51 D2 Balonne r. Austr.
74 B2 Balotra India
77 D2 Balpyk Bi Kazakh.
75 C2 Balrampur India
52 B2 Balranald Austr.

110 B2 Balş Romania
151 E3 Balsas Brazil
145 C3 Balsas Mex.
145 B3 Balsas r. Mex.
90 B2 Balta Ukr.
90 B2 Bălţi Moldova
93 G4 Baltic Sea g. Europe
80 B2 Baltīm Egypt
97 B3 Baltimore Rep. of Ireland
123 C1 Baltimore S. Africa
141 D3 Baltimore U.S.A.
97 C2 Baltinglass Rep. of Ireland
88 A3 Baltiysk Rus. Fed.
75 D2 Balu India
52 A2 Balumbah Austr.
88 C2 Balvi Latvia
77 D2 Balykchy Kyrg.
87 E4 Balykshi Kazakh.
79 C2 Bam Iran
71 A3 Bama China
130 A2 Bamaga Austr.
114 B3 Bamako Mali
118 C2 Bambari C.A.R.
101 E3 Bamberg Ger.
119 C2 Bambili Dem. Rep. Congo
118 B2 Bambio C.A.R.
119 C2 Bambouti C.A.R.
155 C2 Bambuí Brazil
98 C2 Bamburgh U.K.
118 B2 Bamenda Cameroon
77 C3 Bāmīān Afgh.
118 C2 Bamingui C.A.R.
79 D2 Bampūr Iran
79 C2 Bampūr watercourse Iran
48 H4 Banaba i. Kiribati
152 B1 Bañados del Izozog swamp Bol.
119 C2 Banalia Dem. Rep. Congo
71 A3 Banan China
151 D4 Bananal, Ilha do i. Brazil
74 B2 Banas r. India
111 C3 Banaz Turkey
62 B2 Ban Ban Laos
97 C1 Banbridge U.K.
99 C3 Banbury U.K.
96 C2 Banchory U.K.
130 C3 Bancroft Can.
Bancroft Zambia see Chililabombwe
119 C2 Banda Dem. Rep. Congo
75 C2 Banda India
59 C3 Banda, Kepulauan is Indon.
60 A1 Banda Aceh Indon.
Bandar India see Machilipatnam
Bandar Abbās Iran see Bandar-e 'Abbās
75 D2 Bandarban Bangl.
79 C2 Bandar-e 'Abbās Iran
79 C2 Bandar-e Anzalī Iran
79 C2 Bandar-e Chārak Iran
81 C2 Bandar-e Emām Khomeynī Iran
79 C2 Bandar-e Lengeh Iran
79 C2 Bandar-e Maqām Iran
Bandar-e Pahlavī Iran see Bandar-e Anzalī
Bandar-e Shāhpūr Iran see Bandar-e Emām Khomeynī
Bandar Lampung Indon. see Telukbetung
Bandjarmasin Indon. see Banjarmasin
61 C1 Bandar Seri Begawan Brunei
59 C3 Banda Sea Indon.
155 D2 Bandeiras, Pico de mt. Brazil
123 D1 Bandelierkop S. Africa
144 B2 Banderas, Bahía de b. Mex.
114 B3 Bandiagara Mali
111 C3 Bandırma Turkey
97 B3 Bandon Rep. of Ireland
97 B3 Bandon r. Rep. of Ireland
118 B3 Bandundu Dem. Rep. Congo
60 B2 Bandung Indon.
128 C2 Banff Can.
96 C2 Banff U.K.
114 B3 Banfora Burkina
64 B3 Banga Phil.
73 B3 Bangalore India
118 C2 Bangassou C.A.R.
61 D2 Banggai Indon.
61 D2 Banggai, Kepulauan is Indon.

59 C3 Banggai, Kepulauan is Indon.
61 C1 Banggi i. Sabah Malaysia
115 E1 Banghāzī Libya
60 B2 Bangka i. Indon.
60 B2 Bangka, Selat sea chan. Indon.
61 C2 Bangkalan Indon.
60 B1 Bangkinang Indon.
60 B2 Bangko Indon.
63 B2 Bangkok Thai.
75 C2 Bangladesh country Asia
97 D1 Bangor Northern Ireland U.K.
98 A3 Bangor Wales U.K.
141 F2 Bangor U.S.A.
63 A2 Bang Saphan Yai Thai.
64 B2 Bangued Phil.
118 B2 Bangui C.A.R.
64 B2 Bangui Phil.
121 B2 Bangweulu, Lake Zambia
62 B1 Ban Houayxay Laos
118 C2 Bani C.A.R.
115 D1 Banī Walīd Libya
80 B2 Bāniyās Syria
109 C2 Banja Luka Bos.-Herz.
61 C2 Banjarmasin Indon.
114 A3 Banjul Gambia
63 A3 Ban Khok Kloi Thai.
128 A2 Banks Island B.C. Can.
126 D2 Banks Island N.W.T. Can.
48 H5 Banks Islands Vanuatu
129 E1 Banks Lake Can.
54 B2 Banks Peninsula N.Z.
51 D4 Banks Strait Austr.
75 C2 Bankura India
62 A1 Banmauk Myanmar
62 B2 Ban Mouang Laos
97 C1 Bann r. U.K.
62 B2 Ban Napè Laos
63 A3 Ban Na San Thai.
146 C2 Bannerman Town Bahamas
Banningville Dem. Rep. Congo see Bandundu
71 A4 Ban Nong Kung Thai.
74 B1 Bannu Pak.
103 D2 Banská Bystrica Slovakia
111 B2 Bansko Bulg.
74 B2 Banswara India
62 B2 Ban Taviang Laos
63 A3 Ban Tha Kham Thai.
62 A2 Ban Tha Song Yang Thai.
63 B2 Ban Tôp Laos
97 B3 Bantry Rep. of Ireland
97 B3 Bantry Bay Rep. of Ireland
60 A1 Banyak, Pulau-pulau is Indon.
118 B2 Banyo Cameroon
107 D1 Banyoles Spain
61 C2 Banyuwangi Indon.
Banzyville Dem. Rep. Congo see Mobayi-Mbongo
Bao'an China see Shenzhen
70 B1 Baochang China
70 B2 Baoding China
70 A2 Baoji China
63 B2 Bao Lôc Vietnam
66 B1 Baoqing China
118 B2 Baoro C.A.R.
62 A1 Baoshan China
70 B1 Baotou China
74 B2 Bap India
81 C2 Ba'qūbah Iraq
90 B2 Bar Ukr.
109 C2 Bar Yugo.
116 B3 Bara Sudan
117 C4 Baraawe Somalia
147 C2 Baracoa Cuba
53 C2 Baradine Austr.
147 C3 Barahona Dom. Rep.
116 B3 Baraka watercourse Eritrea/Sudan
106 C1 Barakaldo Spain
61 C1 Baram r. Sarawak Malaysia
150 D2 Baramanni Guyana
89 D3 Baran' Belarus
74 B2 Baran India
88 C3 Baranavichy Belarus
90 B1 Baranivka Ukr.
128 A2 Baranof Island U.S.A.
Baranowicze Belarus see Baranavichy
59 C3 Barat Daya, Kepulauan is Indon.
155 D2 Barbacena Brazil
147 E3 Barbados country West Indies

107 D1 Barbastro Spain
106 B2 Barbate de Franco Spain
123 D2 Barberton S. Africa
104 B2 Barbezieux-St-Hilaire France
51 D2 Barcaldine Austr.
107 D1 Barcelona Spain
150 C1 Barcelona Venez.
105 D3 Barceloneta France
150 C3 Barcelos Brazil
114 B4 Barclayville Liberia
51 D2 Barcoo watercourse Austr.
Barcoo Creek watercourse Austr. see Cooper Creek
103 D2 Barcs Hungary
92 □B3 Bárðarbunga mt. Iceland
75 C2 Barddhamān India
103 E2 Bardejov Slovakia
Bardera Somalia see Baardheere
79 C2 Bardsīr Iran
75 B2 Bareilly India
82 D1 Barents Sea Arctic Ocean
78 A3 Barentu Eritrea
108 B2 Barga Italy
75 C2 Barh India
52 B3 Barham Austr.
141 F2 Bar Harbor U.S.A.
109 C2 Bari Italy
107 E2 Barika Alg.
74 B1 Barikot Afgh.
150 B2 Barinas Venez.
75 C2 Baripada India
75 D2 Barisal Bangl.
60 B2 Barisan, Pegunungan mts Indon.
61 C2 Barito r. Indon.
79 C2 Barkā Oman
88 C2 Barkava Latvia
74 A2 Barkhan Pak.
51 C1 Barkly Tableland reg. Austr.
122 B2 Barkly West S. Africa
68 C2 Barkol China
110 C1 Bârlad Romania
105 D2 Bar-le-Duc France
50 A2 Barlee, Lake salt flat Austr.
109 C2 Barletta Italy
53 C2 Barmedman Austr.
Barmen-Elberfeld Ger. see Wuppertal
74 B2 Barmer India
52 B2 Barmera Austr.
99 A3 Barmouth U.K.
101 D1 Barmstedt Ger.
98 C2 Barnard Castle U.K.
53 B2 Barnato Austr.
82 G3 Barnaul Rus. Fed.
127 H2 Barnes Icecap Can.
100 B1 Barneveld Neth.
98 C3 Barnsley U.K.
99 A4 Barnstaple U.K.
Barnstaple Bay U.K. see Bideford Bay
143 D2 Barnwell U.S.A.
Baroda India see Vadodara
150 C1 Barquisimeto Venez.
96 A2 Barra r. U.K.
53 D2 Barraba Austr.
151 D4 Barra do Bugres Brazil
151 E3 Barra do Corda Brazil
154 B1 Barra do Garças Brazil
150 D3 Barra do São Manuel Brazil
Barraigh i. U.K. see Barra
150 B4 Barranca Peru
150 B3 Barranca Peru
152 C2 Barranqueras Arg.
150 B1 Barranquilla Col.
105 D3 Barre des Ecrins mt. France
151 E4 Barreiras Brazil
63 A2 Barren Island India
154 C2 Barretos Brazil
128 C2 Barrhead Can.
130 C3 Barrie Can.
128 B2 Barrière Can.
52 B2 Barrier Range hills Austr.
53 D2 Barrington, Mount Austr.
129 D2 Barrington Lake Can.
53 C1 Barringun Austr.
97 C2 Barrow r. Rep. of Ireland
126 B2 Barrow U.S.A.
126 B2 Barrow, Point U.S.A.
51 C2 Barrow Creek Austr.
98 B2 Barrow-in-Furness U.K.
50 A2 Barrow Island Austr.
126 F2 Barrow Strait Can.
99 B4 Barry U.K.

122 B3 Barrydale S. Africa
130 C3 Barrys Bay Can.
74 B2 Barsalpur India
101 D1 Barsinghausen Ger.
135 C4 Barstow U.S.A.
105 C2 Bar-sur-Aube France
102 C1 Barth Ger.
80 B1 Bartın Turkey
51 D1 Bartle Frere, Mount Austr.
139 D1 Bartlesville U.S.A.
137 D2 Bartlett NE U.S.A.
142 C1 Bartlett TN U.S.A.
98 C3 Barton-upon-Humber U.K.
103 E1 Bartoszyce Pol.
61 C2 Barung i. Indon.
69 D1 Baruun Urt Mongolia
91 D2 Barvinkove Ukr.
53 C2 Barwon r. Austr.
88 C3 Barysaw Belarus
118 B2 Basankusu Dem. Rep. Congo
110 C2 Basarabi Romania
104 B3 Basauri Spain
64 B1 Basco Phil.
105 D2 Basel Switz.
71 C3 Bashi Channel Taiwan
91 C2 Bashtanka Ukr.
64 B3 Basilan i. Phil.
99 D4 Basildon U.K.
99 C4 Basingstoke U.K.
81 C2 Başkale Turkey
130 C3 Baskatong, Réservoir resr Can.
Basle Switz. see Basel
118 C2 Basoko Dem. Rep. Congo
81 C2 Basra Iraq
128 C2 Bassano Can.
114 C4 Bassar Togo
63 A2 Bassein Myanmar
147 D3 Basse-Terre Guadeloupe
147 D3 Basseterre St Kitts and Nevis
114 B3 Bassikounou Maur.
114 C4 Bassila Benin
51 D3 Bass Strait Austr.
79 C2 Bastak Iran
101 E2 Bastheim Ger.
75 C2 Basti India
105 D3 Bastia Corsica France
100 B2 Bastogne Belgium
142 B2 Bastrop U.S.A.
Basuo China see Dongfang
117 C4 Basutoland country Africa see Lesotho
118 A2 Bata Equat. Guinea
146 B2 Batabanó, Golfo de b. Cuba
83 J2 Batagay Rus. Fed.
154 B2 Bataguaçu Brazil
74 B1 Batala India
106 B2 Batalha Port.
64 B1 Batan i. Phil.
118 B2 Batangafo C.A.R.
60 B2 Batanghari r. Indon.
64 B1 Batan Islands Phil.
154 C2 Batatais Brazil
141 D2 Batavia U.S.A.
91 D2 Bataysk Rus. Fed.
130 B3 Batchawana Mountain hill Can.
50 C1 Batchelor U.S.A.
63 B2 Bătdâmbâng Cambodia
118 B3 Batéké, Plateaux Congo
53 D3 Batemans Bay Austr.
142 B1 Batesville AR U.S.A.
142 C2 Batesville MS U.S.A.
89 D2 Batetskiy Rus. Fed.
99 B4 Bath U.K.
96 C3 Bathgate U.K.
74 B1 Bathinda India
53 C2 Bathurst Austr.
131 D3 Bathurst Can.
Bathurst Gambia see Banjul
Bathurst Inlet Can.
126 E2 Bathurst Inlet inlet Can.
126 E2 Bathurst Island Austr.
50 C1 Bathurst Island Can.
126 F1 Bâtin, Wādī al watercourse Asia
78 B1 Batley U.K.
53 C3 Batman Turkey
81 C2 Baton Rouge U.S.A.
115 C1 Batouri Cameroon
154 B1 Batovi Brazil

Batrā' tourist site Jordan see Petra
92 I1 Båtsfjord Norway
73 C4 Batticaloa Sri Lanka
109 B2 Battipaglia Italy
128 D2 Battle r. Can.
140 B2 Battle Creek U.S.A.
135 C2 Battle Mountain U.S.A.
74 B1 Battura Glacier Jammu and Kashmir
117 B4 Batu mt. Eth.
60 A2 Batu, Pulau-pulau is Indon.
61 D2 Batudaka i. Indon.
64 B3 Batulaki Phil.
Batum Georgia see Bat'umi
81 C1 Bat'umi Georgia
60 B1 Batu Pahat Malaysia
61 D2 Baubau Indon.
115 C3 Bauchi Nigeria
137 E1 Baudette U.S.A.
Baudouinville Dem. Rep. Congo see Moba
104 B2 Baugé France
105 D2 Baume-les-Dames France
154 C2 Bauru Brazil
154 B1 Baús Brazil
88 B2 Bauska Latvia
102 C1 Bautzen Ger.
144 B2 Bavispe r. Mex.
87 E3 Bavly Rus. Fed.
62 A1 Bawdwin Myanmar
61 C2 Bawean i. Indon.
116 A2 Bawiti Egypt
114 B3 Bawku Ghana
Baxian China see Banan
146 C2 Bayamo Cuba
Bayan Gol China see Dengkou
68 C1 Bayanhongor Mongolia
70 A2 Bayan Hot China
70 A1 Bayan Obo Kuangqu China
136 C2 Bayard NE U.S.A.
138 B2 Bayard NM U.S.A.
64 B3 Bayawan Phil.
81 C1 Bayburt Turkey
140 C2 Bay City MI U.S.A.
139 D3 Bay City TX U.S.A.
86 F2 Baydaratskaya Guba Rus. Fed.
117 C4 Baydhabo Somalia
136 B3 Bayeux France
136 B3 Bayfield U.S.A.
78 B3 Bayhan al Qişab Yemen
Bay Islands is Hond. see La Bahía, Islas de
81 C2 Bayjī Iraq
Baykal, Ozero l. Rus. Fed. see Baikal, Lake
Baykal Range mts Rus. Fed. see Baykal'skiy Khrebet
83 I3 Baykal'skiy Khrebet mts Rus. Fed.
76 C2 Baykonur Kazakh.
87 E3 Baymak Rus. Fed.
64 B2 Bayombong Phil.
104 B3 Bayonne France
76 C3 Bayramaly Turkm.
111 C3 Bayramiç Turkey
101 E3 Bayreuth Ger.
78 B3 Bayt al Faqīh Yemen
139 D3 Baytown U.S.A.
106 C2 Baza Spain
106 C2 Baza, Sierra de mts Spain
76 A2 Bazardyuzi, Gora mt. Azer./Rus. Fed.
104 B3 Bazas France
74 A2 Bazdar Pak.
70 A2 Bazhong China
79 D2 Bazmān Iran
79 D2 Bazmān, Küh-e mt. Iran
Bé, Nossi i. Madag. see Nosy Bé
136 C1 Beach U.S.A.
52 B3 Beachport Austr.
99 D4 Beachy Head hd U.S.A.
123 C3 Beacon Bay S. Africa
50 B1 Beagle Gulf Austr.
121 □D2 Bealanana Madag.
121 □D3 Beampingaratra mts Madag.
134 D2 Bear r. U.S.A.
130 B3 Beardmore Can.
53 C1 Beardmore Reservoir Austr.
82 C2 Bear Island Arctic Ocean

134 E1 Bear Paw Mountain U.S.A.
147 C3 Beata, Cabo c. Dom. Rep.
147 C3 Beata, Isla i. Dom. Rep.
137 D2 Beatrice U.S.A.
135 C3 Beatty U.S.A.
53 D1 Beaudesert Austr.
52 B3 Beaufort Austr.
61 C1 Beaufort Sabah Malaysia
143 D2 Beaufort U.S.A.
126 D2 Beaufort Sea Can./U.S.A.
122 B3 Beaufort West S. Africa
96 B2 Beauly U.K.
96 B2 Beauly r. U.K.
100 B2 Beaumont Belgium
54 A3 Beaumont N.Z.
139 E2 Beaumont U.S.A.
105 C2 Beaune France
100 B2 Beauraing Belgium
129 E2 Beauséjour Can.
104 C2 Beauvais France
129 D2 Beauval Can.
129 D2 Beaver r. Can.
135 D3 Beaver U.S.A.
128 A1 Beaver Creek Can.
140 B2 Beaver Dam U.S.A.
129 E2 Beaver Hill Lake Can.
140 B1 Beaver Island U.S.A.
128 C2 Beaverlodge Can.
74 B2 Beawar India
154 C2 Bebedouro Brazil
101 D2 Bebra Ger.
99 D3 Beccles U.K.
109 D1 Bečej Yugo.
106 B1 Becerreá Spain
114 B1 Béchar Alg.
Bechuanaland country Africa see Botswana
140 C3 Beckley U.S.A.
117 B4 Bedelē Eth.
99 C3 Bedford U.K.
140 B3 Bedford U.S.A.
98 C2 Bedlington U.K.
100 C1 Bedum Neth.
53 C3 Beechworth Austr.
53 D2 Beecroft Peninsula Austr.
101 F1 Beelitz Ger.
53 D1 Beenleigh Austr.
Beersheba Israel see Be'ér Sheva'
80 B2 Be'ér Sheva' Israel
139 D3 Beeville U.S.A.
121 □D2 Befandriana Avaratra Madag.
53 C3 Bega Austr.
107 D1 Begur, Cap de c. Spain
81 D2 Behbehān Iran
81 D2 Behshahr Iran
69 E1 Bei'an China
71 A3 Beihai China
70 B2 Beijing China
100 C1 Beilen Neth.
118 B2 Béinamar Chad
96 B3 Beinn an Oir hill U.K.
96 A2 Beinn Mhòr hill U.K.
Beinn na Faoghla i. U.K. see Benbecula
121 C2 Beira Moz.
80 B2 Beirut Lebanon
123 C1 Beitbridge Zimbabwe
106 B2 Beja Port.
115 C1 Bejaïa Alg.
106 B1 Béjar Spain
74 A2 Beji r. Pak.
76 B2 Bekdash Turkm.
103 E2 Békés Hungary
103 E2 Békéscsaba Hungary
121 □D3 Bekily Madag.
66 D2 Bekkai Japan
114 B4 Bekwai Ghana
75 C2 Bela India
74 A2 Bela Pak.
123 C1 Bela-Bela S. Africa
118 B2 Bélabo Cameroon
109 D2 Bela Crkva Yugo.
61 C1 Belaga Sarawak Malaysia
60 C2 Belangiran Indon.
88 C3 Belarus country Europe
121 C3 Bela Vista Moz.
60 A1 Belawan Indon.
83 M2 Belaya r. Rus. Fed.
Belchatow Pol. see Bełchatów
103 D1 Bełchatów Pol.
130 C2 Belcher Islands Can.
87 E3 Belebey Rus. Fed.
117 C4 Beledweyne Somalia
118 B2 Bélèl Cameroon
151 E3 Belém Brazil
138 B2 Belen U.S.A.
110 C2 Belene Bulg.

89 E3	**Belev** Rus. Fed.	
97 D1	**Belfast** U.K.	
141 F2	**Belfast** U.S.A.	
136 C1	**Belfield** U.S.A.	
105 D2	**Belfort** France	
73 B3	**Belgaum** India	
	Belgian Congo country	
	Africa see	
	Congo, Democratic	
	Republic of	
100 B2	**Belgium** country Europe	
91 D1	**Belgorod** Rus. Fed.	
134 D1	**Belgrade** U.S.A.	
109 D2	**Belgrade** Yugo.	
115 D4	**Beli** Nigeria	
109 C1	**Beli Manastir** Croatia	
60 B2	**Belinyu** Indon.	
60 B2	**Belitung** i. Indon.	
118 B3	**Belize** Angola	
146 B3	**Belize** Belize	
146 B3	**Belize** country	
	Central America	
83 K1	**Bel'kovskiy, Ostrov** i.	
	Rus. Fed.	
128 B2	**Bella Bella** Can.	
104 C2	**Bellac** France	
128 B2	**Bella Coola** Can.	
73 B3	**Bellary** India	
53 C1	**Bellata** Austr.	
140 C2	**Bellefontaine** U.S.A.	
136 C2	**Belle Fourche** U.S.A.	
136 C2	**Belle Fourche** r. U.S.A.	
143 D3	**Belle Glade** U.S.A.	
104 B2	**Belle-Île** i. France	
131 E2	**Belle Isle** i. Can.	
131 E2	**Belle Isle, Strait of** Can.	
130 C3	**Belleville** Can.	
140 B3	**Belleville** IL U.S.A.	
137 D3	**Belleville** KS U.S.A.	
134 D2	**Bellevue** ID U.S.A.	
134 B1	**Bellevue** WA U.S.A.	
	Bellin Can. see Kangirsuk	
53 D2	**Bellingen** Austr.	
134 B1	**Bellingham** U.S.A.	
55 R2	**Bellingshausen Sea**	
	Antarctica	
105 D2	**Bellinzona** Switz.	
108 B1	**Belluno** Italy	
122 A3	**Bellville** S. Africa	
53 D2	**Belmont** Austr.	
155 E1	**Belmonte** Brazil	
146 B3	**Belmopan** Belize	
97 B1	**Belmullet** Rep. of Ireland	
69 E1	**Belogorsk** Rus. Fed.	
121 □D3	**Beloha** Madag.	
155 D1	**Belo Horizonte** Brazil	
140 B2	**Beloit** U.S.A.	
86 C2	**Belomorsk** Rus. Fed.	
89 E3	**Beloomut** Rus. Fed.	
91 D3	**Belorechensk** Rus. Fed.	
	Belorechenskaya	
	Rus. Fed. see	
	Belorechensk	
87 E3	**Beloretsk** Rus. Fed.	
	Belorussia country Europe	
	see Belarus	
	Belorusskaya S.S.R.	
	country Europe see	
	Belarus	
	Belostok Pol. see	
	Białystok	
121 □D2	**Belo Tsiribihina** Madag.	
86 F2	**Beloyarskiy** Rus. Fed.	
89 E1	**Beloye, Ozero** l. Rus. Fed.	
	Beloye More sea	
	Rus. Fed. see White Sea	
89 E1	**Belozersk** Rus. Fed.	
52 A2	**Beltana** Austr.	
139 D2	**Belton** U.S.A.	
	Bel'ts' Moldova see Bălţi	
	Bel'tsy Moldova see Bălţi	
97 C1	**Belturbet** Rep. of Ireland	
77 E2	**Belukha, Gora** mt.	
	Kazakh./Rus. Fed.	
86 D2	**Belush'ye** Rus. Fed.	
140 B2	**Belvidere** U.S.A.	
51 D2	**Belyando** r. Austr.	
89 D2	**Belyy** Rus. Fed.	
82 F2	**Belyy, Ostrov** i. Rus. Fed.	
101 F1	**Belzig** Ger.	
137 E1	**Bemidji** U.S.A.	
118 C3	**Bena Dibele**	
	Dem. Rep. Congo	
53 C3	**Benalla** Austr.	
	Benares India see	
	Varanasi	
115 D1	**Ben Arous** Tunisia	
118 C3	**Bena-Sungu**	
	Dem. Rep. Congo	
106 B2	**Benavente** Spain	
96 A2	**Benbecula** i. U.K.	
134 B2	**Bend** U.S.A.	
123 C3	**Bendearg** mt. S. Africa	
	Bender Moldova see	
	Tighina	
	Dendery Moldova see	
	Tighina	
52 B3	**Bendigo** Austr.	
121 C2	**Bene** Moz.	
102 C2	**Benešov** Czech Rep.	
109 B2	**Benevento** Italy	
73 C3	**Bengal, Bay of** sea	
	Indian Ocean	
70 B2	**Bengbu** China	
	Benghazi Libya see	
	Banghāzī	
60 B1	**Bengkalis** Indon.	
60 B1	**Bengkayang** Indon.	
60 B2	**Bengkulu** Indon.	
120 A2	**Benguela** Angola	
80 B2	**Benha** Egypt	
96 B1	**Ben Hope** hill U.K.	
152 B1	**Beni** r. Bol.	
119 C2	**Beni** Dem. Rep. Congo	
114 B1	**Beni-Abbès** Alg.	
107 C2	**Benidorm** Spain	
80 B3	**Benî Mazâr** Egypt	
114 B1	**Beni Mellal** Morocco	
114 C4	**Benin** country Africa	
114 C4	**Benin, Bight of** g. Africa	
115 C4	**Benin City** Nigeria	
107 C2	**Beni-Saf** Alg.	
116 B2	**Benî Suef** Egypt	
153 C3	**Benito Juárez** Arg.	
150 C3	**Benjamim Constant** Brazil	
144 A1	**Benjamin Hill** Mex.	
59 C3	**Benjina** Indon.	
136 C2	**Benkelman** U.S.A.	
96 B2	**Ben Lawers** mt. U.K.	
96 B2	**Ben Lomond** hill U.K.	
96 B2	**Ben Macdui** mt. U.K.	
96 A2	**Ben More** hill U.K.	
96 B2	**Ben More** mt. U.K.	
54 B2	**Benmore, Lake** N.Z.	
96 B1	**Ben More Assynt** hill U.K.	
128 A2	**Bennett** Can.	
83 K1	**Bennetta, Ostrov** i.	
	Rus. Fed.	
	Bennett Island Rus. Fed.	
	see Bennetta, Ostrov	
96 B2	**Ben Nevis** mt. U.K.	
141 E2	**Bennington** U.S.A.	
123 C2	**Benoni** S. Africa	
115 D4	**Bénoy** Chad	
101 D3	**Bensheim** Ger.	
114 B1	**Ben Slimane** Morocco	
138 A2	**Benson** U.S.A.	
61 D2	**Benteng** Indon.	
117 A4	**Bentiu** Sudan	
140 B2	**Benton Harbor** U.S.A.	
142 B1	**Bentonville** U.S.A.	
63 B2	**Bên Tre** Vietnam	
115 C4	**Benue** r. Nigeria	
97 B1	**Benwee Head** hd	
	Rep. of Ireland	
96 B2	**Ben Wyvis** mt. U.K.	
70 C1	**Benxi** China	
	Beograd Yugo. see	
	Belgrade	
75 C2	**Béohari** India	
114 B4	**Béoumi** Côte d'Ivoire	
67 B4	**Beppu** Japan	
109 C2	**Berane** Yugo.	
59 C3	**Berat** Albania	
59 C3	**Berau, Teluk** b. Indon.	
116 B3	**Berber** Sudan	
117 C3	**Berbera** Somalia	
118 B2	**Berbérati** C.A.R.	
104 C1	**Berck** France	
91 D1	**Berdyans'k** Ukr.	
90 B2	**Berdychiv** Ukr.	
91 C2	**Berehove** Ukr.	
59 D3	**Bereina** P.N.G.	
116 B2	**Berenice** Egypt	
129 E2	**Berens River** Can.	
137 D2	**Beresford** U.S.A.	
91 D2	**Berezanskaya** Rus. Fed.	
90 A2	**Berezhany** Ukr.	
90 C2	**Berezivka** Ukr.	
90 B1	**Berezne** Ukr.	
86 D2	**Bereznik** Rus. Fed.	
86 E3	**Berezniki** Rus. Fed.	
	Berezov Rus. Fed. see	
	Berezovo	
86 F2	**Berezovo** Rus. Fed.	
107 D1	**Berga** Spain	
111 C3	**Bergama** Turkey	
108 A1	**Bergamo** Italy	
102 C1	**Bergen** Ger.	
101 D1	**Bergen** Ger.	
100 B1	**Bergen** Neth.	
93 E3	**Bergen** Norway	
100 B2	**Bergen op Zoom** Neth.	
104 C3	**Bergerac** France	
100 C2	**Bergheim (Erft)** Ger.	
100 C2	**Bergisch Gladbach** Ger.	
122 A1	**Bergland** Namibia	
93 G3	**Bergsjö** Sweden	
92 H2	**Bergsviken** Sweden	
	Berhampur India see	
	Baharampur	
83 M3	**Beringa, Ostrov** i.	
	Rus. Fed.	
100 B2	**Beringen** Belgium	
124 A4	**Bering Sea**	
	N. Pacific Ocean	
124 B3	**Bering Strait**	
	Rus. Fed./U.S.A.	
100 C1	**Berkel** r. Neth.	
135 B3	**Berkeley** U.S.A.	
100 B1	**Berkhout** Neth.	
55 B2	**Berkner Island** Antarctica	
110 B2	**Berkovitsa** Bulg.	
92 I1	**Berlevåg** Norway	
101 F1	**Berlin** Ger.	
141 E2	**Berlin** U.S.A.	
101 E2	**Berlingerode** Ger.	
53 D3	**Bermagui** Austr.	
144 B2	**Bermejillo** Mex.	
152 B2	**Bermejo** Bol.	
125 L6	**Bermuda** terr.	
	N. Atlantic Ocean	
105 D2	**Bern** Switz.	
101 E2	**Bernburg (Saale)** Ger.	
127 G2	**Bernier Bay** Can.	
50 A2	**Bernier Island** Austr.	
100 C3	**Bernkastel-Kues** Ger.	
121 □D3	**Beroroha** Madag.	
52 B2	**Berri** Austr.	
115 C1	**Berriane** Alg.	
53 C3	**Berrigan** Austr.	
107 D2	**Berrouaghia** Alg.	
53 D2	**Berry** Austr.	
146 C2	**Berry Islands** Bahamas	
122 A2	**Berseba** Namibia	
101 C1	**Bersenbrück** Ger.	
90 B2	**Bershad'** Ukr.	
131 D2	**Berté, Lac** l. Can.	
118 B2	**Bertoua** Cameroon	
150 C3	**Beruri** Brazil	
98 B2	**Berwick-upon-Tweed**	
	U.K.	
91 C2	**Beryslav** Ukr.	
121 □D2	**Besalampy** Madag.	
105 D2	**Besançon** France	
81 D3	**Beshneh** Iran	
129 D2	**Besnard Lake** Can.	
142 C2	**Bessemer** U.S.A.	
76 B2	**Besshoky, Gora** hill	
	Kazakh.	
100 B2	**Best** Neth.	
121 □D2	**Betafo** Madag.	
106 B1	**Betanzos** Spain	
118 B2	**Betaré Oya** Cameroon	
122 A2	**Bethanie** Namibia	
100 B3	**Béthany** France	
141 D3	**Bethesda** U.S.A.	
123 C2	**Bethlehem** S. Africa	
141 D2	**Bethlehem** U.S.A.	
123 C3	**Bethulie** S. Africa	
105 C1	**Béthune** France	
121 □D3	**Betioky** Madag.	
51 D2	**Betoota** Austr.	
121 □D3	**Betroka** Madag.	
131 D3	**Betsiamites** Can.	
121 □D2	**Betsiboka** r. Madag.	
137 E2	**Bettendorf** U.S.A.	
75 C2	**Bettiah** India	
74 B2	**Betul** India	
74 B2	**Betwa** r. India	
99 B3	**Betws-y-coed** U.K.	
100 C2	**Betzdorf** Ger.	
136 C1	**Beulah** U.S.A.	
98 C3	**Beverley** U.K.	
101 D2	**Beverungen** Ger.	
100 B1	**Beverwijk** Neth.	
99 D4	**Bexhill** U.K.	
111 C2	**Beykoz** Turkey	
114 B4	**Beyla** Guinea	
76 B2	**Beyneu** Kazakh.	
80 B1	**Beypazarı** Turkey	
	Beyrouth Lebanon see	
	Beirut	
80 B2	**Beyşehir** Turkey	
80 B2	**Beyşehir Gölü** l. Turkey	
80 B2	**Beyşug** r. Turkey	
91 D2	**Beysugskiy Liman** lag.	
	Rus. Fed.	
88 C2	**Bezhanitsy** Rus. Fed.	
89 E2	**Bezhetsk** Rus. Fed.	
105 C3	**Béziers** France	
75 C2	**Bhadgaon** Nepal	
75 C2	**Bhadrakh** India	
73 B3	**Bhadravati** India	
75 C2	**Bhagalpur** India	
74 A2	**Bhairi Hol** mt. Pak.	
74 B1	**Bhakkar** Pak.	
	Bhaktapur Nepal see	
	Bhadgaon	
62 A1	**Bhamo** Myanmar	
75 C3	**Bhanjanagar** India	
74 B2	**Bharatpur** India	
74 B2	**Bharuch** India	
74 B2	**Bhavnagar** India	
75 C3	**Bhawanipatna** India	
123 D2	**Bhekuzulu** S. Africa	
74 B1	**Bhera** Pak.	
74 B2	**Bhilwara** India	
73 B3	**Bhima** r. India	
74 B2	**Bhind** India	
74 B2	**Bhiwani** India	
123 C3	**Bhongweni** S. Africa	
74 B2	**Bhopal** India	
75 C2	**Bhubaneshwar** India	
	Bhubaneswar India see	
	Bhubaneshwar	
74 A2	**Bhuj** India	
62 A2	**Bhumiphol Dam** Thai.	
74 B2	**Bhusawal** India	
75 D2	**Bhutan** country Asia	
62 B2	**Bia, Phou** mt. Laos	
	Biafra, Bight of g. Africa	
	see Benin, Bight of	
59 D3	**Biak** Indon.	
59 D3	**Biak** i. Indon.	
103 E1	**Biała Podlaska** Pol.	
103 D1	**Białogard** Pol.	
103 E1	**Białystok** Pol.	
109 C3	**Bianco** Italy	
74 B2	**Biaora** India	
104 B3	**Biarritz** France	
105 D2	**Biasca** Switz.	
66 D2	**Bibai** Japan	
120 A2	**Bibala** Angola	
53 C3	**Bibbenluke** Austr.	
102 B2	**Biberach an der Riß** Ger.	
155 D2	**Bicas** Brazil	
73 B3	**Bid** India	
115 C4	**Bida** Nigeria	
73 B3	**Bidar** India	
141 E2	**Biddeford** U.S.A.	
96 B2	**Bidean nam Bian** mt. U.K.	
99 A4	**Bideford** U.K.	
99 A4	**Bideford Bay** U.K.	
	Bié Angola see Kuito	
101 D2	**Biedenkopf** Ger.	
105 D2	**Biel** Switz.	
101 D1	**Bielefeld** Ger.	
108 A1	**Biella** Italy	
103 D2	**Bielsko-Biała** Pol.	
63 B2	**Biên Hoa** Vietnam	
130 C2	**Bienville, Lac** l. Can.	
120 A2	**Bié Plateau** Angola	
100 B3	**Bièvre** Belgium	
118 B3	**Bifoun** Gabon	
111 C2	**Biga** Turkey	
134 D1	**Big Belt Mountains** U.S.A.	
123 D2	**Big Bend** Swaziland	
129 D2	**Biggar** Can.	
96 C3	**Biggar** U.K.	
99 C3	**Biggleswade** U.K.	
134 D1	**Big Hole** r. U.S.A.	
134 E1	**Bighorn** r. U.S.A.	
136 B1	**Bighorn** r. U.S.A.	
136 B2	**Bighorn Mountains** U.S.A.	
139 C2	**Big Lake** U.S.A.	
140 B2	**Big Rapids** U.S.A.	
129 D2	**Big River** Can.	
129 E2	**Big Sand Lake** Can.	
137 D2	**Big Sioux** r. U.S.A.	
139 C2	**Big Spring** U.S.A.	
134 E1	**Big Timber** U.S.A.	
130 B2	**Big Trout Lake** Can.	
130 A2	**Big Trout Lake** l. Can.	
109 C2	**Bihać** Bos.-Herz.	
75 C2	**Bihar** state India	
75 C2	**Bihar Sharif** India	
110 B1	**Bihor, Vârful** mt. Romania	
114 A3	**Bijagós, Arquipélago dos**	
	is Guinea-Bissau	
73 B3	**Bijapur** India	
81 C2	**Bijār** Iran	
109 C2	**Bijeljina** Bos.-Herz.	
109 C2	**Bijelo Polje** Yugo.	
71 A3	**Bijie** China	
74 B2	**Bikaner** India	
66 B1	**Bikin** Rus. Fed.	
66 B1	**Bikin** r. Rus. Fed.	
118 B3	**Bikoro** Dem. Rep. Congo	
79 C2	**Bilād Banī Bū 'Alī** Oman	
75 C2	**Bilaspur** India	
81 C2	**Bīlāsuvar** Azer.	
90 C2	**Bila Tserkva** Ukr.	

63 A2 **Bilauktaung Range** *mts* Myanmar/Thai.
106 C1 **Bilbao** Spain
109 C2 **Bileća** Bos.-Herz.
111 C2 **Bilecik** Turkey
103 E1 **Biłgoraj** Pol.
119 D3 **Bilharamulo** Tanz.
90 C2 **Bilhorod-Dnistrovs'kyy** Ukr.
119 C2 **Bili** Dem. Rep. Congo
83 M2 **Bilibino** Rus. Fed.
109 D2 **Bilisht** Albania
104 B3 **Billère** France
134 E1 **Billings** U.S.A.
99 B4 **Bill of Portland** *hd* U.K.
138 A1 **Bill Williams Mountain** U.S.A.
115 D3 **Bilma** Niger
51 E2 **Biloela** Austr.
91 C2 **Bilohirs'k** Ukr.
90 B1 **Bilohir″ya** Ukr.
91 C1 **Bilopillya** Ukr.
91 D2 **Bilovods'k** Ukr.
142 C2 **Biloxi** U.S.A.
51 C2 **Bilpa Morea Claypan** *salt flat* Austr.
101 E2 **Bilshausen** Ger.
115 E3 **Biltine** Chad
90 C2 **Bilyayivka** Ukr.
114 C4 **Bimbila** Ghana
143 E3 **Bimini Islands** Bahamas
74 B2 **Bina-Etawa** India
59 C3 **Binaija, Gunung** *mt.* Indon.
53 C1 **Bindle** Austr.
118 B3 **Bindu** Dem. Rep. Congo
121 C2 **Bindura** Zimbabwe
107 D1 **Binéfar** Spain
120 B2 **Binga** Zimbabwe
53 D1 **Bingara** Austr.
100 C3 **Bingen am Rhein** Ger.
114 B4 **Bingerville** Côte d'Ivoire
141 F1 **Bingham** U.S.A.
141 D2 **Binghamton** U.S.A.
115 D2 **Bin Ghanīmah, Jabal** *hills* Libya
81 C2 **Bingöl** Turkey
62 A1 **Bingzhongluo** China
60 A1 **Binjai** Indon.
53 C2 **Binnaway** Austr.
60 B1 **Bintan** *i.* Indon.
60 B2 **Bintuhan** Indon.
61 C1 **Bintulu** *Sarawak* Malaysia
115 C3 **Bin-Yauri** Nigeria
70 B2 **Binzhou** China
118 A2 **Bioco** *i.* Equat. Guinea
109 C2 **Biograd na Moru** Croatia
155 C1 **Biquinhas** Brazil
115 D2 **Birāk** Libya
118 C1 **Birao** C.A.R.
75 C2 **Biratnagar** Nepal
52 B3 **Birchip** Austr.
128 C2 **Birch Mountains** Can.
100 B1 **Birdaard** Neth.
51 C2 **Birdsville** Austr.
80 B2 **Birecik** Turkey
Birendranagar Nepal *see* Surkhet
60 A1 **Bireun** Indon.
75 C2 **Birganj** Nepal
117 B3 **Birhan** *mt.* Eth.
154 B2 **Birigüi** Brazil
118 C2 **Birini** C.A.R.
76 B3 **Birjand** Iran
98 B3 **Birkenhead** U.K.
99 C3 **Birmingham** U.K.
142 C2 **Birmingham** U.S.A.
114 A2 **Bir Mogreïn** Maur.
115 C3 **Birnin-Kebbi** Nigeria
115 C3 **Birnin Konni** Niger
69 E1 **Birobidzhan** Rus. Fed.
97 C2 **Birr** Rep. of Ireland
96 C1 **Birsay** U.K.
78 A2 **Bîr Shalatein** Egypt
88 B2 **Biržai** Lith.
75 B2 **Bisalpur** India
138 B2 **Bisbee** U.S.A.
104 A2 **Biscay, Bay of** *sea* France/Spain
143 D3 **Biscayne Bay** U.S.A.
102 C2 **Bischofshofen** Austria
77 D2 **Bishkek** Kyrg.
123 C3 **Bisho** S. Africa
135 C3 **Bishop** U.S.A.
98 C2 **Bishop Auckland** U.K.
69 E1 **Bishui** China
150 C2 **Bisinaca** Col.
115 C1 **Biskra** Alg.
64 B3 **Bislig** Phil.
136 C1 **Bismarck** U.S.A.

59 D3 **Bismarck Archipelago** *is* P.N.G.
59 D3 **Bismarck Sea** P.N.G.
107 D2 **Bissa, Djebel** *mt.* Alg.
114 A3 **Bissau** Guinea-Bissau
129 E2 **Bissett** Can.
128 C2 **Bistcho Lake** Can.
110 B1 **Bistriţa** Romania
110 C1 **Bistriţa** *r.* Romania
100 C3 **Bitburg** Ger.
105 D2 **Bitche** France
115 D3 **Bitkine** Chad
81 C2 **Bitlis** Turkey
111 B2 **Bitola** Macedonia
Bitolj Macedonia *see* Bitola
109 C2 **Bitonto** Italy
101 F2 **Bitterfeld** Ger.
122 A3 **Bitterfontein** S. Africa
134 D1 **Bitterroot** *r.* U.S.A.
134 C1 **Bitterroot Range** *mts* U.S.A.
89 E3 **Bityug** *r.* Rus. Fed.
115 D3 **Biu** Nigeria
67 C3 **Biwa-ko** *l.* Japan
77 E1 **Biysk** Rus. Fed.
Bizerta Tunisia *see* Bizerte
115 C1 **Bizerte** Tunisia
92 A2 **Bjargtangar** *hd* Iceland
92 G3 **Bjästa** Sweden
109 C1 **Bjelovar** Croatia
92 G2 **Bjerkvik** Norway
Björneborg Fin. *see* Pori
Bjørnøya *i.* Arctic Ocean *see* Bear Island
114 B3 **Bla** Mali
137 E3 **Black** *r.* U.S.A.
51 D2 **Blackall** Austr.
98 B3 **Blackburn** U.K.
134 D2 **Blackfoot** U.S.A.
Black Forest *mts* Ger. *see* Schwarzwald
136 C2 **Black Hills** U.S.A.
96 B2 **Black Isle** *pen.* U.K.
129 D2 **Black Lake** Can.
129 D2 **Black Lake** *l.* Can.
99 B4 **Black Mountains** *hills* U.K.
138 A1 **Black Mountains** U.S.A.
98 B3 **Blackpool** U.K.
138 B2 **Black Range** *mts* U.S.A.
Black River *r.* Vietnam *see* Đa, Sông
140 A2 **Black River Falls** U.S.A.
134 C2 **Black Rock Desert** U.S.A.
140 C3 **Blacksburg** U.S.A.
80 B1 **Black Sea** Asia/Europe
131 D3 **Blacks Harbour** Can.
97 A1 **Blacksod Bay** Rep. of Ireland
97 C2 **Blackstairs Mountains** *hills* Rep. of Ireland
114 B4 **Black Volta** *r.* Africa
51 D2 **Blackwater** Austr.
97 C2 **Blackwater** *r.* Rep. of Ireland
128 B1 **Blackwater Lake** Can.
50 A3 **Blackwood** *r.* Austr.
87 D4 **Blagodarnyy** Rus. Fed.
111 B2 **Blagoevgrad** Bulg.
69 E1 **Blagoveshchensk** Rus. Fed.
129 D2 **Blaine Lake** Can.
137 D2 **Blair** U.S.A.
96 C2 **Blair Atholl** U.K.
96 C2 **Blairgowrie** U.K.
143 D2 **Blakely** U.S.A.
153 B3 **Blanca, Bahía b.** Arg.
52 A1 **Blanche, Lake** *salt flat* Austr.
152 B1 **Blanco** *r.* Bol.
134 B2 **Blanco, Cape** U.S.A.
131 E2 **Blanc-Sablon** Can.
92 A2 **Blanda** *r.* Iceland
99 B4 **Blandford Forum** U.K.
135 E3 **Blanding** U.S.A.
107 D1 **Blanes** Spain
60 A1 **Blangkejeren** Indon.
100 A2 **Blankenberge** Belgium
100 C2 **Blankenheim** Ger.
100 C2 **Blankenrath** Ger.
147 D3 **Blanquilla, Isla** *i.* Venez.
103 D2 **Blansko** Czech Rep.
121 C2 **Blantyre** Malawi
97 B3 **Blarney** Rep. of Ireland
98 C2 **Blaydon** U.K.
53 C2 **Blayney** Austr.
54 B2 **Blenheim** N.Z.
115 C1 **Blida** Alg.
130 B3 **Blind River** Can.
123 C2 **Bloemfontein** S. Africa
123 C2 **Bloemhof** S. Africa

123 C2 **Bloemhof Dam** S. Africa
104 C2 **Blois** France
92 A2 **Blönduós** Iceland
97 B1 **Bloody Foreland** *pt* Rep. of Ireland
138 B1 **Bloomfield** U.S.A.
140 B2 **Bloomington** *IL* U.S.A.
140 B3 **Bloomington** *IN* U.S.A.
102 B2 **Bludenz** Austria
137 E2 **Blue Earth** U.S.A.
140 C3 **Bluefield** U.S.A.
146 B3 **Bluefields** Nic.
53 C2 **Blue Mountains** Austr.
134 C1 **Blue Mountains** U.S.A.
116 B3 **Blue Nile** *r.* Eth./Sudan
126 E2 **Bluenose Lake** Can.
140 C3 **Blue Ridge** *mts* U.S.A.
128 C2 **Blue River** Can.
97 B1 **Blue Stack Mountains** *hills* Rep. of Ireland
54 A3 **Bluff** N.Z.
135 E3 **Bluff** U.S.A.
154 C3 **Blumenau** Brazil
52 A2 **Blyth** Austr.
98 C2 **Blyth** U.K.
135 D4 **Blythe** U.S.A.
142 C1 **Blytheville** U.S.A.
114 A4 **Bo** Sierra Leone
64 B2 **Boac** Phil.
146 B3 **Boaco** Nic.
151 E3 **Boa Esperança, Açude** *resr* Brazil
134 C1 **Boardman** U.S.A.
123 C1 **Boatlaname** Botswana
151 F3 **Boa Viagem** Brazil
150 C2 **Boa Vista** Brazil
53 C2 **Bobadah** Austr.
71 B3 **Bobai** China
121 D2 **Bobaomby, Tanjona** *c.* Madag.
114 B3 **Bobo-Dioulasso** Burkina
121 B3 **Bobonong** Botswana
Bobriki Rus. Fed. *see* Novomoskovsk
89 F3 **Bobrov** Rus. Fed.
91 C1 **Bobrovytsya** Ukr.
91 C2 **Bobrynets'** Ukr.
121 D3 **Boby** *mt.* Madag.
150 C3 **Boca do Acre** Brazil
155 D1 **Bocaiúva** Brazil
154 A2 **Bocajá** Brazil
118 B2 **Bocaranga** C.A.R.
143 D3 **Boca Raton** U.S.A.
146 B4 **Bocas del Toro** Panama
103 E2 **Bochnia** Pol.
100 B2 **Bocholt** Belgium
100 C2 **Bocholt** Ger.
100 C2 **Bochum** Ger.
123 C1 **Bochum** S. Africa
101 E1 **Bockenem** Ger.
110 B1 **Bocşa** Romania
118 B2 **Boda** C.A.R.
83 I3 **Bodaybo** Rus. Fed.
96 D2 **Boddam** U.K.
115 D3 **Bodélé** *reg.* Chad
92 H2 **Boden** Sweden
Bodensee *l.* Ger./Switz. *see* Constance, Lake
99 A4 **Bodmin** U.K.
99 A4 **Bodmin Moor** *moorland* U.K.
92 F2 **Bodø** Norway
111 C3 **Bodrum** Turkey
118 C3 **Boende** Dem. Rep. Congo
63 A2 **Bogale** Myanmar
142 C2 **Bogalusa** U.S.A.
114 B3 **Bogandé** Burkina
118 B2 **Bogangolo** C.A.R.
80 B2 **Boğazlıyan** Turkey
68 B2 **Bogda Shan** *mts* China
53 D1 **Boggabilla** Austr.
53 D2 **Boggabri** Austr.
97 B2 **Boggeragh Mountains** *hills* Rep. of Ireland
92 □A2 **Boghari** Alg. *see* Ksar el Boukhari
59 D3 **Bogia** P.N.G.
100 B3 **Bogny-sur-Meuse** France
97 C2 **Bog of Allen** *reg.* Rep. of Ireland
53 C3 **Bogong, Mount** Austr.
60 B2 **Bogor** Indon.
89 E3 **Bogoroditsk** Rus. Fed.
150 B2 **Bogotá** Col.
83 G3 **Bogotol** Rus. Fed.
Bogoyavlenskoye Rus. Fed. *see* Pervomayskiy
83 H3 **Boguchany** Rus. Fed.
91 E2 **Boguchar** Rus. Fed.
114 A3 **Bogué** Maur.

70 B2 **Bo Hai** *g.* China
100 A3 **Bohain-en-Vermandois** France
70 B2 **Bohai Wan** *b.* China
Bohemian Forest *mts* Ger. *see* Böhmer Wald
123 C2 **Bohlokong** S. Africa
101 F3 **Böhmer Wald** *mts* Ger.
91 D1 **Bohodukhiv** Ukr.
64 B3 **Bohol** *i.* Phil.
64 B3 **Bohol Sea** Phil.
77 E2 **Bohu** China
155 C2 **Boi, Ponta do** *pt* Brazil
123 C2 **Boikhutso** S. Africa
154 B3 **Boi Preto, Serra de** *hills* Brazil
154 B1 **Bois** *r.* Brazil
126 D2 **Bois, Lac des** *l.* Can.
134 C2 **Boise** U.S.A.
139 C1 **Boise City** U.S.A.
129 D3 **Boissevain** Can.
123 C2 **Boitumelong** S. Africa
154 C2 **Boituva** Brazil
101 E1 **Boizenburg** Ger.
76 B3 **Bojnūrd** Iran
75 C2 **Bokaro** India
118 B3 **Bokatola** Dem. Rep. Congo
114 A3 **Boké** Guinea
118 C3 **Bokele** Dem. Rep. Congo
93 E4 **Boknafjorden** *sea chan.* Norway
115 D3 **Bokoro** Chad
63 A2 **Bokpyin** Myanmar
89 D2 **Boksitogorsk** Rus. Fed.
122 B2 **Bokspits** S. Africa
118 C3 **Bokungu** Dem. Rep. Congo
115 D3 **Bol** Chad
114 A3 **Bolama** Guinea-Bissau
104 C2 **Bolbec** France
77 E2 **Bole** China
118 B3 **Boleko** Dem. Rep. Congo
114 B3 **Bolgatanga** Ghana
90 B2 **Bolhrad** Ukr.
66 B1 **Boli** China
118 B3 **Bolia** Dem. Rep. Congo
92 H3 **Boliden** Sweden
110 C2 **Bolintin-Vale** Romania
137 E3 **Bolivar** *MO* U.S.A.
142 C1 **Bolivar** *TN* U.S.A.
150 B2 **Bolívar, Pico** *mt.* Venez.
152 B1 **Bolivia** *country* S. America
89 E3 **Bolkhov** Rus. Fed.
105 C3 **Bollène** France
93 G3 **Bollnäs** Sweden
53 C1 **Bollon** Austr.
101 E2 **Bollstedt** Ger.
93 F4 **Bolmen** *l.* Sweden
118 B3 **Bolobo** Dem. Rep. Congo
108 B2 **Bologna** Italy
89 D2 **Bologovo** Rus. Fed.
89 D2 **Bologoye** Rus. Fed.
123 C2 **Bolokanang** S. Africa
118 B2 **Bolomba** Dem. Rep. Congo
63 B2 **Bolovens, Phouphieng** *plat.* Laos
108 B2 **Bolsena, Lago di** *l.* Italy
83 H1 **Bol'shevik, Ostrov** *i.* Rus. Fed.
86 E2 **Bol'shezemel'skaya Tundra** *lowland* Rus. Fed.
83 L2 **Bol'shoy Aluy** *r.* Rus. Fed.
66 B2 **Bol'shoy Kamen'** Rus. Fed.
Bol'shoy Kavkaz *mts* Asia/Europe *see* Caucasus
83 K2 **Bol'shoy Lyakhovskiy, Ostrov** *i.* Rus. Fed.
Bol'shoy Tokmak Kyrg. *see* Tokmak
Bol'shoy Tokmak Ukr. *see* Tokmak
100 B1 **Bolsward** Neth.
98 B1 **Bolton** U.K.
80 B1 **Bolu** Turkey
59 E3 **Bolubolu** P.N.G.
92 □A2 **Bolungarvík** Iceland
108 B1 **Bolzano** Italy
118 B3 **Boma** Dem. Rep. Congo
53 D2 **Bomaderry** Austr.
53 C3 **Bombala** Austr.
Bombay India *see* Mumbai
155 C1 **Bom Despacho** Brazil
75 C2 **Bomdila** India
154 B1 **Bom Jardim de Goiás** Brazil
151 E4 **Bom Jesus da Lapa** Brazil
155 D2 **Bom Jesus do Itabapoana** Brazil

115 D1 Bon, Cap c. Tunisia
147 D3 Bonaire i. Neth. Antilles
134 C1 Bonaparte, Mount U.S.A.
50 B1 Bonaparte Archipelago is Austr.
131 B1 Bonavista Can.
131 E3 Bonavista Bay Can.
118 C2 Bondo Dem. Rep. Congo
114 B4 Bondoukou Côte d'Ivoire
  Bône Alg. see Annaba
61 D2 Bonerate, Kepulauan is Indon.
155 C1 Bonfinópolis de Minas Brazil
117 B4 Bonga Eth.
75 D2 Bongaigaon India
118 C2 Bongandanga Dem. Rep. Congo
122 B2 Bongani S. Africa
118 C2 Bongo, Massif des mts C.A.R.
121 □D2 Bongolava mts Madag.
115 D3 Bongor Chad
114 B4 Bongouanou Côte d'Ivoire
63 B2 Bông Son Vietnam
139 D2 Bonham U.S.A.
105 D3 Bonifacio Corsica France
108 A2 Bonifacio, Strait of France/Italy
  Bonin Islands Japan see Ogasawara-shotō
100 C2 Bonn Ger.
134 C1 Bonners Ferry U.S.A.
105 D2 Bonneville France
50 A3 Bonnie Rock Austr.
129 C2 Bonnyville Can.
108 A2 Bonorva Sardinia Italy
53 D1 Bonshaw Austr.
61 C1 Bontang Indon.
114 A4 Bonthe Sierra Leone
64 B2 Bontoc Phil.
61 C2 Bontosunggu Indon.
123 C3 Bontrug S. Africa
53 C1 Boolba Austr.
52 B2 Booligal Austr.
53 C1 Boomi Austr.
53 D1 Boonah Austr.
137 E2 Boone U.S.A.
142 C2 Booneville U.S.A.
137 E3 Booneville U.S.A.
52 B2 Booroorban Austr.
53 C2 Boorowa Austr.
117 C3 Boosaaso Somalia
126 G2 Boothia, Gulf of Can.
126 F2 Boothia Peninsula Can.
118 B3 Booué Gabon
100 C2 Boppard Ger.
117 B4 Bor Sudan
80 B2 Bor Turkey
109 D2 Bor Yugo.
93 F4 Borås Sweden
81 D3 Borāzjān Iran
150 D3 Borba Brazil
104 B3 Bordeaux France
126 E1 Borden Island Can.
127 G2 Borden Peninsula Can.
52 B3 Bordertown Austr.
107 D2 Bordj Bou Arréridj Alg.
107 D2 Bordj Bounaama Alg.
114 B2 Bordj Flye Ste-Marie Alg.
115 C1 Bordj Messaouda Alg.
114 C2 Bordj Mokhtar Alg.
  Bordj Omar Driss Alg. see Bordj Omer Driss
115 C2 Bordj Omer Driss Alg.
94 B1 Borðoy i. Faroe Is
94 B1 Borðoy i. Faroe Is
  Borgå Fin. see Porvoo
92 □A3 Borgarnes Iceland
139 C1 Borger U.S.A.
93 G4 Borgholm Sweden
100 B2 Borgloon Belgium
108 A1 Borgosesia Italy
87 D1 Borisoglebsk Rus. Fed.
89 E2 Borisoglebskiy Rus. Fed.
91 D1 Borisovka Rus. Fed.
119 C2 Bo River Post Sudan
100 C2 Borken Ger.
92 G2 Borkenes Norway
100 C1 Borkum Ger.
100 C1 Borkum i. Ger.
93 G3 Borlänge Sweden
101 F2 Borne Neth.
100 C1 Borne Neth.
61 C1 Borneo i. Asia
93 F4 Bornholm i. Denmark
111 C3 Bornova Turkey
90 B1 Borodyanka Ukr.
77 E2 Borohoro Shan mts China
114 B3 Boron Mali
89 D2 Borovichi Rus. Fed.

89 E2 Borovsk Rus. Fed.
76 C1 Borovskoy Kazakh.
51 C1 Borroloola Austr.
110 B1 Borşa Romania
90 B2 Borshchiv Ukr.
69 D1 Borshchovochnyy Khrebet mts Rus. Fed.
101 E1 Börßum Ger.
  Bortala China see Bole
81 C2 Borüjerd Iran
90 A2 Boryslav Ukr.
90 C1 Boryspil' Ukr.
91 C1 Borzna Ukr.
69 D1 Borzya Rus. Fed.
109 C1 Bosanska Dubica Bos.-Herz.
109 C1 Bosanska Gradiška Bos.-Herz.
109 C2 Bosanska Krupa Bos.-Herz.
109 C1 Bosanski Novi Bos.-Herz.
109 C2 Bosansko Grahovo Bos.-Herz.
71 A3 Bose China
123 C2 Boshof S. Africa
109 C2 Bosnia-Herzegovina country Europe
118 B2 Bosobolo Dem. Rep. Congo
111 C2 Bosporus str. Turkey
138 B2 Bosque U.S.A.
118 B2 Bossangoa C.A.R.
118 B2 Bossembélé C.A.R.
142 B2 Bossier City U.S.A.
122 A2 Bossiesvlei Namibia
68 B2 Bosten Hu l. China
99 C3 Boston U.K.
141 E2 Boston U.S.A.
142 B1 Boston Mountains U.S.A.
53 D2 Botany Bay Austr.
120 B3 Boteti r. Botswana
110 B2 Botev mt. Bulg.
80 A1 Botevgrad Bulg.
92 G3 Bothnia, Gulf of Fin./Sweden
110 C1 Botoşani Romania
70 B2 Botou China
123 C2 Botshabelo S. Africa
120 B3 Botswana country Africa
109 C3 Botte Donato, Monte mt. Italy
136 C1 Bottineau U.S.A.
100 C2 Bottrop Ger.
154 C2 Botucatu Brazil
114 B4 Bouaké Côte d'Ivoire
118 B2 Bouar C.A.R.
114 B1 Bouârfa Morocco
131 D3 Bouctouche Can.
107 E2 Bougaa Alg.
48 G4 Bougainville Island P.N.G.
  Bougie Alg. see Bejaïa
114 B3 Bougouni Mali
100 B3 Bouillon Belgium
107 D2 Bouira Alg.
114 A2 Boujdour Western Sahara
50 B3 Boulder Austr.
136 B2 Boulder CO U.S.A.
134 D1 Boulder MT U.S.A.
135 D3 Boulder City U.S.A.
  Boulhaut Morocco see Ben Slimane
51 C2 Boulia Austr.
104 C2 Boulogne-Billancourt France
104 C1 Boulogne-sur-Mer France
118 C2 Boulouba C.A.R.
118 B3 Boumango Gabon
118 B2 Boumba r. Cameroon
107 D2 Boumerdes Alg.
114 B4 Bouna Côte d'Ivoire
114 B4 Boundiali Côte d'Ivoire
134 D2 Bountiful U.S.A.
49 I8 Bounty Islands N.Z.
114 B3 Bourem Mali
104 C2 Bourganeuf France
105 D2 Bourg-en-Bresse France
104 C2 Bourges France
105 D2 Bourgogne reg. France
105 D2 Bourgoin-Jallieu France
53 C2 Bourke Austr.
99 C3 Bourne U.K.
99 C4 Bournemouth U.K.
118 C1 Bourtoutou Chad
115 C1 Bou Saâda Alg.
53 D2 Bousso Chad
104 A2 Boussu Belgium
128 C3 Bow r. Can.
  Bowa China see Muli
51 D2 Bowen Austr.
53 C3 Bowen, Mount Austr.

129 C3 Bow Island Can.
140 B3 Bowling Green KY U.S.A.
137 E3 Bowling Green MO U.S.A.
140 C2 Bowling Green OH U.S.A.
136 C1 Bowman U.S.A.
53 D2 Bowral Austr.
101 D3 Boxberg Ger.
100 B2 Boxtel Neth.
80 B1 Boyabat Turkey
71 B3 Boyang China
97 B2 Boyle Rep. of Ireland
97 C2 Boyne r. Rep. of Ireland
136 B2 Boysen Reservoir U.S.A.
152 B2 Boyuibe Bol.
111 C3 Bozburun Turkey
111 C3 Bozcaada i. Turkey
111 C3 Bozdağ mt. Turkey
111 C3 Boz Dağları mts Turkey
111 C3 Bozdoğan Turkey
134 D1 Bozeman U.S.A.
118 B2 Bozoum C.A.R.
111 D3 Bozüyük Turkey
109 C2 Brač i. Croatia
130 C3 Bracebridge Can.
131 D3 Brachet, Lac au l. Can.
93 G3 Bräcke Sweden
99 C4 Bracknell U.K.
109 C2 Bradano r. Italy
143 D3 Bradenton U.S.A.
98 C3 Bradford U.K.
141 D2 Bradford U.S.A.
139 D2 Brady U.S.A.
96 C2 Braemar U.K.
106 B1 Braga Port.
151 E3 Bragança Brazil
106 B1 Bragança Port.
155 C2 Bragança Paulista Brazil
89 D3 Brahin Belarus
75 D2 Brahmanbaria Bangl.
75 C3 Brahmapur India
62 A1 Brahmaputra r. China/India
53 C3 Braidwood Austr.
110 C1 Brăila Romania
137 E1 Brainerd U.S.A.
99 D4 Braintree U.K.
100 B2 Braives Belgium
101 D1 Brake (Unterweser) Ger.
122 A1 Brakwater Namibia
98 B2 Brampton U.K.
101 D1 Bramsche Ger.
150 C3 Branco r. Brazil
101 F1 Brandenburg Ger.
129 E3 Brandon Can.
142 C2 Brandon U.S.A.
97 A2 Brandon Mountain hill Rep. of Ireland
122 B3 Brandvlei S. Africa
103 D1 Braniewo Pol.
130 B3 Brantford Can.
53 D2 Branxton Austr.
131 D3 Bras d'Or Lake Can.
155 D1 Brasil, Planalto do plat. Brazil
154 C1 Brasilândia Brazil
154 C1 Brasília Brazil
155 D1 Brasília de Minas Brazil
88 C2 Braslaw Belarus
110 C1 Braşov Romania
103 D2 Bratislava Slovakia
83 H3 Bratsk Rus. Fed.
102 C2 Braunau am Inn Austria
101 E1 Braunschweig Ger.
92 □A2 Brautarholt Iceland
  Bravo del Norte, Río r. Mex./U.S.A. see Rio Grande
135 C4 Brawley U.S.A.
97 C2 Bray Rep. of Ireland
150 D2 Brazil country S. America
158 E6 Brazil Basin sea feature S. Atlantic Ocean
139 D3 Brazos r. U.S.A.
118 B3 Brazzaville Congo
109 C2 Brčko Bos.-Herz.
96 C2 Brechin U.K.
100 B2 Brecht Belgium
139 D2 Breckenridge U.S.A.
103 D2 Břeclav Czech Rep.
99 B4 Brecon U.K.
99 B4 Brecon Beacons reg. U.K.
100 B2 Breda Neth.
122 B3 Bredasdorp S. Africa
102 B2 Bregenz Austria
92 H1 Breivikbotn Norway
92 E3 Brekstad Norway
101 D1 Bremen Ger.
100 D1 Bremerhaven Ger.
  Bremersdorp Swaziland see Manzini
134 B1 Bremerton U.S.A.

101 D1 Bremervörde Ger.
139 D2 Brenham U.S.A.
108 B1 Brennero Italy
102 C2 Brenner Pass Austria/Italy
99 D4 Brentwood U.K.
108 B1 Brescia Italy
100 A2 Breskens Neth.
108 B1 Bressanone Italy
96 □ Bressay i. U.K.
104 B2 Bressuire France
88 B3 Brest Belarus
104 B2 Brest France
  Brest-Litovsk Belarus see Brest
104 B2 Bretagne reg. France
142 C3 Breton Sound b. U.S.A.
151 D3 Breves Brazil
53 C1 Brewarrina Austr.
134 C1 Brewster U.S.A.
89 E2 Breytovo Rus. Fed.
  Brezhnev Rus. Fed. see Naberezhnyye Chelny
109 C1 Brezovo Polje hill Croatia
118 C2 Bria C.A.R.
105 D3 Briançon France
90 B2 Briceni Moldova
  Brichany Moldova see Briceni
99 B4 Bridgend U.K.
141 E2 Bridgeport CT U.S.A.
136 C2 Bridgeport NE U.S.A.
147 E3 Bridgetown Barbados
131 D3 Bridgewater Can.
99 B3 Bridgnorth U.K.
99 B4 Bridgwater U.K.
99 B4 Bridgwater Bay U.K.
98 C2 Bridlington U.K.
98 C2 Bridlington Bay U.K.
99 B4 Bridport U.K.
105 D2 Brig Switz.
134 D2 Brigham City U.S.A.
53 C3 Bright Austr.
54 B3 Brighton N.Z.
99 C4 Brighton U.K.
136 C3 Brighton CO U.S.A.
140 C2 Brighton MI U.S.A.
105 D3 Brignoles France
114 A3 Brikama Gambia
101 D2 Brilon Ger.
109 C2 Brindisi Italy
97 B1 Brinlack Rep. of Ireland
53 D1 Brisbane Austr.
99 B4 Bristol U.K.
141 E2 Bristol CT U.S.A.
143 D1 Bristol TN U.S.A.
99 A4 Bristol Channel est. U.K.
128 B2 British Columbia prov. Can.
  British Guiana country S. America see Guyana
  British Honduras country Central America see Belize
56 C6 British Indian Ocean Territory terr. Indian Ocean
  British Solomon Islands country S. Pacific Ocean see Solomon Islands
123 C2 Brits S. Africa
122 B3 Britstown S. Africa
  Brittany reg. France see Bretagne
104 C2 Brive-la-Gaillarde France
106 C1 Briviesca Spain
99 B4 Brixham U.K.
103 D2 Brno Czech Rep.
  Broach India see Bharuch
143 D2 Broad r. Can.
130 C2 Broadback r. Can.
96 A1 Broad Bay U.K.
53 C3 Broadford Austr.
96 B2 Broadford U.K.
96 C3 Broad Law hill U.K.
136 B1 Broadus U.S.A.
129 D2 Brochet Can.
129 D2 Brochet, Lac l. Can.
101 E1 Bröckel Ger.
101 E2 Brocken mt. Ger.
126 E1 Brock Island Can.
130 C3 Brockville Can.
127 G2 Brodeur Peninsula Can.
96 B3 Brodick U.K.
103 D1 Brodnica Pol.
90 B1 Brody Ukr.
139 D1 Broken Arrow U.S.A.
137 D2 Broken Bow U.S.A.
52 B2 Broken Hill Austr.
  Broken Hill Zambia see Kabwe
159 F6 Broken Plateau sea feature Indian Ocean
151 D2 Brokopondo Suriname

99 B3 Bromsgrove U.K.
93 E4 Brønderslev Denmark
123 C2 Bronkhorstspruit S. Africa
92 F2 Brønnøysund Norway
64 A3 Brooke's Point Phil.
142 B2 Brookhaven U.S.A.
134 B2 Brookings *OR* U.S.A.
137 D2 Brookings *SD* U.S.A.
128 C2 Brooks Can.
126 C2 Brooks Range *mts* U.S.A.
143 D3 Brooksville U.S.A.
141 D2 Brookville U.S.A.
96 B2 Broom, Loch *inlet* U.K.
50 B1 Broome Austr.
134 B2 Brothers U.S.A.
Broughton Island Can.
see Qikiqtarjuaq
90 C1 Brovary Ukr.
139 C2 Brownfield U.S.A.
128 C3 Browning U.S.A.
142 C1 Brownsville *TN* U.S.A.
139 D3 Brownsville *TX* U.S.A.
139 D2 Brownwood U.S.A.
92 ▢A2 Brú Iceland
104 C1 Bruay-la-Bussière France
140 B1 Bruce Crossing U.S.A.
130 B3 Bruce Peninsula Can.
103 D2 Bruck an der Mur Austria
100 A2 Bruges Belgium
Brugge Belgium *see*
Bruges
62 A1 Bruint India
128 C2 Brûlé Can.
151 E4 Brumado Brazil
93 F3 Brumunddal Norway
61 C1 Brunei *country* Asia
Brunei Brunei *see*
Bandar Seri Begawan
102 C2 Brunico Italy
Brünn Czech Rep. *see*
Brno
101 D1 Brunsbüttel Ger.
143 D2 Brunswick *GA* U.S.A.
141 F2 Brunswick *ME* U.S.A.
53 D1 Brunswick Head Austr.
123 D2 Bruntville S. Africa
136 C2 Brush U.S.A.
100 B2 Brussels Belgium
Bruxelles Belgium *see*
Brussels
139 D2 Bryan U.S.A.
89 D3 Bryansk Rus. Fed.
91 D2 Bryn'kovskaya Rus. Fed.
91 D2 Bryukhovetskaya Rus. Fed.
103 D1 Brzeg Pol.
Brześć nad Bugiem
Belarus *see* Brest
114 A3 Buba Guinea-Bissau
111 C3 Buca Turkey
80 B2 Bucak Turkey
150 B2 Bucaramanga Col.
90 B2 Buchach Ukr.
53 C3 Buchan Austr.
114 A4 Buchanan Liberia
110 C2 Bucharest Romania
101 D1 Bucholz in der Nordheide Ger.
110 C1 Bucin, Pasul *pass* Romania
101 D1 Bückeburg Ger.
138 A2 Buckeye U.S.A.
96 C2 Buckhaven U.K.
96 C2 Buckie U.K.
99 C3 Buckingham U.K.
51 C1 Buckingham Bay Austr.
51 D2 Buckland Tableland *reg.* Austr.
52 A2 Buckleboo Austr.
141 F2 Bucksport U.S.A.
103 D2 Bučovice Czech Rep.
București Romania *see* Bucharest
89 D3 Buda-Kashalyova Belarus
103 D2 Budapest Hungary
75 B2 Budaun India
108 A2 Buddusò *Sardinia* Italy
99 A4 Bude U.K.
87 D4 Budennovsk Rus. Fed.
Budennoye Rus. Fed. *see*
Krasnogvardeyskoye
89 D2 Budogoshch' Rus. Fed.
108 A2 Budoni *Sardinia* Italy
Budweis Czech Rep. *see*
České Budějovice
118 A2 Buea Cameroon
135 B4 Buellton U.S.A.
150 B2 Buenaventura Col.
144 B2 Buenaventura Mex.
Buena Vista *i.*
N. Mariana Is *see* Tinian

106 C1 Buendia, Embalse de *resr* Spain
155 D1 Buenópolis Brazil
153 C3 Buenos Aires Arg.
153 A4 Buenos Aires, Lago *l.* Arg./Chile
141 D2 Buffalo *NY* U.S.A.
136 C1 Buffalo *SD* U.S.A.
139 D2 Buffalo *TX* U.S.A.
136 B2 Buffalo *WY* U.S.A.
129 D2 Buffalo Narrows Can.
121 C3 Buffalo Range Zimbabwe
122 A2 Buffels *watercourse* S. Africa
123 C1 Buffels Drift S. Africa
110 C2 Buftea Romania
103 E1 Bug *r.* Pol.
61 C2 Bugel, Tanjung *pt* Indon.
109 C2 Bugojno Bos.-Herz.
86 D2 Bugrino Rus. Fed.
64 A3 Bugsuk *i.* Phil.
87 E3 Bugul'ma Rus. Fed.
87 E3 Buguruslan Rus. Fed.
121 C2 Buhera Zimbabwe
110 C1 Buhuşi Romania
99 B3 Builth Wells U.K.
69 D1 Buir Nur *l.* Mongolia
120 A3 Buitepos Namibia
109 D2 Bujanovac Yugo.
119 C3 Bujumbura Burundi
69 D1 Bukachacha Rus. Fed.
120 B2 Bukalo Namibia
119 C3 Bukavu Dem. Rep. Congo
76 C3 Bukhara Uzbek.
60 B2 Bukittinggi Indon.
119 D3 Bukoba Tanz.
103 D1 Bukowiec *hill* Pol.
59 C3 Bula Indon.
53 D2 Bulahdelal Austr.
121 B3 Bulawayo Zimbabwe
111 C3 Buldan Turkey
123 D2 Bulembu Swaziland
68 C1 Bulgan Mongolia
110 C2 Bulgaria *country* Europe
54 B2 Buller *r.* N.Z.
138 A1 Bullhead City U.S.A.
52 B1 Bulloo *watercourse* Austr.
52 B1 Bulloo Downs Austr.
122 A1 Büllsport Namibia
61 C2 Bulukumba Indon.
118 B3 Bulungu Dem. Rep. Congo
118 B3 Bumba Dem. Rep. Congo
118 C2 Bumba Dem. Rep. Congo
62 A1 Bumhkang Myanmar
118 B3 Buna Dem. Rep. Congo
97 B1 Bunbeg Rep. of Ireland
50 A3 Bunbury Austr.
97 C2 Bunclody Rep. of Ireland
97 C1 Buncrana Rep. of Ireland
119 D3 Bunda Tanz.
51 E2 Bundaberg Austr.
53 C1 Bundaleer Austr.
53 D2 Bundarra Austr.
74 B2 Bundi India
97 B1 Bundoran Rep. of Ireland
75 C2 Bundu India
53 C3 Bungendore Austr.
119 D2 Bungoma Kenya
67 B4 Bungo-suidō *sea chan.* Japan
119 D2 Bunia Dem. Rep. Congo
118 C3 Bunianga Dem. Rep. Congo
63 B2 Buôn Mê Thuột Vietnam
119 D3 Bura Kenya
117 C3 Buraan Somalia
75 C1 Burang China
117 C4 Burao Somalia
78 B2 Buraydah Saudi Arabia
101 D2 Burbach Ger.
111 D3 Burdur Turkey
Burdwan India *see*
Barddhaman
117 B3 Burē Eth.
99 D3 Bure *r.* U.K.
69 E1 Bureinskiy Khrebet *mts* Rus. Fed.
101 D2 Büren Ger.
Bureya Range *mts*
Rus. Fed. *see*
Bureinskiy Khrebet
110 C2 Burgas Bulg.
101 E1 Burg bei Magdeburg Ger.
101 E1 Burgdorf Ger.
101 E1 Burgdorf Ger.
131 E2 Burgeo Can.
123 C3 Burgersdorp S. Africa
123 D1 Burgersfort S. Africa
100 A2 Burgh-Haamstede Neth.
101 F3 Burglengenfeld Ger.
145 C2 Burgos Mex.

106 C1 Burgos Spain
Burgundy *reg.* France *see*
Bourgogne
111 C3 Burhaniye Turkey
74 B2 Burhanpur India
75 C2 Burhar-Dhanpuri India
101 D1 Burhave (Butjadingen) Ger.
154 C2 Buri Brazil
60 B2 Buriai Indon.
64 B2 Burias *i.* Phil.
131 E3 Burin Can.
63 B2 Buriram Thai.
154 C1 Buriti Alegre Brazil
151 E3 Buriti Bravo Brazil
155 C1 Buritis Brazil
107 C2 Burjassot Spain
139 D2 Burkburnett U.S.A.
51 C1 Burketown Austr.
114 B3 Burkina *country* Africa
134 D2 Burley U.S.A.
136 C3 Burlington *CO* U.S.A.
137 E2 Burlington *IA* U.S.A.
143 E1 Burlington *NC* U.S.A.
141 E2 Burlington *VT* U.S.A.
134 B2 Burney U.S.A.
51 D4 Burnie Austr.
98 B3 Burnley U.K.
134 C2 Burns U.S.A.
134 C2 Burns Junction U.S.A.
128 B2 Burns Lake Can.
137 E2 Burnsville U.S.A.
101 F1 Burow Ger.
77 E2 Burqin China
52 A2 Burra Austr.
109 D2 Burrel Albania
97 B2 Burren *reg.* Rep. of Ireland
53 C2 Burrendong Reservoir Austr.
53 C2 Burren Junction Austr.
107 C2 Burriana Spain
53 C2 Burrinjuck Reservoir Austr.
144 B2 Burro, Serranías del *mts* Mex.
111 C2 Bursa Turkey
116 B2 Bûr Safâga Egypt
Bûr Sa'îd Egypt *see*
Port Said
Bûr Sudan Sudan *see*
Port Sudan
130 C2 Burton, Lac *l.* Can.
97 B1 Burtonport Rep. of Ireland
99 C3 Burton upon Trent U.K.
52 B2 Burtundy Austr.
59 C3 Buru *i.* Indon.
119 D3 Burundi *country* Africa
119 C3 Bururi Burundi
96 C1 Burwick U.K.
98 B3 Bury U.K.
91 C1 Buryn' Ukr.
76 B2 Burynshyk Kazakh.
99 D3 Bury St Edmunds U.K.
118 C3 Busanga Dem. Rep. Congo
81 D3 Büshehr Iran
119 D3 Bushenyi Uganda
Bushire Iran *see* Büshehr
118 C2 Businga Dem. Rep. Congo
50 A3 Busselton Austr.
139 C3 Bustamante Mex.
108 A1 Busto Arsizio Italy
64 A2 Busuanga Phil.
118 C2 Buta Dem. Rep. Congo
119 C3 Butare Rwanda
96 B3 Bute *i.* U.K.
119 C2 Butembo Dem. Rep. Congo
123 C2 Butha Buthe Lesotho
141 D2 Butler U.S.A.
61 D2 Buton *i.* Indon.
134 D1 Butte U.S.A.
60 B1 Butterworth Malaysia
96 A1 Butt of Lewis *hd* U.K.
129 E2 Button Bay Can.
131 D1 Button Islands Can.
64 B3 Butuan Phil.
89 F3 Buturlinovka Rus. Fed.
75 C2 Butwal Nepal
101 D2 Butzbach Ger.
117 C4 Buulobarde Somalia
117 C5 Buur Gaabo Somalia
117 C4 Buurhabaka Somalia
78 A2 Buwāţah Saudi Arabia
101 D1 Buxtehude Ger.
98 C3 Buxton U.K.
89 F2 Buy Rus. Fed.
87 D4 Buynaksk Rus. Fed.
111 C3 Büyükmenderes *r.* Turkey
65 A1 Buyun Shan *mt.* China
74 B1 Buzai Gumbad Afgh.

110 C1 Buzău Romania
110 C1 Buzău *r.* Romania
121 C2 Búzi Moz.
87 E3 Buzuluk Rus. Fed.
88 C3 Byahoml' Belarus
110 C2 Byala Bulg.
110 C2 Byala Bulg.
88 C3 Byalynichy Belarus
88 D3 Byarezina *r.* Belarus
88 B3 Byaroza Belarus
88 C3 Byarozawka Belarus
103 D1 Bydgoszcz Pol.
Byelorussia *country*
Europe *see* Belarus
88 C3 Byerazino Belarus
88 C2 Byeshankovichy Belarus
89 D3 Bykhaw Belarus
127 G2 Bylot Island Can.
53 C2 Byrock Austr.
53 D1 Byron Bay Austr.
83 J2 Bytantay *r.* Rus. Fed.
103 D1 Bytom Pol.
103 D1 Bytów Pol.

C

120 A2 Caála Angola
154 B2 Caarapó Brazil
155 C1 Caatinga Brazil
106 B1 Cabañaquinta Spain
64 B2 Cabanatuan Phil.
117 C3 Cabdul Qaadir Somalia
154 A1 Cabeceira Rio Manso Brazil
154 C1 Cabeceiras Brazil
106 B2 Cabeza del Buey Spain
152 B1 Cabezas Bol.
150 B1 Cabimas Venez.
120 A1 Cabinda Angola
118 B3 Cabinda *prov.* Angola
151 F3 Cabo Brazil
155 D2 Cabo Frio Brazil
155 D2 Cabo Frio, Ilha do *i.* Brazil
130 C3 Cabonga, Réservoir *resr* Can.
53 D1 Caboolture Austr.
150 B3 Cabo Pantoja Peru
Cabora Bassa, Lake *resr*
Moz. *see*
Cahora Bassa, Lago de
144 A1 Caborca Mex.
131 D3 Cabot Strait Can.
106 C2 Cabra Spain
155 D1 Cabral, Serra do *mts* Brazil
107 D2 Cabrera *i.* Spain
129 D2 Cabri Can.
107 C2 Cabriel *r.* Spain
154 B3 Caçador Brazil
109 D2 Čačak Yugo.
108 A2 Caccia, Capo *c.* Sardinia Italy
151 D4 Cacém Port.
151 D4 Cáceres Brazil
106 B2 Cáceres Spain
128 B2 Cache Creek Can.
114 A3 Cacheu Guinea-Bissau
151 D3 Cachimbo, Serra do *hills* Brazil
154 B1 Cachoeira Alta Brazil
155 D2 Cachoeiro de Itapemirim Brazil
114 A3 Cacine Guinea-Bissau
120 A2 Cacolo Angola
120 A2 Caconda Angola
154 B1 Caçu Brazil
103 D2 Čadca Slovakia
101 D1 Cadenberge Ger.
145 B2 Cadereyta Mex.
140 B2 Cadillac U.S.A.
64 B2 Cadiz Phil.
106 B2 Cádiz Spain
106 B2 Cádiz, Golfo de *g.* Spain
128 C2 Cadotte Lake Can.
104 B2 Caen France
98 A3 Caernarfon U.K.
99 A3 Caernarfon Bay U.K.
Caernarvon U.K. *see*
Caernarfon
152 B2 Cafayate Arg.
154 C2 Cafelândia Brazil
64 B2 Cagayan de Oro Phil.
108 B2 Cagli Italy
108 A3 Cagliari *Sardinia* Italy

108 A3 **Cagliari, Golfo di** b. *Sardinia* Italy
120 A2 **Cahama** Angola
97 B3 **Caha Mountains** hills Rep. of Ireland
97 A3 **Cahermore** Rep. of Ireland
97 A3 **Cahersiveen** Rep. of Ireland
97 C2 **Cahir** Rep. of Ireland
121 C2 **Cahora Bassa, Lago de** resr Moz.
97 C2 **Cahore Point** Rep. of Ireland
104 C3 **Cahors** France
90 B2 **Cahul** Moldova
121 C2 **Caia** Moz.
151 D4 **Caiabis, Serra dos** hills Brazil
120 B2 **Caianda** Angola
154 B1 **Caiapó, Serra do** mts Brazil
154 B1 **Caiapônia** Brazil
147 C2 **Caicos Islands** Turks and Caicos Is
96 C2 **Cairngorm Mountains** U.K.
96 B3 **Cairnryan** U.K.
51 D1 **Cairns** Austr.
116 B1 **Cairo** Egypt
Caisleán an Bharraigh Rep. of Ireland see Castlebar
98 C3 **Caistor** U.K.
120 A2 **Caiundo** Angola
150 B3 **Cajamarca** Peru
109 C1 **Čakovec** Croatia
123 C3 **Cala** S. Africa
115 C4 **Calabar** Nigeria
150 C2 **Calabozo** Venez.
110 B2 **Calafat** Romania
153 A5 **Calafate** Arg.
107 C1 **Calahorra** Spain
120 A2 **Calai** Angola
104 C1 **Calais** France
141 F1 **Calais** U.S.A.
152 B2 **Calama** Chile
64 A2 **Calamian Group** is Phil.
107 C1 **Calamocha** Spain
120 A1 **Calandula** Angola
60 A1 **Calang** Indon.
115 E1 **Calanscio Sand Sea** des. Libya
64 B2 **Calapan** Phil.
110 C2 **Călărași** Romania
107 C1 **Calatayud** Spain
64 B2 **Calauan** i. Phil.
64 B2 **Calbayog** Phil.
151 F3 **Calcanhar, Ponta do** pt Brazil
151 D2 **Calçoene** Brazil
75 C2 **Calcutta** India
106 B2 **Caldas da Rainha** Port.
154 C1 **Caldas Novas** Brazil
152 A2 **Caldera** Chile
51 D2 **Caldervale** Austr.
134 C2 **Caldwell** U.S.A.
123 C3 **Caledon** r. Lesotho/S. Africa
122 A3 **Caledon** S. Africa
153 B4 **Caleta Olivia** Arg.
98 A2 **Calf of Man** i. Isle of Man
128 C2 **Calgary** Can.
150 B2 **Cali** Col.
73 B3 **Calicut** India
135 D3 **Caliente** U.S.A.
135 B2 **California** state U.S.A.
144 A1 **California, Golfo de** g. Mex.
135 B3 **California Aqueduct** canal U.S.A.
81 C2 **Cälilabad** Azer.
122 B3 **Calitzdorp** S. Africa
145 C2 **Calkini** Mex.
52 B1 **Callabonna, Lake** salt flat Austr.
135 C3 **Callaghan, Mount** U.S.A.
97 C2 **Callan** Rep. of Ireland
96 B2 **Callander** U.K.
150 B4 **Callao** Peru
99 A4 **Callington** U.K.
108 B3 **Caltagirone** Sicily Italy
108 B3 **Caltanissetta** Sicily Italy
120 A1 **Calulo** Angola
120 B2 **Calunda** Angola
120 A2 **Caluquembe** Angola
117 D3 **Caluula** Somalia
105 D3 **Calvi** Corsica France
107 D2 **Calvià** Spain
144 B2 **Calvillo** Mex.
122 A3 **Calvinia** S. Africa
109 C2 **Calvo, Monte** mt. Italy

120 A1 **Camabatela** Angola
151 F4 **Camaçari** Brazil
144 B2 **Camacho** Mex.
120 A2 **Camacupa** Angola
146 C2 **Camagüey** Cuba
146 C2 **Camagüey, Archipiélago de** is Cuba
150 B4 **Camana** Peru
120 B2 **Camanongue** Angola
154 B1 **Camapuã** Brazil
145 C2 **Camargo** Mex.
63 B3 **Ca Mau** Vietnam
Cambay India see Khambhat
63 B2 **Cambodia** country Asia
99 A4 **Camborne** U.K.
105 C1 **Cambrai** France
99 B3 **Cambrian Mountains** hills U.K.
140 C2 **Cambridge** Can.
54 C1 **Cambridge** N.Z.
99 D3 **Cambridge** U.K.
141 E2 **Cambridge** MA U.S.A.
141 D3 **Cambridge** MD U.S.A.
137 E1 **Cambridge** MN U.S.A.
140 C2 **Cambridge** OH U.S.A.
126 E2 **Cambridge Bay** Can.
131 D2 **Cambrien, Lac** l. Can.
120 B1 **Cambulo** Angola
53 D2 **Camden** Austr.
142 B2 **Camden** AR U.S.A.
141 F2 **Camden** ME U.S.A.
141 D3 **Camden** NJ U.S.A.
137 E3 **Camdenton** U.S.A.
137 E3 **Cameron** U.S.A.
118 B2 **Cameroon** country Africa
118 A2 **Cameroun, Mont** vol. Cameroon
151 E3 **Cametá** Brazil
64 B3 **Camiguin** i. Phil.
64 B2 **Camiguin** i. Phil.
152 B2 **Camiri** Bol.
151 E3 **Camocim** Brazil
51 C1 **Camooweal** Austr.
63 A3 **Camorta** i. India
153 A4 **Campana, Isla** i. Chile
155 D1 **Campanário** Brazil
155 C2 **Campanha** Brazil
122 B2 **Campbell** S. Africa
64 B2 **Campbell, Cape** N.Z.
54 B2 **Campbell Island** N.Z.
156 D9 **Campbell Plateau** sea feature S. Pacific Ocean
128 B2 **Campbell River** Can.
140 B3 **Campbellsville** U.S.A.
131 D3 **Campbellton** Can.
53 D2 **Campbelltown** Austr.
96 B3 **Campbeltown** U.K.
145 C3 **Campeche** Mex.
145 C3 **Campeche, Bahía de** g. Mex.
52 B3 **Camperdown** Austr.
110 C1 **Câmpina** Romania
151 F3 **Campina Grande** Brazil
154 C2 **Campinas** Brazil
154 C1 **Campina Verde** Brazil
108 B2 **Campobasso** Italy
155 C2 **Campo Belo** Brazil
154 C1 **Campo Florido** Brazil
152 B3 **Campo Gallo** Arg.
154 B2 **Campo Grande** Brazil
151 E3 **Campo Maior** Brazil
106 B2 **Campo Maior** Port.
109 C2 **Campomarino** Italy
154 B2 **Campo Mourão** Brazil
155 D2 **Campos** Brazil
155 C1 **Campos Altos** Brazil
155 C2 **Campos do Jordão** Brazil
110 C1 **Câmpulung** Romania
138 A2 **Camp Verde** U.S.A.
63 B2 **Cam Ranh** Vietnam
63 B2 **Cam Ranh, Vinh** b. Vietnam
Cam Ranh Bay Vietnam see Cam Ranh, Vinh
128 C2 **Camrose** Can.
129 D2 **Camsell Portage** Can.
111 C2 **Çan** Turkey
126 G3 **Canada** country N. America
160 A2 **Canada Basin** sea feature Arctic Ocean
139 C1 **Canadian** U.S.A.
139 D1 **Canadian** r. U.S.A.
111 C2 **Çanakkale** Turkey
144 A1 **Cananea** Mex.
114 C2 **Cananéia** Brazil
114 A2 **Canary Islands** terr. N. Atlantic Ocean

155 C1 **Canastra, Serra da** mts Brazil
154 B1 **Canastra, Serra da** mts Brazil
144 B2 **Canatlán** Mex.
113 D3 **Canaveral, Cape** U.S.A.
155 E1 **Canavieiras** Brazil
53 C2 **Canbelego** Austr.
53 C3 **Canberra** Austr.
145 D2 **Cancún** Mex.
111 C3 **Çandarlı** Turkey
155 C2 **Candeias** Brazil
145 C3 **Candelaria** Mex.
154 B2 **Cândido de Abreu** Brazil
129 D2 **Candle Lake** Can.
137 D1 **Cando** U.S.A.
120 A2 **Cangamba** Angola
106 B1 **Cangas** Spain
106 B1 **Cangas del Narcea** Spain
120 B2 **Cangombe** Angola
152 C3 **Canguçu** Brazil
70 B2 **Cangzhou** China
131 D2 **Caniapiscau** Can.
131 D2 **Caniapiscau** r. Can.
131 C2 **Caniapiscau, Lac** l. Can.
Caniçado Moz. see Guija
108 B3 **Canicattì** Sicily Italy
151 F3 **Canindé** Brazil
144 B2 **Cañitas de Felipe Pescador** Mex.
80 B1 **Çankırı** Turkey
128 C2 **Canmore** Can.
96 A2 **Canna** i. U.K.
73 B3 **Cannanore** India
105 D3 **Cannes** France
99 B3 **Cannock** U.K.
53 C3 **Cann River** Austr.
152 C2 **Canoas** Brazil
129 D2 **Canoe Lake** Can.
154 B3 **Canoinhas** Brazil
136 B3 **Canon City** U.S.A.
52 B2 **Canopus** Austr.
129 D2 **Canora** Can.
53 C2 **Canowindra** Austr.
131 D3 **Canso** Can.
Cantabrian Mountains Spain see Cantábrica, Cordillera
106 B1 **Cantabrian Sea** Spain
106 C1 **Cantábrica, Cordillera** mts Spain
Cantábrico, Mar sea Spain see Cantabrian Sea
99 D4 **Canterbury** U.K.
54 B2 **Canterbury Bight** b. N.Z.
54 B2 **Canterbury Plains** N.Z.
63 B2 **Cân Tho** Vietnam
151 E3 **Canto do Buriti** Brazil
Canton China see Guangzhou
137 E2 **Canton** MO U.S.A.
142 C2 **Canton** MS U.S.A.
141 D2 **Canton** NY U.S.A.
140 C2 **Canton** OH U.S.A.
139 C1 **Canyon** U.S.A.
134 D1 **Canyon Ferry Lake** U.S.A.
134 B2 **Canyonville** U.S.A.
62 B1 **Cao Bằng** Vietnam
109 C2 **Capaccio** Italy
154 C2 **Capão Bonito** Brazil
155 D2 **Caparaó, Serra do** mts Brazil
141 E1 **Cap-de-la-Madeleine** Can.
51 D4 **Cape Barren Island** Austr.
158 F7 **Cape Basin** sea feature S. Atlantic Ocean
52 A3 **Cape Borda** Austr.
131 D3 **Cape Breton Island** Can.
143 D3 **Cape Canaveral** U.S.A.
141 D3 **Cape Charles** U.S.A.
114 B4 **Cape Coast** Ghana
141 E2 **Cape Cod Bay** U.S.A.
143 D3 **Cape Coral** U.S.A.
127 G2 **Cape Dorset** Can.
143 E2 **Cape Fear** r. U.S.A.
137 F3 **Cape Girardeau** U.S.A.
155 D1 **Capelinha** Brazil
100 B2 **Capelle aan de IJssel** Neth.
Capelongo Angola see Kuvango
141 E3 **Cape May Point** U.S.A.
120 A1 **Capenda-Camulemba** Angola
122 A3 **Cape Town** S. Africa
158 E3 **Cape Verde** country N. Atlantic Ocean
158 D4 **Cape Verde Basin** sea feature N. Atlantic Ocean

51 D1 **Cape York Peninsula** Austr.
147 C3 **Cap-Haïtien** Haiti
151 E3 **Capim** r. Brazil
154 A2 **Capitán Bado** Para.
154 B2 **Capivara, Represa** resr Brazil
109 C2 **Čapljina** Bos.-Herz.
109 B3 **Capo d'Orlando** Sicily Italy
108 A2 **Capraia, Isola di** i. Italy
108 A2 **Caprara, Punta** pt Sardinia Italy
108 B2 **Capri, Isola di** i. Italy
51 E2 **Capricorn Channel** Austr.
120 B2 **Caprivi Strip** reg. Namibia
139 C2 **Cap Rock Escarpment** U.S.A.
139 C1 **Caqulin** U.S.A.
150 C3 **Caquetá** r. Col.
110 B2 **Caracal** Romania
150 C2 **Caracaraí** Brazil
150 C1 **Caracas** Venez.
151 E3 **Caracol** Brazil
155 C2 **Caraguatatuba** Brazil
153 A3 **Carahue** Chile
155 D1 **Caraí** Brazil
151 D3 **Carajás, Serra dos** hills Brazil
155 D2 **Carandaí** Brazil
155 D2 **Carangola** Brazil
110 B1 **Caransebeş** Romania
131 D3 **Caraquet** Can.
146 B3 **Caratasca, Laguna** lag. Hond.
155 D1 **Caratinga** Brazil
150 C3 **Carauari** Brazil
107 C2 **Caravaca de la Cruz** Spain
155 E1 **Caravelas** Brazil
129 E3 **Carberry** Can.
144 A2 **Carbó** Mex.
108 A3 **Carbonara, Capo** c. Sardinia Italy
136 B3 **Carbondale** CO U.S.A.
140 B3 **Carbondale** IL U.S.A.
141 D2 **Carbondale** PA U.S.A.
131 E3 **Carbonear** Can.
155 D1 **Carbonita** Brazil
107 C2 **Carcaixent** Spain
104 C3 **Carcassonne** France
128 A1 **Carcross** Can.
146 B2 **Cárdenas** Cuba
145 C3 **Cárdenas** Mex.
99 B4 **Cardiff** U.K.
99 A3 **Cardigan** U.K.
99 A3 **Cardigan Bay** U.K.
154 C2 **Cardoso** Brazil
128 C3 **Cardston** Can.
110 B1 **Carei** Romania
104 B2 **Carentan** France
50 B2 **Carey, Lake** salt flat Austr.
155 D2 **Cariacica** Brazil
146 B3 **Caribbean Sea** N. Atlantic Ocean
128 B2 **Cariboo Mountains** Can.
141 F1 **Caribou** U.S.A.
130 B2 **Caribou Lake** Can.
128 C2 **Caribou Mountains** Can.
144 B2 **Carichic** Mex.
100 B3 **Carignan** France
53 C2 **Carinda** Austr.
107 C1 **Cariñena** Spain
130 C3 **Carleton Place** Can.
123 C2 **Carletonville** S. Africa
135 C2 **Carlin** U.S.A.
97 C1 **Carlingford Lough** inlet Rep. of Ireland/U.K.
140 B3 **Carlinville** U.S.A.
98 B2 **Carlisle** U.K.
141 D2 **Carlisle** U.S.A.
155 D1 **Carlos Chagas** Brazil
97 C2 **Carlow** Rep. of Ireland
96 A1 **Carloway** U.K.
135 C4 **Carlsbad** CA U.S.A.
138 C2 **Carlsbad** NM U.S.A.
129 D3 **Carlyle** Can.
128 A1 **Carmacks** Can.
129 E3 **Carman** Can.
99 A4 **Carmarthen** U.K.
99 A4 **Carmarthen Bay** U.K.
104 C3 **Carmaux** France
145 C3 **Carmelita** Guat.
144 A2 **Carmen, Isla** i. Mex.
155 C1 **Carmo do Paranaíba** Brazil
Carmona Angola see Uige
106 B2 **Carmona** Spain
104 B2 **Carnac** France
50 A2 **Carnarvon** Austr.
122 B3 **Carnarvon** S. Africa

97 C1	Carndonagh
	Rep. of Ireland
129 D3	Carnduff Can.
50 B2	Carnegie, Lake *salt flat*
	Austr.
96 B2	Carn Eighe *mt.* U.K.
55 P2	Carney Island Antarctica
73 D4	Car Nicobar *i.* India
118 B2	Carnot C.A.R.
52 A2	Carnot, Cape Austr.
96 C2	Carnoustie U.K.
97 C2	Carnsore Point
	Rep. of Ireland
151 E3	Carolina Brazil
49 L4	Caroline Island Kiribati
59 D2	Caroline Islands
	N. Pacific Ocean
122 A2	Carolusberg S. Africa
103 D2	Carpathian Mountains
	Europe
110 B1	Carpaţii Meridionali *mts*
	Romania
51 C1	Carpentaria, Gulf of
	Austr.
105 D3	Carpentras France
108 B2	Carpi Italy
143 D3	Carrabelle U.S.A.
97 B3	Carrantuohill *mt.*
	Rep. of Ireland
108 B2	Carrara Italy
97 D1	Carrickfergus U.K.
97 C2	Carrickmacross
	Rep. of Ireland
97 B2	Carrick-on-Shannon
	Rep. of Ireland
97 C2	Carrick-on-Suir
	Rep. of Ireland
137 D1	Carrington U.S.A.
139 D3	Carrizo Springs U.S.A.
138 B2	Carrizozo U.S.A.
137 E2	Carroll U.S.A.
143 C2	Carrollton U.S.A.
129 D2	Carrot River Can.
135 C3	Carson City U.S.A.
135 C3	Carson Sink *l.* U.S.A.
	Carstensz-top *mt.* Indon.
	see Jaya, Puncak
150 B1	Cartagena Col.
107 C2	Cartagena Spain
146 B4	Cartago Costa Rica
54 C2	Carterton N.Z.
137 E3	Carthage *MO* U.S.A.
139 E2	Carthage *TX* U.S.A.
131 E2	Cartwright Can.
151 F3	Caruarú Brazil
150 C1	Carúpano Venez.
52 B1	Caryapundy Swamp
	Austr.
114 B1	Casablanca Morocco
154 C2	Casa Branca Brazil
144 B1	Casa de Janos Mex.
138 A2	Casa Grande U.S.A.
108 A1	Casale Monferrato Italy
109 C2	Casarano Italy
144 B1	Casas Grandes Mex.
134 C2	Cascade U.S.A.
134 B2	Cascade Range *mts*
	Can./U.S.A.
106 B2	Cascais Port.
151 F3	Cascavel Brazil
154 B2	Cascavel Brazil
141 F2	Casco Bay U.S.A.
108 B2	Caserta Italy
117 D3	Caseyr, Raas *c.* Somalia
97 C2	Cashel Rep. of Ireland
153 B3	Casilda Arg.
53 D1	Casino Austr.
	Casnewydd U.K. *see*
	Newport
107 C1	Caspe Spain
136 B2	Casper U.S.A.
	Caspian Lowland
	Kazakh./Rus. Fed. *see*
	Prikaspiyskaya
	Nizmennost'
81 C1	Caspian Sea Asia/Europe
	Cassaigne Alg. *see* Sidi Ali
154 C2	Cássia Brazil
128 B2	Cassiar Can.
128 A2	Cassiar Mountains Can.
154 B1	Cassilândia Brazil
120 A2	Cassinga Angola
108 B2	Cassino Italy
96 B2	Cassley *r.* U.K.
151 E3	Castanhal Brazil
152 B3	Castaño *r.* Arg.
144 B2	Castaños Mex.
104 C3	Casteljaloux France
105 D3	Castellane France
107 C2	Castelló de la Plana
	Spain

155 D2	Castelo Brazil
106 B2	Castelo Branco Port.
104 C3	Castelsarrasin France
108 B3	Castelvetrano *Sicily* Italy
52 B3	Casterton Austr.
108 B2	Castiglione della Pescaia
	Italy
106 C2	Castilla - La Mancha
	aut. comm. Spain
106 C1	Castilla y León
	aut. comm. Spain
97 B2	Castlebar Rep. of Ireland
96 A2	Castlebay U.K.
97 C1	Castleblayney
	Rep. of Ireland
97 C1	Castlederg U.K.
96 C3	Castle Douglas U.K.
128 C3	Castlegar Can.
97 B2	Castleisland
	Rep. of Ireland
52 B3	Castlemaine Austr.
97 C2	Castlepollard
	Rep. of Ireland
97 B2	Castlerea Rep. of Ireland
53 C2	Castlereagh *r.* Austr.
136 C3	Castle Rock U.S.A.
128 C2	Castor Can.
104 C3	Castres France
100 B1	Castricum Neth.
147 D3	Castries St Lucia
154 C2	Castro Brazil
153 A4	Castro Chile
106 B2	Castro Verde Port.
109 C3	Castrovillari Italy
150 A3	Catacaos Peru
155 D2	Cataguases Brazil
154 C1	Catalão Brazil
	Catalonia *aut. comm.*
	Spain *see* Cataluña
107 D1	Cataluña *aut. comm.*
	Spain
152 B2	Catamarca Arg.
64 B2	Catanduanes *i.* Phil.
154 C2	Catanduva Brazil
154 B3	Catanduvas Brazil
109 C3	Catania *Sicily* Italy
109 C3	Catanzaro Italy
64 B2	Catarman Phil.
107 C2	Catarroja Spain
64 B2	Catbalogan Phil.
145 C3	Catemaco Mex.
119 B2	Catete Angola
147 C2	Cat Island Bahamas
130 A2	Cat Lake Can.
145 D2	Catoche, Cabo *c.* Mex.
141 E2	Catskill Mountains U.S.A.
123 D2	Catuane Moz.
64 B3	Cauayan Phil.
131 D2	Caubvick, Mount Can.
150 B2	Cauca *r.* Col.
151 F3	Caucaia Brazil
81 C1	Caucasus *mts*
	Asia/Europe
100 A2	Caudry France
109 C3	Caulonia Italy
120 A1	Caungula Angola
150 C2	Caura *r.* Venez.
131 D3	Causapscal Can.
90 B2	Căuşeni Moldova
105 D3	Cavaillon France
151 E4	Cavalcante Brazil
114 B4	Cavally *r.* Côte d'Ivoire
97 C2	Cavan Rep. of Ireland
154 B3	Cavernoso, Serra do *mts*
	Brazil
151 D2	Caviana, Ilha *i.* Brazil
	Cawnpore India *see*
	Kanpur
151 E3	Caxias Brazil
152 C2	Caxias do Sul Brazil
120 A1	Caxito Angola
151 D2	Cayenne Fr. Guiana
146 B3	Cayman Islands *terr.*
	West Indies
158 C3	Cayman Trench
	sea feature Caribbean Sea
117 C4	Caynabo Somalia
120 B2	Cazombo Angola

51 C3	Ceduna Austr.
117 C4	Ceelbuur Somalia
117 C3	Ceeldheere Somalia
117 C3	Ceerigaabo Somalia
108 B3	Cefalù *Sicily* Italy
145 B2	Celaya Mex.
	Celebes *i.* Indon. *see*
	Sulawesi
156 C5	Celebes Sea Indon./Phil.
145 C2	Celestún Mex.
101 E1	Celle Ger.
95 B3	Celtic Sea
	Rep. of Ireland/U.K.
59 D3	Cenderawasih, Teluk *b.*
	Indon.
142 C2	Center Point U.S.A.
150 B2	Central, Cordillera *mts*
	Col.
150 B4	Central, Cordillera *mts*
	Peru
64 B2	Central, Cordillera *mts*
	Phil.
	Central African Empire
	country Africa *see*
	Central African Republic
118 C2	Central African Republic
	country Africa
74 A2	Central Brahui Range
	mts Pak.
137 D2	Central City U.S.A.
140 B3	Centralia *IL* U.S.A.
134 B1	Centralia *WA* U.S.A.
74 A2	Central Makran Range
	mts Pak.
156 D5	Central Pacific Basin
	sea feature Pacific Ocean
134 B2	Central Point U.S.A.
	Central Provinces *state*
	India *see* Madhya Pradesh
59 D3	Central Range *mts* P.N.G.
	Central Russian Upland
	hills Rus. Fed. *see* Sredne-
	Russkaya Vozvyshennost'
	Central Siberian Plateau
	Rus. Fed. *see* Sredne-
	Sibirskoye Ploskogor'ye
142 C2	Century U.S.A.
	Ceos *i.* Greece *see* Kea
111 B3	Cephalonia *i.* Greece
	Ceram *i.* Indon. *see*
	Seram
	Ceram Sea Indon. *see*
	Seram Sea
101 F3	Čerchov *mt.* Czech Rep.
152 B2	Ceres Arg.
154 C1	Ceres Brazil
122 A3	Ceres S. Africa
105 C3	Céret France
106 C1	Cerezo de Abajo Spain
109 C2	Cerignola Italy
	Cerigo *i.* Greece *see*
	Kythira
110 C2	Cernavodă Romania
145 C2	Cerralvo Mex.
144 B2	Cerralvo, Isla *i.* Mex.
145 B2	Cerritos Mex.
154 C2	Cerro Azul Brazil
145 C2	Cerro Azul Mex.
150 B4	Cerro de Pasco Peru
105 D3	Cervione *Corsica* France
106 B1	Cervo Spain
108 B2	Cesena Italy
108 B2	Cesenatico Italy
88 C2	Cēsis Latvia
102 C2	České Budějovice
	Czech Rep.
101 F3	Český Les *mts*
	Czech Rep./Ger.
111 C3	Çeşme Turkey
53 D2	Cessnock Austr.
104 B2	Cesson-Sévigné France
104 B3	Cestas France
109 C2	Cetinje Yugo.
109 C3	Cetraro Italy
106 B2	Ceuta N. Africa
105 C3	Cévennes *mts* France
	Ceylon *country* Asia *see*
	Sri Lanka
79 D2	Chābahār Iran
75 C1	Chabyêr Caka *salt l.* China
150 B3	Chachapoyas Peru
89 D3	Chachersk Belarus
63 B2	Chachoengsao Thai.
152 C2	Chaco Boreal *reg.* Para.
138 B1	Chaco Mesa *plat.* U.S.A.
115 D3	Chad *country* Africa
115 D3	Chad, Lake Africa
68 C1	Chadaasan Mongolia
68 C1	Chadan Rus. Fed.
123 C1	Chadibe Botswana
153 B3	Chadileo *r.* Arg.
136 C2	Chadron U.S.A.

	Chadyr-Lunga Moldova
	see Ciadâr-Lunga
77 D2	Chaek Kyrg.
65 B2	Chaeryŏng N. Korea
74 A2	Chagai Pak.
77 C3	Chaghcharān Afgh.
89 E2	Chagoda Rus. Fed.
56 I10	Chagos Archipelago *is*
	B.I.O.T.
159 E4	Chagos-Laccadive Ridge
	sea feature Indian Ocean
159 E4	Chagos Trench
	sea feature Indian Ocean
76 B2	Chagyl Turkm.
75 C2	Chaibāsa India
63 B2	Chainat Thai.
63 A3	Chaiya Thai.
63 B2	Chaiyaphum Thai.
152 C3	Chajari Arg.
119 D3	Chake Chake Tanz.
131 D2	Chakonipau, Lake Can.
150 B4	Chala Peru
74 A1	Chalap Dalan *mts* Afgh.
121 C2	Chaláua Moz.
131 D3	Chaleur Bay *inlet* Can.
74 B2	Chalisgaon India
111 C3	Chalki *i.* Greece
111 B3	Chalkida Greece
139 C3	Chalk Mountains U.S.A.
104 B2	Challans France
134 D2	Challis U.S.A.
105 C2	Châlons-en-Champagne
	France
	Châlons-sur-Marne
	France *see* Châlons-en-
	Champagne
105 C2	Chalon-sur-Saône
	France
101 F3	Cham Ger.
138 B1	Chama U.S.A.
121 C2	Chama Zambia
74 A1	Chaman Pak.
74 B1	Chamba India
74 B1	Chambal *r.* India
137 D2	Chamberlain U.S.A.
138 B1	Chambers U.S.A.
141 D3	Chambersburg U.S.A.
105 D2	Chambéry France
121 C2	Chambeshi Zambia
121 B2	Chambeshi *r.* Zambia
	Chamdo China *see* Qamdo
119 D2	Ch'amo Häyk' *l.* Eth.
105 D2	Chamonix-Mont-Blanc
	France
140 B2	Champaign U.S.A.
141 E2	Champlain, Lake
	Can./U.S.A.
145 C3	Champotón Mex.
	Chanak Turkey *see*
	Çanakkale
152 A2	Chañaral Chile
	Chanda India *see*
	Chandrapur
126 C2	Chandalar *r.* U.S.A.
142 C3	Chandeleur Islands
	U.S.A.
74 B1	Chandigarh India
131 D3	Chandler Can.
138 A2	Chandler U.S.A.
75 C2	Chandpur Bangl.
75 B3	Chandrapur India
63 B2	Chang, Ko *i.* Thai.
	Chang'an China *see*
	Rong'an
121 C3	Changane *r.* Moz.
121 C2	Changara Moz.
65 B1	Changbai China
	Changbai Shan *mt.*
	China/N. Korea *see*
	Paekdu-san
65 B1	Changbai Shan *mts*
	China/N. Korea
	Changchow China *see*
	Zhangzhou
	Changchow China *see*
	Changzhou
69 E2	Changchun China
71 B3	Changde China
65 B2	Ch'angdo N. Korea
70 B2	Changge China
71 C3	Changhua Taiwan
65 B3	Changhŭng S. Korea
	Chang Jiang *r.* China *see*
	Yangtze
	Changjiang Kou *r. mouth*
	China *see*
	Yangtze, Mouth of the
65 B1	Changjin China
65 B1	Changjin-gang *r.*
	N. Korea

Changkiang China *see* Zhanjiang
Changning China *see* Xunwu
Ch'ang-pai Shan *mts* China/N. Korea *see* Changbai Shan
71 B3 **Changsha** China
70 C3 **Changshu** China
65 B2 **Changsŏng** S. Korea
Changteh China *see* Changde
71 B3 **Changting** *Fujian* China
66 A2 **Changting** *Heilong.* China
65 A1 **Changtu** China
146 B4 **Changuinola** Panama
65 B2 **Ch'angwŏn** S. Korea
65 B2 **Changyŏn** N. Korea
70 B2 **Changyuan** China
70 B2 **Changzhi** China
70 B2 **Changzhou** China
111 B3 **Chania** Greece
95 C4 **Channel Islands** Europe
135 C4 **Channel Islands** U.S.A.
131 E3 **Channel-Port-aux-Basques** Can.
106 B1 **Chantada** Spain
63 B2 **Chanthaburi** Thai.
104 C2 **Chantilly** France
137 D3 **Chanute** U.S.A.
82 G3 **Chany, Ozero** *salt l.* Rus. Fed.
70 B2 **Chaohu** China
71 B3 **Chaoyang** *Guangdong* China
Chaoyang China *see* Huinan
70 C1 **Chaoyang** *Liaoning* China
71 B3 **Chaozhou** China
144 B2 **Chapala, Laguna de** *l.* Mex.
76 B1 **Chapayevo** Kazakh.
87 D3 **Chapayevsk** Rus. Fed.
152 C2 **Chapecó** Brazil
143 E1 **Chapel Hill** U.S.A.
130 B3 **Chapleau** Can.
89 E3 **Chaplygin** Rus. Fed.
91 C2 **Chaplynka** Ukr.
Chapra India *see* Chhapra
145 B2 **Charcas** Mex.
99 B4 **Chard** U.K.
76 C3 **Chardzhev** Turkm.
Chardzhou Turkm. *see* Chardzhev
104 B2 **Charente** *r.* France
118 B1 **Chari** *r.* Cameroon/Chad
77 C3 **Chārīkār** Afgh.
86 E2 **Charkayuvom** Rus. Fed.
Charkhlik China *see* Ruoqiang
100 B2 **Charleroi** Belgium
141 D3 **Charles, Cape** U.S.A.
141 E1 **Charlesbourg** Can.
137 E2 **Charles City** U.S.A.
140 B3 **Charleston** *IL* U.S.A.
137 F3 **Charleston** *MO* U.S.A.
143 E2 **Charleston** *SC* U.S.A.
140 C3 **Charleston** *WV* U.S.A.
135 C3 **Charleston Peak** U.S.A.
51 D2 **Charleville** Austr.
105 C2 **Charleville-Mézières** France
140 B1 **Charlevoix** U.S.A.
143 D1 **Charlotte** U.S.A.
143 D3 **Charlotte Harbor** *b.* U.S.A.
141 D3 **Charlottesville** U.S.A.
131 D3 **Charlottetown** Can.
52 B3 **Charlton** Austr.
130 C2 **Charlton Island** Can.
51 D2 **Charters Towers** Austr.
104 C2 **Chartres** France
128 C2 **Chase** Can.
88 C3 **Chashniki** Belarus
54 A3 **Chaslands Mistake** *c.* N.Z.
65 B2 **Chasŏng** N. Korea
104 B2 **Chassiron, Pointe de** *pt* France
104 C2 **Châteaubriant** France
104 C2 **Château-du-Loir** France
104 C2 **Châteaudun** France
104 B2 **Château-Gontier** France
104 B2 **Châteaulin** France
105 D3 **Châteauneuf-les-Martigues** France
104 C2 **Châteauneuf-sur-Loire** France
104 C2 **Châteauroux** France
105 C2 **Château-Thierry** France
128 C2 **Chateh** Can.
100 B2 **Châtelet** Belgium

104 C2 **Châtellerault** France
131 D3 **Chatham** *N.B.* Can.
140 C2 **Chatham** *Ont.* Can.
99 D4 **Chatham** U.K.
49 J8 **Chatham Islands** N.Z.
105 C2 **Châtillon-sur-Seine** France
143 D2 **Chattahoochee** *r.* U.S.A.
143 C1 **Chattanooga** U.S.A.
63 B2 **Châu Đốc** Vietnam
62 A1 **Chauk** Myanmar
104 C2 **Chaumont** France
105 C2 **Chauny** France
Chau Phu Vietnam *see* Châu Đốc
151 E3 **Chaves** Brazil
106 B1 **Chaves** Port.
130 C2 **Chavigny, Lac** *l.* Can.
89 D3 **Chavusy** Belarus
89 E2 **Chayevo** Rus. Fed.
86 E3 **Chaykovskiy** Rus. Fed.
142 C2 **Cheaha Mountain** *hill* U.S.A.
102 C1 **Cheb** Czech Rep.
87 D3 **Cheboksary** Rus. Fed.
140 C1 **Cheboygan** U.S.A.
65 B2 **Chech'ŏn** S. Korea
142 A1 **Checotah** U.S.A.
62 A2 **Cheduba Island** Myanmar
Chefoo China *see* Yantai
126 B2 **Chefornak** U.S.A.
114 B2 **Chegga** Maur.
121 C2 **Chegutu** Zimbabwe
134 B1 **Chehalis** U.S.A.
65 B3 **Cheju** S. Korea
65 B3 **Cheju-do** *i.* S. Korea
65 B3 **Cheju-haehyŏp** *sea chan.* S. Korea
89 E2 **Chekhov** Rus. Fed.
Chekiang *prov.* China *see* Zhejiang
134 B1 **Chelan, Lake** U.S.A.
81 D2 **Cheleken** Turkm.
107 D2 **Chélif, Oued** *r.* Alg.
76 B2 **Chelkar** Kazakh.
103 E1 **Chełm** Pol.
99 D4 **Chelmer** *r.* U.K.
103 D1 **Chełmno** Pol.
99 D4 **Chelmsford** U.K.
99 B4 **Cheltenham** U.K.
87 F3 **Chelyabinsk** Rus. Fed.
83 H1 **Chelyuskin** Rus. Fed.
101 F2 **Chemnitz** Ger.
Chemulpo S. Korea *see* Inch'ŏn
134 B2 **Chemult** U.S.A.
74 B2 **Chenab** *r.* India/Pak.
114 B2 **Chenachane** Alg.
134 C1 **Cheney** U.S.A.
Chengchow China *see* Zhengzhou
70 B1 **Chengde** China
70 A2 **Chengdu** China
Chengjiang China *see* Taihe
71 B4 **Chengmai** China
Chengshou China *see* Yingshan
Chengtu China *see* Chengdu
70 A2 **Chengxian** China
Chengxiang China *see* Wuxi
Chengxiang China *see* Mianning
Chengyang China *see* Juxian
73 C3 **Chennai** India
Chenstokhov Pol. *see* Częstochowa
71 B3 **Chenzhou** China
99 B4 **Chepstow** U.K.
143 E2 **Cheraw** U.S.A.
104 B2 **Cherbourg** France
Cherchen China *see* Qiemo
89 E3 **Cheremisinovo** Rus. Fed.
68 C1 **Cheremkhovo** Rus. Fed.
89 E2 **Cherepovets** Rus. Fed.
91 C1 **Cherkasy** Ukr.
87 D4 **Cherkessk** Rus. Fed.
89 E3 **Chern'** Rus. Fed.
91 C1 **Chernihiv** Ukr.
91 D2 **Chernivtsi** Ukr.
68 C1 **Chernogorsk** Rus. Fed.
90 B1 **Chernyakhiv** Ukr.
88 B3 **Chernyakhovsk** Rus. Fed.
89 E3 **Chernyanka** Rus. Fed.
69 D1 **Chernyshevsk** Rus. Fed.
83 I2 **Chernyshevskiy** Rus. Fed.

Chernyy Rynok Rus. Fed. *see* Kochubey
137 D2 **Cherokee** U.S.A.
83 L2 **Cherskiy** Rus. Fed.
83 K2 **Cherskogo, Khrebet** *mts* Rus. Fed.
91 E2 **Chertkovo** Rus. Fed.
Chervonoarmeyskoye Ukr. *see* Vil'nyans'k
Chervonoarmiys'k Ukr. *see* Krasnoarmiys'k
Chervonoarmiys'k Ukr. *see* Radyvyliv
90 A1 **Chervonohrad** Ukr.
88 C3 **Chervyen'** Belarus
89 D3 **Cherykaw** Belarus
141 D3 **Chesapeake Bay** U.S.A.
86 D2 **Cheshskaya Guba** *b.* Rus. Fed.
98 B3 **Chester** U.K.
140 B3 **Chester** *IL* U.S.A.
143 D2 **Chester** *SC* U.S.A.
141 D3 **Chester** *VA* U.S.A.
98 C3 **Chesterfield** U.K.
137 E3 **Chesterfield** U.S.A.
129 E1 **Chesterfield Inlet** Can.
129 E1 **Chesterfield Inlet** *inlet* Can.
141 F1 **Chesuncook Lake** U.S.A.
108 A3 **Chetaïbi** Alg.
131 D3 **Chéticamp** Can.
145 D3 **Chetumal** Mex.
128 B2 **Chetwynd** Can.
98 B2 **Cheviot Hills** U.K.
119 D2 **Che'w Bahir** *salt l.* Eth.
136 C2 **Cheyenne** U.S.A.
136 C2 **Cheyenne** *r.* U.S.A.
136 C3 **Cheyenne Wells** U.S.A.
75 C2 **Chhapra** India
75 B2 **Chhatarpur** India
74 B2 **Chhindwara** India
75 C2 **Chhukha** Bhutan
71 C3 **Chiai** Taiwan
62 A2 **Chiang Dao** Thai.
120 A2 **Chiange** Angola
62 A2 **Chiang Mai** Thai.
62 A2 **Chiang Rai** Thai.
145 C3 **Chiapa** Mex.
108 A1 **Chiavenno** Italy
69 F2 **Chiba** Japan
Chibizovka Rus. Fed. *see* Zherdevka
121 C3 **Chiboma** Moz.
130 C3 **Chibougamau** Can.
123 D1 **Chibuto** Moz.
75 D1 **Chibuzhang Hu** *l.* China
140 B2 **Chicago** U.S.A.
128 A2 **Chichagof Island** U.S.A.
99 C4 **Chichester** U.K.
50 A2 **Chichester Range** *mts* Austr.
139 D1 **Chickasha** U.S.A.
106 B2 **Chiclana de la Frontera** Spain
150 B3 **Chiclayo** Peru
153 B4 **Chico** *r.* Arg.
153 B4 **Chico** *r.* Arg.
135 B3 **Chico** U.S.A.
141 E2 **Chicopee** U.S.A.
64 B2 **Chico Sapocoy, Mount** Phil.
131 C3 **Chicoutimi** Can.
131 D1 **Chidley, Cape** Can.
63 A3 **Chieo Lan Reservoir** Thai.
108 B2 **Chieti** Italy
70 B1 **Chifeng** China
155 D1 **Chifre, Serra do** *mts* Brazil
121 C2 **Chifunde** Moz.
77 D2 **Chiganak** Kazakh.
145 C3 **Chignahuapán** Mex.
121 C3 **Chigubo** Moz.
62 A1 **Chigu Co** *l.* China
144 B2 **Chihuahua** Mex.
77 C2 **Chiili** Kazakh.
88 C2 **Chikhachevo** Rus. Fed.
67 C3 **Chikuma-gawa** *r.* Japan
128 B2 **Chilanko** *r.* Can.
74 B1 **Chilas** Jammu and Kashmir
139 C2 **Childress** U.S.A.
153 A3 **Chile** *country* S. America
158 C6 **Chile Basin** *sea feature* S. Pacific Ocean
152 B2 **Chilecito** Arg.
157 G8 **Chile Rise** *sea feature* S. Pacific Ocean
77 D2 **Chilik** Kazakh.
75 C3 **Chilika Lake** India
121 B2 **Chililabombwe** Zambia
128 B2 **Chilko** *r.* Can.

128 B2 **Chilko Lake** Can.
153 A3 **Chillán** Chile
140 B2 **Chillicothe** *IL* U.S.A.
137 E3 **Chillicothe** *MO* U.S.A.
140 C3 **Chillicothe** *OH* U.S.A.
128 B3 **Chilliwack** Can.
150 A4 **Chiloé, Isla de** *i.* Chile
145 C3 **Chilpancingo** Mex.
53 C3 **Chiltern** Austr.
99 C4 **Chiltern Hills** U.K.
120 B1 **Chiluage** Angola
71 C3 **Chilung** Taiwan
119 D3 **Chimala** Tanz.
121 C2 **Chimanimani** Zimbabwe
152 B3 **Chimbas** Arg.
76 B2 **Chimbay** Uzbek.
150 B3 **Chimborazo** *mt.* Ecuador
150 B3 **Chimbote** Peru
Chimishliya Moldova *see* Cimişlia
Chimkent Kazakh. *see* Shymkent
121 C2 **Chimoio** Moz.
77 C3 **Chimtargha, Qullai** *mt.* Tajik.
68 B2 **China** *country* Asia
145 C2 **China** Mex.
77 C2 **Chinaz** Uzbek.
150 B4 **Chincha Alta** Peru
128 C2 **Chinchaga** *r.* Can.
145 D3 **Chinchorro, Banco** *sea feature* Mex.
121 C2 **Chinde** Moz.
65 B3 **Chindo** S. Korea
65 B3 **Chin-do** *i.* S. Korea
68 C2 **Chindu** China
62 A1 **Chindwin** *r.* Myanmar
Chinese Turkestan *aut. reg.* China *see* Xinjiang Uygur Zizhiqu
65 B2 **Chinghwa** N. Korea
121 B2 **Chingola** Zambia
120 A2 **Chinguar** Angola
65 B2 **Chinhae** S. Korea
121 C2 **Chinhoyi** Zimbabwe
Chini India *see* Kalpa
74 B1 **Chiniot** Pak.
144 B2 **Chinipas** Mex.
65 B2 **Chinju** S. Korea
118 C2 **Chinko** *r.* C.A.R.
138 B1 **Chinle** U.S.A.
71 B3 **Chinmen** Taiwan
Chinnamp'o N. Korea *see* Namp'o
67 C3 **Chino** Japan
135 C4 **Chino** U.S.A.
104 C2 **Chinon** France
134 E1 **Chinook** U.S.A.
138 A2 **Chino Valley** U.S.A.
121 C2 **Chinsali** Zambia
108 B1 **Chioggia** Italy
111 C3 **Chios** Greece
111 C3 **Chios** *i.* Greece
121 C2 **Chipata** Zambia
120 A2 **Chipindo** Angola
Chipinga Zimbabwe *see* Chipinge
121 C3 **Chipinge** Zimbabwe
73 B3 **Chiplun** India
99 B4 **Chippenham** U.K.
140 A2 **Chippewa Falls** U.S.A.
99 C4 **Chipping Norton** U.K.
Chipuriro Zimbabwe *see* Guruve
145 D3 **Chiquimula** Guat.
77 C2 **Chirchik** Uzbek.
121 C3 **Chiredzi** Zimbabwe
138 B2 **Chiricahua Peak** U.S.A.
146 B4 **Chiriquí, Golfo de** *b.* Panama
65 B2 **Chiri-san** *mt.* S. Korea
146 B4 **Chirripo** *mt.* Costa Rica
121 B2 **Chirundu** Zimbabwe
130 C2 **Chisasibi** Can.
137 E1 **Chisholm** U.S.A.
Chisimaio Somalia *see* Kismaayo
90 B2 **Chişinau** Moldova
87 E3 **Chistopol'** Rus. Fed.
69 D1 **Chita** Rus. Fed.
120 A2 **Chitado** Angola
Chitaldrug India *see* Chitradurga
121 C2 **Chitambo** Zambia
120 B1 **Chitato** Angola
121 C1 **Chitipa** Malawi
121 C3 **Chitobe** Moz.
66 D2 **Chitose** Japan

73 B3 **Chitradurga** India
74 B1 **Chitral** Pak.
146 B4 **Chitré** Panama
75 D2 **Chittagong** Bangl.
74 B2 **Chittaurgarh** India
73 B3 **Chittoor** India
Chittorgarh India see
Chittaurgarh
121 C2 **Chitungwiza** Zimbabwe
120 B2 **Chiume** Angola
121 C2 **Chivhu** Zimbabwe
Chkalov Rus. Fed. see
Orenburg
101 F2 **Chodov** Czech Rep.
153 B3 **Choele Choel** Arg.
Chogori Feng mt.
China/Jammu and Kashmir
see K2
48 G4 **Choiseul** i. Solomon Is
144 B2 **Choix** Mex.
102 C1 **Chojna** Pol.
103 D1 **Chojnice** Pol.
117 B3 **Ch'ok'ē Mountains** Eth.
Chokue Moz. see Chókwé
83 K2 **Chokurdakh** Rus. Fed.
121 C3 **Chókwé** Moz.
104 B2 **Cholet** France
145 C3 **Cholula** Mex.
120 B2 **Choma** Zambia
Chomo China see Yadong
102 C1 **Chomutov** Czech Rep.
83 I2 **Chona** r. Rus. Fed.
65 B2 **Ch'ŏnan** S. Korea
58 A2 **Chon Buri** Thai.
150 A3 **Chone** Ecuador
Chong'an China see
Wuyishan
65 B1 **Ch'ŏngjin** N. Korea
65 B2 **Ch'ŏngju** N. Korea
65 B2 **Ch'ŏngju** S. Korea
65 B2 **Chŏngp'yŏng** N. Korea
70 A3 **Chongqing** N. Korea
70 A2 **Chongqing** mun. China
65 B2 **Chŏngŭp** S. Korea
121 B2 **Chongwe** Zambia
71 A3 **Chongzuo** China
65 B2 **Chŏnju** S. Korea
154 B3 **Chopimzinho** Brazil
98 B3 **Chorley** U.K.
91 C2 **Chornobay** Ukr.
90 C1 **Chornobyl'** Ukr.
91 C2 **Chornomors'ke** Ukr.
90 B2 **Chortkiv** Ukr.
65 B2 **Ch'ŏrwŏn** S. Korea
65 B1 **Ch'osan** N. Korea
67 D3 **Chōshi** Japan
153 A3 **Chos Malal** Arg.
103 D1 **Choszczno** Pol.
134 D1 **Choteau** U.S.A.
114 A2 **Choûm** Maur.
69 D1 **Choybalsan** Mongolia
69 D1 **Choyr** Mongolia
54 B2 **Christchurch** N.Z.
99 C4 **Christchurch** U.K.
127 H2 **Christian, Cape** Can.
123 C2 **Christiana** S. Africa
Christianshåb
Greenland see
Qasigiannguit
54 C2 **Christina, Mount** N.Z.
58 B3 **Christmas Island** terr.
Indian Ocean
111 C3 **Chrysi** i. Greece
111 B3 **Chrysoupoli** Greece
Chu Kazakh. see Shu
Chubarovka Ukr. see
Polohy
153 B4 **Chubut** r. Arg.
89 F3 **Chuchkovo** Rus. Fed.
90 B1 **Chudniv** Ukr.
89 D2 **Chudovo** Rus. Fed.
126 C2 **Chugach Mountains**
U.S.A.
67 B4 **Chūgoku-sanchi** mts
Japan
Chuguchak China see
Tacheng
66 B2 **Chuguyevka** Rus. Fed.
91 D2 **Chuhuyiv** Ukr.
Chukchi Peninsula
Rus. Fed. see
Chukotskiy Poluostrov
160 J3 **Chukchi Sea** sea
Rus. Fed./U.S.A.
89 F2 **Chukhloma** Rus. Fed.
83 N2 **Chukotskiy Poluostrov**
pen. Rus. Fed.
Chulaktau Kazakh. see
Karatau
135 C4 **Chula Vista** U.S.A.
82 G3 **Chulym** Rus. Fed.

152 B2 **Chumbicha** Arg.
83 K3 **Chumikan** Rus. Fed.
63 A2 **Chumphon** Thai.
65 B2 **Ch'unch'ŏn** S. Korea
Chungking China see
Chongqing
Ch'ungmu S. Korea see
T'ongyŏng
71 C3 **Chungyang Shanmo** mts
Taiwan
83 H2 **Chunya** r. Rus. Fed.
119 D3 **Chunya** Tanz.
150 B4 **Chuquibamba** Peru
152 B2 **Chuquicamata** Chile
105 D2 **Chur** Switz.
62 A1 **Churachandpur** India
83 J2 **Churapcha** Rus. Fed.
129 E2 **Churchill** Can.
129 E2 **Churchill** r. Man. Can.
131 D2 **Churchill** r. Nfld. Can.
129 E2 **Churchill, Cape** Can.
131 D2 **Churchill Falls** Can.
129 D2 **Churchill Lake** Can.
74 B2 **Churu** India
138 B1 **Chuska Mountains** U.S.A.
86 E3 **Chusovoy** Rus. Fed.
131 C3 **Chute-des-Passes** Can.
48 G3 **Chuuk** is Micronesia
62 B1 **Chuxiong** China
63 B2 **Chư Yang Sin** mt. Vietnam
91 C2 **Chyhyryn** Ukr.
Chymyshliya Moldova see
Cimişlia
90 B2 **Ciadâr-Lunga** Moldova
Ciadîr-Lunga Moldova see
Ciadâr-Lunga
60 B2 **Ciamis** Indon.
60 B2 **Cianjur** Indon.
154 B2 **Cianorte** Brazil
138 A2 **Cibuta, Sierra** mt. Mex.
80 B1 **Cide** Turkey
103 E1 **Ciechanów** Pol.
146 C2 **Ciego de Ávila** Cuba
147 C3 **Ciénaga** Col.
146 B2 **Cienfuegos** Cuba
107 C2 **Cieza** Spain
106 C2 **Cigüela** r. Spain
80 B2 **Cihanbeyli** Turkey
144 B3 **Cihuatlán** Mex.
106 C2 **Cijara, Embalse de** resr
Spain
109 C2 **Çikes, Maja e** mt. Albania
60 B2 **Cilacap** Indon.
Cill Airne Rep. of Ireland
see Killarney
Cill Chainnigh
Rep. of Ireland see
Kilkenny
139 C1 **Cimarron** r. U.S.A.
90 B2 **Cimişlia** Moldova
108 B2 **Cimone, Monte** mt. Italy
Cîmpina Romania see
Câmpina
Cîmpulung Romania see
Câmpulung
60 B2 **Cina, Tanjung** c. Indon.
140 C3 **Cincinnati** U.S.A.
Cinco de Outubro Angola
see Xá-Muteba
111 C3 **Çine** Turkey
100 B2 **Ciney** Belgium
134 C2 **Cinnabar Mountain** U.S.A.
145 C3 **Cintalapa** Mex.
Ciping China see
Jinggangshan
153 B3 **Cipolletti** Arg.
126 C2 **Circle** AK U.S.A.
136 B1 **Circle** MT U.S.A.
60 B2 **Cirebon** Indon.
99 C4 **Cirencester** U.K.
108 A1 **Cirié** Italy
109 C3 **Cirò Marina** Italy
110 B1 **Cisnădie** Romania
109 C2 **Čitluk** Bos.-Herz.
122 A3 **Citrusdal** S. Africa
135 B3 **Citrus Heights** U.S.A.
110 C1 **Ciucaş, Vârful** mt.
Romania
145 B2 **Ciudad Acuña** Mex.
145 B3 **Ciudad Altamirano** Mex.
150 C2 **Ciudad Bolívar** Venez.
127 C4 **Ciudad Bolivia** Venez.
144 B2 **Ciudad Camargo** Mex.
145 C3 **Ciudad Cuauhtémoc** Mex.
145 C3 **Ciudad del Carmen** Mex.
152 C3 **Ciudad del Este** Para.
144 B2 **Ciudad Delicias** Mex.
145 C2 **Ciudad de Valles** Mex.
150 C2 **Ciudad Guayana** Venez.
138 B3 **Ciudad Guerrero** Mex.
144 B3 **Ciudad Guzmán** Mex.

145 C3 **Ciudad Hidalgo** Mex.
145 C3 **Ciudad Ixtepec** Mex.
144 B1 **Ciudad Juárez** Mex.
145 C2 **Ciudad Madero** Mex.
145 C2 **Ciudad Mante** Mex.
145 C2 **Ciudad Mier** Mex.
144 B2 **Ciudad Obregón** Mex.
106 C2 **Ciudad Real** Spain
145 C2 **Ciudad Río Bravo** Mex.
106 B1 **Ciudad Rodrigo** Spain
Ciudad Trujillo Dom. Rep.
see Santo Domingo
145 C2 **Ciudad Victoria** Mex.
107 D1 **Ciutadella de Menorca**
Spain
108 B1 **Cividale del Friuli** Italy
108 B2 **Civitanova Marche** Italy
108 B2 **Civitavecchia** Italy
104 C2 **Civray** France
111 C3 **Çivril** Turkey
70 C2 **Cixi** China
99 D4 **Clacton-on-Sea** U.K.
128 C2 **Claire, Lake** Can.
105 C2 **Clamecy** France
142 C2 **Clanton** U.S.A.
122 A3 **Clanwilliam** S. Africa
97 C2 **Clara** Rep. of Ireland
52 A2 **Clare** Austr.
140 C2 **Clare** U.S.A.
97 A2 **Clare Island**
Rep. of Ireland
141 E2 **Claremont** U.S.A.
97 B2 **Claremorris**
Rep. of Ireland
54 B2 **Clarence** N.Z.
55 B3 **Clarence Island**
Antarctica
131 E3 **Clarenville** Can.
128 C2 **Claresholm** Can.
137 D2 **Clarinda** U.S.A.
144 A3 **Clarión, Isla** i. Mex.
123 C3 **Clarkebury** S. Africa
134 C1 **Clark Fork** r. U.S.A.
143 D2 **Clark Hill Reservoir**
U.S.A.
140 C3 **Clarksburg** U.S.A.
142 B2 **Clarksdale** U.S.A.
134 C1 **Clarkston** U.S.A.
142 B1 **Clarksville** AR U.S.A.
142 C1 **Clarksville** TN U.S.A.
154 B1 **Claro** r. Brazil
139 C1 **Clayton** NM U.S.A.
139 C1 **Clayton** U.S.A.
97 B3 **Clear, Cape**
Rep. of Ireland
126 C3 **Cleare, Cape** U.S.A.
137 E2 **Clear Lake** U.S.A.
135 B3 **Clear Lake** l. U.S.A.
128 C2 **Clearwater** Can.
129 C2 **Clearwater** r. Can.
143 D3 **Clearwater** U.S.A.
134 C1 **Clearwater** r. U.S.A.
139 D2 **Cleburne** U.S.A.
101 E1 **Clenze** Ger.
51 D2 **Clermont** Austr.
105 C2 **Clermont-Ferrand** France
100 C2 **Clervaux** Lux.
52 A2 **Cleve** Austr.
142 B2 **Cleveland** MS U.S.A.
140 C2 **Cleveland** OH U.S.A.
143 D1 **Cleveland** TN U.S.A.
134 D1 **Cleveland, Mount** U.S.A.
154 B3 **Clevelândia** Brazil
97 B2 **Clew Bay** Rep. of Ireland
143 D3 **Clewiston** U.S.A.
97 A2 **Clifden** Rep. of Ireland
53 D1 **Clifton** Austr.
138 B2 **Clifton** U.S.A.
138 B1 **Clines Corners** U.S.A.
128 B2 **Clinton** Can.
137 E2 **Clinton** IA U.S.A.
137 E3 **Clinton** MO U.S.A.
139 D1 **Clinton** OK U.S.A.
125 H8 **Clipperton, Île** terr.
N. Pacific Ocean
96 A2 **Clisham** hill U.K.
98 B3 **Clitheroe** U.K.
97 B3 **Clonakilty** Rep. of Ireland
51 D2 **Cloncurry** Austr.
97 C1 **Clones** Rep. of Ireland
97 C2 **Clonmel** Rep. of Ireland
101 D1 **Cloppenburg** Ger.
137 E1 **Cloquet** U.S.A.
136 B2 **Cloud Peak** U.S.A.
135 C3 **Clovis** CA U.S.A.
139 C2 **Clovis** NM U.S.A.
Cluain Meala
Rep. of Ireland see
Clonmel
129 D2 **Cluff Lake Mine** Can.
110 B1 **Cluj-Napoca** Romania

51 C2 **Cluny** Austr.
105 D2 **Cluses** France
54 A3 **Clutha** r. N.Z.
96 B3 **Clyde** r. U.K.
96 B3 **Clyde, Firth of** est. U.K.
96 B3 **Clydebank** U.K.
127 H2 **Clyde River** Can.
144 B3 **Coalcomán** Mex.
128 C3 **Coaldale** Can.
135 C3 **Coaldale** U.S.A.
128 B2 **Coal River** Can.
150 C3 **Coari** Brazil
150 C3 **Coari** r. Brazil
143 C2 **Coastal Plain** U.S.A.
128 B2 **Coast Mountains** Can.
134 B2 **Coast Ranges** mts U.S.A.
96 B3 **Coatbridge** U.K.
129 F1 **Coats Island** Can.
55 C2 **Coats Land** reg. Antarctica
145 C3 **Coatzacoalcos** Mex.
146 A3 **Cobán** Guat.
53 C2 **Cobar** Austr.
97 B3 **Cóbh** Rep. of Ireland
152 B1 **Cobija** Bol.
Coblenz Ger. see Koblenz
130 C3 **Cobourg** Can.
50 C1 **Cobourg Peninsula** Austr.
53 C3 **Cobram** Austr.
101 E2 **Coburg** Ger.
152 B1 **Cochabamba** Bol.
100 C2 **Cochem** Ger.
73 B4 **Cochin** India
128 C2 **Cochrane** Alta Can.
130 B3 **Cochrane** Ont. Can.
153 A4 **Cochrane** Chile
52 A2 **Cockaleechie** Austr.
52 B2 **Cockburn** Austr.
Cockburn Town
Turks and Caicos Is see
Grand Turk
98 B2 **Cockermouth** U.K.
50 B3 **Cocklebiddy** Austr.
122 B3 **Cockscomb** mt. S. Africa
146 B3 **Coco** r. Hond./Nic.
125 J9 **Coco, Isla de** i.
N. Pacific Ocean
159 F4 **Cocos Basin** sea feature
Indian Ocean
58 A3 **Cocos Islands** terr.
Indian Ocean
144 B2 **Cocula** Mex.
150 B2 **Cocuy, Sierra Nevada del**
mt. Col.
141 E2 **Cod, Cape** U.S.A.
150 C3 **Codajás** Brazil
108 B2 **Codigoro** Italy
131 D2 **Cod Island** Can.
151 E3 **Codó** Brazil
136 B2 **Cody** U.S.A.
51 D1 **Coen** Austr.
100 C2 **Coesfeld** Ger.
113 I6 **Coëtivy** i. Seychelles
134 C1 **Coeur d'Alene** U.S.A.
100 C1 **Coevorden** Neth.
123 C3 **Coffee Bay** S. Africa
137 D3 **Coffeyville** U.S.A.
52 A2 **Coffin Bay** Austr.
53 D2 **Coffs Harbour** Austr.
123 C3 **Cofimvaba** S. Africa
104 B2 **Cognac** France
118 A2 **Cogo** Equat. Guinea
52 B3 **Cohuna** Austr.
146 B4 **Coiba, Isla** i. Panama
153 A4 **Coihaique** Chile
73 B3 **Coimbatore** India
106 B1 **Coimbra** Port.
152 B1 **Coipasa, Salar de** salt flat
Bol.
52 B3 **Colac** Austr.
155 D1 **Colatina** Brazil
136 C3 **Colby** U.S.A.
99 D4 **Colchester** U.K.
129 C2 **Cold Lake** Can.
96 C3 **Coldstream** U.K.
53 C2 **Coleambally** Austr.
139 D2 **Coleman** U.S.A.
52 B3 **Coleraine** Austr.
97 C1 **Coleraine** U.K.
123 C3 **Colesberg** S. Africa
153 A3 **Colico** Chile
144 B3 **Colima** Mex.
144 B3 **Colima, Nevado de** vol.
Mex.
96 A2 **Coll** i. U.K.
53 C1 **Collarenebri** Austr.
139 D2 **College Station** U.S.A.
53 C1 **Collie** Austr.
50 A3 **Collie** Austr.
50 B1 **Collier Bay** Austr.
140 C2 **Collingwood** Can.
54 B2 **Collingwood** N.Z.

126 F2 Collinson Peninsula Can.
101 F2 Collmberg hill Ger.
108 A3 Collo Alg.
97 B1 Collooney Rep. of Ireland
105 D2 Colmar France
98 B3 Colne U.K.
100 C2 Cologne Ger.
 Colomb-Béchar Alg. see Béchar
154 C2 Colômbia Brazil
150 B2 Colombia country S. America
73 B4 Colombo Sri Lanka
104 C3 Colomiers France
152 C3 Colón Arg.
146 C4 Colón Panama
59 D2 Colonia Micronesia
153 B4 Colonia Las Heras Arg.
109 C3 Colonna, Capo c. Italy
96 A2 Colonsay i. U.K.
153 B3 Colorado r. Arg.
138 A2 Colorado r. Mex./U.S.A.
139 D3 Colorado r. U.S.A.
136 B3 Colorado state U.S.A.
135 C4 Colorado Desert U.S.A.
135 E3 Colorado Plateau U.S.A.
136 C3 Colorado Springs U.S.A.
144 B2 Colotlán Mex.
152 B1 Colquiri Bol.
136 B1 Colstrip U.S.A.
140 B3 Columbia KY U.S.A.
141 D3 Columbia MD U.S.A.
137 E3 Columbia MO U.S.A.
143 D2 Columbia SC U.S.A.
142 C1 Columbia TN U.S.A.
134 B1 Columbia r. U.S.A.
128 C2 Columbia, Mount Can.
134 D1 Columbia Falls U.S.A.
128 B2 Columbia Mountains Can.
134 C1 Columbia Plateau U.S.A.
143 D2 Columbus GA U.S.A.
140 B3 Columbus IN U.S.A.
142 C2 Columbus MS U.S.A.
134 E1 Columbus MT U.S.A.
137 D2 Columbus NE U.S.A.
138 B2 Columbus NM U.S.A.
140 C3 Columbus OH U.S.A.
139 D3 Columbus TX U.S.A.
134 C1 Colville U.S.A.
126 B2 Colville r. U.S.A.
126 D2 Colville Lake Can.
98 B3 Colwyn Bay U.K.
108 B2 Comacchio Italy
145 C3 Comalcalco Mex.
110 C1 Comănești Romania
130 C2 Comencho, Lac l. Can.
97 C2 Comeragh Mountains hills Rep. of Ireland
139 D2 Comfort U.S.A.
75 D2 Comilla Bangl.
108 A2 Comino, Capo c. Sardinia Italy
145 C3 Comitán de Domínguez Mex.
105 C2 Commentry France
139 D2 Commerce U.S.A.
127 G2 Committee Bay Can.
108 A1 Como Italy
108 A1 Como, Lago di l. Italy
 Como, Lake Italy see Como, Lago di
153 B4 Comodoro Rivadavia Arg.
145 B2 Comonfort Mex.
121 D2 Comoros country Africa
128 B3 Comox Can.
105 C2 Compiègne France
144 B2 Compostela Mex.
90 B2 Comrat Moldova
114 A4 Conakry Guinea
104 B2 Concarneau France
155 E1 Conceição da Barra Brazil
151 E3 Conceição do Araguaia Brazil
155 D1 Conceição do Mato Dentro Brazil
152 B2 Concepción Arg.
153 A3 Concepción Chile
144 B2 Concepción Mex.
146 B4 Concepción Panama
135 B4 Conception, Point U.S.A.
154 C2 Conchas Brazil
138 C1 Conchas Lake U.S.A.
144 B2 Conchos r. Mex.
145 C2 Conchos r. Mex.
135 B3 Concord CA U.S.A.
141 E2 Concord NH U.S.A.
152 C3 Concordia Arg.
122 A2 Concordia S. Africa
137 D3 Concordia U.S.A.
53 C2 Condobolin Austr.

104 C3 Condom France
134 B1 Condon U.S.A.
108 B1 Conegliano Italy
51 E1 Conflict Group is P.N.G.
104 C2 Confolens France
135 D3 Confusion Range mts U.S.A.
98 B3 Congleton U.K.
118 B3 Congo country Africa
118 B3 Congo r. Congo/Dem. Rep. Congo
118 C3 Congo, Democratic Republic of country Africa see Congo
118 C3 Congo Basin Dem. Rep. Congo
 Congo (Brazzaville) country Africa see Congo
52 B3 Congo Free State country Africa see Congo, Democratic Republic of
 Congo (Kinshasa) country Africa see Congo, Democratic Republic of
129 C2 Conklin Can.
97 B1 Conn, Lough l. Rep. of Ireland
97 B2 Connaught reg. Rep. of Ireland
141 E2 Connecticut r. U.S.A.
141 E2 Connecticut state U.S.A.
96 B2 Connel U.K.
97 B2 Connemara reg. Rep. of Ireland
134 D1 Conrad U.S.A.
159 D7 Conrad Rise sea feature Southern Ocean
139 D2 Conroe U.S.A.
155 D2 Conselheiro Lafaiete Brazil
155 D1 Conselheiro Pena Brazil
100 B3 Consenvoye France
98 C2 Consett U.K.
63 B3 Côn Son i. Vietnam
 Constance see Konstanz
105 D2 Constance, Lake Ger./Switz.
110 C2 Constanța Romania
106 B2 Constantina Spain
115 C1 Constantine Alg.
134 D2 Contact U.S.A.
155 D2 Contagalo Brazil
150 B3 Contamana Peru
153 A5 Contreras, Isla i. Chile
126 E2 Contwoyto Lake Can.
142 B1 Conway AR U.S.A.
141 E2 Conway NH U.S.A.
51 C2 Coober Pedy Austr.
 Cooch Behar India see Koch Bihār
54 B2 Cook, Mount N.Z.
143 C1 Cookeville U.S.A.
126 B2 Cook Inlet sea chan. U.S.A.
49 K5 Cook Islands terr. S. Pacific Ocean
131 E2 Cook's Harbour Can.
97 C1 Cookstown U.K.
54 B2 Cook Strait N.Z.
51 D1 Cooktown Austr.
53 C2 Coolabah Austr.
53 C2 Coolamon Austr.
53 D1 Coolangatta Austr.
50 B3 Coolgardie Austr.
53 C3 Cooma Austr.
52 B2 Coombah Austr.
53 C2 Coonabarabran Austr.
52 A3 Coonalpyn Austr.
53 C1 Coonamble Austr.
53 C1 Coongoola Austr.
137 E1 Coon Rapids U.S.A.
52 A1 Cooper Creek watercourse Austr.
143 E3 Cooper's Town Bahamas
134 B2 Coos Bay U.S.A.
53 C2 Cootamundra Austr.
97 C1 Cootehill Rep. of Ireland
145 C3 Copainalá Mex.
93 F4 Copala Mex.
112 C2 Copenhagen Denmark
109 C2 Copertino Italy
53 D1 Copeton Reservoir Austr.
152 A2 Copiapó Chile
139 D2 Copperas Cove U.S.A.
140 B1 Copper Harbor U.S.A.
 Coppermine Can. see Kugluktuk
126 E2 Coppermine r. Can.
122 B2 Copperton S. Africa

 Coquilhatville Dem. Rep. Congo see Mbandaka
152 A2 Coquimbo Chile
152 A2 Coquimbo, Bahía de b. Chile
110 B2 Corabia Romania
155 D1 Coração de Jesus Brazil
150 B4 Coracora Peru
53 D1 Coraki Austr.
50 A2 Coral Bay Austr.
127 G2 Coral Harbour Can.
156 D7 Coral Sea S. Pacific Ocean
48 G5 Coral Sea Islands Territory terr. Austr.
137 E2 Coralville U.S.A.
52 B3 Corangamite, Lake Austr.
99 C3 Corby U.K.
 Corcaigh Rep. of Ireland see Cork
135 C3 Corcoran U.S.A.
153 A4 Corcovado, Golfo de sea chan. Chile
143 D2 Cordele U.S.A.
64 B2 Cordilleras Range mts Phil.
155 D1 Cordisburgo Brazil
152 B3 Córdoba Arg.
145 C3 Córdoba Mex.
106 C2 Córdoba Spain
153 B3 Córdoba, Sierras de mts Arg.
126 C2 Cordova U.S.A.
51 D2 Corfield Austr.
111 A3 Corfu i. Greece
154 B1 Corguinho Brazil
106 B2 Coria Spain
106 B2 Coria del Río Spain
53 D2 Coricudgy mt. Austr.
 Corinth Greece see Korinthos
142 C2 Corinth U.S.A.
 Corinth, Gulf of sea chan. Greece see Korinthiakos Kolpos
155 D1 Corinto Brazil
97 B3 Cork Rep. of Ireland
111 C2 Çorlu Turkey
154 B2 Cornélio Procópio Brazil
131 E3 Corner Brook Can.
53 C3 Corner Inlet b. Austr.
135 B3 Corning CA U.S.A.
141 D2 Corning NY U.S.A.
 Corn Islands is Nic. see Maíz, Islas del
108 B2 Corno, Monte mt. Italy
130 C3 Cornwall Can.
126 F1 Cornwallis Island Can.
150 C1 Coro Venez.
155 D1 Coroaci Brazil
154 C1 Coromandel Brazil
73 C3 Coromandel Coast India
54 C1 Coromandel Peninsula N.Z.
64 B2 Coron Phil.
129 C2 Coronation Can.
126 E2 Coronation Gulf Can.
55 B3 Coronation Island S. Atlantic Ocean
155 D1 Coronel Fabriciano Brazil
152 C2 Coronel Oviedo Para.
154 B1 Coronel Ponce Brazil
153 B3 Coronel Pringles Arg.
154 A2 Coronel Sapucaia Brazil
153 B3 Coronel Suárez Arg.
109 D2 Corovodë Albania
145 D3 Corozal Belize
139 D3 Corpus Christi U.S.A.
152 B1 Corque Bol.
151 E4 Corrente Brazil
154 B1 Correntes Brazil
151 E4 Correntina Brazil
97 B2 Corrib, Lough l. Rep. of Ireland
152 C2 Corrientes Arg.
153 C3 Corrientes, Cabo c. Arg.
144 B2 Corrientes, Cabo c. Mex.
139 E2 Corrigan U.S.A.
53 C3 Corryong Austr.
 Corse i. France see Corsica
105 D3 Corse, Cap c. Corsica France
105 D3 Corsica i. France
139 D2 Corsicana U.S.A.
105 D3 Corte Corsica France
106 B2 Cortegana Spain
136 B3 Cortez U.S.A.
108 B1 Cortina d'Ampezzo Italy
141 D2 Cortland U.S.A.

108 B2 Cortona Italy
106 B2 Coruche Port.
 Çoruh Turkey see Artvin
80 B1 Çorum Turkey
151 D4 Corumbá Brazil
154 C1 Corumbá r. Brazil
154 C1 Corumbá de Goiás Brazil
100 B1 Corunna Spain see A Coruña
134 B2 Corvallis U.S.A.
99 B3 Corwen U.K.
 Cos i. Greece see Kos
144 B2 Cosalá Mex.
145 C3 Cosamaloapan Mex.
109 C3 Cosenza Italy
105 C2 Cosne-Cours-sur-Loire France
152 B3 Cosquín Arg.
107 C2 Costa Blanca coastal area Spain
107 D1 Costa Brava coastal area Spain
106 B2 Costa de la Luz coastal area Spain
107 C2 Costa del Azahar coastal area Spain
106 B2 Costa del Sol coastal area Spain
146 B3 Costa de Mosquitos coastal area Nic.
107 D1 Costa Dorada coastal area Spain
150 C4 Costa Marques Brazil
154 B1 Costa Rica Brazil
146 B3 Costa Rica country Central America
144 B2 Costa Rica Mex.
 Costermansville Dem. Rep. Congo see Bukavu
110 B2 Costești Romania
64 B3 Cotabato Phil.
137 D1 Coteau des Prairies slope U.S.A.
136 C1 Coteau du Missouri slope U.S.A.
147 C3 Coteaux Haiti
105 D3 Côte d'Azur coastal area France
114 B4 Côte d'Ivoire country Africa
 Côte Française de Somalis country Africa see Djibouti
105 C2 Côtes de Meuse ridge France
150 B3 Cotopaxi, Volcán vol. Ecuador
99 B4 Cotswold Hills U.K.
134 B2 Cottage Grove U.S.A.
102 C1 Cottbus Ger.
105 D3 Cottian Alps mts France/Italy
52 A2 Coüedic, Cape de Austr.
105 C2 Coulommiers France
137 D2 Council Bluffs U.S.A.
88 B2 Courland Lagoon b. Lith./Rus. Fed.
100 A3 Courmelles France
128 B3 Courtenay Can.
104 B2 Coutances France
104 B2 Coutras France
100 B2 Couvin Belgium
99 C3 Coventry U.K.
106 B1 Covilhã Port.
143 D2 Covington GA U.S.A.
140 C3 Covington KY U.S.A.
140 C3 Covington VA U.S.A.
50 B3 Cowan, Lake salt flat Austr.
96 C2 Cowdenbeath U.K.
52 A2 Cowell Austr.
53 C3 Cowes Austr.
134 B1 Cowlitz r. U.S.A.
53 C2 Cowra Austr.
154 B1 Coxim Brazil
154 B1 Coxim r. Brazil
75 D2 Cox's Bazar Bangl.
145 B3 Coyuca de Benítez Mex.
145 D2 Cozumel Mex.
145 D2 Cozumel, Isla de i. Mex.
52 A2 Cradock U.S.A.
123 C3 Cradock S. Africa
136 B2 Craig U.S.A.
102 C2 Crailsheim Ger.
110 B2 Craiova Romania
129 D2 Cranberry Portage Can.
53 C3 Cranbourne Austr.
128 C3 Cranbrook Can.
151 E3 Crateús Brazil
151 F3 Crato Brazil

154 C2 Cravinhos Brazil
136 C2 Crawford U.S.A.
140 B2 Crawfordsville U.S.A.
99 C4 Crawley U.K.
134 D1 Crazy Mountains U.S.A.
129 D2 Cree r. Can.
144 B2 Creel Mex.
129 D2 Cree Lake Can.
129 D2 Creighton Can.
104 C2 Creil France
100 B1 Creil Neth.
108 A1 Crema Italy
108 B1 Cremona Italy
108 B2 Cres i. Croatia
134 B2 Crescent City U.S.A.
53 D2 Crescent Head Austr.
135 E3 Crescent Junction U.S.A.
128 C3 Creston Can.
137 E2 Creston U.S.A.
142 C2 Crestview U.S.A.
111 B3 Crete i. Greece
107 D1 Creus, Cap de c. Spain
107 C2 Crevillente Spain
98 B3 Crewe U.K.
96 B2 Crianlarich U.K.
152 D2 Criciúma Brazil
96 C2 Crieff U.K.
108 B1 Crikvenica Croatia
91 C2 Crimea pen. Ukr.
101 F2 Crimmitschau Ger.
96 B2 Crinan U.K.
118 B2 Cristal, Monts de mts Equat. Guinea/Gabon
154 C1 Cristalina Brazil
110 B1 Crişul Alb r. Romania
101 E1 Crivitz Ger.
Crna Gora aut. rep. Yugo. see Montenegro
109 C1 Črnomelj Slovenia
97 B2 Croagh Patrick hill Rep. of Ireland
109 C1 Croatia country Europe
61 C1 Crocker, Banjaran mts Malaysia
139 D2 Crockett U.S.A.
59 C3 Croker Island Austr.
96 B2 Cromarty U.K.
99 D3 Cromer U.K.
54 A3 Cromwell N.Z.
147 C4 Crooked Island Bahamas
137 D1 Crookston U.S.A.
53 C2 Crookwell Austr.
53 D1 Croppa Creek Austr.
136 C1 Crosby U.K.
143 D3 Cross City U.S.A.
142 B2 Crossett U.S.A.
98 B2 Cross Fell hill U.K.
129 E2 Cross Lake Can.
143 C1 Crossville U.S.A.
109 C3 Crotone Italy
134 E1 Crow Agency U.S.A.
99 D4 Crowborough U.K.
142 B2 Crowley U.S.A.
53 D1 Crows Nest Austr.
128 C3 Crowsnest Pass Can.
159 D7 Crozet, Îles is Indian Ocean
146 C3 Cruz, Cabo c. Cuba
152 C2 Cruz Alta Brazil
152 B3 Cruz del Eje Arg.
155 D2 Cruzeiro Brazil
150 B3 Cruzeiro do Sul Brazil
52 A2 Crystal Brook Austr.
139 D3 Crystal City U.S.A.
140 B1 Crystal Falls U.S.A.
142 B2 Crystal Springs U.S.A.
103 E2 Csongrád Hungary
103 D2 Csorna Hungary
121 C2 Cuamba Moz.
120 B2 Cuando r. Angola/Zambia
120 A2 Cuangar Angola
118 B3 Cuango r. Angola/Dem. Rep. Congo
120 A1 Cuanza r. Angola
144 B2 Cuatro Ciénegas Mex.
144 B2 Cuauhtémoc Mex.
145 C3 Cuautla Mex.
146 B2 Cuba country West Indies
120 A2 Cubal Angola
120 B2 Cubango r. Angola/Namibia
150 B2 Cúcuta Col.
73 B3 Cuddalore India
73 B3 Cuddapah India
50 A2 Cue Austr.
106 C1 Cuéllar Spain
120 A2 Cuemba Angola
150 B3 Cuenca Ecuador
107 C1 Cuenca Spain
107 C1 Cuenca, Serranía de mts Spain

145 C3 Cuernavaca Mex.
139 D3 Cuero U.S.A.
104 C3 Cugnaux France
151 D4 Cuiabá Brazil
151 D4 Cuiabá r. Brazil
96 A2 Cuillin Sound sea chan. U.K.
120 A1 Cuilo Angola
120 B2 Cuito r. Angola
120 A2 Cuito Cuanavale Angola
60 B1 Cukai Malaysia
64 B2 Culasi Phil.
53 C3 Culcairn Austr.
100 B2 Culemborg Neth.
53 C1 Culgoa r. Austr.
144 B2 Culiacán Mex.
64 A2 Culion i. Phil.
107 C2 Cullera Spain
142 C2 Cullman U.S.A.
97 C1 Cullybackey U.K.
141 D3 Culpeper U.S.A.
151 D4 Culuene r. Brazil
54 B2 Culverden N.Z.
150 C1 Cumaná Venez.
141 D3 Cumberland U.S.A.
140 B3 Cumberland r. U.S.A.
143 D2 Cumberland Island U.S.A.
129 D2 Cumberland Lake Can.
127 H2 Cumberland Peninsula Can.
142 C1 Cumberland Plateau U.S.A.
127 H2 Cumberland Sound sea chan. Can.
96 C3 Cumbernauld U.K.
135 B3 Cummings U.S.A.
96 B3 Cumnock U.K.
144 B1 Cumpas Mex.
145 C3 Cunduacán Mex.
120 A2 Cunene r. Angola/Namibia
108 A2 Cuneo Italy
53 C1 Cunnamulla Austr.
108 A1 Cuorgnè Italy
96 C2 Cupar U.K.
110 B2 Ćuprija Yugo.
147 D3 Curaçao i. Neth. Antilles
150 B3 Curaray r. Ecuador
153 A3 Curicó Chile
154 C3 Curitiba Brazil
52 A2 Curnamona Austr.
135 C3 Currant U.S.A.
51 D3 Currie Austr.
135 D2 Currie U.S.A.
51 E2 Curtis Island Austr.
151 D3 Curuá r. Brazil
60 B2 Curup Indon.
151 E3 Cururupu Brazil
155 D1 Curvelo Brazil
150 B4 Cusco Peru
97 C1 Cushendun U.K.
139 D1 Cushing U.S.A.
136 C2 Custer U.S.A.
134 D1 Cut Bank U.S.A.
142 B3 Cut Off U.S.A.
75 C2 Cuttack India
120 A2 Cuvelai Angola
101 D1 Cuxhaven Ger.
64 B2 Cuyo Islands Phil.
Cuzco Peru see Cusco
99 B4 Cwmbran U.K.
119 C3 Cyangugu Rwanda
111 B3 Cyclades is Greece
129 C3 Cypress Hills Can.
80 B2 Cyprus country Asia
80 B2 Cyprus i. Asia
102 C2 Czech Republic country Europe
103 D1 Czersk Pol.
103 D1 Częstochowa Pol.

D

62 B1 Đa, Sông r. Vietnam
69 D2 Daban China
103 D2 Dabas Hungary
114 A3 Dabola Guinea
103 D1 Dąbrowa Górnicza Pol.
110 B2 Dăbuleni Romania
Dacca Bangl. see Dhaka
102 C2 Dachau Ger.
70 A2 Dachuan China
143 D3 Dade City U.S.A.
Dadong China see Donggang
74 B2 Dadra India see Achalpur
Dadra and Nagar Haveli union terr. India
74 A2 Dadu Pak.
64 B2 Daet Phil.

114 A3 Dagana Senegal
119 D2 Daga Post Sudan
88 C2 Dagda Latvia
64 B2 Dagupan Phil.
Dahalach, Isole is Eritrea
Dahlak Archipelago
74 B3 Dahanu India
69 D2 Da Hinggan Ling mts China
116 C3 Dahlak Archipelago is Eritrea
100 C2 Dahlem Ger.
74 B2 Dāhod India
Dahomey country Africa see Benin
Dahra Senegal see Dara
81 C2 Dahūk Iraq
60 B2 Daik Indon.
106 C2 Daimiel Spain
Dairen China see Dalian
51 C2 Dajarra Austr.
70 A2 Dajing China
114 A3 Dakar Senegal
117 C4 Daketa Shet' watercourse Eth.
116 A2 Dakhla Oasis Egypt
63 A3 Dakoank India
88 C3 Dakol'ka r. Belarus
109 D2 Đakovica Yugo.
109 C1 Đakovo Croatia
120 B2 Dala Angola
70 A1 Dalain Hob China
93 G3 Dalälven r. Sweden
111 C3 Dalaman Turkey
111 C3 Dalaman r. Turkey
68 C2 Dalandzadgad Mongolia
64 B2 Dalanganem Islands Phil.
48 I3 Dalap-Uliga-Djarrit Marshall Is
63 B2 Đa Lat Vietnam
74 A2 Dalbandin Pak.
96 C3 Dalbeattie U.K.
53 D1 Dalby Austr.
93 E3 Dale Norway
143 C1 Dale Hollow Lake U.S.A.
53 C3 Dalgety Austr.
139 C1 Dalhart U.S.A.
131 D3 Dalhousie Can.
62 B1 Dali China
70 C2 Dalian China
96 C3 Dalkeith U.K.
139 D2 Dallas U.S.A.
128 A2 Dall Island U.S.A.
109 C2 Dalmacija reg. Croatia
Dalmatia reg. Croatia see Dalmacija
96 B3 Dalmellington U.K.
66 C2 Dal'negorsk Rus. Fed.
66 B1 Dal'nerechensk Rus. Fed.
Dalny China see Dalian
114 B4 Daloa Côte d'Ivoire
71 A3 Dalou Shan mts China
51 D2 Dalrymple, Mount Austr.
92 □A3 Dalsmynni Iceland
75 C2 Dalton India
143 D2 Dalton U.S.A.
Daltenganj India see Daltonganj
60 B1 Daludalu Indon.
71 B3 Daluo Shan mt. China
92 □B2 Dalvík Iceland
96 B2 Dalwhinnie U.K.
50 C1 Daly r. Austr.
51 C1 Daly Waters Austr.
74 B2 Damān India
74 B2 Daman and Diu union terr. India
116 B1 Damanhûr Egypt
59 C3 Damar i. Indon.
118 B2 Damara C.A.R.
80 B2 Damascus Syria
115 D3 Damaturu Nigeria
76 B3 Damāvand, Qolleh-ye mt. Iran
120 A1 Damba Angola
118 B1 Damboa Nigeria
81 D2 Damghan Iran
Damietta Egypt see Dumyât
Dammam Saudi Arabia see Ad Dammām
101 D1 Damme Ger.
75 B2 Damoh India
114 B4 Damongo Ghana
59 C3 Dampir, Selat sea chan. Indon.
62 A1 Damroh India

75 D1 Damxung China
114 B4 Danané Côte d'Ivoire
63 B2 Đa Nẵng Vietnam
141 E2 Danbury U.S.A.
70 C1 Dandong China
117 B3 Dangila Eth.
146 B3 Dangriga Belize
70 B2 Dangshan China
89 F2 Danilov Rus. Fed.
89 E2 Danilovskaya Vozvyshennost' hills Rus. Fed.
70 B2 Danjiangkou China
79 C2 Dank Oman
89 E3 Dankov Rus. Fed.
146 B3 Danlí Hond.
101 E1 Dannenberg (Elbe) Ger.
54 C2 Dannevirke N.Z.
62 B2 Dan Sai Thai.
Dantu China see Zhenjiang
110 A1 Danube r. Europe
Danube Delta Romania see Dunării, Delta
Danubyu Myanmar
140 B2 Danville IL U.S.A.
140 C3 Danville KY U.S.A.
141 D3 Danville VA U.S.A.
Danxian China see Danzhou
71 A4 Danzhou China
Danzig, Gulf of Pol./Rus. Fed. see Gdańsk, Gulf of
Daojiang China see Daoxian
115 D2 Dao Timmi Niger
Daoud Alg. see Aïn Beïda
114 B4 Daoukro Côte d'Ivoire
71 B3 Daoxian China
64 B3 Dapa Phil.
114 C3 Dapaong Togo
68 C2 Da Qaidam Zhen China
69 E1 Daqing China
114 A3 Dara Senegal
80 B2 Dar'ā Syria
81 D3 Dārāb Iran
115 D1 Daraj Libya
81 D2 Dārān Iran
63 B2 Đa Răng, Sông r. Vietnam
109 D2 Đaravica mt. Yugo.
75 C2 Darbhanga India
Dardo China see Kangding
119 D3 Dar es Salaam Tanz.
74 B1 Dargai Pak.
54 B1 Dargaville N.Z.
53 C3 Dargo Austr.
71 B3 Darhan Mongolia
150 B2 Darién, Golfo del g. Col.
Darjeeling India see Dārjiling
75 C2 Dārjiling India
68 C2 Darlag China
52 B2 Darling r. Austr.
53 C1 Darling Downs hills Austr.
50 A3 Darling Range hills Austr.
98 C2 Darlington U.K.
53 C2 Darlington Point Austr.
103 D1 Darłowo Pol.
101 D1 Darmstadt Ger.
115 E1 Darnah Libya
52 B2 Darnick Austr.
55 H3 Darnley, Cape Antarctica
107 C1 Daroca Spain
99 D4 Dartford U.K.
99 A4 Dartmoor hills U.K.
131 D3 Dartmouth Can.
99 B4 Dartmouth U.K.
97 B1 Darty Mountains hills Rep. of Ireland
59 D3 Daru P.N.G.
59 C2 Daruba Indon.
50 C1 Darwin Austr.
79 C2 Dārzīn Iran
65 A1 Dashiqiao China
88 C2 Dashkhovuz Turkm.
74 A2 Dasht r. Pak.
61 C1 Datadian Indon.
111 C3 Datça Turkey
66 D2 Date Japan
71 B3 Datian China
71 B3 Datong China
64 B1 Datu Piang Phil.
74 B1 Daud Khel Pak.
88 C2 Daugava r. Latvia
88 C2 Daugavpils Latvia
100 C2 Daun Ger.
129 D2 Dauphin Can.
129 E2 Dauphin Lake Can.
73 B3 Davangere India
64 B3 Davao Phil.
64 B3 Davao Gulf Phil.

137 E2 Davenport U.S.A.
99 C3 Daventry U.K.
123 C2 Daveyton S. Africa
146 B4 David Panama
129 D2 Davidson Oan.
126 F3 Davidson Lake Can.
135 B3 Davis U.S.A.
131 D2 Davis Inlet Can.
55 I3 Davis Sea sea Antarctica
160 P3 Davis Strait str.
Can./Greenland
105 D2 Davos Switz.
88 C3 Davyd-Haradok Belarus
79 C3 Dawqah Oman
78 B3 Dawqah Saudi Arabia
126 C2 Dawson Can.
143 D2 Dawson U.S.A.
128 B2 Dawson Creek Can.
128 B2 Dawsons Landing Can.
68 C2 Daxian China
Dawukou China see
Shizuishan
79 C2 Dawwah Oman
104 B3 Dax France
Daxian China see Dachuan
68 C2 Daxue Shan mts China
52 B3 Daylesford Austr.
71 B3 Dayong China
81 C2 Dayr az Zawr Syria
140 C3 Dayton U.S.A.
143 D3 Daytona Beach U.S.A.
71 B3 Dayu China
122 B3 De Aar S. Africa
143 D3 Deadman Bay U.S.A.
80 B2 Dead Sea salt l. Asia
99 D4 Deal U.K.
71 B3 De'an China
152 B3 Deán Funes Arg.
128 B2 Dease Lake Can.
126 E2 Dease Strait Can.
135 C3 Death Valley depr. U.S.A.
104 C2 Deauville France
61 C1 Debak Sarawak Malaysia
111 B2 Debar Macedonia
103 E1 Dębica Pol.
103 E1 Deblin Pol.
114 B3 Débo, Lac l. Mali
103 E2 Debrecen Hungary
117 B3 Debre Markos Eth.
119 D2 Debre Sina Eth.
117 B3 Debre Tabor Eth.
117 B4 Debre Zeyit Eth.
142 C2 Decatur AL U.S.A.
140 B3 Decatur IL U.S.A.
73 B3 Deccan plat. India
53 D1 Deception Bay Austr.
71 A3 Dechang China
102 C1 Děčín Czech Rep.
137 E2 Decorah U.S.A.
154 C2 Dedo de Deus mt. Brazil
88 C2 Dedovichi Rus. Fed.
121 C2 Dedza Malawi
99 B3 Dee r. England/Wales U.K.
96 C2 Dee r. Scotland U.K.
130 C3 Deep River Can.
53 D1 Deepwater Austr.
131 E3 Deer Lake Can.
134 D1 Deer Lodge U.S.A.
140 C2 Defiance U.S.A.
142 C2 De Funiak Springs U.S.A.
68 C2 Dêgê China
117 C4 Degeh Bur Eth.
141 F1 Dégelis Can.
102 C2 Deggendorf Ger.
91 E2 Degtevo Rus. Fed.
81 D2 Deh Bīd Iran
81 C2 Dehlorān Iran
74 B1 Dehra Dun India
75 C2 Dehri India
69 E2 Dehui China
100 A2 Deinze Belgium
110 B1 Dej Romania
140 B2 De Kalb U.S.A.
116 B3 Dekemhare Eritrea
118 C3 Dekese Dem. Rep. Congo
118 B2 Dékoa C.A.R.
143 D3 De Land U.S.A.
135 C3 Delano U.S.A.
135 D3 Delano Peak U.S.A.
74 A1 Delārām Afgh.
123 C2 Delareyville S. Africa
129 D2 Delaronde Lake Can.
140 C2 Delaware U.S.A.
141 D3 Delaware r. U.S.A.
141 D3 Delaware state U.S.A.
141 D3 Delaware Bay U.S.A.
53 C3 Delegate Austr.
118 C2 Délembé C.A.R.
105 D2 Delémont Switz.
100 B1 Delft Neth.
100 C1 Delfzijl Neth.

121 D2 Delgado, Cabo c. Moz.
68 C2 Delhi China
74 B2 Delhi India
60 B2 Deli i. Indon.
128 R1 Déline Can.
101 F2 Delitzsch Ger.
107 D2 Dellys Alg.
135 C4 Del Mar U.S.A.
101 D1 Delmenhorst Ger.
109 B1 Delnice Croatia
136 B3 Del Norte U.S.A.
83 L1 De-Longa, Ostrova is
Rus. Fed.
De Long Islands Rus. Fed.
see De-Longa, Ostrova
De Long Strait Rus. Fed.
see Longa, Proliv
129 D3 Deloraine Can.
111 B3 Delphi tourist site Greece
143 D3 Delray Beach U.S.A.
139 C3 Del Rio U.S.A.
136 B3 Delta CO U.S.A.
135 D3 Delta UT U.S.A.
126 C2 Delta Junction U.S.A.
109 D3 Delvinë Albania
Demavend mt. Iran see
Damāvand, Qolleh-ye
118 C3 Demba Dem. Rep. Congo
119 D1 Dembech'a Eth.
117 B4 Dembī Dolo Eth.
Demerara Guyana see
Georgetown
91 C3 Demerdzhi mt. Ukr.
89 D2 Demidov Rus. Fed.
138 B2 Deming U.S.A.
111 C3 Demirci Turkey
111 C2 Demirköy Turkey
102 C1 Demmin Ger.
142 C2 Demopolis U.S.A.
60 B2 Dempo, Gunung vol.
Indon.
89 D2 Demyansk Rus. Fed.
122 B3 De Naawte S. Africa
117 C3 Denakil reg. Eritrea/Eth.
77 C3 Denau Uzbek.
98 B3 Denbigh U.K.
100 B1 Den Burg Neth.
62 B2 Den Chai Thai.
60 B2 Dendang Indon.
100 B2 Dendermonde Belgium
100 B2 Dendre r. Belgium
Dengjiabu China see
Yujiang
70 A1 Dengkou China
Dengxian China see
Dengzhou
70 B2 Dengzhou China see
Penglai
Den Haag Neth. see
The Hague
50 A2 Denham Austr.
100 B1 Den Helder Neth.
107 D2 Denia Spain
52 B3 Deniliquin Austr.
134 C2 Denio U.S.A.
137 D2 Denison IA U.S.A.
139 D2 Denison TX U.S.A.
111 C3 Denizli Turkey
52 D2 Denman Austr.
50 A3 Denmark Austr.
93 F4 Denmark country Europe
84 B2 Denmark Strait
Greenland/Iceland
61 C2 Denpasar Indon.
139 D2 Denton U.S.A.
50 A3 D'Entrecasteaux, Point
Austr.
59 E3 D'Entrecasteaux Islands
P.N.G.
143 D2 Dentsville U.S.A.
136 B3 Denver U.S.A.
75 C2 Deogarh Orissa India
74 B2 Deogarh Rajasthan India
75 C2 Deoghar India
140 B2 De Pere U.S.A.
83 K2 Deputatskiy Rus. Fed.
62 A1 Dêqên China
142 B2 De Queen U.S.A.
74 A1 Dera Bugti Pak.
74 B1 Dera Ghazi Khan Pak.
74 B1 Dera Ismail Khan Pak.
87 D4 Derbent Rus. Fed.
50 B1 Derby Austr.
99 C3 Derby U.K.
137 D3 Derby U.S.A.
97 B2 Derg, Lough l.
Rep. of Ireland
91 D1 Derhachi Ukr.
142 B2 De Ridder U.S.A.

91 D2 Derkul r. Rus. Fed./Ukr.
Dêrub China see Rutog
116 B3 Derudeb Sudan
122 B3 De Rust S. Africa
109 C2 Derventa Bos.-Herz.
50 D1 Darwent r. England U.K.
98 C3 Derwent r. England U.K.
98 B2 Derwent Water l. U.K.
77 C1 Derzhavinsk Kazakh.
Derzhavinskiy Kazakh.
see Derzhavinsk
152 B1 Desaguadero r. Bol.
49 M5 Désappointement, Îles
du is Fr. Polynesia
129 D2 Deschambault Lake Can.
134 B1 Deschutes r. U.S.A.
117 B3 Desē Eth.
153 B4 Deseado Arg.
153 B4 Deseado r. Arg.
138 A2 Desemboque Mex.
137 E2 Des Moines U.S.A.
137 E2 Des Moines r. U.S.A.
91 C1 Desna r. Rus. Fed./Ukr.
89 D3 Desnogorsk Rus. Fed.
101 F2 Dessau Ger.
Dessye Eth. see Desē
128 A1 Destruction Bay Can.
128 C1 Detah Can.
120 B2 Dete Zimbabwe
101 D2 Detmold Ger.
140 C2 Detroit U.S.A.
137 D1 Detroit Lakes U.S.A.
Dett Zimbabwe see Dete
100 B2 Deurne Neth.
110 B1 Deva Romania
100 C1 Deventer Neth.
96 C2 Deveron r. U.K.
103 D2 Devět Skal hill Czech Rep.
137 D1 Devil's Lake U.S.A.
128 A2 Devil's Paw mt. U.S.A.
99 C4 Devizes U.K.
74 B2 Devli India
110 C2 Devnya Bulg.
128 C2 Devon Can.
126 F1 Devon Island Can.
51 D4 Devonport Austr.
74 B2 Dewas India
51 F3 Dexter U.S.A.
70 A2 Deyang China
59 D3 Deyong, Tanjung pt
Indon.
81 C2 Deyyer Iran
81 C2 Dezfūl Iran
70 B2 Dezhou China
79 C2 Dhahran Saudi Arabia
79 B3 Dhaka Bangl.
78 B3 Dhamār Yemen
75 C2 Dhamtari India
75 C2 Dhanbad India
74 B2 Dhandhuka India
75 C2 Dhankuta Nepal
74 B2 Dhar India
75 D2 Dharmanagar India
73 B3 Dharmapuri India
75 C2 Dharmjaygarh India
114 B3 Dhar Oualâta hills Maur.
114 B3 Dhar Tichît hills Maur.
73 B3 Dhārwād India
Dharwar India see
Dhārwād
74 B2 Dhasa India
75 C2 Dhaulagiri mt. Nepal
78 B3 Dhubāb Yemen
74 B2 Dhule India
Dhulia India see Dhule
117 C4 Dhuusa Marreeb Somalia
144 A1 Diablo, Picacho del mt.
Mex.
138 B2 Diablo Plateau U.S.A.
121 D2 Diaca Moz.
51 C2 Diamantina watercourse
Austr.
155 D1 Diamantina Brazil
151 E4 Diamantina, Chapada
plat. Brazil
159 F6 Diamantina Deep
sea feature Indian Ocean
154 B1 Diamantino Brazil
151 D4 Diamantino Brazil
71 B3 Dianbai China
151 E4 Dianópolis Brazil
114 B4 Dianra Côte d'Ivoire
114 C3 Diapaga Burkina
79 C2 Dibā al Ḥiṣn U.A.E.
79 C2 Dibab Oman
118 C3 Dibaya Dem. Rep. Congo
123 B3 Dibeng S. Africa
72 D2 Dibrugarh India
111 C3 Dickinson U.S.A.
142 C1 Dickson U.S.A.
Dicle r. Turkey see Tigris

105 D3 Die France
Diedenhofen France see
Thionville
129 D2 Diefenbaker, Lake Can.
Diégo Suarez Madag. see
Antsiranana
114 B3 Diemā Mali
101 D2 Diemel r. Ger.
62 B1 Điên Biên Phu Vietnam
62 B2 Điên Châu Vietnam
101 D1 Diepholz Ger.
104 C2 Dieppe France
100 B2 Diest Belgium
115 D3 Diffa Niger
131 D3 Digby Can.
105 D3 Digne-les-Bains France
105 C2 Digoin France
64 B3 Digos Phil.
59 D3 Digul r. Indon.
105 D2 Dijon France
115 D4 Dik Chad
117 C3 Dikhil Djibouti
111 C3 Dikili Turkey
100 A2 Diksmuide Belgium
82 G2 Dikson Rus. Fed.
115 D3 Dikwa Nigeria
117 B4 Dila Eth.
59 C3 Dili East Timor
101 D2 Dillenburg Ger.
117 A3 Dilling Sudan
126 B3 Dillingham U.S.A.
134 D1 Dillon MT U.S.A.
143 E2 Dillon SC U.S.A.
118 C4 Dilolo Dem. Rep. Congo
72 D2 Dimapur India
Dimashq Syria see
Damascus
52 B3 Dimboola Austr.
110 C2 Dimitrovgrad Bulg.
87 D3 Dimitrovgrad Rus. Fed.
Dimitrovo Bulg. see Pernik
64 B2 Dinagat i. Phil.
75 C2 Dinajpur Bangl.
104 B2 Dinan France
100 B2 Dinant Belgium
111 D3 Dinar Turkey
81 D2 Dīnār, Kūh-e mt. Iran
104 B2 Dinard France
Dinbych U.K. see Denbigh
73 B3 Dindigul India
118 B1 Dindima Nigeria
123 D1 Dindiza Moz.
101 E2 Dingelstädt Ger.
97 A2 Dingle Rep. of Ireland
97 A2 Dingle Bay Rep. of Ireland
71 B3 Dingnan China
102 C2 Dingolfing Ger.
114 A3 Dinguiraye Guinea
96 B2 Dingwall U.K.
70 A2 Dingxi China
75 C2 Dinngyê China
123 C1 Dinokwe Botswana
91 D2 Dinskaya Rus. Fed.
100 C2 Dinslaken Ger.
135 C3 Dinuba U.S.A.
114 B3 Dioïla Mali
154 B3 Dionísio Cerqueira Brazil
114 A3 Diourbel Senegal
75 D2 Diphu India
64 B3 Dipolog Phil.
74 B1 Dir Pak.
51 D1 Direction, Cape Austr.
117 C4 Dirë Dawa Eth.
120 B2 Dirico Angola
50 A2 Dirk Hartog Island Austr.
53 C1 Dirranbandi Austr.
78 B3 Dirs Saudi Arabia
153 E5 Disappointment, Cape
S. Georgia
134 B1 Disappointment, Cape
U.S.A.
50 B2 Disappointment, Lake
salt flat Austr.
52 B3 Discovery Bay Austr.
127 H2 Disko i. Greenland see
Qeqertarsuaq
143 E1 Dismal Swamp U.S.A.
99 D3 Diss U.K.
108 B3 Dittaino r. Sicily Italy
74 B2 Diu India
155 D2 Divinópolis Brazil
87 D4 Divnoye Rus. Fed.
114 B4 Divo Côte d'Ivoire
80 B2 Divriği Turkey
74 A2 Diwana Pak.
140 B2 Dixon U.S.A.
128 A2 Dixon Entrance sea chan.
Can./U.S.A.
81 C2 Diyarbakır Turkey
74 A2 Diz Pak.
115 D2 Djado Niger

115 D2	Djado, Plateau du Niger
	Djakarta Indon. see
	Jakarta
118 B3	Djambala Congo
115 C2	Djanet Alg.
115 D3	Djédaa Chad
115 C1	Djelfa Alg.
119 C2	Djéma C.A.R.
114 B3	Djenné Mali
114 B3	Djibo Burkina
117 C3	Djibouti country Africa
117 C3	Djibouti Djibouti
	Djidjelli Alg. see Jijel
118 C2	Djolu Dem. Rep. Congo
114 C4	Djougou Benin
118 B2	Djoum Cameroon
92 C3	Djúpivogur Iceland
89 F3	Dmitriyevka Rus. Fed.
89 E3	Dmitriyev-L'govskiy Rus. Fed.
	Dmitriyevsk Ukr. see Makiyivka
89 E2	Dmitrov Rus. Fed.
	Dmytriyevs'k Ukr. see Makiyivka
	Dnepr r. Rus. Fed. see Dnieper
89 D3	Dnieper r. Europe
	Dniester r. Ukr. see Dnister
	Dnipro r. Ukr. see Dnieper
91 C2	Dniprodzerzhyns'k Ukr.
91 D2	Dnipropetrovs'k Ukr.
91 C2	Dniprorudne Ukr.
90 B2	Dnister r. Ukr.
90 C2	Dnistrov'ky Lyman l. Ukr.
88 C2	Dno Rus. Fed.
121 C2	Doa Moz.
115 D4	Doba Chad
88 B2	Dobele Latvia
101 F2	Döbeln Ger.
59 C3	Doberai, Jazirah pen. Indon.
	Doberai Peninsula Indon. see Doberai, Jazirah
59 C3	Dobo Indon.
109 C2	Doboj Bos.-Herz.
103 E1	Dobre Miasto Pol.
110 C2	Dobrich Bulg.
89 F3	Dobrinka Rus. Fed.
89 E3	Dobroye Rus. Fed.
89 D3	Dobrush Belarus
86 E3	Dobryanka Rus. Fed.
155 E1	Doce r. Brazil
145 B2	Doctor Arroyo Mex.
144 B2	Doctor Belisario Domínguez Mex.
	Doctor Petru Groza Romania see Ştei
111 C3	Dodecanese is Greece
	Dodekanisos is Greece see Dodecanese
136 C3	Dodge City U.S.A.
119 D3	Dodoma Tanz.
100 C1	Doesburg Neth.
100 C2	Doetinchem Neth.
59 C3	Dofa Indon.
75 C1	Dogai Coring salt l. China
128 B2	Dog Creek Can.
67 B3	Dōgo i. Japan
115 C3	Dogondoutchi Niger
81 C2	Doğubeyazıt Turkey
79 C2	Doha Qatar
62 A2	Doi Saket Thai.
81 D2	Dokali Iran
100 B1	Dokkum Neth.
88 C3	Dokshytsy Belarus
91 D2	Dokuchayevs'k Ukr.
59 D3	Dolak, Pulau i. Indon.
138 A1	Dolan Springs U.S.A.
130 C3	Dolbeau Can.
104 B2	Dol-de-Bretagne France
105 D2	Dole France
91 D2	Dolgaya, Kosa spit Rus. Fed.
99 B3	Dolgellau U.K.
89 E3	Dolgorukovo Rus. Fed.
89 E3	Dolgoye Rus. Fed.
69 F1	Dolinsk Rus. Fed.
103 D2	Dolný Kubín Slovakia
	Dolomites mts Italy see Dolomiti
108 B1	Dolomiti mts Italy
	Dolonnur China see Duolun
117 C4	Dolo Odo Eth.
144 A2	Dolores Mex.
126 E2	Dolphin and Union Strait Can.
90 A2	Dolyna Ukr.
102 C2	Domažlice Czech Rep.
93 E3	Dombås Norway
103 D2	Dombóvár Hungary
	Dombrovitsa Ukr. see Dubrovytsya
	Dombrowa Pol. see Dąbrowa Górnicza
128 B2	Dome Creek Can.
147 D3	Dominica country West Indies
147 C3	Dominican Republic country West Indies
118 C3	Domiongo Dem. Rep. Congo
117 C4	Domo Eth.
89 E2	Domodedovo Rus. Fed.
111 B3	Domokos Greece
61 C2	Dompu Indon.
138 B3	Don Mex.
89 E3	Don r. Rus. Fed.
96 C2	Don r. U.K.
97 D1	Donaghadee U.K.
52 B3	Donald Austr.
	Donau r. Austria/Ger. see Danube
102 C2	Donauwörth Ger.
106 B2	Don Benito Spain
98 C3	Doncaster U.K.
120 A1	Dondo Angola
121 C2	Dondo Moz.
73 C4	Dondra Head hd Sri Lanka
97 B1	Donegal Rep. of Ireland
97 B1	Donegal Bay Rep. of Ireland
91 D2	Donets'k Ukr.
91 D2	Donets'kyy Kryazh hills Rus. Fed./Ukr.
118 B2	Donga Nigeria
50 A2	Dongara Austr.
71 A3	Dongchuan China
71 A4	Dongfang China
66 B1	Dongfanghong China
61 C2	Donggala Indon.
65 A2	Donggang China
	Donggou China see Donggang
62 B2	Đông Ha Vietnam
	N. Pacific Ocean see East China Sea
62 B2	Đông Hới Vietnam
116 B3	Dongola Sudan
118 B2	Dongou Congo
63 B2	Dong Phraya Fai mts Thai.
63 B2	Dong Phraya Yen esc. Thai.
	Dongping China see Anhua
71 B3	Dongshan China
70 B2	Dongsheng China
70 C2	Dongtai China
71 B3	Dongting Hu l. China
	Dong Ujimqin Qi China see Uliastai
71 C3	Dongyang China
70 B2	Dongying China
139 D3	Donna U.S.A.
54 B1	Donnellys Crossing N.Z.
100 C3	Donnersberg hill Ger.
107 C1	Donostia - San Sebastián Spain
81 D1	Donyztau, Sor dry lake Kazakh.
51 C1	Doomadgee Austr.
140 B2	Door Peninsula U.S.A.
117 C4	Dooxo Nugaaleed val. Somalia
50 B2	Dora, Lake salt flat Austr.
99 B4	Dorchester U.K.
122 A1	Dordabis Namibia
104 B2	Dordogne r. France
100 B2	Dordrecht Neth.
123 C3	Dordrecht S. Africa
122 A1	Doreenville Namibia
129 C2	Doré Lake Can.
101 D1	Dorfmark Ger.
114 B3	Dori Burkina
122 A3	Doring r. S. Africa
100 C2	Dormagen Ger.
96 B2	Dornoch U.K.
96 B2	Dornoch Firth est. U.K.
89 D3	Dorogobuzh Rus. Fed.
110 C1	Dorohoi Romania
68 C1	Döröö Nuur salt l. Mongolia
92 G3	Dorotea Sweden
50 A2	Dorre Island Austr.
53 D2	Dorrigo Austr.
118 B2	Dorsale Camerounaise slope Cameroon/Nigeria
100 C2	Dorsten Ger.
100 C2	Dortmund Ger.
100 C2	Dortmund-Ems-Kanal canal Ger.
153 B4	Dos Bahías, Cabo c. Arg.
101 F1	Dosse r. Ger.
114 C3	Dosso Niger
143 C2	Dothan U.S.A.
101 D1	Dötlingen Ger.
105 C1	Douai France
118 A2	Douala Cameroon
104 B2	Douarnenez France
105 D2	Doubs r. France/Switz.
54 A3	Doubtful Sound N.Z.
114 B3	Douentza Mali
98 A2	Douglas Isle of Man
122 B2	Douglas S. Africa
128 A2	Douglas AK U.S.A.
138 B2	Douglas AZ U.S.A.
143 D2	Douglas GA U.S.A.
136 B2	Douglas WY U.S.A.
104 C1	Doullens France
154 B1	Dourada, Serra hills Brazil
154 B2	Dourados Brazil
154 B2	Dourados r. Brazil
154 B2	Dourados, Serra dos hills Brazil
106 B1	Douro r. Port.
99 D4	Dover U.K.
141 D3	Dover U.S.A.
95 D3	Dover, Strait of France/U.K.
141 F1	Dover-Foxcroft U.S.A.
121 C2	Dowa Malawi
81 D3	Dowlatābād Iran
79 C2	Dowlatābād Iran
97 D1	Downpatrick U.K.
81 C2	Dow Rūd Iran
77 C3	Dowshī Afgh.
67 B3	Dōzen is Japan
130 C3	Dozois, Réservoir resr Can.
154 B2	Dracena Brazil
100 C1	Drachten Neth.
110 B2	Drăgăneşti-Olt Romania
110 B2	Drăgăşani Romania
105 D3	Draguignan France
88 C3	Drahichyn Belarus
123 C2	Drakensberg mts Lesotho/S. Africa
123 C2	Drakensberg mts S. Africa
149 C8	Drake Passage S. Atlantic Ocean
111 B2	Drama Greece
93 F4	Drammen Norway
109 C1	Drava r. Europe
128 C2	Drayton Valley Can.
101 D2	Dreieich Ger.
111 B3	Drepano, Akra pt Greece
102 C1	Dresden Ger.
104 C2	Dreux France
100 B1	Driemond Neth.
98 C2	Driffield U.K.
137 D1	Drift Prairie reg. U.S.A.
109 C2	Drina r. Bos.-Herz./Yugo.
142 B2	Driskill Mountain hill U.S.A.
109 C2	Drissa Belarus Vyerkhnyadzvinsk
110 B2	Drobeta-Turnu Severin Romania
90 B2	Drochia Moldova
101 D1	Drochtersen Ger.
97 C2	Drogheda Rep. of Ireland
90 A2	Drohobych Ukr.
99 B3	Droitwich U.K.
	Drokiya Moldova see Drochia
97 C1	Dromahair Rep. of Ireland
97 C1	Dromore U.K.
100 B1	Dronten Neth.
74 B1	Drosh Pak.
53 C3	Drouin Austr.
128 C2	Drumheller Can.
140 C1	Drummond Island U.S.A.
131 C3	Drummondville Can.
96 B3	Drummore U.K.
96 B2	Drumnadrochit U.K.
	Druskieniki Lith. see Druskininkai
88 B3	Druskininkai Lith.
88 C2	Druya Belarus
91 D2	Druzhkivka Ukr.
88 D2	Druzhnaya Gorka Rus. Fed.
89 D3	Drybin Belarus
130 A3	Dryden Can.
50 B1	Drysdale r. Austr.
147 D3	Duarte, Pico mt. Dom. Rep.
78 A2	Dubā Saudi Arabia
79 C2	Dubai U.A.E.
90 B2	Dubăsari Moldova
129 D1	Dubawnt Lake Can.
	Dubayy U.A.E. see Dubai
78 A2	Dubbagh, Jabal ad mt. Saudi Arabia
53 C2	Dubbo Austr.
	Dubesar' Moldova see Dubăsari
97 C2	Dublin Rep. of Ireland
143 D2	Dublin U.S.A.
89 E2	Dubna Rus. Fed.
90 B1	Dubno Ukr.
141 D2	Du Bois U.S.A.
	Dubossary Moldova see Dubăsari
114 A4	Dubréka Guinea
109 C2	Dubrovnik Croatia
90 B1	Dubrovytsya Ukr.
89 D3	Dubrowna Belarus
137 E2	Dubuque U.S.A.
135 D2	Duchesne U.S.A.
129 D2	Duck Bay Can.
63 B2	Đưc Trong Vietnam
101 E2	Duderstadt Ger.
82 G2	Dudinka Rus. Fed.
99 B3	Dudley U.K.
106 B1	Duero r. Spain
48 H4	Duff Islands Solomon Is
96 C2	Dufftown U.K.
131 C2	Dufreboy, Lac l. Can.
109 C2	Dugi Otok i. Croatia
109 C2	Dugi Rat Croatia
100 C2	Duisburg Ger.
123 D1	Duiwelskloof S. Africa
123 C3	Dukathole S. Africa
117 B4	Duk Fadiat Sudan
79 C2	Dukhān Qatar
89 D2	Dukhovshchina Rus. Fed.
	Dukou China see Panzhihua
88 C2	Dūkštas Lith.
68 C2	Dulan China
152 B3	Dulce r. Arg.
138 B1	Dulce U.S.A.
97 C2	Duleek Rep. of Ireland
100 C2	Dülmen Ger.
110 C2	Dulovo Bulg.
137 E1	Duluth U.S.A.
64 B3	Dumaguete Phil.
60 B1	Dumai Indon.
64 B2	Dumaran i. Phil.
142 B2	Dumas AR U.S.A.
139 C1	Dumas TX U.S.A.
96 B3	Dumbarton U.K.
103 D2	Đumbier mt. Slovakia
96 C3	Dumfries U.K.
89 E3	Duminichi Rus. Fed.
75 C2	Dumka India
55 L3	Dumont d'Urville Sea Antarctica
116 B1	Dumyât Egypt
	Duna r. Hungary see Danube
	Dunaburg Latvia see Daugavpils
103 D2	Dunakeszi Hungary
97 C2	Dunany Point Rep. of Ireland
	Dunărea r. Romania see Danube
110 C1	Dunării, Delta Romania
103 D2	Dunaújváros Hungary
	Dunav r. Bulg./Croatia/Yugo. see Danube
90 B2	Dunayivtsi Ukr.
96 B2	Dunbar U.K.
96 C1	Dunbeath U.K.
128 B3	Duncan Can.
139 D2	Duncan U.S.A.
96 C1	Duncansby Head hd U.K.
88 B2	Dundaga Latvia
97 C1	Dundalk Rep. of Ireland
141 D3	Dundalk U.S.A.
97 C2	Dundalk Bay Rep. of Ireland
	Dundas Greenland see Uummannaq
	Dún Dealgan Rep. of Ireland see Dundalk
123 D2	Dundee S. Africa
96 C2	Dundee U.K.
97 D1	Dundrum Bay U.K.
54 B3	Dunedin N.Z.
53 C2	Dunedoo Austr.
96 C2	Dunfermline U.K.
97 C1	Dungannon U.K.
74 B2	Dungarpur India

97 C2 Dungarvan Rep. of Ireland
99 D4 Dungeness hd U.K.
97 C1 Dungiven U.K.
53 D2 Dungog Austr.
119 C2 Dungu Dem. Rep. Congo
60 B1 Dungun Malaysia
116 B2 Dungunab Sudan
69 E2 Dunhua China
68 C2 Dunhuang China
96 C2 Dunkeld U.K.
Dunkerque France see
Dunkirk
104 C1 Dunkirk France
141 D2 Dunkirk U.S.A.
97 C2 Dún Laoghaire
Rep. of Ireland
97 B3 Dunmanway
Rep. of Ireland
97 D1 Dunmurry U.K.
96 C1 Dunnet Head hd U.K.
96 C3 Duns U.K.
134 B2 Dunsmuir U.S.A.
99 C4 Dunstable U.K.
100 B3 Dun-sur-Meuse France
96 A2 Dunvegan U.K.
70 B1 Duolun China
Duperré Alg. see Aïn Defla
110 B2 Dupnitsa Bulg.
136 C1 Dupree U.S.A.
Duque de Bragança
Angola see Calandula
140 B3 Du Quoin U.S.A.
50 B1 Durack r. Austr.
105 C3 Durance r. France
144 B2 Durango Mex.
106 C1 Durango Spain
136 B3 Durango U.S.A.
139 D2 Durant U.S.A.
153 C3 Durazno Uru.
Durazzo Albania see
Durrës
123 D2 Durban S. Africa
105 C3 Durban-Corbières
France
122 A3 Durbanville S. Africa
100 B2 Durbuy Belgium
100 C3 Düren Ger.
75 C2 Durg India
98 C2 Durham U.K.
143 E1 Durham U.S.A.
60 B1 Duri Indon.
109 C2 Durmitor mt. Yugo.
96 B1 Durness U.K.
109 C2 Durrës Albania
97 A3 Dursey Island
Rep. of Ireland
111 C3 Dursunbey Turkey
117 C4 Durukhsi Somalia
59 D3 D'Urville, Tanjung pt
Indon.
54 B2 D'Urville Island N.Z.
71 A3 Dushan China
77 C2 Dushanbe Tajik.
100 C2 Düsseldorf Ger.
Dutch East Indies country
Asia see Indonesia
Dutch Guiana country
S. America see Suriname
Dutch West Indies terr.
West Indies see
Netherlands Antilles
Duvno Bos.-Herz. see
Tomislavgrad
71 A3 Duyun China
80 B1 Düzce Turkey
91 D2 Dvorichna Ukr.
74 A2 Dwarka India
123 C1 Dwarsberg S. Africa
134 C1 Dworshak Reservoir
U.S.A.
89 D3 Dyat'kovo Rus. Fed.
96 C2 Dyce U.K.
127 H2 Dyer, Cape Can.
142 C1 Dyersburg U.S.A.
99 B3 Dyfi r. U.K.
103 D2 Dyje r. Austria/Czech Rep.
103 D1 Dylewska Góra hill Pol.
91 D2 Dymytrov Ukr.
123 C3 Dyoki S. Africa
51 D2 Dysart Austr.
122 B3 Dysselsdorp S. Africa
87 E3 Dyurtyuli Rus. Fed.
69 D2 Dzamin Üüd Mongolia
91 D2 Dzerzhyns'k Ukr.
Dzhaltyr Kazakh. see
Zhaltyr
Dzhambul Kazakh. see
Taraz
81 D2 Dzhanga Turkm.
76 B2 Dzhangala Kazakh.
91 C2 Dzhankoy Ukr.

76 A2 Dzhanybek Kazakh.
76 C1 Dzharkent Kazakh. see
Zharkent
81 D2 Dzhebel Turkm.
Dzhetygara Kazakh. see
Zhitikara
Dzhezkazgan Kazakh. see
Zhezkazgan
77 C2 Dzhizak Uzbek.
91 D3 Dzhubga Rus. Fed.
83 K3 Dzhugdzhur, Khrebet mts
Rus. Fed.
77 D2 Dzhungarskiy Alatau,
Khrebet mts
China/Kazakh.
76 C2 Dzhusaly Kazakh.
103 E1 Działdowo Pol.
145 D2 Dzilam de Bravo Mex.
69 D1 Dzuunmod Mongolia
88 C3 Dzyarzhynsk Belarus
88 C3 Dzyatlavichy Belarus

E

131 E2 Eagle r. Can.
134 C1 Eagle Cap mt. U.S.A.
130 A3 Eagle Lake Can.
134 B2 Eagle Lake U.S.A.
139 C3 Eagle Pass U.S.A.
126 C2 Eagle Plain Can.
Eap i. Micronesia see Yap
130 A2 Ear Falls Can.
135 C3 Earlimart U.S.A.
96 C2 Earn r. U.K.
55 J2 East Antarctica reg.
Antarctica
East Bengal country Asia
see Bangladesh
99 D4 Eastbourne U.K.
59 D2 East Caroline Basin
sea feature
N. Pacific Ocean
69 E2 East China Sea
N. Pacific Ocean
54 B1 East Coast Bays N.Z.
99 D3 East Dereham U.K.
129 D3 Eastend Can.
157 G7 Easter Island
S. Pacific Ocean
123 C3 Eastern Cape prov.
S. Africa
116 B2 Eastern Desert Egypt
73 B3 Eastern Ghats mts India
Eastern Samoa terr.
S. Pacific Ocean see
American Samoa
Eastern Sayan
Mountains Rus. Fed. see
Vostochnyy Sayan
Eastern Transvaal prov.
S. Africa see Mpumalanga
129 E2 Easterville Can.
153 C5 East Falkland i.
Falkland Is
100 C1 East Frisian Islands Ger.
135 C3 Eastgate U.S.A.
137 D1 East Grand Forks U.S.A.
96 B3 East Kilbride U.K.
140 C2 East Lansing U.S.A.
99 C4 Eastleigh U.K.
96 C3 East Linton U.K.
140 C2 East Liverpool U.S.A.
123 C3 East London S. Africa
130 C2 Eastmain Can.
130 C2 Eastmain r. Can.
143 D2 Eastman U.S.A.
157 G8 East Pacific Rise
sea feature
N. Pacific Ocean
East Pakistan country
Asia see Bangladesh
140 A3 East St Louis U.S.A.
83 K2 East Siberian Sea
Rus. Fed.
53 C2 East Timor terr. Asia
59 C3 East Toorale Austr.
141 D2 East York Can.
140 A2 Eau Claire U.S.A.
59 D2 Eauripik atoll Micronesia
145 C2 Ebano Mex.
99 B4 Ebbw Vale U.K.
118 B2 Ebebiyin Equat. Guinea
102 C1 Eberswalde-Finow Ger.
66 C1 Ebetsu Japan
77 C2 Ebinur Hu salt l. China
118 C2 Ebola r. Dem. Rep. Congo
109 C2 Eboli Italy
118 B2 Ebolowa Cameroon
107 D1 Ebro r. Spain

107 C1 Echarri-Aranaz Spain
114 C1 Ech Chélif Alg.
Echeng China see Ezhou
144 A2 Echeverria, Pico mt. Mex.
129 E2 Echoing r. Can.
100 C3 Echternach Lux.
52 B3 Echuca Austr.
106 B2 Écija Spain
102 B1 Eckernförde Ger.
127 G2 Eclipse Sound sea chan.
Can.
150 B3 Ecuador country
S. America
116 C3 Ed Eritrea
96 C1 Eday i. U.K.
117 A3 Ed Da'ein Sudan
117 B3 Ed Damazin Sudan
116 B3 Ed Damer Sudan
116 B3 Ed Debba Sudan
116 B3 Ed Dueim Sudan
51 D4 Eddystone Point Austr.
100 B1 Ede Neth.
118 B2 Edéa Cameroon
154 C1 Edéia Brazil
53 C3 Eden Austr.
98 B2 Eden r. U.K.
139 D2 Eden U.S.A.
123 C2 Edenburg S. Africa
97 C2 Edenderry Rep. of Ireland
52 B3 Edenhope Austr.
143 E1 Edenton U.S.A.
111 B2 Edessa Greece
141 E2 Edgartown U.S.A.
Edge Island Svalbard see
Edgeøya
82 C1 Edgeøya i. Svalbard
143 D3 Edgewater U.S.A.
140 C2 Edinboro U.S.A.
139 D3 Edinburg U.S.A.
96 C3 Edinburgh U.K.
90 B2 Edineţ Moldova
111 C2 Edirne Turkey
Edith Ronne Land
ice feature Antarctica see
Ronne Ice Shelf
128 C2 Edmonton Can.
131 D3 Edmundston Can.
111 C3 Edremit Turkey
111 C3 Edremit Körfezi b. Turkey
128 C2 Edson Can.
119 C3 Edward, Lake
Dem. Rep. Congo/Uganda
Edwardesabad Pak. see
Bannu
139 D2 Edwards Plateau U.S.A.
55 C2 Edward VII Peninsula
Antarctica
96 C2 Edzell U.K.
100 A3 Eeklo Belgium
135 B2 Eel r. U.S.A.
100 C1 Eemskanaal canal Neth.
100 C1 Eenrum Neth.
140 B3 Effingham U.S.A.
135 C3 Egan Range mts U.S.A.
103 E2 Eger Hungary
93 E4 Egersund Norway
100 B2 Eghezée Belgium
92 □C2 Egilsstaðir Iceland
80 B2 Eğirdir Turkey
80 B2 Eğirdir Gölü l. Turkey
104 C2 Égletons France
54 B1 Egmont, Mount vol. N.Z.
83 M2 Egvekinot Rus. Fed.
116 B2 Egypt country Africa
70 A2 Ehen Hudag China
106 C1 Eibar Spain
100 C1 Eibergen Neth.
100 C2 Eifel hills Ger.
96 A2 Eigg i. U.K.
73 B4 Eight Degree Channel
India/Maldives
50 B1 Eighty Mile Beach Austr.
Eilat Israel see Elat
101 F2 Eilenburg Ger.
101 D2 Einbeck Ger.
100 B2 Eindhoven Neth.
160 N4 Eirik Ridge sea feature
N. Atlantic Ocean
150 C3 Eirunepé Brazil
120 B2 Eiseb watercourse
Namibia
101 E2 Eisenach Ger.
101 E2 Eisenberg Ger.
102 C1 Eisenhüttenstadt Ger.
103 D2 Eisenstadt Austria
101 E2 Eisleben Lutherstadt Ger.
107 D2 Eivissa Spain
Eivissa i. Spain see Ibiza
107 C1 Ejea de los Caballeros
Spain
121 □D3 Ejeda Madag.

Ejin Qi China see
Dalain Hob
93 H4 Ekenäs Fin.
77 D1 Ekibastuz Kazakh.
92 J2 Ekostrovskaya Imandra,
Ozero l. Rus. Fed.
93 I4 Eksjö Sweden
122 A2 Eksteenfontein S. Africa
130 B2 Ekwan r. Can.
62 A2 Ela Myanmar
El Aaiún Western Sahara
see Laâyoune
80 A2 El 'Amirîya Egypt
123 C2 Elandsdoorn S. Africa
El Araïche Morocco see
Larache
80 B2 El 'Arish Egypt
El Asnam Alg. see
Ech Chélif
111 B3 Elassona Greece
80 B3 Elat Israel
80 B2 Elazığ Turkey
108 B2 Elba, Isola d' i. Italy
150 B2 El Banco Col.
109 D2 Elbasan Albania
150 C2 El Baúl Venez.
114 C1 El Bayadh Alg.
101 D1 Elbe r. Ger.
136 B3 Elbert, Mount U.S.A.
143 D2 Elberton U.S.A.
104 C2 Elbeuf France
80 B2 Elbistan Turkey
103 D1 Elbląg Pol.
153 A4 El Bolsón Arg.
87 D4 Elbrus mt. Rus. Fed.
Elburz Mountains Iran see
Alborz, Reshteh-ye
150 C2 El Callao Venez.
139 D3 El Campo U.S.A.
135 C4 El Centro U.S.A.
152 B1 El Cerro Bol.
107 C2 Elche Spain
107 C2 Elda Spain
119 D2 Eldama Ravine Kenya
137 E3 Eldon U.S.A.
154 B3 Eldorado Arg.
154 B2 Eldorado Brazil
144 B2 El Dorado Mex.
142 B2 El Dorado AR U.S.A.
137 D3 El Dorado KS U.S.A.
134 D1 Electric Peak U.S.A.
114 B2 El Eglab plat. Alg.
106 C2 El Ejido Spain
89 E2 Elektrostal' Rus. Fed.
150 B3 El Encanto Col.
146 C2 Eleuthera i. Bahamas
80 B3 El Faiyûm Egypt
116 A3 El Fasher Sudan
144 B2 El Fuerte Mex.
117 A3 El Fula Sudan
116 A3 El Geneina Sudan
116 B3 El Geteina Sudan
96 C2 Elgin U.K.
140 B2 Elgin U.S.A.
83 K2 El'ginskiy Rus. Fed.
116 B2 El Gîza Egypt
115 C1 El Goléa Alg.
144 A1 El Golfo de Santa Clara
Mex.
119 D2 Elgon, Mount Uganda
80 A2 El Hadjar Alg.
80 A2 El Hammâm Egypt
114 A2 El Hammâmi reg. Maur.
114 A2 El Hank esc. Mali/Maur.
114 A2 El Hierro i. Canary Is
145 C2 El Higo Mex.
114 C2 El Homr Alg.
Elichpur India see
Achalpur
126 B2 Elim U.S.A.
Élisabethville
Dem. Rep. Congo see
Lubumbashi
El Iskandarîya Egypt see
Alexandria
87 D4 Elista Rus. Fed.
141 E2 Elizabeth U.S.A.
143 E1 Elizabeth City U.S.A.
140 B3 Elizabethtown U.S.A.
114 B1 El Jadida Morocco
103 E1 Ełk Pol.
108 A3 El Kala Alg.
88 C2 Elkas kalns hill Latvia
139 D1 Elk City U.S.A.
114 B1 El Kelaâ des Srarhna
Morocco
103 E1 Elkford Can.
116 B2 El Khârga Egypt
140 B2 Elkhart U.S.A.
El Khartûm Sudan see
Khartoum

110 C2 Elkhovo Bulg.
141 D3 Elkins U.S.A.
128 C3 Elko Can.
134 C2 Elko U.S.A.
129 C2 Elk Point Can.
137 E1 Elk River U.S.A.
126 F1 Ellef Ringnes Island Can.
137 D1 Ellendale U.S.A.
134 B1 Ellensburg U.S.A.
54 B2 Ellesmere, Lake N.Z.
127 G1 Ellesmere Island Can.
98 B3 Ellesmere Port U.K.
126 F2 Ellice r. Can.
Ellice Islands country
S. Pacific Ocean see
Tuvalu
123 C3 Elliotdale S. Africa
140 C1 Elliot Lake Can.
123 C1 Ellisras S. Africa
96 C2 Ellon U.K.
141 F2 Ellsworth U.S.A.
55 R2 Ellsworth Mountains
Antarctica
116 B2 El Maks el Bahari Egypt
111 C3 Elmalı Turkey
80 B2 El Mansûra Egypt
115 C1 El Meghaïer Alg.
116 B2 El Minya Egypt
141 D2 Elmira U.S.A.
107 C2 El Moral Spain
101 D1 Elmshorn Ger.
117 A3 El Muglad Sudan
150 B2 El Nevado, Cerro mt. Col.
64 A2 El Nido Phil.
116 B3 El Obeid Sudan
144 B2 El Oro Mex.
115 C1 El Oued Alg.
138 A2 Eloy U.S.A.
El Paso U.S.A. see Derby
138 B2 El Paso U.S.A.
145 D3 El Pinalón, Cerro mt.
Guat.
144 B1 El Porvenir Mex.
107 D1 El Prat de Llobregat
Spain
106 B2 El Puerto de Santa María
Spain
El Qâhira Egypt see Cairo
116 A2 El Qasr Egypt
El Quds Israel/West Bank
see Jerusalem
139 D1 El Reno U.S.A.
128 A1 Elsa Can.
145 B2 El Salado Mex.
144 B2 El Salto Mex.
146 B3 El Salvador country
Central America
152 B2 El Salvador Chile
145 B2 El Salvador Mex.
138 B3 El Sauz Mex.
144 A1 El Socorro Mex.
138 B3 El Sueco Mex.
El Suweis Egypt see Suez
108 A3 El Tarf Alg.
106 B1 El Teleno mt. Spain
145 C2 El Temascal Mex.
150 C2 El Tigre Venez.
147 D4 El Tocuyo Venez.
116 B2 El Tûr Egypt
El Uqsur Egypt see Luxor
73 C3 Eluru India
88 C2 Elva Estonia
106 B2 Elvas Port.
93 F3 Elverum Norway
119 E2 El Wak Kenya
99 D3 Ely U.K.
137 E1 Ely MN U.S.A.
135 D3 Ely NV U.S.A.
81 D2 Emāmrūd Iran
93 G4 Emån r. Sweden
76 B2 Emba Kazakh.
76 B2 Emba r. Kazakh.
123 C2 Embalenhle S. Africa
118 B2 Embondo
Dem. Rep. Congo
154 C1 Emborcação, Represa de
resr Brazil
119 D3 Embu Kenya
100 C1 Emden Ger.
51 D2 Emerald Austr.
129 E3 Emerson Can.
111 C3 Emet Turkey
123 D2 eMgwenya S. Africa
123 D2 eMijindini S. Africa
115 D3 Emi Koussi mt. Chad
145 C3 Emiliano Zapata Mex.
110 C2 Emine, Nos pt Bulg.
80 B2 Emirdağ Turkey
88 B2 Emmaste Estonia
100 B1 Emmeloord Neth.
100 C2 Emmelshausen Ger.

100 C1 Emmen Neth.
139 C3 Emory Peak U.S.A.
144 A2 Empalme Mex.
123 D2 Empangeni S. Africa
156 D2 Emperor Trough
sea feature
N. Pacific Ocean
108 B2 Empoli Italy
111 C3 Emponas Greece
137 D3 Emporia KS U.S.A.
141 D3 Emporia VA U.S.A.
Empty Quarter des.
Saudi Arabia see
Rub' al Khālī
100 C1 Ems r. Ger.
100 C1 Emsdetten Ger.
88 C2 Emumägi hill Estonia
123 C2 Emzinoni S. Africa
59 D3 Enarotali Indon.
144 B2 Encarnación Mex.
152 C2 Encarnación Para.
155 D1 Encruzilhada Brazil
60 B1 Endau Malaysia
61 D2 Endeh Indon.
55 G2 Enderby Land reg.
Antarctica
126 B2 Endicott Mountains
U.S.A.
50 A2 Eneabba Austr.
91 C2 Enerhodar Ukr.
111 C2 Enez Turkey
97 C2 Enfield Rep. of Ireland
87 D3 Engel's Rus. Fed.
60 B2 Enggano i. Indon.
99 C3 England admin. div. U.K.
130 C3 Englehart Can.
143 D3 Englewood U.S.A.
130 A2 English r. Can.
English Bazar India see
Ingrāj Bāzār
95 C4 English Channel
France/U.K.
139 D1 Enid U.S.A.
Enkeldoorn Zimbabwe see
Chivhu
100 B1 Enkhuizen Neth.
93 G4 Enköping Sweden
108 B3 Enna Sicily Italy
129 D1 Ennadai Lake Can.
116 A3 En Nahud Sudan
115 E3 Ennedi, Massif mts Chad
53 C1 Enngonia Austr.
97 B2 Ennis Rep. of Ireland
139 D2 Ennis U.S.A.
97 C2 Enniscorthy
Rep. of Ireland
97 C2 Enniskerry Rep. of Ireland
97 C1 Enniskillen U.K.
97 B2 Ennistymon
Rep. of Ireland
102 C2 Enns Austria
102 C2 Enns r. Austria
92 J3 Eno Fin.
92 H2 Enontekiö Fin.
53 C3 Ensay Austr.
100 C1 Enschede Neth.
144 A1 Ensenada Mex.
70 A2 Enshi China
119 D2 Entebbe Uganda
121 C3 Enterprise Can.
142 D2 Enterprise AL U.S.A.
134 C1 Enterprise OR U.S.A.
152 B2 Entre Ríos Bol.
106 B2 Entroncamento Port.
115 C4 Enugu Nigeria
150 B3 Envira Brazil
118 B2 Epéna Congo
105 C2 Épernay France
135 D3 Ephraim U.S.A.
134 C1 Ephrata U.S.A.
105 D2 Épinal France
99 D4 Epping U.K.
99 C4 Epsom U.K.
118 A2 Equatorial Guinea
country Africa
104 B2 Équerdreville-Hainneville
France
101 D3 Erbach Ger.
101 F3 Erbendorf Ger.
100 C3 Erbeskopf hill Ger.
81 C2 Erciş Turkey
80 B2 Erciyes Dağı mt. Turkey
103 D2 Érd Hungary
Erdaobaihe China see
Baihe
65 B1 Erdao Jiang r. China
111 C2 Erdek Turkey
80 B2 Erdemli Turkey
154 B2 Eré, Campos hills Brazil
55 M2 Erebus, Mount vol.
Antarctica

152 C2 Erechim Brazil
69 D1 Ereentsav Mongolia
80 B2 Ereğli Turkey
80 B1 Ereğli Turkey
69 D2 Erenhot China
Erevan Armenia see
Yerevan
101 E2 Erfurt Ger.
80 B2 Ergani Turkey
114 B2 'Erg Chech des. Alg./Mali
115 D3 Erg du Djourab des. Chad
115 D3 Erg du Ténéré des. Niger
111 C2 Ergene r. Turkey
114 B2 Erg Iabès des. Alg.
114 B2 Erg Iguidi des. Alg./Maur.
78 A3 Erheib Sudan
96 B2 Ericht, Loch l. U.K.
140 C2 Erie U.S.A.
140 C2 Erie, Lake Can./U.S.A.
66 D2 Erimo-misaki c. Japan
116 B3 Eritrea country Africa
101 E3 Erlangen Ger.
50 C2 Erldunda Austr.
123 C2 Ermelo S. Africa
80 B2 Ermenek Turkey
111 B3 Ermoupoli Greece
73 B4 Ernakulam India
97 B1 Erne r. Rep. of Ireland/U.K.
73 B3 Erode India
100 B2 Erp Neth.
114 B1 Er Rachidia Morocco
116 B3 Er Rahad Sudan
97 B1 Errigal hill Rep. of Ireland
97 A1 Erris Head hd
Rep. of Ireland
48 H5 Erromango i. Vanuatu
109 D2 Ersekë Albania
89 F3 Ertil' Rus. Fed.
101 D2 Erwitte Ger.
101 F2 Erzgebirge mts
Czech Rep./Ger.
80 B2 Erzincan Turkey
81 C2 Erzurum Turkey
66 D2 Esashi Japan
93 E4 Esbjerg Denmark
135 D3 Escalante U.S.A.
135 D3 Escalante Desert U.S.A.
144 B2 Escalón Mex.
140 B1 Escanaba U.S.A.
145 C3 Escárcega Mex.
107 C1 Escatrón Spain
100 A2 Escaut r. Belgium
101 E1 Eschede Ger.
100 B3 Esch-sur-Alzette Lux.
101 E2 Eschwege Ger.
100 C2 Eschweiler Ger.
135 C4 Escondido U.S.A.
144 B2 Escuinapa Mex.
111 C3 Eşen Turkey
81 D2 Eşfahān Iran
123 D2 Eshowe S. Africa
123 D2 Esikhawini S. Africa
98 B2 Esk r. U.K.
131 D2 Esker Can.
92 □C2 Eskifjörður Iceland
93 G4 Eskilstuna Sweden
Eskimo Point Can. see
Arviat
111 D3 Eskişehir Turkey
81 C2 Eslāmābād-e Gharb Iran
111 C3 Esler Dağı mt. Turkey
111 C3 Eşme Turkey
146 C2 Esmeralda Cuba
150 B2 Esmeraldas Ecuador
79 D2 Espakeh Iran
105 C3 Espalion France
130 B3 Espanola Can.
138 B1 Espanola U.S.A.
50 B3 Esperance Austr.
153 A5 Esperanza Arg.
144 B2 Esperanza Mex.
106 B2 Espichel, Cabo c. Port.
154 B3 Espigão, Serra do mts
Brazil
139 C3 Espinazo Mex.
155 D1 Espinhaço, Serra do mts
Brazil
151 E4 Espinosa Brazil
Espírito Santo Brazil see
Vila Velha
48 H5 Espíritu Santo i. Vanuatu
144 A2 Espíritu Santo, Isla i.
Mex.
93 H3 Espoo Fin.
153 A4 Esquel Arg.
114 B1 Essaouira Morocco
114 A2 Es Semara
Western Sahara
100 C2 Essen Ger.
150 D2 Essequibo r. Guyana
141 E2 Essex Junction U.S.A.

83 L3 Esso Rus. Fed.
106 B1 Estaca de Bares, Punta
da pt Spain
81 D3 Eştahbān Iran
151 F4 Estância Brazil
123 C2 Estcourt S. Africa
107 C1 Estella Spain
106 B2 Estepona Spain
106 C1 Esteras de Medinaceli
Spain
129 D2 Esterhazy Can.
152 B2 Esteros Para.
136 B2 Estes Park U.S.A.
129 D3 Estevan Can.
137 E2 Estherville U.S.A.
129 D2 Eston Can.
88 C2 Estonia country Europe
Estonskaya S.S.R.
country Europe see Estonia
106 B1 Estrela, Serra da mts
Port.
106 B2 Estremoz Port.
52 A1 Etadunna Austr.
104 C2 Étampes France
104 C1 Étaples France
75 B2 Etawah India
123 D2 eThandakukhanya
S. Africa
122 B2 E'Thembini S. Africa
117 B4 Ethiopia country Africa
109 C3 Etna, Monte vol. Sicily
Italy
109 C3 Etna, Mount vol. Italy see
Etna, Monte
93 E4 Etne Norway
128 A2 Etolin Island U.S.A.
120 A2 Etosha Pan salt pan
Namibia
110 B2 Etropole Bulg.
100 C3 Ettelbruck Lux.
100 B2 Etten-Leur Neth.
99 D4 Eu France
99 C3 Euabalong Austr.
Euboea i. Greece see
Evvoia
50 B3 Eucla Austr.
140 C2 Euclid U.S.A.
142 C2 Eufaula U.S.A.
139 D1 Eufaula Lake resr U.S.A.
134 B2 Eugene U.S.A.
144 A2 Eugenia, Punta pt Mex.
53 C1 Eulo Austr.
53 C2 Eumungerie Austr.
139 C2 Eunice U.S.A.
81 C2 Euphrates r. Asia
134 B2 Eureka CA U.S.A.
134 C1 Eureka MT U.S.A.
135 C3 Eureka NV U.S.A.
52 B2 Euriowie Austr.
53 C3 Euroa Austr.
106 B2 Europa Point Gibraltar
142 C2 Eutaw U.S.A.
128 B2 Eutsuk Lake Can.
123 C2 Evander S. Africa
130 C2 Evans, Lac l. Can.
53 D1 Evans Head Austr.
127 G2 Evans Strait Can.
134 A2 Evanston IL U.S.A.
140 B3 Evanston WY U.S.A.
140 B3 Evansville U.S.A.
Eva Perón Arg. see
La Plata
123 C2 Evaton S. Africa
79 C2 Evaz Iran
83 L2 Evensk Rus. Fed.
50 C2 Everard Range hills Austr.
75 C2 Everest, Mount
China/Nepal
134 B1 Everett U.S.A.
100 A2 Evergem Belgium
143 D3 Everglades swamp U.S.A.
142 C2 Evergreen U.S.A.
99 C3 Evesham U.K.
118 B2 Evinayong Equat. Guinea
93 E4 Evje Norway
106 B2 Évora Port.
69 F1 Evoron, Ozero l. Rus. Fed.
111 B3 Evosmo Greece
104 C2 Évreux France
111 C2 Evros r. Greece/Turkey
111 B3 Evrotas r. Greece
104 C2 Évry France
80 B2 Evrychou Cyprus
111 B3 Evvoia i. Greece
119 E2 Ewaso Ngiro r. Kenya
152 B1 Exaltación Bol.
99 B4 Exe r. U.K.
99 B4 Exeter U.K.
99 B4 Exmoor hills U.K.
50 A2 Exmouth Austr.
99 B4 Exmouth U.K.

50 A2 **Exmouth Gulf** Austr.
106 B2 **Extremadura** *aut. comm.*
Spain
146 C2 **Exuma Cays** *is* Bahamas
91 D2 **Eya** *r.* Rus. Fed.
118 C3 **Eyangu** Dem. Rep. Congo
119 D3 **Eyasi, Lake** *salt l.* Tanz.
96 C3 **Eyemouth** U.K.
92 □B2 **Eyjafjörður** *inlet* Iceland
117 C4 **Eyl** Somalia
52 A1 **Eyre, Lake** *salt flat* Austr.
52 A2 **Eyre Peninsula** Austr.
94 B1 **Eysturoy** *i.* Faroe Is
94 B1 **Eysturoy** *i.* Faroe Is
123 D2 **Ezakheni** S. Africa
123 C2 **Ezenzeleni** S. Africa
70 B2 **Ezhou** China
86 E2 **Ezhva** Rus. Fed.
111 C3 **Ezine** Turkey

F

138 B2 **Fabens** U.S.A.
102 C1 **Fåborg** Denmark
108 B2 **Fabriano** Italy
115 D3 **Fachi** Niger
114 C3 **Fada-Ngourma** Burkina
108 B2 **Faenza** Italy
Faeroes *terr.*
N. Atlantic Ocean *see*
Faroe Islands
59 C3 **Fafanlap** Indon.
110 B1 **Făgăraş** Romania
49 J5 **Fagatogo** American Samoa
93 E3 **Fagernes** Norway
93 G4 **Fagersta** Sweden
153 B5 **Fagnano, Lago** *l.*
Arg./Chile
114 B3 **Faguibine, Lac** *l.* Mali
92 □B3 **Fagurhólsmýri** Iceland
126 C2 **Fairbanks** U.S.A.
137 D2 **Fairbury** U.S.A.
135 B3 **Fairfield** *CA* U.S.A.
140 C3 **Fairfield** *OH* U.S.A.
96 □ **Fair Isle** *i.* U.K.
137 E2 **Fairmont** *MN* U.S.A.
140 C3 **Fairmont** *WV* U.S.A.
128 C2 **Fairview** Can.
128 A2 **Fairweather, Mount**
Can./U.S.A.
59 D2 **Fais** *i.* Micronesia
74 B1 **Faisalabad** Pak.
136 C1 **Faith** U.S.A.
75 C2 **Faizabad** India
156 E6 **Fakaofo** *atoll* Tokelau
99 D3 **Fakenham** U.K.
59 C3 **Fakfak** Indon.
65 A1 **Faku** China
114 A4 **Falaba** Sierra Leone
97 B1 **Falcarragh** Rep. of Ireland
139 D3 **Falcon Lake** Mex./U.S.A.
Faleshty Moldova *see*
Făleşti
90 B2 **Făleşti** Moldova
139 D3 **Falfurrias** U.S.A.
128 C2 **Falher** Can.
101 F2 **Falkenberg** Ger.
93 F4 **Falkenberg** Sweden
101 F1 **Falkensee** Ger.
96 C3 **Falkirk** U.K.
158 D8 **Falkland Escarpment**
sea feature
S. Atlantic Ocean
153 C5 **Falkland Islands** *terr.*
S. Atlantic Ocean
157 I9 **Falkland Plateau**
sea feature
S. Atlantic Ocean
93 F4 **Falköping** Sweden
101 D1 **Fallingbostel** Ger.
135 C3 **Fallon** U.S.A.
141 E2 **Fall River** U.S.A.
137 D2 **Falls City** U.S.A.
99 A4 **Falmouth** U.K.
122 A3 **False Bay** S. Africa
144 B2 **Falso, Cabo** *c.* Mex.
93 F5 **Falster** *i.* Denmark
110 C1 **Fălticeni** Romania
93 G3 **Falun** Sweden
152 B2 **Famailla** Arg.
121 □D3 **Fandriana** Madag.
Fangcheng China *see*
Fangchenggang
71 A3 **Fangchenggang** China
71 C3 **Fangshan** Taiwan
66 A1 **Fangzheng** China
108 B2 **Fano** Italy
62 B1 **Fan Si Pan** *mt.* Vietnam
119 C2 **Faradje** Dem. Rep. Congo

121 □D3 **Farafangana** Madag.
116 A2 **Farafra Oasis** Egypt
76 C3 **Farāh** Afgh.
114 A3 **Faranah** Guinea
70 C3 **Fararah** Oman
78 B3 **Farasān, Jazā'ir** *is*
Saudi Arabia
59 D2 **Faraulep** *atoll* Micronesia
Farewell, Cape Greenland
see Nunap Isua
54 B2 **Farewell, Cape** N.Z.
137 D1 **Fargo** U.S.A.
137 E2 **Faribault** U.S.A.
130 C2 **Faribault, Lac** *l.* Can.
74 B2 **Faridabad** India
75 C2 **Faridpur** Bangl.
141 E2 **Farmington** *ME* U.S.A.
138 B1 **Farmington** *NM* U.S.A.
141 D3 **Farmville** U.S.A.
99 C4 **Farnborough** U.K.
128 C2 **Farnham, Mount** Can.
128 A1 **Faro** Can.
106 B2 **Faro** Port.
88 A2 **Fårö** *i.* Sweden
147 C3 **Faro, Punta** *pt* Col.
106 B1 **Faro, Serra do** *mts* Spain
94 B1 **Faroe Islands** *terr.*
N. Atlantic Ocean
113 I6 **Farquhar Group** *atoll*
Seychelles
81 D3 **Farrāshband** Iran
Farrukhabad India *see*
Fatehgarh
79 C3 **Fartak, Ra's** *c.* Yemen
154 B3 **Fartura, Serra da** *mts*
Brazil
Farvel, Kap *c.* Greenland
see Nunap Isua
139 C2 **Farwell** U.S.A.
79 C2 **Fāryāb** Iran
79 C2 **Fāryāb** Iran
81 D3 **Fasā** Iran
109 C2 **Fasano** Italy
90 B1 **Fastiv** Ukr.
119 D2 **Fataki** Dem. Rep. Congo
75 B2 **Fatehgarh** India
75 C2 **Fatehpur** India
114 A3 **Fatick** Senegal
131 D3 **Fatima** Can.
123 C2 **Fauresmith** S. Africa
92 G2 **Fauske** Norway
92 □A3 **Faxaflói** *b.* Iceland
92 G3 **Faxälven** *r.* Sweden
115 D3 **Faya** Chad
142 B1 **Fayetteville** *AR* U.S.A.
143 E1 **Fayetteville** *NC* U.S.A.
142 C1 **Fayetteville** *TN* U.S.A.
74 B1 **Fazilka** India
114 A2 **Fdérik** Maur.
143 E2 **Fear, Cape** U.S.A.
54 C2 **Featherston** N.Z.
104 C2 **Fécamp** France
Federated Malay States
country Asia *see* Malaysia
48 G3 **Federated States of**
Micronesia *country*
N. Pacific Ocean
102 C1 **Fehmarn** *i.* Ger.
101 F1 **Fehrbellin** Ger.
155 D2 **Feia, Lagoa** *lag.* Brazil
150 B3 **Feijó** Brazil
54 C2 **Feilding** N.Z.
151 F4 **Feira de Santana** Brazil
107 D2 **Felanitx** Spain
101 F1 **Feldberg** Ger.
145 D3 **Felipe C. Puerto** Mex.
155 D1 **Felixlândia** Brazil
99 D4 **Felixstowe** U.K.
101 D2 **Felsberg** Ger.
108 B1 **Feltre** Italy
93 F3 **Femunden** *l.* Norway
Fénérive Madag. *see*
Fenoarivo Atsinanana
Fengcheng China *see*
Fengshan
71 B3 **Fengcheng** *Jiangxi* China
65 A1 **Fengcheng** *Liaoning* China
62 A1 **Fengqing** China
71 A3 **Fengshan** China
Fengshan China *see*
Fengqing
70 B2 **Fengxian** *Jiangsu* China
70 A2 **Fengxian** *Shaanxi* China
Fengxiang China *see*
Lincang
Fengyi China *see*
Zhengʼan
71 C3 **Fengyüan** Taiwan
70 B2 **Fengzhen** China
105 D3 **Feno, Capo di** *c. Corsica*
France

121 □D2 **Fenoarivo Atsinanana**
Madag.
70 B2 **Fenyang** China
91 D2 **Feodosiya** Ukr.
108 A3 **Fer, Cap de** *c.* Alg.
77 D2 **Fergana** Uzbek.
137 D1 **Fergus Falls** U.S.A.
51 E1 **Fergusson Island** P.N.G.
114 B4 **Ferkessédougou**
Côte d'Ivoire
108 B2 **Fermo** Italy
131 D2 **Fermont** Can.
106 B1 **Fermoselle** Spain
97 B2 **Fermoy** Rep. of Ireland
143 D2 **Fernandina Beach** U.S.A.
154 B2 **Fernandópolis** Brazil
Fernando Poó *i.*
Equat. Guinea *see* Bioco
134 B1 **Ferndale** U.S.A.
99 C4 **Ferndown** U.K.
128 C3 **Fernie** Can.
135 C3 **Fernley** U.S.A.
97 C2 **Ferns** Rep. of Ireland
Ferozepore India *see*
Firozpur
108 B2 **Ferrara** Italy
154 B2 **Ferreiros** Brazil
108 A2 **Ferro, Capo** *c. Sardinia*
Italy
106 B1 **Ferrol** Spain
Ferryville Tunisia *see*
Menzel Bourguiba
100 B1 **Ferwerd** Neth.
114 B1 **Fès** Morocco
118 B3 **Feshi** Dem. Rep. Congo
137 E3 **Festus** U.S.A.
110 C2 **Feteşti** Romania
97 C2 **Fethard** Rep. of Ireland
111 C3 **Fethiye** Turkey
96 □ **Fetlar** *i.* U.K.
130 C2 **Feuilles, Rivière aux** *r.*
Can.
77 D3 **Feyzābād** Afgh.
Fez Morocco *see* Fès
121 □D3 **Fianarantsoa** Madag.
115 D4 **Fianga** Chad
117 B4 **Fichê** Eth.
109 C2 **Fier** Albania
96 C2 **Fife Ness** *pt* U.K.
104 C3 **Figeac** France
106 B1 **Figueira da Foz** Port.
107 D1 **Figueres** Spain
114 B1 **Figuig** Morocco
49 I5 **Fiji** *country*
S. Pacific Ocean
152 B2 **Filadélfia** Para.
55 B2 **Filchner Ice Shelf**
Antarctica
98 C2 **Filey** U.K.
108 B3 **Filicudi, Isola** *i.* Italy
114 C3 **Filingué** Niger
111 B3 **Filippiada** Greece
93 F4 **Filipstad** Sweden
92 E3 **Fillan** Norway
135 D3 **Fillmore** U.S.A.
119 E2 **Filtu** Eth.
55 D2 **Fimbul Ice Shelf**
Antarctica
96 C2 **Findhorn** *r.* U.K.
140 C2 **Findlay** U.S.A.
51 D4 **Fingal** Austr.
141 D2 **Finger Lakes** U.S.A.
111 D3 **Finike** Turkey
Finisterre, Cape Spain
see Fisterra, Cabo
93 I3 **Finland** *country* Europe
93 H4 **Finland, Gulf of** Europe
128 B2 **Finlay** *r.* Can.
53 C3 **Finley** Austr.
134 C1 **Finley** U.S.A.
101 E2 **Finne** *ridge* Ger.
92 H2 **Finnmarksvidda** *reg.*
Norway
92 G2 **Finnsnes** Norway
93 G4 **Finspång** Sweden
97 C1 **Fintona** U.K.
96 A2 **Fionnphort** U.K.
Fırat *r.* Turkey *see*
Euphrates
Firenze Italy *see* Florence
105 C2 **Firminy** France
74 B2 **Firozabad** India
74 B1 **Firozpur** India
81 D3 **Fīrūzābād** Iran
122 A2 **Fish** *watercourse* Namibia
122 B3 **Fish** *r.* S. Africa
129 F1 **Fisher Strait** Can.
99 A4 **Fishguard** U.K.
105 C2 **Fismes** France
106 B1 **Fisterra, Cabo** *c.* Spain
141 E2 **Fitchburg** U.S.A.

128 C2 **Fitzgerald** Can.
143 D2 **Fitzgerald** U.S.A.
50 B1 **Fitzroy Crossing** Austr.
Fiume Croatia *see* Rijeka
54 A3 **Five Rivers** N.Z.
108 B2 **Fivizzano** Italy
119 C3 **Fizi** Dem. Rep. Congo
93 F3 **Fjallnäs** Sweden
92 G3 **Fjällsjöälven** *r.* Sweden
123 C3 **Flagstaff** S. Africa
138 A1 **Flagstaff** U.S.A.
130 C2 **Flaherty Island** Can.
98 C2 **Flamborough Head** *hd*
U.K.
101 F1 **Fläming** *hills* Ger.
136 B2 **Flaming Gorge Reservoir**
U.S.A.
134 D1 **Flathead** *r.* U.S.A.
134 D1 **Flathead Lake** U.S.A.
51 D1 **Flattery, Cape** Austr.
134 B1 **Flattery, Cape** U.S.A.
98 B3 **Fleetwood** U.K.
93 E4 **Flekkefjord** Norway
102 B1 **Flensburg** Ger.
104 B2 **Flers** France
100 B2 **Fleurus** Belgium
104 C2 **Fleury-les-Aubrais** France
51 D1 **Flinders** *r.* Austr.
50 A3 **Flinders Bay** Austr.
51 D3 **Flinders Island** Austr.
52 A2 **Flinders Ranges** *mts*
Austr.
129 D2 **Flin Flon** Can.
98 B3 **Flint** U.K.
140 C2 **Flint** U.S.A.
49 L5 **Flint Island** Kiribati
101 F2 **Flöha** Ger.
107 D1 **Florac** France
100 C1 **Florange** France
108 B2 **Florence** Italy
142 C2 **Florence** *AL* U.S.A.
138 A2 **Florence** *AZ* U.S.A.
134 B2 **Florence** *OR* U.S.A.
143 E2 **Florence** *SC* U.S.A.
150 B2 **Florencia** Col.
146 B3 **Flores** Guat.
61 D2 **Flores** *i.* Indon.
Floreshty Moldova *see*
Floreşti
61 C2 **Flores Sea** Indon.
151 F3 **Floresta** Brazil
90 B2 **Floreşti** Moldova
139 D3 **Floresville** U.S.A.
151 E3 **Floriano** Brazil
152 D2 **Florianópolis** Brazil
153 C3 **Florida** Uru.
143 D2 **Florida** *state* U.S.A.
143 D4 **Florida, Straits of**
Bahamas/U.S.A.
143 D4 **Florida Bay** U.S.A.
143 D4 **Florida Keys** *is* U.S.A.
111 B2 **Florina** Greece
93 E3 **Florø** Norway
129 D2 **Foam Lake** Can.
109 C2 **Foča** Bos.-Herz.
110 C1 **Focşani** Romania
71 B3 **Fogang** China
109 C2 **Foggia** Italy
131 E3 **Fogo Island** Can.
104 C3 **Foix** France
89 D3 **Fokino** Rus. Fed.
130 B3 **Foleyet** Can.
108 B2 **Foligno** Italy
99 D4 **Folkestone** U.K.
143 D2 **Folkston** U.S.A.
108 B2 **Follonica** Italy
129 D2 **Fond-du-Lac** Can.
129 D2 **Fond du Lac** *r.* Can.
140 B2 **Fond du Lac** U.S.A.
106 B1 **Fondevila** Spain
108 B2 **Fondi** Italy
146 B3 **Fonseca, Golfo de** *b.*
Central America
150 B2 **Fonte Boa** Brazil
104 B2 **Fontenay-le-Comte**
France
92 □C2 **Fontur** *pt* Iceland
Foochow China *see*
Fuzhou
53 C2 **Forbes** Austr.
75 C2 **Forbesganj** India
101 E3 **Forchheim** Ger.
93 E3 **Forde** Norway
53 C1 **Fords Bridge** Austr.
142 B2 **Fordyce** U.S.A.
142 C2 **Forest** U.S.A.
53 C3 **Forest Hill** Austr.
131 D3 **Forestville** Can.
96 C2 **Forfar** U.K.
134 B1 **Forks** U.S.A.
108 B2 **Forlì** Italy

107 D2 Formentera i. Spain
107 D2 Formentor, Cap de c. Spain
155 C2 Formiga Brazil
152 C2 Formosa Arg.
Formosa Asia see Taiwan
154 C1 Formosa Brazil
Formosa Strait China/Taiwan see Taiwan Strait
Føroyar terr. N. Atlantic Ocean see Faroe Islands
96 C2 Forres U.K.
50 B3 Forrest Austr.
142 B1 Forrest City U.S.A.
51 D1 Forsayth Austr.
93 H3 Forssa Fin.
53 D2 Forster Austr.
136 B1 Forsyth U.S.A.
74 B2 Fort Abbas Pak.
130 B2 Fort Albany Can.
151 F3 Fortaleza Brazil
Fort Archambault Chad see Sarh
128 C2 Fort Assiniboine Can.
96 B2 Fort Augustus U.K.
123 C3 Fort Beaufort S. Africa
134 D1 Fort Benton U.S.A.
Fort Brabant Can. see Tuktoyaktuk
135 B3 Fort Bragg U.S.A.
Fort Carnot Madag. see Ikongo
Fort Charlet Alg. see Djanet
Fort Chimo Can. see Kuujjuaq
129 C2 Fort Chipewyan Can.
136 B2 Fort Collins U.S.A.
Fort Crampel C.A.R. see Kaga Bandoro
Fort-Dauphin Madag. see Tôlañaro
147 D3 Fort-de-France Martinique
Fort de Polignac Alg. see Illizi
137 E2 Fort Dodge U.S.A.
141 D2 Fort Erie Can.
Fort Flatters Alg. see Bordj Omer Driss
Fort Foureau Cameroon see Kousséri
130 A3 Fort Frances Can.
Fort Franklin Can. see Déline
Fort Gardel Alg. see Zaouatallaz
Fort George Can. see Chisasibi
126 D2 Fort Good Hope Can.
Fort Gouraud Maur. see Fdérik
96 C2 Forth r. U.K.
96 C2 Forth, Firth of est. U.K.
Fort Hall Kenya see Muranga
Fort Hertz Myanmar see Putao
152 C2 Fortín Madrejón Para.
Fort Jameson Zambia see Chipata
Fort Johnston Malawi see Mangochi
Fort Lamy Chad see Ndjamena
Fort Laperrine Alg. see Tamanrasset
143 D3 Fort Lauderdale U.S.A.
128 B1 Fort Liard Can.
128 C2 Fort Mackay Can.
137 E2 Fort Madison U.S.A.
Fort Manning Malawi see Mchinji
128 C2 Fort McMurray Can.
126 D2 Fort McPherson Can.
136 C2 Fort Morgan U.S.A.
143 D3 Fort Myers U.S.A.
128 B2 Fort Nelson Can.
128 B2 Fort Nelson r. Can.
Fort Norman Can. see Tulit'a
142 C2 Fort Payne U.S.A.
136 B1 Fort Peck U.S.A.
136 B1 Fort Peck Reservoir U.S.A.
143 D3 Fort Pierce U.S.A.
119 D2 Fort Portal Uganda
128 C1 Fort Providence Can.
129 D2 Fort Qu'Appelle Can.

128 C1 Fort Resolution Can.
96 B2 Fortrose U.K.
Fort Rosebery Zambia see Mansa
Fort Rousset Congo see Owando
Fort Rupert Can. see Waskaganish
128 B2 Fort St James Can.
Fort Sandeman Pak. see Zhob
128 B2 Fort St John Can.
128 C2 Fort Saskatchewan Can.
137 E3 Fort Scott U.S.A.
130 B2 Fort Severn Can.
76 B2 Fort-Shevchenko Kazakh.
128 B1 Fort Simpson Can.
128 C1 Fort Smith Can.
142 B1 Fort Smith U.S.A.
139 C2 Fort Stockton U.S.A.
138 C2 Fort Sumner U.S.A.
Fort Trinquet Maur. see Bîr Mogreïn
134 B2 Fortuna U.S.A.
131 E3 Fortune Bay Can.
128 C2 Fort Vermilion Can.
Fort Victoria Zimbabwe see Masvingo
Fort Walton Beach see Fort Walton Beach
142 C2 Fort Walton Beach U.S.A.
136 B2 Fort Washakie U.S.A.
140 B2 Fort Wayne U.S.A.
96 B2 Fort William U.K.
139 D2 Fort Worth U.S.A.
126 C2 Fort Yukon U.S.A.
71 B3 Foshan China
92 F3 Fosna pen. Norway
93 E3 Fosnavåg Norway
92 □B3 Foss Iceland
92 □A2 Fossá Iceland
108 A2 Fossano Italy
137 D1 Fosston U.S.A.
53 C3 Foster Austr.
118 B3 Fougamou Gabon
104 B2 Fougères France
96 □ Foula i. U.K.
99 D4 Foulness Point U.K.
118 B2 Foumban Cameroon
111 C3 Fournoi i. Greece
114 A3 Fouta Djallon reg. Guinea
54 A3 Foveaux Strait N.Z.
136 C3 Fowler U.S.A.
50 C3 Fowlers Bay Austr.
81 C2 Fowman Iran
128 C2 Fox Creek Can.
127 G2 Foxe Basin g. Can.
127 G2 Foxe Channel Can.
127 G2 Foxe Peninsula Can.
54 B2 Fox Glacier N.Z.
128 C2 Fox Lake Can.
128 A1 Fox Mountain Can.
54 C2 Foxton N.Z.
129 D2 Fox Valley Can.
97 C1 Foyle r. Rep. of Ireland/U.K.
97 C1 Foyle, Lough b. Rep. of Ireland/U.K.
97 B2 Foynes Rep. of Ireland
154 B3 Foz de Areia, Represa de resr Brazil
120 A2 Foz do Cunene Angola
154 B3 Foz do Iguaçu Brazil
107 D1 Fraga Spain
100 A2 Frameries Belgium
154 C2 Franca Brazil
109 C2 Francavilla Fontana Italy
104 C2 France country Europe
118 B3 Franceville Gabon
137 D2 Francis Case, Lake U.S.A.
155 D1 Francisco Sá Brazil
123 B3 Francistown Botswana
128 B2 François Lake Can.
100 B1 Franeker Neth.
101 D2 Frankenberg (Eder) Ger.
101 D3 Frankenthal (Pfalz) Ger.
101 E2 Frankenwald mts Ger.
140 C3 Frankfort KY U.S.A.
140 B2 Frankfort MI U.S.A.
101 D2 Frankfurt am Main Ger.
102 C1 Frankfurt an der Oder Ger.
102 C2 Fränkische Alb hills Ger.
101 E3 Fränkische Schweiz reg. Ger.
141 E2 Franklin NH U.S.A.
141 D3 Franklin PA U.S.A.
142 C1 Franklin TN U.S.A.
126 D2 Franklin Bay Can.
134 C1 Franklin D. Roosevelt Lake U.S.A.

128 B1 Franklin Mountains Can.
126 F2 Franklin Strait Can.
53 C3 Frankston Austr.
54 B2 Franz Josef Glacier N.Z.
Franz Josef Land is Rus. Fed. see Zemlya Frantsa-Iosifa
108 A3 Frasca, Capo della c. Sardinia Italy
128 B3 Fraser r. B.C. Can.
131 D2 Fraser r. Nfld. Can.
122 B3 Fraserburg S. Africa
96 C2 Fraserburgh U.K.
130 B3 Fraserdale Can.
51 E2 Fraser Island Austr.
128 B2 Fraser Lake Can.
128 B2 Fraser Plateau Can.
153 C3 Fray Bentos Uru.
93 E4 Fredericia Denmark
139 D2 Frederick U.S.A.
139 D2 Fredericksburg TX U.S.A.
141 D3 Fredericksburg VA U.S.A.
128 A2 Frederick Sound sea chan. U.S.A.
131 D3 Fredericton Can.
Frederikshåb Greenland see Paamiut
93 F4 Frederikshavn Denmark
Fredrikshamn Fin. see Hamina
93 F4 Fredrikstad Norway
140 B2 Freeport IL U.S.A.
139 D3 Freeport TX U.S.A.
146 C2 Freeport City Bahamas
139 D3 Freer U.S.A.
123 C2 Free State prov. S. Africa
114 A4 Freetown Sierra Leone
106 B2 Fregenal de la Sierra Spain
104 B2 Fréhel, Cap c. France
102 B2 Freiburg im Breisgau Ger.
102 C2 Freising Ger.
102 C2 Freistadt Austria
105 D3 Fréjus France
50 A3 Fremantle Austr.
135 B3 Fremont CA U.S.A.
137 D2 Fremont NE U.S.A.
140 C2 Fremont OH U.S.A.
French Congo country Africa see Congo
151 D2 French Guiana terr. S. America
French Guinea country Africa see Guinea
134 E1 Frenchman r. U.S.A.
49 M5 French Polynesia terr. S. Pacific Ocean
French Somaliland country Africa see Djibouti
French Sudan country Africa see Mali
French Territory of the Afars and Issas country Africa see Djibouti
151 D3 Fresco r. Brazil
144 B2 Fresnillo Mex.
135 C3 Fresno U.S.A.
107 D2 Freu, Cap des c. Spain
105 D2 Freyming-Merlebach France
114 A3 Fria Guinea
152 B2 Frías Arg.
101 D2 Friedberg (Hessen) Ger.
102 B2 Friedrichshafen Ger.
101 F1 Friesack Ger.
100 C1 Friesoythe Ger.
139 C3 Friona U.S.A.
136 B3 Frisco U.S.A.
Frobisher Bay Can. see Iqaluit
127 H2 Frobisher Bay b. Can.
101 F2 Frohburg Ger.
87 D4 Frolovo Rus. Fed.
103 D1 Frombork Pol.
99 B4 Frome U.K.
52 A2 Frome, Lake salt flat Austr.
52 A2 Frome Downs Austr.
100 C2 Fröndenberg Ger.
139 C3 Frontera Mex.
145 C3 Frontera Mex.
144 B1 Fronteras Mex.
141 D3 Front Royal U.S.A.
108 B2 Frosinone Italy
92 E3 Frøya i. Norway
Frunze Kyrg. see Bishkek
154 C2 Frutal Brazil
105 D2 Frutigen Switz.
103 D2 Frýdek-Místek Czech Rep.
71 B3 Fu'an China

71 C3 Fuding China
106 C1 Fuenlabrada Spain
152 C2 Fuerte Olimpo Para.
114 A2 Fuerteventura i. Canary Is
64 B2 Fuga i. Phil.
79 C2 Fujairah U.A.E.
67 C3 Fuji Japan
71 B3 Fujian prov. China
67 C3 Fujinomiya Japan
67 C3 Fuji-san vol. Japan
Fukien prov. China see Fujian
67 A4 Fukue Japan
67 A4 Fukue-jima i. Japan
67 C3 Fukui Japan
67 B4 Fukuoka Japan
67 D3 Fukushima Japan
101 D2 Fulda Ger.
101 D2 Fulda r. Ger.
70 A3 Fuling China
137 E3 Fulton U.S.A.
105 C2 Fumay France
49 I4 Funafuti atoll Tuvalu
114 A1 Funchal Madeira
155 D1 Fundão Brazil
106 B1 Fundão Port.
131 D3 Fundy, Bay of g. Can.
121 C3 Funhalouro Moz.
70 B2 Funing Jiangsu China
71 A3 Funing Yunnan China
115 C3 Funtua Nigeria
79 C2 Fürgun, Küh-e mt. Iran
89 F2 Furmanov Rus. Fed.
Furmanovka Kazakh. see Moyynkum
Furmanovo Kazakh. see Zhalpaktal
155 C2 Furnas, Represa resr Brazil
51 D4 Furneaux Group is Austr.
Furong China see Wan'an
100 C1 Fürstenau Ger.
101 E3 Fürth Ger.
66 D3 Furukawa Japan
127 G2 Fury and Hecla Strait Can.
70 C1 Fushun China
65 B1 Fusong China
79 C2 Fuwayriṭ Qatar
Fuxian China see Wafangdian
70 A2 Fuxian China
70 C1 Fuxin China
70 B2 Fuyang China
69 E1 Fuyu China
Fuyu China see Songyuan
68 B1 Fuyun China
71 B3 Fuzhou China
Fuzhou China see Linchuan
93 F4 Fyn i. Denmark
96 B3 Fyne, Loch inlet U.K.
F.Y.R.O.M. country Europe see Macedonia

G

117 C4 Gaalkacyo Somalia
120 A2 Gabela Angola
Gaberones Botswana see Gaborone
115 D1 Gabès Tunisia
115 D1 Gabès, Golfe de g. Tunisia
118 B3 Gabon country Africa
123 C1 Gaborone Botswana
79 C2 Gäbrīk Iran
110 C2 Gabrovo Bulg.
114 A3 Gabú Guinea-Bissau
73 B3 Gadag India
101 E1 Gadebusch Ger.
142 C2 Gadsden U.S.A.
118 B2 Gadzi C.A.R.
110 C2 Găeşti Romania
108 B2 Gaeta Italy
108 B2 Gaeta, Golfo di g. Italy
143 D1 Gaffney U.S.A.
115 C1 Gafsa Tunisia
89 E2 Gagarin Rus. Fed.
109 C3 Gagliano del Capo Italy
114 B4 Gagnoa Côte d'Ivoire
131 D2 Gagnon Can.
81 C1 Gagra Georgia
122 A2 Gaiab watercourse Namibia
104 C3 Gaillac France
Gaillimh Rep. of Ireland see Galway

143 D3 Gainesville FL U.S.A.
143 D2 Gainesville GA U.S.A.
139 D2 Gainesville TX U.S.A.
98 C3 Gainsborough U.K.
52 A2 Gairdner, Lake salt flat Austr.
96 B2 Gairloch U.K.
122 B2 Gakarosa mt. S. Africa
119 E3 Galana r. Kenya
103 D2 Galanta Slovakia
Galápagos, Islas is Pacific Ocean see
125 I10 Galapagos Islands is Pacific Ocean
157 G6 Galapagos Rise sea feature Pacific Ocean
96 C3 Galashiels U.K.
110 C1 Galaţi Romania
93 E3 Galdhøpiggen mt. Norway
145 B2 Galeana Mex.
128 C2 Galena Bay Can.
140 A2 Galesburg U.S.A.
122 B2 Galeshewe S. Africa
89 F2 Galich Rus. Fed.
106 B1 Galicia aut. comm. Spain
80 B2 Galilee, Sea of l. Israel
78 A3 Gallabat Sudan
142 C1 Gallatin U.S.A.
73 C4 Galle Sri Lanka
157 G6 Gallego Rise sea feature Pacific Ocean
150 B1 Gallinas, Punta pt Col.
109 C2 Gallipoli Italy
Gallipoli Turkey see Gelibolu
92 H2 Gällivare Sweden
138 B1 Gallup U.S.A.
114 A2 Galtat Zemmour Western Sahara
97 B2 Galtymore hill Rep. of Ireland
139 E3 Galveston U.S.A.
139 E3 Galveston Bay U.S.A.
139 E3 Galveston Island U.S.A.
97 B2 Galway Rep. of Ireland
97 B2 Galway Bay Rep. of Ireland
154 C1 Gamá Brazil
123 D3 Gamalakhe S. Africa
117 B4 Gambēla Eth.
114 A3 Gambia r. Gambia
49 N6 Gambier, Îles is Fr. Polynesia
52 A3 Gambier Islands Austr.
131 E3 Gambo Can.
118 B3 Gamboma Congo
92 H2 Gammelstaden Sweden
138 B1 Gamōka Iran
81 D3 Ganāveh Iran
81 C1 Gäncä Azer.
Gand Belgium see Gent
61 C2 Gandadiwata, Bukit mt. Indon.
118 C3 Gandajika Dem. Rep. Congo
106 B1 Gándara Spain
131 E3 Gander Can.
131 E3 Gander r. Can.
131 E3 Ganderkesee Ger.
107 D1 Gandesa Spain
74 B2 Gāndhidhām India
74 B2 Gandhinagar India
74 B2 Gāndhi Sāgar resr India
107 C2 Gandia Spain
76 C4 Gand-i-Zureh plain Afgh.
Ganga r. Bangl./India see Ganges
153 B4 Gangán Arg.
74 B2 Ganganagar India
62 A1 Gangaw Myanmar
68 C2 Gangca China
75 C1 Gangdisê Shan mts China
75 D2 Ganges r. Bangl./India
105 C3 Ganges France
75 C2 Ganges, Mouths of the Bangl./India
159 E2 Ganges Cone sea feature Indian Ocean
75 C2 Gangtok India
75 C3 Ganjam India
71 B3 Gan Jiang r. China
71 A3 Ganluo China
105 C2 Gannat France
136 B2 Gannett Peak U.S.A.
70 A1 Gansbaai S. Africa
70 B2 Gansu prov. China
115 D4 Ganye Nigeria
71 B3 Ganzhou China
114 B3 Gao Mali

Gaoleshan China see Xianfeng
114 B3 Gaoua Burkina
114 A3 Gaoual Guinea
70 B2 Gaoyou China
70 B2 Gaoyou Hu l. China
105 D3 Gap France
64 B2 Gapan Phil.
107 C2 Gap Carbon hd Alg.
75 C1 Gar China
97 B2 Gara, Lough l. Rep. of Ireland
117 C4 Garacad Somalia
53 C1 Garah Austr.
151 F3 Garanhuns Brazil
123 C2 Ga-Rankuwa S. Africa
118 C1 Garar, Plaine de plain Chad
117 C4 Garbahaarey Somalia
135 B2 Garberville U.S.A.
81 D2 Garbosh, Kūh-e mt. Iran
101 D1 Garbsen Ger.
154 C2 Garça Brazil
154 B2 Garcias Brazil
108 B1 Garda, Lago di l. Italy
108 A3 Garde, Cap de c. Alg.
101 E1 Gardelegen Ger.
137 D3 Garden City U.S.A.
129 E2 Garden Hill Can.
77 C3 Gardez Afgh.
141 F2 Gardiner U.S.A.
Gardner atoll Micronesia see Faraulep
135 C3 Gardnerville U.S.A.
136 B3 Garfield U.S.A.
88 B2 Gargždai Lith.
75 C2 Garhchiroli India
123 C3 Gariep Dam resr S. Africa
122 A3 Garies S. Africa
119 D3 Garissa Kenya
88 B2 Garkalne Latvia
139 D2 Garland U.S.A.
102 C2 Garmisch-Partenkirchen Ger.
77 D3 Garmo, Qullai mt. Tajik.
52 B2 Garnpung Lake imp. l. Austr.
104 B3 Garonne r. France
117 C4 Garoowe Somalia
74 B2 Garoth India
118 B2 Garoua Cameroon
118 B2 Garoua Boulaï Cameroon
Garqêntang China see Sogxian
96 B2 Garry r. U.K.
81 D2 Garrygala Turkm.
126 F2 Garry Lake Can.
119 E3 Garsen Kenya
122 A2 Garub Namibia
60 B2 Garut Indon.
140 B2 Gary U.S.A.
145 B2 Garza García Mex.
68 C2 Garzê China
104 B3 Gascogne reg. France
104 B3 Gascogne, Golfe de g. France/Spain see Gascony, Gulf of
53 C3 Gascony reg. France see Gascogne
104 B3 Gascony, Gulf of France/Spain
50 A2 Gascoyne r. Austr.
118 B2 Gashaka Nigeria
115 D3 Gashua Nigeria
59 E3 Gasmata P.N.G.
131 D3 Gaspé Can.
131 D3 Gaspé, Péninsule de pen. Can.
143 E1 Gaston, Lake U.S.A.
143 D1 Gastonia U.S.A.
107 C2 Gata, Cabo de c. Spain
88 D2 Gatchina Rus. Fed.
98 C2 Gateshead U.K.
139 D2 Gatesville U.S.A.
141 D1 Gatineau Can.
130 C3 Gatineau r. Can.
Gatooma Zimbabwe see Kadoma
53 C1 Gatton Austr.
129 E2 Gauer Lake Can.
93 E4 Gausta mt. Norway
123 C2 Gauteng prov. S. Africa
79 C2 Gâvbandī Iran
111 B3 Gavdos i. Greece
104 B3 Gave r. France
93 G3 Gävle Sweden
93 G3 Gävlebukten b. Sweden
89 F2 Gavrilov Posad Rus. Fed.
89 E2 Gavrilov-Yam Rus. Fed.
122 A2 Gawachab Namibia
62 A1 Gawai Myanmar

52 A2 Gawler Austr.
52 A2 Gawler Ranges hills Austr.
75 C2 Gaya India
114 C3 Gaya Niger
114 C3 Gayéri Burkina
140 C1 Gaylord U.S.A.
86 E2 Gayny Rus. Fed.
116 B1 Gaza terr. Asia
80 B2 Gaza Gaza
76 C2 Gaz-Achak Turkm.
76 B3 Gazandzhyk Turkm.
80 B2 Gaziantep Turkey
114 B4 Gbarnga Liberia
118 A2 Gboko Nigeria
103 D1 Gdańsk Pol.
88 A3 Gdańsk, Gulf of Pol./Rus. Fed.
88 C2 Gdov Rus. Fed.
103 D1 Gdynia Pol.
116 B3 Gedaref Sudan
101 D2 Gedern Ger.
111 C3 Gediz Turkey
111 C3 Gediz r. Turkey
102 C1 Gedser Denmark
100 B2 Geel Belgium
52 B3 Geelong Austr.
101 E1 Geesthacht Ger.
75 C1 Gê'gyai China
129 D2 Geikie r. Can.
93 E3 Geilo Norway
119 D3 Geita Tanz.
71 A3 Gejiu China
108 B3 Gela Sicily Italy
108 B3 Gela, Golfo di g. Sicily Italy
91 D3 Gelendzhik Rus. Fed.
111 C2 Gelibolu Turkey
100 C2 Gelsenkirchen Ger.
118 B2 Gemena Dem. Rep. Congo
111 C2 Gemlik Turkey
108 B1 Gemona del Friuli Italy
78 A2 Gemsa Egypt
117 C4 Genalē Wenz r. Eth.
153 B3 General Acha Arg.
153 B3 General Alvear Arg.
153 C3 General Belgrano Arg.
144 B2 General Cepeda Mex.
General Freire Angola see Muxaluando
General Machado Angola see Camacupa
153 B3 General Pico Arg.
153 B3 General Roca Arg.
154 B2 General Salgado Brazil
64 B3 General Santos Phil.
141 D2 Genesee r. U.S.A.
141 D2 Geneseo IL U.S.A.
141 D2 Geneseo NY U.S.A.
Geneva Switz. see Genève
141 D2 Geneva U.S.A.
Geneva, Lake France/Switz. see Léman, Lac
105 D2 Genève Switz.
106 B2 Genil r. Spain
100 B2 Genk Belgium
108 A2 Genoa Austr.
108 A2 Genoa Italy
Genova Italy see Genoa
108 A2 Genova, Golfo di g. Italy
100 A2 Gent Belgium
61 C2 Genteng i. Indon.
101 F1 Genthin Ger.
50 A3 Geographe Bay Austr.
131 D2 George r. Can.
122 B3 George S. Africa
52 A3 George, Lake Austr.
143 D3 George, Lake FL U.S.A.
141 E2 George, Lake NY U.S.A.
146 C2 George Town Bahamas
114 A3 Georgetown Gambia
151 D2 Georgetown Guyana
60 B1 George Town Malaysia
140 C3 Georgetown KY U.S.A.
143 E2 Georgetown SC U.S.A.
139 D2 Georgetown TX U.S.A.
55 L2 George V Land reg. Antarctica
81 C1 Georgia country Asia
143 D2 Georgia state U.S.A.
130 B3 Georgian Bay Can.
51 C2 Georgina watercourse Austr.
Georgiu-Dezh Rus. Fed. see Liski
77 E2 Georgiyevka Kazakh.
87 D4 Georgiyevsk Rus. Fed.
101 F2 Gera Ger.
151 E4 Geral de Goiás, Serra hills Brazil
54 B2 Geraldine N.Z.

50 A2 Geraldton Austr.
80 B1 Gerede Turkey
76 C3 Gereshk Afgh.
102 C2 Geretsried Ger.
135 C2 Gerlach U.S.A.
103 F2 Gerlachovský štit mt. Slovakia
141 D3 Germantown U.S.A.
102 C1 Germany country Europe
100 C2 Gerolstein Ger.
101 E3 Gerolzhofen Ger.
53 D2 Gerringong Austr.
101 D2 Gersfeld (Rhön) Ger.
Géryville Alg. see El Bayadh
75 C1 Gêrzê China
106 C1 Getafe Spain
141 D3 Gettysburg PA U.S.A.
136 D1 Gettysburg SD U.S.A.
55 P2 Getz Ice Shelf Antarctica
111 B2 Gevgelija Macedonia
106 C1 Gexto Spain
111 C3 Geyikli Turkey
122 B2 Ghaap Plateau S. Africa
Ghadamés Libya see Ghadāmis
115 C1 Ghadāmis Libya
75 C2 Ghaghara r. India
76 C2 Ghalkarteniz, Solonchak salt marsh Kazakh.
114 B4 Ghana country Africa
120 B3 Ghanzi Botswana
115 C1 Ghardaïa Alg.
78 A2 Ghârib, Gebel mt. Egypt
115 D1 Gharyān Libya
115 D2 Ghāt Libya
75 C2 Ghatal India
75 C2 Ghazipur India
77 C3 Ghaznī Afgh.
78 B2 Ghazzālah Saudi Arabia
Ghent Belgium see Gent
Gheorghe Gheorghiu-Dej Romania see Oneşti
110 C1 Gheorgheni Romania
110 B1 Gherla Romania
105 D3 Ghisonaccia Corsica France
74 B2 Ghotāru India
74 A2 Ghotki Pak.
75 C2 Ghuari r. India
76 C3 Ghurian Afgh.
91 E3 Giaginskaya Rus. Fed.
97 C1 Giant's Causeway lava field U.K.
61 C2 Gianyar Indon.
109 C3 Giarre Sicily Italy
108 A1 Giaveno Italy
122 A2 Gibeon Namibia
106 B2 Gibraltar terr. Europe
106 B2 Gibraltar, Strait of Morocco/Spain
142 B2 Gibsland U.S.A.
50 B2 Gibson Desert Austr.
68 C1 Gichgeniyn Nuruu mts Mongolia
118 B4 Gīdolē Eth.
105 C2 Gien France
101 D2 Gießen Ger.
101 E1 Gifhorn Ger.
128 C2 Gift Lake Can.
67 C3 Gifu Japan
96 B3 Gigha i. U.K.
106 B1 Gijón Spain
138 A2 Gila r. U.S.A.
138 A2 Gila Bend U.S.A.
51 D1 Gilbert r. Austr.
48 I4 Gilbert Islands country Pacific Ocean
156 D5 Gilbert Ridge sea feature Pacific Ocean
151 E3 Gilbués Brazil
134 C1 Gildford U.S.A.
116 A2 Gilf Kebir Plateau Egypt
53 C2 Gilgandra Austr.
74 B1 Gilgit Jammu and Kashmir
74 B1 Gilgit r. Jammu and Kashmir
53 C2 Gilgunnia Austr.
129 E2 Gillam Can.
136 B2 Gillette U.S.A.
99 D4 Gillingham U.K.
130 C2 Gilmour Island Can.
135 B3 Gilroy U.S.A.
129 E2 Gimli Can.
64 B3 Gingoog Phil.
117 C4 Gīnīr Eth.
109 C2 Ginosa Italy
109 C2 Gioia del Colle Italy
53 C3 Gippsland reg. Austr.
74 A2 Girdar Dhor r. Pak.
79 D1 Girdi Iran

80 B1 Giresun Turkey
116 B2 Girga Egypt
Girgenti Italy see
Agrigento
53 C2 Girilambone Austr.
Giron Sweden see Kiruna
107 D1 Girona Spain
104 B2 Gironde est. France
53 C2 Girral Austr.
96 B3 Girvan U.K.
54 C1 Gisborne N.Z.
93 F4 Gislaved Sweden
119 C3 Gitarama Rwanda
119 C3 Gitega Burundi
Giuba r. Somalia see
Jubba
108 B2 Giulianova Italy
110 C2 Giurgiu Romania
110 C1 Giuvala, Pasul pass
Romania
105 C2 Givors France
123 D1 Giyani S. Africa
119 D2 Giyon Eth.
Giza Egypt see El Gîza
80 B3 Giza Pyramids tourist site
Egypt
76 C2 Gizhduvan Uzbek.
103 E1 Giżycko Pol.
109 D2 Gjirokastër Albania
126 F2 Gjoa Haven Can.
93 F3 Gjøvik Norway
131 E3 Glace Bay Can.
134 B1 Glacier Peak vol. U.S.A.
139 E2 Gladewater U.S.A.
51 E2 Gladstone Qld Austr.
52 A2 Gladstone S.A. Austr.
92 □A2 Gláma mts Iceland
109 C2 Glamoč Bos.-Herz.
100 C3 Glan r. Ger.
97 B2 Glanaruddery Mountains
hills Rep. of Ireland
96 B3 Glasgow U.K.
140 B3 Glasgow KY U.S.A.
136 B1 Glasgow MT U.S.A.
99 B4 Glastonbury U.K.
101 F2 Glauchau Ger.
86 E3 Glazov Rus. Fed.
89 E3 Glazunovka Rus. Fed.
123 D2 Glencoe S. Africa
96 B2 Glen Coe val. U.K.
138 A2 Glendale AZ U.S.A.
140 B2 Glendale WI U.S.A.
53 D2 Glen Davis Austr.
51 D2 Glenden Austr.
136 C1 Glendive U.S.A.
52 B3 Glenelg r. Austr.
96 B2 Glenfinnan U.K.
53 D1 Glen Innes Austr.
96 B2 Glen More val. U.K.
53 C1 Glenmorgan Austr.
126 C2 Glennallen U.S.A.
134 C2 Glenns Ferry U.S.A.
136 B2 Glenrock U.S.A.
96 C2 Glenrothes U.K.
141 E2 Glens Falls U.S.A.
96 C2 Glen Shee val. U.K.
97 B1 Glenties Rep. of Ireland
138 B2 Glenwood U.S.A.
136 B3 Glenwood Springs U.S.A.
101 E1 Glinde Ger.
103 D1 Gliwice Pol.
138 A2 Globe U.S.A.
103 D1 Głogów Pol.
92 F2 Glomfjord Norway
93 F4 Glomma r. Norway
53 D2 Gloucester Austr.
99 B4 Gloucester U.K.
131 E3 Glovertown Can.
101 F1 Glöwen Ger.
77 E1 Glubokoye Kazakh.
101 D1 Glückstadt Ger.
103 C2 Gmünd Austria
102 C2 Gmunden Austria
101 D1 Gnarrenburg Ger.
103 D1 Gniezno Pol.
109 D2 Gnjilane Yugo.
75 D2 Goalpara India
96 B3 Goat Fell hill U.K.
117 C4 Goba Eth.
122 A1 Gobabis Namibia
153 A4 Gobernador Gregores
Arg.
152 C2 Gobernador Virasoro Arg.
68 D2 Gobi des. China/Mongolia
67 C4 Gobō Japan
100 C2 Goch Ger.
122 A1 Gochas Namibia
74 B3 Godavari r. India
73 C3 Godavari, Mouths of the
India
75 C2 Godda India

117 C4 Godē Eth.
130 B3 Goderich Can.
Godhavn Greenland see
Qeqertarsuaq
74 B2 Godhra India
129 E2 Gods r. Can.
129 E2 Gods Lake Can.
Godthåb Greenland see
Nuuk
Godwin-Austen, Mount
China/Jammu and Kashmir
see K2
Goedgegun Swaziland see
Nhlangano
130 C3 Goéland, Lac au l. Can.
131 D2 Goélands, Lac aux l. Can.
100 A2 Goes Neth.
140 B1 Gogebic Range hills
U.S.A.
88 C1 Gogland, Ostrov i.
Rus. Fed.
Gogra r. India see
Ghaghara
119 C2 Gogrial Sudan
154 C1 Goianira Brazil
154 C1 Goianésia Brazil
154 C1 Goiânia Brazil
154 B1 Goiás Brazil
154 C1 Goiatuba Brazil
154 B2 Goio-Erê Brazil
111 C2 Gökçeada i. Turkey
111 C3 Gökçedağ Turkey
121 B2 Gokwe Zimbabwe
93 E3 Gol Norway
62 A1 Golaghat India
111 C2 Gölcük Turkey
103 E1 Gołdap Pol.
101 F1 Goldberg Ger.
Gold Coast country Africa
see Ghana
53 D1 Gold Coast Austr.
114 B4 Gold Coast coastal area
Ghana
128 C2 Golden Can.
54 B2 Golden Bay N.Z.
134 B1 Goldendale U.S.A.
128 B3 Golden Hinde mt. Can.
97 B2 Golden Vale lowland
Rep. of Ireland
135 C3 Goldfield U.S.A.
128 B3 Gold River Can.
143 E1 Goldsboro U.S.A.
103 C1 Goleniów Pol.
135 C4 Goleta U.S.A.
Golfe du St-Laurent g.
Can. see
St Lawrence, Gulf of
111 C3 Gölhisar Turkey
Gollel Swaziland see
Lavumisa
75 D1 Golmud China
81 D2 Golpäyegän Iran
96 C2 Golspie U.K.
Golyshi Rus. Fed. see
Vetluzhskiy
119 C3 Goma Dem. Rep. Congo
75 C2 Gomati r. India
115 D3 Gombe Nigeria
115 D3 Gombi Nigeria
Gomel' Belarus see
Homyel'
144 B2 Gómez Palacio Mex.
81 D2 Gomīshän Iran
75 C1 Gomo China
147 C3 Gonaïves Haiti
81 D2 Gonbad-e Kavus Iran
74 B2 Gondal India
Gondar Eth. see Gonder
116 B3 Gonder Eth.
75 C2 Gondia India
111 C2 Gönen Turkey
62 A1 Gonggar China
70 A3 Gongga Shan mt. China
68 C2 Gonghe China
115 D4 Gongola r. Nigeria
53 C2 Gongolgon Austr.
Gongtang China see
Damxung
123 C3 Gonubie S. Africa
145 C2 Gonzáles Mex.
139 D3 Gonzales U.S.A.
122 A3 Good Hope, Cape of
S. Africa
134 D2 Gooding U.S.A.
136 C3 Goodland U.S.A.
53 C1 Goodooga Austr.
98 C3 Goole U.K.
53 C2 Goolgowi Austr.
52 A3 Goolwa Austr.
53 D1 Goondiwindi Austr.
134 B2 Goose Lake U.S.A.

102 B2 Göppingen Ger.
75 C2 Gorakhpur India
109 C2 Goražde Bos.-Herz.
111 C3 Gördes Turkey
89 D3 Gordeyevka Rus. Fed.
136 C2 Gordon U.S.A.
51 D4 Gordon, Lake Austr.
115 D4 Goré Chad
117 B4 Gorē Eth.
54 A3 Gore N.Z.
97 C2 Gorey Rep. of Ireland
81 D2 Gorgān Iran
81 C1 Gori Georgia
100 B2 Gorinchem Neth.
108 B1 Gorizia Italy
Gor'kiy Rus. Fed. see
Nizhniy Novgorod
89 F2 Gor'kovskoye
Vodokhranilishche resr
Rus. Fed.
103 E2 Gorlice Pol.
103 C1 Görlitz Ger.
Gorna Dzhumaya Bulg.
see Blagoevgrad
109 D2 Gornji Milanovac Yugo.
109 C2 Gornji Vakuf Bos.-Herz.
77 E1 Gorno-Altaysk Rus. Fed.
86 F2 Gornopravdinsk Rus. Fed.
110 C2 Gornotrakiyska Nizina
lowland Bulg.
66 D1 Gornozavodsk Rus. Fed.
77 E1 Gornyak Rus. Fed.
59 D3 Goroka P.N.G.
52 B3 Goroke Austr.
114 B3 Gorom Gorom Burkina
121 C2 Gorongosa Moz.
61 D1 Gorontalo Indon.
89 E3 Gorshechnoye Rus. Fed.
97 B2 Gorumna Island
Rep. of Ireland
91 D3 Goryachiy Klyuch
Rus. Fed.
103 D1 Gorzów Wielkopolski Pol.
59 E3 Goschen Strait P.N.G.
53 D2 Gosford Austr.
74 A2 Goshanak Pak.
66 D2 Goshogawara Japan
101 E2 Goslar Ger.
109 C2 Gospić Croatia
99 C4 Gosport U.K.
111 B2 Gostivar Macedonia
Göteborg Sweden see
Gothenburg
101 E2 Gotha Ger.
93 F4 Gothenburg Sweden
136 C2 Gothenburg U.S.A.
93 G4 Gotland i. Sweden
111 B2 Gotse Delchev Bulg.
93 G4 Gotska Sandön i. Sweden
67 B4 Gōtsu Japan
101 D2 Göttingen Ger.
128 B2 Gott Peak Can.
Gottwaldow Czech Rep.
see Zlín
Gotval'd Ukr. see Zmiyiv
100 B1 Gouda Neth.
114 A3 Goudiri Senegal
115 D3 Goudoumania Niger
158 E7 Gough Island
S. Atlantic Ocean
130 C3 Gouin, Réservoir resr
Can.
53 C2 Goulburn Austr.
53 B3 Goulburn r. N.S.W. Austr.
53 B3 Goulburn r. Vic. Austr.
114 B3 Goundam Mali
107 D2 Gouraya Alg.
114 B3 Gourcy Burkina
104 C3 Gourdon France
115 D3 Gouré Niger
122 B3 Gourits r. S. Africa
114 B3 Gourma-Rharous Mali
53 C3 Gourock Range mts Austr.
155 D1 Governador Valadares
Brazil
143 E3 Governor's Harbour
Bahamas
68 C2 Govĭ Altayn Nuruu mts
Mongolia
75 C2 Govind Ballash Pant
Sägar resr India
99 A3 Gower pen. U.K.
152 C2 Goya Arg.
81 C1 Göycay Azer.
80 B1 Göynük Turkey
115 E3 Goz-Beïda Chad
75 C1 Gozha Co salt l. China
122 B3 Graaff-Reinet S. Africa
122 A3 Graafwater S. Africa
101 E1 Grabow Ger.
109 C2 Gračac Croatia

87 E3 Grachevka Rus. Fed.
109 C2 Gradačac Bos.-Herz.
104 B3 Gradignan France
101 F2 Gräfenhainichen Ger.
53 D1 Grafton Austr.
137 D1 Grafton U.S.A.
139 D2 Graham U.S.A.
138 B2 Graham, Mount U.S.A.
Graham Bell Island
Rus. Fed. see
Greem-Bell, Ostrov
128 A2 Graham Island Can.
55 A3 Graham Land reg.
Antarctica
123 C3 Grahamstown S. Africa
97 C2 Graiguenamanagh
Rep. of Ireland
151 E3 Grajaú Brazil
103 E1 Grajewo Pol.
111 B2 Grámmos mt. Greece
96 B2 Grampian Mountains U.K.
52 B3 Grampians mts Austr.
146 B3 Granada Nic.
107 D2 Granada Spain
97 C2 Granard Rep. of Ireland
141 E1 Granby Can.
114 A2 Gran Canaria i. Canary Is
152 B3 Gran Chaco reg.
Arg./Para.
136 F2 Grand r. MO U.S.A.
136 C1 Grand r. SD U.S.A.
146 C2 Grand Bahama i.
Bahamas
131 E3 Grand Bank Can.
158 D2 Grand Banks of
Newfoundland sea feature
N. Atlantic Ocean
Grand Canary i. Canary Is
see Gran Canaria
138 A1 Grand Canyon U.S.A.
138 A1 Grand Canyon gorge
U.S.A.
146 B3 Grand Cayman i.
Cayman Is
129 C2 Grand Centre Can.
134 C1 Grand Coulee U.S.A.
152 B1 Grande r. Bol.
154 B2 Grande r. Brazil
153 B5 Grande, Bahía b. Arg.
155 D2 Grande, Ilha i. Brazil
150 C2 Grande, Serra mt. Brazil
128 C2 Grande Cache Can.
121 D2 Grande Comore i.
Comoros
128 C2 Grande Prairie Can.
115 D3 Grand Erg de Bilma des.
Niger
114 B1 Grand Erg Occidental
des. Alg.
115 C2 Grand Erg Oriental des.
Alg.
131 D3 Grande-Rivière Can.
130 C2 Grande Rivière de la
Baleine r. Can.
152 B3 Grandes, Salinas
salt marsh Arg.
128 C1 Grandin, Lac l. Can.
137 D2 Grand Island U.S.A.
142 B3 Grand Isle U.S.A.
136 B3 Grand Junction U.S.A.
114 B4 Grand-Lahou Côte d'Ivoire
131 D3 Grand Lake N.B. Can.
131 E3 Grand Lake Nfld. Can.
137 D1 Grand Marais U.S.A.
130 C3 Grand-Mère Can.
106 B2 Grândola Port.
129 E2 Grand Rapids Can.
140 B2 Grand Rapids MI U.S.A.
137 E1 Grand Rapids MN U.S.A.
136 A2 Grand Teton mt. U.S.A.
147 C2 Grand Turk
Turks and Caicos Is
129 D2 Grandview Can.
134 C1 Grandview U.S.A.
134 C1 Grangeville U.S.A.
128 B2 Granisle Can.
137 D2 Granite Falls U.S.A.
134 E1 Granite Peak MT U.S.A.
134 C1 Granite Peak NV U.S.A.
108 B3 Granitola, Capo c. Sicily
Italy
93 F4 Gränna Sweden
101 F1 Gransee Ger.
99 C3 Grantham U.K.
96 C2 Grantown-on-Spey U.K.
138 B1 Grants U.S.A.

134 B2 Grants Pass U.S.A.
104 B2 Granville France
129 D2 Granville Lake Can.
155 D1 Grão Mogol Brazil
123 D1 Graskop S. Africa
105 D3 Grasse France
50 B3 Grass Patch Austr.
107 D1 Graus Spain
92 F2 Gravdal Norway
104 B2 Grave, Pointe de *pt* France
129 D3 Gravelbourg Can.
130 C3 Gravenhurst Can.
53 D1 Gravesend Austr.
99 D4 Gravesend U.K.
105 D2 Gray France
143 D1 Gray U.S.A.
140 C2 Grayling U.S.A.
99 D4 Grays U.K.
103 D2 Graz Austria
146 C2 Great Abaco *i.* Bahamas
50 B3 Great Australian Bight *g.* Austr.
146 C2 Great Bahama Bank *sea feature* Bahamas
54 C1 Great Barrier Island N.Z.
51 D1 Great Barrier Reef Austr.
135 C3 Great Basin U.S.A.
128 C1 Great Bear Lake Can.
Great Belt *sea chan.* Denmark *see* Store Bælt
137 D3 Great Bend U.S.A.
63 A2 Great Coco Island Cocos Is
53 B3 Great Dividing Range *mts* Austr.
Great Eastern Erg *des.* Alg. *see* Grand Erg Oriental
146 B2 Greater Antilles *is* Caribbean Sea
Greater Khingan Mountains China *see* Da Hinggan Ling
134 D1 Great Falls U.S.A.
123 C3 Great Fish *r.* S. Africa
123 C3 Great Fish Point S. Africa
147 C2 Great Inagua *i.* Bahamas
122 B3 Great Karoo *plat.* S. Africa
123 C3 Great Kei *r.* S. Africa
99 B3 Great Malvern U.K.
73 D4 Great Nicobar *i.* India
98 B3 Great Ormes Head *hd* U.K.
99 D3 Great Ouse *r.* U.K.
136 C2 Great Plains U.S.A.
119 D3 Great Rift Valley Africa
119 D3 Great Ruaha *r.* Tanz.
134 D2 Great Salt Lake U.S.A.
134 D2 Great Salt Lake Desert U.S.A.
116 A2 Great Sand Sea *des.* Egypt/Libya
50 B2 Great Sandy Desert Austr.
128 C1 Great Slave Lake Can.
143 D1 Great Smoky Mountains U.S.A.
99 A4 Great Torrington U.K.
50 B2 Great Victoria Desert Austr.
70 B1 Great Wall *tourist site* China
Great Western Erg *des.* Alg. *see* Grand Erg Occidental
99 D3 Great Yarmouth U.K.
Grebenkovskiy Ukr. *see* Hrebinka
106 C1 Gredos, Sierra de *mts* Spain
111 B3 Greece *country* Europe
136 C2 Greeley U.S.A.
82 F1 Greem-Bell, Ostrov *i.* Rus. Fed.
140 F1 Green *r.* Can.
140 B3 Green *r. KY* U.S.A.
136 B3 Green *r. WY* U.S.A.
140 B2 Green Bay U.S.A.
140 B1 Green Bay *b.* U.S.A.
140 C3 Greenbrier *r.* U.S.A.
140 B3 Greencastle U.S.A.
143 D1 Greeneville U.S.A.
141 E2 Greenfield U.S.A.
129 D2 Green Lake Can.
127 J2 Greenland *terr.* N. America
160 L2 Greenland Basin *sea feature* Arctic Ocean
160 R2 Greenland Sea *sea* Greenland/Svalbard
96 B3 Greenock U.K.
97 C1 Greenore Rep. of Ireland

135 D3 Green River *UT* U.S.A.
136 B2 Green River *WY* U.S.A.
140 B3 Greensburg *IN* U.S.A.
141 D2 Greensburg *PA* U.S.A.
143 E2 Green Swamp U.S.A.
138 A2 Green Valley U.S.A.
114 B4 Greenville Liberia
142 C2 Greenville *AL* U.S.A.
141 F1 Greenville *ME* U.S.A.
142 B2 Greenville *MS* U.S.A.
143 E1 Greenville *NC* U.S.A.
143 D2 Greenville *SC* U.S.A.
139 D2 Greenville *TX* U.S.A.
53 D2 Greenwell Point Austr.
131 D3 Greenwood Can.
142 B2 Greenwood *MS* U.S.A.
143 D2 Greenwood *SC* U.S.A.
50 B2 Gregory, Lake *salt flat* Austr.
51 D1 Gregory Range *hills* Austr.
102 C1 Greifswald Ger.
101 F2 Greiz Ger.
86 C2 Gremikha Rus. Fed.
93 F4 Grenå Denmark
142 E2 Grenada U.S.A.
147 D3 Grenada *country* West Indies
104 C3 Grenade France
93 F4 Grenen *spit* Denmark
53 C2 Grenfell Austr.
129 D2 Grenfell Can.
105 D2 Grenoble France
51 D1 Grenville, Cape Austr.
134 B1 Gresham U.S.A.
142 B3 Gretna *LA* U.S.A.
141 D3 Gretna *VA* U.S.A.
100 C1 Greven Ger.
111 B2 Grevena Greece
100 C2 Grevenbroich Ger.
101 E1 Grevesmühlen Ger.
136 B2 Greybull U.S.A.
128 A1 Grey Hunter Peak Can.
131 E2 Grey Islands Can.
54 B2 Greymouth N.Z.
52 B1 Grey Range *hills* Austr.
97 C2 Greystones Rep. of Ireland
123 D2 Greytown S. Africa
91 E1 Gribanovskiy Rus. Fed.
118 B2 Gribingui *r.* C.A.R.
101 D3 Griesheim Ger.
143 D2 Griffin U.S.A.
53 C2 Griffith Austr.
88 C3 Grigiškes Lith.
118 C2 Grimari C.A.R.
101 F2 Grimma Ger.
102 C1 Grimmen Ger.
98 C3 Grimsby U.K.
128 C2 Grimshaw Can.
92 □B2 Grímsstaðir Iceland
93 E4 Grimstad Norway
92 □A3 Grindavík Iceland
93 E4 Grindsted Denmark
137 E2 Grinnell U.S.A.
123 C3 Griqualand East *reg.* S. Africa
122 B2 Griqualand West *reg.* S. Africa
122 B2 Griquatown S. Africa
127 G1 Grise Fiord Can.
Grishino Ukr. *see* Krasnoarmiys'k
99 D4 Gris Nez, Cap *c.* France
96 C1 Gritley U.K.
123 C2 Groblersdal S. Africa
123 C3 Groblershoop S. Africa
66 B2 Grodekovo Rus. Fed.
Grodno Belarus *see* Hrodna
103 D1 Grodzisk Wielkopolski Pol.
92 □A3 Gróf Iceland
104 B2 Groix, Île de *i.* France
100 C1 Gronau (Westfalen) Ger.
92 F3 Grong Norway
100 C1 Groningen Neth.
122 B3 Groot Brakrivier S. Africa
122 B2 Grootdrink S. Africa
51 C1 Groote Eylandt *i.* Austr.
120 A2 Grootfontein Namibia
122 A2 Groot Karas Berg *plat.* Namibia
122 B3 Groot Swartberge *mts* S. Africa
122 B2 Grootvloer *salt pan* S. Africa
123 C3 Groot Winterberg *mt.* S. Africa
101 D2 Großenlüder Ger.
101 E2 Großer Beerberg *hill* Ger.
102 C2 Großer Rachel *mt.* Ger.

103 C2 Grosser Speikkogel *mt.* Austria
108 B2 Grosseto Italy
101 D3 Groß-Gerau Ger.
102 C2 Großglockner *mt.* Austria
100 C1 Groß-Hesepe Ger.
101 E2 Großlohra Ger.
122 A1 Gross Ums Namibia
136 A2 Gros Ventre Range *mts* U.S.A.
131 E2 Groswater Bay Can.
130 B3 Groundhog *r.* Can.
135 B3 Grover Beach U.S.A.
142 B3 Groves U.S.A.
141 E2 Groveton U.S.A.
87 D4 Groznyy Rus. Fed.
109 C1 Grubišno Polje Croatia
Grudovo Bulg. *see* Sredets
103 D1 Grudziądz Pol.
122 A2 Grünau Namibia
92 □A3 Grundarfjörður Iceland
Gruzinskaya S.S.R. *country* Asia *see* Georgia
89 E3 Gryazi Rus. Fed.
89 F2 Gryazovets Rus. Fed.
103 D1 Gryfice Pol.
102 C1 Gryfino Pol.
153 E5 Grytviken S. Georgia
146 C2 Guacanayabo, Golfo de *b.* Cuba
144 B2 Guadalajara Mex.
106 C1 Guadalajara Spain
48 H4 Guadalcanal *i.* Solomon Is
107 C1 Guadalope *r.* Spain
106 B2 Guadalquivir *r.* Spain
132 B4 Guadalupe *i.* Mex.
106 B2 Guadalupe, Sierra de *mts* Spain
138 C2 Guadalupe Peak U.S.A.
144 B2 Guadalupe Victoria Mex.
144 B2 Guadalupe y Calvo Mex.
106 C1 Guadarrama, Sierra de *mts* Spain
147 D3 Guadeloupe *terr.* West Indies
147 D3 Guadeloupe Passage Caribbean Sea
106 B2 Guadiana *r.* Port./Spain
106 C2 Guadix Spain
154 B2 Guaíra Brazil
147 C3 Guajira, Península de la *pen.* Col.
150 B3 Gualaceo Ecuador
59 D2 Guam *terr.* N. Pacific Ocean
144 B2 Guamúchil Mex.
144 B2 Guanacevi Mex.
151 E4 Guanambi Brazil
150 C2 Guanare Venez.
146 B2 Guane Cuba
70 A2 Guang'an China
71 B3 Guangchang China
71 B3 Guangdong *prov.* China
Guanghua China *see* Laohekou
71 A3 Guangxi Zhuangzu Zizhiqu *aut. reg.* China
70 A2 Guangyuan China
71 B3 Guangzhou China
155 D1 Guanhães Brazil
147 D4 Guanipa *r.* Venez.
71 A3 Guanling China
65 A1 Guanshui China
Guansuo China *see* Guanling
147 C2 Guantánamo Cuba
155 C2 Guapé Brazil
150 D3 Guaporé *r.* Bol./Brazil
155 B2 Guarapari Brazil
154 B3 Guarapuava Brazil
154 C3 Guaraqueçaba Brazil
155 C2 Guaratinguetá Brazil
154 C3 Guaratuba Brazil
106 B1 Guarda Port.
Guardafui, Cape Somalia *see* Caseyr, Raas
154 C1 Guarda Mor Brazil
106 C1 Guardo Spain
155 C2 Guarujá Brazil
144 B2 Guasave Mex.
146 A3 Guatemala *country* Central America
146 A3 Guatemala Guat.
157 G5 Guatemala Basin *sea feature* N. Pacific Ocean
Guatemala City Guat. *see* Guatemala
150 C2 Guaviare *r.* Col.
155 C2 Guaxupé Brazil
150 B3 Guayaquil Ecuador

150 A3 Guayaquil, Golfo de *g.* Ecuador
152 B1 Guayaramerin Bol.
144 A2 Guaymas Mex.
117 B3 Guba Eth.
86 E1 Guba Dolgaya Rus. Fed.
108 B2 Gubbio Italy
89 E3 Gubkin Rus. Fed.
73 C3 Gudivada India
105 D2 Guebwiller France
114 A2 Guelb er Rîchât *hill* Maur.
115 C1 Guelma Alg.
114 A2 Guelmine Morocco
130 B3 Guelph Can.
145 C2 Guémez Mex.
104 B2 Guérande France
115 E2 Guerende Libya
104 C2 Guéret France
95 C4 Guernsey *i.* Channel Is
95 C4 Guernsey *terr.* Channel Is
144 A2 Guerrero Negro Mex.
131 D2 Guers, Lac *l.* Can.
158 D4 Guiana Basin *sea feature* N. Atlantic Ocean
70 B2 Guichi China
118 B2 Guider Cameroon
108 B2 Guidonia-Montecelio Italy
71 A3 Guigang China
100 A3 Guignicourt France
123 D1 Guija Moz.
99 C4 Guildford U.K.
71 B3 Guilin China
130 C2 Guillaume-Delisle, Lac *l.* Can.
106 B1 Guimarães Port.
114 A3 Guinea *country* Africa
113 D5 Guinea, Gulf of Africa
114 A3 Guinea-Bissau *country* Africa
104 B2 Guingamp France
104 B2 Guipavas France
154 B1 Guiratinga Brazil
150 C1 Güiria Venez.
151 D2 Guisanbourg Fr. Guiana
98 C2 Guisborough U.K.
100 A3 Guise France
64 B2 Guiuan Phil.
71 A3 Guiyang China
71 A3 Guizhou *prov.* China
104 B3 Gujan-Mestras France
74 B2 Gujarat *state* India
Gujarat *state* India *see* Gujarat
74 B1 Gujranwala Pak.
74 B1 Gujrat Pak.
91 D2 Gukovo Rus. Fed.
76 B2 Gulabie Uzbek.
70 A2 Gulang China
53 C2 Gulargambone Austr.
73 B3 Gulbarga India
88 C2 Gulbene Latvia
Gulf of California Mex. *see* California, Golfo de
Gulf of Chihli China *see* Bo Hai
142 C2 Gulfport U.S.A.
53 C2 Gulgong Austr.
69 E1 Gulian China
77 C2 Gulistan Uzbek.
Gulja China *see* Yining
129 D2 Gull Lake Can.
111 C3 Güllük Turkey
Gulü China *see* Xincai
119 D2 Gulu Uganda
120 B2 Gumare Botswana
76 B3 Gumdag Turkm.
115 C3 Gumel Nigeria
75 C2 Gumla India
100 C2 Gummersbach Ger.
87 C4 Gümüşhane Turkey
74 B2 Guna India
Gunan China *see* Qijiang
53 C3 Gundagai Austr.
111 C3 Güney Turkey
118 B3 Gungu Dem. Rep. Congo
129 E2 Gunisao *r.* Can.
53 D2 Gunnedah Austr.
136 B3 Gunnison *CO* U.S.A.
135 D3 Gunnison *UT* U.S.A.
136 B3 Gunnison *r.* U.S.A.
73 B3 Guntakal India
73 C3 Guntur India
51 C1 Gunungsitoli Indon.
60 A1 Gunungtua Indon.
102 C2 Günzburg Ger.
102 C2 Gunzenhausen Ger.
Guoluezhen China *see* Lingbao
74 B2 Gurgaon India
151 E3 Gurgueia *r.* Brazil

150 C2 Guri, Embalse de resr Venez.
154 C1 Gurinhatã Brazil
121 C2 Guro Moz.
151 E4 Gurupi Brazil
151 E3 Gurupi r. Brazil
74 B2 Guru Sikhar mt. India
121 C2 Guruve Zimbabwe
Gur'yev Kazakh. see Atyrau
115 C3 Gusau Nigeria
88 B3 Gusev Rus. Fed.
65 A2 Gushan China
74 A1 Gushgy Turkm.
70 B2 Gushi China
83 I3 Gusinoozersk Rus. Fed.
89 F2 Gus'-Khrustal'nyy Rus. Fed.
108 A3 Guspini Sardinia Italy
128 A2 Gustavus U.S.A.
101 F1 Güstrow Ger.
101 D2 Gütersloh Ger.
139 D1 Guthrie U.S.A.
152 B1 Gutiérrez Bol.
121 C2 Gutu Zimbabwe
75 D2 Guwahati India
150 D2 Guyana country S. America
Guyi China see Sanjiang
139 C1 Guymon U.S.A.
53 D2 Guyra Austr.
70 A2 Guyuan China
77 C3 Guzar Uzbek.
Guzhou China see Rongjiang
144 B1 Guzmán Mex.
144 B1 Guzmán, Lago de l. Mex.
88 B3 Gvardeysk Rus. Fed.
74 A2 Gwadar Pak.
Gwador Pak. see Gwadar
74 B2 Gwalior India
121 B3 Gwanda Zimbabwe
97 B1 Gweebarra Bay Rep. of Ireland
97 B1 Gweedore Rep. of Ireland
Gwelo Zimbabwe see Gweru
121 B2 Gweru Zimbabwe
115 D3 Gwoza Nigeria
53 D2 Gwydir r. Austr.
Gya'gya China see Saga
Gyandzha Azer. see Gäncä
Gyangkar China see Dinngyê
Gyangtse China see Gyangzê
75 C2 Gyangzê China
75 C1 Gyaring Co l. China
68 C2 Gyaring Hu l. China
86 G1 Gydanskiy Poluostrov pen. Rus. Fed.
Gyêgu China see Yushu
Gyixong China see Gonggar
51 E2 Gympie Austr.
62 A2 Gyobingauk Myanmar
103 D2 Gyöngyös Hungary
103 D2 Győr Hungary
136 B3 Gypsum U.S.A.
129 E2 Gypsumville Can.
131 D2 Gyrfalcon Islands Can.
111 B3 Gytheio Greece
103 E2 Gyula Hungary
81 C1 Gyumri Armenia
76 B3 Gyzylarbat Turkm.
Gzhatsk Rus. Fed. see Gagarin

H

88 B2 Haapsalu Estonia
100 B1 Haarlem Neth.
122 B3 Haarlem S. Africa
101 C2 Haarstrang ridge Ger.
54 A2 Haast N.Z.
74 A2 Hab r. Pak.
79 C3 Habarūt Oman
78 B3 Habbān Yemen
81 C2 Habbānīyah, Hawr al l. Iraq
70 B1 Habirag China
67 C4 Hachijō-jima i. Japan
66 D2 Hachinohe Japan
67 C3 Hachiōji Japan
121 C3 Hacufera Moz.
79 C2 Hadd, Ra's al pt Oman
96 C3 Haddington U.K.
115 D3 Hadejia Nigeria
93 E4 Haderslev Denmark

78 B2 Hādhah Saudi Arabia
79 B3 Hadramawt reg. Yemen
79 B3 Hadramawt, Wādī watercourse Yemen
91 C1 Hadyach Ukr.
65 B2 Haeju N. Korea
65 B2 Haeju-man b. N. Korea
65 B3 Haenam S. Korea
78 B2 Hafar al Bāțin Saudi Arabia
74 B1 Hafizabad Pak.
75 D2 Hāflong India
92 □A3 Hafnarfjörður Iceland
78 A3 Hagar Nish Plateau Eritrea
59 D2 Hagåtña Guam
101 F1 Hagelberg hill Ger.
100 C2 Hagen Ger.
101 E1 Hagenow Ger.
128 B2 Hagensborg Can.
141 D3 Hagerstown U.S.A.
93 F3 Hagfors Sweden
134 D1 Haggin, Mount U.S.A.
67 B4 Hagi Japan
62 B1 Ha Giang Vietnam
97 B2 Hag's Head hd Rep. of Ireland
69 F3 Hahajima-rettō is Japan
119 D3 Hai Tanz.
Haicheng China see Haifeng
70 C1 Haicheng China
62 B1 Hai Dương Vietnam
Haifa Israel see Hefa
71 B3 Haifeng China
Haikang China see Leizhou
71 B3 Haikou China
78 B2 Hā'il Saudi Arabia
69 D1 Hailar China
Hailong China see Meihekou
92 H2 Hailuoto i. Fin.
69 D3 Hainan i. China
71 A4 Hainan prov. China
128 A2 Haines U.S.A.
128 A1 Haines Junction Can.
101 E2 Hainich ridge Ger.
101 E2 Hainleite ridge Ger.
62 B1 Hai Phong Vietnam
Haiphong Vietnam see Hai Phong
147 C3 Haiti country West Indies
116 B3 Haiya Sudan
103 E2 Hajdúböszörmény Hungary
103 E2 Hajdúszoboszló Hungary
67 C3 Hajiki-zaki pt Japan
78 B3 Hajjah Yemen
81 D3 Hājjīābād Iran
103 E1 Hajnówka Pol.
62 A1 Haka Myanmar
81 C2 Hakkârı Turkey
66 D2 Hakodate Japan
122 B2 Hakseen Pan salt pan S. Africa
78 B2 Halab Syria see Aleppo
81 C2 Halabja Iraq
116 B2 Halaib Sudan
78 A2 Halaib Triangle terr. Egypt/Sudan
79 C3 Halāniyāt, Juzur al is Oman
78 A2 Hālat 'Ammār Saudi Arabia
68 C1 Halban Mongolia
101 E2 Halberstadt Ger.
64 B2 Halcon, Mount Phil.
93 F4 Halden Norway
101 E1 Haldensleben Ger.
75 B2 Haldwani India
79 C2 Hāleh Iran
54 A3 Halfmoon Bay N.Z.
141 D1 Haliburton Highlands hills Can.
131 D3 Halifax Can.
98 C3 Halifax U.K.
141 D3 Halifax U.S.A.
65 B3 Halla-san mt. S. Korea
127 G2 Hall Beach Can.
100 B2 Halle Belgium
102 C2 Hallein Austria
101 E2 Halle-Neustadt Ger.
101 E2 Halle (Saale) Ger.
48 G3 Hall Islands Micronesia
137 D1 Hallock U.S.A.
127 H2 Hall Peninsula Can.
50 B1 Halls Creek Austr.
59 C2 Halmahera i. Indon.
93 F4 Halmstad Sweden

Hälsingborg Sweden see Helsingborg
100 B2 Halsteren Neth.
98 B2 Haltwhistle U.K.
67 B4 Hamada Japan
81 C2 Hamadān Iran
80 B2 Hamāh Syria
67 C4 Hamamatsu Japan
93 F3 Hamar Norway
116 B2 Hamāta, Gebel mt. Egypt
73 C4 Hambantota Sri Lanka
101 D1 Hamburg Ger.
123 C3 Hamburg S. Africa
142 B2 Hamburg U.S.A.
78 A2 Hamd, Wādī al watercourse Saudi Arabia
78 B3 Hamdah Saudi Arabia
141 E2 Hamden U.S.A.
93 H3 Hämeenlinna Fin.
101 D1 Hameln Ger.
50 A2 Hamersley Range mts Austr.
65 B1 Hamgyŏng-sanmaek mts N. Korea
65 B2 Hamhŭng N. Korea
68 C2 Hami China
116 B2 Hamid Sudan
52 B3 Hamilton Austr.
130 C3 Hamilton Can.
Hamilton r. Can. see Churchill
54 C1 Hamilton N.Z.
96 B3 Hamilton U.K.
142 C2 Hamilton AL U.S.A.
134 D1 Hamilton MT U.S.A.
140 C3 Hamilton OH U.S.A.
115 E1 Hamim, Wādī al watercourse Libya
93 I3 Hamina Fin.
100 C2 Hamm Ger.
114 B2 Hammada du Drâa plat. Alg.
115 D1 Hammamet, Golfe de g. Tunisia
81 C2 Hammār, Hawr al imp. l. Iraq
101 D2 Hammelburg Ger.
92 G3 Hammerdal Sweden
92 H1 Hammerfest Norway
142 B2 Hammond U.S.A.
141 E3 Hammonton U.S.A.
141 D3 Hampton U.S.A.
141 E2 Hampton Bays U.S.A.
79 C2 Hāmūn-e Jaz Mūriān salt marsh Iran
74 A2 Hamun-i-Lora dry lake Pak.
74 A2 Hamun-i-Mashkel salt flat Pak.
78 A2 Hanalc Saudi Arabia
66 D3 Hanamaki Japan
101 D2 Hanau Ger.
70 B2 Hancheng China
140 B1 Hancock U.S.A.
70 B2 Handan China
119 D3 Handeni Tanz.
135 C3 Hanford U.S.A.
68 C1 Hangayn Nuruu mts Mongolia
Hangchow China see Hangzhou
Hanggin Houqi China see Xamba
Hangö Fin. see Hanko
70 B2 Hangu China
70 C2 Hangzhou China
70 C2 Hangzhou Wan b. China
79 B2 Hanīdh Saudi Arabia
Hanjia China see Pengshui
Hanjiang China see Yangzhou
93 H4 Hanko Fin.
135 D3 Hanksville U.S.A.
54 B2 Hanmer Springs N.Z.
52 B2 Hanna Can.
130 C1 Hanna Can.
137 E3 Hannibal U.S.A.
101 D1 Hannover Ger.
101 D2 Hannoversch Münden Ger.
93 F4 Hanöbukten b. Sweden
Hanoi Vietnam see Ha Nôi
62 B1 Ha Nôi Vietnam
130 B3 Hanover Can.
122 B3 Hanover S. Africa
141 E2 Hanover NH U.S.A.
141 D3 Hanover PA U.S.A.
92 G2 Hansnes Norway
93 E4 Hanstholm Denmark

88 C3 Hantsavichy Belarus
75 C2 Hanumana India
74 B2 Hanumangarh India
70 A2 Hanzhong China
49 M5 Hao atoll Fr. Polynesia
75 C2 Hāora India
92 H2 Haparanda Sweden
100 B2 Hapert Neth.
131 D2 Happy Valley-Goose Bay Can.
78 A2 Haql Saudi Arabia
79 B2 Haradh Saudi Arabia
88 C2 Haradok Belarus
78 B3 Harajā Saudi Arabia
121 C2 Harare Zimbabwe
79 C3 Harāsis, Jiddat al des. Oman
69 D1 Har-Ayrag Mongolia
115 E3 Haraze-Mangueigne Chad
114 A4 Harbel Liberia
69 E1 Harbin China
140 C2 Harbor Beach U.S.A.
131 E3 Harbour Breton Can.
74 B2 Harda Khās India
61 C1 Harden, Bukit mt. Indon.
100 C1 Hardenberg Neth.
100 B1 Harderwijk Neth.
122 A3 Hardeveld mts S. Africa
134 E1 Hardin U.S.A.
128 C1 Hardisty Lake Can.
93 E3 Hareid Norway
100 C1 Haren (Ems) Ger.
117 C4 Härer Eth.
117 C4 Hargeysa Somalia
110 C1 Harghita-Mădăraș, Vârful mt. Romania
68 C2 Har Hu l. China
88 B2 Hari kurk sea chan. Estonia
74 B1 Haripur Pak.
74 A1 Hari Rūd r. Afgh./Iran
110 C1 Hârlău Romania
100 B1 Harlingen Neth.
139 D3 Harlingen U.S.A.
99 D4 Harlow U.K.
134 E1 Harlowton U.S.A.
134 C2 Harney Basin U.S.A.
134 C2 Harney Lake U.S.A.
93 G3 Härnösand Sweden
69 E1 Har Nur China
97 B1 Har Nuur l. Mongolia
96 □ Haroldswick U.K.
114 B4 Harper Liberia
101 D1 Harpstedt Ger.
130 C2 Harricanaw r. Can.
53 D2 Harrington Austr.
131 E2 Harrington Harbour Can.
96 A2 Harris pen. U.K.
96 A2 Harris, Sound of sea chan. U.K.
140 B3 Harrisburg IL U.S.A.
134 B2 Harrisburg OR U.S.A.
141 D2 Harrisburg PA U.S.A.
123 C2 Harrismith S. Africa
142 B1 Harrison U.S.A.
131 E2 Harrison, Cape Can.
126 B2 Harrison Bay U.S.A.
141 D3 Harrisonburg U.S.A.
128 B3 Harrison Lake Can.
137 E3 Harrisonville U.S.A.
98 C3 Harrogate U.K.
110 C2 Hârșova Romania
92 G2 Harstad Norway
122 B2 Hartbees watercourse S. Africa
103 D2 Hartberg Austria
141 E2 Hartford CT U.S.A.
137 D2 Hartford SD U.S.A.
99 A4 Hartland Point U.K.
98 C2 Hartlepool U.K.
Hartley Zimbabwe see Chegutu
128 B2 Hartley Bay Can.
123 B3 Harts r. S. Africa
143 D2 Hartwell Reservoir U.S.A.
68 C1 Har Us Nuur l. Mongolia
136 C1 Harvey U.S.A.
99 D4 Harwich U.K.
74 B2 Haryana state India
101 E2 Harz hills Ger.
101 E2 Harzgerode Ger.
78 B2 Hasan, Jabal hill Saudi Arabia
80 B2 Hasan Dağı mts Turkey
99 C4 Haslemere U.K.
73 B3 Hassan India
100 B2 Hasselt Belgium
101 E2 Haßfurt Ger.
115 C2 Hassi Bel Guebbour Alg.
115 C1 Hassi Messaoud Alg.
93 F4 Hässleholm Sweden

100 B2 **Hastière-Lavaux** Belgium
53 C3 **Hastings** *Vic.* Austr.
53 C3 **Hastings** *Vic.* Austr.
54 C1 **Hastings** N.Z.
99 D4 **Hastings** U.K.
137 E2 **Hastings** *MN* U.S.A.
137 D2 **Hastings** *NE* U.S.A.
Hatay Turkey *see* Antakya
138 B2 **Hatch** U.S.A.
129 D2 **Hatchet Lake** Can.
110 B1 **Haţeg** Romania
52 B2 **Hatfield** Austr.
68 C1 **Hatgal** Mongolia
62 B2 **Ha Tinh** Vietnam
52 B2 **Hattah** Austr.
143 E1 **Hatteras, Cape** U.S.A.
157 H3 **Hatteras Abyssal Plain**
    sea feature
    S. Atlantic Ocean
142 C2 **Hattiesburg** U.S.A.
100 C2 **Hattingen** Ger.
63 B3 **Hat Yai** Thai.
117 C4 **Haud** *reg.* Eth.
93 E4 **Haugesund** Norway
93 E4 **Haukeligrend** Norway
92 I2 **Haukipudas** Fin.
54 C1 **Hauraki Gulf** N.Z.
54 A3 **Hauroko, Lake** N.Z.
114 B1 **Haut Atlas** *mts* Morocco
131 D3 **Hauterive** Can.
    Haute-Volta *country* Africa
    see Burkina
114 B1 **Hauts Plateaux** Alg.
146 B2 **Havana** Cuba
99 C4 **Havant** U.K.
101 E1 **Havel** *r.* Ger.
101 F1 **Havelberg** Ger.
54 B2 **Havelock** N.Z.
    Havelock Swaziland *see*
    Bulembu
54 C1 **Havelock North** N.Z.
99 A4 **Haverfordwest** U.K.
100 C2 **Havixbeck** Ger.
103 D2 **Havlíčkův Brod**
    Czech Rep.
92 H1 **Havøysund** Norway
111 C3 **Havran** Turkey
134 E1 **Havre** U.S.A.
131 D3 **Havre Aubert** Can.
131 D2 **Havre-St-Pierre** Can.
49 L2 **Hawaii** *i.* U.S.A.
124 A5 **Hawaiian Islands** *is*
    N. Pacific Ocean
78 B2 **Hawalli** Kuwait
98 B3 **Hawarden** U.K.
54 A2 **Hawea, Lake** N.Z.
54 B1 **Hawera** N.Z.
98 B2 **Hawes** U.K.
96 C3 **Hawick** U.K.
54 C1 **Hawke Bay** N.Z.
52 A2 **Hawker** Austr.
52 B1 **Hawkers Gate** Austr.
122 A3 **Hawston** S. Africa
135 C3 **Hawthorne** U.S.A.
52 B2 **Hay** Austr.
128 C1 **Hay** *r.* Can.
70 A1 **Haya** China
100 C3 **Hayange** France
81 C2 **Haydarābād** Iran
134 C1 **Hayden** U.S.A.
129 E2 **Hayes** *r. Man.* Can.
126 F2 **Hayes** *r. Nunavut* Can.
79 C3 **Haymā'** Oman
111 C2 **Hayrabolu** Turkey
128 C1 **Hay River** Can.
137 D3 **Hays** U.S.A.
78 B3 **Hays** Yemen
90 B2 **Haysyn** Ukr.
135 B3 **Hayward** U.S.A.
99 C4 **Haywards Heath** U.K.
74 A1 **Hazarajat** *reg.* Afgh.
140 C3 **Hazard** U.S.A.
75 C2 **Hazārībāg** India
75 C2 **Hazaribagh Range** *mts*
    India
104 C1 **Hazebrouck** France
128 B2 **Hazelton** Can.
141 D2 **Hazleton** U.S.A.
135 B3 **Healdsburg** U.S.A.
53 C3 **Healesville** Austr.
159 E7 **Heard Island** Indian Ocean
139 D2 **Hearne** U.S.A.
130 B3 **Hearst** Can.
55 A3 **Hearst Island** Antarctica
70 B2 **Hebei** *prov.* China
53 C1 **Hebel** Austr.
142 B1 **Heber Springs** U.S.A.
70 B2 **Hebi** China
131 D2 **Hebron** Can.
128 A2 **Hecate Strait** Can.
71 A3 **Hechi** China

100 B2 **Hechtel** Belgium
54 C2 **Hector, Mount** N.Z.
93 F3 **Hede** Sweden
100 C1 **Heerde** Neth.
100 B1 **Heerenveen** Neth.
100 D1 **Heerhugowaard** Neth.
100 B2 **Heerlen** Neth.
80 B2 **Hefa** Israel
70 B2 **Hefei** China
70 B3 **Hefeng** China
69 E1 **Hegang** China
119 D1 **Heiban** Sudan
102 B1 **Heide** Ger.
122 A1 **Heide** Namibia
101 D3 **Heidelberg** Ger.
122 B3 **Heidelberg** S. Africa
69 E1 **Heihe** China
102 B2 **Heilbronn** Ger.
69 E1 **Heilong Jiang** *r.*
    China/Rus. Fed.
93 I3 **Heinola** Fin.
    Hejaz *reg.* Saudi Arabia
    see Hijaz
92 F3 **Helagsfjället** *mt.* Sweden
70 A2 **Helan Shan** *mts* China
142 B2 **Helena** *AR* U.S.A.
134 D1 **Helena** *MT* U.S.A.
96 B2 **Helensburgh** U.K.
102 B1 **Helgoland** *i.* Ger.
102 B1 **Helgoländer Bucht** *b.* Ger.
    Heligoland *i.* Ger. *see*
    Helgoland
    Heligoland Bight *b.* Ger.
    see Helgoländer Bucht
    Helixi China *see* Ningguo
92 □A3 **Hella** Iceland
100 B2 **Hellevoetsluis** Neth.
107 C2 **Hellín** Spain
    Hell-Ville Madag. *see*
    Andoany
76 C3 **Helmand** *r.* Afgh.
101 E2 **Helmbrechts** Ger.
122 A2 **Helmeringhausen**
    Namibia
100 B2 **Helmond** Neth.
96 C1 **Helmsdale** U.K.
96 C1 **Helmsdale** *r.* U.K.
98 C2 **Helmsley** U.K.
101 E1 **Helmstedt** Ger.
65 B1 **Helong** China
139 D3 **Helotes** U.S.A.
93 F4 **Helsingborg** Sweden
    Helsingfors Fin. *see*
    Helsinki
93 F4 **Helsingør** Denmark
93 H3 **Helsinki** Fin.
99 A4 **Helston** U.K.
97 C2 **Helvick Head** *hd*
    Rep. of Ireland
99 C4 **Hemel Hempstead** U.K.
101 D1 **Hemmoor** Ger.
92 F2 **Hemnesberget** Norway
70 B2 **Henan** *prov.* China
111 D2 **Hendek** Turkey
140 B3 **Henderson** *KY* U.S.A.
143 E1 **Henderson** *NC* U.S.A.
135 D3 **Henderson** *NV* U.S.A.
139 E2 **Henderson** *TX* U.S.A.
49 O6 **Henderson Island**
    Pitcairn Is
143 D1 **Hendersonville** U.S.A.
99 C4 **Hendon** U.K.
62 A1 **Hengduan Shan** *mts*
    China
100 C1 **Hengelo** Neth.
    Hengnan China *see*
    Hengyang
71 B3 **Hengshan** China
70 B2 **Hengshui** China
71 A3 **Hengxian** China
71 B3 **Hengyang** China
    Hengzhou China *see*
    Hengyang
91 C2 **Heniches'k** Ukr.
141 D1 **Henlopen, Cape** U.S.A.
100 C2 **Hennef (Sieg)** Ger.
130 B2 **Henrietta Maria, Cape**
    Can.
    Henrique de Carvalho
    Angola *see* Saurimo
147 C3 **Henryetta** U.S.A.
51 D1 **Henry Kater, Cape** Can.
52 B3 **Henstedt-Ulzburg** Ger.
74 A1 **Henties Baai** Namibia
73 B3 **Henzada** Myanmar
134 C2 **Heppenheim (Bergstraße)**
    Ger.

54 C2 **Herbertville** N.Z.
101 D2 **Herbstein** Ger.
109 C2 **Herceg-Novi** Yugo.
99 B3 **Hereford** U.K.
139 C2 **Hereford** U.S.A.
101 D1 **Herford** Ger.
100 C2 **Herkenbosch** Neth.
96 □ **Herma Ness** *hd* U.K.
122 A3 **Hermanus** S. Africa
53 C2 **Hermidale** Austr.
134 C1 **Hermiston** U.S.A.
59 D3 **Hermit Islands** P.N.G.
144 A2 **Hermosillo** Mex.
154 B3 **Hernandarias** Para.
100 C2 **Herne** Ger.
93 E4 **Herning** Denmark
104 B2 **Hérouville-St-Clair** France
106 B2 **Herrera del Duque** Spain
141 D2 **Hershey** U.S.A.
99 C4 **Hertford** U.K.
123 C2 **Hertzogville** S. Africa
51 E2 **Hervey Bay** Austr.
101 F2 **Herzberg** Ger.
101 E3 **Herzogenaurach** Ger.
71 A3 **Heshan** China
135 C4 **Hesperia** U.S.A.
128 A1 **Hess** *r.* Can.
101 D2 **Hessen** *land* Ger.
101 D2 **Hessisch Lichtenau** Ger.
136 C1 **Hettinger** U.S.A.
101 E2 **Hettstedt** Ger.
98 C2 **Hexham** U.K.
71 B3 **Hexian** China
98 B2 **Heysham** U.K.
71 B3 **Heyuan** China
52 B3 **Heywood** Austr.
70 B2 **Heze** China
143 D3 **Hialeah** U.S.A.
137 D3 **Hiawatha** U.S.A.
137 E1 **Hibbing** U.S.A.
143 D1 **Hickory** U.S.A.
54 C1 **Hicks Bay** N.Z.
66 D2 **Hidaka-sanmyaku** *mts*
    Japan
139 D3 **Hidalgo** Mex.
145 C2 **Hidalgo** Mex.
144 B2 **Hidalgo del Parral** Mex.
154 C1 **Hidrolândia** Brazil
67 A4 **Higashi-suidō** *sea chan.*
    Japan
    High Atlas *mts* Morocco
    see Haut Atlas
134 B2 **High Desert** U.S.A.
128 C2 **High Level** Can.
143 E1 **High Point** U.S.A.
128 C2 **High Prairie** Can.
128 C2 **High River** Can.
129 D2 **Highrock Lake** Can.
    High Tatras *mts*
    Pol./Slovakia *see*
    Tatra Mountains
99 C4 **High Wycombe** U.K.
88 B2 **Hiiumaa** *i.* Estonia
78 A2 **Hijaz** *reg.* Saudi Arabia
54 C1 **Hikurangi** *mt.* N.Z.
101 E2 **Hildburghausen** Ger.
100 C2 **Hilden** Ger.
101 E2 **Hilders** Ger.
101 D1 **Hildesheim** Ger.
    Hillah Iraq *see* Al Ḥillah
100 B1 **Hillegom** Neth.
100 C2 **Hillesheim** Ger.
140 C3 **Hillsboro** *OH* U.S.A.
139 D2 **Hillsboro** *TX* U.S.A.
53 C2 **Hillston** Austr.
96 □ **Hillswick** U.K.
49 L2 **Hilo** U.S.A.
143 D2 **Hilton Head Island** U.S.A.
100 B1 **Hilversum** Neth.
74 B1 **Himachal Pradesh** *state*
    India
68 B2 **Himalaya** *mts* Asia
74 B2 **Himatnagar** India
67 B4 **Himeji** Japan
123 C2 **Himeville** S. Africa
67 C3 **Himi** Japan
80 B2 **Ḥimş** Syria
147 C3 **Hinche** Haiti
51 D1 **Hinchinbrook Island**
    Austr.
52 B3 **Hindmarsh, Lake** *dry lake*
    Austr.
74 A1 **Hindu Kush** *mts*
    Afgh./Pak.
73 B3 **Hindupur** India
134 C2 **Hines** U.S.A.
74 B2 **Hinganghat** India
81 C2 **Hınıs** Turkey
92 G2 **Hinnøya** *i.* Norway
106 B2 **Hinojosa del Duque** Spain

100 C1 **Hinte** Ger.
128 C2 **Hinton** Can.
75 C2 **Hirakud Reservoir** India
    Hîrlău Romania *see* Hârlău
66 D2 **Hiroo** Japan
66 D2 **Hirosaki** Japan
67 B4 **Hiroshima** Japan
101 E3 **Hirschaid** Ger.
101 E2 **Hirschberg** Ger.
105 C2 **Hirson** France
    Hîrșova Romania *see*
    Hârșova
93 E4 **Hirtshals** Denmark
74 B2 **Hisar** India
147 C2 **Hispaniola** *i.*
    Caribbean Sea
81 C2 **Hīt** Iraq
67 D3 **Hitachi** Japan
67 D3 **Hitachinaka** Japan
92 E3 **Hitra** *i.* Norway
49 N4 **Hiva Oa** *i.* Fr. Polynesia
93 G4 **Hjälmaren** *l.* Sweden
129 D1 **Hjalmar Lake** Can.
93 F4 **Hjørring** Denmark
123 D2 **Hlabisa** S. Africa
92 □B2 **Hlíð** Iceland
91 C2 **Hlobyne** Ukr.
123 C2 **Hlohlowane** S. Africa
123 C2 **Hlotse** Lesotho
91 C1 **Hlukhiv** Ukr.
88 C3 **Hlusk** Belarus
88 C2 **Hlybokaye** Belarus
114 C4 **Ho** Ghana
122 A1 **Hoachanas** Namibia
120 A2 **Hoanib** *watercourse*
    Namibia
120 A2 **Hoarusib** *watercourse*
    Namibia
51 D4 **Hobart** Austr.
139 D1 **Hobart** U.S.A.
139 C2 **Hobbs** U.S.A.
93 E4 **Hobro** Denmark
117 C4 **Hobyo** Somalia
63 B2 **Hô Chi Minh** Vietnam
    Ho Chi Minh City Vietnam
    see Hô Chi Minh
114 B3 **Hôd** *reg.* Maur.
117 D3 **Hodda** *mt.* Somalia
    Hodeidah Yemen *see*
    Al Ḩudaydah
103 E2 **Hódmezővásárhely**
    Hungary
100 B3 **Hoek van Holland** Neth.
65 B2 **Hoeyang** N. Korea
101 E2 **Hof** Ger.
101 E2 **Hofheim in Unterfranken**
    Ger.
92 □A2 **Höfn** Iceland
92 □A2 **Höfn** Iceland
92 □B3 **Hofsjökull** *ice cap* Iceland
67 B4 **Höfu** Japan
115 C2 **Hoggar** *plat.* Alg.
93 G4 **Högsby** Sweden
93 E3 **Høgste Breakulen** *mt.*
    Norway
101 D2 **Hohe Rhön** *mts* Ger.
100 C2 **Hohe Venn** *moorland*
    Belgium
75 C1 **Hoh Xil Shan** *mts* China
63 B2 **Hôi An** Vietnam
119 D2 **Hoima** Uganda
62 B1 **Hôi Xuân** Vietnam
75 D2 **Hojai** India
54 B2 **Hokitika** N.Z.
66 D2 **Hokkaidō** *i.* Japan
91 C2 **Hola Prystan'** Ukr.
128 B2 **Holbæk** Den.
53 C3 **Holbrook** Austr.
138 A2 **Holbrook** U.S.A.
137 D2 **Holdrege** U.S.A.
146 C2 **Holguín** Cuba
92 □B2 **Hóll** Iceland
103 D2 **Hollabrunn** Austria
140 B2 **Holland** U.S.A.
    Hollandia Indon. *see*
    Jayapura
135 B3 **Hollister** U.S.A.
103 E2 **Hollóháza** Hungary
93 I3 **Hollola** Fin.
100 B1 **Hollum** Neth.
142 C2 **Holly Springs** U.S.A.
143 D3 **Hollywood** U.S.A.
92 F2 **Holm** Norway
126 E2 **Holman** Can.
92 H3 **Holmsund** Sweden
122 A2 **Holoog** Namibia
93 E4 **Holstebro** Denmark
143 D1 **Holston** *r.* U.S.A.
98 A3 **Holyhead** U.K.
98 C2 **Holy Island** *England* U.K.
98 A3 **Holy Island** *Wales* U.K.

136 C2 Holyoke U.S.A.
Holy See Europe *see*
Vatican City
101 D2 Holzminden Ger.
62 A1 Homalin Myanmar
101 D2 Homberg (Efze) Ger.
114 B3 Hombori Mali
100 C3 Homburg Ger.
127 H2 Home Bay Can.
142 B2 Homer U.S.A.
143 D3 Homestead U.S.A.
92 F3 Hommelvik Norway
143 D3 Homosassa Springs
U.S.A.
Homs Syria *see* Ḥimṣ
89 D3 Homyel' Belarus
Honan *prov.* China *see*
Henan
122 A3 Hondeklipbaai S. Africa
145 D3 Hondo *r.* Belize/Mex.
138 B2 Hondo *NM* U.S.A.
139 D3 Hondo *TX* U.S.A.
146 B3 Honduras *country*
Central America
146 B3 Honduras, Gulf of
Belize/Hond.
93 F3 Hønefoss Norway
135 B2 Honey Lake U.S.A.
104 C2 Honfleur France
62 B1 Hông Gai Vietnam
70 B3 Honghu China
71 A3 Hongjiang China
69 D3 Hong Kong China
71 B3 Hong Kong
special admin. reg. China
Hongqizhen China *see*
Tongshi
131 D3 Honguedo, Détroit d'
sea chan. Can.
65 B1 Hongwǒn N. Korea
70 B2 Hongze Hu *l.* China
48 H4 Honiara Solomon Is
99 B4 Honiton U.K.
66 D3 Honjō Japan
92 I1 Honningsvåg Norway
49 L1 Honolulu U.S.A.
67 B3 Honshū *i.* Japan
134 B1 Hood, Mount *vol.* U.S.A.
50 A3 Hood Point Austr.
134 B1 Hood River U.S.A.
100 B2 Hoogeheide Neth.
100 C1 Hoogeveen Neth.
100 C1 Hoogezand-Sappemeer
Neth.
100 C2 Hoog-Keppel Neth.
Hook of Holland Neth. *see*
Hoek van Holland
128 A2 Hoonah U.S.A.
123 C2 Hoopstad S. Africa
100 B1 Hoorn Neth.
49 J5 Hoorn, Îles de *is*
Wallis and Futuna Is
128 B3 Hope Can.
142 B2 Hope U.S.A.
83 N2 Hope, Point U.S.A.
131 D2 Hopedale Can.
Hopei *prov.* China *see*
Hebei
145 D3 Hopelchén Mex.
131 D2 Hope Mountains Can.
Hopes Advance Bay Can.
see Aupaluk
52 B3 Hopetoun Austr.
122 B2 Hopetown S. Africa
141 D3 Hopewell U.S.A.
130 C2 Hopewell Islands Can.
50 B2 Hopkins, Lake *salt flat*
Austr.
140 B3 Hopkinsville U.S.A.
134 B1 Hoquiam U.S.A.
81 C1 Horasan Turkey
93 F4 Hörby Sweden
89 D3 Horki Belarus
91 D2 Horlivka Ukr.
79 D2 Hormak Iran
79 C2 Hormuz, Strait of
Iran/Oman
103 D2 Horn Austria
92 □A2 Horn *c.* Iceland
153 B5 Horn, Cape Chile
141 D2 Hornell U.S.A.
130 B3 Hornepayne Can.
Hornos, Cabo de *c.* Chile
see Horn, Cape
53 D2 Hornsby Austr.
98 C3 Hornsea U.K.
90 B2 Horodenka Ukr.
91 C1 Horodnya Ukr.
90 B2 Horodok Ukr.
90 A2 Horodok Ukr.
90 A1 Horokhiv Ukr.

Horqin Youyi Qianqi
China *see* Ulanhot
131 E2 Horse Islands Can.
52 B3 Horsham Austr.
99 C4 Horsham U.K.
93 F4 Horten Norway
126 D2 Horton *r.* Can.
117 B4 Hosa'ina Eth.
74 A2 Hoshab Pak.
74 B1 Hoshiarpur India
138 B1 Hosta Butte *mt.* U.S.A.
75 C1 Hotan China
122 B2 Hotazel S. Africa
92 G3 Hoting Sweden
142 B2 Hot Springs *AR* U.S.A.
Hot Springs *SD* U.S.A. *see*
Truth or Consequences
136 C2 Hot Springs *SD* U.S.A.
128 C1 Hottah Lake Can.
100 B2 Houffalize Belgium
140 B1 Houghton U.S.A.
141 F1 Houlton U.S.A.
70 B2 Houma China
142 B3 Houma U.S.A.
128 B2 Houston Can.
139 D3 Houston U.S.A.
50 A2 Houtman Abrolhos *is*
Austr.
122 B3 Houwater S. Africa
68 C1 Hovd Mongolia
99 C4 Hove U.K.
90 A2 Hoverla, Hora *mt.* Ukr.
68 C1 Hövsgöl Nuur *l.* Mongolia
68 C2 Hövüün Mongolia
116 A3 Howar, Wadi *watercourse*
Sudan
98 C3 Howden U.K.
53 C3 Howe, Cape Austr.
123 D2 Howick S. Africa
49 J3 Howland Island *terr.*
N. Pacific Ocean
53 C3 Howlong Austr.
Howrah India *see* Hāora
142 B1 Hoxie U.S.A.
101 D2 Höxter Ger.
96 C1 Hoy *i.* U.K.
93 E3 Høyanger Norway
102 C1 Hoyerswerda Ger.
103 D1 Hradec Králové
Czech Rep.
109 C2 Hrasnica Bos.-Herz.
92 □B2 Hraun Iceland
91 C1 Hrebinka Ukr.
88 B3 Hrodna Belarus
62 A1 Hsi-hseng Myanmar
71 C3 Hsinchu Taiwan
71 C3 Hsinying Taiwan
62 A1 Hsipaw Myanmar
70 A2 Huachi China
150 B4 Huacho Peru
70 B1 Huade China
65 B1 Huadian China
70 B2 Huaibei China
70 B2 Huai He *r.* China
71 A3 Huaihua China
70 B2 Huainan China
70 B2 Huaiyang China
70 B2 Huaiyin China
145 C3 Huajuápan de León Mex.
59 C3 Huaki Indon.
71 C3 Hualien Taiwan
150 B3 Huallaga *r.* Peru
120 A2 Huambo Angola
150 B4 Huancavelica Peru
150 B4 Huancayo Peru
Huangcaoba China *see*
Xingyi
70 B2 Huangchuan China
Huang Hai *sea*
N. Pacific Ocean *see*
Yellow Sea
70 B2 Huang He *r.* China
71 A4 Huangliu China
70 B3 Huangshan China
70 B2 Huangshi China
70 A2 Huangtu Gaoyuan *plat.*
China
71 C3 Huangyan China
70 A2 Huangzhong China
65 B1 Huanren China
150 B3 Huánuco Peru
152 B1 Huanuni Bol.
150 B4 Huaral Peru
150 B4 Huarmey Peru
152 A2 Huasco Chile
152 A2 Huasco *r.* Chile
144 B2 Huatabampo Mex.
145 C3 Huatusco Mex.
71 A3 Huayuan China
70 B2 Hubei *prov.* China

73 B3 Hubli India
100 C2 Hückelhoven Ger.
99 C3 Hucknall U.K.
98 C3 Huddersfield U.K.
93 G3 Hudiksvall Sweden
141 E2 Hudson *r.* U.S.A.
129 D2 Hudson Bay Can.
127 G3 Hudson Bay *sea* Can.
128 B2 Hudson's Hope Can.
127 H2 Hudson Strait Can.
63 B2 Huê Vietnam
146 A3 Huehuetenango Guat.
144 B2 Huehueto, Cerro *mt.* Mex.
145 C2 Huejutla Mex.
106 B2 Huelva Spain
107 C2 Huércal-Overa Spain
107 C1 Huesca Spain
106 C2 Huéscar Spain
51 D2 Hughenden Austr.
50 B3 Hughes Austr.
75 C2 Hugli *r. mouth* India
139 D2 Hugo U.S.A.
Huhehot China *see* Huhhot
70 B1 Huhhot China
122 B2 Huhudi S. Africa
122 A2 Huib-Hoch Plateau
Namibia
71 B3 Huichang China
Huicheng China *see* Huilai
65 B1 Huich'ŏn N. Korea
71 B3 Huilai China
120 A2 Huila Plateau Angola
71 A3 Huili China
70 B2 Huimin China
69 E2 Huinan China
Huinan China *see* Nanhui
93 H3 Huittinen Fin.
145 C3 Huixtla Mex.
Huiyang China *see*
Huizhou
71 A3 Huize China
71 B3 Huizhou China
68 C1 Hujirt Mongolia
78 B2 Hujr Saudi Arabia
122 B1 Hukuntsi Botswana
78 B2 Hulayfah Saudi Arabia
66 B1 Hulin China
130 C3 Hull Can.
70 C1 Huludao China
Hulun China *see* Hailar
69 D1 Hulun Nur *l.* China
91 D2 Hulyaypole Ukr.
69 E1 Huma China
150 C3 Humaitá Brazil
122 B3 Humansdorp S. Africa
98 C2 Humber *est.* U.K.
139 D3 Humble U.S.A.
129 D2 Humboldt Can.
135 C2 Humboldt *NV* U.S.A.
142 C1 Humboldt *TN* U.S.A.
135 C2 Humboldt *r.* U.S.A.
103 E2 Humenné Slovakia
53 C3 Hume Reservoir Austr.
138 A1 Humphreys Peak U.S.A.
65 A1 Hun *r.* China
115 D2 Hūn Libya
92 □A2 Húnaflói *b.* Iceland
71 B3 Hunan *prov.* China
65 C1 Hunchun China
110 B1 Hunedoara Romania
101 D2 Hünfeld Ger.
103 D2 Hungary *country* Europe
52 B1 Hungerford Austr.
65 B2 Hǔngnam N. Korea
Hunjiang China *see*
Baishan
99 D3 Hunstanton U.K.
101 D1 Hunte *r.* Ger.
48 I6 Hunter Island
S. Pacific Ocean
51 D4 Hunter Islands Austr.
99 C3 Huntingdon U.K.
140 B2 Huntington *IN* U.S.A.
140 C3 Huntington *WV* U.S.A.
135 C4 Huntington Beach U.S.A.
54 C1 Huntly N.Z.
96 C2 Huntly U.K.
130 C3 Huntsville Can.
142 C2 Huntsville *AL* U.S.A.
139 D2 Huntsville *TX* U.S.A.
Hunyani *r.* Moz./Zimbabwe
see Manyame
59 D3 Huon Peninsula P.N.G.
Huoxian China *see*
Huozhou
70 B2 Huozhou China
Hupeh *prov.* China *see*
Hubei
116 B2 Hurghada Egypt
137 D2 Huron U.S.A.
140 C2 Huron, Lake Can./U.S.A.

135 D3 Hurricane U.S.A.
100 C2 Hürth Ger.
92 □B1 Húsavík Iceland
110 C1 Huşi Romania
126 B2 Huslia U.S.A.
78 B3 Husn Āl 'Abr Yemen
102 B1 Husum Ger.
68 C1 Hutag Mongolia
60 A1 Hutanopan Indon.
137 D3 Hutchinson U.S.A.
143 D3 Hutchinson Island U.S.A.
70 B2 Hutuo *r.* China
100 B2 Huy Belgium
70 C2 Huzhou China
92 □C3 Hvalnes Iceland
92 □B3 Hvannadalshnúkur *vol.*
Iceland
109 C2 Hvar Croatia
109 C2 Hvar *i.* Croatia
91 C2 Hvardiys'ke Ukr.
120 B2 Hwange Zimbabwe
Hwang Ho *r.* China *see*
Huang He
136 C2 Hyannis U.S.A.
68 C1 Hyargas Nuur *salt l.*
Mongolia
50 A3 Hyden Austr.
73 B3 Hyderabad India
74 A2 Hyderabad Pak.
Hydra *i.* Greece *see* Ydra
105 D3 Hyères France
105 D3 Hyères, Îles d' *is* France
65 B1 Hyesan N. Korea
128 B2 Hyland Post Can.
67 B3 Hyōno-sen *mt.* Japan
99 D4 Hythe U.K.
67 B4 Hyūga Japan
93 H3 Hyvinkää Fin.

I

150 C3 Iaco *r.* Brazil
110 C2 Ialomiţa *r.* Romania
110 C1 Ianca Romania
110 C1 Iaşi Romania
64 A2 Iba Phil.
115 C4 Ibadan Nigeria
150 B2 Ibagué Col.
154 B2 Ibaiti Brazil
150 B2 Ibarra Ecuador
78 B3 Ibb Yemen
100 C1 Ibbenbüren Ger.
115 C4 Ibi Nigeria
107 C2 Ibi Spain
155 C1 Ibiá Brazil
155 D1 Ibiaí Brazil
151 D3 Ibiraçu Brazil
107 D2 Ibiza *i.* Spain
151 E4 Ibotirama Brazil
79 C2 Ibrā' Oman
79 C2 Ibri Oman
150 B4 Ica Peru
Icaria *i.* Greece *see* Ikaria
80 B2 İçel Turkey
92 □A2 Iceland *country* Europe
160 M4 Iceland Basin *sea feature*
N. Atlantic Ocean
160 L3 Icelandic Plateau
sea feature
N. Atlantic Ocean
67 C3 Ichinoseki Japan
91 C1 Ichnya Ukr.
65 B2 Ich'ŏn N. Korea
151 F3 Icó Brazil
155 D2 Iconha Brazil
139 E2 Idabel U.S.A.
115 C4 Idah Nigeria
134 D2 Idaho *state* U.S.A.
134 D2 Idaho Falls U.S.A.
100 C3 Idar-Oberstein Ger.
68 C1 Ideriyn Gol *r.* Mongolia
116 B2 Idfu Egypt
115 D2 Idhān Awbārī *des.* Libya
115 D2 Idhān Murzūq *des.* Libya
Idi Amin Dada, Lake
Dem. Rep. Congo/Uganda
see Edward, Lake
118 B3 Idiofa Dem. Rep. Congo
80 B2 Idlib Syria
123 C3 Idutywa S. Africa
88 B2 Iecava Latvia
154 B2 Iepê Brazil
100 A2 Ieper Belgium
111 C3 Ierapetra Greece
119 D3 Ifakara Tanz.
121 □D3 Ifanadiana Madag.
115 C4 Ife Nigeria
114 C3 Ifôghas, Adrar des *hills*
Mali

Itanagar
191

118 C3 **Ifumo** Dem. Rep. Congo
61 C1 **Igan** *Sarawak* Malaysia
119 D2 **Iganga** Uganda
154 C2 **Igarapava** Brazil
82 G2 **Igarka** Rus. Fed.
154 A2 **Igatimí** Para.
74 B3 **Igatpuri** India
81 C2 **Iğdır** Turkey
108 A3 **Iglesias** *Sardinia* Italy
127 G2 **Igloolik** Can.
Igluligaarjuk Can. *see* **Chesterfield Inlet**
130 A3 **Ignace** Can.
88 C2 **Ignalina** Lith.
111 C2 **İğneada** Turkey
110 C2 **İğneada Burnu** *pt* Turkey
111 B3 **Igoumenitsa** Greece
86 E3 **Igra** Rus. Fed.
86 F2 **Igrim** Rus. Fed.
154 B3 **Iguaçu** *r.* Brazil
154 B3 **Iguaçu Falls** Arg./Brazil
145 C3 **Iguala** Mex.
107 D1 **Igualada** Spain
154 C2 **Iguape** Brazil
154 B2 **Iguatemi** Brazil
154 B2 **Iguatemi** *r.* Brazil
151 F3 **Iguatu** Brazil
118 A3 **Iguéla** Gabon
119 D3 **Igunga** Tanz.
121 □D2 **Iharaña** Madag.
69 D2 **Ihbulag** Mongolia
121 □D3 **Ihosy** Madag.
92 I2 **Iijoki** *r.* Fin.
92 I3 **Iisalmi** Fin.
67 B4 **Iizuka** Japan
115 C4 **Ijebu-Ode** Nigeria
100 B1 **IJmuiden** Neth.
100 B1 **IJssel** *r.* Neth.
100 B1 **IJsselmeer** *l.* Neth.
152 C2 **Ijuí** Brazil
Ikaahuk Can. *see* **Sachs Harbour**
123 C2 **Ikageleng** S. Africa
123 C2 **Ikageng** S. Africa
111 C3 **Ikaria** *i.* Greece
118 C3 **Ikela** Dem. Rep. Congo
110 B2 **Ikhtiman** Bulg.
67 A4 **Iki** *i.* Japan
118 A2 **Ikom** Nigeria
121 □D3 **Ikongo** Madag.
65 B2 **Iksan** S. Korea
119 D3 **Ikungu** Tanz.
114 C2 **Ilaferh, Oued** *watercourse* Alg.
64 B2 **Ilagan** Phil.
81 C2 **Īlām** Iran
75 C2 **Ilam** Nepal
103 D1 **Iława** Pol.
79 C2 **Ilazārān, Kūh-e** *mt.* Iran
129 D2 **Île-à-la-Crosse** Can.
129 D2 **Île-à-la-Crosse, Lac** *l.* Can.
118 C3 **Ilebo** Dem. Rep. Congo
119 D2 **Ileret** Kenya
99 D4 **Ilford** U.K.
99 A4 **Ilfracombe** U.K.
155 C2 **Ilhabela** Brazil
155 D2 **Ilha Grande, Baía da** *b.* Brazil
154 B2 **Ilha Grande, Represa** *resr* Brazil
154 B2 **Ilha Solteíra, Represa** *resr* Brazil
106 B1 **Ílhavo** Port.
151 F4 **Ilhéus** Brazil
Ili Kazakh. *see* **Kapchagay**
126 B3 **Iliamna Lake** U.S.A.
64 B3 **Iligan** Phil.
Iliysk Kazakh. *see* **Kapchagay**
98 C3 **Ilkley** U.K.
152 A3 **Illapel** Chile
90 C2 **Illichivs'k** Ukr.
140 A3 **Illinois** *r.* U.S.A.
140 B3 **Illinois** *state* U.S.A.
90 B2 **Illintsi** Ukr.
115 C2 **Illizi** Alg.
89 D2 **Il'men', Ozero** *l.* Rus. Fed.
101 E2 **Ilmenau** Ger.
150 B4 **Ilo** Peru
64 B2 **Iloilo** Phil.
92 J3 **Ilomantsi** Fin.
115 C4 **Ilorin** Nigeria
87 D4 **Ilovlya** Rus. Fed.
53 D1 **Iluka** Austr.
127 I2 **Ilulissat** Greenland
Iman Rus. Fed. *see* **Dal'nerechensk**
66 B1 **Iman** *r.* Rus. Fed.
67 A4 **Imari** Japan
93 I3 **Imatra** Fin.
imeni Petra Stuchki Latvia *see* **Aizkraukle**
117 C4 **Īmī** Eth.
65 B2 **Imjin-gang** *r.* N. Korea/S. Korea
143 D3 **Immokalee** U.S.A.
108 B2 **Imola** Italy
151 E3 **Imperatriz** Brazil
108 A2 **Imperia** Italy
136 C2 **Imperial** U.S.A.
118 B2 **Impfondo** Congo
72 D2 **Imphal** India
111 C2 **İmroz** Turkey
67 C3 **Ina** Japan
150 C4 **Inambari** *r.* Peru
115 C2 **In Aménas** Alg.
115 C2 **In Amguel** Alg.
54 B2 **Inangahua Junction** N.Z.
59 C3 **Inanwatan** Indon.
92 I2 **Inari** Fin.
92 I2 **Inarijärvi** *l.* Fin.
67 D3 **Inawashiro-ko** *l.* Japan
80 B1 **İnce Burun** *pt* Turkey
65 B2 **Inch'ŏn** S. Korea
121 C2 **Inchope** Moz.
123 D2 **Incomati** *r.* Moz.
116 B3 **Inda Silasē** Eth.
144 B2 **Indé** Mex.
135 C3 **Independence** *CA* U.S.A.
137 E2 **Independence** *IA* U.S.A.
137 D3 **Independence** *KS* U.S.A.
137 E3 **Independence** *MO* U.S.A.
134 C2 **Independence Mountains** U.S.A.
76 B2 **Inderborskiy** Kazakh.
72 D2 **India** *country* Asia
141 D2 **Indiana** U.S.A.
140 B2 **Indiana** *state* U.S.A.
140 B3 **Indianapolis** U.S.A.
129 D2 **Indian Head** Can.
159 **Indian Ocean**
137 E2 **Indianola** *IA* U.S.A.
142 B2 **Indianola** *MS* U.S.A.
135 D3 **Indian Peak** U.S.A.
135 C3 **Indian Springs** U.S.A.
86 D2 **Indiga** Rus. Fed.
83 K2 **Indigirka** *r.* Rus. Fed.
109 D1 **Inđija** Yugo.
135 C4 **Indio** U.S.A.
58 B3 **Indonesia** *country* Asia
74 B2 **Indore** India
60 B2 **Indramayu, Tanjung** *pt* Indon.
Indrapura, Gunung *vol.* Indon. *see* **Kerinci, Gunung**
75 C3 **Indravati** *r.* India
104 C2 **Indre** *r.* France
74 A2 **Indus** *r.* China/Pak.
74 A2 **Indus, Mouths of the** Pak.
159 E2 **Indus Cone** *sea feature* Indian Ocean
80 B1 **İnebolu** Turkey
111 C2 **İnegöl** Turkey
Infantes Spain *see* **Villanueva de los Infantes**
144 B3 **Infiernillo, Presa** *resr* Mex.
51 D1 **Ingham** Austr.
53 D1 **Inglewood** Austr.
102 C2 **Ingolstadt** Ger.
75 C2 **Ingrāj Bāzār** India
123 D2 **Ingwavuma** S. Africa
120 B2 **Ingwe** Zambia
123 D2 **Inhaca** Moz.
121 C3 **Inhambane** Moz.
121 C2 **Inhaminga** Moz.
151 D2 **Inini** Fr. Guiana
Inis Rep. of Ireland *see* **Ennis**
97 A2 **Inishbofin** *i.* Rep. of Ireland
97 B2 **Inishmore** *i.* Rep. of Ireland
97 C1 **Inishowen** *pen.* Rep. of Ireland
54 B2 **Inland Kaikoura Range** *mts* N.Z.
Inland Sea Japan *see* **Seto-naikai**
102 C2 **Inn** *r.* Europe
127 H1 **Innaanganeq** *c.* Greenland
52 B1 **Innamincka** Austr.
Inner Mongolia *aut. reg.* China *see* **Nei Mongol Zizhiqu**
96 B2 **Inner Sound** *sea chan.* U.K.
51 D1 **Innisfail** Austr.
102 C2 **Innsbruck** Austria
97 C2 **Inny** *r.* Rep. of Ireland
154 B1 **Inocência** Brazil
118 B3 **Inongo** Dem. Rep. Congo
111 D3 **İnönü** Turkey
Inoucdjouac Can. *see* **Inukjuak**
103 D1 **Inowrocław** Pol.
114 C2 **In Salah** Alg.
62 A2 **Insein** Myanmar
110 C2 **Însurăţei** Romania
86 F2 **Inta** Rus. Fed.
105 D2 **Interlaken** Switz.
137 E1 **International Falls** U.S.A.
63 A2 **Interview Island** India
130 C2 **Inukjuak** Can.
126 D2 **Inuvik** Can.
96 B2 **Inveraray** U.K.
96 C2 **Inverbervie** U.K.
54 A3 **Invercargill** N.Z.
53 D1 **Inverell** Austr.
96 B2 **Invergordon** U.K.
128 C2 **Invermere** Can.
131 D3 **Inverness** Can.
96 B2 **Inverness** U.K.
96 C2 **Inverurie** U.K.
159 F4 **Investigator Ridge** *sea feature* Indian Ocean
52 A3 **Investigator Strait** Austr.
77 E1 **Inya** Rus. Fed.
Inyanga Zimbabwe *see* **Nyanga**
119 D3 **Inyonga** Tanz.
87 D3 **Inza** Rus. Fed.
111 B3 **Ioannina** Greece
137 D3 **Iola** U.S.A.
96 A2 **Iona** *i.* U.K.
111 B3 **Ionian Islands** Greece
109 C3 **Ionian Sea** Greece/Italy
Ionioi Nisoi *is* Greece *see* **Ionian Islands**
111 C3 **Ios** *i.* Greece
137 E2 **Iowa** *state* U.S.A.
137 E2 **Iowa City** U.S.A.
154 C1 **Ipameri** Brazil
155 D1 **Ipatinga** Brazil
81 C1 **Ipatovo** Rus. Fed.
123 C2 **Ipelegeng** S. Africa
150 B2 **Ipiales** Col.
151 F4 **Ipiaú** Brazil
154 B3 **Ipiranga** Brazil
150 B3 **Ipixuna** Brazil
60 B1 **Ipoh** Malaysia
154 B1 **Iporá** Brazil
118 C2 **Ippy** C.A.R.
111 C2 **İpsala** Turkey
53 D1 **Ipswich** Austr.
99 D3 **Ipswich** U.K.
127 H2 **Iqaluit** Can.
152 A2 **Iquique** Chile
150 B3 **Iquitos** Peru
Irakleio Greece *see* **Iraklion**
111 C3 **Iraklion** Greece
81 D2 **Iran** *country* Asia
61 C1 **Iran, Pegunungan** *mts* Indon.
79 D2 **Īrānshahr** Iran
144 B2 **Irapuato** Mex.
81 C2 **Iraq** *country* Asia
154 B3 **Irati** Brazil
88 B2 **Irbe Strait** Estonia/Latvia
80 B2 **Irbid** Jordan
86 F3 **Irbit** Rus. Fed.
151 E4 **Irecê** Brazil
97 C2 **Ireland, Republic of** *country* Europe
118 C3 **Irema** Dem. Rep. Congo
76 C2 **Irgiz** Kazakh.
Iri S. Korea *see* **Iksan**
59 D3 **Irian Jaya** *reg.* Indon.
115 E3 **Iriba** Chad
114 B3 **Irîgui** *reg.* Mali/Maur.
119 D3 **Iringa** Tanz.
151 D3 **Iriri** *r.* Brazil
Irish Free State *country* Europe *see* **Ireland, Republic of**
95 B3 **Irish Sea** Rep. of Ireland/U.K.
68 C1 **Irkutsk** Rus. Fed.
160 M4 **Irminger Basin** *sea feature* N. Atlantic Ocean
141 D2 **Irondequoit** U.S.A.
52 A2 **Iron Knob** Austr.
140 B1 **Iron Mountain** U.S.A.
140 C3 **Ironton** U.S.A.
140 A1 **Ironwood** U.S.A.
130 B3 **Iroquois Falls** Can.
64 B2 **Irosin** Phil.
67 C4 **Irō-zaki** *pt* Japan
90 C1 **Irpin'** Ukr.
62 A2 **Irrawaddy** *r.* Myanmar
63 A2 **Irrawaddy, Mouths of the** Myanmar
86 F2 **Irtysh** *r.* Kazakh./Rus. Fed.
107 C1 **Irún** Spain
96 B3 **Irvine** U.K.
139 D2 **Irving** U.S.A.
64 B3 **Isabela** Phil.
146 B3 **Isabelia, Cordillera** *mts* Nic.
92 □A2 **Ísafjarðardjúp** *est.* Iceland
92 □A2 **Ísafjörður** Iceland
67 B4 **Isahaya** Japan
102 C2 **Isar** *r.* Ger.
96 □ **Isbister** U.K.
108 B2 **Ischia, Isola d'** *i.* Italy
67 C4 **Ise** Japan
118 C2 **Isengi** Dem. Rep. Congo
105 C3 **Isère** *r.* France
100 C2 **Iserlohn** Ger.
101 D1 **Isernhagen** Ger.
67 C4 **Ise-wan** *b.* Japan
114 C4 **Iseyin** Nigeria
Isfahan Iran *see* **Eşfahān**
66 D2 **Ishikari-wan** *b.* Japan
77 D1 **Ishim** *r.* Kazakh./Rus. Fed.
82 F3 **Ishim** Rus. Fed.
67 D3 **Ishinomaki** Japan
67 D3 **Ishioka** Japan
67 B4 **Ishizuchi-san** *mt.* Japan
74 B1 **Ishkoshim** Tajik.
140 B1 **Ishpeming** U.S.A.
111 C2 **Işıklar Dağı** *mts* Turkey
111 C3 **Işıklı** Turkey
123 D2 **Isipingo** S. Africa
119 C2 **Isiro** Dem. Rep. Congo
80 B2 **İskenderun** Turkey
82 G3 **Iskitim** Rus. Fed.
110 B2 **Iskŭr** *r.* Bulg.
117 D3 **Iskushuban** Somalia
128 A2 **Iskut** *r.* Can.
74 B1 **Islamabad** Pak.
143 D4 **Islamorada** U.S.A.
52 A2 **Island Lagoon** *salt flat* Austr.
129 E2 **Island Lake** Can.
54 B1 **Islands, Bay of** N.Z.
Islas Canarias *is* N. Atlantic Ocean *see* **Canary Islands**
96 A3 **Islay** *i.* U.K.
98 A2 **Isle of Man** *i.* Irish Sea
Ismail Ukr. *see* **Izmayil**
116 B1 **Ismâ'ilîya** Egypt
116 B2 **Isna** Egypt
121 □D3 **Isoanala** Madag.
121 C2 **Isoka** Zambia
93 H3 **Isokyrö** Fin.
109 C3 **Isola di Capo Rizzuto** Italy
Ispahan Iran *see* **Eşfahān**
80 B2 **Isparta** Turkey
110 C2 **Isperikh** Bulg.
Ispisar Tajik. *see* **Khŭjand**
80 B2 **Israel** *country* Asia
50 B3 **Israelite Bay** Austr.
105 C2 **Issoire** France
Issyk-Kul' Kyrg. *see* **Balykchy**
111 C2 **İstanbul** Turkey
İstanbul Boğazı *str.* Turkey *see* **Bosporus**
103 D2 **Isten dombja** *hill* Hungary
111 B3 **Istiaia** Greece
143 D3 **Istokpoga, Lake** U.S.A.
108 B1 **Istra** *pen.* Croatia
105 C3 **Istres** France
Istria *pen.* Croatia *see* **Istra**
155 D2 **Itabapoana** Brazil
151 E4 **Itaberaba** Brazil
154 C1 **Itaberaí** Brazil
155 D1 **Itabira** Brazil
155 D2 **Itabirito** Brazil
151 F4 **Itabuna** Brazil
150 D3 **Itacoatiara** Brazil
155 D2 **Itaguaí** Brazil
154 B2 **Itaguajé** Brazil
154 C2 **Itaí** Brazil
154 C3 **Itaiópolis** Brazil
154 B3 **Itaipu, Represa de** *resr* Brazil
151 D3 **Itaituba** Brazil
154 C3 **Itajaí** Brazil
155 C2 **Itajubá** Brazil
108 B2 **Italy** *country* Europe
155 E1 **Itamaraju** Brazil
155 D1 **Itamarandiba** Brazil
155 D1 **Itambacuri** Brazil
155 D1 **Itambé, Pico de** *mt.* Brazil
75 D2 **Itanagar** India

154 C2 Itanhaém Brazil
155 D1 Itanhém Brazil
155 D1 Itaobim Brazil
154 C1 Itapajipe Brazil
155 E1 Itapebi Brazil
155 D2 Itapemirim Brazil
155 D2 Itaperuna Brazil
155 D1 Itapetinga Brazil
154 C2 Itapetininga Brazil
154 C2 Itapeva Brazil
151 F4 Itapicuru r. Brazil
151 E3 Itapicuru Mirim Brazil
155 C2 Itapira Brazil
154 C2 Itaporanga Brazil
154 C1 Itapuranga Brazil
154 C2 Itararé Brazil
74 B2 Itarsi India
154 B1 Itarumã Brazil
155 D2 Itaúna Brazil
155 E1 Itaúnas Brazil
64 B1 Itbayat i. Phil.
141 D2 Ithaca U.S.A.
101 D1 Ith Hils ridge Ger.
118 C2 Itimbiri r.
   Dem. Rep. Congo
155 D1 Itinga Brazil
154 B1 Itiquira Brazil
154 A1 Itiquira r. Brazil
67 C4 Itō Japan
154 C2 Itu Brazil
150 B3 Itui r. Brazil
154 C1 Ituiutaba Brazil
119 C3 Itula Dem. Rep. Congo
154 C1 Itumbiara Brazil
154 C1 Itumbiara, Barragem resr
   Brazil
154 B1 Iturama Brazil
101 D1 Itzehoe Ger.
83 N2 Iul'tin Rus. Fed.
155 D2 Iúna Brazil
154 B2 Ivaí r. Brazil
92 I2 Ivalo Fin.
88 C3 Ivanava Belarus
109 C1 Ivanec Croatia
   Ivangrad Yugo. see Berane
52 B2 Ivanhoe Austr.
90 B1 Ivankiv Ukr.
90 A2 Ivano-Frankivs'k Ukr.
89 F2 Ivanovo Rus. Fed.
88 C3 Ivatsevichy Belarus
111 C2 Ivaylovgrad Bulg.
86 F2 Ivdel' Rus. Fed.
110 C1 Iveşti Romania
154 B2 Ivinheima Brazil
154 B2 Ivinheima r. Brazil
127 I2 Ivittuut Greenland
   Iviza i. Spain see Ibiza
89 E3 Ivnya Rus. Fed.
   Ivory Coast country Africa
   see Côte d'Ivoire
108 A1 Ivrea Italy
111 C3 İvrindi Turkey
   Ivujivik Can. see Ivujivik
127 G2 Ivujivik Can.
67 D3 Iwaki Japan
67 B4 Iwakuni Japan
66 D2 Iwamizawa Japan
66 C2 Iwanai Japan
66 D3 Iwate-san vol. Japan
88 C3 Iwye Belarus
123 D3 Ixopo S. Africa
144 B2 Ixtlán Mex.
146 B3 Izabal, Lago de l. Guat.
145 D2 Izamal Mex.
81 C1 Izberbash Rus. Fed.
86 E3 Izhevsk Rus. Fed.
86 E2 Izhma Rus. Fed.
   Izhma Rus. Fed. see
   Sosnogorsk
89 E3 Izmalkovo Rus. Fed.
90 B2 Izmayil Ukr.
111 C3 İzmir Turkey
   İzmit Turkey see Kocaeli
111 C2 İznik Gölü l. Turkey
145 C3 Izúcar de Matamoros
   Mex.
67 A4 Izuhara Japan
67 B3 Izumo Japan
156 C4 Izu-Ogasawara Trench
   sea feature
   N. Pacific Ocean
67 C4 Izu-shotō is Japan
90 B1 Izyaslav Ukr.
91 D2 Izyum Ukr.

J

74 A1 Jabal as Sirāj Afgh.
106 C2 Jabalón r. Spain

75 B2 Jabalpur India
50 C1 Jabiru Austr.
109 C2 Jablanica Bos.-Herz.
151 E2 Jaboatão Brazil
154 C2 Jaboticabal Brazil
107 C1 Jaca Spain
145 C2 Jacala Mex.
151 D3 Jacareacanga Brazil
155 C2 Jacareí Brazil
154 B1 Jaciara Brazil
155 D1 Jacinto Brazil
141 E1 Jackman U.S.A.
142 C2 Jackson AL U.S.A.
140 C2 Jackson MI U.S.A.
142 B2 Jackson MS U.S.A.
142 C1 Jackson TN U.S.A.
136 A2 Jackson WY U.S.A.
54 A2 Jackson Head hd N.Z.
142 B2 Jacksonville AR U.S.A.
143 D2 Jacksonville FL U.S.A.
140 A3 Jacksonville IL U.S.A.
143 E2 Jacksonville NC U.S.A.
139 D2 Jacksonville TX U.S.A.
147 C3 Jacmel Haiti
74 A2 Jacobabad Pak.
151 E4 Jacobina Brazil
131 D3 Jacques Cartier, Mont
   mt. Can.
151 E3 Jacunda Brazil
154 C2 Jacupiranga Brazil
101 D1 Jadebusen b. Ger.
   Jadotville
   Dem. Rep. Congo see
   Likasi
109 C2 Jadovnik mt. Bos.-Herz.
150 B3 Jaén Peru
106 C2 Jaén Spain
   Jaffa Israel see
   Tel Aviv-Yafo
52 A3 Jaffa, Cape Austr.
73 B4 Jaffna Sri Lanka
75 C3 Jagdalpur India
123 C2 Jagersfontein S. Africa
79 C2 Jaghin Iran
152 C3 Jaguarão Uru.
154 C2 Jaguariaíva Brazil
81 D3 Jahrom Iran
74 B2 Jaipur India
74 B2 Jaisalmer India
74 B2 Jaitgarh hill India
75 C2 Jajarkot Nepal
109 C2 Jajce Bos.-Herz.
   Jajnagar state India see
   Orissa
60 B2 Jakarta Indon.
128 A1 Jakes Corner Can.
92 G2 Jäkkvik Sweden
   Jakobshavn Greenland
   see Ilulissat
92 H3 Jakobstad Fin.
77 D3 Jalālābād Afgh.
77 D2 Jalal-Abad Kyrg.
74 B1 Jalandhar India
145 C3 Jalapa Enríquez Mex.
154 B2 Jales Brazil
74 B2 Jalgaon India
115 D4 Jalingo Nigeria
74 B3 Jalna India
74 B2 Jalor India
144 B2 Jalostotitlán Mex.
144 B2 Jalpa Mex.
75 C2 Jalpaiguri India
145 C2 Jalpan Mex.
115 E2 Jālū Libya
146 C3 Jamaica country
   West Indies
146 C3 Jamaica Channel
   Haiti/Jamaica
75 C2 Jamalpur Bangl.
60 B2 Jambi Indon.
137 D2 James r. ND/SD U.S.A.
141 D3 James r. VA U.S.A.
130 B2 James Bay Can.
52 A2 Jamestown Austr.
   Jamestown Can. see
   Wawa
123 C3 Jamestown S. Africa
137 D1 Jamestown ND U.S.A.
141 D2 Jamestown NY U.S.A.
74 B1 Jammu
   Jammu and Kashmir
74 B1 Jammu and Kashmir terr.
   Asia
74 B2 Jamnagar India
74 B2 Jampur Pak.
93 I3 Jämsä Fin.
75 C2 Jamshedpur India
75 C2 Jamuna r. Bangl.
75 C2 Janakpur Nepal
155 D1 Janaúba Brazil
81 D2 Jandaq Iran

114 A2 Jandía hill Canary Is
135 B2 Janesville CA U.S.A.
140 B2 Janesville WI U.S.A.
154 A2 Jango Brazil
82 A2 Jan Mayen i. Arctic Ocean
122 B3 Jansenville S. Africa
155 D1 Januária Brazil
74 B2 Jaora India
66 C3 Japan country Asia
66 B3 Japan, Sea of
   N. Pacific Ocean
150 C3 Japurá r. Brazil
154 C1 Jaraguá Brazil
154 C3 Jaraguá, Serra mts Brazil
154 C3 Jaraguá do Sul Brazil
154 B2 Jaraguari Brazil
152 C2 Jardim Brazil
69 D1 Jargalant Mongolia
103 D1 Jarocin Pol.
103 E1 Jarosław Pol.
92 F3 Järpen Sweden
70 A2 Jartai China
150 C4 Jarú Brazil
   Jarud China see Lubei
88 C1 Järvenpää Fin.
49 K4 Jarvis Island terr.
   S. Pacific Ocean
93 G3 Järvsö Sweden
79 C2 Jāsk Iran
103 E2 Jasło Pol.
55 A3 Jason Peninsula
   Antarctica
128 C2 Jasper Can.
142 C2 Jasper AL U.S.A.
140 B3 Jasper IN U.S.A.
139 E2 Jasper TX U.S.A.
   Jassy Romania see Iaşi
103 D2 Jastrzębie-Zdrój Pol.
103 D2 Jászberény Hungary
154 B1 Jataí Brazil
154 C2 Jaú Brazil
150 C3 Jaú r. Brazil
145 C2 Jaumave Mex.
75 C2 Jaunpur India
154 B1 Jauru Brazil
61 B2 Java i. Indon.
107 C1 Javalambre, Sierra de
   mts Spain
69 D1 Javarthushuu Mongolia
60 C2 Java Sea Indon.
156 B6 Java Trench sea feature
   Indian Ocean
117 C4 Jawhar Somalia
103 D1 Jawor Pol.
103 D1 Jaworzno Pol.
59 D3 Jaya, Puncak mt. Indon.
59 D3 Jayapura Indon.
128 B1 Jean Marie River Can.
131 D2 Jeannin, Lac l. Can.
   Jebel, Bahr el r.
   Sudan/Uganda see
   White Nile
116 A3 Jebel Abyad Plateau
   Sudan
96 C3 Jedburgh U.K.
78 A2 Jeddah Saudi Arabia
108 A3 Jedeida Tunisia
101 E1 Jeetze r. Ger.
137 E2 Jefferson U.S.A.
135 C2 Jefferson, Mount U.S.A.
137 E3 Jefferson City U.S.A.
122 B3 Jeffrey's Bay S. Africa
88 C2 Jēkabpils Latvia
103 D1 Jelenia Góra Pol.
88 B2 Jelgava Latvia
60 B1 Jemaja i. Indon.
61 C2 Jember Indon.
101 E2 Jena Ger.
77 E2 Jengish Chokusu mt.
   China/Kyrg.
80 B2 Jenin West Bank
142 B2 Jennings U.S.A.
151 E4 Jequié Brazil
155 D1 Jequitaí Brazil
155 D1 Jequitinhonha Brazil
155 E1 Jequitinhonha r. Brazil
147 C3 Jérémie Haiti
144 B2 Jerez Mex.
106 B2 Jerez de la Frontera
   Spain
109 D3 Jergucat Albania
115 C1 Jerid, Chott el salt l.
   Tunisia
134 D2 Jerome U.S.A.
95 C4 Jersey i. Channel Is
95 C4 Jersey terr. Channel Is
151 E3 Jerumenha Brazil
80 B2 Jerusalem
   Israel/West Bank

53 D3 Jervis Bay Territory
   admin. div. Austr.
108 B1 Jesenice Slovenia
108 B2 Jesi Italy
   Jesselton Malaysia see
   Kota Kinabalu
101 F2 Jessen Ger.
75 C2 Jessore Bangl.
143 D2 Jesup U.S.A.
137 D3 Jesus, Mount hill U.S.A.
145 C3 Jesús Carranza Mex.
100 C1 Jever Ger.
74 B2 Jhalawar India
74 B1 Jhang Pak.
74 B2 Jhansi India
75 C2 Jharsuguda India
74 B1 Jhelum r. India/Pak.
74 B1 Jhelum Pak.
74 B2 Jhunjhunūn India
70 C2 Jiading China
69 E1 Jiamusi China
71 B3 Ji'an Jiangxi China
65 B1 Ji'an Jilin China
   Jianchang China see
   Nancheng
62 A1 Jianchuan China
   Jiandaoyu China see
   Zigui
70 B3 Jiande China
71 B3 Jiangling China see
   Jingzhou
71 B3 Jiangmen China
70 B2 Jiangsu prov. China
71 B3 Jiangxi prov. China
70 A2 Jiangyou China
70 B3 Jianli China
71 B3 Jianyang Fujian China
70 A2 Jianyang Sichuan China
70 B2 Jiaohe Hebei China
69 E2 Jiaohe Jilin China
   Jiaojiang China see
   Taizhou
70 C2 Jiaozhou China
70 B2 Jiaozuo China
   Jiashan China see
   Mingguang
70 C2 Jiaxing China
68 C2 Jiayuguan China
   Jiddah Saudi Arabia see
   Jeddah
92 G2 Jiehkkevarri mt. Norway
70 B2 Jiexiu China
70 A2 Jigzhi China
103 D2 Jihlava Czech Rep.
115 C1 Jijel Alg.
117 C4 Jijiga Eth.
117 C4 Jilib Somalia
69 E2 Jilin China
65 B1 Jilin prov. China
65 A1 Jilin Handa Ling mts
   China
117 B4 Jima Eth.
110 B1 Jimbolia Romania
144 B2 Jiménez Mex.
139 C3 Jiménez Mex.
145 C2 Jiménez Mex.
70 B2 Jinan China
70 A2 Jinchang China
70 B2 Jincheng China
   Jinchuan China see
   Jinchang
53 C3 Jindabyne Austr.
103 D2 Jindřichův Hradec
   Czech Rep.
   Jin'e China see
   Longchang
70 A2 Jingbian China
71 B3 Jingdezhen China
62 B1 Jinggang China
53 C3 Jingellic Austr.
71 B3 Jinggangshan China
62 B1 Jinghong China
70 B2 Jingmen China
70 A2 Jingning China
70 A2 Jingtai China
71 A3 Jingxi China
   Jingxian China see
   Jingzhou
65 B1 Jingyu China
70 A2 Jingyuan China
70 B2 Jingzhou Hubei China
71 A3 Jingzhou Hunan China
73 B3 Jinhua China
70 B1 Jining Nei Mongol China
70 B2 Jining Shandong China
119 D2 Jinja Uganda
117 B4 Jinka Eth.
146 B3 Jinotega Nic.
146 B3 Jinotepe Nic.
71 A3 Jinping China

Jinsha Jiang *r.* China *see* Yangtze
Jinshi China *see* Xinning
70 B3 **Jinshi** China
Jinxi China *see* Lianshan
70 C1 **Jinzhou** China
150 C3 **Jiparaná** *r.* Brazil
Jirang China *see* Burang
79 C2 **Jiroft** Iran
79 C2 **Jirwan** Saudi Arabia
71 A3 **Jishou** China
110 B2 **Jiu** *r.* Romania
70 A2 **Jiuding Shan** *mt.* China
70 B3 **Jiujiang** China
Jiulian China *see* Mojiang
79 D2 **Jiwani** Pak.
66 B1 **Jixi** China
78 B3 **Jīzān** Saudi Arabia
155 D1 **Joaima** Brazil
João Belo Moz. *see* Xai-Xai
151 F3 **João Pessoa** Brazil
155 C1 **João Pinheiro** Brazil
74 B2 **Jodhpur** India
92 I3 **Joensuu** Fin.
67 C3 **Jōetsu** Japan
121 C3 **Jofane** Moz.
88 C2 **Jõgeva** Estonia
Jogjakarta Indon. *see* Yogyakarta
123 C2 **Johannesburg** S. Africa
134 C2 **John Day** U.S.A.
134 B1 **John Day** *r.* U.S.A.
128 C2 **John d'Or Prairie** Can.
143 E1 **John H. Kerr Reservoir** U.S.A.
96 C1 **John o'Groats** U.K.
143 D1 **Johnson City** U.S.A.
128 A1 **Johnson's Crossing** Can.
50 B3 **Johnston, Lake** *salt flat* Austr.
49 J2 **Johnston Atoll** N. Pacific Ocean
96 B3 **Johnstone** U.K.
Johnstone Lake Can. *see* Old Wives Lake
141 D2 **Johnstown** U.S.A.
60 B1 **Johor Bahru** Malaysia
88 C2 **Jõhvi** Estonia
154 C3 **Joinville** Brazil
105 D2 **Joinville** France
55 B3 **Joinville Island** Antarctica
92 G2 **Jokkmokk** Sweden
92 □B2 **Jökulsá á Fjöllum** *r.* Iceland
140 B2 **Joliet** U.S.A.
130 C3 **Joliette** Can.
64 B3 **Jolo** Phil.
64 B3 **Jolo** *i.* Phil.
61 C2 **Jombang** Indon.
75 C2 **Jomsom** Nepal
88 B2 **Jonava** Lith.
142 B1 **Jonesboro** *AR* U.S.A.
142 B2 **Jonesboro** *LA* U.S.A.
141 F2 **Jonesport** U.S.A.
127 G1 **Jones Sound** *sea chan.* Can.
93 F4 **Jönköping** Sweden
131 C3 **Jonquière** Can.
145 C3 **Jonuta** Mex.
137 E3 **Joplin** U.S.A.
80 B2 **Jordan** *country* Asia
80 B2 **Jordan** *r.* Asia
134 E1 **Jordan** U.S.A.
155 D1 **Jordânia** Brazil
134 C2 **Jordan Valley** U.S.A.
72 A2 **Jorhat** India
101 D1 **Jork** Ger.
93 E4 **Jørpeland** Norway
115 C4 **Jos** Nigeria
145 C3 **José Cardel** Mex.
131 D2 **Joseph, Lac** *l.* Can.
50 B1 **Joseph Bonaparte Gulf** Austr.
115 C4 **Jos Plateau** Nigeria
93 E3 **Jotunheimen** *mts* Norway
122 B3 **Joubertina** S. Africa
123 C2 **Jouberton** S. Africa
104 C2 **Joué-lès-Tours** France
93 I3 **Joutseno** Fin.
134 B1 **Juan de Fuca Strait** Can./U.S.A.
149 B6 **Juan Fernández Islands** S. Pacific Ocean
Juanshui China *see* Tongcheng
145 B2 **Juárez** Mex.
144 A1 **Juárez, Sierra de** *mts* Mex.
151 E3 **Juàzeiro** Brazil
151 F3 **Juàzeiro do Norte** Brazil

117 B4 **Juba** Sudan
117 C5 **Jubba** *r.* Somalia
78 B2 **Jubbah** Saudi Arabia
117 A3 **Jubbulpore** India *see* Jabalpur
107 C2 **Júcar** *r.* Spain
154 B1 **Juçara** Brazil
145 C3 **Juchitán** Mex.
155 E1 **Jucuruçu** Brazil
102 C2 **Judenburg** Austria
155 E1 **Juerana** Brazil
101 D2 **Jühnde** Ger.
146 B3 **Juigalpa** Nic.
150 D4 **Juina** Brazil
100 C1 **Juist** *i.* Ger.
155 D2 **Juiz de Fora** Brazil
136 C2 **Julesburg** U.S.A.
150 B4 **Juliaca** Peru
Julianatop *mt.* Indon. *see* Mandala, Puncak
151 D2 **Juliana Top** *mt.* Suriname
Jullundur India *see* Jalandhar
107 C2 **Jumilla** Spain
75 C2 **Jumla** Nepal
Jumna *r.* India *see* Yamuna
74 B2 **Junagadh** India
139 D2 **Junction** U.S.A.
137 D3 **Junction City** U.S.A.
154 C2 **Jundiaí** Brazil
128 A2 **Juneau** U.S.A.
53 C2 **Junee** Austr.
105 D2 **Jungfrau** *mt.* Switz.
141 D2 **Juniata** *r.* U.S.A.
153 B3 **Junín** Arg.
92 G3 **Junsele** Sweden
134 C2 **Juntura** U.S.A.
Junxi China *see* Datian
Junxian China *see* Danjiangkou
154 B2 **Jupia, Represa** *resr* Brazil
143 D3 **Jupiter** U.S.A.
154 C2 **Juquiá** Brazil
117 A4 **Jur** *r.* Sudan
105 D2 **Jura** *mts* France/Switz.
96 B2 **Jura** *i.* U.K.
96 B3 **Jura, Sound of** *sea chan.* U.K.
88 B2 **Jurbarkas** Lith.
88 B2 **Jūrmala** Latvia
150 B3 **Juruá** *r.* Brazil
150 D3 **Juruena** *r.* Brazil
154 C2 **Jurumirim, Represa de** *resr* Brazil
151 D3 **Juruti** Brazil
150 C3 **Jutaí** *r.* Brazil
101 F2 **Jüterbog** Ger.
154 B2 **Juti** Brazil
145 D3 **Jutiapa** Guat.
Jutland *pen.* Denmark *see* Jylland
70 B2 **Juxian** China
81 D3 **Jüyom** Iran
122 B1 **Jwaneng** Botswana
93 E4 **Jylland** *pen.* Denmark
93 I3 **Jyväskylä** Fin.

K

74 B1 **K2** *mt.* China/Jammu and Kashmir
Kaakhka Turkm. *see* Kaka
92 I2 **Kaamanen** Fin.
61 D2 **Kabaena** *i.* Indon.
119 C3 **Kabalo** Dem. Rep. Congo
119 C3 **Kabambare** Dem. Rep. Congo
119 C3 **Kabare** Dem. Rep. Congo
130 B3 **Kabinakagami Lake** Can.
118 C3 **Kabinda** Dem. Rep. Congo
118 B2 **Kabo** C.A.R.
120 B2 **Kabompo** Zambia
119 C3 **Kabongo** Dem. Rep. Congo
77 C3 **Kābul** Afgh.
64 B3 **Kaburuang** *i.* Indon.
121 B2 **Kabwe** Zambia
109 D2 **Kačanik** Yugo.
74 A2 **Kachchh, Gulf of** India
83 I3 **Kachug** Rus. Fed.
81 C1 **Kaçkar Dağı** *mt.* Turkey
111 C3 **Kadıköy** Turkey
52 A2 **Kadina** Austr.
114 B3 **Kadiolo** Mali
Kadiyevka Ukr. *see* Stakhanov
73 B3 **Kadmat** *i.* India

89 F2 **Kadnikov** Rus. Fed.
121 B2 **Kadoma** Zimbabwe
63 A2 **Kadonkani** Myanmar
117 A3 **Kadugli** Sudan
115 C3 **Kaduna** Nigeria
89 E2 **Kaduy** Rus. Fed.
86 E2 **Kadzherom** Rus. Fed.
114 A3 **Kaédi** Maur.
118 B1 **Kaélé** Cameroon
65 B2 **Kaesŏng** N. Korea
118 C3 **Kafakumba** Dem. Rep. Congo
114 A3 **Kaffrine** Senegal
111 B3 **Kafireas, Akra** *pt* Greece
80 B2 **Kafr el Sheikh** Egypt
121 B2 **Kafue** Zambia
120 B2 **Kafue** *r.* Zambia
67 C3 **Kaga** Japan
118 B2 **Kaga Bandoro** C.A.R.
91 E2 **Kagal'nitskaya** Rus. Fed.
Kaganovichi Pervyye Ukr. *see* Polis'ke
60 A2 **Kagologolo** Indon.
67 B4 **Kagoshima** Japan
Kagul Moldova *see* Cahul
119 D3 **Kahama** Tanz.
90 C2 **Kaharlyk** Ukr.
61 C2 **Kahayan** *r.* Indon.
118 B3 **Kahemba** Dem. Rep. Congo
101 E2 **Kahla** Ger.
79 C2 **Kahnūj** Iran
92 H2 **Kahperusvaarat** *mts* Fin.
80 B2 **Kahramanmaraş** Turkey
79 C2 **Kahūrak** Iran
59 C3 **Kai, Kepulauan** *is* Indon.
115 C4 **Kaiama** Nigeria
54 B2 **Kaiapoi** N.Z.
59 C3 **Kai Besar** *i.* Indon.
70 B2 **Kaifeng** China
Kaihua China *see* Wenshan
122 B2 **Kaiingveld** *reg.* S. Africa
59 C3 **Kai Kecil** *i.* Indon.
54 B2 **Kaikoura** N.Z.
114 A4 **Kailahun** Sierra Leone
Kailas Range *mts* China *see* Gangdisê Shan
71 A3 **Kaili** China
59 C3 **Kaimana** Indon.
54 C1 **Kaimanawa Mountains** N.Z.
72 C2 **Kaimur Range** *hills* India
88 B2 **Käina** Estonia
67 C4 **Kainan** Japan
115 C3 **Kainji Reservoir** Nigeria
54 B1 **Kaipara Harbour** N.Z.
74 B2 **Kairana** India
115 D1 **Kairouan** Tunisia
100 C3 **Kaiserslautern** Ger.
55 I2 **Kaiser Wilhelm II Land** *reg.* Antarctica
54 B1 **Kaitaia** N.Z.
54 C1 **Kaitawa** N.Z.
Kaitong China *see* Tongyu
59 C3 **Kaiwatu** Indon.
65 A1 **Kaiyuan** *Liaoning* China
71 A3 **Kaiyuan** *Yunnan* China
92 I3 **Kajaani** Fin.
51 D2 **Kajabbi** Austr.
76 B3 **Kaka** Turkm.
122 B2 **Kakamas** S. Africa
119 D2 **Kakamega** Kenya
114 A4 **Kakata** Liberia
91 C2 **Kakhovka** Ukr.
91 C2 **Kakhovs'ke Vodoskhovyshche** *resr* Ukr.
73 C3 **Kākināda** India
128 C1 **Kakisa** Can.
67 B4 **Kakogawa** Japan
119 C3 **Kakoswa** Dem. Rep. Congo
126 C2 **Kaktovik** U.S.A.
Kalaallit Nunaat *terr.* N. America *see* Greenland
59 C3 **Kalabahi** Indon.
120 B2 **Kalabo** Zambia
91 E1 **Kalach** Rus. Fed.
119 D2 **Kalacha Dida** Kenya
87 D4 **Kalach-na-Donu** Rus. Fed.
62 A1 **Kaladan** *r.* India/Myanmar
120 B3 **Kalahari Desert** Africa
92 H3 **Kalajoki** Fin.
123 C1 **Kalamare** Botswana
111 B3 **Kalamaria** Greece
111 B3 **Kalamata** Greece
140 B2 **Kalamazoo** U.S.A.
111 B3 **Kalampaka** Greece
88 B2 **Kalana** Estonia

91 C2 **Kalanchak** Ukr.
61 D2 **Kalao** *i.* Indon.
61 D2 **Kalaotoa** *i.* Indon.
63 B2 **Kalasin** Thai.
79 C2 **Kalāt** Iran
74 A2 **Kalat** Pak.
50 A2 **Kalbarri** Austr.
111 C3 **Kale** Turkey
80 B1 **Kalecik** Turkey
118 C3 **Kalema** Dem. Rep. Congo
119 C3 **Kalémié** Dem. Rep. Congo
62 A1 **Kalemyo** Myanmar
86 C2 **Kalevala** Rus. Fed.
Kalgan China *see* Zhangjiakou
50 B3 **Kalgoorlie** Austr.
109 C2 **Kali** Croatia
110 C2 **Kaliakra, Nos** *pt* Bulg.
60 A2 **Kaliet** Indon.
119 C3 **Kalima** Dem. Rep. Congo
61 C2 **Kalimantan** *reg.* Indon.
Kalinin Rus. Fed. *see* Tver'
88 B3 **Kaliningrad** Rus. Fed.
91 D2 **Kalininskaya** Rus. Fed.
88 C3 **Kalinkavichy** Belarus
134 D1 **Kalispell** U.S.A.
103 D1 **Kalisz** Pol.
91 E2 **Kalitva** *r.* Rus. Fed.
92 H2 **Kalix** Sweden
92 H2 **Kalixälven** *r.* Sweden
111 C3 **Kalkan** Turkey
120 A3 **Kalkfeld** Namibia
100 C2 **Kall** Ger.
92 I3 **Kallavesi** *l.* Fin.
92 F3 **Kallsjön** *l.* Sweden
93 G4 **Kalmar** Sweden
93 G4 **Kalmarsund** *sea chan.* Sweden
73 C4 **Kalmunai** Sri Lanka
119 C3 **Kalole** Dem. Rep. Congo
120 B2 **Kalomo** Zambia
128 B2 **Kalone Peak** Can.
74 B1 **Kalpa** India
73 B3 **Kalpeni** *i.* India
75 B2 **Kalpi** India
126 B2 **Kaltag** U.S.A.
101 D1 **Kaltenkirchen** Ger.
118 B2 **Kaltungo** Nigeria
89 E3 **Kaluga** Rus. Fed.
93 F4 **Kalundborg** Denmark
74 B1 **Kalur Kot** Pak.
90 A2 **Kalush** Ukr.
74 B3 **Kalyan** India
89 E2 **Kalyazin** Rus. Fed.
111 C3 **Kalymnos** Greece
111 C3 **Kalymnos** *i.* Greece
119 C3 **Kama** Dem. Rep. Congo
62 A2 **Kama** Myanmar
86 E3 **Kama** *r.* Rus. Fed.
66 D3 **Kamaishi** Japan
80 B2 **Kaman** Turkey
120 A2 **Kamanjab** Namibia
78 B3 **Kamarán Island** Yemen
Kamaran Island Yemen *see* Kamarán
74 A2 **Kamarod** Pak.
50 B3 **Kambalda** Austr.
119 C4 **Kambove** Dem. Rep. Congo
160 C4 **Kamchatka Basin** *sea feature* Bering Sea
110 C2 **Kamchiya** *r.* Bulg.
108 B2 **Kamenjak, Rt** *pt* Croatia
76 B1 **Kamenka** Kazakh.
86 D2 **Kamenka** Rus. Fed.
87 D3 **Kamenka** Rus. Fed.
66 C2 **Kamenka** Rus. Fed.
91 D1 **Kamenka** Rus. Fed.
Kamenka-Strumilovskaya Ukr. *see* Kam"yanka-Buz'ka
91 E3 **Kamennomostskiy** Rus. Fed.
91 E2 **Kamenolomni** Rus. Fed.
Kamenongue Angola *see* Camanongue
83 M2 **Kamenskoye** Rus. Fed.
Kamenskoye Ukr. *see* Dniprodzerzhyns'k
91 E2 **Kamensk-Shakhtinskiy** Rus. Fed.
86 F3 **Kamensk-Ural'skiy** Rus. Fed.
89 F2 **Kameshkovo** Rus. Fed.
75 B1 **Kamet** *mt.* China
122 A3 **Kamiesberge** *mts* S. Africa
122 A3 **Kamieskroon** S. Africa
129 D1 **Kamilukuak Lake** Can.
119 C3 **Kamina** Dem. Rep. Congo
129 E1 **Kaminak Lake** Can.

90 A1 Kamin'-Kashyrs'kyy Ukr.
119 C3 Kamituga
Dem. Rep. Congo
128 B2 Kamloops Can.
54 B1 Kamo N.Z.
116 B3 Kamob Sanha Sudan
118 C3 Kamonia
Dem. Rep. Congo
119 D2 Kampala Uganda
60 B1 Kampar r. Indon.
60 B1 Kampar Malaysia
100 B1 Kampen Neth.
119 C3 Kampene
Dem. Rep. Congo
63 A2 Kamphaeng Phet Thai.
63 B2 Kâmpóng Cham
Cambodia
63 B2 Kâmpóng Chhnăng
Cambodia
Kâmpóng Saôm
Cambodia see
Sihanoukville
63 B2 Kâmpóng Spoe Cambodia
63 B2 Kâmpôt Cambodia
Kampuchea country Asia
see Cambodia
129 D2 Kamsack Can.
86 E3 Kamskoye
Vodokhranilishche resr
Rus. Fed.
117 C4 Kamsuuma Somalia
90 B2 Kam"yanets'-Podil's'kyy
Ukr.
90 A1 Kam"yanka-Buz'ka Ukr.
88 B3 Kamyanyets Belarus
91 D2 Kamyshevatskaya
Rus. Fed.
87 D3 Kamyshin Rus. Fed.
135 D3 Kanab U.S.A.
118 C3 Kananga
Dem. Rep. Congo
87 D3 Kanash Rus. Fed.
140 C3 Kanawha r. U.S.A.
67 C3 Kanazawa Japan
62 A1 Kanbalu Myanmar
63 A2 Kanchanaburi Thai.
73 B3 Kanchipuram India
77 C3 Kandahār Afgh.
86 C2 Kandalaksha Rus. Fed.
61 C2 Kandangan Indon.
74 A2 Kandhkot Pak.
114 C3 Kandi Benin
74 A2 Kandiaro Pak.
74 B2 Kandla India
53 C2 Kandos Austr.
121 D2 Kandreho Madag.
73 C4 Kandy Sri Lanka
76 B2 Kandyagash Kazakh.
127 H1 Kane Bassin b. Greenland
91 D2 Kanevskaya Rus. Fed.
122 B1 Kang Botswana
127 I2 Kangaatsiaq Greenland
114 B3 Kangaba Mali
80 B2 Kangal Turkey
79 C2 Kangān Iran
60 B1 Kangar Malaysia
52 A3 Kangaroo Island Austr.
93 H3 Kangasala Fin.
81 C2 Kangāvar Iran
75 C2 Kangchenjunga mt.
India/Nepal
70 A2 Kangding China
65 B2 Kangdong N. Korea
61 C2 Kangean, Kepulauan is
Indon.
119 D2 Kangen r. Sudan
127 J2 Kangeq c. Greenland
127 J2 Kangerlussuaq inlet
Greenland
127 I2 Kangerlussuaq inlet
Greenland
127 I2 Kangersuatsiaq
Greenland
65 B1 Kanggye N. Korea
131 D2 Kangiqsualujjuaq Can.
127 H2 Kangiqsujuaq Can.
131 C1 Kangirsuk Can.
75 C2 Kangmar China
65 B2 Kangnŭng S. Korea
65 A1 Kangping China
72 D2 Kangto mt. China/India
62 A1 Kani Myanmar
118 C3 Kaniama
Dem. Rep. Congo
61 C1 Kanibongan Sabah
Malaysia
86 D2 Kanin, Poluostrov pen.
Rus. Fed.
86 D2 Kanin Nos Rus. Fed.
86 D2 Kanin Nos, Mys c.
Rus. Fed.

91 C2 Kaniv Ukr.
52 B3 Kaniva Austr.
93 H3 Kankaanpää Fin.
140 B2 Kankakee U.S.A.
114 B3 Kankan Guinea
75 C2 Kanker India
Kannur India see
Cannanore
115 C3 Kano Nigeria
122 B3 Kanonpunt pt S. Africa
67 B4 Kanoya Japan
75 C2 Kanpur India
136 C3 Kansas r. U.S.A.
137 D3 Kansas state U.S.A.
137 E3 Kansas City KS U.S.A.
137 E3 Kansas City MO U.S.A.
83 H3 Kansk Rus. Fed.
Kansu prov. China see
Gansu
63 B2 Kantaralak Thai.
114 C3 Kantchari Burkina
91 D2 Kantemirovka Rus. Fed.
49 J4 Kanton i. Kiribati
97 B2 Kanturk Rep. of Ireland
123 D2 KaNyamazane S. Africa
123 C1 Kanye Botswana
71 C3 Kaohsiung Taiwan
120 A2 Kaokoveld plat. Namibia
114 A3 Kaolack Senegal
120 B2 Kaoma Zambia
118 C3 Kapanga
Dem. Rep. Congo
88 C3 Kapatkyevichy Belarus
77 D2 Kapchagay Kazakh.
77 D2 Kapchagayskoye
Vodokhranilishche resr
Kazakh.
100 B2 Kapellen Belgium
121 B2 Kapiri Mposhi Zambia
127 I2 Kapisillit Greenland
130 B2 Kapiskau r. Can.
61 C1 Kapit Sarawak Malaysia
63 A3 Kapoe Thai.
117 B4 Kapoeta Sudan
103 D2 Kaposvár Hungary
102 B1 Kappeln Ger.
65 B1 Kapsan N. Korea
Kapsukas Lith. see
Marijampolė
61 B2 Kapuas r. Indon.
52 A2 Kapunda Austr.
130 B3 Kapuskasing Can.
53 D2 Kaputar mt. Austr.
103 D2 Kapuvár Hungary
88 C3 Kapyl' Belarus
77 D3 Kaqung China
114 C4 Kara Togo
115 C3 Kara Ada i. Turkey
77 D2 Kara-Balta Kyrg.
76 C3 Karabil', Vozvyshennost'
hills Turkm.
Kara-Bogaz-Gol Turkm.
see Karabogazkel'
76 B2 Kara-Bogaz Gol, Zaliv b.
Turkm.
76 B2 Karabogazkel' Turkm.
80 B1 Karabük Turkey
76 C2 Karabutak Kazakh.
111 C2 Karacabey Turkey
111 C2 Karacaköy Turkey
81 C1 Karachayevsk Rus. Fed.
89 D3 Karachev Rus. Fed.
74 A2 Karachi Pak.
77 D2 Karaganda Kazakh.
77 D2 Karagayly Kazakh.
83 L3 Karaginskiy Zaliv b.
Rus. Fed.
81 D2 Karaj Iran
Kara-Kala Turkm. see
Garrygala
76 B2 Karakalpakiya Kazakh.
64 B3 Karakelong i. Indon.
Karaklis Armenia see
Vanadzor
77 D2 Kara-Köl Kyrg.
77 D2 Karakol Kyrg.
74 B1 Karakoram mts Asia
72 B1 Karakoram Range mts
Asia
117 B3 Kara K'orē Eth.
76 B2 Karakum, Peski des.
Kazakh.
76 C3 Karakum Desert Turkm.
Karakumy, Peski des.
Turkm. see
Karakum Desert
80 B2 Karaman Turkey
77 E2 Karamay China
54 B2 Karamea N.Z.
54 B2 Karamea Bight b. N.Z.
80 B2 Karapınar Turkey

122 A2 Karasburg Namibia
86 F1 Kara Sea Rus. Fed.
92 I2 Karasjok Norway
Kara Strait Rus. Fed. see
Karskiye Vorota, Proliv
111 D2 Karasu Turkey
Karasubazar Ukr. see
Bilohirs'k
77 D1 Karasuk Rus. Fed.
77 D2 Karatau Kazakh.
77 C2 Karatau, Khrebet mts
Kazakh.
86 F2 Karatayka Rus. Fed.
67 A4 Karatsu Japan
111 B3 Karavas Greece
60 B2 Karawang Indon.
81 C2 Karbalā' Iraq
103 E2 Karcag Hungary
Kardeljevo Croatia see
Ploče
111 B3 Karditsa Greece
88 B2 Kärdla Estonia
122 B3 Kareeberge mts S. Africa
75 B2 Kareli India
88 C3 Karelichy Belarus
92 H2 Kareseuando Sweden
Karghalik China see
Yecheng
74 B1 Kargil Jammu and Kashmir
Kargilik China see
Yecheng
86 C2 Kargopol' Rus. Fed.
118 B1 Kari Nigeria
121 B2 Kariba Zimbabwe
121 B2 Kariba, Lake resr
Zambia/Zimbabwe
60 B2 Karimata, Pulau-pulau is
Indon.
60 B2 Karimata, Selat str. Indon.
73 B3 Karimnagar India
61 C2 Karimunjawa, Pulau-
pulau is Indon.
91 C2 Karkinits'ka Zatoka g.
Ukr.
91 D2 Karlivka Ukr.
Karl-Marx-Stadt Ger. see
Chemnitz
109 C1 Karlovac Croatia
102 C1 Karlovy Vary Czech Rep.
Karlsburg Romania see
Alba Iulia
93 F4 Karlshamn Sweden
93 F4 Karlskoga Sweden
93 G4 Karlskrona Sweden
102 B2 Karlsruhe Ger.
93 F4 Karlstad Sweden
101 D3 Karlstadt Ger.
89 D3 Karma Belarus
93 E4 Karmøy i. Norway
75 D2 Karnafuli Reservoir
Bangl.
74 B2 Karnal India
110 C2 Karnobat Bulg.
74 A2 Karodi Pak.
121 B2 Karoi Zimbabwe
121 C1 Karonga Malawi
116 B3 Karora Eritrea
111 C3 Karpathos Greece
111 C3 Karpathos i. Greece
111 B3 Karpenisi Greece
Karpilovka Belarus see
Aktsyabrski
86 D2 Karpogory Rus. Fed.
50 A2 Karratha Austr.
81 C1 Kars Turkey
88 C2 Kārsava Latvia
76 B2 Karshi Rus. Fed.
77 C3 Karshi Uzbek.
111 C3 Karşıyaka Turkey
86 E2 Karskiye Vorota, Proliv
str. Rus. Fed.
Karskoye More sea
Rus. Fed. see Kara Sea
101 E1 Karstädt Ger.
111 C2 Kartal Turkey
87 F3 Kartaly Rus. Fed.
81 C2 Kārūn, Rūd-e r. Iran
73 B3 Karwar India
83 I3 Karymskoye Rus. Fed.
111 B3 Karystos Greece
111 C3 Kaş Turkey
130 B2 Kasabonika Lake Can.
118 C3 Kasai, Plateau du
Dem. Rep. Congo
118 C4 Kasaji Dem. Rep. Congo
121 C2 Kasama Zambia
120 B2 Kasane Botswana
118 B3 Kasangulu
Dem. Rep. Congo
73 B3 Kasaragod India
129 D1 Kasba Lake Can.

120 B2 Kasempa Zambia
119 C4 Kasenga
Dem. Rep. Congo
119 C3 Kasese Dem. Rep. Congo
119 D2 Kasese Uganda
Kasevo Rus. Fed. see
Neftekamsk
81 D2 Kāshān Iran
Kashgar China see Kashi
77 D3 Kashi China
67 D3 Kashima-nada b. Japan
89 E2 Kashin Rus. Fed.
89 E3 Kashira Rus. Fed.
89 E3 Kashirskoye Rus. Fed.
67 C3 Kashiwazaki Japan
76 B3 Kāshmar Iran
Kashmir terr. Asia see
Jammu and Kashmir
74 A2 Kashmor Pak.
119 C3 Kashyukulu
Dem. Rep. Congo
89 F3 Kasimov Rus. Fed.
140 B3 Kaskaskia r. U.S.A.
93 H3 Kaskinen Fin.
119 C3 Kasongo
Dem. Rep. Congo
118 B3 Kasongo-Lunda
Dem. Rep. Congo
111 C3 Kasos i. Greece
Kaspiyskiy Rus. Fed. see
Lagan'
116 B3 Kassala Sudan
101 D2 Kassel Ger.
115 C1 Kasserine Tunisia
80 B1 Kastamonu Turkey
111 B3 Kastelli Greece
Kastellorizon i. Greece
see Megisti
116 B3 Kastoria Greece
89 D3 Kastsyukovichy Belarus
119 D3 Kasulu Tanz.
121 C2 Kasungu Malawi
141 F1 Katahdin, Mount U.S.A.
118 C3 Katako-Kombe
Dem. Rep. Congo
119 D2 Katakwi Uganda
50 A3 Katanning Austr.
63 A3 Katchall i. India
111 B2 Katerini Greece
119 D3 Katesh Tanz.
128 A2 Kate's Needle mt.
Can./U.S.A.
121 C2 Katete Zambia
62 A1 Katha Myanmar
80 B3 Katherîna, Gebel mt.
Egypt
50 C1 Katherine Austr.
50 C1 Katherine r. Austr.
74 B2 Kathiawar pen. India
123 C2 Kathlehong S. Africa
75 C2 Kathmandu Nepal
122 B2 Kathu S. Africa
74 B1 Kathua
Jammu and Kashmir
114 B3 Kati Mali
75 C2 Katihar India
54 C1 Katikati N.Z.
123 C3 Kati-Kati S. Africa
120 B2 Katima Mulilo Namibia
114 B4 Katiola Côte d'Ivoire
Katmandu Nepal see
Kathmandu
111 B3 Kato Achaïa Greece
119 C3 Katompi Dem. Rep. Congo
53 D2 Katoomba Austr.
103 D1 Katowice Pol.
93 G4 Katrineholm Sweden
115 C3 Katsina Nigeria
115 C4 Katsina-Ala Nigeria
67 D3 Katsuura Japan
77 C3 Kattakurgan Uzbek.
93 F4 Kattegat str.
Denmark/Sweden
100 B1 Katwijk aan Zee Neth.
101 D3 Katzenbuckel hill Ger.
49 L1 Kauai i. U.S.A.
93 H3 Kauhajoki Fin.
88 B3 Kaunas Lith.
115 C3 Kaura-Namoda Nigeria
Kaushany Moldova see
Căuşeni
92 H2 Kautokeino Norway
109 D2 Kavadarci Macedonia
109 C2 Kavajë Albania
111 B2 Kavala Greece
66 C2 Kavalerovo Rus. Fed.
73 C3 Kavali India
73 B3 Kavaratti i. India
110 C2 Kavarna Bulg.
59 E3 Kavieng P.N.G.
81 D2 Kavīr, Dasht-e des. Iran

67 C3 **Kawagoe** Japan
54 B1 **Kawakawa** N.Z.
121 B1 **Kawambwa** Zambia
67 C3 **Kawanishi** Japan
130 C3 **Kawartha Lakes** Can.
67 C3 **Kawasaki** Japan
54 C1 **Kawerau** N.Z.
63 A2 **Kawkareik** Myanmar
62 A1 **Kawlin** Myanmar
63 A2 **Kawmapyin** Myanmar
63 A2 **Kawthaung** Myanmar
Kaxgar China *see* Kashi
77 D3 **Kaxgar He** *r.* China
114 B3 **Kaya** Burkina
111 C3 **Kayacı Dağı** *hill* Turkey
121 C1 **Kayambi** Zambia
61 C1 **Kayan** *r.* Indon.
136 B2 **Kaycee** U.S.A.
Kaydanovo Belarus *see* Dzyarzhynsk
138 A1 **Kayenta** U.S.A.
114 A3 **Kayes** Mali
77 D2 **Kaynar** Kazakh.
80 B2 **Kayseri** Turkey
134 D2 **Kaysville** U.S.A.
60 B2 **Kayuagung** Indon.
Kazakhskaya S.S.R. *country* Asia *see* Kazakhstan
77 D1 **Kazakhskiy Melkosopochnik** *plain* Kazakh.
76 B2 **Kazakhskiy Zaliv** *b.* Kazakh.
76 E2 **Kazakhstan** *country* Asia
Kazakhstan Kazakh. *see* Aksay
87 D3 **Kazan'** Rus. Fed.
Kazandzhik Turkm. *see* Gazandzhyk
110 C2 **Kazanlŭk** Bulg.
69 F3 **Kazan-rettō** *is* Japan
76 A2 **Kazbek** *mt.* Georgia/Rus. Fed.
81 D3 **Kāzerūn** Iran
103 E2 **Kazincbarcika** Hungary
118 C3 **Kazumba** Dem. Rep. Congo
66 D2 **Kazuno** Japan
86 F2 **Kazymsky Mys** Rus. Fed.
111 B3 **Kea** *i.* Greece
97 C1 **Keady** U.K.
137 D2 **Kearney** U.S.A.
138 A2 **Kearny** U.S.A.
115 C1 **Kebili** Tunisia
116 A3 **Kebkabiya** Sudan
92 G2 **Kebnekaise** *mt.* Sweden
117 C4 **K'ebri Dehar** Eth.
60 B2 **Kebumen** Indon.
128 B2 **Kechika** *r.* Can.
111 D3 **Keçiborlu** Turkey
103 D2 **Kecskemét** Hungary
88 B2 **Kėdainiai** Lith.
114 A3 **Kédougou** Senegal
103 D1 **Kędzierzyn-Koźle** Pol.
128 B1 **Keele** *r.* Can.
128 A1 **Keele Peak** Can.
Keelung Taiwan *see* Chilung
141 E2 **Keene** U.S.A.
122 A2 **Keetmanshoop** Namibia
129 E3 **Keewatin** Can.
Kefallonia *i.* Greece *see* Cephalonia
59 C3 **Kefamenanu** Indon.
92 □A3 **Keflavík** Iceland
77 D2 **Kegen** Kazakh.
128 C2 **Keg River** Can.
88 C2 **Kehra** Estonia
62 A1 **Kehsi Mansam** Myanmar
98 C3 **Keighley** U.K.
88 B2 **Keila** Estonia
122 B2 **Keimoes** S. Africa
92 I3 **Keitele** *l.* Fin.
52 B3 **Keith** Austr.
96 C2 **Keith** U.K.
128 B1 **Keith Arm** *b.* Can.
134 B2 **Keizer** U.S.A.
103 E2 **Kékes** *mt.* Hungary
117 C4 **K'elafo** Eth.
60 B1 **Kelang** Malaysia
92 J2 **Keles-Uayv, Gora** *hill* Rus. Fed.
102 C2 **Kelheim** Ger.
76 C3 **Kelifskiy Uzboy** *marsh* Turkm.
80 B1 **Kelkit** *r.* Turkey
128 B1 **Keller Lake** Can.
134 C1 **Kellogg** U.S.A.
92 I2 **Kelloselkä** Fin.
97 C2 **Kells** Rep. of Ireland

88 B2 **Kelmė** Lith.
115 D4 **Kelo** Chad
128 C3 **Kelowna** Can.
96 C3 **Kelso** U.K.
134 B1 **Kelso** U.S.A.
60 B1 **Keluang** Malaysia
129 D2 **Kelvington** Can.
86 C2 **Kem'** Rus. Fed.
Ke Macina Mali *see* Massina
128 B2 **Kemano** Can.
118 C2 **Kembé** C.A.R.
111 C3 **Kemer** Turkey
82 G3 **Kemerovo** Rus. Fed.
92 H2 **Kemi** Fin.
92 I2 **Kemijärvi** Fin.
92 I2 **Kemijärvi** *l.* Fin.
92 I2 **Kemijoki** *r.* Fin.
136 A2 **Kemmerer** U.S.A.
92 I3 **Kempele** Fin.
55 G2 **Kemp Land** *reg.* Antarctica
55 A2 **Kemp Peninsula** Antarctica
53 D2 **Kempsey** Austr.
130 C3 **Kempt, Lac** *l.* Can.
102 C2 **Kempten (Allgäu)** Ger.
123 C2 **Kempton Park** S. Africa
61 C2 **Kemujan** *i.* Indon.
126 B2 **Kenai** U.S.A.
129 D2 **Kenaston** Can.
98 B2 **Kendal** U.K.
143 D3 **Kendall** U.S.A.
61 D2 **Kendari** Indon.
60 C2 **Kendawangan** Indon.
115 D3 **Kendégué** Chad
75 C2 **Kendujhargarh** India
114 A4 **Kenema** Sierra Leone
118 B3 **Kenge** Dem. Rep. Congo
62 A1 **Kengtung** Myanmar
122 B2 **Kenhardt** S. Africa
114 B1 **Kénitra** Morocco
97 B3 **Kenmare** Rep. of Ireland
136 C1 **Kenmare** U.S.A.
97 A3 **Kenmare River** *inlet* Rep. of Ireland
100 C1 **Kenn** Ger.
139 C2 **Kenna** U.S.A.
141 F2 **Kennebec** *r.* U.S.A.
Kennedy, Cape U.S.A. *see* Canaveral, Cape
142 B3 **Kenner** U.S.A.
99 C4 **Kennet** *r.* U.K.
137 E3 **Kennett** U.S.A.
134 C1 **Kennewick** U.S.A.
130 A3 **Kenora** Can.
140 B2 **Kenosha** U.S.A.
138 C2 **Kent** U.S.A.
Kentau Kazakh.
140 B3 **Kentucky** *r.* U.S.A.
140 C3 **Kentucky** *state* U.S.A.
140 B3 **Kentucky Lake** U.S.A.
142 B2 **Kentwood** U.S.A.
119 D2 **Kenya** *country* Africa
Kenya, Mount Kenya *see* Kirinyaga
60 B1 **Kenyir, Tasik** *resr* Malaysia
137 E2 **Keokuk** U.S.A.
111 C3 **Kepsut** Turkey
52 B3 **Kerang** Austr.
91 D2 **Kerch** Ukr.
59 D3 **Keremeos** P.N.G.
128 C3 **Keremeos** Can.
116 B3 **Keren** Eritrea
81 C2 **Kerend** Iran
159 E7 **Kerguélen, Îles** *is* Indian Ocean
159 E7 **Kerguelen Plateau** *sea feature* Indian Ocean
119 D3 **Kericho** Kenya
54 B1 **Kerikeri** N.Z.
60 B2 **Kerinci, Gunung** *vol.* Indon.
Kerintji *vol.* Indon. *see* Kerinci, Gunung
77 C3 **Kerki** Turkm.
100 C2 **Kerkrade** Neth.
111 A3 **Kerkyra** Greece
Kerkyra *i.* Greece *see* Corfu
116 B3 **Kerma** Sudan
49 J7 **Kermadec Islands** S. Pacific Ocean
79 C2 **Kermān** Iran
81 C2 **Kermānshāh** Iran
139 C2 **Kermit** U.S.A.
135 C3 **Kern** *r.* U.S.A.
114 B4 **Kérouané** Guinea
100 C2 **Kerpen** Ger.
129 D2 **Kerrobert** Can.

139 D2 **Kerrville** U.S.A.
97 B2 **Kerry Head** *hd* Rep. of Ireland
80 B2 **Keryneia** Cyprus
130 B2 **Kesagami Lake** Can.
111 C2 **Keşan** Turkey
66 D3 **Kesennuma** Japan
74 B2 **Keshod** India
100 C2 **Kessel** Neth.
98 B2 **Keswick** U.K.
103 D2 **Keszthely** Hungary
82 G3 **Ket'** *r.* Rus. Fed.
60 C2 **Ketapang** Indon.
128 A2 **Ketchikan** U.S.A.
134 D2 **Ketchum** U.S.A.
114 B4 **Kete Krachi** Ghana
118 B2 **Kétté** Cameroon
99 C3 **Kettering** U.K.
140 C3 **Kettering** U.S.A.
134 C1 **Kettle River Range** *mts* U.S.A.
93 H3 **Keuruu** Fin.
100 C2 **Kevelaer** Ger.
140 B2 **Kewanee** U.S.A.
140 B1 **Keweenaw Bay** U.S.A.
140 B1 **Keweenaw Peninsula** U.S.A.
143 D3 **Key Largo** U.S.A.
99 B4 **Keynsham** U.K.
141 D3 **Keyser** U.S.A.
143 D4 **Key West** U.S.A.
123 C2 **Kgotsong** S. Africa
69 F1 **Khabarovsk** Rus. Fed.
91 D3 **Khadyzhensk** Rus. Fed.
75 D2 **Khagrachari** Bangl.
74 A2 **Khairpur** Pak.
122 B1 **Khakhea** Botswana
75 D2 **Khalilabad** Iran
86 F2 **Khal'mer-Yu** Rus. Fed.
68 C1 **Khamar-Daban, Khrebet** *mts* Rus. Fed.
74 B2 **Khambhat** India
74 B2 **Khambhat, Gulf of** India
74 B2 **Khamgaon** India
79 C2 **Khamir** Iran
78 B3 **Khamir** Yemen
78 B3 **Khamis Mushayt** Saudi Arabia
77 C3 **Khānābād** Afgh.
74 B2 **Khandwa** India
75 D2 **Khandyga** Rus. Fed.
74 B1 **Khanewal** Pak.
Khan Hung Vietnam *see* Soc Trăng
83 J3 **Khani** Rus. Fed.
66 B2 **Khanka, Lake** China/Rus. Fed.
115 C2 **Khannfoussa** *hill* Alg.
74 B2 **Khanpur** Pak.
77 D2 **Khantau** Kazakh.
83 H2 **Khantayskoye, Ozero** *l.* Rus. Fed.
86 F2 **Khanty-Mansiysk** Rus. Fed.
63 A3 **Khao Chum Thong** Thai.
63 A2 **Khao Laem Reservoir** Thai.
74 B1 **Khapalu** Jammu and Kashmir
87 D4 **Kharabali** Rus. Fed.
75 C2 **Kharagpur** India
79 C2 **Khārān** *r.* Iran
Kharga Oasis Egypt *see* The Great Oasis
74 B2 **Khargon** India
91 D2 **Kharkiv** Ukr.
Khar'kov Ukr. *see* Kharkiv
111 C2 **Kharmanli** Bulg.
89 F2 **Kharovsk** Rus. Fed.
116 B3 **Khartoum** Sudan
87 D4 **Khasav'yurt** Rus. Fed.
79 D2 **Khāsh** Iran
78 A3 **Khashm el Girba** Sudan
78 A3 **Khashm el Girba Dam** Sudan
81 C1 **Khashuri** Georgia
75 C2 **Khāsi Hills** India
111 C2 **Khaskovo** Bulg.
83 H2 **Khatanga** Rus. Fed.
123 C3 **Khayamnandi** S. Africa
77 C2 **Khayatbashi, Gora** *mt.* Uzbek.
78 A2 **Khaybar** Saudi Arabia
122 A3 **Khayelitsha** S. Africa
62 B2 **Khê Bo** Vietnam
107 D2 **Khemis Miliana** Alg.
63 B2 **Khemmarat** Thai.
115 C1 **Khenchela** Alg.
81 D3 **Kherāmeh** Iran
91 C2 **Kherson** Ukr.

83 H2 **Kheta** *r.* Rus. Fed.
69 D1 **Khilok** Rus. Fed.
89 E2 **Khimki** Rus. Fed.
89 E3 **Khlevnoye** Rus. Fed.
63 B2 **Khlung** Thai.
90 B2 **Khmel'nyts'kyy** Ukr.
Khmer Republic *country* Asia *see* Cambodia
76 B1 **Khobda** Kazakh.
76 B2 **Khodzheyli** Uzbek.
89 E3 **Khokhol'skiy** Rus. Fed.
74 B2 **Khokhropar** Pak.
74 A1 **Kholm** Afgh.
89 D2 **Kholm** Rus. Fed.
89 D2 **Kholm-Zhirkovskiy** Rus. Fed.
122 A1 **Khomas Highland** *hills* Namibia
89 E3 **Khomutovo** Rus. Fed.
79 C2 **Khonj** Iran
63 B2 **Khon Kaen** Thai.
62 A1 **Khonsa** India
83 K2 **Khonuu** Rus. Fed.
86 E2 **Khoreyver** Rus. Fed.
69 D1 **Khorinsk** Rus. Fed.
120 A3 **Khorixas** Namibia
66 B2 **Khorol** Rus. Fed.
91 C2 **Khorol** Ukr.
81 C2 **Khorramābād** Iran
81 C2 **Khorramshahr** Iran
77 D3 **Khorugh** Tajik.
Khotan China *see* Hotan
90 B2 **Khotyn** Ukr.
114 B1 **Khouribga** Morocco
77 C3 **Khowst** Afgh.
88 C3 **Khoyniki** Belarus
62 A1 **Khreum** Myanmar
76 B1 **Khromtau** Kazakh.
Khrushchev Ukr. *see* Svitlovods'k
90 B2 **Khrystynivka** Ukr.
123 B1 **Khudumelapye** Botswana
77 C2 **Khŭjand** Tajik.
63 B2 **Khu Khan** Thai.
78 A2 **Khulays** Saudi Arabia
75 C2 **Khulna** Bangl.
Khŭninshahr Iran *see* Khorramshahr
81 D2 **Khunsar** Iran
79 B2 **Khurayş** Saudi Arabia
74 B1 **Khushab** Pak.
90 A2 **Khust** Ukr.
123 C2 **Khutsong** S. Africa
74 A2 **Khuzdar** Pak.
81 D3 **Khvormūj** Iran
81 C2 **Khvoy** Iran
89 D2 **Khvoynaya** Rus. Fed.
77 D3 **Khyber Pass** Afgh./Pak.
53 D2 **Kiama** Austr.
64 B3 **Kiamba** Phil.
119 C3 **Kiambi** Dem. Rep. Congo
Kiangsi *prov.* China *see* Jiangxi
Kiangsu *prov.* China *see* Jiangsu
119 D3 **Kibaha** Tanz.
119 D3 **Kibaya** Tanz.
119 C3 **Kibiti** Tanz.
119 C3 **Kibombo** Dem. Rep. Congo
119 D3 **Kibondo** Tanz.
119 D2 **Kibre Mengist** Eth.
119 D3 **Kibungo** Rwanda
111 B2 **Kičevo** Macedonia
114 C3 **Kidal** Mali
99 B3 **Kidderminster** U.K.
114 A3 **Kidira** Senegal
74 B1 **Kidmang** Jammu and Kashmir
54 C1 **Kidnappers, Cape** N.Z.
102 C1 **Kiel** Ger.
103 E1 **Kielce** Pol.
98 B2 **Kielder Water** *resr* U.K.
119 C4 **Kienge** Dem. Rep. Congo
90 C1 **Kiev** Ukr.
114 A3 **Kiffa** Maur.
119 D3 **Kigali** Rwanda
119 C3 **Kigoma** Tanz.
88 B2 **Kihnu** *i.* Estonia
92 I2 **Kiiminki** Fin.
67 B4 **Kii-suidō** *sea chan.* Japan
109 D1 **Kikinda** Yugo.
119 C3 **Kikondja** Dem. Rep. Congo
59 D3 **Kikori** P.N.G.
59 D3 **Kikori** *r.* P.N.G.
118 B3 **Kikwit** Dem. Rep. Congo
65 B1 **Kilchu** N. Korea
97 C2 **Kilcock** Rep. of Ireland
97 C2 **Kildare** Rep. of Ireland
118 B3 **Kilembe** Dem. Rep. Congo

139 E2 Kilgore U.S.A.
119 D3 Kilifi Kenya
119 D3 Kilimanjaro *vol.* Tanz.
119 D3 Kilindoni Tanz.
80 B2 Kılıs Turkey
90 B2 Kiliya Ukr.
97 B2 Kilkee Rep. of Ireland
97 D1 Kilkeel U.K.
97 C2 Kilkenny Rep. of Ireland
111 B2 Kilkis Greece
97 B1 Killala Rep. of Ireland
97 B1 Killala Bay Rep. of Ireland
97 B2 Killaloe Rep. of Ireland
128 C2 Killam Can.
97 B2 Killarney Rep. of Ireland
139 D2 Killeen U.S.A.
96 B2 Killin U.K.
131 D1 Killinig Can.
97 B2 Killorglin Rep. of Ireland
97 B1 Killybegs Rep. of Ireland
96 B3 Kilmarnock U.K.
53 B3 Kilmore Austr.
119 D3 Kilosa Tanz.
97 B2 Kilrush Rep. of Ireland
119 C3 Kilwa Dem. Rep. Congo
119 D3 Kilwa Masoko Tanz.
119 D3 Kimambi Tanz.
52 A2 Kimba Austr.
136 C2 Kimball U.S.A.
59 E3 Kimbe P.N.G.
128 C3 Kimberley Can.
122 B2 Kimberley S. Africa
50 B1 Kimberley Plateau Austr.
65 B1 Kimch'aek N. Korea
65 B2 Kimch'ŏn S. Korea
65 B2 Kimhae S. Korea
127 H2 Kimmirut Can.
89 E3 Kimovsk Rus. Fed.
118 C3 Kimpanga
           Dem. Rep. Congo
118 B3 Kimpese
           Dem. Rep. Congo
89 E2 Kimry Rus. Fed.
61 C1 Kinabalu, Gunung *mt.*
           Sabah Malaysia
128 C2 Kinbasket Lake Can.
96 C1 Kinbrace U.K.
130 B3 Kincardine Can.
62 A1 Kinchang Myanmar
119 C3 Kinda Dem. Rep. Congo
98 C3 Kinder Scout *hill* U.K.
129 D2 Kindersley Can.
114 A3 Kindia Guinea
119 C3 Kindu Dem. Rep. Congo
89 F2 Kineshma Rus. Fed.
118 B3 Kingandu
           Dem. Rep. Congo
51 E2 Kingaroy Austr.
135 B3 King City U.S.A.
130 C2 King George Islands
           Can.
88 C2 Kingisepp Rus. Fed.
51 D3 King Island Austr.
           Kingisseppa Estonia *see*
           Kuressaare
50 B1 King Leopold Ranges *hills*
           Austr.
138 A1 Kingman U.S.A.
135 B3 Kings *r.* U.S.A.
52 A3 Kingscote Austr.
97 C2 Kingscourt Rep. of Ireland
99 D3 King's Lynn U.K.
50 B1 King Sound *b.* Austr.
134 D2 Kings Peak U.S.A.
143 D1 Kingsport U.S.A.
51 D2 Kingston Austr.
130 C3 Kingston Can.
146 C3 Kingston Jamaica
141 E2 Kingston U.S.A.
52 A3 Kingston South East
           Austr.
98 C3 Kingston upon Hull U.K.
147 D3 Kingstown St Vincent
139 D3 Kingsville U.S.A.
99 B4 Kingswood U.K.
96 B2 Kingussie U.K.
126 F2 King William Island Can.
123 C3 King William's Town
           S. Africa
67 D3 Kinka-san *i.* Japan
96 B2 Kinlochleven U.K.
93 F4 Kinna Sweden
97 B3 Kinsale Rep. of Ireland
118 B3 Kinshasa
           Dem. Rep. Congo
143 E1 Kinston U.S.A.
88 B2 Kintai Lith.
114 B4 Kintampo Ghana
96 C2 Kintore U.K.
96 B3 Kintyre *pen.* U.K.
119 D3 Kiomboi Tanz.

130 C3 Kipawa, Lac *l.* Can.
119 D3 Kipembawe Tanz.
119 D3 Kipengere Range *mts*
           Tanz.
129 D2 Kipling Can.
           Kipling Station Can. *see*
           Kipling
119 C4 Kipushi Dem. Rep. Congo
119 C4 Kipushia
           Dem. Rep. Congo
101 D2 Kirchhain Ger.
101 D3 Kirchheim-Bolanden
           Ger.
83 I3 Kirenga *r.* Rus. Fed.
83 I3 Kirensk Rus. Fed.
89 E3 Kireyevsk Rus. Fed.
           Kirghizia *country* Asia *see*
           Kyrgyzstan
77 D2 Kirghiz Range *mts* Asia
           Kirgizskaya S.S.R.
           country Asia *see*
           Kyrgyzstan
49 J4 Kiribati *country*
           Pacific Ocean
80 B2 Kırıkkale Turkey
89 E2 Kirillov Rus. Fed.
           Kirin China *see* Jilin
           Kirin *prov.* China *see* Jilin
119 D3 Kirinyaga *mt.* Kenya
89 D2 Kirishi Rus. Fed.
48 L3 Kiritimati *i.* Kiribati
111 C3 Kırkağaç Turkey
98 B3 Kirkby U.K.
98 B2 Kirkby Stephen U.K.
96 C2 Kirkcaldy U.K.
96 B3 Kirkcudbright U.K.
92 J2 Kirkenes Norway
88 B1 Kirkkonummi Fin.
130 B3 Kirkland Lake Can.
111 C2 Kırklareli Turkey
137 E2 Kirksville U.S.A.
81 C2 Kirkūk Iraq
96 C1 Kirkwall U.K.
           Kirov Kazakh. *see*
           Balpyk Bi
89 D3 Kirov Rus. Fed.
86 D3 Kirov Rus. Fed.
           Kirovabad Azer. *see* Gäncä
           Kirovakan Armenia *see*
           Vanadzor
           Kirovo Ukr. *see* Kirovohrad
86 E3 Kirovo-Chepetsk
           Rus. Fed.
           Kirovo-Chepetskiy
           Rus. Fed. *see* Kirovo-
           Chepetsk
91 C2 Kirovohrad Ukr.
86 C2 Kirovsk Rus. Fed.
91 D2 Kirovs'ke Ukr.
           Kirovskiy Kazakh. *see*
           Balpyk Bi
66 B1 Kirovskiy Rus. Fed.
96 C2 Kirriemuir U.K.
86 E3 Kirs Rus. Fed.
87 D3 Kirsanov Rus. Fed.
80 B2 Kırşehir Turkey
74 A2 Kirthar Range *mts* Pak.
92 H2 Kiruna Sweden
67 C3 Kiryū Japan
89 E2 Kirzhach Rus. Fed.
119 D3 Kisaki Tanz.
119 C2 Kisangani
           Dem. Rep. Congo
118 B3 Kisantu Dem. Rep. Congo
60 A1 Kisaran Indon.
82 G3 Kiselevsk Rus. Fed.
75 C2 Kishanganj India
           Kishinev Moldova *see*
           Chişinău
67 C4 Kishiwada Japan
77 D1 Kishkenekol' Kazakh.
75 D2 Kishorganj Bangl.
74 B1 Kishtwar
           Jammu and Kashmir
115 C4 Kisi Nigeria
119 D3 Kisii Kenya
103 D2 Kiskunfélegyháza
           Hungary
103 D2 Kiskunhalas Hungary
87 D4 Kislovodsk Rus. Fed.
117 C5 Kismaayo Somalia
           Kismayu Somalia *see*
           Kismaayo
119 C3 Kisoro Uganda
114 A4 Kissidougou Guinea
143 D3 Kissimmee U.S.A.
143 D3 Kissimmee, Lake U.S.A.
129 D2 Kississing Lake Can.
           Kistna *r.* India *see* Krishna
119 D3 Kisumu Kenya
103 E2 Kisvárda Hungary

           Kisykkamys Kazakh. *see*
           Dzhangala
114 B3 Kita Mali
67 D3 Kitaibaraki Japan
66 D3 Kitakami Japan
66 D3 Kitakami-gawa *r.* Japan
67 B4 Kita-Kyūshū Japan
119 D2 Kitale Kenya
66 D2 Kitami Japan
130 B3 Kitchener Can.
93 J3 Kitee Fin.
119 D2 Kitgum Uganda
128 B2 Kitimat Can.
118 B3 Kitona Dem. Rep. Congo
92 H2 Kittilä Fin.
143 E1 Kitty Hawk U.S.A.
119 D3 Kitunda Tanz.
128 B2 Kitwanga Can.
121 B2 Kitwe Zambia
102 C2 Kitzbühel Austria
101 E3 Kitzingen Ger.
59 D3 Kiunga P.N.G.
92 I3 Kiuruvesi Fin.
92 I2 Kivalo *ridge* Fin.
90 B1 Kivertsi Ukr.
88 C2 Kiviõli Estonia
91 D2 Kivsharivka Ukr.
119 C3 Kivu, Lake
           Dem. Rep. Congo/Rwanda
111 C2 Kıyıköy Turkey
86 E3 Kizel Rus. Fed.
111 C3 Kızılca Dağ *mt.* Turkey
80 B1 Kızılırmak *r.* Turkey
87 D4 Kizlyar Rus. Fed.
           Kizyl-Arbat Turkm. *see*
           Gyzylarbat
92 I1 Kjøllefjord Norway
92 G2 Kjøpsvik Norway
102 C1 Kladno Czech Rep.
102 C2 Klagenfurt Austria
88 B2 Klaipėda Lith.
94 B1 Klaksvík Faroe Is
134 B2 Klamath *r.* U.S.A.
134 B2 Klamath Falls U.S.A.
134 B2 Klamath Mountains
           U.S.A.
           Klang Malaysia *see* Kelang
102 C2 Klatovy Czech Rep.
122 B2 Klawer S. Africa
122 A3 Klawock U.S.A.
128 B2 Kleena Kleene Can.
122 B2 Kleinbegin S. Africa
122 A2 Klein Karas Namibia
122 A2 Kleinsee S. Africa
123 C2 Klerksdorp S. Africa
90 B1 Klesiv Ukr.
89 D3 Kletnya Rus. Fed.
100 C2 Kleve Ger.
88 C3 Klichaw Belarus
89 D3 Klimavichy Belarus
89 D3 Klimovo Rus. Fed.
89 E2 Klimovsk Rus. Fed.
89 E2 Klin Rus. Fed.
101 F2 Klingenthal Ger.
101 F2 Klinovec *mt.* Czech Rep.
93 G4 Klintehamn Sweden
89 D3 Klintsy Rus. Fed.
109 C2 Ključ Bos.-Herz.
103 D1 Kłodzko Pol.
100 C1 Kloosterhaar Neth.
103 D2 Klosterneuburg Austria
101 E1 Kloster (Altmark) Ger.
128 A1 Kluane Lake Can.
           Kluang Malaysia *see*
           Keluang
103 D1 Kluczbork Pol.
           Klukhori Rus. Fed. *see*
           Karachayevsk
128 A2 Klukwan U.S.A.
74 A2 Klupro Pak.
89 F2 Klyaz'ma *r.* Rus. Fed.
88 C3 Klyetsk Belarus
83 L3 Klyuchi Rus. Fed.
98 C2 Knaresborough U.K.
93 F3 Knästen *hill* Sweden
129 E2 Knee Lake Can.
101 E1 Knesebeck Ger.
101 E3 Knetzgau Ger.
109 C2 Knin Croatia
103 C2 Knittelfeld Austria
109 D2 Knjaževac Yugo.
           Knob Lake Can. *see*
           Schefferville
97 B3 Knockaboy *hill*
           Rep. of Ireland
100 A2 Knokke-Heist Belgium
143 D1 Knoxville U.S.A.
127 H1 Knud Rasmussen Land
           reg. Greenland
122 B3 Knysna S. Africa
60 B2 Koba Indon.

67 C4 Kōbe Japan
           København Denmark *see*
           Copenhagen
100 C2 Koblenz Ger.
59 C3 Kobroör *i.* Indon.
88 B3 Kobryn Belarus
111 C2 Kocaeli Turkey
111 B2 Kočani Macedonia
111 C2 Kocasu *r.* Turkey
109 B1 Kočevje Slovenia
75 C2 Koch Bihār India
89 F3 Kochetovka Rus. Fed.
           Kochi India *see* Cochin
67 B4 Kōchi Japan
87 D4 Kochubey Rus. Fed.
75 C2 Kodarma India
126 B3 Kodiak U.S.A.
126 B3 Kodiak Island U.S.A.
123 C1 Kodibeleng Botswana
117 B4 Kodok Sudan
90 B2 Kodyma Ukr.
111 C2 Kodzhaele *mt.*
           Bulg./Greece
122 A2 Koës Namibia
122 C2 Koffiefontein S. Africa
114 B4 Koforidua Ghana
67 C3 Kōfu Japan
131 D2 Kogaluk *r.* Can.
114 B3 Kogoni Mali
74 B1 Kohat Pak.
72 D2 Kohima India
88 C2 Kohtla-Järve Estonia
128 A1 Koidern Can.
77 D2 Kokand Uzbek.
88 B2 Kōkar Fin.
           Kokchetav Kazakh. *see*
           Kokshetau
122 A2 Kokerboom Namibia
122 C2 Kokhanava Belarus
89 F2 Kokhma Rus. Fed.
92 H3 Kokkola Fin.
88 C2 Koknese Latvia
140 B2 Kokomo U.S.A.
121 B3 Kokong Botswana
123 C2 Kokosi S. Africa
77 E2 Kokpekti Kazakh.
77 C1 Kokshetau Kazakh.
131 D2 Koksoak *r.* Can.
123 C3 Kokstad S. Africa
           Koktokay China *see* Fuyun
61 D2 Kolaka Indon.
86 C2 Kola Peninsula Rus. Fed.
92 H2 Kolari Fin.
           Kolarovgrad Bulg. *see*
           Shumen
114 A3 Kolda Senegal
93 E4 Kolding Denmark
119 C2 Kole Dem. Rep. Congo
107 D2 Koléa Alg.
86 D2 Kolguyev, Ostrov *i.*
           Rus. Fed.
73 B3 Kolhapur India
88 B2 Kolkasrags *pt* Latvia
           Kolkata India *see* Calcutta
           Kollam India *see* Quilon
100 C1 Kollum Neth.
           Köln Ger. *see* Cologne
103 D1 Koło Pol.
103 D1 Kołobrzeg Pol.
114 B3 Kolokani Mali
89 E2 Kolomna Rus. Fed.
90 B2 Kolomyya Ukr.
114 B3 Kolondiéba Mali
61 D2 Kolonedale Indon.
122 B2 Kolonkwane Botswana
89 E3 Kolpny Rus. Fed.
           Kol'skiy Poluostrov *pen.*
           Rus. Fed. *see*
           Kola Peninsula
78 B3 Koluli Eritrea
92 F3 Kolvereid Norway
119 C4 Kolwezi Dem. Rep. Congo
83 L2 Kolyma *r.* Rus. Fed.
           Kolyma Lowland
           Rus. Fed. *see*
           Kolymskaya Nizmennost'
           Kolyma Range *mts*
           Rus. Fed. *see*
           Kolymskiy, Khrebet
83 L2 Kolymskaya Nizmennost'
           lowland Rus. Fed.
83 M2 Kolymskiy, Khrebet *mts*
           Rus. Fed.
78 A3 Komaggas S. Africa
67 C3 Komaki Japan
83 M3 Komandorskiye Ostrova
           is Rus. Fed.
123 D2 Komárno Slovakia
123 D2 Komati *r.* Swaziland
123 D2 Komatipoort S. Africa

Kugluktuk 197

67 C3 **Komatsu** Japan
120 A2 **Kombat** Namibia
119 C3 **Kombe** Dem. Rep. Congo
Komintern Ukr. *see* **Marhanets'**
90 C2 **Kominternivs'ke** Ukr.
109 C2 **Komiža** Croatia
103 D2 **Komló** Hungary
Kommunarsk Ukr. *see* **Alchevs'k**
116 B2 **Kôm Ombo** Egypt
118 B3 **Komono** Congo
111 C2 **Komotini** Greece
Kompong Som Cambodia *see* **Sihanoukville**
Komrat Moldova *see* **Comrat**
122 B3 **Komsberg** *mts* S. Africa
76 C1 **Komsomolets** Kazakh.
83 H1 **Komsomolets, Ostrov** *i.* Rus. Fed.
89 F2 **Komsomol'sk** Rus. Fed.
91 C2 **Komsomol's'k** Ukr.
83 M2 **Komsomol'skiy** Rus. Fed.
Komsomol'skiy Rus. Fed. *see* **Yugorsk**
87 D4 **Komsomol'skiy** Rus. Fed.
83 K3 **Komsomol'sk-na-Amure** Rus. Fed.
89 E2 **Konakovo** Rus. Fed.
75 C3 **Kondagaon** India
86 F2 **Kondinskoye** Rus. Fed.
Kondinskoye Rus. Fed. *see* **Oktyabr'skoye**
119 D3 **Kondoa** Tanz.
86 C2 **Kondopoga** Rus. Fed.
89 E3 **Kondrovo** Rus. Fed.
127 J2 **Kong Christian IX Land** *reg.* Greenland
127 K2 **Kong Christian X Land** *reg.* Greenland
127 J2 **Kong Frederik VI Kyst** *coastal area* Greenland
65 B2 **Kongju** S. Korea
119 C3 **Kongolo** Dem. Rep. Congo
93 E4 **Kongsberg** Norway
93 F3 **Kongsvinger** Norway
77 D3 **Kongur Shan** *mt.* China
100 C2 **Königswinter** Ger.
103 D1 **Konin** Pol.
109 C2 **Konjic** Bos.-Herz.
122 A2 **Konkiep** *watercourse* Namibia
86 D2 **Konosha** Rus. Fed.
91 C1 **Konotop** Ukr.
103 E1 **Końskie** Pol.
Konstantinograd Ukr. *see* **Krasnohrad**
102 B2 **Konstanz** Ger.
115 C3 **Kontagora** Nigeria
63 B2 **Kon Tum** Vietnam
63 B2 **Kontum, Plateau du** Vietnam
80 B2 **Konya** Turkey
77 D2 **Konyrat** Kazakh.
100 C3 **Konz** Ger.
86 E3 **Konzhakovskiy Kamen', Gora** *mt.* Rus. Fed.
134 C1 **Kooskia** U.S.A.
128 C3 **Kootenay Lake** Can.
53 D2 **Kootingal** Austr.
122 B3 **Kootjieskolk** S. Africa
92 □B2 **Kópasker** Iceland
108 B1 **Koper** Slovenia
93 G4 **Köping** Sweden
123 C1 **Kopong** Botswana
93 G4 **Kopparberg** Sweden
109 C1 **Koprivnica** Croatia
89 F3 **Korablino** Rus. Fed.
73 C3 **Koraput** India
75 C2 **Korba** India
101 D2 **Korbach** Ger.
109 D2 **Korçë** Albania
109 C2 **Korčula** Croatia
109 C2 **Korčula** *i.* Croatia
65 B1 **Korea, North** *country* Asia
65 B2 **Korea, South** *country* Asia
70 C2 **Korea Bay** *g.* China/N. Korea
65 B3 **Korea Strait** Japan/S. Korea
89 D3 **Korenevo** Rus. Fed.
91 D2 **Korenovsk** Rus. Fed.
Korenovskaya Rus. Fed. *see* **Korenovsk**
90 B1 **Korets'** Ukr.
111 C2 **Körfez** Turkey
114 B4 **Korhogo** Côte d'Ivoire
111 B3 **Korinthiakos Kolpos** *sea chan.* Greece
111 B3 **Korinthos** Greece
103 D2 **Kőris-hegy** *hill* Hungary
109 D2 **Koritnik** *mt.* Albania
Koritsa Albania *see* **Korçë**
67 D3 **Kōriyama** Japan
87 F3 **Korkino** Rus. Fed.
111 D3 **Korkuteli** Turkey
77 E2 **Korla** China
103 D2 **Körmend** Hungary
49 I5 **Koro** *i.* Fiji
114 B3 **Koro** Mali
131 D2 **Koroc** *r.* Can.
91 D1 **Korocha** Rus. Fed.
119 D3 **Korogwe** Tanz.
59 C2 **Koror** Palau
103 E2 **Körös** *r.* Romania
90 B1 **Korosten'** Ukr.
90 B1 **Korostyshiv** Ukr.
115 D3 **Koro Toro** Chad
93 H3 **Korpo** Fin.
66 D1 **Korsakov** Rus. Fed.
91 C2 **Korsun'-Shevchenkivs'kyy** Ukr.
103 E1 **Korsze** Pol.
116 B3 **Korti** Sudan
100 A2 **Kortrijk** Belgium
83 L3 **Koryakskaya, Sopka** *vol.* Rus. Fed.
83 M2 **Koryakskiy Khrebet** *mts* Rus. Fed.
86 D2 **Koryazhma** Rus. Fed.
65 B2 **Koryŏng** S. Korea
91 C1 **Koryukivka** Ukr.
111 C3 **Kos** Greece
111 C3 **Kos** Greece
111 C3 **Kos** *i.* Greece
91 D2 **Kosa Biryuchyy Ostriv** *i.* Ukr.
65 B2 **Kosan** N. Korea
103 D1 **Kościan** Pol.
Kosciusko, Mount Austr. *see* **Kosciuszko, Mount**
53 C3 **Kosciuszko, Mount** Austr.
77 E2 **Kosh-Agach** Rus. Fed.
67 A4 **Koshikijima-rettō** *is* Japan
103 E2 **Košice** Slovakia
92 H2 **Koskullskulle** Sweden
65 B2 **Kosŏng** N. Korea
109 D2 **Kosovo** *prov.* Yugo.
109 D2 **Kosovska Mitrovica** Yugo.
48 H3 **Kosrae** *atoll* Micronesia
114 B4 **Kossou, Lac de** *l.* Côte d'Ivoire
76 C1 **Kostanay** Kazakh.
110 B2 **Kostenets** Bulg.
123 C2 **Koster** S. Africa
116 B3 **Kosti** Sudan
92 J3 **Kostomuksha** Rus. Fed.
90 B1 **Kostopil'** Ukr.
89 F2 **Kostroma** Rus. Fed.
89 F2 **Kostroma** *r.* Rus. Fed.
102 C1 **Kostrzyn** Pol.
91 D2 **Kostyantynivka** Ukr.
103 D1 **Koszalin** Pol.
103 D2 **Kőszeg** Hungary
74 B2 **Kota** India
60 B2 **Kotaagung** Indon.
61 C2 **Kotabaru** Indon.
61 C1 **Kota Belud** *Sabah* Malaysia
60 B1 **Kota Bharu** Malaysia
60 B2 **Kotabumi** Indon.
61 C1 **Kota Kinabalu** *Sabah* Malaysia
75 C3 **Kotapārh** India
61 C1 **Kota Samarahan** *Sarawak* Malaysia
86 D3 **Kotel'nich** Rus. Fed.
87 D4 **Kotel'nikovo** Rus. Fed.
83 K1 **Kotel'nyy, Ostrov** *i.* Rus. Fed.
91 C1 **Kotel'va** Ukr.
101 E2 **Köthen (Anhalt)** Ger.
119 D2 **Kotido** Uganda
93 I3 **Kotka** Fin.
86 D2 **Kotlas** Rus. Fed.
126 B2 **Kotlik** U.S.A.
115 C3 **Kotorkoshi** Nigeria
109 C2 **Kotor Varoš** Bos.-Herz.
87 D3 **Kotovo** Rus. Fed.
91 E1 **Kotovsk** Rus. Fed.
90 B2 **Kotovs'k** Ukr.
73 C3 **Kottagudem** India
118 C2 **Kotto** *r.* C.A.R.
83 H2 **Kotuy** *r.* Rus. Fed.
126 B2 **Kotzebue** U.S.A.
126 B2 **Kotzebue Sound** *sea chan.* U.S.A.
114 A3 **Koubia** Guinea
100 A2 **Koudekerke** Neth.
114 B3 **Koudougou** Burkina
122 B3 **Kougaberge** *mts* S. Africa
118 B3 **Koulamoutou** Gabon
114 B3 **Koulikoro** Mali
118 B2 **Koum** Cameroon
118 B2 **Koumra** Chad
114 A3 **Koundâra** Guinea
Kounradskiy Kazakh. *see* **Konyrat**
151 D2 **Kourou** Fr. Guiana
114 B3 **Kouroussa** Guinea
115 D3 **Kousséri** Cameroon
114 B3 **Koutiala** Mali
93 I3 **Kouvola** Fin.
109 D1 **Kovačica** Yugo.
92 J2 **Kovdor** Rus. Fed.
90 A1 **Kovel'** Ukr.
Kovno Lith. *see* **Kaunas**
89 F2 **Kovrov** Rus. Fed.
51 D1 **Kowanyama** Austr.
54 B2 **Kowhitirangi** N.Z.
71 B3 **Kowloon** China
111 C3 **Köyceğiz** Turkey
86 D2 **Koyda** Rus. Fed.
126 B2 **Koyukuk** *r.* U.S.A.
111 B2 **Kozani** Greece
90 C1 **Kozelets'** Ukr.
89 E3 **Kozel'sk** Rus. Fed.
Kozhikode India *see* **Calicut**
90 B2 **Kozyatyn** Ukr.
114 C4 **Kpalimé** Togo
63 A2 **Kra, Isthmus of** Thai.
63 A3 **Krabi** Thai.
63 A2 **Kra Buri** Thai.
63 B2 **Krâchéh** Cambodia
93 E4 **Kragerø** Norway
100 B1 **Kraggenburg** Neth.
109 D2 **Kragujevac** Yugo.
60 B2 **Krakatau** *i.* Indon.
103 D1 **Kraków** Pol.
109 D2 **Kraljevo** Yugo.
91 D2 **Kramators'k** Ukr.
93 G3 **Kramfors** Sweden
111 B3 **Kranidi** Greece
102 C2 **Kranj** Slovenia
123 D2 **Kranskop** S. Africa
86 E1 **Krasino** Rus. Fed.
88 C2 **Krāslava** Latvia
101 F2 **Kraslice** Czech Rep.
89 D3 **Krasnapollye** Belarus
89 D3 **Krasnaya Gora** Rus. Fed.
89 F2 **Krasnaya Gorbatka** Rus. Fed.
Krasnoarmeysk Kazakh. *see* **Tayynsha**
87 D3 **Krasnoarmeysk** Rus. Fed.
Krasnoarmeyskaya Rus. Fed. *see* **Poltavskaya**
91 D2 **Krasnoarmiys'k** Ukr.
86 D2 **Krasnoborsk** Rus. Fed.
91 D2 **Krasnodar** Rus. Fed.
91 D2 **Krasnodon** Ukr.
88 C2 **Krasnogorodskoye** Rus. Fed.
91 D1 **Krasnogvardeyskoye** Rus. Fed.
91 D2 **Krasnohrad** Ukr.
91 C2 **Krasnohvardiys'ke** Ukr.
86 E3 **Krasnokamsk** Rus. Fed.
89 D2 **Krasnomayskiy** Rus. Fed.
91 C2 **Krasnoperekops'k** Ukr.
87 D3 **Krasnoslobodsk** Rus. Fed.
86 F3 **Krasnotur'insk** Rus. Fed.
86 E3 **Krasnoufimsk** Rus. Fed.
86 E2 **Krasnovishersk** Rus. Fed.
Krasnovodsk Turkm. *see* **Turkmenbashi**
83 H3 **Krasnoyarsk** Rus. Fed.
89 E3 **Krasnoye** Rus. Fed.
83 M2 **Krasnoye, Ozero** *l.* Rus. Fed.
89 F2 **Krasnoye-na-Volge** Rus. Fed.
103 E1 **Krasnystaw** Pol.
89 D3 **Krasnyy** Rus. Fed.
Krasnyy Kamyshanik Rus. Fed. *see* **Komsomol'skiy**
89 E2 **Krasnyy Kholm** Rus. Fed.
91 D2 **Krasnyy Luch** Ukr.
91 E2 **Krasnyy Sulin** Rus. Fed.
90 B2 **Krasyliv** Ukr.
Kraulshavn Greenland *see* **Nuussuaq**
100 C2 **Krefeld** Ger.
91 C2 **Kremenchuk** Ukr.
91 C2 **Kremenchuts'ka Vodoskhovyshche** *resr* Ukr.
90 B1 **Kremenets'** Ukr.
103 D2 **Křemešník** *hill* Czech Rep.
Kremges Ukr. *see* **Svitlovods'k**
91 D2 **Kreminna** Ukr.
136 B2 **Kremmling** U.S.A.
103 D2 **Krems an der Donau** Austria
89 D2 **Kresttsy** Rus. Fed.
88 B2 **Kretinga** Lith.
100 C2 **Kreuzau** Ger.
101 C2 **Kreuztal** Ger.
118 A2 **Kribi** Cameroon
123 C2 **Kriel** S. Africa
111 B3 **Krikellos** Greece
66 D1 **Kril'on, Mys** *c.* Rus. Fed.
111 B3 **Krios, Akra** *pt* Greece
73 C3 **Krishna** *r.* India
73 C3 **Krishna, Mouths of the** India
75 C2 **Krishnanagar** India
93 E4 **Kristiansand** Norway
93 F4 **Kristianstad** Sweden
92 E3 **Kristiansund** Norway
93 F4 **Kristinehamn** Sweden
Kristinopol' Ukr. *see* **Chervonohrad**
Kriti *i.* Greece *see* **Crete**
110 B2 **Kriva Palanka** Macedonia
Krivoy Rog Ukr. *see* **Kryvyy Rih**
109 C1 **Križevci** Croatia
108 B1 **Krk** *i.* Croatia
92 F3 **Krokom** Sweden
91 C1 **Krolevets'** Ukr.
89 E3 **Kromy** Rus. Fed.
101 E2 **Kronach** Ger.
63 B2 **Krŏng Kaôh Kŏng** Cambodia
127 J2 **Kronprins Frederik Bjerge** *nunataks* Greenland
123 C2 **Kroonstad** S. Africa
91 E2 **Kropotkin** Rus. Fed.
103 E2 **Krosno** Pol.
103 D1 **Krotoszyn** Pol.
60 B2 **Krui** Indon.
122 B3 **Kruisfontein** S. Africa
109 C2 **Krujë** Albania
111 C2 **Krumovgrad** Bulg.
Krung Thep Thai. *see* **Bangkok**
88 C3 **Krupki** Belarus
109 D2 **Kruševac** Yugo.
101 E2 **Krušné Hory** *mts* Czech Rep.
128 A2 **Kruzof Island** U.S.A.
89 D3 **Krychaw** Belarus
91 D2 **Krylovskaya** Rus. Fed.
91 D3 **Krymsk** Rus. Fed.
Krymskaya Rus. Fed. *see* **Krymsk**
Kryms'kyy Pivostriv *pen.* Ukr. *see* **Crimea**
Krystynopol Ukr. *see* **Chervonohrad**
111 C3 **Krytiko Pelagos** *sea* Greece
91 C2 **Kryvyy Rih** Ukr.
90 B2 **Kryzhopil'** Ukr.
114 B2 **Ksabi** Alg.
107 D2 **Ksar el Boukhari** Alg.
114 B1 **Ksar el Kebir** Morocco
Ksar-es-Souk Morocco *see* **Er Rachidia**
89 E3 **Kshenskiy** Rus. Fed.
78 B2 **Kū', Jabal al** *hill* Saudi Arabia
61 C1 **Kuala Belait** Brunei
Kuala Dungun Malaysia *see* **Dungun**
60 B1 **Kuala Kangsar** Malaysia
60 B1 **Kuala Kerai** Malaysia
60 B1 **Kuala Lipis** Malaysia
60 B1 **Kuala Lumpur** Malaysia
61 C2 **Kualapembuang** Indon.
60 B1 **Kuala Terengganu** Malaysia
60 B2 **Kualatungal** Indon.
61 C1 **Kuamut** *Sabah* Malaysia
65 A1 **Kuandian** China
60 B1 **Kuantan** Malaysia
91 D2 **Kuban'** *r.* Rus. Fed.
89 E2 **Kubenskoye, Ozero** *l.* Rus. Fed.
110 C2 **Kubrat** Bulg.
60 B2 **Kubu** Indon.
61 C1 **Kubuang** Indon.
60 C1 **Kuching** *Sarawak* Malaysia
109 C2 **Kuçovë** Albania
61 C2 **Kudus** Indon.
102 C2 **Kufstein** Austria
91 D2 **Kugey** Rus. Fed.
126 E2 **Kugluktuk** Can.

126 D2 Kugmallit Bay Can.
92 I3 Kuhmo Fin.
79 C2 Kührän, Küh-e mt. Iran
122 A1 Kuis Namibia
Kuitin China see Kuytun
120 A2 Kuito Angola
128 A2 Kuiu Island U.S.A.
92 I2 Kuivaniemi Fin.
65 B2 Kujang N. Korea
66 D2 Kuji Japan
67 B4 Kujū-san vol. Japan
109 D2 Kukës Albania
76 B3 Kukurtli Turkm.
111 C3 Kula Turkey
75 D2 Kula Kangri mt. Bhutan
76 B2 Kulandy Kazakh.
88 B2 Kuldiga Latvia
Kuldja China see Yining
122 B1 Kule Botswana
101 E2 Kulmbach Ger.
77 C3 Külöb Tajik.
76 B2 Kul'sary Kazakh.
111 D3 Kulübe Tepe mt. Turkey
77 D1 Kulunda Rus. Fed.
77 D1 Kulundinskoye, Ozero salt l. Rus. Fed.
127 J2 Kulusuk Greenland
67 C3 Kumagaya Japan
67 B4 Kumamoto Japan
67 C4 Kumano Japan
110 B2 Kumanovo Macedonia
114 B4 Kumasi Ghana
118 A2 Kumba Cameroon
Kum-Dag Turkm. see Gumdag
78 B2 Kumdah Saudi Arabia
87 E3 Kumertau Rus. Fed.
65 B2 Kumi S. Korea
119 D2 Kumi Uganda
111 C3 Kumkale Turkey
93 G4 Kumla Sweden
115 D3 Kumo Nigeria
62 A1 Kumon Range mts Myanmar
62 B2 Kumphawapi Thai.
Kumul China see Hami
66 D2 Kunashir, Ostrov i. Rus. Fed.
61 C1 Kundat Sabah Malaysia
77 D2 Kungei Alatau mts Kazakh./Kyrg.
76 B2 Kungrad Uzbek.
93 F4 Kungsbacka Sweden
118 B2 Kungu Dem. Rep. Congo
86 E3 Kungur Rus. Fed.
62 A1 Kunhing Myanmar
62 A1 Kunlong Myanmar
75 B1 Kunlun Shan mts China
71 A3 Kunming China
65 B2 Kunsan S. Korea
50 B1 Kununurra Austr.
101 D3 Künzelsau Ger.
92 I3 Kuopio Fin.
109 C1 Kupa r. Croatia/Slovenia
59 C3 Kupang Indon.
88 B2 Kupiškis Lith.
111 C2 Küplü Turkey
128 A2 Kupreanof Island U.S.A.
91 D2 Kup"yans'k Ukr.
77 E2 Kuqa China
81 C2 Kür r. Azer.
67 B4 Kurashiki Japan
75 C2 Kurasia India
67 B3 Kurayoshi Japan
89 E3 Kurchatov Rus. Fed.
77 E2 Kurchum Kazakh.
111 C2 Kürdzhali Bulg.
67 B4 Kure Japan
57 T7 Kure Atoll U.S.A.
88 B2 Kuressaare Estonia
87 F3 Kurgan Rus. Fed.
Kuria Muria Islands Oman see Ḩalāniyāt, Juzur al
93 H3 Kurikka Fin.
156 C2 Kuril Basin sea feature Sea of Okhotsk
Kuril Islands Rus. Fed. see Kuril'skiye Ostrova
69 F1 Kuril'sk Rus. Fed.
69 F1 Kuril'skiye Ostrova is Rus. Fed.
156 C3 Kuril Trench sea feature N. Pacific Ocean
89 E3 Kurkino Rus. Fed.
Kurmashkino Kazakh. see Kurchum
117 B3 Kurmuk Sudan
73 B3 Kurnool India
67 D3 Kuroiso Japan
101 E2 Kurort Schmalkalden Ger.

53 D2 Kurri Kurri Austr.
88 B2 Kuršėnai Lith.
78 B2 Kursh, Jabal hill Saudi Arabia
89 E3 Kursk Rus. Fed.
109 D2 Kuršumlija Yugo.
122 B2 Kuruman S. Africa
122 B2 Kuruman watercourse S. Africa
67 B4 Kurume Japan
83 I3 Kurumkan Rus. Fed.
73 C4 Kurunegala Sri Lanka
81 D1 Kuryk Kazakh.
111 C3 Kuşadası Turkey
111 C3 Kuşadası Körfezi b. Turkey
63 B2 Kut, Ko i. Thai.
111 C3 Kütahya Turkey
81 C1 K'ut'aisi Georgia
Kutaraja Indon. see Banda Aceh
Kutch, Gulf of India see Kachchh, Gulf of
109 C1 Kutjevo Croatia
103 D1 Kutno Pol.
118 B3 Kutu Dem. Rep. Congo
116 A3 Kutum Sudan
126 E2 Kuujjua r. Can.
131 D2 Kuujjuaq Can.
130 C2 Kuujjuarapik Can.
92 I2 Kuusamo Fin.
62 A2 Kuvango Angola
89 D2 Kuvshinovo Rus. Fed.
78 B2 Kuwait country Asia
78 B2 Kuwait Kuwait
82 G3 Kuybyshev Rus. Fed.
Kuybyshev Rus. Fed. see Samara
91 D2 Kuybysheve Ukr.
Kuybyshevka-Vostochnaya Rus. Fed. see Belogorsk
87 D3 Kuybyshevskoye Vodokhranilishche resr Rus. Fed.
77 E2 Kuytun China
111 C3 Kuyucak Turkey
87 D3 Kuznetsk Rus. Fed.
90 B1 Kuznetsovs'k Ukr.
86 C2 Kuzomen' Rus. Fed.
92 H1 Kvalsund Norway
123 D2 KwaMashu S. Africa
61 D1 Kwandang Indon.
Kwangchow China see Guangzhou
65 B2 Kwangju S. Korea
Kwangsi Chuang Autonomous Region aut. reg. China see Guangxi Zhuangzu Zizhiqu
Kwangtung prov. China see Guangdong
65 B1 Kwanmo-bong mt. N. Korea
123 C3 Kwanobuhle S. Africa
123 C3 KwaNojoli S. Africa
122 B3 Kwanonzame S. Africa
123 C3 Kwatinidubu S. Africa
123 C2 KwaZamokhule S. Africa
122 B3 Kwazamukucinga S. Africa
123 C2 KwaZanele S. Africa
123 D2 Kwazulu-Natal prov. S. Africa
Kweichow prov. China see Guizhou
Kweiyang China see Guiyang
121 B2 Kwekwe Zimbabwe
118 B3 Kwenge r. Dem. Rep. Congo
123 C3 Kwezi-Naledi S. Africa
103 D1 Kwidzyn Pol.
59 D3 Kwikila P.N.G.
118 B3 Kwilu r. Angola/Dem. Rep. Congo
59 C3 Kwoka mt. Indon.
118 B2 Kyabé Chad

53 C3 Kyabram Austr.
62 A2 Kyaikto Myanmar
63 A2 Kya-in Seikkyi Myanmar
68 D1 Kyakhta Rus. Fed.
52 A2 Kyancutta Austr.
62 A1 Kyaukpadaung Myanmar
62 A2 Kyaukpyu Myanmar
88 B3 Kybartai Lith.
62 A2 Kyebogyi Myanmar
54 B3 Kyeburn N.Z.
62 A2 Kyeintali Myanmar
74 B1 Kyelang India
Kyiv Ukr. see Kiev
Kyklades is Greece see Cyclades
129 D2 Kyle Can.
96 B2 Kyle of Lochalsh U.K.
100 C3 Kyll r. Ger.
111 B3 Kyllini mt. Greece
111 B3 Kymi Greece
52 B3 Kyneton Austr.
119 D2 Kyoga, Lake Uganda
53 D1 Kyogle Austr.
65 B2 Kyŏnggi-man b. S. Korea
65 B2 Kyŏngju S. Korea
67 C4 Kyoto Japan
111 B3 Kyparissia Greece
111 B3 Kyparissiakos Kolpos b. Greece
77 C1 Kypshak, Ozero salt l. Kazakh.
111 B3 Kyra Panagia i. Greece
Kyrenia Cyprus see Keryneia
77 C2 Kyrgyzstan country Asia
101 F1 Kyritz Ger.
93 H3 Kyrönjoki r. Fin.
86 E2 Kyrta Rus. Fed.
86 D2 Kyssa Rus. Fed.
83 J2 Kytalyktakh Rus. Fed.
111 B3 Kythira i. Greece
111 B3 Kythnos i. Greece
128 B2 Kyuquot Can.
67 B4 Kyūshū i. Japan
110 B2 Kyustendil Bulg.
62 A2 Kywebwe Myanmar
90 C1 Kyyivs'ke Vodoskhovyshche resr Ukr.
92 H3 Kyyjärvi Fin.
68 C1 Kyzyl Rus. Fed.
76 C2 Kyzylkum Desert Kazakh./Uzbek.
77 C2 Kyzyl-Orda Kazakh. see Kyzylorda
Kzyltu Kazakh. see Kishkenekol'

L

145 C3 La Angostura, Presa de resr Mex.
117 C4 Laascaanood Somalia
145 D3 La Ascensión, Bahía de b. Mex.
117 C3 Laasgoray Somalia
150 C1 La Asunción Venez.
114 A2 Laâyoune Western Sahara
87 D4 Laba r. Rus. Fed.
144 B2 La Babia Mex.
123 C3 La Bahia, Islas de is Hond.
61 D2 Labala Indon.
131 D2 La Baleine, Rivière à r. Can.
152 B2 La Banda Arg.
61 C1 Labang Sarawak Malaysia
104 B2 La Baule-Escoublac France
102 C1 Labe r. Czech Rep.
114 A3 Labé Guinea
128 A1 Laberge, Lake Can.
128 C2 La Biche, Lac l. Can.
108 B1 Labin Croatia
87 D4 Labinsk Rus. Fed.
64 B2 Labo Phil.
144 B2 La Boquilla, Presa de resr Mex.
61 D2 Labala Indon.
131 D2 La Baleine, Rivière à r. Can.
104 B2 Labouheyre France
153 B3 Laboulaye Arg.
131 D2 Labrador reg. Can.
131 D2 Labrador City Can.
127 I2 Labrador Sea Can./Greenland
151 E2 Lábrea Brazil
61 C1 Labuan Malaysia
61 C2 Labuhanbajo Indon.
60 B1 Labuhanbilik Indon.

59 C3 Labuna Indon.
63 A2 Labutta Myanmar
86 F2 Labytnangi Rus. Fed.
109 C2 Laç Albania
106 B1 La Cabrera, Sierra de mts Spain
La Calle Alg. see El Kala
105 C2 La Capelle France
131 D2 Lac Bermen l. Can.
73 B3 Laccadive Islands India
129 E2 Lac du Bonnet Can.
146 B3 La Ceiba Hond.
52 A3 Lacepede Bay Austr.
134 B1 Lacey U.S.A.
105 D2 La Chaux-de-Fonds Switz.
53 B2 Lachlan r. Austr.
146 C4 La Chorrera Panama
141 E1 Lachute Can.
105 D3 La Ciotat France
128 C2 Lac la Biche Can.
Lac la Martre Can. see Wha Ti
141 E1 Lac-Mégantic Can.
128 C2 Lacombe Can.
145 C3 La Concordia Mex.
108 A3 Laconi Sardinia Italy
141 E2 Laconia U.S.A.
104 B2 La Coubre, Pointe de pt France
128 C2 La Crete Can.
140 A2 La Crosse U.S.A.
144 B2 La Cruz Mex.
144 B2 La Cuesta Mex.
155 D1 Ladainha Brazil
74 B1 Ladakh Range mts India
106 C1 La Demanda, Sierra de mts Spain
122 B3 Ladismith S. Africa
79 D2 Lādīz Iran
89 D1 Ladoga, Lake Rus. Fed.
Ladozhskoye Ozero l. Rus. Fed. see Ladoga, Lake
143 D2 Ladson U.S.A.
123 C3 Lady Grey S. Africa
128 B3 Ladysmith Can.
123 C2 Ladysmith S. Africa
59 D3 Lae P.N.G.
62 B2 Lae Thai.
139 C3 La Encantada, Sierra mts Mex.
152 B2 La Esmeralda Bol.
93 F4 Læsø i. Denmark
Lafayette Alg. see Bougaa
143 C2 La Fayette U.S.A.
140 C2 Lafayette IN U.S.A.
142 B2 Lafayette LA U.S.A.
115 C4 Lafia Nigeria
104 B2 La Flèche France
143 D1 La Follette U.S.A.
130 C2 Laforge Can.
79 C2 Läft Iran
108 A3 La Galite i. Tunisia
87 D4 Lagan' Rus. Fed.
151 F4 Lagarto Brazil
118 B2 Lagdo, Lac de l. Cameroon
119 E2 Lagh Bor watercourse Kenya/Somalia
114 B3 Laghouat Alg.
152 B3 Lagoa Santa Brazil
114 A2 La Gomera i. Canary Is
147 C3 La Gonâve, Île de i. Haiti
114 C4 Lagos Nigeria
106 B2 Lagos Port.
134 C1 La Grande U.S.A.
130 C2 La Grande 2, Réservoir resr Can.
130 C2 La Grande 3, Réservoir resr Can.
130 C2 La Grande 4, Réservoir resr Can.
50 B1 Lagrange Austr.
143 C2 La Grange U.S.A.
150 C2 La Gran Sabana plat. Venez.
152 D2 Laguna Brazil
152 A2 Lagunas Peru
147 C3 Lagunillas Venez.
La Habana Cuba see Havana
61 C1 Lahad Datu Sabah Malaysia
104 B2 La Hague, Cap de c. France
60 B2 Lahat Indon.
78 B3 Lahij Yemen
81 C2 Lāhījān Iran
100 C2 Lahnstein Ger.
74 B1 Lahore Pak.

74 A2	Lahri Pak.
93 I3	Lahti Fin.
115 D4	Laï Chad
53 D1	Laidley Austr.
104 C2	L'Aigle France
122 B3	Laingsburg S. Africa
92 H2	Lainioälven r. Sweden
115 C3	L'Aïr, Massif de mts Niger
96 B1	Lairg U.K.
108 B1	Laives Italy
70 B2	Laiwu China
70 C2	Laiyang China
70 B2	Laiyuan China
70 B2	Laizhou China
70 B2	Laizhou Wan b. China
50 C1	Lajamanu Austr.
152 C2	Lajes Brazil
144 B2	La Junta Mex.
136 C3	La Junta U.S.A.
146 B2	La Juventud, Isla de i. Cuba
53 C2	Lake Cargelligo Austr.
53 D2	Lake Cathie Austr.
142 B2	Lake Charles U.S.A.
143 D2	Lake City FL U.S.A.
143 E2	Lake City SC U.S.A.
128 B3	Lake Cowichan Can.
	Lake Harbour Can. see Kimmirut
138 A2	Lake Havasu City U.S.A.
139 D3	Lake Jackson U.S.A.
50 A3	Lake King Austr.
143 D3	Lakeland U.S.A.
128 C2	Lake Louise Can.
134 B1	Lake Oswego U.S.A.
54 A2	Lake Paringa N.Z.
142 B2	Lake Providence U.S.A.
54 B2	Lake Pukaki N.Z.
53 C3	Lakes Entrance Austr.
134 B2	Lakeview U.S.A.
137 E2	Lakeville U.S.A.
136 B3	Lakewood CO U.S.A.
141 E2	Lakewood NJ U.S.A.
143 D3	Lake Worth U.S.A.
74 A2	Lakhpat India
74 B1	Lakki Pak.
111 B3	Lakonikos Kolpos b. Greece
114 B4	Lakota Côte d'Ivoire
92 H1	Lakselv Norway
144 A2	La Laguna, Picacho de mt. Mex.
146 A3	La Libertad Guat.
106 B1	Lalin Spain
106 B2	La Línea de la Concepción Spain
74 B2	Lalitpur India
	Lalitpur Nepal see Patan
129 D2	La Loche Can.
100 B2	La Louvière Belgium
108 A2	La Maddalena Sardinia Italy
131 D3	La Madeleine, Îles de is Can.
61 C1	Lamag Sabah Malaysia
	La Manche str. France/U.K. see English Channel
136 C3	Lamar U.S.A.
79 C2	Lamard Iran
108 A3	La Marmora, Punta mt. Sardinia Italy
128 C1	La Martre, Lac l. Can.
104 B2	Lamballe France
118 B3	Lambaréné Gabon
122 A3	Lambert's Bay S. Africa
92 □A2	Lambeyri Iceland
106 B1	Lamego Port.
131 D3	La Mauricie, Île i. Can.
150 B4	La Merced Peru
52 B3	Lameroo Austr.
139 C2	Lamesa U.S.A.
111 B3	Lamia Greece
137 E2	Lamoni U.S.A.
62 A2	Lampang Thai.
139 D2	Lampasas U.S.A.
145 B2	Lampazos Mex.
99 A3	Lampeter U.K.
62 A2	Lamphun Thai.
119 E3	Lamu Kenya
105 D3	La Mure France
107 D2	La Nao, Cabo de c. Spain
96 C3	Lanark U.K.
63 A2	Lanbi Kyun i. Myanmar
62 A1	Lancang China
	Lancang Jiang r. China see Mekong
98 B2	Lancaster U.K.
135 C4	Lancaster CA U.S.A.
140 C3	Lancaster OH U.S.A.
141 D2	Lancaster PA U.S.A.
143 D2	Lancaster SC U.S.A.
127 G2	Lancaster Sound str. Can.
50 A3	Lancelin Austr.
	Lanchow China see Lanzhou
102 C2	Landeck Austria
136 B2	Lander U.S.A.
99 A4	Land's End pt U.K.
102 C2	Landshut Ger.
93 F4	Landskrona Sweden
143 C2	Lanett U.S.A.
122 B2	Langberg mts S. Africa
137 D1	Langdon U.S.A.
93 F4	Langeland i. Denmark
101 D1	Langen Ger.
100 C1	Langeoog Ger.
100 C1	Langeoog i. Ger.
82 G2	Langepas Rus. Fed.
70 B2	Langfang China
101 D2	Langgöns Ger.
96 C3	Langholm U.K.
92 □A3	Langjökull ice cap Iceland
60 A1	Langkawi i. Malaysia
105 C3	Langogne France
104 B3	Langon France
106 B1	Langreo Spain
105 D2	Langres France
60 A1	Langsa Indon.
62 B1	Lang Son Vietnam
105 C3	Languedoc reg. France
101 D1	Langwedel Ger.
129 D2	Lanigan Can.
153 A3	Lanin, Volcán vol. Arg./Chile
81 C2	Länkäran Azer.
104 B2	Lannion France
140 B1	L'Anse U.S.A.
141 E1	L'Anse-St-Jean Can.
140 C2	Lansing U.S.A.
71 B3	Lanxi China
117 B4	Lanya Sudan
114 A2	Lanzarote i. Canary Is
70 A2	Lanzhou China
64 B2	Laoag Phil.
62 B1	Lao Cai Vietnam
70 B2	Laohekou China
	Laojunmiao China see Yumen
65 B1	Laoling China
65 B1	Lao Ling mts China
105 C2	Laon France
62 B2	Laos country Asia
65 B1	Laotougou China
66 A2	Laoye Ling mts China
154 C3	Lapa Brazil
114 A2	La Palma i. Canary Is
146 C4	La Palma Panama
150 C2	La Paragua Venez.
152 B1	La Paz Bol.
145 D3	La Paz Mex.
144 A2	La Paz Mex.
150 C3	La Pedrera Col.
140 C2	Lapeer U.S.A.
66 D1	La Pérouse Strait Japan/Rus. Fed.
145 C2	La Pesca Mex.
144 B2	La Piedad Mex.
153 C3	La Plata Arg.
153 C3	La Plata, Río de sea chan. Arg./Uru.
92 H3	Lappajärvi l. Fin.
93 I3	Lappeenranta Fin.
92 G2	Lappland reg. Europe
111 C2	Lâpseki Turkey
	Laptev Rus. Fed. see Yasnogorsk
83 J1	Laptev Sea Rus. Fed.
	Laptevykh, More sea Rus. Fed. see Laptev Sea
93 H3	Lapua Fin.
152 B2	La Quiaca Arg.
108 B2	L'Aquila Italy
135 C4	La Quinta U.S.A.
79 C2	Lār Iran
114 B1	Larache Morocco
136 B2	Laramie U.S.A.
136 B2	Laramie Mountains U.S.A.
154 B3	Laranjeiras do Sul Brazil
61 D2	Larantuka Indon.
59 C3	Larat i. Indon.
107 D2	Larba Alg.
106 C1	Laredo Spain
139 D3	Laredo U.S.A.
153 A5	La Reina Adelaida, Archipiélago de is Chile
143 D3	Largo U.S.A.
96 B3	Largs U.K.
115 D1	L'Ariana Tunisia
152 B2	La Rioja Arg.
111 B3	Larisa Greece
74 A2	Larkana Pak.
	Larnaca Cyprus see Larnaka
80 B2	Larnaka Cyprus
97 D1	Larne U.K.
100 B2	La Roche-en-Ardenne Belgium
104 B2	La Rochelle France
104 B2	La Roche-sur-Yon France
107 C2	La Roda Spain
147 D3	La Romana Dom. Rep.
129 D2	La Ronge Can.
129 D2	La Ronge, Lac l. Can.
50 C1	Larrimah Austr.
55 A3	Larsen Ice Shelf Antarctica
93 F4	Larvik Norway
136 C3	Las Animas U.S.A.
	Las Anod Somalia see Laascaanood
130 C3	La Sarre Can.
138 B2	Las Cruces U.S.A.
152 A2	La Serena Chile
153 C3	Las Flores Arg.
153 B3	Las Heras Arg.
62 A1	Lashio Myanmar
76 B3	Lashkar Gāh Afgh.
109 C3	La Sila reg. Italy
152 B2	Las Lomitas Arg.
106 B2	Las Marismas marsh Spain
145 D3	Las Minas, Cerro de mt. Hond.
144 B2	Las Nieves Mex.
114 A2	Las Palmas de Gran Canaria Canary Is
108 A2	La Spezia Italy
153 C3	Las Piedras Uru.
150 C4	Las Piedras, Río de r. Peru
153 B4	Las Plumas Arg.
155 D1	Lassance Brazil
129 D2	Last Mountain Lake Can.
152 B2	Las Tórtolas, Cerro mt. Chile
118 B3	Lastoursville Gabon
109 C2	Lastovo i. Croatia
144 A2	Las Tres Vírgenes, Volcán vol. Mex.
146 C2	Las Tunas Cuba
144 B2	Las Varas Mex.
144 B2	Las Varas Mex.
138 B1	Las Vegas NM U.S.A.
135 C3	Las Vegas NV U.S.A.
131 E2	La Tabatière Can.
	Latakia Syria see Al Lādhiqīyah
108 B2	La Teste France
108 B2	Latina Italy
147 D3	La Tortuga, Isla i. Venez.
64 B2	La Trinidad Phil.
89 E2	Latskoye Rus. Fed.
130 C3	La Tuque Can.
88 B2	Latvia country Europe
	Latviyskaya S.S.R. country Europe see Latvia
59 E3	Lau P.N.G.
102 C1	Lauchhammer Ger.
101 E3	Lauf an der Pegnitz Ger.
105 D2	Laufen Switz.
92 □A3	Laugarás Iceland
127 H1	Lauge Koch Kyst reg. Greenland
138 C1	Laughlin Peak U.S.A.
51 D4	Launceston Austr.
99 A4	Launceston U.K.
62 A1	Launggyaung Myanmar
153 A4	La Unión Chile
51 D1	Laura Austr.
142 C2	Laurel MS U.S.A.
134 E1	Laurel MT U.S.A.
96 C2	Laurencekirk U.K.
109 C2	Lauria Italy
143 E2	Laurinburg U.S.A.
105 D2	Lausanne Switz.
61 C2	Laut i. Indon.
61 C2	Laut i. Indon.
101 D2	Lautersbach (Hessen) Ger.
61 C2	Laut Kecil, Kepulauan is Indon.
100 C1	Lauwersmeer l. Neth.
141 E1	Laval Can.
104 B2	Laval France
81 D2	Lävar Meydän salt marsh Iran
50 B2	Laverton Austr.
154 B3	La Victoria, Sierra de hills Arg.
155 D2	Lavras Brazil
123 D2	Lavumisa Swaziland
61 C1	Lawas Sarawak Malaysia
78 B3	Lawdar Yemen
62 A1	Lawksawk Myanmar
114 B3	Lawra Ghana
140 B3	Lawrence IN U.S.A.
137 D3	Lawrence KS U.S.A.
141 E2	Lawrence MA U.S.A.
142 C1	Lawrenceburg U.S.A.
143 D2	Lawrenceville U.S.A.
139 D2	Lawton U.S.A.
78 A2	Lawz, Jabal al mt. Saudi Arabia
93 F4	Laxå Sweden
122 B2	Laxey U.K.
78 B2	Laylá Saudi Arabia
109 D2	Lazarevac Yugo.
144 A1	Lázaro Cárdenas Mex.
144 B3	Lázaro Cárdenas Mex.
88 B3	Lazdijai Lith.
66 B2	Lazo Rus. Fed.
83 K2	Lazo Rus. Fed.
136 C2	Lead U.S.A.
129 D2	Leader Can.
136 B3	Leadville U.S.A.
	Leaf Bay Can. see Tasiujaq
129 D2	Leaf Rapids Can.
139 D3	League City U.S.A.
139 D3	Leakey U.S.A.
99 C3	Leamington Spa, Royal U.K.
97 B2	Leane, Lough l. Rep. of Ireland
130 C2	L'Eau Claire, Lac à l. Can.
137 E3	Leavenworth U.S.A.
64 B3	Lebak Phil.
80 B2	Lebanon country Asia
137 E3	Lebanon MO U.S.A.
141 E2	Lebanon NH U.S.A.
134 B2	Lebanon OR U.S.A.
141 D2	Lebanon PA U.S.A.
142 C1	Lebanon TN U.S.A.
89 E3	Lebedyan' Rus. Fed.
91 C1	Lebedyn Ukr.
130 C3	Lebel-sur-Quévillon Can.
104 C2	Le Blanc France
103 D1	Lębork Pol.
123 C1	Lebowakgomo S. Africa
106 B2	Lebrija Spain
153 A3	Lebu Chile
104 C3	Le Bugue France
109 C2	Lecce Italy
108 A1	Lecco Italy
102 B2	Lech r. Austria/Ger.
111 B3	Lechaina Greece
71 B3	Lechang China
102 B1	Leck Ger.
142 B2	Lecompte U.S.A.
105 C2	Le Creusot France
104 C3	Lectoure France
104 B2	Ledesma Spain
104 C2	Le Dorat France
128 C2	Leduc Can.
97 B3	Lee r. Rep. of Ireland
137 E1	Leech Lake U.S.A.
98 C1	Leeds U.K.
99 B3	Leek U.K.
97 B2	Leenane Rep. of Ireland
100 C1	Leer (Ostfriesland) Ger.
143 D3	Leesburg U.S.A.
142 B2	Leesville U.S.A.
53 C2	Leeton Austr.
122 B3	Leeu-Gamka S. Africa
100 B1	Leeuwarden Neth.
50 A3	Leeuwin, Cape Austr.
147 D3	Leeward Islands Caribbean Sea
111 B3	Lefkada Greece
111 B3	Lefkada i. Greece
	Lefkosia Cyprus see Nicosia
64 B2	Legaspi Phil.
103 E1	Legionowo Pol.
108 B1	Legnago Italy
103 D1	Legnica Pol.
74 B1	Leh Jammu and Kashmir
104 C2	Le Havre France
101 E1	Lehre Ger.
122 B1	Lehututu Botswana
74 B1	Leiah Pak.
103 D2	Leibnitz Austria
99 C3	Leicester U.K.
51 C1	Leichhardt r. Austr.
51 D2	Leichhardt Range mts Austr.
100 B1	Leiden Neth.
100 A2	Leie r. Belgium
52 A2	Leigh Creek Austr.

97 C2 **Leighlinbridge**
Rep. of Ireland
99 C4 **Leighton Buzzard** U.K.
93 E3 **Leikanger** Norway
101 D1 **Leine** r. Ger.
50 B2 **Leinster** Austr.
97 C2 **Leinster** reg.
Rep. of Ireland
97 C2 **Leinster, Mount** hill
Rep. of Ireland
101 F2 **Leipzig** Ger.
92 F2 **Leiranger** Norway
106 B2 **Leiria** Port.
93 E4 **Leirvik** Norway
97 C2 **Leixlip** Rep. of Ireland
71 B3 **Leiyang** China
71 B3 **Leizhou** China
71 A3 **Leizhou Bandao** pen.
China
118 B3 **Lékana** Congo
122 A2 **Lekkersing** S. Africa
142 B2 **Leland** U.S.A.
Leli China see Tianlin
100 B1 **Lelystad** Neth.
153 B5 **Le Maire, Estrecho de**
sea chan. Arg.
105 D2 **Léman, Lac** l.
France/Switz.
104 C2 **Le Mans** France
137 D2 **Le Mars** U.S.A.
102 B2 **Lemberg** mt. Ger.
154 C2 **Leme** Brazil
80 B2 **Lemesos** Cyprus
101 D1 **Lemförde** Ger.
127 H2 **Lemieux Islands** Can.
136 C1 **Lemmon** U.S.A.
135 C3 **Lemoore** U.S.A.
131 D2 **Le Moyne, Lac** l. Can.
62 A1 **Lemro** r. Myanmar
109 C2 **Le Murge** hills Italy
83 J2 **Lena** r. Rus. Fed.
100 C1 **Lengerich** Ger.
70 A2 **Lenglong Ling** mts China
71 B3 **Lengshuijiang** China
71 B3 **Lengshuitan** China
Leninabad Tajik. see
Khŭjand
Leninakan Armenia see
Gyumri
91 D2 **Lenine** Ukr.
Leningrad Rus. Fed. see
St Petersburg
91 D2 **Leningradskaya** Rus. Fed.
Leninobod Tajik. see
Khŭjand
77 E1 **Leninogorsk** Kazakh.
77 D3 **Lenin Peak** Kyrg./Tajik.
Leninsk Kazakh. see
Baykonur
89 E3 **Leninskiy** Rus. Fed.
53 D1 **Lennox Head** Austr.
143 D1 **Lenoir** U.S.A.
100 A2 **Lens** Belgium
105 C1 **Lens** France
83 I2 **Lensk** Rus. Fed.
103 D2 **Lenti** Hungary
109 C3 **Lentini** Sicily Italy
114 B3 **Léo** Burkina
103 D2 **Leoben** Austria
Leodhais, Eilean i. U.K.
see Lewis, Isle of
99 B3 **Leominster** U.K.
144 B2 **León** Mex.
146 B3 **León** Nic.
106 B1 **León** Spain
122 A1 **Leonardville** Namibia
108 B3 **Leonforte** Sicily Italy
53 C3 **Leongatha** Austr.
50 B2 **Leonora** Austr.
155 D2 **Leopoldina** Brazil
Léopoldville
Dem. Rep. Congo see
Kinshasa
90 B2 **Leova** Moldova
Leovo Moldova see Leova
123 C1 **Lephepe** Botswana
123 C3 **Lephoi** S. Africa
71 B3 **Leping** China
77 D2 **Lepsy** Kazakh.
105 C2 **Le-Puy-en-Velay** France
123 C1 **Lerala** Botswana
123 C2 **Leratswana** S. Africa
150 B3 **Lérida** Col.
Lérida Spain see Lleida
106 C1 **Lerma** Spain
111 C3 **Leros** i. Greece
130 C2 **Le Roy, Lac** l. Can.
93 F4 **Lerum** Sweden

96 □ **Lerwick** U.K.
111 C3 **Lesbos** i. Greece
147 C3 **Les Cayes** Haiti
104 C3 **Les Escaldes** Andorra
141 F1 **Les Escoumins** Can.
107 D1 **Le Seu d'Urgell** Spain
70 A3 **Leshan** China
104 B2 **Les Herbiers** France
86 D2 **Leshukonskoye** Rus. Fed.
Leskhimstroy Ukr. see
Syeverodonets'k
109 D2 **Leskovac** Yugo.
104 B2 **Lesneven** France
Lesnoy Rus. Fed. see
Umba
89 E2 **Lesnoye** Rus. Fed.
83 H3 **Lesosibirsk** Rus. Fed.
123 C2 **Lesotho** country Africa
66 B1 **Lesozavodsk** Rus. Fed.
104 B2 **Les Sables-d'Olonne**
France
147 D3 **Lesser Antilles** is
Caribbean Sea
Lesser Caucasus mts
Asia see Malyy Kavkaz
Lesser Khingan
Mountains China see
Xiao Hinggan Ling
128 C2 **Lesser Slave Lake** Can.
105 C3 **Les Vans** France
Lesvos i. Greece see
Lesbos
103 D1 **Leszno** Pol.
123 D1 **Letaba** S. Africa
99 C4 **Letchworth** U.K.
128 C3 **Lethbridge** Can.
150 D2 **Lethem** Guyana
59 C3 **Leti, Kepulauan** is Indon.
150 C3 **Leticia** Col.
120 B3 **Letlhakane** Botswana
123 C1 **Letlhakeng** Botswana
104 C1 **Le Touquet-Paris-Plage**
France
99 D4 **Le Tréport** France
123 D1 **Letsitele** S. Africa
63 A2 **Letsok-aw Kyun** i.
Myanmar
123 C2 **Letsopa** S. Africa
97 C1 **Letterkenny**
Rep. of Ireland
105 C3 **Leucate, Étang de** l.
France
Leukas Greece see
Lefkada
60 A1 **Leuser, Gunung** mt.
Indon.
100 B2 **Leuven** Belgium
111 B3 **Levadeia** Greece
92 F3 **Levanger** Norway
139 C2 **Levelland** U.S.A.
50 B1 **Lévêque, Cape** Austr.
96 A2 **Leverburgh** U.K.
100 C2 **Leverkusen** Ger.
103 D2 **Levice** Slovakia
54 C2 **Levin** N.Z.
131 C3 **Lévis** Can.
141 E2 **Levittown** U.S.A.
89 E3 **Lev Tolstoy** Rus. Fed.
99 D4 **Lewes** U.K.
96 A1 **Lewis, Isle of** i. U.K.
140 D2 **Lewisburg** PA U.S.A.
142 C1 **Lewisburg** TN U.S.A.
140 C3 **Lewisburg** WV U.S.A.
134 D1 **Lewis Range** mts U.S.A.
134 C1 **Lewiston** ID U.S.A.
141 E2 **Lewiston** ME U.S.A.
134 E1 **Lewistown** U.S.A.
140 C3 **Lexington** KY U.S.A.
136 D2 **Lexington** NE U.S.A.
139 D1 **Lexington** OK U.S.A.
141 D3 **Lexington** VA U.S.A.
64 B2 **Leyte** i. Phil.
109 C2 **Lezhë** Albania
89 F2 **Lezhnevo** Rus. Fed.
89 E3 **L'gov** Rus. Fed.
75 C2 **Lhagoi Kangri** mt. China
Lharigarbo China see
Amdo
75 D2 **Lhasa** China
75 C2 **Lhazê** China
60 A1 **Lhokseumawe** Indon.
62 A1 **Lhünzê** China
67 B3 **Liancourt Rocks** i.
N. Pacific Ocean
70 B2 **Liangzu Hu** l. China
Liangzhou China see
Wuwei
Lianhe China see
Qianjiang
71 B3 **Lianhua** China
71 B3 **Lianjiang** China

70 C1 **Lianran** China see Anning
Lianshan China
Liantang China see
Nanchang
Lianxian China see
Lianzhou
70 B2 **Lianyungang** China
71 B3 **Lianzhou** China
Lianzhou China see Hepu
65 A1 **Liao** r. China
70 B2 **Liaocheng** China
70 C1 **Liaodong Bandao** pen.
China
70 C1 **Liaodong Wan** b. China
70 C1 **Liaoning** prov. China
70 C1 **Liaoyang** China
65 B1 **Liaoyuan** China
128 B1 **Liard** r. Can.
134 C1 **Libby** U.S.A.
118 B2 **Libenge** Dem. Rep. Congo
136 C3 **Liberal** U.S.A.
103 D1 **Liberec** Czech Rep.
114 B4 **Liberia** country Africa
146 B3 **Liberia** Costa Rica
150 C2 **Libertad** Venez.
137 E3 **Libin** Belgium
100 B3 **Libin** Belgium
64 B2 **Libmanan** Phil.
71 A3 **Libo** China
123 C3 **Libode** S. Africa
119 E2 **Liboi** Kenya
104 B3 **Libourne** France
100 B3 **Libramont** Belgium
138 A3 **Libre, Sierra** mts Mex.
118 A2 **Libreville** Gabon
115 D2 **Libya** country Africa
115 E2 **Libyan Desert** Egypt/Libya
116 A1 **Libyan Plateau** Egypt
108 B3 **Licata** Sicily Italy
Licheng China see Lipu
99 C3 **Lichfield** U.K.
121 C2 **Lichinga** Moz.
101 E2 **Lichte** Ger.
123 C2 **Lichtenburg** S. Africa
101 E2 **Lichtenfels** Ger.
88 C3 **Lida** Belarus
93 F4 **Lidköping** Sweden
50 C2 **Liebig, Mount** Austr.
105 D2 **Liechtenstein** country
Europe
100 B2 **Liège** Belgium
92 J3 **Lieksa** Fin.
119 C2 **Lienart** Dem. Rep. Congo
102 C2 **Lienz** Austria
88 B2 **Liepāja** Latvia
100 B2 **Lier** Belgium
102 C2 **Liezen** Austria
97 C2 **Liffey** r. Rep. of Ireland
97 C1 **Lifford** Rep. of Ireland
53 C1 **Lightning Ridge** Austr.
121 C2 **Ligonha** r. Moz.
105 D3 **Ligurian Sea** France/Italy
119 C4 **Likasi** Dem. Rep. Congo
118 C2 **Likati** Dem. Rep. Congo
128 B2 **Likely** Can.
Likhachevo Ukr. see
Pervomays'kyy
Likhachyovo Ukr. see
Pervomays'kyy
89 E2 **Likhoslavl'** Rus. Fed.
60 B1 **Liku** Indon.
105 D3 **L'Île-Rousse** Corsica
France
71 B3 **Liling** China
93 F4 **Lilla Edet** Sweden
100 B3 **Lille** Belgium
105 C1 **Lille** France
93 E4 **Lille Bælt** sea chan.
Denmark
93 F3 **Lillehammer** Norway
93 F4 **Lillestrøm** Norway
128 B2 **Lillooet** Can.
121 C2 **Lilongwe** Malawi
64 B3 **Liloy** Phil.
150 B4 **Lima** Peru
140 C2 **Lima** U.S.A.
155 D2 **Lima Duarte** Brazil
79 C2 **Limah** Oman
Limassol Cyprus see
Lemesos
97 C1 **Limavady** U.K.
153 B3 **Limay** r. Arg.
101 F2 **Limbach-Oberfrohna** Ger.
88 B2 **Limbaži** Latvia
118 A2 **Limbe** Cameroon
101 D2 **Limburg an der Lahn** Ger.
122 B2 **Lime Acres** S. Africa
154 C2 **Limeira** Brazil
97 B2 **Limerick** Rep. of Ireland
93 E4 **Limfjorden** sea chan.
Denmark

92 I3 **Liminka** Fin.
111 C3 **Limnos** i. Greece
104 C2 **Limoges** France
146 B3 **Limón** Costa Rica
136 C3 **Limon** U.S.A.
104 C2 **Limousin, Plateaux du**
France
104 C3 **Limoux** France
121 C3 **Limpopo** r.
S. Africa/Zimbabwe
64 A2 **Linapacan** i. Phil.
153 A3 **Linares** Chile
145 C2 **Linares** Mex.
106 C2 **Linares** Spain
108 A3 **Linas, Monte** mt. Sardinia
Italy
62 B1 **Lincang** China
71 B3 **Linchuan** China
98 C3 **Lincoln** U.K.
140 B2 **Lincoln** IL U.S.A.
141 F1 **Lincoln** ME U.S.A.
137 D2 **Lincoln** NE U.S.A.
134 B2 **Lincoln City** U.S.A.
151 D2 **Linden** Guyana
142 C1 **Linden** U.S.A.
119 C2 **Lindi** r. Dem. Rep. Congo
119 D3 **Lindi** Tanz.
Lindisfarne i. U.K. see
Holy Island
111 C3 **Lindos** Greece
130 C3 **Lindsay** Can.
48 K3 **Line Islands** Kiribati
70 B2 **Linfen** China
64 B2 **Lingayen** Phil.
70 B2 **Lingbao** China
Lingcheng China see
Lingshan
Lingcheng China see
Lingshui
123 C3 **Lingelethu** S. Africa
123 C3 **Lingelihle** S. Africa
100 C1 **Lingen (Ems)** Ger.
60 B2 **Lingga** i. Indon.
60 B2 **Lingga, Kepulauan** is
Indon.
71 A3 **Lingshan** China
71 A4 **Lingshui** China
114 A3 **Linguère** Senegal
155 D1 **Linhares** Brazil
70 A1 **Linhe** China
Linjiang China see
Shanghang
65 B1 **Linjiang** China
93 G4 **Linköping** Sweden
66 B1 **Linkou** China
71 B3 **Linli** China
96 B2 **Linnhe, Loch** inlet U.K.
70 B2 **Linqing** China
154 C2 **Lins** Brazil
136 C1 **Linton** U.S.A.
69 D2 **Linxi** China
70 A2 **Linxia** China
70 B2 **Linyi** Shandong China
70 B2 **Linyi** Shandong China
70 B2 **Linying** China
102 C2 **Linz** Austria
90 A1 **Lioboml'** Ukr.
105 C3 **Lion, Golfe du** g. France
Lions, Gulf of France see
Lion, Golfe du
109 B3 **Lipari** Italy
108 B3 **Lipari, Isole** is Italy
89 E3 **Lipetsk** Rus. Fed.
110 B1 **Lipova** Romania
101 D2 **Lippstadt** Ger.
53 C3 **Liptrap, Cape** Austr.
71 B3 **Lipu** China
119 D2 **Lira** Uganda
108 B2 **Liri** r. Italy
76 C1 **Lisakovsk** Kazakh.
118 C2 **Lisala** Dem. Rep. Congo
Lisboa Port. see Lisbon
106 B2 **Lisbon** Port.
97 C1 **Lisburn** U.K.
97 B2 **Liscannor Bay**
Rep. of Ireland
97 B2 **Lisdoonvarna**
Rep. of Ireland
71 B3 **Lishi** China
71 B3 **Lishui** China
104 C2 **Lisieux** France
99 A4 **Liskeard** U.K.
89 E3 **Liski** Rus. Fed.
53 D1 **Lismore** Austr.
97 C2 **Lismore** Rep. of Ireland
97 C1 **Lisnaskea** U.K.
97 B2 **Listowel** Rep. of Ireland
71 A3 **Litang** Guangxi China
68 C2 **Litang** Sichuan China
140 B3 **Litchfield** IL U.S.A.
137 E1 **Litchfield** MN U.S.A.

53 D2 Lithgow Austr.
111 B3 Lithino, Akra pt Greece
88 B2 Lithuania country Europe
111 B3 Litochoro Greece
102 C1 Litoměřice Czech Rep.
Litovskaya S.S.R. country Europe see Lithuania
146 C2 Little Abaco i. Bahamas
73 D3 Little Andaman i. India
143 E3 Little Bahama Bank sea feature Bahamas
Little Belt sea chan. Denmark see Lille Bælt
146 B3 Little Cayman i. Cayman Is
138 A1 Little Colorado r. U.S.A.
140 C1 Little Current Can.
137 E1 Little Falls U.S.A.
139 C2 Littlefield U.S.A.
99 C4 Littlehampton U.K.
122 A2 Little Karas Berg plat. Namibia
122 B3 Little Karoo plat. S. Africa
96 A2 Little Minch sea chan. U.K.
136 C1 Little Missouri r. U.S.A.
73 D4 Little Nicobar i. India
142 B2 Little Rock U.S.A.
141 E2 Littleton U.S.A.
121 C2 Litunde Moz.
90 B2 Lityn Ukr.
Liuchow China see Liuzhou
70 B2 Liujiachang China
Liupanshui China see Lupanshui
121 C2 Liupo Moz.
71 A3 Liuzhou China
88 C2 Līvāni Latvia
143 D2 Live Oak U.S.A.
50 B1 Liveringa Austr.
138 C2 Livermore, Mount U.S.A.
53 D2 Liverpool Austr.
131 D3 Liverpool Can.
98 B3 Liverpool U.K.
127 G2 Liverpool, Cape Can.
53 C2 Liverpool Range mts Austr.
96 C3 Livingston U.K.
134 D1 Livingston MT U.S.A.
139 E2 Livingston TX U.S.A.
139 D2 Livingstone, Lake U.S.A.
120 B2 Livingstone Zambia
55 A3 Livingston Island Antarctica
109 C2 Livno Bos.-Herz.
89 E3 Livny Rus. Fed.
140 C2 Livonia U.S.A.
108 B2 Livorno Italy
119 D3 Liwale Tanz.
70 B2 Liyang China
99 A5 Lizard Point U.K.
108 B1 Ljubljana Slovenia
93 G3 Ljungan r. Sweden
93 F4 Ljungby Sweden
93 G3 Ljusdal Sweden
93 G3 Ljusnan r. Sweden
99 B4 Llandeilo U.K.
99 B4 Llandovery U.K.
99 B3 Llandrindod Wells U.K.
99 B3 Llandudno U.K.
99 A4 Llanelli U.K.
106 C1 Llanes Spain
98 A3 Llangefni U.K.
99 B3 Llangollen U.K.
99 B3 Llangurig U.K.
139 C2 Llano Estacado plain U.S.A.
150 C2 Llanos reg. Col./Venez.
107 D1 Lleida Spain
99 A3 Lleyn Peninsula U.K.
107 C2 Lliria Spain
106 C1 Llodio Spain
128 C2 Lloyd George, Mount Can.
129 D2 Lloyd Lake Can.
129 C2 Lloydminster Can.
152 B2 Llullaillaco, Volcán vol. Chile
154 B2 Loanda Brazil
123 C2 Lobatse Botswana
103 D1 Łobez Pol.
120 A2 Lobito Angola
101 F1 Loburg Ger.
96 B2 Lochaber mts U.K.
96 B2 Lochaline U.K.
Loch Baghasdail U.K. see Lochboisdale
96 A2 Lochboisdale U.K.
104 C2 Loches France
96 B2 Lochgilphead U.K.

96 B1 Lochinver U.K.
96 A2 Lochmaddy U.K.
96 C2 Lochnagar mt. U.K.
Loch nam Madadh U.K. see Lochmaddy
96 B3 Lochranza U.K.
52 A2 Lock U.K.
96 C3 Lockerbie U.K.
53 C3 Lockhart Austr.
139 D3 Lockhart U.S.A.
51 D1 Lockhart River Austr.
141 D2 Lock Haven U.S.A.
141 D2 Lockport U.S.A.
63 B2 Lộc Ninh Vietnam
105 C3 Lodève France
86 C2 Lodeynoye Pole Rus. Fed.
74 B2 Lodhran Pak.
108 A1 Lodi Italy
135 B3 Lodi U.S.A.
92 F2 Løding Norway
92 G2 Lødingen Norway
118 C3 Lodja Dem. Rep. Congo
119 D2 Lodwar Kenya
103 D1 Łódź Pol.
62 B2 Loei Thai.
122 A3 Loeriesfontein S. Africa
92 F2 Lofoten is Norway
134 D2 Logan U.S.A.
128 A1 Logan, Mount Can.
140 B2 Logansport U.S.A.
108 B1 Logatec Slovenia
118 B2 Logone r. Africa
106 C1 Logroño Spain
93 H3 Lohja Fin.
101 D1 Löhne Ger.
101 D1 Lohne (Oldenburg) Ger.
62 A2 Loikaw Myanmar
62 A2 Loi Lan mt. Myanmar/Thai.
93 H3 Loimaa Fin.
104 B2 Loire r. France
150 B3 Loja Ecuador
106 C2 Loja Spain
92 I2 Lokan tekojärvi l. Fin.
100 B2 Lokeren Belgium
122 B1 Lokgwabe Botswana
91 C1 Lokhvytsya Ukr.
119 D2 Lokichar Kenya
119 D2 Lokichokio Kenya
93 E4 Løkken Denmark
89 D2 Loknya Rus. Fed.
115 C4 Lokoja Nigeria
89 D3 Lokot' Rus. Fed.
88 C2 Loksa Estonia
127 H2 Loks Land i. Can.
114 B4 Lola Guinea
93 F5 Lolland i. Denmark
119 D3 Lollondo Tanz.
118 C2 Lolo Dem. Rep. Congo
122 B2 Lolwane S. Africa
110 B2 Lom Bulg.
93 E3 Lom Norway
119 C2 Lomami r. Dem. Rep. Congo
100 B2 Lommel Belgium
96 B2 Lomond, Loch l. U.K.
160 A1 Lomonosov Ridge sea feature Arctic Ocean
88 C2 Lomonosov Rus. Fed.
61 C2 Lompobattang, Gunung mt. Indon.
135 B4 Lompoc U.S.A.
63 B2 Lom Sak Thai.
103 E1 Łomża Pol.
130 B3 London Can.
99 C4 London U.K.
140 C3 London U.S.A.
97 C1 Londonderry U.K.
50 B1 Londonderry, Cape Austr.
154 C3 Londrina Brazil
135 C3 Lone Pine U.S.A.
83 M2 Longa, Proliv sea chan. Rus. Fed.
61 C1 Long Akah Sarawak Malaysia
143 E2 Long Bay U.S.A.
135 C4 Long Beach U.S.A.
71 A3 Longchuan China
99 C3 Long Eaton U.K.
97 C2 Longford Rep. of Ireland
96 C1 Longhope U.K.
119 D3 Longido Tanz.
61 C2 Longiram Indon.
147 C2 Long Island Bahamas

130 C2 Long Island Can.
59 D3 Long Island P.N.G.
141 E2 Long Island U.S.A.
130 B3 Longlac Can.
130 B3 Long Lake Can.
71 A3 Longli China
71 A3 Longming China
136 B2 Longmont U.S.A.
Longping China see Luodian
140 C2 Long Point Can.
71 B3 Longquan China
131 E3 Long Range Mountains Can.
51 D2 Longreach Austr.
Longshan China see Longli
99 D3 Long Stratton U.K.
98 B2 Longtown U.K.
105 D2 Longuyon France
139 E2 Longview TX U.S.A.
134 B1 Longview WA U.S.A.
61 C1 Longwai Indon.
70 A2 Longxi China
Longxian China see Wengyuan
71 B3 Longxi Shan mt. China
63 B2 Long Xuyên Vietnam
71 B3 Longyan China
82 C1 Longyearbyen Svalbard
108 B1 Lonigo Italy
100 C1 Löningen Ger.
105 D2 Lons-le-Saunier France
143 E2 Lookout, Cape U.S.A.
119 D3 Loolmalasin vol. crater Tanz.
50 B3 Loongana Austr.
97 B2 Loop Head hd Rep. of Ireland
Lopasnya Rus. Fed. see Chekhov
63 B2 Lop Buri Thai.
64 B2 Lopez Phil.
118 A3 Lopez, Cap c. Gabon
68 C2 Lop Nur salt l. China
118 B2 Lopori r. Dem. Rep. Congo
92 H1 Lopphavet b. Norway
106 B2 Lora del Río Spain
140 C2 Lorain U.S.A.
74 A1 Loralai Pak.
107 C2 Lorca Spain
51 E3 Lord Howe Island Austr.
138 B2 Lordsburg U.S.A.
155 C2 Lorena Brazil
59 D3 Lorengau P.N.G.
59 D3 Lorentz r. Indon.
152 B1 Loreto Bol.
144 A2 Loreto Mex.
104 B2 Lorient France
96 B2 Lorn, Firth of est. U.K.
52 B3 Lorne Austr.
139 C3 Lorraine reg. France
139 C3 Los Alamitos, Sierra de mt. Mex.
138 B1 Los Alamos U.S.A.
139 D3 Los Aldamas Mex.
153 A3 Los Angeles Chile
135 C4 Los Angeles U.S.A.
135 B3 Los Banos U.S.A.
152 B2 Los Blancos Arg.
144 B2 Los Caballos Mesteños, Llano de plain Mex.
153 A4 Los Chonos, Archipiélago de is Chile
149 C5 Los Desventurados, Islas de is S. Pacific Ocean
153 B5 Los Estados, Isla de i. Arg.
89 F3 Losevo Rus. Fed.
108 B2 Lošinj i. Croatia
144 B2 Los Mochis Mex.
146 B4 Los Mosquitos, Golfo de b. Panama
118 B2 Losombo Dem. Rep. Congo
106 B2 Los Pedroches plat. Spain
147 D3 Los Roques, Islas is Venez.
96 C2 Lossiemouth U.K.
150 C1 Los Teques Venez.
59 E3 Losuia P.N.G.
152 A3 Los Vilos Chile
104 C3 Lot r. France
96 C1 Loth U.K.
134 D1 Lothair U.S.A.
Lothringen reg. France see Lorraine
119 D2 Lotikipi Plain Kenya
118 C3 Loto Dem. Rep. Congo
89 E2 Lotoshino Rus. Fed.
62 B1 Louang Namtha Laos

62 B2 Louangphrabang Laos
118 B3 Loubomo Congo
104 B2 Loudéac France
71 B3 Loudi China
114 A3 Louga Senegal
99 C3 Loughborough U.K.
97 B2 Loughrea Rep. of Ireland
105 D2 Louhans France
97 B2 Louisburgh Rep. of Ireland
51 E1 Louisiade Archipelago is P.N.G.
142 B2 Louisiana state U.S.A.
123 C1 Louis Trichardt S. Africa
140 B3 Louisville KY U.S.A.
142 C2 Louisville MS U.S.A.
86 C2 Loukhi Rus. Fed.
118 B3 Loukoléla Congo
106 B2 Loulé Port.
118 A2 Loum Cameroon
130 C2 Loups-Marins, Lacs des lakes Can.
104 B3 Lourdes France
151 D2 Lourenço Brazil
Lourenço Marques Moz. see Maputo
106 B1 Lousã Port.
53 C2 Louth Austr.
98 C3 Louth U.K.
Louvain Belgium see Leuven
122 A1 Louwater-Suid Namibia
89 D2 Lovat' r. Rus. Fed.
110 B2 Lovech Bulg.
136 B2 Loveland U.S.A.
136 B2 Lovell U.S.A.
135 C2 Lovelock U.S.A.
88 C1 Loviisa Fin.
139 C2 Lovington U.S.A.
86 C2 Lovozero Rus. Fed.
119 C3 Lowa Dem. Rep. Congo
141 E2 Lowell U.S.A.
119 D2 Lowelli Sudan
128 C3 Lower Arrow Lake Can.
Lower California pen. Mex. see Baja California
54 B2 Lower Hutt N.Z.
97 C1 Lower Lough Erne l. U.K.
128 B2 Lower Post Can.
137 E1 Lower Red Lake U.S.A.
Lower Tunguska r. Rus. Fed. see Nizhnyaya Tunguska
99 D3 Lowestoft U.K.
103 D1 Łowicz Pol.
141 D2 Lowville U.S.A.
52 B2 Loxton Austr.
48 H6 Loyalty Islands New Caledonia
Loyang China see Luoyang
89 D3 Loyew Belarus
92 F2 Leypskardtinden mt. Norway
109 C2 Loznica Yugo.
91 D2 Lozova Ukr.
120 B2 Luacano Angola
70 B2 Lu'an China
120 A1 Luanda Angola
121 C2 Luangwa r. Zambia
121 B2 Luanshya Zambia
Luao Angola see Luau
106 B1 Luarca Spain
120 B2 Luau Angola
103 E1 Lubaczów Pol.
120 A2 Lubango Angola
119 C3 Lubao Dem. Rep. Congo
103 E1 Lubartów Pol.
101 D1 Lübbecke Ger.
102 C1 Lübben Ger.
139 C2 Lubbock U.S.A.
101 E1 Lübeck Ger.
69 E2 Lubei China
76 B1 Lubenka Kazakh.
119 C3 Lubero Dem. Rep. Congo
103 D1 Lubin Pol.
103 E1 Lublin Pol.
91 C1 Lubny Ukr.
61 C1 Lubok Antu Sarawak Malaysia
101 E1 Lübow Ger.
101 E1 Lübtheen Ger.
119 C3 Lubudi Dem. Rep. Congo
60 B2 Lubuklinggau Indon.
119 C4 Lubumbashi Dem. Rep. Congo
120 B2 Lubungu Zambia
119 C3 Lububu Dem. Rep. Congo
120 A1 Lucala Angola
97 C2 Lucan Rep. of Ireland

120 B1 Lucapa Angola
108 B2 Lucca Italy
96 B3 Luce Bay U.K.
154 B2 Lucélia Brazil
64 B2 Lucena Phil.
106 C2 Lucena Spain
103 D2 Lučenec Slovakia
109 C2 Lucera Italy
　Lucerne Switz. see Luzern
66 B1 Luchegorsk Rus. Fed.
101 E1 Lüchow Ger.
120 A2 Lucira Angola
　Łuck Ukr. see Luts'k
101 F1 Luckenwalde Ger.
122 B2 Luckhoff S. Africa
75 C2 Lucknow India
120 A1 Lucunga Angola
120 B2 Lucusse Angola
　Lüda China see Dalian
100 C2 Lüdenscheid Ger.
101 E1 Lüder Ger.
120 A3 Lüderitz Namibia
119 D4 Ludewa Tanz.
74 B1 Ludhiana India
140 B2 Ludington U.S.A.
99 B3 Ludlow U.K.
135 C4 Ludlow U.S.A.
110 C2 Ludogorie reg. Bulg.
93 G3 Ludvika Sweden
102 B2 Ludwigsburg Ger.
101 F1 Ludwigsfelde Ger.
101 D3 Ludwigshafen am Rhein Ger.
101 E1 Ludwigslust Ger.
88 C2 Ludza Latvia
118 C3 Luebo Dem. Rep. Congo
120 A2 Luena Angola
70 A2 Lüeyang China
71 B3 Lufeng China
119 C3 Lufira r. Dem. Rep. Congo
139 E2 Lufkin U.S.A.
88 C2 Luga Rus. Fed.
88 C2 Luga r. Rus. Fed.
105 D2 Lugano Switz.
121 C2 Lugenda r. Moz.
106 B1 Lugo Spain
110 B1 Lugoj Romania
91 D2 Luhans'k Ukr.
119 D3 Luhombero Tanz.
90 B1 Luhyny Ukr.
120 B2 Luiana Angola
　Luichow Peninsula China see Leizhou Bandao
118 C3 Luilaka r. Dem. Rep. Congo
　Luimneach Rep. of Ireland see Limerick
105 D2 Luino Italy
92 I2 Luiro r. Fin.
118 C3 Luiza Dem. Rep. Congo
70 B2 Lujiang China
　Lukapa Angola see Lucapa
109 C2 Lukavac Bos.-Herz.
118 B3 Lukenie r. Dem. Rep. Congo
138 A2 Lukeville U.S.A.
89 E3 Lukhovitsy Rus. Fed.
　Lukou China see Zhuzhou
103 E1 Łuków Pol.
120 B2 Lukulu Zambia
92 H2 Luleå Sweden
92 H2 Luleälven r. Sweden
111 C2 Lüleburgaz Turkey
70 B2 Lüliang Shan mts China
139 D3 Luling U.S.A.
　Luluabourg Dem. Rep. Congo see Kananga
61 C2 Lumajang Indon.
75 C1 Lumajangdong Co salt l. China
　Lumbala Angola see Lumbala Kaquengue
　Lumbala Kaquengue Angola see Lumbala N'guimbo
120 B2 Lumbala Kaquengue Angola
120 B2 Lumbala N'guimbo Angola
142 C2 Lumberton MS U.S.A.
143 E2 Lumberton NC U.S.A.
61 C1 Lumbis Indon.
106 B1 Lumbrales Spain
63 B2 Lumphăt Cambodia
129 D2 Lumsden Can.
54 A3 Lumsden N.Z.
93 F4 Lund Sweden
121 C2 Lundazi Zambia
99 A4 Lundy Island U.K.
101 E1 Lüneburg Ger.

101 E1 Lüneburger Heide reg. Ger.
100 C2 Lünen Ger.
105 D2 Lunéville France
120 B2 Lunga r. Zambia
114 A4 Lungi Sierra Leone
　Lungleh India see Lunglei
75 D2 Lunglei India
97 C2 Lungnaquilla Mountain hill Rep. of Ireland
120 B2 Lungwebungu r. Zambia
74 B2 Luni r. India
88 C3 Luninyets Belarus
104 C3 L'Union France
114 A4 Lunsar Sierra Leone
77 E2 Luntai China
71 A3 Luodian China
71 B3 Luoding China
70 B2 Luohe China
70 B2 Luoyang China
118 B3 Luozi Dem. Rep. Congo
121 B2 Lupane Zimbabwe
71 A3 Lupanshui China
110 B1 Lupeni Romania
121 C2 Lupilichi Moz.
101 F2 Luppa Ger.
95 B3 Lurgan U.K.
　Luring China see Gêrzê
121 C3 Lúrio Moz.
121 D2 Lurio r. Moz.
92 F2 Lurøy Norway
121 B2 Lusaka Zambia
118 C3 Lusambo Dem. Rep. Congo
109 C2 Lushnjë Albania
70 C2 Lushunkou China
123 C3 Lusikisiki S. Africa
136 C2 Lusk U.S.A.
　Luso Angola see Luena
76 B3 Lut, Dasht-e des. Iran
101 F2 Lutherstadt Wittenberg Ger.
99 C4 Luton U.K.
61 C1 Lutong Sarawak Malaysia
129 C1 Łutselk'e Can.
90 B1 Luts'k Ukr.
55 F3 Lützow-Holm Bay Antarctica
122 B2 Lutzputs S. Africa
122 A3 Lutzville S. Africa
117 C4 Luuq Somalia
137 D2 Luverne U.S.A.
119 C3 Luvua r. Dem. Rep. Congo
120 B2 Luvuei Angola
123 D1 Luvuvhu r. S. Africa
119 D3 Luwegu r. Tanz.
119 D2 Luwero Uganda
61 D2 Luwuk Indon.
100 C3 Luxembourg country Europe
100 C3 Luxembourg Lux.
105 D2 Luxeuil-les-Bains France
62 A1 Luxi China
123 C3 Luxolweni S. Africa
116 B2 Luxor Egypt
100 B2 Luyksgestel Neth.
86 D2 Luza Rus. Fed.
105 D2 Luzern Switz.
62 B1 Luzhai China
71 A3 Luzhi China
71 A3 Luzhou China
154 C1 Luziânia Brazil
151 E3 Luzilândia Brazil
64 B2 Luzon i. Phil.
64 B1 Luzon Strait Phil.
109 C3 Luzzi Italy
90 A2 L'viv Ukr.
　L'vov Ukr. see L'viv
　Lwów Ukr. see L'viv
88 C3 Lyakhavichy Belarus
　Lyallpur Pak. see Faisalabad
89 D2 Lychkovo Rus. Fed.
92 G3 Lycksele Sweden
55 C2 Lyddan Island Antarctica
123 D2 Lydenburg S. Africa
88 C3 Lyel'chytsy Belarus
88 C3 Lyepyel' Belarus
136 A2 Lyman U.S.A.
99 B4 Lyme Bay U.K.
99 B4 Lyme Regis U.K.
141 D3 Lynchburg U.S.A.
52 A2 Lyndhurst Austr.
129 E2 Lynn Lake Can.
134 B1 Lynnwood U.S.A.
129 D1 Lynx Lake Can.
105 C2 Lyon France
　Lyons France see Lyon
89 D2 Lyozna Belarus
103 E1 Lysica hill Pol.
86 E3 Lys'va Rus. Fed.

91 D2 Lysychans'k Ukr.
87 D3 Lysyye Gory Rus. Fed.
98 B3 Lytham St Anne's U.K.
88 C3 Lyuban' Belarus
90 C2 Lyubashivka Ukr.
89 E2 Lyubertsy Rus. Fed.
90 B1 Lyubeshiv Ukr.
89 F2 Lyubim Rus. Fed.
91 D2 Lyubotyn Ukr.
89 D2 Lyubytino Rus. Fed.
89 D3 Lyudinovo Rus. Fed.

M

80 B2 Ma'an Jordan
70 B2 Ma'anshan China
88 C2 Maardu Estonia
78 B3 Ma'ārid, Bani des. Saudi Arabia
80 B2 Ma'arrat an Nu'mān Syria
100 B1 Maarssen Neth.
100 B2 Maas r. Neth.
100 B2 Maaseik Belgium
64 B2 Maasin Phil.
100 B2 Maastricht Neth.
121 C3 Mabalane Moz.
78 B3 Ma'bar Yemen
150 D2 Mabaruma Guyana
98 D3 Mablethorpe U.K.
123 C2 Mabopane S. Africa
121 C3 Mabote Moz.
122 B2 Mabule Botswana
122 B1 Mabutsane Botswana
155 D2 Macaé Brazil
121 C2 Macaloge Moz.
126 F2 MacAlpine Lake Can.
151 D2 Macapá Brazil
150 B3 Macará Ecuador
155 D1 Macarani Brazil
　Macassar Indon. see Ujung Pandang
61 C2 Macassar Strait Indon.
121 C2 Macatanja Moz.
151 F3 Macau Brazil
69 D3 Macau China
71 B3 Macau special admin. reg. China
121 C3 Maccaretane Moz.
98 B3 Macclesfield U.K.
50 B2 Macdonald, Lake salt flat Austr.
50 C2 Macdonnell Ranges mts Austr.
130 A2 MacDowell Lake Can.
96 C2 Macduff U.K.
106 B1 Macedo de Cavaleiros Port.
52 B3 Macedon mt. Austr.
111 B2 Macedonia country Europe
151 F3 Maceió Brazil
108 B2 Macerata Italy
52 A2 Macfarlane, Lake salt flat Austr.
97 B3 Macgillycuddy's Reeks mts Rep. of Ireland
74 A2 Mach Pak.
155 C2 Machado Brazil
121 C3 Machaila Moz.
119 D3 Machakos Kenya
150 B3 Machala Ecuador
121 C3 Machanga Moz.
　Machaze Moz. see Chitobe
70 B2 Macheng China
140 B2 Machesney Park U.S.A.
141 F2 Machias U.S.A.
73 C3 Machilipatnam India
121 C2 Machinga Malawi
150 B1 Machiques Venez.
150 B4 Machupicchu Peru
99 B3 Machynlleth U.K.
123 D2 Macia Moz.
　Macias Nguema i. Equat. Guinea see Bioco
110 C1 Măcin Romania
53 D1 Macintyre r. Austr.
51 D2 Mackay Austr.
50 B2 Mackay, Lake salt flat Austr.
128 C1 MacKay Lake Can.
128 B2 Mackenzie Can.
128 A1 Mackenzie r. Can.
　Mackenzie Guyana see Linden
　Mackenzie atoll Micronesia see Ulithi
55 H3 Mackenzie Bay Antarctica

126 C2 Mackenzie Bay Can.
126 E1 Mackenzie King Island Can.
128 A1 Mackenzie Mountains Can.
　Mackillop, Lake salt flat Austr. see Yamma Yamma, Lake
129 D2 Macklin Can.
53 D2 Macksville Austr.
53 D1 Maclean Austr.
123 C3 Maclear S. Africa
50 A2 MacLeod, Lake imp. l. Austr.
140 A2 Macomb U.S.A.
108 A2 Macomer Sardinia Italy
121 D2 Macomia Moz.
105 C2 Mâcon France
143 D2 Macon GA U.S.A.
137 E3 Macon MO U.S.A.
142 C2 Macon MS U.S.A.
53 C2 Macquarie r. Austr.
48 G9 Macquarie Island S. Pacific Ocean
53 C2 Macquarie Marshes Austr.
53 C2 Macquarie Mountain Austr.
156 D9 Macquarie Ridge sea feature S. Pacific Ocean
55 H2 Mac. Robertson Land reg. Antarctica
97 B3 Macroom Rep. of Ireland
52 A1 Macumba watercourse Austr.
145 C3 Macuspana Mex.
144 B2 Macuzari, Presa resr Mex.
123 D2 Madadeni S. Africa
121 □D3 Madagascar country Africa
159 D5 Madagascar Ridge sea feature Indian Ocean
115 D2 Madama Niger
111 B2 Madan Bulg.
59 D3 Madang P.N.G.
141 D1 Madawaska r. Can.
62 A1 Madaya Myanmar
151 D3 Madeira r. Brazil
114 A1 Madeira terr. N. Atlantic Ocean
115 E2 Madeira is Port.
99 B3 Madeley U.K.
144 B2 Madera Mex.
135 B3 Madera U.S.A.
73 B3 Madgaon India
74 B2 Madhya Pradesh state India
123 C2 Madibogo S. Africa
118 B3 Madingou Congo
121 □D2 Madirovalo Madag.
140 B3 Madison IN U.S.A.
137 D2 Madison SD U.S.A.
140 B3 Madison WI U.S.A.
140 C3 Madison WV U.S.A.
134 D1 Madison r. U.S.A.
140 B3 Madisonville U.S.A.
61 C2 Madiun Indon.
119 D2 Mado Gashi Kenya
68 C2 Madoi China
88 C2 Madona Latvia
78 A2 Madrakah Saudi Arabia
79 C3 Madrakah, Ra's c. Oman
　Madras India see Chennai
134 B2 Madras U.S.A.
145 C2 Madre, Laguna lag. Mex.
139 D3 Madre, Laguna lag. U.S.A.
152 B1 Madre de Dios r. Peru
145 B3 Madre del Sur, Sierra mts Mex.
144 B2 Madre Occidental, Sierra mts Mex.
145 B2 Madre Oriental, Sierra mts Mex.
106 C1 Madrid Spain
106 C2 Madridejos Spain
61 C2 Madura i. Indon.
61 C2 Madura, Selat sea chan. Indon.
73 B4 Madurai India
121 □D2 Madziwadzido Zimbabwe
67 C3 Maebashi Japan
62 A2 Mae Hong Son Thai.
62 A2 Mae Sariang Thai.
99 B4 Maesteg U.K.
62 A2 Mae Suai Thai.
121 □D2 Maevatanana Madag.
　Mafeking S. Africa see Mafikeng
123 C2 Mafeteng Lesotho
53 C3 Maffra Austr.

119 D3 **Mafia Island** Tanz.
123 C2 **Mafikeng** S. Africa
119 D3 **Mafinga** Tanz.
154 C3 **Mafra** Brazil
83 L3 **Magadan** Rus. Fed.
Magallanes Chile see Punta Arenas
153 A5 **Magallanes, Estrecho de** sea chan. Chile
150 B2 **Magangue** Col.
142 B1 **Magazine Mountain** hill U.S.A.
114 A4 **Magburaka** Sierra Leone
69 E1 **Magdagachi** Rus. Fed.
144 A1 **Magdalena** Mex.
138 B2 **Magdalena** U.S.A.
144 A2 **Magdalena, Bahia** b. Mex.
101 E1 **Magdeburg** Ger.
Magellan, Strait of Chile see Magallanes, Estrecho de
108 A1 **Maggiore, Lago** l. Italy
Maggiore, Lake Italy see Maggiore, Lago
116 B2 **Maghagha** Egypt
97 C1 **Magherafelt** U.K.
87 E3 **Magnitogorsk** Rus. Fed.
142 B2 **Magnolia** U.S.A.
121 C2 **Magoe** Moz.
130 C3 **Magog** Can.
131 D2 **Magpie, Lac** l. Can.
114 A3 **Magta' Lahjar** Maur.
119 D3 **Magu** Tanz.
151 E3 **Maguarinho, Cabo** c. Brazil
123 D2 **Magude** Moz.
90 B2 **Magura, Dealul** hill Moldova
62 A1 **Magwe** Myanmar
81 C2 **Mahabad** Iran
74 B2 **Mahajan** India
121 □D2 **Mahajanga** Madag.
61 C2 **Mahakam** r. Indon.
123 C1 **Mahalapye** Botswana
121 □D2 **Mahalevona** Madag.
75 C2 **Mahanadi** r. India
121 □D2 **Mahanoro** Madag.
74 B3 **Maharashtra** state India
63 B2 **Maha Sarakham** Thai.
121 □D2 **Mahavavy** r. Madag.
68 B3 **Mahbubnagar** India
78 B2 **Mahd adh Dhahab** Saudi Arabia
107 D2 **Mahdia** Alg.
150 D2 **Mahdia** Guyana
113 I6 **Mahe** i. Seychelles
75 C3 **Mahendragiri** mt. India
119 D3 **Mahenge** Tanz.
54 B3 **Maheno** N.Z.
74 B2 **Mahesana** India
74 B2 **Mahi** r. India
54 C1 **Mahia Peninsula** N.Z.
89 D3 **Mahilyow** Belarus
107 D2 **Mahon** Spain
114 B3 **Mahou** Mali
Mahsana India see Mahesana
74 B2 **Mahuva** India
111 C2 **Mahya Dagi** mt. Turkey
106 B1 **Maia** Port.
Maiaia Moz. see Nacala
147 C3 **Maicao** Col.
129 D2 **Maidstone** Can.
99 D4 **Maidstone** U.K.
115 D3 **Maiduguri** Nigeria
75 D2 **Maijdi** Bangl.
75 C2 **Mailani** India
101 D2 **Main** r. Ger.
118 B3 **Mai-Ndombe, Lac** l. Dem. Rep. Congo
101 E3 **Main-Donau-Kanal** canal Ger.
141 F1 **Maine** state U.S.A.
131 D3 **Maine, Gulf of** Can./U.S.A.
62 A1 **Maingkwan** Myanmar
96 C1 **Mainland** i. Scotland U.K.
96 □ **Mainland** i. Scotland U.K.
121 □D2 **Maintirano** Madag.
101 D2 **Mainz** Ger.
150 C1 **Maiquetia** Venez.
120 B3 **Maitengwe** Botswana
53 D2 **Maitland** N.S.W. Austr.
52 A2 **Maitland** S.A. Austr.
146 B3 **Maiz, Islas del** is Nic.
67 C3 **Maizuru** Japan
109 C2 **Maja Jezerce** mt. Albania
61 C2 **Majene** Indon.
119 D2 **Maji** Eth.
Majorca i. Spain see Mallorca

Majunga Madag. see Mahajanga
123 C2 **Majwemasweu** S. Africa
118 B3 **Makabana** Congo
61 C2 **Makale** Indon.
119 C3 **Makamba** Burundi
77 E2 **Makanchi** Kazakh.
118 B2 **Makanza** Dem. Rep. Congo
90 B1 **Makariv** Ukr.
69 F1 **Makarov** Rus. Fed.
160 B1 **Makarov Basin** sea feature Arctic Ocean
109 C2 **Makarska** Croatia
Makassar Indon. see Ujung Pandang
76 B2 **Makat** Kazakh.
119 D3 **Makatapora** Tanz.
123 D2 **Makatini Flats** lowland S. Africa
114 A4 **Makeni** Sierra Leone
120 B3 **Makgadikgadi** salt pan Botswana
87 D4 **Makhachkala** Rus. Fed.
76 B2 **Makhambet** Kazakh.
119 D3 **Makindu** Kenya
77 D1 **Makinsk** Kazakh.
91 D2 **Makiyivka** Ukr.
Makkah Saudi Arabia see Mecca
131 E1 **Makkovik** Can.
103 E2 **Mako** Hungary
118 B2 **Makokou** Gabon
119 D3 **Makongolosi** Tanz.
122 B2 **Makopong** Botswana
119 C2 **Makoro** Dem. Rep. Congo
118 B3 **Makoua** Congo
111 B3 **Makrakomi** Greece
79 D2 **Makran** reg. Iran/Pak.
89 E2 **Maksatikha** Rus. Fed.
81 C2 **Maku** Iran
62 A1 **Makum** India
67 B4 **Makurazaki** Japan
115 C4 **Makurdi** Nigeria
92 G2 **Mala** Sweden
146 B4 **Mala, Punta** pt Panama
73 B3 **Malabar Coast** India
118 A2 **Malabo** Equat. Guinea
155 D1 **Malacacheta** Brazil
Malacca Malaysia see Melaka
60 B1 **Malacca, Strait of** Indon./Malaysia
134 D2 **Malad City** U.S.A.
88 C3 **Maladzyechna** Belarus
106 C2 **Malaga** Spain
Malagasy Republic country Africa see Madagascar
121 □D3 **Malaimbandy** Madag.
48 H4 **Malaita** i. Solomon Is
117 B4 **Malakal** Sudan
48 H5 **Malakula** i. Vanuatu
61 D2 **Malamala** Indon.
61 C2 **Malang** Indon.
Malange Angola see Malanje
120 A1 **Malanje** Angola
93 G4 **Malaren** l. Sweden
153 B3 **Malargue** Arg.
130 C3 **Malartic** Can.
88 B3 **Malaryta** Belarus
80 B2 **Malatya** Turkey
121 C2 **Malawi** country Africa
Malawi, Lake Africa see Nyasa, Lake
89 D2 **Malaya Vishera** Rus. Fed.
64 B3 **Malaybalay** Phil.
81 C2 **Malayer** Iran
60 B1 **Malaysia** country Asia
60 B1 **Malaysia, Semenanjung** pen. Malaysia
81 C2 **Malazgirt** Turkey
103 D1 **Malbork** Pol.
101 F1 **Malchin** Ger.
100 A2 **Maldegem** Belgium
48 L4 **Malden Island** Kiribati
56 C5 **Maldives** country Indian Ocean
99 D4 **Maldon** U.K.
153 C3 **Maldonado** Uru.
56 I9 **Male** Maldives
111 B3 **Maleas, Akra** pt Greece
103 D2 **Male Karpaty** hills Slovakia
119 C3 **Malela** Dem. Rep. Congo
116 A3 **Maleh** Sudan
134 C2 **Malheur Lake** U.S.A.
114 A3 **Mali** country Africa
114 A3 **Mali** Guinea
59 C3 **Maliana** East Timor

58 C3 **Malili** Indon.
97 C1 **Malin** Rep. of Ireland
119 E3 **Malindi** Kenya
97 C1 **Malin Head** hd Rep. of Ireland
97 B1 **Malin More** Rep. of Ireland
111 C2 **Malkara** Turkey
88 C3 **Mal'kavichy** Belarus
110 C2 **Malko Turnovo** Bulg.
53 C3 **Mallacoota** Austr.
53 C3 **Mallacoota Inlet** b. Austr.
96 B2 **Mallaig** U.K.
116 B2 **Mallawi** Egypt
128 A1 **Mallery Lake** Can.
107 D2 **Mallorca** i. Spain
97 B2 **Mallow** Rep. of Ireland
92 F3 **Malm** Norway
92 H2 **Malmberget** Sweden
100 C2 **Malmedy** Belgium
122 A3 **Malmesbury** S. Africa
93 F4 **Malmo** Sweden
71 A3 **Malong** China
118 C4 **Malonga** Dem. Rep. Congo
86 D2 **Maloshuyka** Rus. Fed.
93 E3 **Maloy** Norway
89 E2 **Maloyaroslavets** Rus. Fed.
89 E2 **Maloye Borisovo** Rus. Fed.
86 D2 **Malozemel'skaya Tundra** lowland Rus. Fed.
125 J9 **Malpelo, Isla de** i. N. Pacific Ocean
84 F5 **Malta** country Europe
88 C2 **Malta** Latvia
134 E1 **Malta** U.S.A.
122 A1 **Maltahohe** Namibia
98 C2 **Malton** U.K.
59 C3 **Maluku** is Indon.
93 F3 **Malung** Sweden
123 C2 **Maluti Mountains** Lesotho
73 B3 **Malvan** India
142 B2 **Malvern** U.S.A.
117 B4 **Malwal** Sudan
90 B1 **Malyn** Ukr.
83 L2 **Malyy Anyuy** r. Rus. Fed.
81 C1 **Malyy Kavkaz** mts Asia
83 K2 **Malyy Lyakhovskiy, Ostrov** i. Rus. Fed.
123 C2 **Mamafubedu** S. Africa
151 F3 **Mamanguape** Brazil
64 B3 **Mambajao** Phil.
119 C2 **Mambasa** Dem. Rep. Congo
118 B2 **Mambere** r. C.A.R.
64 B2 **Mamburao** Phil.
123 C2 **Mamelodi** S. Africa
118 A2 **Mamfe** Cameroon
135 C3 **Mammoth Lakes** U.S.A.
88 A3 **Mamonovo** Rus. Fed.
150 C4 **Mamore** r. Bol./Brazil
114 A3 **Mamou** Guinea
114 B4 **Mampong** Ghana
61 C2 **Mamuju** Indon.
114 B4 **Man** Cote d'Ivoire
150 C3 **Manacapuru** Brazil
107 D2 **Manacor** Spain
59 C2 **Manado** Indon.
146 B3 **Managua** Nic.
121 □D3 **Manakara** Madag.
78 B3 **Manakhah** Yemen
79 C2 **Manama** Bahrain
59 D3 **Manam Island** P.N.G.
121 □D2 **Mananara** r. Madag.
121 □D2 **Mananara Avaratra** Madag.
121 □D3 **Mananjary** Madag.
114 A3 **Manantali, Lac de** l. Mali
54 A3 **Manapouri, Lake** N.Z.
77 E2 **Manas Hu** l. China
75 C2 **Manaslu** mt. Nepal
Manastir Macedonia see Bitola
59 C3 **Manatuto** East Timor
150 C3 **Manaus** Brazil
80 B2 **Manavgat** Turkey
116 A3 **Manawashei** Sudan
98 B3 **Manchester** U.K.
141 E2 **Manchester** CT U.S.A.
141 E2 **Manchester** NH U.S.A.
142 C1 **Manchester** TN U.S.A.
81 D3 **Mand, Rud-e** r. Iran
117 A4 **Manda, Jebel** mt. Sudan
121 □D3 **Mandabe** Madag.
93 E4 **Mandal** Norway
59 D3 **Mandala, Puncak** mt. Indon.
62 A1 **Mandalay** Myanmar
68 D1 **Mandalgovi** Mongolia
136 C1 **Mandan** U.S.A.
118 B1 **Mandara Mountains** Cameroon/Nigeria

108 A3 **Mandas** Sardinia Italy
119 E2 **Mandera** Kenya
100 C2 **Manderscheid** Ger.
74 B1 **Mandi** India
114 B3 **Mandiana** Guinea
74 B1 **Mandi Burewala** Pak.
Mandidzuzure Zimbabwe see Chimanimani
75 C2 **Mandla** India
121 □D2 **Mandritsara** Madag.
74 B2 **Mandsaur** India
50 A3 **Mandurah** Austr.
73 B3 **Mandya** India
108 B1 **Manerbio** Italy
90 B1 **Manevychi** Ukr.
109 C2 **Manfredonia** Italy
109 C2 **Manfredonia, Golfo di** g. Italy
114 B3 **Manga** Burkina
118 B3 **Mangai** Dem. Rep. Congo
49 L6 **Mangaia** i. Cook Is
54 C1 **Mangakino** N.Z.
110 C2 **Mangalia** Romania
73 B3 **Mangalore** India
123 C2 **Mangaung** S. Africa
60 B2 **Manggar** Indon.
Mangghyshlaq Kazakh. see Mangistau
76 B2 **Mangistau** Kazakh.
61 C1 **Mangkalihat, Tanjung** pt Indon.
68 C2 **Mangnai** China
121 C2 **Mangochi** Malawi
121 □D3 **Mangoky** r. Madag.
59 C3 **Mangole** i. Indon.
54 B1 **Mangonui** N.Z.
106 B1 **Mangualde** Port.
154 B3 **Mangueirinha** Brazil
69 E1 **Mangui** China
Mangyshlak Kazakh. see Mangistau
137 D3 **Manhattan** U.S.A.
121 C3 **Manhica** Moz.
155 D2 **Manhuacu** Brazil
121 □D2 **Mania** r. Madag.
108 B1 **Maniago** Italy
121 C2 **Maniamba** Moz.
150 C3 **Manicore** Brazil
131 D3 **Manicouagan** r. Can.
131 D3 **Manicouagan, Reservoir** resr Can.
79 B2 **Manifah** Saudi Arabia
49 K5 **Manihiki** atoll Cook Is
53 D2 **Manilla** Austr.
111 C3 **Manisa** Turkey
107 C2 **Manises** Spain
140 B2 **Manistee** U.S.A.
140 B1 **Manistique** U.S.A.
129 E2 **Manitoba** prov. Can.
129 E2 **Manitoba, Lake** Can.
140 B1 **Manitou Islands** U.S.A.
130 B3 **Manitoulin Island** Can.
136 C3 **Manitou Springs** U.S.A.
130 B3 **Manitouwadge** Can.
140 B2 **Manitowoc** U.S.A.
130 C3 **Maniwaki** Can.
150 B2 **Manizales** Col.
121 □D3 **Manja** Madag.
121 C3 **Manjacaze** Moz.
137 E2 **Mankato** U.S.A.
114 B4 **Mankono** Cote d'Ivoire
129 D3 **Mankota** Can.
73 C4 **Mankulam** Sri Lanka
74 B2 **Manmad** India
52 A2 **Mannahill** Austr.
73 B4 **Mannar** Sri Lanka
73 B4 **Mannar, Gulf of** India/Sri Lanka
101 D3 **Mannheim** Ger.
128 C2 **Manning** Can.
52 A2 **Mannum** Austr.
129 C2 **Mannville** Can.
59 C3 **Manokwari** Indon.
119 C3 **Manono** Dem. Rep. Congo
63 A2 **Manoron** Myanmar
105 D3 **Manosque** France
131 C2 **Manouane, Lac** l. Can.
65 B1 **Manp'o** N. Korea
107 D1 **Manresa** Spain
121 B2 **Mansa** Zambia
127 G2 **Mansel Island** Can.
92 I2 **Mansel'kya** ridge Fin./Rus. Fed.
53 C3 **Mansfield** Austr.
98 C3 **Mansfield** U.K.
142 B1 **Mansfield** AR U.S.A.
142 B2 **Mansfield** LA U.S.A.
140 C2 **Mansfield** OH U.S.A.

141 D2 **Mansfield** *PA* U.S.A.
150 A3 **Manta** Ecuador
64 A3 **Mantalingajan, Mount** Phil.
155 D1 **Mantena** Brazil
143 E1 **Manteo** U.S.A.
104 C2 **Mantes-la-Jolie** France
155 C2 **Mantiqueira, Serra da** *mts* Brazil
108 B1 **Mantova** Italy
88 C1 **Mäntsälä** Fin.
    Mantua Italy *see* **Mantova**
86 D3 **Manturovo** Rus. Fed.
151 D3 **Manuelzinho** Brazil
61 D2 **Manui** *i.* Indon.
54 B1 **Manukau** N.Z.
59 D3 **Manus Island** P.N.G.
142 B2 **Many** U.S.A.
121 C2 **Manyame** *r.* Moz./Zimbabwe
119 D3 **Manyara, Lake** *salt l.* Tanz.
    Manyas Gölü *l.* Turkey *see* **Kuş Gölü**
87 D4 **Manych-Gudilo, Ozero** *l.* Rus. Fed.
138 B1 **Many Farms** U.S.A.
119 D3 **Manyoni** Tanz.
106 C2 **Manzanares** Spain
146 C2 **Manzanillo** Cuba
144 B3 **Manzanillo** Mex.
119 C3 **Manzanza** Dem. Rep. Congo
69 D1 **Manzhouli** China
123 D2 **Manzini** Swaziland
115 D3 **Mao** Chad
    Maó Spain *see* **Mahón**
59 D3 **Maoke, Pegunungan** *mts* Indon.
123 C2 **Maokeng** S. Africa
65 A1 **Maokui Shan** *mt.* China
70 A2 **Maomao Shan** *mt.* China
71 B3 **Maoming** China
121 C3 **Mapai** Moz.
75 C1 **Mapam Yumco** *l.* China
61 D2 **Mapane** Indon.
145 C3 **Mapastepec** Mex.
144 B2 **Mapimí** Mex.
144 B2 **Mapimí, Bolsón de** *des.* Mex.
64 A3 **Mapin** *i.* Phil.
121 C3 **Mapinhane** Moz.
129 D3 **Maple Creek** Can.
156 D4 **Mapmakers Seamounts** *sea feature* N. Pacific Ocean
59 D3 **Maprik** P.N.G.
123 D1 **Maputo** Moz.
121 C3 **Maputo** Moz.
123 D2 **Maputo** *r.* Moz./S. Africa
123 C2 **Maputsoe** Lesotho
114 A2 **Maqteïr** *reg.* Maur.
75 C2 **Maquan He** *r.* China
120 A1 **Maquela do Zombo** Angola
153 B4 **Maquinchao** Arg.
137 E2 **Maquoketa** U.S.A.
123 C1 **Mara** S. Africa
150 B1 **Mara** Venez.
150 C3 **Maraã** Brazil
151 E3 **Maraba** Brazil
151 D2 **Maracá, Ilha de** *i.* Brazil
150 B1 **Maracaibo** Venez.
150 B2 **Maracaibo, Lago de** *l.* Venez.
    Maracaibo, Lake Venez. *see* **Maracaibo, Lago de**
154 A2 **Maracaju** Brazil
154 A2 **Maracaju, Serra de** *hills* Brazil
150 C1 **Maracay** Venez.
115 D2 **Marādah** Libya
115 C3 **Maradi** Niger
81 C2 **Marāgheh** Iran
150 C2 **Marahuaca, Cerro** *mt.* Venez.
151 E3 **Marajó, Baía de** *est.* Brazil
151 D3 **Marajó, Ilha de** *i.* Brazil
79 C2 **Marākī** Iran
119 D2 **Maralal** Kenya
    Maralbashi China *see* **Bachu**
50 C3 **Maralinga** Austr.
    Maralwexi China *see* **Bachu**
138 A2 **Marana** U.S.A.
81 C2 **Marand** Iran
    Marandellas Zimbabwe *see* **Marondera**
150 B3 **Marañón** *r.* Peru
    Maraş Turkey *see* **Kahramanmaraş**

110 C1 **Mărăşeşti** Romania
130 B3 **Marathon** Can.
143 D4 **Marathon** U.S.A.
106 C2 **Marbella** Spain
50 A2 **Marble Bar** Austr.
123 C1 **Marble Hall** S. Africa
123 D3 **Marburg** S. Africa
101 D2 **Marburg an der Lahn** Ger.
103 D2 **Marcali** Hungary
137 E3 **Marceline** U.S.A.
99 D3 **March** U.K.
100 B2 **Marche-en-Famenne** Belgium
106 B2 **Marchena** Spain
152 B3 **Mar Chiquita, Lago** *l.* Arg.
150 B4 **Marcona** Peru
141 E2 **Marcy, Mount** U.S.A.
74 B1 **Mardan** Pak.
153 C3 **Mar del Plata** Arg.
96 B2 **Mardin** Turkey
51 D1 **Maree, Loch** *l.* U.K.
108 B3 **Mareeba** Austr.
    Marettimo, Isola *i.* Sicily Italy
89 D2 **Marevo** Rus. Fed.
138 C2 **Marfa** U.S.A.
    Margao India *see* **Madgaon**
50 A3 **Margaret River** Austr.
150 C1 **Margarita, Isla de** *i.* Venez.
123 D3 **Margate** S. Africa
99 D4 **Margate** U.K.
62 A1 **Margherita** India
    Margherita, Lake Eth. *see* **Ābaya Hāyk'**
119 C2 **Margherita Peak** Dem. Rep. Congo/Uganda
76 C3 **Margo, Dasht-i** *des.* Afgh.
91 C2 **Marhanets'** Ukr.
62 A1 **Mari** Myanmar
152 B2 **Maria Elena** Chile
156 C5 **Mariana Trench** *sea feature* N. Pacific Ocean
    Mariánica, Cordillera *mts* Spain *see* **Morena, Sierra**
142 B2 **Marianna** *AR* U.S.A.
143 C2 **Marianna** *FL* U.S.A.
102 C2 **Mariánské Lázně** Czech Rep.
144 B2 **Marias, Islas** *is* Mex.
78 B3 **Ma'rib** Yemen
109 C1 **Maribor** Slovenia
    Maricourt Can. *see* **Kangiqsujuaq**
119 C2 **Maridi** Sudan
117 A4 **Maridi** *watercourse* Sudan
55 P2 **Marie Byrd Land** *reg.* Antarctica
147 D3 **Marie-Galante** *i.* Guadeloupe
93 G3 **Mariehamn** Fin.
122 A1 **Mariental** Namibia
93 F4 **Mariestad** Sweden
143 D2 **Marietta** *GA* U.S.A.
140 C3 **Marietta** *OH* U.S.A.
105 D3 **Marignane** France
83 K3 **Marii, Mys** *pt* Rus. Fed.
88 B3 **Marijampolė** Lith.
154 C2 **Marília** Brazil
106 B1 **Marin** Spain
135 B3 **Marina** U.S.A.
109 C3 **Marina di Gioiosa Ionica** Italy
88 C3 **Mar"ina Horka** Belarus
140 B1 **Marinette** U.S.A.
154 B2 **Maringá** Brazil
106 B2 **Marinha Grande** Port.
140 B2 **Marion** *IN* U.S.A.
140 C2 **Marion** *OH* U.S.A.
143 E2 **Marion** *SC* U.S.A.
140 C3 **Marion** *VA* U.S.A.
143 D2 **Marion, Lake** U.S.A.
52 A3 **Marion Bay** Austr.
152 B2 **Mariscal Estigarribia** Para.
105 D3 **Maritime Alps** *mts* France/Italy
110 C2 **Maritsa** *r.* Bulg.
91 D2 **Mariupol'** Ukr.
117 C4 **Marka** Somalia
68 C3 **Markam** China
123 C1 **Marken** S. Africa
100 B1 **Markermeer** *l.* Neth.
98 C3 **Market Rasen** U.K.
98 C3 **Market Weighton** U.K.
83 I2 **Markha** *r.* Rus. Fed.
141 D2 **Markham** Can.
91 D2 **Markivka** Ukr.
118 B2 **Markounda** C.A.R.

142 B2 **Marksville** U.S.A.
101 D3 **Marktheidenfeld** Ger.
101 F2 **Marktredwitz** Ger.
100 C2 **Marl** Ger.
51 C2 **Marla** Austr.
100 A3 **Marle** France
139 D2 **Marlin** U.S.A.
53 C3 **Marlo** Austr.
104 C3 **Marmande** France
    Marmara, Sea of *g.* Turkey *see* **Marmara Denizi**
111 C2 **Marmara Denizi** *g.* Turkey
111 C3 **Marmaris** Turkey
105 C2 **Marne** *r.* France
105 C2 **Marne-la-Vallée** France
118 B2 **Maro** Chad
121 □D2 **Maroantsetra** Madag.
54 B1 **Marokopa** N.Z.
101 E2 **Maroldsweisach** Ger.
121 □D2 **Maromokotro** *mt.* Madag.
121 C2 **Marondera** Zimbabwe
151 D2 **Maroni** *r.* Fr. Guiana
51 E2 **Maroochydore** Austr.
61 C2 **Maros** Indon.
    Marotiri *is* Fr. Polynesia
118 B1 **Maroua** Cameroon
121 □D2 **Marovoay** Madag.
49 N4 **Marquesas Islands** Fr. Polynesia
143 D4 **Marquesas Keys** *is* U.S.A.
155 D2 **Marquês de Valença** Brazil
140 B1 **Marquette** U.S.A.
116 A3 **Marra, Jebel** *mt.* Sudan
123 D2 **Marracuene** Moz.
114 B1 **Marrakech** Morocco
    Marrakesh Morocco *see* **Marrakech**
116 A3 **Marra Plateau** Sudan
52 A1 **Marree** Austr.
86 F2 **Marresale** Rus. Fed.
121 C2 **Marromeu** Moz.
121 C2 **Marrupa** Moz.
115 D1 **Marsa Alam** Egypt
115 D1 **Marsa al Burayqah** Libya
119 D2 **Marsabit** Kenya
78 A2 **Marsa Delwein** Sudan
108 B3 **Marsala** Sicily Italy
116 A1 **Marsa Matrûh** Egypt
101 D2 **Marsberg** Ger.
108 B2 **Marsciano** Italy
53 C2 **Marsden** Austr.
100 B1 **Marsdiep** *sea chan.* Neth.
105 D3 **Marseille** France
    Marseilles France *see* **Marseille**
142 B1 **Marshall** *AR* U.S.A.
137 D2 **Marshall** *MN* U.S.A.
137 E3 **Marshall** *MO* U.S.A.
139 E2 **Marshall** *TX* U.S.A.
48 H2 **Marshall Islands** *country* N. Pacific Ocean
137 E2 **Marshalltown** U.S.A.
140 A2 **Marshfield** U.S.A.
146 C2 **Marsh Harbour** Bahamas
142 B3 **Marsh Island** U.S.A.
93 G4 **Märsta** Sweden
63 A2 **Martaban** Myanmar
63 A2 **Martaban, Gulf of** Myanmar
61 C2 **Martapura** Indon.
61 B2 **Martapura** Indon.
141 E2 **Martha's Vineyard** *i.* U.S.A.
105 D2 **Martigny** Switz.
103 D2 **Martin** Slovakia
136 C2 **Martin** U.S.A.
145 C2 **Martínez** Mex.
143 D2 **Martínez** U.S.A.
155 C1 **Martinho Campos** Brazil
147 D3 **Martinique** *terr.* West Indies
147 D3 **Martinique Passage** Dominica/Martinique
141 D3 **Martinsburg** U.S.A.
140 D3 **Martinsville** U.S.A.
54 C2 **Marton** N.Z.
107 D1 **Martorell** Spain
106 C2 **Martos** Spain
76 B1 **Marv Dasht** Iran
105 C3 **Marvejols** France
76 C3 **Mary** Turkm.
51 E2 **Maryborough** Austr.
122 B2 **Marydale** S. Africa
141 D3 **Maryland** *state* U.S.A.
98 B2 **Maryport** U.K.
137 D2 **Marysville** U.S.A.
137 E2 **Maryville** *MO* U.S.A.
143 D1 **Maryville** *TN* U.S.A.
119 D3 **Masai Steppe** *plain* Tanz.

119 D3 **Masaka** Uganda
61 C2 **Masalembu Besar** *i.* Indon.
61 C2 **Masamba** Indon.
65 B2 **Masan** S. Korea
119 D4 **Masasi** Tanz.
64 B2 **Masbate** Phil.
64 B2 **Masbate** *i.* Phil.
107 D2 **Mascara** Alg.
155 E1 **Mascote** Brazil
123 C2 **Maseru** Lesotho
    Mashaba Zimbabwe *see* **Mashava**
121 C3 **Mashava** Zimbabwe
76 B3 **Mashhad** Iran
123 C3 **Masibambane** S. Africa
79 C3 **Maşīlah, Wādī al** *watercourse* Yemen
123 C3 **Masilo** S. Africa
118 B3 **Masi-Manimba** Dem. Rep. Congo
119 D2 **Masindi** Uganda
122 B3 **Masinyusane** S. Africa
    Masira, Gulf of Oman *see* **Maşīrah, Gulf of**
79 C2 **Maşīrah** *i.* Oman
79 C3 **Maşīrah, Gulf of** Oman
81 C2 **Masjed Soleymān** Iran
97 B2 **Mask, Lough** *l.* Rep. of Ireland
121 □E2 **Masoala, Tanjona** *c.* Madag.
137 E2 **Mason City** U.S.A.
    Masqat Oman *see* **Muscat**
108 B2 **Massa** Italy
141 E2 **Massachusetts** *state* U.S.A.
141 E2 **Massachusetts Bay** U.S.A.
115 D3 **Massaguet** Chad
115 D3 **Massakory** Chad
121 C3 **Massangena** Moz.
120 A1 **Massango** Angola
116 B3 **Massawa** Eritrea
141 E2 **Massena** U.S.A.
115 D3 **Massenya** Chad
128 A2 **Masset** Can.
105 C2 **Massif Central** *mts* France
140 C2 **Massillon** U.S.A.
114 B3 **Massina** Mali
121 C3 **Massinga** Moz.
123 D1 **Massingir** Moz.
78 A2 **Mastābah** Saudi Arabia
54 C2 **Masterton** N.Z.
74 B1 **Mastuj** Pak.
74 A2 **Mastung** Pak.
78 A2 **Masturah** Saudi Arabia
88 B3 **Masty** Belarus
67 B4 **Masuda** Japan
    Masuku Gabon *see* **Franceville**
121 C3 **Masvingo** Zimbabwe
119 D3 **Maswe** Tanz.
118 B3 **Matadi** Dem. Rep. Congo
146 B3 **Matagalpa** Nic.
130 C3 **Matagami** Can.
130 C3 **Matagami, Lac** *l.* Can.
139 D3 **Matagorda Island** U.S.A.
139 D3 **Matagorda Peninsula** U.S.A.
120 A2 **Matala** Angola
114 A3 **Matam** Senegal
54 C1 **Matamata** N.Z.
144 B2 **Matamoros** Mex.
145 C2 **Matamoros** Mex.
119 D3 **Matandu** *r.* Tanz.
131 D3 **Matane** Can.
146 B2 **Matanzas** Cuba
73 C4 **Matara** Sri Lanka
61 C2 **Mataram** Indon.
50 C1 **Mataranka** Austr.
107 D1 **Mataró** Spain
123 C3 **Matatiele** S. Africa
54 A3 **Mataura** N.Z.
54 A3 **Mataura** *r.* N.Z.
54 C1 **Matawai** N.Z.
152 B1 **Mategua** Bol.
145 B2 **Matehuala** Mex.
109 C2 **Matera** Italy
114 C1 **Mateur** Tunisia
129 E2 **Matheson Island** Can.
139 D3 **Mathis** U.S.A.
74 B2 **Mathura** India
64 B3 **Mati** Phil.
145 C3 **Matias Romero** Mex.
98 C3 **Matlock** U.K.
150 D4 **Mato Grosso** Brazil

154 B1 **Mato Grosso, Planalto do** *plat.* Brazil
123 D2 **Matola** Moz.
106 B1 **Matosinhos** Port.
Matou China *see* **Pingguo**
79 C2 **Matraḥ** Oman
67 B3 **Matsue** Japan
66 D2 **Matsumae** Japan
67 C3 **Matsumoto** Japan
67 C4 **Matsusaka** Japan
71 C3 **Matsu Tao** *i.* Taiwan
67 B4 **Matsuyama** Japan
130 B2 **Mattagami** *r.* Can.
130 C3 **Mattawa** Can.
105 D2 **Matterhorn** *mt.* Italy/Switz.
134 C2 **Matterhorn** *mt.* U.S.A.
143 D1 **Matthews** U.S.A.
79 C2 **Maṭṭi, Sabkhat** *salt pan* Saudi Arabia
140 B3 **Mattoon** U.S.A.
150 C2 **Maturín** Venez.
91 D2 **Matveyev Kurgan** Rus. Fed.
123 C2 **Matwabeng** S. Africa
75 C2 **Mau** India
105 C1 **Maubeuge** France
104 C3 **Maubourguet** France
55 E3 **Maud Seamount** *sea feature* S. Atlantic Ocean
49 L1 **Maui** *i.* U.S.A.
143 D2 **Mauldin** U.S.A.
140 C2 **Maumee** *r.* U.S.A.
61 D2 **Maumere** Indon.
120 B2 **Maun** Botswana
123 C1 **Maunatlala** Botswana
62 A1 **Maungdaw** Myanmar
75 B2 **Mau Rampur** India
50 C2 **Maurice, Lake** *salt flat* Austr.
114 A3 **Mauritania** *country* Africa
113 I8 **Mauritius** *country* Indian Ocean
120 B2 **Mavinga** Angola
123 C3 **Mavuya** S. Africa
78 B2 **Māwān, Khashm** *hill* Saudi Arabia
118 B3 **Mawanga** Dem. Rep. Congo
71 B3 **Mawei** China
62 A1 **Mawkmai** Myanmar
62 A1 **Mawlaik** Myanmar
78 B2 **Mawqaq** Saudi Arabia
55 L3 **Mawson Peninsula** Antarctica
78 B3 **Mawza** Yemen
108 A3 **Maxia, Punta** *mt.* Sardinia Italy
121 C3 **Maxixe** Moz.
54 B1 **Maxwell** N.Z.
83 J2 **Maya** *r.* Rus. Fed.
147 C2 **Mayaguana** *i.* Bahamas
147 D3 **Mayagüez** Puerto Rico
81 D2 **Mayamey** Iran
96 B3 **Maybole** U.K.
116 B3 **Maych'ew** Eth.
117 C3 **Maydh** Somalia
100 C2 **Mayen** Ger.
104 C2 **Mayenne** France
104 B2 **Mayenne** *r.* France
128 C2 **Mayerthorpe** Can.
140 B3 **Mayfield** U.S.A.
91 E3 **Maykop** Rus. Fed.
62 A1 **Maymyo** Myanmar
128 A1 **Mayo** *r.* Can.
118 B3 **Mayo** Congo
Mayo Landing Can. *see* **Mayo**
64 B2 **Mayon** *vol.* Phil.
121 D2 **Mayotte** *terr.* Africa
83 J3 **Mayskiy** Rus. Fed.
140 C3 **Maysville** U.S.A.
118 B3 **Mayumba** Gabon
137 D1 **Mayville** U.S.A.
120 B2 **Mazabuka** Zambia
Mazagan Morocco *see* **El Jadida**
151 D3 **Mazagão** Brazil
104 C3 **Mazamet** France
74 B1 **Mazar** China
108 B3 **Mazara del Vallo** Sicily Italy
77 C3 **Mazār-e Sharīf** Afgh.
107 C2 **Mazarrón** Spain
107 C2 **Mazarrón, Golfo de** *b.* Spain
144 A2 **Mazatán** Mex.
146 A3 **Mazatenango** Guat.
144 B2 **Mazatlán** Mex.
88 B2 **Mažeikiai** Lith.
88 B2 **Mazirbe** Latvia

121 B3 **Mazunga** Zimbabwe
103 E1 **Mazurskie, Pojezierze** *reg.* Pol.
88 C3 **Mazyr** Belarus
123 D2 **Mbabane** Swaziland
118 B2 **Mbaïki** C.A.R.
118 B2 **Mbakaou, Lac de** *l.* Cameroon
121 C1 **Mbala** Zambia
121 B3 **Mbalabala** Zimbabwe
119 D2 **Mbale** Uganda
118 B2 **Mbalmayo** Cameroon
118 B3 **Mbandaka** Dem. Rep. Congo
118 B2 **Mbandjok** Cameroon
118 A2 **Mbanga** Cameroon
120 A1 **M'banza Congo** Angola
118 B3 **Mbanza-Ngungu** Dem. Rep. Congo
119 D3 **Mbarara** Uganda
118 B2 **Mbé** Cameroon
119 D3 **Mbeya** Tanz.
119 D4 **Mbinga** Tanz.
119 D3 **Mbizi Mountains** Tanz.
119 C3 **Mboki** C.A.R.
118 B2 **Mbomo** Congo
118 B2 **Mbouda** Cameroon
114 A3 **Mbour** Senegal
114 A3 **Mbout** Maur.
118 C3 **Mbuji-Mayi** Dem. Rep. Congo
119 D3 **Mbuyuni** Tanz.
141 F1 **McAdam** Can.
139 D2 **McAlester** U.S.A.
139 D3 **McAllen** U.S.A.
128 B2 **McBride** Can.
134 C2 **McCall** U.S.A.
139 C2 **McCamey** U.S.A.
126 F2 **McClintock Channel** Can.
126 E2 **McClure Strait** Can.
142 B2 **McComb** U.S.A.
136 C2 **McConaughy, Lake** U.S.A.
136 C2 **McCook** U.S.A.
134 C2 **McDermitt** U.S.A.
159 E7 **McDonald Islands** Indian Ocean
134 D1 **McDonald Peak** U.S.A.
135 D3 **McGill** U.S.A.
126 B2 **McGrath** U.S.A.
134 D1 **McGuire, Mount** U.S.A.
121 C2 **Mchinji** Malawi
142 C1 **McKenzie** U.S.A.
51 D2 **McKinlay** Austr.
134 B2 **McKinleyville** U.S.A.
128 C2 **McLennan** Can.
128 B2 **McLeod Lake** Can.
134 B1 **McMinnville** *OR* U.S.A.
142 C1 **McMinnville** *TN* U.S.A.
137 D3 **McPherson** U.S.A.
128 C1 **McTavish Arm** *b.* Can.
123 C3 **Mdantsane** S. Africa
135 D3 **Mead, Lake** *resr* U.S.A.
136 C3 **Meade** U.S.A.
129 D2 **Meadow Lake** Can.
140 C2 **Meadville** U.S.A.
66 D2 **Meaken-dake** *vol.* Japan
106 B1 **Mealhada** Port.
131 E2 **Mealy Mountains** Can.
128 C2 **Meander River** Can.
78 A2 **Mecca** Saudi Arabia
141 D3 **Mechanicsville** U.S.A.
100 B2 **Mechelen** Belgium
100 B2 **Mechelen** Neth.
100 C2 **Mechernich** Ger.
100 C2 **Meckenheim** Ger.
101 E1 **Mecklenburgische Seenplatte** *reg.* Ger.
106 B1 **Meda** Port.
60 A1 **Medan** Indon.
153 B4 **Medanosa, Punta** *pt* Arg.
73 C4 **Medawachchiya** Sri Lanka
107 D2 **Médéa** Alg.
150 B2 **Medellín** Col.
115 D1 **Medenine** Tunisia
134 B2 **Medford** U.S.A.
110 C2 **Medgidia** Romania
110 B1 **Mediaş** Romania
136 B2 **Medicine Bow Mountains** U.S.A.
136 B2 **Medicine Bow Peak** U.S.A.
129 C2 **Medicine Hat** Can.
137 D3 **Medicine Lodge** U.S.A.
155 D1 **Medina** Brazil
78 A2 **Medina** Saudi Arabia
106 C1 **Medinaceli** Spain
106 C1 **Medina del Campo** Spain
106 B1 **Medina de Rioseco** Spain
75 C2 **Medinipur** India
84 E5 **Mediterranean Sea**

129 C2 **Medley** Can.
87 E3 **Mednogorsk** Rus. Fed.
62 A1 **Mêdog** China
88 B2 **Medvêgalio kalnis** *hill* Lith.
83 L2 **Medvezh'i, Ostrova** *is* Rus. Fed.
86 C2 **Medvezh'yegorsk** Rus. Fed.
50 A2 **Meekatharra** Austr.
136 B2 **Meeker** U.S.A.
74 B2 **Meerut** India
100 A2 **Meetkerke** Belgium
119 D2 **Mêga** Eth.
119 D2 **Mega Escarpment** Eth./Kenya
111 B3 **Megalopoli** Greece
75 D2 **Meghalaya** *state* India
75 C2 **Meghāsani** *mt.* India
111 C3 **Megisti** *i.* Greece
92 I1 **Mehamn** Norway
50 A2 **Meharry, Mount** Austr.
137 E3 **Mehlville** U.S.A.
79 C2 **Mehrān** *watercourse* Iran
74 B1 **Mehtar Lām** Afgh.
119 D3 **Meia Meia** Tanz.
154 C1 **Meia Ponte** *r.* Brazil
118 B2 **Meiganga** Cameroon
65 B1 **Meihekou** China
Meijiang China *see* **Ningdu**
62 A1 **Meiktila** Myanmar
101 E2 **Meiningen** Ger.
102 C1 **Meißen** Ger.
Meixian China *see* **Meizhou**
71 B3 **Meizhou** China
152 B2 **Mejicana** *mt.* Arg.
152 A2 **Mejillones** Chile
118 B2 **Mékambo** Gabon
116 B3 **Mek'elê** Eth.
114 C2 **Mekerrhane, Sebkha** *salt pan* Alg.
114 B1 **Meknès** Morocco
63 B2 **Mekong** *r.* Asia
63 B3 **Mekong, Mouths of the** Vietnam
60 B1 **Melaka** Malaysia
156 D6 **Melanesia** International Feature
156 D5 **Melanesian Basin** *sea feature* Pacific Ocean
53 B3 **Melbourne** Austr.
143 D3 **Melbourne** U.S.A.
108 A2 **Mele, Capo** *c.* Italy
Melekess Rus. Fed. *see* **Dimitrovgrad**
89 F2 **Melenki** Rus. Fed.
131 C2 **Mélèzes, Rivière aux** *r.* Can.
115 D3 **Mélfi** Chad
109 C2 **Melfi** Italy
129 D2 **Melfort** Can.
92 F3 **Melhus** Norway
106 B1 **Melide** Spain
114 B1 **Melilla** N. Africa
129 D3 **Melita** Can.
91 D2 **Melitopol'** Ukr.
119 D2 **Melka Guba** Eth.
101 D1 **Melle** Ger.
93 F4 **Mellerud** Sweden
101 D1 **Mellrichstadt** Ger.
101 D1 **Mellum** *i.* Ger.
123 D2 **Melmoth** S. Africa
152 C3 **Melo** Uru.
115 C1 **Melrhir, Chott** *salt l.* Alg.
96 C3 **Melrose** U.K.
Melsetter Zimbabwe *see* **Chimanimani**
52 B3 **Melton** Austr.
99 C3 **Melton Mowbray** U.K.
105 C2 **Melun** France
129 D2 **Melville** Can.
51 D1 **Melville, Cape** Austr.
131 E2 **Melville, Lake** Can.
50 C1 **Melville Island** Austr.
126 E1 **Melville Island** Can.
127 G2 **Melville Peninsula** Can.
61 C2 **Memboro** Indon.
102 C2 **Memmingen** Ger.
60 B1 **Mempawah** Indon.
80 B3 **Memphis** *tourist site* Egypt
142 B1 **Memphis** *TN* U.S.A.
139 C2 **Memphis** *TX* U.S.A.
91 C1 **Mena** Ukr.
142 B2 **Mena** U.S.A.
121 □D3 **Menabe** *mts* Madag.
114 C3 **Ménaka** Mali
Mènam Khong *r.* Laos/Thai. *see* **Mekong**
105 C3 **Mende** France
117 B4 **Mendebo Mountains** Eth.

116 B3 **Mendefera** Eritrea
160 B1 **Mendeleyev Ridge** *sea feature* Arctic Ocean
145 C2 **Méndez** Mex.
117 B4 **Mendī** Eth.
59 D3 **Mendi** P.N.G.
99 B4 **Mendip Hills** U.K.
140 B2 **Mendota** U.S.A.
153 B3 **Mendoza** Arg.
111 C3 **Menemen** Turkey
100 A2 **Menen** Belgium
70 B2 **Mengcheng** China
60 B2 **Menggala** Indon.
71 A3 **Mengzi** China
131 D2 **Menihek** Can.
52 B2 **Menindee** Austr.
52 B2 **Menindee Lake** Austr.
52 A3 **Meningie** Austr.
104 C2 **Mennecy** France
140 B1 **Menominee** U.S.A.
120 A2 **Menongue** Angola
107 D1 **Menorca** *i.* Spain
61 C1 **Mensalong** Indon.
60 A2 **Mentawai, Kepulauan** *is* Indon.
60 B2 **Mentok** Indon.
61 C1 **Menyapa, Gunung** *mt.* Indon.
108 A3 **Menzel Bourguiba** Tunisia
50 B2 **Menzies** Austr.
144 B2 **Meoqui** Mex.
100 C1 **Meppel** Neth.
100 C1 **Meppen** Ger.
121 C3 **Mepuze** Moz.
123 C2 **Meqheleng** S. Africa
140 B2 **Mequon** U.S.A.
108 B1 **Merano** Italy
59 D3 **Merauke** Indon.
52 B2 **Merbein** Austr.
Merca Somalia *see* **Marka**
107 D2 **Mercadal** Spain
135 B3 **Merced** U.S.A.
152 C2 **Mercedes** Arg.
153 B3 **Mercedes** Arg.
139 D3 **Mercedes** U.S.A.
127 H2 **Mercy, Cape** Can.
139 C1 **Meredith, Lake** U.S.A.
91 D2 **Merefa** Ukr.
116 A3 **Merga Oasis** Sudan
63 A2 **Mergui** Myanmar
63 A2 **Mergui Archipelago** *is* Myanmar
110 C2 **Meriç** *r.* Greece/Turkey
111 C2 **Meriç** Turkey
145 D2 **Mérida** Mex.
106 B2 **Mérida** Spain
150 B2 **Mérida** Venez.
147 C4 **Mérida, Cordillera de** *mts* Venez.
134 C2 **Meridian** *ID* U.S.A.
142 C2 **Meridian** *MS* U.S.A.
139 D2 **Meridian** *TX* U.S.A.
104 B3 **Mérignac** France
93 H3 **Merikarvia** Fin.
53 C3 **Merimbula** Austr.
88 B3 **Merkinė** Lith.
116 B3 **Merowe** Sudan
50 A3 **Merredin** Austr.
96 B3 **Merrick** *hill* U.K.
140 B1 **Merrill** U.S.A.
140 B2 **Merrillville** U.S.A.
136 C2 **Merriman** U.S.A.
128 B2 **Merritt** Can.
53 C2 **Merrygoen** Austr.
116 C3 **Mersa Fatma** Eritrea
100 C3 **Mersch** Lux.
101 E2 **Merseburg (Saale)** Ger.
98 B2 **Mersey** *r.* U.K.
Mersin Turkey *see* **İçel**
60 B1 **Mersing** Malaysia
99 C4 **Mers-les-Bains** France
74 B2 **Merta** India
99 B4 **Merthyr Tydfil** U.K.
119 D2 **Merti Plateau** Kenya
106 B2 **Mértola** Port.
119 D3 **Meru** *vol.* Tanz.
122 B3 **Merweville** S. Africa
80 B1 **Merzifon** Turkey
100 C3 **Merzig** Ger.
138 A2 **Mesa** *AZ* U.S.A.
138 C2 **Mesa** *NM* U.S.A.
137 E1 **Mesabi Range** *hills* U.S.A.
109 C2 **Mesagne** Italy
138 B2 **Mescalero** U.S.A.
139 C2 **Mescalero Ridge** U.S.A.
101 D2 **Meschede** Ger.
89 E3 **Meshchovsk** Rus. Fed.
Meshed Iran *see* **Mashhad**
91 E2 **Meshkovskaya** Rus. Fed.
138 B2 **Mesilla** U.S.A.
111 B2 **Mesimeri** Greece

111 B3 **Mesolongi** Greece
115 C1 **Messaad** Alg.
121 D2 **Messalo** r. Moz.
109 C3 **Messina** Sicily Italy
123 D1 **Messina** S. Africa
Messina, Strait of Italy *see* **Messina, Stretta di**
109 C3 **Messina, Stretta di** str. Italy
111 B3 **Messini** Greece
111 B3 **Messiniakos Kolpos** b. Greece
111 B2 **Mesta** r. Bulg.
Mesta r. Greece *see* **Nestos**
150 C2 **Meta** r. Col./Venez.
130 C3 **Métabetchouan** Can.
127 H2 **Meta Incognita Peninsula** Can.
142 B3 **Metairie** U.S.A.
152 B2 **Metán** Arg.
111 B3 **Methoni** Greece
109 C3 **Metković** Croatia
121 C2 **Metoro** Moz.
60 C1 **Metro** Indon.
100 C3 **Mettlach** Ger.
135 C3 **Mettler** U.S.A.
117 B4 **Metu** Eth.
105 D2 **Metz** France
100 B2 **Meuse** r. Belgium/France
139 D2 **Mexia** U.S.A.
144 A1 **Mexicali** Mex.
144 A1 **Mexico** country Central America
145 C3 **México** Mex.
137 E3 **Mexico** U.S.A.
125 I7 **Mexico, Gulf of** Mex./U.S.A.
Mexico City Mex. *see* **México**
81 D2 **Meybod** Iran
101 F1 **Meyenburg** Ger.
76 C3 **Meymaneh** Afgh.
83 M2 **Meynypil'gyno** Rus. Fed.
86 D2 **Mezen'** Rus. Fed.
86 D2 **Mezen'** r. Rus. Fed.
86 E1 **Mezhdusharskiy, Ostrov** i. Rus. Fed.
103 E2 **Mezőtúr** Hungary
132 C4 **Mezquital** r. Mex.
144 B2 **Mezquitic** Mex.
88 C2 **Mežvidi** Latvia
121 C2 **Mfuwe** Zambia
89 D3 **Mglin** Rus. Fed.
123 D2 **Mhlume** Swaziland
74 B2 **Mhow** India
145 C3 **Miahuatlán** Mex.
106 B2 **Miajadas** Spain
143 D3 **Miami** FL U.S.A.
139 E1 **Miami** OK U.S.A.
143 D3 **Miami Beach** U.S.A.
81 C2 **Miandowāb** Iran
121 □D2 **Miandrivazo** Madag.
81 C2 **Miāneh** Iran
71 A3 **Mianning** China
74 B1 **Mianwali** Pak.
Mianyang China *see* **Xiantao**
70 A2 **Mianyang** China
121 □D2 **Miarinarivo** Madag.
87 F3 **Miass** Rus. Fed.
103 D1 **Miastko** Pol.
128 C2 **Mica Creek** Can.
103 E2 **Michalovce** Slovakia
140 B1 **Michigan** state U.S.A.
140 B2 **Michigan City** U.S.A.
140 B2 **Michigan, Lake** U.S.A.
140 B1 **Michipicoten Bay** Can.
130 B3 **Michipicoten Island** Can.
130 B3 **Michipicoten River** Can.
Michurin Bulg. *see* **Tsarevo**
89 F3 **Michurinsk** Rus. Fed.
156 D5 **Micronesia** is Pacific Ocean
158 E6 **Mid-Atlantic Ridge** sea feature Atlantic Ocean
100 A2 **Middelburg** Neth.
123 C3 **Middelburg** S. Africa
123 C2 **Middelburg** S. Africa
100 B2 **Middelharnis** Neth.
134 B2 **Middle Alkali Lake** U.S.A.
73 D3 **Middle Andaman** i. India
Middle Congo country Africa *see* **Congo**
136 D2 **Middle Loup** r. U.S.A.
140 C3 **Middlesboro** U.S.A.
98 C2 **Middlesbrough** U.K.
141 E2 **Middletown** NY U.S.A.
140 C3 **Middletown** OH U.S.A.

78 B3 **Midi** Yemen
130 C3 **Midland** Can.
140 C2 **Midland** MI U.S.A.
139 C2 **Midland** TX U.S.A.
97 B3 **Midleton** Rep. of Ireland
Midnapore India *see* **Medinipur**
94 B1 **Miðvágur** Faroe Is
Midway Oman *see* **Thamarīt**
57 T7 **Midway Islands** terr. N. Pacific Ocean
109 D2 **Midzhur** mt. Bulg./Yugo.
103 E1 **Mielec** Pol.
110 C1 **Miercurea-Ciuc** Romania
106 B1 **Mieres** Spain
101 E1 **Mieste** Ger.
145 C3 **Miguel Alemán, Presa** resr Mex.
144 B2 **Miguel Auza** Mex.
144 B2 **Miguel Hidalgo, Presa** resr Mex.
63 A2 **Migyaunglaung** Myanmar
67 B4 **Mihara** Japan
89 E3 **Mikhaylov** Rus. Fed.
Mikhaylovgrad Bulg. *see* **Montana**
66 B2 **Mikhaylovka** Rus. Fed.
Mikhaylovka Rus. Fed. *see* **Kimovsk**
87 D3 **Mikhaylovka** Rus. Fed.
77 D1 **Mikhaylovskiy** Rus. Fed.
93 I3 **Mikkeli** Fin.
86 E2 **Mikun'** Rus. Fed.
67 C3 **Mikuni-sanmyaku** mts Japan
73 B4 **Miladhunmadulu Atoll** Maldives
108 A1 **Milan** Italy
121 C2 **Milange** Moz.
Milano Italy *see* **Milan**
111 C3 **Milas** Turkey
137 D1 **Milbank** U.S.A.
99 D3 **Mildenhall** U.K.
52 B2 **Mildura** Austr.
71 A3 **Mile** China
136 B1 **Miles City** U.S.A.
141 D3 **Milford** DE U.S.A.
135 D3 **Milford** UT U.S.A.
99 A4 **Milford Haven** U.K.
54 A2 **Milford Sound** N.Z.
Milh, Baḥr al l. Iraq *see* **Razāzah, Buḥayrat ar**
107 D2 **Miliana** Alg.
50 C1 **Milikapiti** Austr.
51 C1 **Milingimbi** Austr.
134 E1 **Milk** r. U.S.A.
116 B3 **Milk, Wadi el** watercourse Sudan
83 L3 **Mil'kovo** Rus. Fed.
128 C3 **Milk River** Can.
105 C3 **Millau** France
143 D2 **Milledgeville** U.S.A.
137 E1 **Mille Lacs** lakes U.S.A.
130 A3 **Mille Lacs, Lac des** l. Can.
137 D2 **Miller** U.S.A.
91 E2 **Millerovo** Rus. Fed.
52 A2 **Millers Creek** Austr.
96 B3 **Milleur Point** U.K.
52 B3 **Millicent** Austr.
142 C1 **Millington** U.S.A.
141 F1 **Millinocket** U.S.A.
55 J3 **Mill Island** Antarctica
53 D1 **Millmerran** Austr.
98 B2 **Millom** U.K.
136 B2 **Mills** U.S.A.
128 C1 **Mills Lake** Can.
111 B3 **Milos** i. Greece
89 E3 **Miloslavskoye** Rus. Fed.
91 E2 **Milove** Ukr.
52 B1 **Milparinka** Austr.
54 A3 **Milton** N.Z.
99 C3 **Milton Keynes** U.K.
140 B2 **Milwaukee** U.S.A.
158 C3 **Milwaukee Deep** sea feature Caribbean Sea
111 B2 **Mimizan** France
118 B3 **Mimongo** Gabon
155 D2 **Mimoso do Sul** Brazil
79 C2 **Mīnāb** Iran
61 D1 **Minahasa, Semenanjung** pen. Indon.
Minahasa, Semenanjung Indon. *see* **Minahassa Peninsula**
79 C2 **Mina Jebel Ali** U.A.E.
60 B1 **Minas** Indon.

153 C3 **Minas** Uru.
79 B2 **Minā' Sa'ūd** Kuwait
155 D1 **Minas Novas** Brazil
145 C3 **Minatitlán** Mex.
62 A1 **Minbu** Myanmar
64 B3 **Mindanao** i. Phil.
52 B2 **Mindarie** Austr.
101 D1 **Minden** Ger.
142 B2 **Minden** LA U.S.A.
137 D2 **Minden** NE U.S.A.
64 B2 **Mindoro** i. Phil.
64 A2 **Mindoro Strait** Phil.
118 B3 **Mindouli** Congo
99 B4 **Minehead** U.K.
154 B1 **Mineiros** Brazil
139 D2 **Mineral Wells** U.S.A.
75 C1 **Minfeng** China
119 C4 **Minga** Dem. Rep. Congo
81 C1 **Mingāçevir** Azer.
131 D2 **Mingan** Can.
52 B2 **Mingary** Austr.
70 B2 **Mingguang** China
62 A1 **Mingin** Myanmar
107 C2 **Minglanilla** Spain
119 D4 **Mingoyo** Tanz.
69 E1 **Mingshui** China
96 A2 **Mingulay** i. U.K.
71 B3 **Mingxi** China
Mingzhou China *see* **Suide**
70 A2 **Minhe** China
73 B4 **Minicoy** i. India
50 C1 **Minilya** Austr.
114 B3 **Mininian** Côte d'Ivoire
131 D2 **Minipi Lake** Can.
130 A2 **Miniss Lake** Can.
52 A2 **Minlaton** Austr.
115 C4 **Minna** Nigeria
129 E2 **Minnedosa** Can.
137 E2 **Minneapolis** U.S.A.
137 E1 **Minnesota** r. U.S.A.
137 E1 **Minnesota** state U.S.A.
106 B1 **Miño** r. Port./Spain
Minorca i. Spain *see* **Menorca**
136 C1 **Minot** U.S.A.
88 C3 **Minsk** Belarus
103 E1 **Mińsk Mazowiecki** Pol.
96 D2 **Mintlaw** U.K.
131 D3 **Minto** Can.
130 C2 **Minto, Lac** l. Can.
68 C1 **Minusinsk** Rus. Fed.
62 A1 **Minutang** India
70 A2 **Minxian** China
155 D1 **Mirabela** Brazil
155 D1 **Miralta** Brazil
111 C3 **Mirampelou, Kolpos** b. Greece
152 C2 **Miranda** Brazil
152 C1 **Miranda** r. Brazil
Miranda Moz. *see* **Macaloge**
106 C1 **Miranda de Ebro** Spain
106 B1 **Mirandela** Port.
154 B2 **Mirandópolis** Brazil
154 B2 **Mirante, Serra do** hills Brazil
79 C2 **Mirbāṭ** Oman
61 C1 **Miri** Sarawak Malaysia
153 C1 **Mirim, Lagoa** l. Brazil
79 D2 **Mirjāveh** Iran
89 D3 **Mirny** Rus. Fed.
83 I2 **Mirnyy** Rus. Fed.
101 F1 **Mirow** Ger.
74 A2 **Mirpur Khas** Pak.
Mirtoan Sea Greece *see* **Mirtoö Pelagos**
111 B3 **Mirtoö Pelagos** sea Greece
65 B2 **Miryang** S. Korea
Mirzachirla Turkm. *see* **Murzechirla**
Mirzachul Uzbek. *see* **Gulistan**
75 C2 **Mirzapur** India
77 E3 **Misalay** China
66 B1 **Mishan** China
51 E1 **Misima Island** P.N.G.
146 B3 **Miskitos, Cayos** is Nic.
103 E2 **Miskolc** Hungary
59 C3 **Misoöl** i. Indon.
115 D1 **Miṣrātah** Libya
130 B2 **Missinaibi** r. Can.
130 B3 **Missinaibi Lake** Can.
128 B3 **Mission** Can.
130 B3 **Missisa Lake** Can.
142 C3 **Mississippi** r. U.S.A.
142 C3 **Mississippi** state U.S.A.
142 C3 **Mississippi Delta** U.S.A.
142 C2 **Mississippi Sound** sea chan. U.S.A.

153 C3 **Missolonghi** Greece *see* **Mesolongi**
134 D1 **Missoula** U.S.A.
137 E3 **Missouri** r. U.S.A.
137 E3 **Missouri** state U.S.A.
130 C3 **Mistassibi** r. Can.
130 C2 **Mistassini, Lac** l. Can.
131 D2 **Mistassini** Can.
103 D2 **Mistelbach** Austria
131 D2 **Mistinibi, Lac** l. Can.
130 C2 **Mistissini** Can.
51 D2 **Mitchell** Austr.
51 D1 **Mitchell** r. Austr.
136 C2 **Mitchell** NE U.S.A.
137 D2 **Mitchell** SD U.S.A.
97 B2 **Mitchelstown** Rep. of Ireland
74 A2 **Mithi** Pak.
67 D3 **Mito** Japan
119 D3 **Mitole** Tanz.
53 D2 **Mittagong** Austr.
101 E2 **Mittelhausen** Ger.
101 D1 **Mittellandkanal** canal Ger.
101 F3 **Mitterteich** Ger.
Mittimatalik Can. *see* **Pond Inlet**
150 B2 **Mitú** Col.
119 C4 **Mitumba, Chaîne des** mts Dem. Rep. Congo
119 C3 **Mitumba, Monts** mts Dem. Rep. Congo
119 C3 **Mitwaba** Dem. Rep. Congo
118 B2 **Mitzic** Gabon
78 B2 **Miyah, Wādī al** watercourse Saudi Arabia
67 C4 **Miyake-jima** i. Japan
66 D3 **Miyako** Japan
67 B4 **Miyakonojō** Japan
76 B2 **Miyaly** Kazakh.
Miyang China *see* **Mile**
67 B4 **Miyazaki** Japan
67 C3 **Miyazu** Japan
115 D1 **Mizdah** Libya
97 B3 **Mizen Head** hd Rep. of Ireland
90 A2 **Mizhhir"ya** Ukr.
Mizo Hills state India *see* **Mizoram**
75 D2 **Mizoram** state India
93 G4 **Mjölby** Sweden
93 F3 **Mjøsa** l. Norway
119 D3 **Mkomazi** Tanz.
103 C1 **Mladá Boleslav** Czech Rep.
109 D2 **Mladenovac** Yugo.
103 E1 **Mława** Pol.
109 C2 **Mljet** i. Croatia
123 C3 **Mlungisi** S. Africa
90 B1 **Mlyniv** Ukr.
123 C2 **Mmabatho** S. Africa
123 C2 **Mmathethe** Botswana
93 E3 **Mo** Norway
123 C2 **Moab** U.S.A.
135 E3 **Moab** U.S.A.
123 D2 **Moamba** Moz.
54 B2 **Moana** N.Z.
118 B3 **Moanda** Gabon
97 C2 **Moate** Rep. of Ireland
119 C3 **Moba** Dem. Rep. Congo
118 C2 **Mobayi-Mbongo** Dem. Rep. Congo
137 E3 **Moberly** U.S.A.
142 C2 **Mobile** U.S.A.
142 C2 **Mobile Bay** U.S.A.
142 C2 **Mobile Point** U.S.A.
136 C1 **Mobridge** U.S.A.
Mobutu, Lake Dem. Rep. Congo/Uganda *see* **Albert, Lake**
Mobutu Sese Seko, Lake Dem. Rep. Congo/Uganda *see* **Albert, Lake**
121 C2 **Moçambicano, Planalto** plat. Moz.
121 D2 **Moçambique** Moz.
Moçâmedes Angola *see* **Namibe**
62 B1 **Mộc Châu** Vietnam
Mocha Yemen *see* **Al Mukhā**
123 C1 **Mochudi** Botswana
121 D2 **Mocimboa da Praia** Moz.
101 D3 **Möckmühl** Ger.
150 B2 **Mococa** Col.
154 C2 **Mococa** Brazil
144 B2 **Mocorito** Mex.
144 B1 **Moctezuma** Mex.
144 B2 **Moctezuma** Mex.
144 B2 **Moctezuma** Mex.
121 C2 **Mocuba** Moz.

05 D2 Modane France
22 B2 Modder r. S. Africa
08 B2 Modena Italy
35 B3 Modesto U.S.A.
09 B3 Modica Sicily Italy
53 C3 Moe Austr.
Moero, Lake
Dem. Rep. Congo/Zambia
see Mweru, Lake
00 C2 Moers Ger.
96 C3 Moffat U.K.
Mogadishu Somalia see
Muqdisho
Mogador Morocco see
Essaouira
06 B1 Mogadouro, Serra de mts
Port.
23 C1 Mogalakwena r. S. Africa
62 A1 Mogaung Myanmar
Mogilev Belarus see
Mahilyow
154 C2 Mogi-Mirim Brazil
83 I3 Mogocha Rus. Fed.
123 C1 Mogoditshane Botswana
62 A1 Mogok Myanmar
38 A2 Mogollon Plateau U.S.A.
13 D2 Mohács Hungary
123 C3 Mohale's Hoek Lesotho
07 D2 Mohammadia Alg.
138 A2 Mohave Mountains U.S.A.
141 E2 Mohawk r. U.S.A.
62 A1 Mohnyin Myanmar
19 D3 Mohoro Tanz.
90 B2 Mohyliv Podil's'kyy Ukr.
23 C1 Moijabana Botswana
10 C1 Moineşti Romania
Mointy Kazakh. see
Moyynty
92 F2 Mo i Rana Norway
88 C2 Mõisaküla Estonia
04 C3 Moissac France
35 C3 Mojave U.S.A.
35 C3 Mojave Desert U.S.A.
62 B1 Mojiang China
155 C2 Moji das Cruzes Brazil
154 C2 Moji-Guaçu r. Brazil
09 C2 Mojkovac Yugo.
54 B1 Mokau N.Z.
23 C2 Mokhotlong Lesotho
83 J2 Mokhsogollokh
Rus. Fed.
118 B1 Mokolo Cameroon
65 B3 Mokp'o S. Korea
09 C2 Mola di Bari Italy
145 C2 Molango Mex.
Moldavia country Europe
see Moldova
Moldavskaya S.S.R.
country Europe see
Moldova
93 E3 Molde Norway
90 B2 Moldova country Europe
10 B2 Moldova Nouă Romania
10 B1 Moldoveanu, Vârful mt.
Romania
10 B1 Moldovei, Podişul plat.
Romania
90 B2 Moldovei Centrale,
Podişul plat. Moldova
23 C1 Molepolole Botswana
88 C2 Molėtai Lith.
09 C2 Molfetta Italy
Molière Alg. see
Bordj Bounaama
07 C1 Molina de Aragón Spain
07 C2 Molina de Segura Spain
19 D3 Moliro Dem. Rep. Congo
50 B4 Mollendo Peru
93 F4 Mölnlycke Sweden
91 D2 Molochna r. Ukr.
89 E2 Molokovo Rus. Fed.
53 C2 Molong Austr.
122 B2 Molopo watercourse
Botswana/S. Africa
Molotov Rus. Fed. see
Perm'
Molotovsk Rus. Fed. see
Severodvinsk
Molotovsk Rus. Fed. see
Nolinsk
118 B2 Moloundou Cameroon
Moluccas is Indon. see
Maluku
59 C3 Molucca Sea Indon.
52 B2 Momba Austr.
19 D3 Mombasa Kenya
154 B1 Mombuca, Serra da hills
Brazil
111 C2 Momchilgrad Bulg.
93 F4 Møn i. Denmark
105 D3 Monaco country Europe

96 B2 Monadhliath Mountains
U.K.
97 C1 Monaghan Rep. of Ireland
139 C2 Monahans U.S.A.
147 D3 Mona Passage
Dom. Rep./Puerto Rico
120 A1 Mona Quimbundo Angola
Monastir Macedonia see
Bitola
89 D3 Monastyrshchina
Rus. Fed.
90 B2 Monastyryshche Ukr.
118 B2 Monatélé Cameroon
66 D2 Monbetsu Japan
108 A1 Moncalieri Italy
86 C2 Monchegorsk Rus. Fed.
100 C2 Mönchengladbach Ger.
144 B2 Monclova Mex.
131 D3 Moncton Can.
106 B1 Mondego r. Port.
118 C2 Mondjamboli
Dem. Rep. Congo
123 D2 Mondlo S. Africa
108 A2 Mondovì Italy
106 C1 Mondragón Spain
111 B3 Monemvasia Greece
66 D1 Moneron, Ostrov i.
Rus. Fed.
141 D1 Monet Can.
137 E3 Monett U.S.A.
108 B1 Monfalcone Italy
106 B1 Monforte Spain
119 D2 Mongbwalu
Dem. Rep. Congo
62 B1 Mông Cai Vietnam
62 A1 Mong Hang Myanmar
Monghyr India see Munger
62 B1 Mong Lin Myanmar
62 A1 Mong Nawng Myanmar
90 B2 Mongo Chad
115 D3 Mongolia country Asia
68 C1 Mongora Pak.
74 B1 Mongora Pak.
62 A1 Mong Pawk Myanmar
62 A1 Mong Ping Myanmar
120 B2 Mongu Zambia
135 C3 Monitor Range mts U.S.A.
103 E1 Mońki Pol.
99 B4 Monmouth U.K.
114 C4 Mono r. Togo
135 C3 Mono Lake U.S.A.
109 C2 Monopoli Italy
107 C1 Monreal del Campo Spain
142 B2 Monroe LA U.S.A.
140 C2 Monroe MI U.S.A.
140 B2 Monroe WI U.S.A.
142 C2 Monroeville U.S.A.
114 A4 Monrovia Liberia
100 A2 Mons Belgium
155 E1 Monsarás, Ponta de pt
Brazil
100 C3 Montabaur Ger.
122 B3 Montagu S. Africa
109 C3 Montalto mt. Italy
110 B2 Montana Bulg.
134 E1 Montana state U.S.A.
105 C2 Montargis France
104 C3 Montauban France
141 E2 Montauk Point U.S.A.
123 C2 Mont-aux-Sources mt.
Lesotho
105 C2 Montbard France
105 D2 Montbéliard France
105 D2 Mont Blanc mt.
France/Italy
105 C2 Montbrison France
100 B3 Montcornet France
104 B3 Mont-de-Marsan France
104 C2 Montdidier France
151 D3 Monte Alegre Brazil
154 C1 Monte Alegre de Minas
Brazil
141 E1 Montebello Can.
154 B3 Montecarlo Arg.
105 D3 Monte-Carlo Monaco
154 C1 Monte Carmelo Brazil
152 C3 Monte Caseros Arg.
123 C1 Monte Christo S. Africa
146 C3 Montego Bay Jamaica
105 C2 Montélimar France
145 C2 Montemorelos Mex.
104 B2 Montendre France
109 C2 Montenegro aut. rep.
Yugo.
121 C2 Montepuez Moz.
108 B2 Montepulciano Italy
135 B3 Monterey U.S.A.
135 B3 Monterey Bay U.S.A.
150 B2 Montería Col.
152 B1 Montero Bol.
145 B2 Monterrey Mex.

109 C2 Montesano sulla
Marcellana Italy
109 C2 Monte Sant'Angelo Italy
151 F4 Monte Santo Brazil
108 A2 Monte Santu, Capo di c.
Sardinia Italy
155 D1 Montes Claros Brazil
153 C3 Montevideo Uru.
137 D2 Montevideo U.S.A.
136 B3 Monte Vista U.S.A.
142 C2 Montgomery U.S.A.
100 B3 Monthermé France
105 D2 Monthey Switz.
142 B2 Monticello AR U.S.A.
143 D2 Monticello FL U.S.A.
135 E3 Monticello UT U.S.A.
104 C2 Montignac France
100 B2 Montignies-le-Tilleul
Belgium
106 B2 Montijo Port.
106 B2 Montijo Spain
106 C2 Montilla Spain
154 B1 Montividiu Brazil
131 D3 Mont-Joli Can.
130 C3 Mont-Laurier Can.
104 C2 Montluçon France
131 C3 Montmagny Can.
104 C2 Montmorillon France
51 E2 Monto Austr.
134 D2 Montpelier ID U.S.A.
141 E2 Montpelier VT U.S.A.
105 C3 Montpellier France
130 C3 Montréal Can.
Montreal Can. see
Montréal
129 D2 Montreal Lake Can.
129 D2 Montreal Lake l. Can.
99 D4 Montreuil France
105 D2 Montreux Switz.
96 C2 Montrose U.K.
136 B3 Montrose U.S.A.
147 D3 Montserrat terr.
West Indies
62 A1 Monywa Myanmar
108 A1 Monza Italy
107 D1 Monzón Spain
123 C1 Mookane Botswana
52 A1 Moolawatana Austr.
52 B1 Moomba Austr.
53 D1 Moonie Austr.
53 C1 Moonie r. Austr.
52 A2 Moonta Austr.
50 A3 Moora Austr.
50 A2 Moore, Lake salt flat
Austr.
137 D1 Moorhead U.S.A.
53 C3 Mooroopna Austr.
122 A3 Mooreesburg S. Africa
130 B2 Moose r. Can.
130 B2 Moose Factory Can.
141 F1 Moosehead Lake U.S.A.
129 D2 Moose Jaw Can.
137 E1 Moose Lake U.S.A.
129 D2 Moosomin Can.
130 B2 Moosonee Can.
52 B2 Mootwingee Austr.
107 E2 M'Ooukal Alg.
123 C1 Mopane S. Africa
114 B3 Mopti Mali
150 B4 Moquegua Peru
103 D2 Mór Hungary
118 B3 Mora Cameroon
93 F3 Mora Sweden
137 E1 Mora U.S.A.
74 B2 Moradabad India
121 D2 Morafenobe Madag.
121 D2 Moramanga Madag.
136 A2 Moran U.S.A.
51 D2 Moranbah Austr.
103 D2 Morava r. Europe
96 B2 Moray Firth b. U.K.
100 C3 Morbach Ger.
74 B2 Morbi India
93 G4 Mörbylånga Sweden
104 B3 Morcenx France
69 E1 Mordaga China
129 E3 Morden Can.
89 F3 Mordovo Rus. Fed.
98 B2 Morecambe U.K.
98 B2 Morecambe Bay U.K.
53 C1 Moree Austr.
59 D3 Morehead P.N.G.
140 C3 Morehead U.S.A.
143 E2 Morehead City U.S.A.
145 B3 Morelia Mex.
107 C1 Morella Spain
74 B2 Morena India
106 B2 Morena, Sierra mts Spain
110 C2 Moreni Romania
138 A3 Moreno Mex.
128 A2 Moresby, Mount Can.

128 A2 Moresby Island Can.
53 D1 Moreton Island Austr.
52 A2 Morgan Austr.
142 B3 Morgan City U.S.A.
143 D1 Morganton U.S.A.
141 D3 Morgantown U.S.A.
105 D2 Morges Switz.
68 C2 Mori China
66 D2 Mori Japan
53 C1 Moriarty's Range hills
Austr.
128 B2 Morice Lake Can.
66 D3 Morioka Japan
53 D2 Morisset Austr.
104 B2 Morlaix France
98 C3 Morley U.K.
157 G9 Mornington Abyssal Plain
sea feature
S. Atlantic Ocean
51 C1 Mornington Island Austr.
59 D3 Morobe P.N.G.
114 B1 Morocco country Africa
119 D3 Morogoro Tanz.
64 B3 Moro Gulf Phil.
122 B2 Morokweng S. Africa
121 □D3 Morombe Madag.
68 C1 Mörön Mongolia
121 □D3 Morondava Madag.
106 B2 Morón de la Frontera
Spain
121 D2 Moroni Comoros
59 C2 Morotai i. Indon.
119 D2 Moroto Uganda
98 C2 Morpeth U.K.
142 B1 Morrilton U.S.A.
154 C1 Morrinhos Brazil
54 C1 Morrinsville N.Z.
129 E3 Morris Can.
137 D1 Morris U.S.A.
143 D1 Morristown U.S.A.
154 C2 Morro Agudo Brazil
155 E1 Morro d'Anta Brazil
55 K3 Morse, Cape Antarctica
87 D3 Morshanka Rus. Fed.
Morshansk Rus. Fed. see
Morshanka
154 B1 Mortes, Rio das r. Brazil
52 B3 Mortlake Austr.
48 G3 Mortlock Islands
Micronesia
140 B2 Morton U.S.A.
53 C2 Morundah Austr.
53 D3 Moruya Austr.
96 B2 Morvern reg. U.K.
Morvi India see Morbi
53 C3 Morwell Austr.
101 D3 Mosbach Ger.
89 E2 Moscow Rus. Fed.
134 C1 Moscow U.S.A.
100 C2 Mosel r. Ger.
122 B2 Moselebe watercourse
Botswana
105 D2 Moselle r. France
134 C1 Moses Lake U.S.A.
92 □A3 Mosfellsbær Iceland
54 B3 Mosgiel N.Z.
88 C2 Moshchnyy, Ostrov i.
Rus. Fed.
89 D2 Moshenskoye Rus. Fed.
119 D3 Moshi Tanz.
92 F2 Mosjøen Norway
Moskva Rus. Fed. see
Moscow
89 E2 Moskva r. Rus. Fed.
103 D2 Mosonmagyaróvár
Hungary
93 F4 Moss Norway
Mossâmedes Angola see
Namibe
122 B3 Mossel Bay S. Africa
122 B3 Mossel Bay b. S. Africa
118 B3 Mossendjo Congo
52 B2 Mossgiel Austr.
51 D1 Mossman Austr.
151 F3 Mossoró Brazil
53 D2 Moss Vale Austr.
111 C4 Most Czech Rep.
107 C2 Mostaganem Alg.
109 C2 Mostar Bos.-Herz.
152 C3 Mostardas Brazil
106 C1 Móstoles Spain
Mosul Iraq see Al Mawşil
145 D3 Motagua r. Guat.
93 G4 Motala Sweden
123 C2 Moteetma S. Africa
96 C3 Motherwell U.K.
75 C2 Motihari India
107 C2 Motilla del Palancar
Spain
122 B1 Motokwe Botswana
106 C2 Motril Spain

Motru
208

110 B2 Motru Romania
136 C1 Mott U.S.A.
54 B2 Motueka N.Z.
145 D2 Motul Mex.
49 L5 Motu One atoll Fr. Polynesia
114 A3 Moudjéria Maur.
111 C3 Moudros Greece
118 B3 Mouila Gabon
52 B3 Moulamein Austr.
105 C2 Moulins France
63 A2 Moulmein Myanmar
143 D2 Moultrie U.S.A.
143 E2 Moultrie, Lake U.S.A.
140 B3 Mound City U.S.A.
115 D4 Moundou Chad
140 C3 Moundsville U.S.A.
137 E3 Mountain Grove U.S.A.
142 B1 Mountain Home AR U.S.A.
134 C2 Mountain Home ID U.S.A.
143 D1 Mount Airy U.S.A.
123 C3 Mount Ayliff S. Africa
52 A3 Mount Barker Austr.
53 C3 Mount Beauty Austr.
97 B2 Mount Bellew Rep. of Ireland
121 C2 Mount Darwin Zimbabwe
141 F2 Mount Desert Island U.S.A.
123 C3 Mount Fletcher S. Africa
123 C3 Mount Frere S. Africa
52 B3 Mount Gambier Austr.
59 D3 Mount Hagen P.N.G.
53 C2 Mount Hope Austr.
51 C2 Mount Isa Austr.
52 A3 Mount Lofty Range mts Austr.
50 A2 Mount Magnet Austr.
52 B2 Mount Manara Austr.
54 C1 Mount Maunganui N.Z.
97 C2 Mountmellick Rep. of Ireland
137 E2 Mount Pleasant IA U.S.A.
140 C2 Mount Pleasant MI U.S.A.
143 E2 Mount Pleasant SC U.S.A.
139 E2 Mount Pleasant TX U.S.A.
135 D3 Mount Pleasant UT U.S.A.
99 A4 Mount's Bay U.K.
134 B2 Mount Shasta U.S.A.
54 B2 Mount Somers N.Z.
140 B3 Mount Vernon IL U.S.A.
140 C2 Mount Vernon OH U.S.A.
134 B1 Mount Vernon WA U.S.A.
51 D2 Moura Austr.
106 B2 Moura Port.
115 E3 Mourdi, Dépression du depr. Chad
97 C1 Mourne Mountains hills U.K.
100 A2 Mouscron Belgium
115 D3 Moussoro Chad
61 D1 Moutong Indon.
115 C2 Mouydir, Monts du plat. Alg.
100 B3 Mouzon France
97 B1 Moy r. Rep. of Ireland
117 B4 Moyale Eth.
Moyen Congo country Africa see Congo
123 C3 Moyeni Lesotho
119 D2 Moyo Uganda
77 D2 Moyynkum Kazakh.
77 D2 Moyynty Kazakh.
121 C3 Mozambique country Africa
113 G8 Mozambique Channel Africa
81 C1 Mozdok Rus. Fed.
89 E2 Mozhaysk Rus. Fed.
119 D3 Mpanda Tanz.
121 C2 Mpika Zambia
118 B2 Mpoko r. C.A.R.
121 C1 Mporokoso Zambia
123 C2 Mpumalanga prov. S. Africa
119 D3 Mpwapwa Tanz.
115 D1 M'Saken Tunisia
119 D3 Msambweni Kenya
119 D3 Msata Tanz.
88 C2 Mshinskaya Rus. Fed.
115 C1 M'Sila Alg.
89 D2 Msta r. Rus. Fed.
89 D2 Mstinskiy Most Rus. Fed.
89 D3 Mstsislaw Belarus
Mtoko Zimbabwe see Mutoko
89 E3 Mtsensk Rus. Fed.
123 D2 Mtubatuba S. Africa
119 E4 Mtwara Tanz.
151 E3 Muana Brazil
118 B3 Muanda Dem. Rep. Congo
62 B1 Muang Hiam Laos
62 B2 Muang Hinboun Laos
62 B2 Muang Khammouan Laos
63 B2 Muang Không Laos
63 B2 Muang Khôngxédôn Laos
62 B1 Muang Ngoy Laos
62 B2 Muang Pakbeng Laos
62 B2 Muang Pakxan Laos
63 B2 Muang Phalan Laos
62 B2 Muang Phôn-Hông Laos
62 B1 Muang Sing Laos
62 B2 Muang Vangviang Laos
62 B2 Muang Xaignabouri Laos
60 B1 Muar Malaysia
60 B2 Muarabungo Indon.
60 B2 Muaradua Indon.
61 C2 Muaralaung Indon.
60 A2 Muarasiberut Indon.
60 B2 Muaratembesi Indon.
61 C2 Muarateweh Indon.
Muara Tuang Malaysia see Kota Samarahan
119 D2 Mubende Uganda
115 D3 Mubi Nigeria
120 B2 Muconda Angola
120 A2 Mucope Angola
121 C2 Mucubela Moz.
155 E1 Mucuri Brazil
155 E1 Mucuri r. Brazil
66 A2 Mudanjiang China
66 A1 Mudan Jiang r. China
111 C2 Mudanya Turkey
136 B2 Muddy Gap U.S.A.
101 E1 Müden (Örtze) Ger.
53 C2 Mudgee Austr.
63 A2 Mudon Myanmar
80 B1 Mudurnu Turkey
121 C2 Mueda Moz.
121 B2 Mufulira Zambia
120 B2 Mufumbwe Zambia
111 C3 Muğla Turkey
116 B2 Muhammad Qol Sudan
Muhammarah Iran see Khorramshahr
101 F2 Mühlberg Ger.
101 E2 Mühlhausen (Thüringen) Ger.
88 B2 Muhu i. Estonia
63 B3 Mui Ca Mau c. Vietnam
97 C2 Muine Bheag Rep. of Ireland
96 B3 Muirkirk U.K.
121 C2 Muite Moz.
65 B2 Muju S. Korea
Mukačevo Ukr. see Mukacheve
90 A2 Mukacheve Ukr.
61 C1 Mukah Sarawak Malaysia
Mukalla Yemen see Al Mukallā
63 B2 Mukdahan Thai.
Mukden China see Shenyang
Mukhtuya Rus. Fed. see Lensk
50 A3 Mukinbudin Austr.
60 B2 Mukomuko Indon.
121 C2 Mulanje, Mount Malawi
101 F2 Mulde r. Ger.
119 D3 Muleba Tanz.
144 A2 Mulegé Mex.
139 C2 Muleshoe U.S.A.
106 C2 Mulhacén mt. Spain
100 C2 Mülheim an der Ruhr Ger.
105 D2 Mulhouse France
62 B1 Muli China
66 B2 Muling China
66 B1 Muling r. China
96 B2 Mull i. U.K.
53 C2 Mullaley Austr.
136 C2 Mullen U.S.A.
61 C1 Muller, Pegunungan mts Indon.
50 A2 Mullewa Austr.
97 C2 Mullingar Rep. of Ireland
96 B3 Mull of Galloway c. U.K.
96 B3 Mull of Kintyre hd U.K.
96 A3 Mull of Oa hd U.K.
53 D1 Mullumbimby Austr.
120 B2 Mulobezi Zambia
74 B1 Multan Pak.
86 F2 Mulym'ya Rus. Fed.
74 B3 Mumbai India
120 B2 Mumbeji Zambia
120 B2 Mumbwa Zambia
61 D2 Muna i. Indon.
145 D2 Muna Mex.
101 E2 Münchberg Ger.
München Ger. see Munich
München-Gladbach Ger. see Mönchengladbach
140 B2 Muncie U.S.A.
50 B3 Mundrabilla Austr.
140 B3 Munfordville U.S.A.
119 C2 Mungbere Dem. Rep. Congo
75 C2 Munger India
52 A1 Mungeranie Austr.
53 C1 Mungindi Austr.
75 C2 Mungla Bangl.
102 C2 Munich Ger.
155 D2 Muniz Freire Brazil
101 E1 Münster Ger.
100 C2 Münster Ger.
97 B2 Munster reg. Rep. of Ireland
100 C2 Münsterland reg. Ger.
62 B1 Mương Nhie Vietnam
92 H2 Muonio Fin.
92 H2 Muonioälven r. Fin./Sweden
117 C4 Muqdisho Somalia
155 D2 Muqui Brazil
103 D2 Mur r. Austria
67 C3 Murakami Japan
119 C3 Muramvya Burundi
119 D3 Muranga Kenya
86 D3 Murashi Rus. Fed.
81 B2 Murat r. Turkey
111 C2 Muratlı Turkey
67 D3 Murayama Japan
50 A2 Murchison watercourse Austr.
107 C2 Murcia Spain
107 C2 Murcia aut. comm. Spain
136 C2 Murdo U.S.A.
131 D3 Murdochville Can.
111 C2 Mürefte Turkey
110 B1 Mureș r. Romania
104 C3 Muret France
142 C1 Murfreesboro U.S.A.
77 C3 Murghab r. Afgh.
77 D3 Murghob Tajik.
155 D2 Muriaé Brazil
120 B1 Muriege Angola
101 F1 Müritz l. Ger.
92 J2 Murmansk Rus. Fed.
86 C2 Murmanskiy Bereg coastal area Rus. Fed.
87 D3 Murom Rus. Fed.
66 D2 Muroran Japan
106 B1 Muros Spain
67 B4 Muroto Japan
67 B4 Muroto-zaki pt Japan
143 D1 Murphy U.S.A.
53 C1 Murra Murra Austr.
52 A3 Murray r. Austr.
128 B2 Murray r. Can.
140 B3 Murray U.S.A.
59 D3 Murray, Lake P.N.G.
143 D2 Murray, Lake U.S.A.
52 A3 Murray Bridge Austr.
122 B3 Murraysburg S. Africa
52 B3 Murrayville Austr.
52 B2 Murrumbidgee r. Austr.
53 C2 Murrumburrah Austr.
121 C2 Murrupula Moz.
53 D2 Murrurundi Austr.
109 C1 Murska Sobota Slovenia
54 C1 Murupara N.Z.
49 N6 Mururoa atoll Fr. Polynesia
75 C2 Murwara India
53 D1 Murwillumbah Austr.
76 C3 Murzechirla Turkm.
115 D2 Murzūq Libya
103 D2 Mürzzuschlag Austria
81 C2 Muş Turkey
110 B2 Musala mt. Bulg.
65 B1 Musan N. Korea
78 B3 Musaymir Yemen
79 C2 Muscat Oman
Muscat and Oman country Asia see Oman
137 E2 Muscatine U.S.A.
50 C2 Musgrave Ranges mts Austr.
118 B3 Mushie Dem. Rep. Congo
60 B2 Musi r. Indon.
140 B2 Muskegon U.S.A.
140 B2 Muskegon r. U.S.A.
140 C3 Muskingum r. U.S.A.
139 D1 Muskogee U.S.A.
141 D1 Muskoka, Lake Can.
128 B2 Muskwa r. Can.
74 A1 Muslimbagh Pak.
116 B3 Musmar Sudan
119 D3 Musoma Tanz.
59 D3 Mussau Island P.N.G.
96 C3 Musselburgh U.K.
117 C4 Mustahīl Eth.
88 B2 Mustjala Estonia
53 D2 Muswellbrook Austr.
116 A2 Mut Egypt
121 C2 Mutare Zimbabwe
121 C2 Mutoko Zimbabwe
66 D2 Mutsu Japan
66 D2 Mutsu-wan b. Japan
121 C2 Mutuali Moz.
155 D1 Mutum Brazil
92 I2 Muurola Fin.
70 A2 Mu Us Shamo des. China
120 A1 Muxaluando Angola
86 C2 Muyezerskiy Rus. Fed.
119 D3 Muyinga Burundi
76 B2 Muynak Uzbek.
74 B1 Muzaffargarh Pak.
75 C2 Muzaffarpur India
123 D1 Muzamane Moz.
155 C2 Muzambinho Brazil
144 B2 Múzquiz Mex.
75 C1 Muztag mt. Xinjiang China
117 A4 Mvolo Sudan
119 C3 Mwanza Dem. Rep. Congo
119 D3 Mwanza Tanz.
118 C3 Mweka Dem. Rep. Congo
121 B2 Mwenda Zambia
118 C3 Mwene-Ditu Dem. Rep. Congo
121 C3 Mwenezi Zimbabwe
121 C3 Mwenezi r. Zimbabwe
119 C3 Mweru, Lake Dem. Rep. Congo/Zambia
121 B1 Mweru Wantipa, Lake Zambia
118 C3 Mwimba Dem. Rep. Congo
120 B2 Mwinilunga Zambia
88 C3 Myadzyel Belarus
62 A2 Myanaung Myanmar
62 A1 Myanmar country Asia
63 A2 Myaungmya Myanmar
62 A1 Myingyan Myanmar
62 A1 Myitkyina Myanmar
90 A2 Mykolayiv Ukr.
91 C2 Mykolayiv Ukr.
111 C3 Mykonos Greece
111 C3 Mykonos i. Greece
86 E2 Myla Rus. Fed.
75 D2 Mymensingh Bangl.
62 A1 Myohaung Myanmar
65 B1 Myŏnggan N. Korea
88 C2 Myory Belarus
92 □B3 Mýrdalsjökull ice cap Iceland
92 G2 Myre Norway
91 C2 Myrhorod Ukr.
111 C3 Myrina Greece
90 C2 Myronivka Ukr.
143 E2 Myrtle Beach U.S.A.
53 C3 Myrtleford Austr.
134 B2 Myrtle Point U.S.A.
89 E2 Myshkin Rus. Fed.
Myshkino Rus. Fed. see Myshkin
103 C1 Myślibórz Pol.
73 B3 Mysore India
83 N2 Mys Shmidta Rus. Fed.
63 B2 My Tho Vietnam
111 C3 Mytilini Greece
89 E3 Mytishchi Rus. Fed.
123 C3 Mzamomhle S. Africa
121 C2 Mzimba Malawi
121 C2 Mzuzu Malawi

N

101 F3 Naab r. Ger.
100 B1 Naarden Neth.
97 C2 Naas Rep. of Ireland
122 A2 Nababeep S. Africa
87 E3 Naberezhnyye Chelny Rus. Fed.
59 D3 Nabire Indon.
80 B2 Nāblus West Bank
123 C1 Naboomspruit S. Africa
121 D2 Nacala Moz.
119 D4 Nachingwea Tanz.
103 D1 Náchod Czech Rep.
73 D3 Nachuge India
139 E2 Nacogdoches U.S.A.
144 B1 Nacozari de García Mex.
Nada China see Danzhou
74 B2 Nadiad India
90 A2 Nadvirna Ukr.
86 C2 Nadvoitsy Rus. Fed.
86 G2 Nadym Rus. Fed.
93 F4 Næstved Denmark
111 B3 Nafpaktos Greece
111 B3 Nafplio Greece
115 D1 Nafūsah, Jabal hills Libya
78 B2 Nafy Saudi Arabia
64 B2 Naga Phil.

Nerang
209

130 B2 Nagagami *r.* Can.
67 C3 Nagano Japan
67 C3 Nagaoka Japan
75 D2 Nagaon India
74 B1 Nagar India
74 B2 Nagar Parkar Pak.
67 A4 Nagasaki Japan
67 B4 Nagato Japan
74 B2 Nagaur India
73 B4 Nagercoil India
74 A2 Nagha Kalat Pak.
74 B2 Nagina India
67 C3 Nagoya Japan
75 B2 Nagpur India
75 D1 Nagqu China
143 E1 Nags Head U.S.A.
82 E1 Nagurskoye Rus. Fed.
103 D2 Nagyatád Hungary
103 D2 Nagykanizsa Hungary
128 B1 Nahanni Butte Can.
81 C2 Nahāvand Iran
101 E1 Nahrendorf Ger.
153 A4 Nahuel Huapí, Lago *l.* Arg.
143 D2 Nahunta U.S.A.
131 D2 Nain Can.
81 D2 Nā'īn Iran
121 C2 Naiopué Moz.
96 C2 Nairn U.K.
119 D3 Nairobi Kenya
Naissus Yugo. *see* Niš
119 D3 Naivasha Kenya
81 D2 Najafābād Iran
78 B2 Najd *reg.* Saudi Arabia
106 C1 Nájera Spain
65 C1 Najin N. Korea
78 B3 Najrān Saudi Arabia
119 D2 Nakasongola Uganda
67 C3 Nakatsugawa Japan
78 A3 Nakfa Eritrea
66 B2 Nakhodka Rus. Fed.
63 B2 Nakhon Nayok Thai.
63 B2 Nakhon Pathom Thai.
62 B2 Nakhon Phanom Thai.
63 B2 Nakhon Ratchasima Thai.
63 B2 Nakhon Sawan Thai.
63 A3 Nakhon Si Thammarat Thai.
Nakhrachi Rus. Fed. *see* Kondinskoye
130 B2 Nakina Can.
126 B3 Naknek U.S.A.
121 C1 Nakonde Zambia
93 F5 Nakskov Denmark
119 D3 Nakuru Kenya
128 C2 Nakusp Can.
75 D2 Nalbari India
87 D4 Nal'chik Rus. Fed.
115 D1 Nālūt Libya
123 D2 Namaacha Moz.
123 C2 Namahadi S. Africa
81 D2 Namak, Daryācheh-ye *salt flat* Iran
76 B3 Namak, Kavīr-i- *salt flat* Iran
79 C1 Namakzar-e Shadad *salt flat* Iran
77 D2 Namangan Uzbek.
119 D3 Namanyere Tanz.
122 A2 Namaqualand *reg.* Namibia
122 A2 Namaqualand *reg.* S. Africa
51 E2 Nambour Austr.
53 D2 Nambucca Heads Austr.
63 B3 Năm Căn Vietnam
65 B2 Namch'ŏn N. Korea
63 A2 Nam Chon Reservoir Thai.
75 D1 Nam Co *salt l.* China
62 B1 Nam Đinh Vietnam
121 C2 Namialo Moz.
120 A3 Namib Desert Namibia
120 A2 Namibe Angola
120 A3 Namibia *country* Africa
72 D2 Namjagbarwa Feng *mt.* China
59 C3 Namlea Indon.
62 B2 Nam Ngum Reservoir Laos
53 C2 Namoi *r.* Austr.
134 C2 Nampa U.S.A.
114 B3 Nampala Mali
65 B2 Namp'o N. Korea
121 C2 Nampula Moz.
72 D2 Namrup India
62 A1 Namsang Myanmar
92 F3 Namsos Norway
92 F3 Namsskogan Norway
63 A2 Nam Tok Thai.
83 J2 Namtsy Rus. Fed.
62 A1 Namtu Myanmar
121 C2 Namuno Moz.
100 B2 Namur Belgium
120 B2 Namwala Zambia
65 B2 Namwŏn S. Korea
62 A1 Namya Ra Myanmar
62 B2 Nan Thai.
128 B3 Nanaimo Can.
71 B3 Nan'an China
122 A1 Nananib Plateau Namibia
Nan'ao China *see* Dayu
67 C3 Nanao Japan
71 B3 Nanchang *Jiangxi* China
71 B3 Nanchang *Jiangxi* China
71 B3 Nancheng China
70 A2 Nanchong China
63 A3 Nancowry *i.* India
105 D2 Nancy France
75 C1 Nanda Devi *mt.* India
71 A3 Nandan China
74 B3 Nānded India
Nander India *see* Nānded
53 D2 Nandewar Range *mts* Austr.
74 B2 Nandurbar India
73 B3 Nandyal India
71 B3 Nanfeng China
62 A1 Nang China
118 B2 Nanga Eboko Cameroon
61 C2 Nangahpinoh Indon.
77 D3 Nanga Parbat *mt.* Jammu and Kashmir
61 C2 Nangatayap Indon.
63 A2 Nangin Myanmar
65 B1 Nangnim-sanmaek *mts* N. Korea
70 B2 Nangong China
119 D3 Nangulangwa Tanz.
70 C2 Nanhui China
70 B2 Nanjing China
Nanking China *see* Nanjing
67 B4 Nankoku Japan
120 A2 Nankova Angola
70 B2 Nanle China
71 B3 Nan Ling *mts* China
71 A3 Nanning China
127 I2 Nanortalik Greenland
71 A3 Nanpan Jiang *r.* China
75 C2 Nanpara India
71 B3 Nanping China
Nanpu China *see* Pucheng
69 E3 Nansei-shotō *is* Japan
160 I1 Nansen Basin *sea feature* Arctic Ocean
126 F1 Nansen Sound *sea chan.* Can.
104 B2 Nantes France
70 C2 Nantong China
141 E2 Nantucket U.S.A.
141 F2 Nantucket Island U.S.A.
99 B3 Nantwich U.K.
49 I4 Nanumea *i.* Tuvalu
155 D1 Nanuque Brazil
64 B3 Nanusa, Kepulauan *is* Indon.
71 B3 Nanxiong China
70 B2 Nanyang China
119 D3 Nanyuki Kenya
70 B2 Nanzhang China
Nanzhao China *see* Zhao'an
131 C2 Naococane, Lac *l.* Can.
74 A2 Naokot Pak.
71 B3 Naozhou Dao *i.* China
135 B3 Napa U.S.A.
126 E2 Napaktulik Lake Can.
141 D2 Napanee Can.
127 I2 Napasoq Greenland
137 F2 Naperville U.S.A.
54 C1 Napier N.Z.
108 B2 Naples Italy
143 D3 Naples U.S.A.
150 B3 Napo *r.* Ecuador
Napoli Italy *see* Naples
Napug China *see* Gê'gyai
114 B3 Nara Mali
88 C3 Narach Belarus
52 B3 Naracoorte Austr.
53 C2 Naradhan Austr.
145 C2 Naranjos Mex.
63 B3 Narathiwat Thai.
74 B3 Narayangaon India
105 C3 Narbonne France
63 A2 Narcondam Island India
127 H1 Nares Strait Can./Greenland
103 E1 Narew *r.* Pol.
122 A1 Narib Namibia
87 D4 Narimanov Rus. Fed.
67 D3 Narita Japan
74 B2 Narmada *r.* India
74 B2 Narnaul India
108 B2 Narni Italy
86 F2 Narodnaya, Gora *mt.* Rus. Fed.
90 B1 Narodychi Ukr.
89 E2 Naro-Fominsk Rus. Fed.
53 D3 Narooma Austr.
88 C3 Narowlya Belarus
93 H3 Närpes Fin.
53 C2 Narrabri Austr.
53 C2 Narrandera Austr.
53 C2 Narromine Austr.
67 B4 Naruto Japan
88 C2 Narva Estonia
88 C2 Narva Bay Estonia/Rus. Fed.
92 G2 Narvik Norway
88 C2 Narvskoye Vodokhranilishche *resr* Estonia/Rus. Fed.
86 E2 Nar'yan-Mar Rus. Fed.
77 D2 Naryn Kyrg.
74 B2 Nashik India
141 E2 Nashua U.S.A.
142 C1 Nashville U.S.A.
137 E1 Nashwauk U.S.A.
109 C1 Našice Croatia
117 B4 Nasir Sudan
Nasirabad Bangl. *see* Mymensingh
119 C4 Nasondoye Dem. Rep. Congo
76 B3 Naṣrābād Iran
128 B2 Nass *r.* Can.
146 C2 Nassau Bahamas
116 B2 Nasser, Lake *resr* Egypt
93 F4 Nässjö Sweden
130 C2 Nastapoca *r.* Can.
130 C2 Nastapoka Islands Can.
89 D2 Nasva Rus. Fed.
120 B3 Nata Botswana
151 F3 Natal Brazil
60 A1 Natal Indon.
Natal *prov.* S. Africa *see* Kwazulu-Natal
159 D6 Natal Basin *sea feature* Indian Ocean
139 D3 Natalia U.S.A.
131 D2 Natashquan Can.
131 D2 Natashquan *r.* Can.
142 B2 Natchez U.S.A.
142 B2 Natchitoches U.S.A.
53 C3 Nathalia Austr.
107 D1 Nati, Punta *pt* Spain
114 C3 Natitingou Benin
151 E4 Natividade Brazil
67 D3 Natori Japan
119 D3 Natron, Lake *salt l.* Tanz.
60 B1 Natuna, Kepulauan *is* Indon.
60 B1 Natuna Besar *i.* Indon.
122 A1 Nauchas Namibia
101 F1 Nauen Ger.
64 B2 Naujan Phil.
88 B2 Naujoji Akmenė Lith.
101 E2 Naumburg (Saale) Ger.
48 H34 Nauru *country* S. Pacific Ocean
150 B3 Nauta Peru
145 C2 Nautla Mex.
88 C3 Navahrudak Belarus
106 B2 Navalmoral de la Mata Spain
106 B2 Navalvillar de Pela Spain
97 C2 Navan Rep. of Ireland
Navangar India *see* Jamnagar
88 C2 Navapolatsk Belarus
83 M2 Navarin, Mys *c.* Rus. Fed.
153 B5 Navarino, Isla *i.* Chile
107 C1 Navarra *aut. comm.* Spain
Navarre *aut. comm.* Spain *see* Navarra
96 B1 Naver *r.* U.K.
89 D3 Navlya Rus. Fed.
110 C2 Năvodari Romania
77 C2 Navoi Uzbek.
144 B2 Navojoa Mex.
144 B2 Navolato Mex.
74 A2 Nawabshah Pak.
75 C2 Nawada India
62 A1 Nawnghkio Myanmar
62 A1 Nawngleng Myanmar
81 C2 Naxçıvan Azer.
111 C3 Naxos Greece
111 C3 Naxos *i.* Greece
144 B2 Nayar Mex.
66 D2 Nayoro Japan
80 B2 Nazareth Israel
144 B2 Nazas Mex.
144 B2 Nazas *r.* Mex.
150 B4 Nazca Peru
157 H7 Nazca Ridge *sea feature* S. Pacific Ocean
111 C3 Nazilli Turkey
117 B4 Nazrēt Eth.
79 C2 Nazwá Oman
121 B1 Nchelenge Zambia
122 B1 Ncojane Botswana
120 A1 N'dalatando Angola
118 C2 Ndélé C.A.R.
118 B3 Ndendé Gabon
115 D3 Ndjamena Chad
118 A3 Ndogo, Lagune *lag.* Gabon
121 B2 Ndola Zambia
97 C1 Neagh, Lough *l.* U.K.
50 C2 Neale, Lake *salt flat* Austr.
111 B3 Neapoli Greece
111 B2 Nea Roda Greece
99 B4 Neath U.K.
119 D2 Nebbi Uganda
53 C1 Nebine Creek *r.* Austr.
76 B3 Nebitdag Turkm.
150 C2 Neblina, Pico da *mt.* Brazil
135 D3 Nebo, Mount U.S.A.
89 D2 Nebolchi Rus. Fed.
136 C2 Nebraska *state* U.S.A.
137 D2 Nebraska City U.S.A.
108 B3 Nebrodi, Monti *mts Sicily* Italy
139 E3 Neches *r.* U.S.A.
156 E4 Necker Island U.S.A.
153 C3 Necochea Arg.
139 E3 Nederland U.S.A.
100 B2 Neder Rijn *r.* Neth.
130 C2 Nedlouc, Lac *l.* Can.
141 E2 Needham U.S.A.
135 D4 Needles U.S.A.
Neemuch India *see* Nimach
129 E2 Neepawa Can.
87 E3 Neftekamsk Rus. Fed.
82 F2 Nefteyugansk Rus. Fed.
108 A3 Nefza Tunisia
120 A1 Negage Angola
117 B4 Negēlē Eth.
109 D2 Negotin Yugo.
111 B2 Negotino Macedonia
150 A3 Negra, Punta *pt* Peru
155 D1 Negra, Serra *mts* Brazil
63 A2 Negrais, Cape Myanmar
153 B4 Negro *r.* Arg.
150 D3 Negro *r.* S. America
152 C3 Negro *r.* Uru.
106 B2 Negro, Cabo *c.* Morocco
64 B3 Negros *i.* Phil.
79 D1 Nehbandān Iran
69 E1 Nehe China
70 A3 Neijiang China
129 D2 Neilburg Can.
70 A1 Nei Mongol Zizhiqu *aut. reg.* China
150 B2 Neiva Col.
129 E2 Nejanilini Lake Can.
Nejd *reg.* Saudi Arabia *see* Najd
117 B4 Nek'emtē Eth.
89 F2 Nekrasovskoye Rus. Fed.
89 D2 Nelidovo Rus. Fed.
73 B3 Nellore India
128 C3 Nelson Can.
129 E2 Nelson *r.* Can.
54 B2 Nelson N.Z.
52 B3 Nelson, Cape Austr.
53 D2 Nelson Bay Austr.
129 E2 Nelson House Can.
134 E1 Nelson Reservoir U.S.A.
123 D2 Nelspruit S. Africa
114 B3 Néma Maur.
88 B2 Neman Rus. Fed.
105 C2 Nemours France
66 D2 Nemuro Japan
90 B2 Nemyriv Ukr.
97 B2 Nenagh Rep. of Ireland
99 D3 Nene *r.* U.K.
69 E1 Nenjiang China
137 E3 Neosho U.S.A.
75 C2 Nepal *country* Asia
75 C2 Nepalganj Nepal
141 D1 Nepean Can.
135 D3 Nephi U.S.A.
97 B1 Nephin *hill* Rep. of Ireland
97 B1 Nephin Beg Range *hills* Rep. of Ireland
131 D3 Nepisiguit *r.* Can.
119 C2 Nepoko *r.* Dem. Rep. Congo
141 E2 Neptune U.S.A.
108 B2 Nera *r.* Italy
104 C3 Nérac France
53 D1 Nerang Austr.

Nerchinsk
210

69 D1 **Nerchinsk** Rus. Fed.
89 F2 **Nerekhta** Rus. Fed.
109 C2 **Neretva** *r.* Bos.-Herz./Croatia
120 B2 **Neriquinha** Angola
88 B3 **Neris** *r.* Lith.
89 E2 **Nerl'** *r.* Rus. Fed.
86 F2 **Nerokhi** Rus. Fed.
154 C1 **Nerópolis** Brazil
83 J3 **Neryungri** Rus. Fed.
92 □C2 **Neskaupstaður** Iceland
96 B2 **Ness, Loch** *l.* U.K.
136 D3 **Ness City** U.S.A.
Nesterov Ukr. *see* **Zhovkva**
111 B2 **Nestos** *r.* Greece
100 B1 **Netherlands** *country* Europe
147 D3 **Netherlands Antilles** *terr.* West Indies
127 H2 **Nettilling Lake** Can.
101 F1 **Neubrandenburg** Ger.
105 D2 **Neuchâtel** Switz.
105 D2 **Neuchâtel, Lac de** *l.* Switz.
100 C2 **Neuerburg** Ger.
100 B3 **Neufchâteau** Belgium
105 D2 **Neufchâteau** France
104 C2 **Neufchâtel-en-Bray** France
101 D2 **Neuhof** Ger.
101 E3 **Neumarkt in der Oberpfalz** Ger.
102 B1 **Neumünster** Ger.
100 C3 **Neunkirchen** Ger.
153 B3 **Neuquén** Arg.
153 B3 **Neuquén** *r.* Arg.
101 F1 **Neuruppin** Ger.
100 C2 **Neuss** Ger.
101 D1 **Neustadt am Rübenberge** Ger.
101 E3 **Neustadt an der Aisch** Ger.
Neustadt an der Hardt Ger. *see* **Neustadt an der Weinstraße**
101 D3 **Neustadt an der Weinstraße** Ger.
101 E1 **Neustadt-Glewe** Ger.
101 F1 **Neustrelitz** Ger.
99 D5 **Neuville-lès-Dieppe** France
100 C2 **Neuwied** Ger.
137 E3 **Nevada** U.S.A.
135 C3 **Nevada** *state* U.S.A.
106 C2 **Nevada, Sierra** *mts* Spain
135 B2 **Nevada, Sierra** *mts* U.S.A.
88 C2 **Nevaišių kalnis** *hill* Lith.
88 C2 **Nevel'** Rus. Fed.
105 C2 **Nevers** France
53 C2 **Nevertire** Austr.
109 C2 **Nevesinje** Bos.-Herz.
87 D4 **Nevinnomyssk** Rus. Fed.
80 B2 **Nevşehir** Turkey
99 C4 **New Addington** U.K.
128 B2 **New Aiyansh** Can.
119 D4 **Newala** Tanz.
140 B3 **New Albany** U.S.A.
151 D2 **New Amsterdam** Guyana
141 E2 **Newark** *NJ* U.S.A.
140 C2 **Newark** *OH* U.S.A.
99 C3 **Newark-on-Trent** U.K.
141 E2 **New Bedford** U.S.A.
143 E1 **New Bern** U.S.A.
140 B1 **Newberry** *MI* U.S.A.
143 D2 **Newberry** *SC* U.S.A.
139 E2 **New Boston** U.S.A.
139 D3 **New Braunfels** U.S.A.
97 C2 **Newbridge** Rep. of Ireland
59 D3 **New Britain** *i.* P.N.G.
131 D3 **New Brunswick** *prov.* Can.
99 C4 **Newbury** U.K.
48 H6 **New Caledonia** *terr.* S. Pacific Ocean
156 D7 **New Caledonia Trough** *sea feature* Tasman Sea
53 D2 **Newcastle** Austr.
131 D3 **Newcastle** Can.
123 C2 **Newcastle** S. Africa
97 D1 **Newcastle** U.K.
140 C2 **New Castle** U.S.A.
136 C2 **Newcastle** U.S.A.
99 B3 **Newcastle-under-Lyme** U.K.
98 C2 **Newcastle upon Tyne** U.K.
51 C1 **Newcastle Waters** Austr.
97 B2 **Newcastle West** Rep. of Ireland
74 B2 **New Delhi** India
128 C3 **New Denver** Can.
53 D2 **New England Range** *mts* Austr.
157 H3 **New England Seamounts** *sea feature* N. Atlantic Ocean
131 E3 **Newfoundland** *i.* Can.
131 E2 **Newfoundland** *prov.* Can.
96 B3 **New Galloway** U.K.
48 G4 **New Georgia Islands** Solomon Is
131 D3 **New Glasgow** Can.
59 D3 **New Guinea** *i.* Indon./P.N.G.
78 A3 **New Halfa** Sudan
141 E2 **New Hampshire** *state* U.S.A.
59 E3 **New Hanover** *i.* P.N.G.
141 E2 **New Haven** U.S.A.
128 B2 **New Hazelton** Can.
New Hebrides *country* S. Pacific Ocean *see* Vanuatu
156 D7 **New Hebrides Trench** *sea feature* S. Pacific Ocean
142 B2 **New Iberia** U.S.A.
59 E3 **New Ireland** *i.* P.N.G.
141 E3 **New Jersey** *state* U.S.A.
130 C3 **New Liskeard** Can.
140 B2 **New London** U.S.A.
50 A2 **Newman** Austr.
54 C2 **Newman** N.Z.
97 B2 **Newmarket** Rep. of Ireland
99 D3 **Newmarket** U.K.
97 B2 **Newmarket-on-Fergus** Rep. of Ireland
138 B2 **New Mexico** *state* U.S.A.
143 D2 **Newnan** U.S.A.
142 B3 **New Orleans** U.S.A.
140 C2 **New Philadelphia** U.S.A.
54 B1 **New Plymouth** N.Z.
99 C4 **Newport** *England* U.K.
99 B4 **Newport** *Wales* U.K.
142 B1 **Newport** *AR* U.S.A.
134 B2 **Newport** *OR* U.S.A.
141 E2 **Newport** *RI* U.S.A.
143 D1 **Newport** *TN* U.S.A.
141 E2 **Newport** *VT* U.S.A.
134 C1 **Newport** *WA* U.S.A.
141 D3 **Newport News** U.S.A.
143 E3 **New Providence** *i.* Bahamas
99 A4 **Newquay** U.K.
142 B2 **New Roads** U.S.A.
97 C2 **New Ross** Rep. of Ireland
97 C1 **Newry** U.K.
New Siberia Islands Rus. Fed. *see* Novosibirskiye Ostrova
52 B2 **New South Wales** *state* Austr.
137 E2 **Newton** *IA* U.S.A.
137 D3 **Newton** *KS* U.S.A.
99 B4 **Newton Abbot** U.K.
98 C2 **Newton Aycliffe** U.K.
96 B3 **Newton Mearns** U.K.
96 B2 **Newtonmore** U.K.
96 B3 **Newton Stewart** U.K.
97 B2 **Newtown** Rep. of Ireland
99 B3 **Newtown** U.K.
136 C1 **New Town** U.S.A.
97 D1 **Newtownabbey** U.K.
97 D1 **Newtownards** U.K.
Newtownbarry Rep. of Ireland *see* Bunclody
97 C1 **Newtownbutler** U.K.
96 C3 **Newtown St Boswells** U.K.
97 C1 **Newtownstewart** U.K.
137 E2 **New Ulm** U.S.A.
141 E2 **New York** U.S.A.
141 D2 **New York** *state* U.S.A.
54 B2 **New Zealand** *country* Oceania
86 D3 **Neya** Rus. Fed.
81 D3 **Neyrīz** Iran
76 B3 **Neyshābūr** Iran
145 C3 **Nezahualcóyotl, Presa** *resr* Mex.
60 B1 **Ngabang** Indon.
118 B3 **Ngabé** Congo
75 C2 **Ngamring** China
119 D2 **Ngangala** Sudan
75 C1 **Ngangla Ringco** *salt l.* China
75 C1 **Nganglong Kangri** *mt.* China
75 C1 **Nganglong Kangri** *mts* China
75 C1 **Ngangzê Co** *salt l.* China
62 A2 **Ngao** Thai.
118 B2 **Ngaoundal** Cameroon
118 B2 **Ngaoundéré** Cameroon
54 C1 **Ngaruawahia** N.Z.
62 A2 **Ngathainggyaung** Myanmar
Ngiva Angola *see* **Ondjiva**
118 B3 **Ngo** Congo
63 B2 **Ngoc Linh** *mt.* Vietnam
115 D4 **Ngol Bembo** Nigeria
68 C2 **Ngoring Hu** *l.* China
115 D3 **Ngourti** Niger
115 D3 **Nguigmi** Niger
59 D2 **Ngulu** *atoll* Micronesia
61 C2 **Ngunut** Indon.
Ngunza Angola *see* **Sumbe**
Ngunza-Kabolu Angola *see* **Sumbe**
115 D3 **Nguru** Nigeria
62 B1 **Nguyên Binh** Vietnam
123 C2 **Ngwathe** S. Africa
123 D2 **Ngwelezana** S. Africa
121 C2 **Nhamalabué** Moz.
120 A2 **N'harea** Angola
63 B2 **Nha Trang** Vietnam
52 B3 **Nhill** Austr.
123 D2 **Nhlangano** Swaziland
51 C1 **Nhulunbuy** Austr.
141 D2 **Niagara Falls** Can.
114 C3 **Niamey** Niger
119 C2 **Niangara** Dem. Rep. Congo
114 B3 **Niangay, Lac** *l.* Mali
119 C2 **Nia-Nia** Dem. Rep. Congo
60 A1 **Nias** *i.* Indon.
88 B2 **Nīca** Latvia
146 B3 **Nicaragua** *country* Central America
146 B3 **Nicaragua, Lago de** *l.* Nic.
Nicaragua, Lake Nic. *see* Nicaragua, Lago de
109 C3 **Nicastro** Italy
105 D3 **Nice** France
73 D4 **Nicobar Islands** India
80 B2 **Nicosia** Cyprus
146 B4 **Nicoya, Golfo de** *b.* Costa Rica
88 B2 **Nida** Lith.
103 E1 **Nidzica** Pol.
102 B1 **Niebüll** Ger.
101 D2 **Niederaula** Ger.
118 B2 **Niefang** Equat. Guinea
101 F1 **Niemegk** Ger.
101 D1 **Nienburg (Weser)** Ger.
103 C1 **Niesky** Ger.
100 B1 **Nieuwegein** Neth.
100 B1 **Nieuwe-Niedorp** Neth.
151 D2 **Nieuw Nickerie** Suriname
122 A3 **Nieuwoudtville** S. Africa
100 A2 **Nieuwpoort** Belgium
80 B2 **Niğde** Turkey
115 D3 **Niger** *country* Africa
115 C4 **Niger** *r.* Africa
115 C4 **Niger, Mouths of the** Nigeria
115 C4 **Nigeria** *country* Africa
130 B3 **Nighthawk Lake** Can.
111 B2 **Nigrita** Greece
67 C3 **Niigata** Japan
67 B4 **Niihama** Japan
67 C4 **Nii-jima** *i.* Japan
67 B4 **Niimi** Japan
67 C3 **Niitsu** Japan
107 C2 **Níjar** Spain
100 B1 **Nijkerk** Neth.
100 B2 **Nijmegen** Neth.
100 C1 **Nijverdal** Neth.
92 J2 **Nikel'** Rus. Fed.
Nikolayev Ukr. *see* Mykolayiv
87 D3 **Nikolayevsk** Rus. Fed.
Nikolayevskiy Rus. Fed. *see* **Nikolayevsk**
86 D3 **Nikol'sk** Rus. Fed.
Nikol'skiy Kazakh. *see* Satpayev
83 M3 **Nikol'skoye** Rus. Fed.
Nikol'skoye Rus. Fed. *see* Sheksna
91 C2 **Nikopol'** Ukr.
80 B1 **Niksar** Turkey
79 D2 **Nīkshahr** Iran
109 C2 **Nikšić** Yugo.
Nīl, Bahr el *r.* Africa *see* Nile
135 C4 **Niland** U.S.A.
116 B1 **Nile** *r.* Africa
140 B2 **Niles** U.S.A.
74 B2 **Nimach** India
105 C3 **Nîmes** France
53 C3 **Nimmitabel** Austr.
117 B4 **Nimule** Sudan
Nimwegen Neth. *see* Nijmegen
53 C1 **Nindigully** Austr.
73 B4 **Nine Degree Channel** India
53 C3 **Ninety Mile Beach** Austr.
54 B1 **Ninety Mile Beach** N.Z.
70 C3 **Ningbo** China
71 B3 **Ningde** China
71 B3 **Ningdu** China
70 B2 **Ningguo** China
71 C3 **Ninghai** China
Ninghsia Hui Autonomous Region *aut. reg.* China *see* **Ningxia**
72 D2 **Ninging** India
Ningjiang China *see* Songyuan
68 C2 **Ningjing Shan** *mts* China
70 A2 **Ningxia** *aut. reg.* China
70 B2 **Ningyang** China
62 B1 **Ninh Binh** Vietnam
63 B2 **Ninh Hoa** Vietnam
66 D2 **Ninohe** Japan
137 D2 **Niobrara** *r.* U.S.A.
62 A1 **Nioko** India
114 B3 **Niono** Mali
114 B3 **Nioro** Mali
104 B2 **Niort** France
129 D2 **Nipawin** Can.
130 B3 **Nipigon** Can.
130 B3 **Nipigon, Lake** Can.
131 D2 **Nipishish Lake** Can.
130 C3 **Nipissing, Lake** Can.
135 C3 **Nipton** U.S.A.
151 E4 **Niquelândia** Brazil
74 B3 **Nirmal** India
109 D2 **Niš** Yugo.
109 D2 **Nišava** *r.* Yugo.
108 B3 **Niscemi** *Sicily* Italy
67 B4 **Nishino-omote** Japan
90 B2 **Nisporeni** Moldova
155 D2 **Niterói** Brazil
96 C3 **Nith** *r.* U.K.
103 D2 **Nitra** Slovakia
49 K5 **Niue** *terr.* S. Pacific Ocean
92 H3 **Nivala** Fin.
100 B2 **Nivelles** Belgium
73 B3 **Nizamabad** India
87 E3 **Nizhnekamsk** Rus. Fed.
87 E3 **Nizhnekamskoye Vodokhranilishche** *resr* Rus. Fed.
83 H3 **Nizhneudinsk** Rus. Fed.
82 G2 **Nizhnevartovsk** Rus. Fed.
Nizhnevolzhsk Rus. Fed. *see* **Narimanov**
83 K2 **Nizhneyansk** Rus. Fed.
Nizhniye Kresty Rus. Fed. *see* **Cherskiy**
Nizhniye Ustriki Pol. *see* Ustrzyki Dolne
89 F3 **Nizhniy Kislyay** Rus. Fed.
87 D3 **Nizhniy Lomov** Rus. Fed.
87 D3 **Nizhniy Novgorod** Rus. Fed.
86 E2 **Nizhniy Odes** Rus. Fed.
86 E3 **Nizhniy Tagil** Rus. Fed.
83 G2 **Nizhnyaya Tunguska** *r.* Rus. Fed.
86 E3 **Nizhnyaya Tura** Rus. Fed.
91 C1 **Nizhyn** Ukr.
103 E1 **Nizina** *reg.* Pol.
Njazidja *i.* Comoros *see* Grande Comore
119 D3 **Njinjo** Tanz.
119 D3 **Njombe** Tanz.
118 B2 **Nkambe** Cameroon
119 D4 **Nkhata Bay** Malawi
121 C2 **Nkhotakota** Malawi
118 A3 **Nkomi, Lagune** *lag.* Gabon
119 D3 **Nkondwe** Tanz.
118 A2 **Nkongsamba** Cameroon
123 C3 **Nkululeko** S. Africa
123 C3 **Nkwenkwezi** S. Africa
67 B4 **Nobeoka** Japan
140 B2 **Noblesville** U.S.A.
52 B1 **Noccundra** Austr.
144 A1 **Nogales** Mex.
138 A2 **Nogales** U.S.A.
104 C2 **Nogent-le-Rotrou** France
83 H2 **Noginsk** Rus. Fed.
89 E2 **Noginsk** Rus. Fed.
83 K3 **Nogliki** Rus. Fed.
74 B2 **Nohar** India
100 C3 **Nohfelden** Ger.
104 B2 **Noires, Montagnes** *hills* France

104 B2 Noirmoutier, Île de i. France
104 B2 Noirmoutier-en-l'Île France
67 C4 Nojima-zaki c. Japan
74 B2 Nokha India
93 H3 Nokia Fin.
74 A2 Nok Kundi Pak.
118 B2 Nola C.A.R.
86 D3 Nolinsk Rus. Fed.
126 A2 Nome U.S.A.
123 C3 Nomonde S. Africa
123 D2 Nondweni S. Africa
Nonghui China see Guang'an
62 B2 Nong Khai Thai.
75 D2 Nongstoin India
52 A2 Nonning Austr.
144 B2 Nonoava Mex.
65 B2 Nonsan S. Korea
63 B2 Nonthaburi Thai.
122 B3 Nonzwakazi S. Africa
100 B1 Noordwijk-Binnen Neth.
77 C3 Norak Tajik.
130 C3 Noranda Can.
82 C1 Nordaustlandet i. Svalbard
128 C2 Nordegg Can.
100 C1 Norden Ger.
83 H1 Nordenshel'da, Arkhipelag is Rus. Fed.
Nordenskjold Archipelago is Rus. Fed. see
Nordenshel'da, Arkhipelag
100 C1 Norderney Ger.
100 C1 Norderney i. Ger.
101 E1 Norderstedt Ger.
93 E3 Nordfjordeid Norway
102 B1 Nordfriesische Inseln is Ger.
101 E2 Nordhausen Ger.
101 D1 Nordholz Ger.
100 C1 Nordhorn Ger.
92 I1 Nordkapp c. Norway
92 F3 Nordli Norway
102 C2 Nördlingen Ger.
92 G3 Nordmaling Sweden
94 B1 Norðoyar i. Faroe Is
97 C2 Nore r. Rep. of Ireland
88 B3 Noreikiškės Lith.
137 D2 Norfolk NE U.S.A.
141 D3 Norfolk VA U.S.A.
48 H6 Norfolk Island terr. S. Pacific Ocean
93 E3 Norheimsund Norway
82 G2 Noril'sk Rus. Fed.
139 D1 Norman U.S.A.
Normandes, Îles is Europe see Channel Islands
150 D2 Normandia Brazil
104 B2 Normandie reg. France
Normandy reg. France see Normandie
51 D1 Normanton Austr.
128 B1 Norman Wells Can.
93 G4 Norrköping Sweden
93 G4 Norrtälje Sweden
50 B3 Norseman Austr.
92 G3 Norsjö Sweden
55 M2 North, Cape Antarctica
98 C2 Northallerton U.K.
50 A3 Northam Austr.
50 A2 Northampton U.K.
99 C3 Northampton U.K.
73 D3 North Andaman i. India
159 F4 North Australian Basin sea feature Indian Ocean
129 D2 North Battleford Can.
130 C3 North Bay Can.
130 C2 North Belcher Islands Can.
96 C2 North Berwick U.K.
North Borneo state Malaysia see Sabah
North Cape Norway see Nordkapp
54 B1 North Cape N.Z.
130 A2 North Caribou Lake Can.
143 E1 North Carolina state U.S.A.
130 B3 North Channel lake channel Can.
96 A3 North Channel U.K.
143 E2 North Charleston U.S.A.
128 B3 North Cowichan Can.
136 C1 North Dakota state U.S.A.
99 C4 North Downs hills U.K.
157 E3 Northeast Pacific Basin sea feature N. Pacific Ocean

143 E3 Northeast Providence Channel Bahamas
101 D2 Northeim Ger.
123 C1 Northern prov. S. Africa
122 A2 Northern Cape prov. S. Africa
Northern Dvina r. Rus. Fed. see Severnaya Dvina
129 E2 Northern Indian Lake Can.
97 C1 Northern Ireland prov. U.K.
59 D1 Northern Mariana Islands terr. N. Pacific Ocean
Northern Rhodesia country Africa see Zambia
50 C1 Northern Territory admin. div. Austr.
Northern Transvaal prov. S. Africa see Northern
96 C2 North Esk r. U.K.
137 E2 Northfield U.S.A.
99 D4 North Foreland c. U.K.
North Frisian Islands Ger. see Nordfriesische Inseln
160 O2 North Geomagnetic Pole Greenland
54 B1 North Island N.Z.
129 E2 North Knife Lake Can.
72 D2 North Lakhimpur India
North Land is Rus. Fed. see Severnaya Zemlya
160 Q2 North Magnetic Pole Can.
136 C2 North Platte U.S.A.
136 C2 North Platte r. U.S.A.
96 C1 North Ronaldsay i. U.K.
129 D2 North Saskatchewan r. Can.
94 D2 North Sea Europe
63 A2 North Sentinel Island India
130 A2 North Spirit Lake Can.
53 D1 North Stradbroke Island Austr.
131 D3 North Sydney Can.
54 B1 North Taranaki Bight b. N.Z.
130 C2 North Twin Island Can.
98 B2 North Tyne r. U.K.
96 A2 North Uist i. U.K.
131 D3 Northumberland Strait Can.
99 D3 North Walsham U.K.
123 C2 North West prov. S. Africa
158 D1 Northwest Atlantic Mid-Ocean Channnel sea chan. N. Atlantic Ocean
50 A2 North West Cape Austr.
156 D3 Northwest Pacific Basin sea feature N. Pacific Ocean
143 E3 Northwest Providence Channel Bahamas
131 E2 North West River Can.
128 B1 Northwest Territories admin. div. Can.
98 C2 North York Moors moorland U.K.
140 C3 Norton U.S.A.
121 C2 Norton Zimbabwe
Norton de Matos Angola see Balombo
126 B2 Norton Sound sea chan. U.S.A.
55 D2 Norvegia, Cape Antarctica
140 C2 Norwalk U.S.A.
93 F3 Norway country Europe
129 E2 Norway House Can.
160 L3 Norwegian Basin sea feature N. Atlantic Ocean
92 E2 Norwegian Sea N. Atlantic Ocean
99 D3 Norwich U.K.
141 E2 Norwich CT U.S.A.
141 D2 Norwich NY U.S.A.
66 D2 Noshiro Japan
91 C1 Nosivka Ukr.
122 B2 Nosop watercourse Africa
86 E2 Nosovaya Rus. Fed.
79 C2 Noşratābād Iran
121 □E2 Nosy Boraha i. Madag.
91 E1 Noteć r. Pol.
93 E4 Notodden Norway
67 C3 Noto-hantō pen. Japan
131 D3 Notre Dame, Monts mts Can.

131 E3 Notre Dame Bay Can.
130 C2 Nottaway r. Can.
99 C3 Nottingham U.K.
114 A2 Nouâdhibou Maur.
114 A3 Nouakchott Maur.
114 A3 Nouâmghâr Maur.
63 D2 Nouei Vietnam
48 H6 Nouméa New Caledonia
114 B3 Nouna Burkina
122 B3 Noupoort S. Africa
Nouveau-Comptoir Can. see Wemindji
Nouvelle Anvers Dem. Rep. Congo see Makanza
Nouvelles Hébrides country S. Pacific Ocean see Vanuatu
154 B2 Nova Chaves Angola see Muconda
154 B2 Nova Esperança Brazil
154 C1 Nova Freixa Moz. see Cuamba
155 D2 Nova Friburgo Brazil
109 C1 Nova Gradiška Croatia
154 C2 Nova Granada Brazil
155 D2 Nova Iguaçu Brazil
91 C2 Nova Kakhovka Ukr.
155 D1 Nova Lima Brazil
Nova Lisboa Angola see Huambo
154 B2 Nova Londrina Brazil
91 C2 Nova Odesa Ukr.
154 C1 Nova Paraíso Brazil
154 C1 Nova Ponte Brazil
108 A1 Novara Italy
151 E3 Nova Remanso Brazil
131 D3 Nova Scotia prov. Can.
155 D1 Nova Venécia Brazil
83 K1 Novaya Sibir', Ostrov i. Rus. Fed.
86 E1 Novaya Zemlya is Rus. Fed.
107 C2 Novelda Spain
103 D2 Nové Zámky Slovakia
Novgorod Rus. Fed. see Velikiy Novgorod
91 C1 Novhorod-Sivers'kyy Ukr.
110 B2 Novi Iskŭr Bulg.
66 D1 Novikovo Rus. Fed.
108 A2 Novi Ligure Italy
109 D2 Novi Pazar Yugo.
109 C1 Novi Sad Yugo.
Novoalekseyevka Kazakh. see Khobda
87 D3 Novoanninskiy Rus. Fed.
150 C3 Novo Aripuanã Brazil
91 D2 Novoazovs'k Ukr.
91 E2 Novocherkassk Rus. Fed.
86 D2 Novodugino Rus. Fed.
86 D2 Novodvinsk Rus. Fed.
Novoekonomicheskoye Ukr. see Dymytrov
152 C2 Novo Hamburgo Brazil
154 C2 Novo Horizonte Brazil
90 B1 Novohrad-Volyns'kyy Ukr.
Novokazalinsk Kazakh. see Ayteke Bi
91 E1 Novokhopersk Rus. Fed.
68 B1 Novokuznetsk Rus. Fed.
109 C1 Novo Mesto Slovenia
91 D3 Novomikhaylovskiy Rus. Fed.
89 E3 Novomoskovsk Rus. Fed.
91 D2 Novomoskovs'k Ukr.
91 C2 Novomyrhorod Ukr.
Novonikolayevsk Rus. Fed. see Novosibirsk
91 C2 Novooleksiyivka Ukr.
91 E2 Novopokrovskaya Rus. Fed.
91 D2 Novopskov Ukr.
Novo Redondo Angola see Sumbe
91 D2 Novorossiysk Rus. Fed.
89 E2 Novorzhev Rus. Fed.
87 E3 Novosergiyevka Rus. Fed.
91 D2 Novoshakhtinsk Rus. Fed.
82 G3 Novosibirsk Rus. Fed.
83 K1 Novosibirskiye Ostrova is Rus. Fed.
89 E3 Novosil' Rus. Fed.
89 D2 Novosokol'niki Rus. Fed.
91 C2 Novotroyits'ke Ukr.
91 C2 Novoukrayinka Ukr.
90 A1 Novovolyns'k Ukr.
89 E3 Novovoronezh Rus. Fed.
Novovoronezhskiy Rus. Fed. see Novovoronezh

89 D3 Novozybkov Rus. Fed.
103 D2 Nový Jičin Czech Rep.
86 E2 Novyy Bor Rus. Fed.
91 C2 Novyy Buh Ukr.
Novyy Donbass Ukr. see Dymytrov
Novyye Petushki Rus. Fed. see Petushki
Novyy Margelan Uzbek. see Fergana
89 E2 Novyy Nekouz Rus. Fed.
91 D1 Novyy Oskol Rus. Fed.
86 G2 Novyy Port Rus. Fed.
86 G2 Novyy Urengoy Rus. Fed.
69 E1 Novyy Urgal Rus. Fed.
Novyy Uzen' Kazakh. see Zhanaozen
103 D1 Nowogard Pol.
Noworadomsk Pol. see Radomsko
53 D2 Nowra Austr.
81 D2 Now Shahr Iran
74 B1 Nowshera Pak.
103 E2 Nowy Sącz Pol.
103 E2 Nowy Targ Pol.
82 G2 Noyabr'sk Rus. Fed.
105 C2 Noyon France
121 C2 Nsanje Malawi
121 B2 Nsombo Zambia
118 B3 Ntandembele Dem. Rep. Congo
123 C2 Ntha S. Africa
118 A2 Ntoum Gabon
119 D3 Ntungamo Uganda
Nuanetsi r. Zimbabwe see Mwenezi
79 C2 Nu'aym reg. Oman
116 B2 Nubian Desert Sudan
150 B4 Nudo Coropuna mt. Peru
139 D3 Nueces r. U.S.A.
129 E1 Nueltin Lake Can.
150 B2 Nueva Loja Ecuador
153 A4 Nueva Lubecka Arg.
145 B2 Nueva Rosita Mex.
144 B1 Nuevo Casas Grandes Mex.
144 B2 Nuevo Ideal Mex.
145 C2 Nuevo Laredo Mex.
117 C4 Nugaal watercourse Somalia
105 C2 Nuits-St-Georges France
62 A1 Nu Jiang r. China
Nukha Azer. see Şäki
49 J6 Nuku'alofa Tonga
49 M4 Nuku Hiva i. Fr. Polynesia
48 G4 Nukumanu Islands P.N.G.
76 B2 Nukus Uzbek.
50 B2 Nullagine Austr.
50 C3 Nullarbor Austr.
50 B3 Nullarbor Plain Austr.
115 D4 Numan Nigeria
67 C3 Numazu Japan
51 C1 Numbulwar Austr.
93 E3 Numedal val. Norway
59 C3 Numfoor i. Indon.
53 C3 Numurkah Austr.
127 J2 Nunap Isua c. Greenland
129 E1 Nunavut admin. div. Can.
99 C3 Nuneaton U.K.
126 A3 Nunivak Island U.S.A.
106 B1 Nuñomoral Spain
108 A2 Nuoro Sardinia Italy
78 B2 Nuqrah Saudi Arabia
77 C1 Nura r. Kazakh.
Nuremberg Ger. see Nürnberg
52 A2 Nuriootpa Austr.
92 I3 Nurmes Fin.
101 E3 Nürnberg Ger.
53 C2 Nurri, Mount hill Austr.
62 A1 Nu Shan mts China
74 A2 Nushki Pak.
127 I2 Nuuk Greenland
127 I2 Nuussuaq Greenland
127 I2 Nuussuaq pen. Greenland
80 B3 Nuweiba el Muzeina Egypt
122 A3 Nuwerus S. Africa
122 B3 Nuweveldberge mts S. Africa
86 F2 Nyagan' Rus. Fed.
75 D1 Nyainqêntanglha Feng mt. China
75 D2 Nyainqêntanglha Shan mts China
Nyakh Rus. Fed. see Nyagan'
117 A3 Nyala Sudan
75 C2 Nyalam China
119 D4 Nyamtumbo Tanz.

Nyande Zimbabwe see Masvingo
86 D2 Nyandoma Rus. Fed.
118 B3 Nyanga Congo
118 B3 Nyanga r. Gabon
121 C2 Nyanga Zimbabwe
121 C1 Nyasa, Lake Africa
Nyasaland country Africa see Malawi
88 C3 Nyasvizh Belarus
62 A2 Nyaunglebin Myanmar
93 F4 Nyborg Denmark
92 I1 Nyborg Norway
93 G4 Nybro Sweden
Nyenchen Tanglha Range mts China see Nyaingêntanglha Shan
119 D3 Nyeri Kenya
75 C1 Nyima China
68 C3 Nyingchi China
103 E2 Nyíregyháza Hungary
93 F5 Nykøbing Denmark
93 G4 Nyköping Sweden
123 C1 Nylstroom S. Africa
53 C2 Nymagee Austr.
93 G4 Nynäshamn Sweden
53 C2 Nyngan Austr.
88 B3 Nyoman r. Belarus/Lith.
105 D3 Nyons France
86 E2 Nyrob Rus. Fed.
103 D1 Nysa Pol.
134 C2 Nyssa U.S.A.
119 C3 Nyunzu Dem. Rep. Congo
83 I2 Nyurba Rus. Fed.
91 C2 Nyzhni Sirohozy Ukr.
91 C2 Nyzhn'ohirs'kyy Ukr.
118 B3 Nzambi Congo
119 D3 Nzega Tanz.
114 B4 Nzérékoré Guinea
120 A1 N'zeto Angola

O

136 C2 Oahe, Lake U.S.A.
49 L1 Oahu i. U.S.A.
52 B2 Oakbank Austr.
142 B2 Oakdale U.S.A.
53 D1 Oakey Austr.
140 B3 Oak Grove U.S.A.
99 C3 Oakham U.K.
134 B1 Oak Harbor U.S.A.
140 C3 Oak Hill U.S.A.
135 B3 Oakland CA U.S.A.
141 D3 Oakland MD U.S.A.
140 B2 Oak Lawn U.S.A.
136 C3 Oakley U.S.A.
50 B2 Oakover r. Austr.
134 B2 Oakridge U.S.A.
143 D1 Oak Ridge U.S.A.
54 B3 Oamaru N.Z.
64 B2 Oas Phil.
145 C3 Oaxaca Mex.
86 F2 Ob' r. Rus. Fed.
Ob, Gulf of sea chan. Rus. Fed. see Obskaya Guba
88 C2 Obal' Belarus
118 B2 Obala Cameroon
96 B2 Oban U.K.
106 B1 O Barco Spain
Obbia Somalia see Hobyo
136 C3 Oberlin U.S.A.
53 C2 Oberon Austr.
101 F3 Oberviechtach Ger.
59 C3 Obi i. Indon.
151 D3 Óbidos Brazil
66 D2 Obihiro Japan
69 E1 Obluch'ye Rus. Fed.
89 E2 Obninsk Rus. Fed.
119 C2 Obo C.A.R.
117 C3 Obock Djibouti
103 D1 Oborniki Pol.
118 B3 Obouya Congo
89 E3 Oboyan' Rus. Fed.
86 D2 Obozerskiy Rus. Fed.
144 B2 Obregón, Presa resr Mex.
109 D2 Obrenovac Yugo.
134 B2 O'Brien U.S.A.
87 E3 Obshchiy Syrt hills Rus. Fed.
86 G2 Obskaya Guba sea chan. Rus. Fed.
114 B4 Obuasi Ghana
90 C1 Obukhiv Ukr.
86 D2 Ob"yachevo Rus. Fed.
143 D3 Ocala U.S.A.
144 B2 Ocampo Mex.
106 C2 Ocaña Spain

150 B2 Occidental, Cordillera mts Col.
150 B4 Occidental, Cordillera mts Peru
141 D3 Ocean City MD U.S.A.
141 E3 Ocean City NJ U.S.A.
128 B2 Ocean Falls Can.
135 C4 Oceanside U.S.A.
91 C2 Ochakiv Ukr.
86 E3 Ocher Rus. Fed.
101 E3 Ochsenfurt Ger.
110 B1 Ocna Mureş Romania
90 B2 Ocniţa Moldova
143 D2 Oconee r. U.S.A.
145 C3 Ocosingo Mex.
143 E1 Ocracoke Island U.S.A.
October Revolution Island Rus. Fed. see Oktyabr'skoy Revolyutsii, Ostrov
116 B2 Oda, Jebel mt. Sudan
66 D2 Ōdate Japan
67 C3 Odawara Japan
93 E3 Odda Norway
106 B2 Odemira Port.
111 C3 Ödemiş Turkey
93 F4 Odense Denmark
101 D3 Odenwald reg. Ger.
102 C1 Oder r. Ger.
102 C1 Oderbucht b. Ger.
90 C2 Odesa Ukr.
139 C2 Odessa U.S.A.
114 B4 Odienné Côte d'Ivoire
89 E3 Odoyev Rus. Fed.
103 D1 Odra r. Pol.
151 E3 Oeiras Brazil
101 D2 Oelde Ger.
136 C2 Oelrichs U.S.A.
101 F2 Oelsnitz Ger.
100 B1 Oenkerk Neth.
137 E3 O'Fallon U.S.A.
109 C2 Ofanto r. Italy
101 D2 Offenbach am Main Ger.
102 B2 Offenburg Ger.
66 C3 Oga Japan
117 C4 Ogadēn reg. Eth.
66 C3 Oga-hantō pen. Japan
67 C3 Ōgaki Japan
136 C2 Ogallala U.S.A.
69 F3 Ogasawara-shotō is Japan
115 C4 Ogbomoso Nigeria
134 D2 Ogden U.S.A.
141 D2 Ogdensburg U.S.A.
126 C2 Ogilvie r. Can.
126 C2 Ogilvie Mountains Can.
143 D2 Oglethorpe, Mount U.S.A.
130 B2 Ogoki r. Can.
130 B2 Ogoki Reservoir Can.
88 B2 Ogre Latvia
109 C1 Ogulin Croatia
81 D2 Ogurchinskiy, Ostrov i. Turkm.
115 C2 Ohanet Alg.
140 B3 Ohio r. U.S.A.
140 C2 Ohio state U.S.A.
101 E2 Ohrdruf Ger.
101 F2 Ohře r. Czech Rep.
111 B2 Ohrid Macedonia
151 D2 Oiapoque Brazil
141 D2 Oil City U.S.A.
100 A3 Oise r. France
67 B4 Ōita Japan
144 B2 Ojinaga Mex.
152 B2 Ojos del Salado, Nevado mt. Arg./Chile
89 F2 Oka r. Rus. Fed.
120 A3 Okahandja Namibia
120 A3 Okakarara Namibia
128 C3 Okanagan Falls Can.
128 C3 Okanagan Lake Can.
134 C1 Okanogan U.S.A.
134 C1 Okanogan r. U.S.A.
74 B1 Okara Pak.
120 B2 Okavango r. Botswana/Namibia
120 B2 Okavango Delta swamp Botswana
67 C3 Okaya Japan
67 B4 Okayama Japan
67 C4 Okazaki Japan
143 D3 Okeechobee U.S.A.
143 D3 Okeechobee, Lake U.S.A.
143 D2 Okefenokee Swamp U.S.A.
99 A4 Okehampton U.K.
115 C4 Okene Nigeria
101 E1 Oker r. Ger.
74 A2 Okha India
83 K3 Okha Rus. Fed.
75 C2 Okhaldhunga Nepal

83 K3 Okhotka r. Rus. Fed.
83 K3 Okhotsk Rus. Fed.
83 K3 Okhotsk, Sea of Japan/Rus. Fed.
Okhotskoye More sea Japan/Rus. Fed. see Okhotsk, Sea of
91 C1 Okhtyrka Ukr.
69 E3 Okinawa i. Japan
67 B3 Oki-shotō is Japan
139 D1 Oklahoma state U.S.A.
139 D1 Oklahoma City U.S.A.
139 D1 Okmulgee U.S.A.
91 C1 Oknitsa Moldova see Ocniţa
78 A2 Oko, Wadi watercourse Sudan
118 B3 Okondja Gabon
118 B3 Okotoks Can.
89 D3 Okovskiy Les for. Rus. Fed.
118 B3 Okoyo Congo
92 H1 Øksfjord Norway
62 A2 Oktwin Myanmar
Oktyabr' Kazakh. see Kandyagash
Oktyabr'sk Kazakh. see Kandyagash
86 D2 Oktyabr'skiy Rus. Fed.
83 L3 Oktyabr'skiy Rus. Fed.
87 E3 Oktyabr'skiy Rus. Fed.
86 F2 Oktyabr'skoye Rus. Fed.
83 H1 Oktyabr'skoy Revolyutsii, Ostrov i. Rus. Fed.
89 D2 Okulovka Rus. Fed.
66 C2 Okushiri-tō i. Japan
92 □B2 Ólafsfjörður Iceland
92 □A3 Ólafsvík Iceland
88 B2 Olaine Latvia
93 G4 Öland i. Sweden
52 B2 Olary Austr.
136 B3 Olathe CO U.S.A.
137 E3 Olathe KS U.S.A.
153 B3 Olavarría Arg.
103 D1 Oława Pol.
108 A2 Olbia Sardinia Italy
126 C2 Old Crow Can.
101 D1 Oldenburg Ger.
102 C1 Oldenburg in Holstein Ger.
100 C1 Oldenzaal Neth.
98 B3 Oldham U.K.
97 B3 Old Head of Kinsale hd Rep. of Ireland
96 C2 Oldmeldrum U.K.
128 C2 Olds Can.
129 D2 Old Wives Lake Can.
141 D2 Olean U.S.A.
103 E1 Olecko Pol.
83 J2 Olekminsk Rus. Fed.
91 C2 Oleksandrivka Ukr.
Oleksandrivs'k Ukr. see Zaporizhzhya
91 C2 Oleksandriya Ukr.
86 C2 Olenegorsk Rus. Fed.
83 I2 Olenek Rus. Fed.
83 I2 Olenek r. Rus. Fed.
89 D2 Olenivs'ki Kar"yery Ukr. see Dokuchayevs'k
Olenya Rus. Fed. see Olenegorsk
Oleshky Ukr. see Tsyurupyns'k
103 D1 Olesno Pol.
90 B1 Olevs'k Ukr.
106 B2 Olhão Port.
122 A2 Olifants watercourse Namibia
123 D1 Olifants S. Africa
122 A3 Olifants r. S. Africa
122 A3 Olifants r. S. Africa
122 B2 Olifantshoek S. Africa
154 C2 Olímpia Brazil
151 F3 Olinda Brazil
123 C1 Oliphants Drift S. Africa
107 C2 Oliva Spain
155 D2 Oliveira Brazil
Olivença Moz. see Lupilichi
106 B2 Olivenza Spain
142 B2 Olla U.S.A.
152 A3 Ollagüe Chile
106 C1 Olmedo Spain
105 D3 Olmeto Corsica France
150 B2 Olmos Peru
140 B3 Olney U.S.A.
103 D2 Olomouc Czech Rep.
86 C2 Olonets Rus. Fed.
64 B2 Olongapo Phil.
104 B3 Oloron-Ste-Marie France

107 D1 Olot Spain
69 D1 Olovyannaya Rus. Fed.
100 C2 Olpe Ger.
103 E1 Olsztyn Pol.
110 B2 Olt r. Romania
110 C2 Olteniţa Romania
139 C2 Olton U.S.A.
81 C1 Oltu Turkey
Ol'viopol' Ukr. see Pervomays'k
111 B3 Olympia tourist site Greece
134 B1 Olympia U.S.A.
111 B2 Olympos mt. Greece
Olympus, Mount Greece see Olympos
134 B1 Olympus, Mount U.S.A.
83 M2 Olyutorskiy Rus. Fed.
83 M3 Olyutorskiy, Mys c. Rus. Fed.
66 D2 Ōma Japan
97 C1 Omagh U.K.
137 D2 Omaha U.S.A.
79 C3 Oman country Asia
79 C2 Oman, Gulf of Asia
54 A2 Omarama N.Z.
120 A3 Omaruru Namibia
120 B2 Omatako watercourse Namibia
122 B2 Omaweneno Botswana
116 B3 Omdurman Sudan
53 C3 Omeo Austr.
145 C3 Ometepec Mex.
78 A3 Om Hajēr Eritrea
81 C2 Omīdīyeh Iran
128 B2 Omineca Mountains Can.
120 A3 Omitara Namibia
67 C3 Ōmiya Japan
100 C1 Ommen Neth.
83 L2 Omolon r. Rus. Fed.
100 B3 Omont France
82 F3 Omsk Rus. Fed.
83 L2 Omsukchan Rus. Fed.
110 C1 Omu, Vârful mt. Romania
67 A4 Ōmura Japan
140 A2 Onalaska U.S.A.
141 D3 Onancock U.S.A.
140 C1 Onaping Lake Can.
131 C3 Onatchiway, Lac l. Can.
63 A2 Onbingwin Myanmar
120 A2 Oncócua Angola
122 B3 Onderstedorings S. Africa
120 A2 Ondjiva Angola
69 D1 Öndörhaan Mongolia
122 B1 One Botswana
86 C2 Onega Rus. Fed.
86 C2 Onega r. Rus. Fed.
86 C2 Onega, Lake Rus. Fed.
128 B2 One Hundred Mile House Can.
141 D2 Oneida Lake U.S.A.
137 D2 O'Neill U.S.A.
141 D2 Oneonta U.S.A.
110 C1 Oneşti Romania
Onezhskoye Ozero l. Rus. Fed. see Onega, Lake
122 B2 Ongers watercourse S. Africa
65 B2 Ongjin N. Korea
73 C3 Ongole India
121 □D3 Onilahy r. Madag.
115 C4 Onitsha Nigeria
120 A3 Onjati Mountain Namibia
67 C3 Ōno Japan
156 D6 Onotoa atoll Kiribati
122 A2 Onseepkans S. Africa
50 A2 Onslow Austr.
143 E2 Onslow Bay U.S.A.
130 A2 Ontario prov. Can.
134 C2 Ontario U.S.A.
141 D2 Ontario, Lake Can./U.S.A.
107 C2 Ontinyent Spain
51 C2 Oodnadatta Austr.
Oostende Belgium see Ostend
100 B2 Oosterhout Neth.
100 A2 Oosterschelde est. Neth.
100 B1 Oost-Vlieland Neth.
128 B2 Ootsa Lake Can.
128 B2 Ootsa Lake l. Can.
118 C3 Opala Dem. Rep. Congo
130 C2 Opataca, Lac l. Can.
103 D2 Opava Czech Rep.
143 C2 Opelika U.S.A.
142 B2 Opelousas U.S.A.
117 A4 Opienge Dem. Rep. Congo
130 C2 Opinaca, Réservoir resr Can.
131 D2 Opiscotéo, Lac l. Can.
88 C2 Opochka Rus. Fed.
144 A2 Opodepe Mex.

103 D1	Opole Pol.
76 B2	Opornyy Kazakh.
106 B1	Oporto Port.
54 C1	Opotiki N.Z.
93 E3	Oppdal Norway
134 C1	Opportunity U.S.A.
54 B1	Opunake N.Z.
120 A2	Opuwo Namibia
110 B1	Oradea Romania
109 D2	Orahovac Yugo.
114 B1	Oran Alg.
152 B2	Orán Arg.
65 B1	Örang N. Korea
53 C2	Orange Austr.
105 C3	Orange France
122 A2	Orange r. Namibia/S. Africa
139 E2	Orangeburg U.S.A.
143 D2	Orangeburg U.S.A.
	Orange Free State prov. S. Africa see Free State
143 D2	Orange Park U.S.A.
140 C2	Orangeville Can.
145 D3	Orange Walk Belize
101 F1	Oranienburg Ger.
122 A2	Oranjemund Namibia
147 C3	Oranjestad Aruba
120 B3	Orapa Botswana
110 B1	Orǎştie Romania
	Oraşul Stalin Romania see Braşov
108 B2	Orbetello Italy
53 C3	Orbost Austr.
143 D3	Orchid Island U.S.A.
111 B3	Orchomenos Greece
50 B1	Ord, Mount hill Austr.
106 B1	Ordes Spain
80 B1	Ordu Turkey
	Ordzhonikidze Rus. Fed. see Vladikavkaz
91 C2	Ordzhonikidze Ukr.
93 G4	Örebro Sweden
134 B2	Oregon state U.S.A.
134 B1	Oregon City U.S.A.
143 E1	Oregon Inlet U.S.A.
87 C3	Orekhovo-Zuyevo Rus. Fed.
89 E3	Orel Rus. Fed.
83 K3	Orel', Ozero l. Rus. Fed.
135 D2	Orem U.S.A.
111 C3	Ören Turkey
87 E3	Orenburg Rus. Fed.
54 A3	Orepuki N.Z.
111 C2	Orestiada Greece
93 F4	Öresund str. Denmark/Sweden
	Oretana, Cordillera mts Spain see Toledo, Montes de
99 D3	Orford Ness hd U.K.
89 F2	Orgtrud Rus. Fed.
74 A1	Orgün Afgh.
111 C3	Orhaneli Turkey
111 C2	Orhangazi Turkey
68 D1	Orhon Gol r. Mongolia
152 B1	Oriental, Cordillera mts Bol.
150 B2	Oriental, Cordillera mts Col.
150 B4	Oriental, Cordillera mts Peru
107 C2	Orihuela Spain
91 D2	Orikhiv Ukr.
130 C3	Orillia Can.
93 I3	Orimattila Fin.
150 C2	Orinoco r. Col./Venez.
150 C2	Orinoco Delta Venez.
75 C2	Orissa state India
88 B2	Orissaare Estonia
108 A3	Oristano Sardinia Italy
93 I3	Orivesi l. Fin.
151 D3	Oriximiná Brazil
145 C3	Orizaba Mex.
145 C3	Orizaba, Pico de vol. Mex.
154 C1	Orizona Brazil
92 E3	Orkanger Norway
93 F4	Örkelljunga Sweden
93 E3	Orkla r. Norway
96 C1	Orkney Islands U.K.
154 C2	Orlândia Brazil
143 D3	Orlando U.S.A.
104 C2	Orléans France
141 F2	Orleans U.S.A.
141 E1	Orléans, Île d' i. Can.
	Orléansville Alg. see Ech Chélif
74 A2	Ormara Pak.
64 B2	Ormoc Phil.
143 D3	Ormond Beach U.S.A.
98 B3	Ormskirk U.K.
104 B2	Orne r. France

92 F2	Ørnes Norway
92 G3	Örnsköldsvik Sweden
114 B3	Orodara Burkina
134 C1	Orofino U.S.A.
141 F2	Orono U.S.A.
	Oroqen Zizhiqi China see Alihe
64 B3	Oroquieta Phil.
108 A2	Orosei Sardinia Italy
108 A2	Orosei, Golfo di b. Sardinia Italy
103 E2	Orosháza Hungary
135 B3	Oroville U.S.A.
52 A2	Orroroo Austr.
93 F3	Orsa Sweden
89 D3	Orsha Belarus
87 E3	Orsk Rus. Fed.
110 B2	Orşova Romania
93 E3	Ørsta Norway
106 B1	Ortegal, Cabo c. Spain
104 B3	Orthez France
106 B1	Ortigueira Spain
108 B1	Ortles mt. Italy
108 B2	Ortona Italy
137 D1	Ortonville U.S.A.
83 J2	Orulgan, Khrebet mts Rus. Fed.
81 C2	Orūmīyeh Iran
81 C2	Orūmīyeh, Daryācheh-ye salt l. Iran
152 B1	Oruro Bol.
104 B2	Orvault France
108 B2	Orvieto Italy
93 F3	Os Norway
146 B4	Osa, Península de pen. Costa Rica
137 E3	Osage r. U.S.A.
137 E3	Osage City U.S.A.
67 C4	Ōsaka Japan
77 D1	Osakarovka Kazakh.
101 E1	Oschersleben (Bode) Ger.
108 A2	Oschiri Sardinia Italy
140 C2	Oscoda U.S.A.
89 E3	Osetr r. Rus. Fed.
141 D1	Osgoode Can.
77 D2	Osh Kyrg.
120 A2	Oshakati Namibia
130 C3	Oshawa Can.
120 A2	Oshikango Namibia
66 C2	Ō-shima i. Japan
67 C4	Ō-shima i. Japan
140 B2	Oshkosh U.S.A.
81 C2	Oshnoviyeh Iran
115 C4	Oshogbo Nigeria
118 B3	Oshwe Dem. Rep. Congo
109 C1	Osijek Croatia
128 C1	Osilinka r. Can.
108 B2	Osimo Italy
	Osipenko Ukr. see Berdyans'k
123 D2	Osizweni S. Africa
137 E2	Oskaloosa U.S.A.
93 G4	Oskarshamn Sweden
89 E3	Oskol r. Rus. Fed.
93 F4	Oslo Norway
93 F4	Oslofjorden sea chan. Norway
80 B1	Osmancık Turkey
111 C2	Osmaneli Turkey
80 B2	Osmaniye Turkey
88 C2	Os'mino Rus. Fed.
101 D1	Osnabrück Ger.
153 A4	Osorno Chile
106 C1	Osorno Spain
128 C3	Osoyoos Can.
100 B2	Oss Neth.
51 D4	Ossa, Mount Austr.
83 L3	Ossora Rus. Fed.
89 D2	Ostashkov Rus. Fed.
101 D1	Oste r. Ger.
100 A2	Ostend Belgium
101 E1	Osterburg (Altmark) Ger.
93 F3	Österdalälven l. Sweden
101 D1	Osterholz-Scharmbeck Ger.
101 E2	Osterode am Harz Ger.
92 F3	Östersund Sweden
	Ostfriesische Inseln is Ger. see East Frisian Islands
100 C1	Ostfriesland reg. Ger.
93 G3	Östhammar Sweden
103 D2	Ostrava Czech Rep.
103 D1	Stróda Pol.
89 E3	Ostrogozhsk Rus. Fed.
90 B1	Ostroh Ukr.
103 E1	Ostrołęka Pol.
101 F2	Ostrov Czech Rep.
88 C2	Ostrov Rus. Fed.
	Ostrovets Pol. see Ostrowiec Świętokrzyski

89 F2	Ostrovskoye Rus. Fed.
103 E1	Ostrowiec Świętokrzyski Pol.
103 E1	Ostrów Mazowiecka Pol.
	Ostrowo Pol. see Ostrów Wielkopolski
103 D1	Ostrów Wielkopolski Pol.
109 C2	Ostuni Italy
110 B2	Osŭm r. Bulg.
67 B4	Ōsumi-kaikyō sea chan. Japan
67 B4	Ōsumi-shotō is Japan
106 B2	Osuna Spain
141 D2	Oswego U.S.A.
99 B3	Oswestry U.K.
67 C3	Ōta Japan
54 B3	Otago Peninsula N.Z.
54 C2	Otaki N.Z.
77 D2	Otar Kazakh.
66 D2	Otaru Japan
120 A2	Otavi Namibia
67 D3	Ōtawara Japan
92 G2	Oteren Norway
134 C1	Othello U.S.A.
120 A2	Otjiwarongo Namibia
109 C2	Otočac Croatia
	Otog Qi China see Ulan
117 B3	Otoro, Jebel mt. Sudan
	Otpor Rus. Fed. see Zabaykal'sk
93 E4	Otra r. Norway
109 C2	Otranto, Strait of Albania/Italy
67 C3	Ōtsu Japan
93 E3	Otta Norway
130 C3	Ottawa Can.
130 C3	Ottawa r. Can.
140 B2	Ottawa IL U.S.A.
137 D3	Ottawa KS U.S.A.
130 B2	Ottawa Islands Can.
98 B2	Otterburn U.K.
130 B2	Otter Rapids Can.
100 B2	Ottignies Belgium
137 E2	Ottumwa U.S.A.
150 B3	Otuzco Peru
52 B3	Otway, Cape Austr.
142 B2	Ouachita r. U.S.A.
142 B2	Ouachita, Lake U.S.A.
142 B2	Ouachita Mountains U.S.A.
118 C2	Ouadda C.A.R.
115 D3	Ouaddaï reg. Chad
114 B3	Ouagadougou Burkina
114 B3	Ouahigouya Burkina
114 B3	Oualâta Maur.
118 C2	Ouanda-Djalié C.A.R.
114 B2	Ouarâne reg. Maur.
115 C1	Ouargla Alg.
114 B1	Ouarzazate Morocco
100 A2	Oudenaarde Belgium
122 B3	Oudtshoorn S. Africa
107 C2	Oued Tlélat Alg.
114 B1	Oued Zem Morocco
104 A2	Ouessant, Île d' i. France
118 B2	Ouésso Congo
97 B2	Oughterard Rep. of Ireland
118 B2	Ouham r. C.A.R./Chad
114 B1	Oujda Morocco
92 H3	Oulainen Fin.
107 D2	Ouled Farès Alg.
92 I2	Oulu Fin.
92 I3	Oulujärvi l. Fin.
108 A1	Oulx Italy
115 E3	Oum-Chalouba Chad
115 D3	Oum-Hadjer Chad
115 E3	Ounianga Kébir Chad
100 B2	Oupeye Belgium
100 C3	Our, Vallée de l' val. Ger./Lux.
106 B1	Ourense Spain
154 C2	Ourinhos Brazil
155 D2	Ouro Preto Brazil
100 B2	Ourthe r. Belgium
98 C3	Ouse r. U.K.
	Outaouais, Rivière des r. Can. see Ottawa
131 D3	Outardes r. Can.
131 D2	Outardes Quatre, Réservoir resr Can.
96 A2	Outer Hebrides is U.K.
	Outer Mongolia country Asia see Mongolia
120 A3	Outjo Namibia
129 D2	Outlook Can.
92 I3	Outokumpu Fin.
52 B3	Ouyen Austr.
108 A2	Ovace, Punta d' mt. Corsica France
153 A3	Ovalle Chile
106 B1	Ovar Port.
92 H2	Överkalix Sweden

137 E3	Overland Park U.S.A.
135 D3	Overton U.S.A.
92 H2	Övertorneå Sweden
106 B1	Oviedo Spain
143 D3	Oviedo U.S.A.
88 B2	Ovišrags hd Latvia
93 E3	Øvre Årdal Norway
93 F3	Øvre Rendal Norway
90 B1	Ovruch Ukr.
118 B3	Owando Congo
67 C4	Owase Japan
139 D1	Owasso U.S.A.
137 E2	Owatonna U.S.A.
141 D2	Owego U.S.A.
140 B3	Owensboro U.S.A.
135 C3	Owens Lake U.S.A.
130 B3	Owen Sound Can.
51 D1	Owen Stanley Range mts P.N.G.
115 C4	Owerri Nigeria
115 C4	Owo Nigeria
140 C2	Owosso U.S.A.
134 C2	Owyhee U.S.A.
134 C2	Owyhee r. U.S.A.
129 D3	Oxbow Can.
54 B2	Oxford N.Z.
99 C4	Oxford U.K.
142 C2	Oxford U.S.A.
129 E2	Oxford Lake Can.
145 D2	Oxkutzcab Mex.
52 B2	Oxley Austr.
	Ox Mountains hills Rep. of Ireland see Slieve Gamph
135 C4	Oxnard U.S.A.
67 C3	Oyama Japan
118 B2	Oyem Gabon
129 C2	Oyen Can.
105 D2	Oyonnax France
64 B3	Ozamiz Phil.
142 C2	Ozark AL U.S.A.
137 E3	Ozark MO U.S.A.
137 E3	Ozark Plateau U.S.A.
137 E3	Ozarks, Lake of the U.S.A.
83 L3	Ozernovskiy Rus. Fed.
88 B3	Ozersk Rus. Fed.
89 E3	Ozery Rus. Fed.
87 D3	Ozinki Rus. Fed.

P

127 I2	Paamiut Greenland
122 A3	Paarl S. Africa
103 D1	Pabianice Pol.
75 C2	Pabna Bangl.
88 C3	Pabradė Lith.
74 A2	Pab Range mts Pak.
150 C2	Pacaraima Mountains mts Brazil
150 B3	Pacasmayo Peru
138 B2	Pacheco Mex.
109 C3	Pachino Sicily Italy
145 C2	Pachuca Mex.
135 B3	Pacifica U.S.A.
157 E9	Pacific-Antarctic Ridge sea feature S. Pacific Ocean
156	Pacific Ocean
61 C2	Pacitan Indon.
52 B2	Packsaddle Austr.
103 D1	Paczków Pol.
60 B2	Padang Indon.
60 B2	Padangpanjang Indon.
60 A1	Padangsidimpuan Indon.
101 D2	Paderborn Ger.
	Padova Italy see Padua
139 D3	Padre Island U.S.A.
99 A4	Padstow U.K.
52 B3	Padthaway Austr.
108 B1	Padua Italy
140 B3	Paducah KY U.S.A.
139 C2	Paducah TX U.S.A.
65 B1	Paegam N. Korea
65 B1	Paekdu-san mt. China/N. Korea
65 A2	Paengnyŏng-do i. S. Korea
54 C1	Paeroa N.Z.
80 B2	Pafos Cyprus
109 C2	Pag Croatia
109 C2	Pag i. Croatia
64 B3	Pagadian Phil.
60 B2	Pagai Selatan i. Indon.
60 B2	Pagai Utara i. Indon.
59 D1	Pagan i. N. Mariana Is
61 C2	Pagatan Indon.
138 A1	Page U.S.A.
88 B2	Pagėgiai Lith.

153 E5 **Paget, Mount** S. Georgia
136 B3 **Pagosa Springs** U.S.A.
88 C2 **Paide** Estonia
99 B4 **Paignton** U.K.
93 I3 **Päijänne** *l.* Fin.
75 C2 **Paikü Co** *l.* China
60 B2 **Painan** Indon.
140 C2 **Painesville** U.S.A.
138 A1 **Painted Desert** U.S.A.
Paint Hills Can. *see* Wemindji
96 B3 **Paisley** U.K.
92 H2 **Pajala** Sweden
150 A3 **Pajan** Ecuador
150 D2 **Pakaraima Mountains** Guyana
74 A2 **Pakistan** *country* Asia
62 A1 **Pakokku** Myanmar
88 B2 **Pakruojis** Lith.
103 D2 **Paks** Hungary
130 A2 **Pakwash Lake** Can.
63 B2 **Pakxé** Laos
115 D4 **Pala** Chad
60 B2 **Palabuhanratu, Teluk** *b.* Indon.
111 C3 **Palaikastro** Greece
111 B3 **Palaiochora** Greece
Palakkat India *see* Palghat
122 B1 **Palamakoloi** Botswana
107 D1 **Palamós** Spain
83 L3 **Palana** Rus. Fed.
64 B2 **Palanan** Phil.
61 C2 **Palangkaraya** Indon.
74 B2 **Palanpur** India
123 C1 **Palapye** Botswana
83 L2 **Palatka** Rus. Fed.
143 D3 **Palatka** U.S.A.
59 C2 **Palau** *country* N. Pacific Ocean
156 C5 **Palau Islands** Palau
63 A2 **Palaw** Myanmar
64 A3 **Palawan** *i.* Phil.
64 A3 **Palawan Passage** *str.* Phil.
88 B2 **Paldiski** Estonia
89 F2 **Palekh** Rus. Fed.
60 B2 **Palembang** Indon.
106 C1 **Palencia** Spain
145 C3 **Palenque** Mex.
108 B3 **Palermo** Sicily Italy
139 D2 **Palestine** U.S.A.
62 A1 **Paletwa** Myanmar
73 B3 **Palghat** India
74 B2 **Pali** India
48 G4 **Palikir** Micronesia
109 C2 **Palinuro, Capo** *c.* Italy
111 B3 **Paliouri, Akra** *pt* Greece
100 B3 **Paliseul** Belgium
92 I3 **Paljakka** *hill* Fin.
88 C2 **Palkino** Rus. Fed.
73 B4 **Palk Strait** India/Sri Lanka
Palla Bianca *mt.* Austria/Italy *see* Weißkugel
54 C2 **Palliser, Cape** N.Z.
157 F7 **Palliser, Îles** *is* Fr. Polynesia
106 B2 **Palma del Río** Spain
107 D2 **Palma de Mallorca** Spain
154 B3 **Palmas** Brazil
154 B3 **Palmas, Campos de** *hills* Brazil
114 B4 **Palmas, Cape** Liberia
143 D3 **Palm Bay** U.S.A.
135 C4 **Palmdale** U.S.A.
154 C3 **Palmeira** Brazil
151 E3 **Palmeirais** Brazil
126 C2 **Palmer** U.S.A.
55 A2 **Palmer Land** *reg.* Antarctica
49 K5 **Palmerston** *atoll* Cook Is
54 C2 **Palmerston North** N.Z.
109 C3 **Palmi** Italy
145 C2 **Palmillas** Mex.
150 B2 **Palmira** Col.
154 B2 **Palmital** Brazil
135 C4 **Palm Springs** U.S.A.
Palmyra Syria *see* Tadmur
49 K3 **Palmyra Atoll** N. Pacific Ocean
135 B3 **Palo Alto** U.S.A.
117 B3 **Paloich** Sudan
145 C3 **Palomares** Mex.
61 D2 **Palopo** Indon.
107 C2 **Palos, Cabo de** *c.* Spain
92 I3 **Paltamo** Fin.
61 C2 **Palu** Indon.
83 N2 **Palyavaam** *r.* Rus. Fed.
150 B3 **Pamar** Col.
121 C3 **Pambarra** Moz.
104 C3 **Pamiers** France
77 D3 **Pamir** *mts* Asia

143 E1 **Pamlico Sound** *sea chan.* U.S.A.
152 B1 **Pampa Grande** Bol.
153 B3 **Pampas** *reg.* Arg.
150 B2 **Pamplona** Col.
107 C1 **Pamplona** Spain
111 D2 **Pamukova** Turkey
60 B2 **Panaitan** *i.* Indon.
73 B3 **Panaji** India
146 B4 **Panama** *country* Central America
146 C4 **Panamá** Panama
146 C4 **Panamá, Golfo de** *g.* Panama
Panama, Gulf of Panama *see* Panamá, Golfo de
146 C4 **Panama Canal** *canal* Panama
Panama City Panama *see* Panamá
142 C2 **Panama City** U.S.A.
135 C3 **Panamint Range** *mts* U.S.A.
60 B1 **Panarik** Indon.
64 B2 **Panay** *i.* Phil.
109 D2 **Pančevo** Yugo.
64 B2 **Pandan** Phil.
64 B2 **Pandan** Phil.
75 C2 **Pandaria** India
73 B3 **Pandharpur** India
88 B2 **Panevėžys** Lith.
Panfilov Kazakh. *see* Zharkent
61 C2 **Pangkalanbuun** Indon.
60 A1 **Pangkalansusu** Indon.
60 B2 **Pangkalpinang** Indon.
61 D2 **Pangkalsiang, Tanjung** *pt* Indon.
127 H2 **Pangnirtung** Can.
86 G2 **Pangody** Rus. Fed.
89 F3 **Panino** Rus. Fed.
74 B2 **Panipat** India
74 A2 **Panjgur** Pak.
Panjim India *see* Panaji
118 A2 **Pankshin** Nigeria
65 C1 **Pan Ling** *mts* China
75 C2 **Panna** India
50 A2 **Pannawonica** Austr.
154 B2 **Panorama** Brazil
65 B1 **Panshi** China
145 C2 **Pánuco** Mex.
145 C2 **Pánuco** *r.* Mex.
71 A3 **Panxian** China
62 B1 **Panzhihua** China
109 C3 **Paola** Italy
118 B2 **Paoua** C.A.R.
63 B2 **Paôy Pêt** Cambodia
103 D2 **Pápa** Hungary
54 B1 **Papakura** N.Z.
145 C2 **Papantla** Mex.
96 □ **Papa Stour** *i.* U.K.
54 B1 **Papatoetoe** N.Z.
49 M5 **Papeete** Fr. Polynesia
100 C1 **Papenburg** Ger.
Paphos Cyprus *see* Pafos
137 D2 **Papillion** U.S.A.
59 D3 **Papua, Gulf of** P.N.G.
59 D3 **Papua New Guinea** *country* Oceania
62 A2 **Papun** Myanmar
89 F3 **Para** *r.* Rus. Fed.
50 A2 **Paraburdoo** Austr.
154 C1 **Paracatu** Brazil
155 C1 **Paracatu** *r.* Brazil
52 A2 **Parachilna** Austr.
109 D2 **Paraćin** Yugo.
155 D1 **Pará de Minas** Brazil
151 D2 **Paradise** Guyana
135 B3 **Paradise** U.S.A.
142 B1 **Paragould** U.S.A.
151 D3 **Paraguai** *r.* Brazil
147 D3 **Paraguaná, Península de** *pen.* Venez.
152 C2 **Paraguay** *r.* Arg./Para.
152 C2 **Paraguay** *country* S. America
155 D2 **Paraíba do Sul** *r.* Brazil
154 B1 **Paraíso** Brazil
145 C3 **Paraíso** Mex.
114 C4 **Parakou** Benin
52 A2 **Parakylia** Austr.
151 D2 **Paramaribo** Suriname
83 L3 **Paramushir, Ostrov** *i.* Rus. Fed.
152 B3 **Paraná** Arg.
154 A3 **Paraná** *r.* S. America
154 C1 **Paraná, Serra do** *hills* Brazil
154 C3 **Paranaguá** Brazil
154 B1 **Paranaíba** Brazil
154 B2 **Paranaíba** *r.* Brazil

154 B2 **Paranapanema** *r.* Brazil
154 B2 **Paranapiacaba, Serra** *mts* Brazil
154 B2 **Paranavaí** Brazil
90 A2 **Parângul Mare, Vârful** *mt.* Romania
54 B2 **Paraparaumu** N.Z.
155 D2 **Parati** Brazil
52 A2 **Paratoo** Austr.
151 D3 **Parauaquara, Serra** *hill* Brazil
154 B1 **Paraúna** Brazil
105 C2 **Paray-le-Monial** France
74 B2 **Parbati** *r.* India
74 B3 **Parbhani** India
101 E1 **Parchim** Ger.
103 E1 **Parczew** Pol.
155 E1 **Pardo** *r.* Brazil
154 B2 **Pardo** *r.* Brazil
154 C2 **Pardo** *r.* Brazil
103 D1 **Pardubice** Czech Rep.
152 C1 **Parecis, Serra dos** *hills* Brazil
150 C4 **Parecis, Serra dos** *hills* Brazil
130 C3 **Parent** Can.
130 C3 **Parent, Lac** *l.* Can.
61 C2 **Parepare** Indon.
89 D2 **Parfino** Rus. Fed.
111 B3 **Parga** Greece
109 C3 **Parghelia** Italy
147 D3 **Paria, Gulf of** Trin. and Tob./Venez.
150 C2 **Parima, Serra** *mts* Brazil
151 D3 **Parintins** Brazil
104 C2 **Paris** France
142 C1 **Paris** *TN* U.S.A.
139 D2 **Paris** *TX* U.S.A.
93 H3 **Parkano** Fin.
138 A2 **Parker** U.S.A.
140 C3 **Parkersburg** U.S.A.
53 C2 **Parkes** Austr.
140 A1 **Park Falls** U.S.A.
134 B1 **Parkland** U.S.A.
137 D1 **Park Rapids** U.S.A.
106 C1 **Parla** Spain
108 B2 **Parma** Italy
134 C2 **Parma** U.S.A.
151 E3 **Parnaíba** Brazil
151 E3 **Parnaíba** *r.* Brazil
111 B3 **Parnassos** *mt.* Greece
54 B2 **Parnassus** N.Z.
111 B3 **Parnon** *mts* Greece
88 B2 **Pärnu** Estonia
65 B2 **P'aro-ho** *l.* S. Korea
52 B2 **Paroo** *watercourse* Austr.
76 C3 **Paropamisus** *mts* Afgh.
111 C3 **Paros** *i.* Greece
135 D3 **Parowan** U.S.A.
153 A3 **Parral** Chile
53 D2 **Parramatta** Austr.
144 B2 **Parras** Mex.
126 D2 **Parry, Cape** Can.
126 E1 **Parry Islands** Can.
130 B3 **Parry Sound** Can.
137 D3 **Parsons** U.S.A.
108 B3 **Partanna** Sicily Italy
101 D2 **Partenstein** Ger.
104 C2 **Parthenay** France
108 B3 **Partinico** Sicily Italy
66 B2 **Partizansk** Rus. Fed.
97 B2 **Partry Mountains** *hills* Rep. of Ireland
151 D3 **Paru** *r.* Brazil
131 E3 **Pasadena** Can.
135 C4 **Pasadena** *CA* U.S.A.
139 D3 **Pasadena** *TX* U.S.A.
62 A2 **Pasawng** Myanmar
142 C2 **Pascagoula** U.S.A.
110 C1 **Pașcani** Romania
134 C1 **Pasco** U.S.A.
155 E1 **Pascoal, Monte** *hill* Brazil
Pascua, Isla de *i.* S. Pacific Ocean *see* Easter Island
Pas de Calais *str.* France/U.K. *see* Dover, Strait of
102 C1 **Pasewalk** Ger.
129 D2 **Pasfield Lake** Can.
89 D1 **Pasha** Rus. Fed.
64 B2 **Pasig** Phil.
60 B1 **Pasir Putih** Malaysia
103 D1 **Pasłęk** Pol.
74 A2 **Pasni** Pak.
153 A4 **Paso Rio Mayo** Arg.
135 B3 **Paso Robles** U.S.A.
97 B3 **Passage West** Rep. of Ireland
155 D2 **Passa Tempo** Brazil
102 C2 **Passau** Ger.

152 C2 **Passo Fundo** Brazil
155 C2 **Passos** Brazil
88 C2 **Pastavy** Belarus
150 B3 **Pastaza** *r.* Peru
150 B2 **Pasto** Col.
74 B1 **Pasu** Jammu and Kashmir
61 C2 **Pasuruan** Indon.
88 B2 **Pasvalys** Lith.
103 D2 **Pásztó** Hungary
153 A5 **Patagonia** *reg.* Arg.
75 C2 **Patan** Nepal
54 B1 **Patea** N.Z.
141 E2 **Paterson** U.S.A.
74 B1 **Pathankot** India
Pathein Myanmar *see* Bassein
136 B2 **Pathfinder Reservoir** U.S.A.
61 C2 **Pati** Indon.
74 B1 **Patiala** India
62 A1 **Pätkai Bum** *mts* India/Myanmar
111 C3 **Patmos** *i.* Greece
75 C2 **Patna** India
81 C2 **Patnos** Turkey
154 B3 **Pato Branco** Brazil
152 C3 **Patos, Lagoa dos** *l.* Brazil
155 C1 **Patos de Minas** Brazil
152 B3 **Patquia** Arg.
111 B3 **Patra** Greece
Patras Greece *see* Patra
75 C2 **Patratu** India
154 C1 **Patrocínio** Brazil
63 B3 **Pattani** Thai.
63 B2 **Pattaya** Thai.
128 B2 **Pattullo, Mount** Can.
129 D2 **Patuanak** Can.
146 B3 **Patuca** *r.* Hond.
144 B3 **Pátzcuaro** Mex.
104 B3 **Pau** France
104 B3 **Pauillac** France
150 C3 **Pauini** Brazil
62 A1 **Pauk** Myanmar
126 D2 **Paulatuk** Can.
Paulis Dem. Rep. Congo *see* Isiro
151 E3 **Paulistana** Brazil
151 F3 **Paulo Afonso** Brazil
123 D2 **Paulpietersburg** S. Africa
139 D2 **Pauls Valley** U.S.A.
62 A2 **Paungde** Myanmar
155 D1 **Pavão** Brazil
108 A1 **Pavia** Italy
88 B2 **Pāvilosta** Latvia
110 C2 **Pavlikeni** Bulg.
77 D1 **Pavlodar** Kazakh.
91 D2 **Pavlohrad** Ukr.
91 E1 **Pavlovsk** Rus. Fed.
91 D2 **Pavlovskaya** Rus. Fed.
141 E2 **Pawtucket** U.S.A.
111 B3 **Paxoi** *i.* Greece
60 B2 **Payakumbuh** Indon.
134 C2 **Payette** U.S.A.
134 C2 **Payette** *r.* U.S.A.
86 F2 **Pay-Khoy, Khrebet** *hills* Rus. Fed.
Payne Can. *see* Kangirsuk
130 C2 **Payne, Lac** *l.* Can.
152 C3 **Paysandú** Uru.
81 C1 **Pazar** Turkey
110 B2 **Pazardzhik** Bulg.
111 C3 **Pazarköy** Turkey
108 B1 **Pazin** Croatia
63 A2 **Pe** Myanmar
128 C2 **Peace** *r.* Can.
128 C2 **Peace River** Can.
53 C2 **Peak Hill** *N.S.W.* Austr.
50 A2 **Peak Hill** *W.A.* Austr.
135 E3 **Peale, Mount** U.S.A.
142 C2 **Pearl** *r.* U.S.A.
139 D3 **Pearsall** U.S.A.
126 F1 **Peary Channel** Can.
121 C2 **Pebane** Moz.
109 D2 **Peć** Yugo.
155 D1 **Peçanha** Brazil
154 C3 **Peças, Ilha das** *i.* Brazil
92 J2 **Pechenga** Rus. Fed.
86 E2 **Pechora** Rus. Fed.
86 E2 **Pechora** *r.* Rus. Fed.
Pechora Sea Rus. Fed. *see* Pechorskoye More
86 E2 **Pechorskoye More** *sea* Rus. Fed.
88 C2 **Pechory** Rus. Fed.
138 B1 **Pecos** *NM* U.S.A.
138 B2 **Pecos** *TX* U.S.A.
139 C2 **Pecos** *r.* U.S.A.
103 D2 **Pécs** Hungary
144 B2 **Pedernales** Mex.
155 D1 **Pedra Azul** Brazil
154 C2 **Pedregulho** Brazil

151 E3 Pedreiras Brazil
73 C4 Pedro, Point Sri Lanka
151 E3 Pedro Afonso Brazil
152 B2 Pedro de Valdivia Chile
154 B1 Pedro Gomes Brazil
152 C2 Pedro Juan Caballero Para.
106 B1 Pedroso Port.
96 C3 Peebles U.K.
143 E2 Pee Dee r. U.S.A.
126 D2 Peel r. Can.
98 A2 Peel Isle of Man
128 C2 Peerless Lake Can.
54 B2 Pegasus Bay N.Z.
101 E3 Pegnitz Ger.
62 A2 Pegu Myanmar
62 A2 Pegu Yoma mts Myanmar
153 B3 Pehuajó Arg.
101 E1 Peine Ger.
88 C2 Peipus, Lake Estonia/Rus. Fed.
111 B3 Peiraias Greece
154 B2 Peixe r. Brazil
151 D4 Peixoto de Azevedo Brazil
123 C2 Peka Lesotho
60 B2 Pekalongan Indon.
60 B1 Pekan Malaysia
60 B1 Pekanbaru Indon.
Peking China see Beijing
130 B3 Pelee Island Can.
61 D2 Peleng i. Indon.
103 D2 Pelhřimov Czech Rep.
92 I2 Pelkosenniemi Fin.
122 A2 Pella S. Africa
137 E2 Pella U.S.A.
59 D3 Pelleluhu Islands P.N.G.
92 H2 Pello Fin.
128 A1 Pelly r. Can.
127 G2 Pelly Bay Can.
128 A1 Pelly Mountains Can.
152 C3 Pelotas Brazil
152 C2 Pelotas, Rio das r. Brazil
141 F1 Pemadumcook Lake U.S.A.
60 B1 Pemangkat Indon.
60 A1 Pematangsiantar Indon.
121 D2 Pemba Moz.
120 B2 Pemba Zambia
119 D3 Pemba Island Tanz.
128 B2 Pemberton Can.
137 D1 Pembina r. Can.
137 D1 Pembina r. U.S.A.
130 C3 Pembroke Can.
99 A4 Pembroke U.K.
143 D3 Pembroke Pines U.S.A.
106 C1 Peña Cerredo mt. Spain
106 C1 Peñalara mt. Spain
145 C2 Peña Nevada, Cerro mt. Mex.
154 B2 Penápolis Brazil
106 B1 Peñaranda de Bracamonte Spain
107 C1 Peñarroya mt. Spain
106 B2 Peñarroya-Pueblonuevo Spain
106 B1 Peñas, Cabo de c. Spain
153 A4 Penas, Golfo de g. Chile
106 B1 Peña Ubiña mt. Spain
111 C2 Pendik Turkey
134 C1 Pendleton U.S.A.
128 B2 Pendleton Bay Can.
134 C1 Pend Oreille Lake U.S.A.
Penfro U.K. see Pembroke
74 B3 Penganga r. India
118 C3 Penge Dem. Rep. Congo
123 D1 Penge S. Africa
70 C2 Penglai China
71 A3 Pengshui China
106 B2 Peniche Port.
96 C3 Penicuik U.K.
108 B2 Penne Italy
52 A3 Penneshaw Austr.
98 B2 Pennines hills U.K.
141 D2 Pennsylvania state U.S.A.
127 H2 Penny Icecap Can.
89 D2 Peno Rus. Fed.
141 F2 Penobscot r. U.S.A.
52 B3 Penola Austr.
50 C3 Penong Austr.
157 E6 Penrhyn Basin sea feature S. Pacific Ocean
53 D2 Penrith Austr.
98 B2 Penrith U.K.
142 C2 Pensacola U.S.A.
55 B1 Pensacola Mountains Antarctica
61 C1 Pensiangan Sabah Malaysia
128 C3 Penticton Can.
96 C1 Pentland Firth sea chan. U.K.

99 B3 Penygadair hill U.K.
87 D3 Penza Rus. Fed.
99 A4 Penzance U.K.
83 L2 Penzhinskaya Guba b. Rus. Fed.
138 A2 Peoria AZ U.S.A.
140 B2 Peoria IL U.S.A.
107 C1 Perales del Alfambra Spain
111 B3 Perama Greece
131 D3 Percé Can.
50 B2 Percival Lakes salt flat Austr.
51 E2 Percy Isles Austr.
107 D1 Perdido, Monte mt. Spain
154 C1 Perdizes Brazil
86 F2 Peregrebnoye Rus. Fed.
150 B2 Pereira Col.
154 B2 Pereira Barreto Brazil
Pereira de Eça Angola see Ondjiva
90 A2 Peremyshlyany Ukr.
89 E2 Pereslavl'-Zalesskiy Rus. Fed.
91 C1 Pereyaslav-Khmel'nyts'kyy Ukr.
153 B3 Pergamino Arg.
92 H3 Perhonjoki r. Fin.
131 C2 Péribonca, Lac l. Can.
152 B2 Perico Arg.
144 B2 Pericos Mex.
104 C2 Périgueux France
150 B2 Perija, Sierra de mts Venez.
111 B3 Peristerio Greece
153 A4 Perito Moreno Arg.
101 E1 Perleberg Ger.
86 E3 Perm' Rus. Fed.
109 D2 Përmet Albania
Pernambuco Brazil see Recife
52 A2 Pernatty Lagoon salt flat Austr.
110 B2 Pernik Bulg.
Pernov Estonia see Pärnu
105 C2 Péronne France
145 C3 Perote Mex.
105 C3 Perpignan France
99 A4 Perranporth U.K.
Perrégaux Alg. see Mohammadia
143 D3 Perry FL U.S.A.
143 D2 Perry GA U.S.A.
137 E2 Perry IA U.S.A.
139 D1 Perry OK U.S.A.
140 C2 Perrysburg U.S.A.
139 C1 Perryton U.S.A.
137 F3 Perryville U.S.A.
Pershnotravnevoye Ukr. see Pershotravens'k
99 B3 Pershore U.K.
91 D2 Pershotravens'k Ukr.
Persia country Asia see Iran
50 A3 Perth Austr.
96 C2 Perth U.K.
159 F5 Perth Basin sea feature Indian Ocean
86 C2 Pertominsk Rus. Fed.
105 D3 Pertuis France
108 A2 Pertusato, Capo c. Corsica France
150 B3 Peru country S. America
140 B2 Peru U.S.A.
157 H6 Peru Basin sea feature S. Pacific Ocean
157 H7 Peru-Chile Trench sea feature S. Pacific Ocean
108 B2 Perugia Italy
154 C2 Peruíbe Brazil
100 A2 Péruwelz Belgium
90 C2 Pervomays'k Ukr.
91 C2 Pervomays'ke Ukr.
Pervomayskiy Rus. Fed. see Novodvinsk
89 F3 Pervomayskiy Rus. Fed.
91 D2 Pervomays'kyy Ukr.
108 B2 Pesaro Italy
108 B2 Pescara Italy
108 B2 Pescara r. Italy
74 B1 Peshawar Pak.
109 D2 Peshkopi Albania
109 C1 Pesnica Slovenia
104 B3 Pessac France
89 E2 Pestovo Rus. Fed.
142 C2 Petal U.S.A.
100 B3 Pétange Lux.
147 D3 Petare Venez.
144 B3 Petatlán Mex.

121 C2 Petauke Zambia
130 C3 Petawawa Can.
140 B2 Petenwell Lake U.S.A.
52 A2 Peterborough Austr.
130 C3 Peterborough Can.
99 C3 Peterborough U.K.
96 D2 Peterhead U.K.
55 R3 Peter I Island Antarctica
129 E1 Peter Lake Can.
50 B2 Petermann Ranges mts Austr.
129 D2 Peter Pond Lake Can.
128 A2 Petersburg AK U.S.A.
141 D3 Petersburg VA U.S.A.
101 D1 Petershagen Ger.
Peter the Great Bay Rus. Fed. see Petra Velikogo, Zaliv
131 D2 Petitjean Morocco see Sidi Kacem
Petit Lac Manicouagan l. Can.
131 C2 Petit Mécatina r. Can.
145 D2 Peto Mex.
140 C1 Petoskey U.S.A.
80 B2 Petra tourist site Jordan
66 B2 Petra Velikogo, Zaliv b. Rus. Fed.
111 B2 Petrich Bulg.
Petroaleksandrovsk Uzbek. see Turtkul'
88 C2 Petrodvorets Rus. Fed.
Petrokov Pol. see Piotrków Trybunalski
151 E3 Petrolina Brazil
77 C1 Petropavlovsk Kazakh.
83 L3 Petropavlovsk-Kamchatskiy Rus. Fed.
110 B1 Petroşani Romania
Petrovskoye Rus. Fed. see Svetlograd
89 F3 Petrovskoye Rus. Fed.
89 E2 Petrovskoye Rus. Fed.
69 D1 Petrovsk-Zabaykal'skiy Rus. Fed.
86 C2 Petrozavodsk Rus. Fed.
123 C2 Petrusburg S. Africa
123 C2 Petrus Steyn S. Africa
122 B3 Petrusville S. Africa
Petsamo Rus. Fed. see Pechenga
87 F3 Petukhovo Rus. Fed.
89 E2 Petushki Rus. Fed.
60 A1 Peureula Indon.
83 M2 Pevek Rus. Fed.
102 B2 Pforzheim Ger.
102 C2 Pfunds Austria
101 D3 Pfungstadt Ger.
123 C2 Phahameng S. Africa
123 C1 Phahameng S. Africa
123 C1 Phalaborwa S. Africa
74 B2 Phalodi India
63 B2 Phangnga Thai.
63 B2 Phan Rang Vietnam
63 B2 Phan Thiết Vietnam
63 B3 Phatthalung Thai.
62 A2 Phayao Thai.
129 D2 Phelps Lake Can.
143 C2 Phenix City U.S.A.
63 A2 Phet Buri Thai.
62 B2 Phetchabun Thai.
63 B2 Phichit Thai.
141 D3 Philadelphia U.S.A.
136 C2 Philip U.S.A.
Philip Atoll Micronesia see Sorol
Philippeville Alg. see Skikda
100 B2 Philippeville Belgium
51 C2 Philippi, Lake salt flat Austr.
100 A2 Philippine Neth.
156 C4 Philippine Basin sea feature N. Pacific Ocean
Philippines country Asia
64 B2 Philippine Sea N. Pacific Ocean
126 C2 Philip Smith Mountains U.S.A.
122 B3 Philipstown S. Africa
53 C3 Phillip Island Austr.
137 D3 Phillipsburg U.S.A.
63 B2 Phimun Mangsahan Thai.
123 C2 Phiritona S. Africa
63 B2 Phitsanulok Thai.
Phnom Penh Cambodia see Phnum Pénh
63 B2 Phnum Pénh Cambodia
138 A2 Phoenix U.S.A.
49 J4 Phoenix Islands Kiribati

63 B2 Phon Thai.
62 B2 Phong Nha Vietnam
62 B1 Phôngsali Laos
62 B1 Phong Thô Vietnam
62 B2 Phrae Thai.
Phu Cuong Vietnam see Thu Dâu Môt
120 B3 Phuduhudu Botswana
63 A3 Phuket Thai.
63 B2 Phumĭ Kâmpóng Trâlach Cambodia
63 B2 Phumĭ Sâmraông Cambodia
63 B2 Phu Nhon Vietnam
63 B2 Phu Quôc, Đao i. Vietnam
123 C2 Phuthaditjhaba S. Africa
Phu Vinh Vietnam see Tra Vinh
108 A1 Piacenza Italy
108 A1 Pianosa, Isola i. Italy
110 C1 Piatra Neamţ Romania
151 E3 Piauí r. Brazil
108 B1 Piave r. Italy
117 B4 Pibor r. Sudan
117 B4 Pibor Post Sudan
104 C2 Picardie reg. France
Picardy reg. France see Picardie
142 C2 Picayune U.S.A.
152 B2 Pichanal Arg.
144 A2 Pichilingue Mex.
98 C2 Pickering U.K.
130 A2 Pickle Lake Can.
151 E3 Picos Brazil
153 B4 Pico Truncado Arg.
53 D2 Picton Austr.
54 B2 Picton N.Z.
73 C4 Pidurutalagala mt. Sri Lanka
154 C2 Piedade Brazil
145 C3 Piedras Negras Guat.
145 B2 Piedras Negras Mex.
93 I3 Pieksämäki Fin.
92 I3 Pielinen l. Fin.
136 C2 Pierre U.S.A.
105 C3 Pierrelatte France
123 D2 Pietermaritzburg S. Africa
Pietersaari Fin. see Jakobstad
123 C1 Pietersburg S. Africa
123 D2 Piet Retief S. Africa
110 B1 Pietrosa mt. Romania
110 C1 Pietrosu, Vârful mt. Romania
128 C2 Pigeon Lake Can.
137 F1 Pigeon River Can.
153 B3 Pigüé Arg.
93 I3 Pihlajavesi l. Fin.
92 I3 Pihtipudas Fin.
145 C3 Pijijiapan Mex.
89 D2 Pikalevo Rus. Fed.
130 A2 Pikangikum Can.
136 C3 Pikes Peak U.S.A.
122 A3 Piketberg S. Africa
140 C3 Pikeville U.S.A.
103 D1 Piła Pol.
153 C3 Pilar Arg.
152 C2 Pilar Para.
75 B2 Pilibhit India
53 C2 Pilliga Austr.
154 C1 Pilões, Serra dos mts Brazil
150 C4 Pimenta Bueno Brazil
88 C3 Pina i. Belarus
153 C3 Pinamar Arg.
80 B2 Pınarbaşı Turkey
146 B2 Pinar del Río Cuba
64 B2 Pinatubo, Mount vol. Phil.
103 E1 Pińczów Pol.
151 E3 Pindaré r. Brazil
111 B2 Pindos mts Greece
Pindus Mountains Greece see Pindos
142 B2 Pine Bluff U.S.A.
136 C2 Pine Bluffs U.S.A.
50 C1 Pine Creek Austr.
136 B2 Pinedale U.S.A.
86 D2 Pinega Rus. Fed.
129 D2 Pinehouse Lake Can.
111 B3 Pineios r. Greece
143 D3 Pine Islands FL U.S.A.
143 D4 Pine Islands FL U.S.A.
128 C1 Pine Point Can.
136 C2 Pine Ridge U.S.A.
108 A2 Pinerolo Italy
Pines, Isle of i. Cuba see La Juventud, Isla de
123 D2 Pinetown S. Africa
142 B2 Pineville U.S.A.
70 B2 Pingdingshan China
70 B2 Pingdu China

62 B1 **Pingguo** China
71 B3 **Pingjiang** China
70 A2 **Pingliang** China
70 B1 **Pingquan** China
71 C3 **P'ingtung** Taiwan
Pingxi China see Yuping
71 A3 **Pingxiang** Guangxi China
71 B3 **Pingxiang** Jiangxi China
70 B2 **Pingyin** China
155 C2 **Pinhal** Brazil
151 E3 **Pinheiro** Brazil
52 B3 **Pinnaroo** Austr.
101 D1 **Pinneberg** Ger.
Pinos, Isla de i. Cuba see
La Juventud, Isla de
145 C3 **Pinotepa Nacional** Mex.
48 H6 **Pins, Île des** i.
New Caledonia
88 C3 **Pinsk** Belarus
152 B2 **Pinto** Arg.
135 D3 **Pioche** U.S.A.
119 C3 **Piodi** Dem. Rep. Congo
108 B2 **Piombino** Italy
86 F2 **Pionerskiy** Rus. Fed.
103 E1 **Pionki** Pol.
103 D1 **Piotrków Trybunalski** Pol.
137 D2 **Pipestone** U.S.A.
131 C3 **Pipmuacan, Réservoir**
resr Can.
154 B2 **Piquiri** r. Brazil
154 C1 **Piracanjuba** Brazil
154 C2 **Piracicaba** Brazil
155 D1 **Piracicaba** r. Brazil
154 C2 **Piraçununga** Brazil
Piraeus Greece see
Peiraias
154 C2 **Piraí do Sul** Brazil
154 C2 **Piraju** Brazil
154 C2 **Pirajuí** Brazil
154 B1 **Piranhas** Brazil
151 F3 **Piranhas** r. Brazil
155 D1 **Pirapora** Brazil
154 C1 **Pirenópolis** Brazil
154 C1 **Pires do Rio** Brazil
Pirineos mts Europe see
Pyrenees
151 E3 **Piripiri** Brazil
109 D2 **Pirot** Yugo.
59 C3 **Piru** Indon.
108 B2 **Pisa** Italy
152 A1 **Pisagua** Chile
150 B4 **Pisco** Peru
102 C2 **Písek** Czech Rep.
79 D2 **Pishin** Iran
74 A1 **Pishin** Pak.
145 D2 **Pisté** Mex.
109 C2 **Pisticci** Italy
108 B2 **Pistoia** Italy
106 C1 **Pisuerga** r. Spain
134 B2 **Pit** r. U.S.A.
114 A3 **Pita** Guinea
154 B2 **Pitanga** Brazil
155 D1 **Pitangui** Brazil
49 O6 **Pitcairn Islands** terr.
S. Pacific Ocean
49 O6 **Pitcairn Islands** terr.
S. Pacific Ocean
92 H2 **Piteå** Sweden
92 H2 **Piteälven** r. Sweden
110 B2 **Piteşti** Romania
75 C2 **Pithoragarh** India
138 A2 **Pithquito** Mex.
86 C2 **Pitkyaranta** Rus. Fed.
96 C2 **Pitlochry** U.K.
128 B2 **Pitt Island** Can.
137 E3 **Pittsburg** U.S.A.
140 D2 **Pittsburgh** U.S.A.
141 E2 **Pittsfield** U.S.A.
53 D1 **Pittsworth** Austr.
155 C2 **Piumhi** Brazil
150 A3 **Piura** Peru
90 C2 **Pivdennyy Buh** r. Ukr.
131 E3 **Placentia** Can.
135 B3 **Placerville** U.S.A.
146 C2 **Placetas** Cuba
139 C2 **Plains** U.S.A.
139 C2 **Plainview** U.S.A.
60 B2 **Plaju** Indon.
61 C2 **Plampang** Indon.
154 C1 **Planaltina** Brazil
137 D2 **Plankinton** U.S.A.
139 D2 **Plano** U.S.A.
154 C2 **Planura** Brazil
142 B2 **Plaquemine** U.S.A.
106 B1 **Plasencia** Spain
109 C1 **Plaški** Croatia
147 C4 **Plato** Col.
137 D2 **Platte** r. U.S.A.
140 A2 **Platteville** U.S.A.
141 E2 **Plattsburgh** U.S.A.
101 F1 **Plau** Ger.

101 F2 **Plauen** Ger.
101 F1 **Plauer See** l. Ger.
89 E3 **Plavsk** Rus. Fed.
106 B2 **Playa de Castilla**
coastal area Spain
63 B2 **Plây Cu** Vietnam
129 E2 **Playgreen Lake** Can.
153 B3 **Plaza Huincul** Arg.
139 D3 **Pleasanton** U.S.A.
54 D2 **Pleasant Point** N.Z.
140 B3 **Pleasure Ridge Park**
U.S.A.
104 C2 **Pleaux** France
130 B2 **Pledger Lake** Can.
54 C1 **Plenty, Bay of** g. N.Z.
136 C1 **Plentywood** U.S.A.
86 D2 **Plesetsk** Rus. Fed.
131 C2 **Pletipi, Lac** l. Can.
100 C2 **Plettenberg** Ger.
122 B3 **Plettenberg Bay** S. Africa
110 B2 **Pleven** Bulg.
Plevna Bulg. see Pleven
109 C2 **Pljevlja** Yugo.
108 A2 **Ploaghe** Sardinia Italy
109 C2 **Ploče** Croatia
103 D1 **Płock** Pol.
109 C2 **Pločno** mt. Bos.-Herz.
104 B2 **Ploemeur** France
Ploeşti Romania see
Ploieşti
110 C2 **Ploieşti** Romania
89 F2 **Ploskoye** Rus. Fed.
104 B2 **Plouzané** France
110 B2 **Plovdiv** Bulg.
Plozk Pol. see Płock
121 B3 **Plumtree** Zimbabwe
88 B2 **Plunge** Lith.
144 B2 **Plutarco Elías Calles,**
Presa resr Mex.
88 C3 **Plyeshchanitsy** Belarus
147 D3 **Plymouth** Montserrat
99 A4 **Plymouth** U.K.
140 B2 **Plymouth** U.S.A.
99 B3 **Plynlimon** hill U.K.
88 C2 **Plyussa** Rus. Fed.
102 C2 **Plzeň** Czech Rep.
114 B3 **Pô** Burkina
108 B1 **Po** r. Italy
61 C1 **Po, Tanjong** pt Malaysia
Pobeda Peak China/Kyrg.
see Jengish Chokusu
Pobedy, Pik mt.
China/Kyrg. see
Jengish Chokusu
142 B1 **Pocahontas** U.S.A.
134 D2 **Pocatello** U.S.A.
90 B1 **Pochayiv** Ukr.
89 D3 **Pochep** Rus. Fed.
89 D3 **Pochinok** Rus. Fed.
145 C3 **Pochutla** Mex.
141 D3 **Pocomoke City** U.S.A.
155 C2 **Poços de Caldas** Brazil
89 D2 **Poddor'ye** Rus. Fed.
91 D1 **Podgorenskiy** Rus. Fed.
109 C2 **Podgorica** Yugo.
82 G3 **Podgornoye** Rus. Fed.
83 H2 **Podkamennaya Tunguska**
r. Rus. Fed.
89 E2 **Podol'sk** Rus. Fed.
109 D2 **Podujevo** Yugo.
122 A2 **Pofadder** S. Africa
89 D3 **Pogar** Rus. Fed.
105 E3 **Poggibonsi** Italy
109 D2 **Pogradec** Albania
Po Hai g. China see Bo Hai
65 B2 **P'ohang** S. Korea
48 G3 **Pohnpei** atoll Micronesia
90 B2 **Pohrebyshche** Ukr.
110 B2 **Poiana Mare** Romania
118 C3 **Poie** Dem. Rep. Congo
118 B3 **Pointe-Noire** Congo
160 B3 **Point Hope** U.S.A.
128 C1 **Point Lake** Can.
140 C3 **Point Pleasant** U.S.A.
104 C2 **Poitiers** France
104 C2 **Poitou, Plaines et Seuil**
du plain France
74 B2 **Pokaran** India
53 C1 **Pokataroo** Austr.
75 C2 **Pokhara** Nepal
119 C2 **Poko** Dem. Rep. Congo
83 J2 **Pokrovsk** Rus. Fed.
91 D2 **Pokrovskoye** Rus. Fed.
Pola Croatia see Pula
138 A1 **Polacca** U.S.A.
106 B1 **Pola de Lena** Spain
106 B1 **Pola de Siero** Spain
103 D1 **Poland** country Europe
55 C1 **Polar Plateau** Antarctica
80 B2 **Polatlı** Turkey
88 C2 **Polatsk** Belarus

77 C3 **Pol-e Khomrī** Afgh.
61 C2 **Polewali** Indon.
118 B2 **Poli** Cameroon
102 C1 **Police** Pol.
109 C2 **Policoro** Italy
105 D2 **Poligny** France
64 B2 **Polillo Islands** Phil.
80 B2 **Polis** Cyprus
90 B1 **Polis'ke** Ukr.
109 C2 **Polistena** Italy
103 D1 **Polkowice** Pol.
107 D2 **Pollença** Spain
109 C3 **Pollino, Monte** mt. Italy
86 F2 **Polnovat** Rus. Fed.
91 D2 **Polohy** Ukr.
90 B1 **Polonne** Ukr.
134 D1 **Polson** U.S.A.
91 C2 **Poltava** Ukr.
66 B2 **Poltava** Rus. Fed.
91 D2 **Poltavskaya** Rus. Fed.
88 C2 **Pôltsamaa** Estonia
88 C2 **Põlva** Estonia
Polyanovgrad Bulg. see
Karnobat
92 J2 **Polyarnyy** Rus. Fed.
86 C2 **Polyarnyye Zori** Rus. Fed.
111 B2 **Polygyros** Greece
111 B2 **Polykastro** Greece
156 E6 **Polynesia**
International Feature
106 B2 **Pombal** Port.
108 B2 **Pomezia** Italy
92 I2 **Pomokaira** reg. Fin.
110 C2 **Pomorie** Bulg.
102 C1 **Pomorska, Zatoka** b. Pol.
155 D1 **Pompéu** Brazil
139 D1 **Ponca City** U.S.A.
147 D3 **Ponce** Puerto Rico
73 B3 **Pondicherry** India
127 G2 **Pond Inlet** Can.
Ponds Bay Can. see
Pond Inlet
106 B1 **Ponferrada** Spain
117 A4 **Pongo** watercourse Sudan
123 D2 **Pongola** r. S. Africa
123 D2 **Pongolapoort Dam** l.
S. Africa
128 C2 **Ponoka** Can.
154 B3 **Ponta Grossa** Brazil
154 C1 **Pontalina** Brazil
105 D2 **Pont-à-Mousson** France
154 A2 **Ponta Porã** Brazil
105 D2 **Pontarlier** France
102 B2 **Pontcharra** France
142 B2 **Pontchartrain, Lake**
U.S.A.
154 B1 **Ponte de Pedra** Brazil
106 B2 **Ponte de Sor** Port.
154 B1 **Ponte do Rio Verde** Brazil
98 C3 **Pontefract** U.K.
129 D3 **Ponteix** Can.
154 B1 **Ponte Nova** Brazil
150 D4 **Pontes-e-Lacerda** Brazil
106 B1 **Pontevedra** Spain
Ponthierville
Dem. Rep. Congo see
Ubundu
140 B2 **Pontiac** IL U.S.A.
140 C2 **Pontiac** MI U.S.A.
60 B2 **Pontianak** Indon.
Pontine Islands is Italy
see Ponziane, Isole
104 B2 **Pontivy** France
157 D2 **Pontoetoe** Suriname
104 C2 **Pontoise** France
129 E2 **Ponton** Can.
99 B4 **Pontypool** U.K.
99 B4 **Pontypridd** U.K.
108 B2 **Ponziane, Isole** is Italy
99 C4 **Poole** U.K.
Poona India see Pune
52 B2 **Pooncarie** Austr.
152 B1 **Poopó, Lago de** l. Bol.
150 B2 **Popayán** Col.
83 I2 **Popigay** r. Rus. Fed.
52 B2 **Popiltah** U.K.
52 B2 **Popiltah** N.S.W. Austr.
129 E2 **Poplar** r. Can.
137 E3 **Poplar Bluff** U.S.A.
118 B3 **Popokabaka**
Dem. Rep. Congo
Popovichskaya Rus. Fed.
see Kalininskaya
110 C2 **Popovo** Bulg.
103 E2 **Poprad** Slovakia
151 E4 **Porangatu** Brazil
74 A2 **Porbandar** India
126 C2 **Porcupine** r. Can./U.S.A.
108 B1 **Pordenone** Italy
109 C1 **Poreč** Croatia
154 B2 **Porecatu** Brazil

114 C3 **Porga** Benin
93 H3 **Pori** Fin.
54 B2 **Porirua** N.Z.
88 C2 **Porkhov** Rus. Fed.
104 B2 **Pornic** France
83 K3 **Poronaysk** Rus. Fed.
Porong China see
Baingoin
111 B3 **Poros** Greece
92 I1 **Porsangen** sea chan.
Norway
93 E4 **Porsgrunn** Norway
111 D3 **Porsuk** r. Turkey
97 C1 **Portadown** U.K.
97 D1 **Portaferry** U.K.
140 B2 **Portage** U.S.A.
129 E3 **Portage la Prairie** Can.
128 B3 **Port Alberni** Can.
106 B2 **Portalegre** Port.
139 C2 **Portales** U.S.A.
128 A2 **Port Alexander** U.S.A.
128 B2 **Port Alice** Can.
142 B2 **Port Allen** U.S.A.
134 B1 **Port Angeles** U.S.A.
97 C2 **Portarlington**
Rep. of Ireland
51 D4 **Port Arthur** Austr.
Port Arthur China see
Lushunkou
139 E3 **Port Arthur** U.S.A.
96 A3 **Port Askaig** U.K.
52 A2 **Port Augusta** Austr.
147 C3 **Port-au-Prince** Haiti
131 E2 **Port aux Choix** Can.
122 B3 **Port Beaufort** S. Africa
73 D3 **Port Blair** India
52 B3 **Port Campbell** Austr.
131 D2 **Port-Cartier** Can.
54 B3 **Port Chalmers** N.Z.
143 D3 **Port Charlotte** U.S.A.
147 C3 **Port-de-Paix** Haiti
128 A2 **Port Edward** Can.
155 D1 **Porteirinha** Brazil
151 D3 **Portel** Brazil
130 B3 **Port Elgin** Can.
123 C3 **Port Elizabeth** S. Africa
96 A3 **Port Ellen** U.K.
98 A2 **Port Erin** Isle of Man
122 A3 **Porterville** S. Africa
135 C3 **Porterville** U.S.A.
Port Étienne Maur. see
Nouâdhibou
52 B3 **Port Fairy** Austr.
54 C1 **Port Fitzroy** N.Z.
Port Francqui
Dem. Rep. Congo see Ilebo
118 A3 **Port-Gentil** Gabon
115 C4 **Port Harcourt** Nigeria
128 B2 **Port Hardy** Can.
Port Harrison Can. see
Inukjuak
131 D3 **Port Hawkesbury** Can.
99 B4 **Porthcawl** U.K.
50 A2 **Port Hedland** Austr.
Port Herald Malawi see
Nsanje
99 A3 **Porthmadog** U.K.
131 E2 **Port Hope Simpson** Can.
140 C2 **Port Huron** U.S.A.
106 B2 **Portimão** Port.
Port Keats Austr. see
Wadeye
Port Láirge Rep. of Ireland
see Waterford
53 C2 **Portland** N.S.W. Austr.
52 B3 **Portland** Vic. Austr.
141 E2 **Portland** ME U.S.A.
134 B1 **Portland** OR U.S.A.
139 D3 **Portland** TX U.S.A.
99 B4 **Portland, Isle of** pen. U.K.
128 A2 **Portland Canal** inlet Can.
97 C2 **Portlaoise** Rep. of Ireland
139 D3 **Port Lavaca** U.S.A.
52 A2 **Port Lincoln** Austr.
114 A4 **Port Loko** Sierra Leone
113 I8 **Port Louis** Mauritius
Port-Lyautrey Morocco
see Kénitra
52 B3 **Port MacDonnell** Austr.
53 D2 **Port Macquarie** Austr.
Portmadoc U.K. see
Porthmadog
128 B2 **Port McNeill** Can.
131 D3 **Port-Menier** Can.
59 D3 **Port Moresby** P.N.G.
96 A3 **Portnahaven** U.K.
96 A1 **Port Nis** U.K.
122 A2 **Port Nolloth** S. Africa
Port-Nouveau-Québec
Can. see Kangiqsualujjuaq
Porto Port. see Oporto

150 C3	Porto Acre Brazil
154 B2	Porto Alegre Brazil
152 C3	Porto Alegre Brazil
	Porto Alexandre Angola see Tombua
	Porto Amélia Moz. see Pemba
151 D4	Porto Artur Brazil
154 B2	Porto Camargo Brazil
151 D4	Porto dos Gaúchos Óbidos Brazil
150 D4	Porto Esperidião Brazil
108 B2	Portoferraio Italy
151 E3	Porto Franco Brazil
147 D3	Port of Spain Trin. and Tob.
108 B1	Portogruaro Italy
108 B2	Portomaggiore Italy
154 B2	Porto Mendes Brazil
152 C2	Porto Murtinho Brazil
151 E4	Porto Nacional Brazil
114 C4	Porto-Novo Benin
154 B2	Porto Primavera, Represa resr Brazil
134 B2	Port Orford U.S.A.
151 D3	Porto Santana Brazil
154 B2	Porto São José Brazil
108 A3	Portoscuso Sardinia Italy
155 E1	Porto Seguro Brazil
108 B2	Porto Tolle Italy
108 A2	Porto Torres Sardinia Italy
154 B3	Porto União Brazil
105 D3	Porto-Vecchio Corsica France
150 C3	Porto Velho Brazil
150 A3	Portoviejo Ecuador
96 B3	Portpatrick U.K.
52 B3	Port Phillip Bay Austr.
52 A2	Port Pirie Austr.
96 A2	Portree U.K.
128 B3	Port Renfrew Can.
97 C1	Portrush U.K.
116 B1	Port Said Egypt
143 C3	Port St Joe U.S.A.
123 C3	Port St Johns S. Africa
143 D3	Port Saint Lucie City U.S.A.
123 D3	Port Shepstone S. Africa
99 C4	Portsmouth U.K.
141 E2	Portsmouth NH U.S.A.
140 C3	Portsmouth OH U.S.A.
141 D3	Portsmouth VA U.S.A.
153 B5	Port Stephens Falkland Is
97 C1	Portstewart U.K.
116 B3	Port Sudan Sudan
142 C3	Port Sulphur U.S.A.
99 B4	Port Talbot U.K.
134 B1	Port Townsend U.S.A.
106 B2	Portugal country Europe
	Portugália Angola see Chitato
	Portuguese Guinea country Africa see Guinea-Bissau
	Portuguese Timor terr. Asia see East Timor
	Portuguese West Africa country Africa see Angola
97 B2	Portumna Rep. of Ireland
105 C3	Port-Vendres France
48 H5	Port Vila Vanuatu
52 A2	Port Wakefield Austr.
50 B1	Port Warrender Austr.
153 A5	Porvenir Chile
93 I3	Porvoo Fin.
65 B2	Poryŏng S. Korea
152 C2	Posadas Arg.
89 E2	Poshekon'ye Rus. Fed.
	Poshekon'ye-Volodarsk Rus. Fed. see Poshekon'ye
92 I2	Posio Fin.
61 D2	Poso Indon.
151 E4	Posse Brazil
101 E2	Pößneck Ger.
139 C2	Post U.S.A.
	Poste-de-la-Baleine Can. see Kuujjuarapik
122 B2	Postmasburg S. Africa
108 B1	Postojna Slovenia
114 C2	Post Weygand Alg.
	Postysheve Ukr. see Krasnoarmiys'k
109 C2	Posušje Bos.-Herz.
123 C2	Potchefstroom S. Africa
139 E1	Poteau U.S.A.
108 B2	Potenza Italy
108 B2	Potenza r. Italy
123 A3	Potgietersrus S. Africa
151 E3	Poti r. Brazil
81 C1	P'ot'i Georgia
155 E1	Potiraguá Brazil
115 D3	Potiskum Nigeria
141 D3	Potomac, South Branch r. U.S.A.
152 B1	Potosí Bol.
64 B2	Pototan Phil.
138 C3	Potrero del Llano Mex.
101 F1	Potsdam Ger.
141 E2	Potsdam U.S.A.
141 D2	Pottstown U.S.A.
141 D2	Pottsville U.S.A.
131 E3	Pouch Cove Can.
141 E2	Poughkeepsie U.S.A.
98 B3	Poulton-le-Fylde U.K.
155 C2	Pouso Alegre Brazil
63 B2	Poŭthĭsăt Cambodia
103 D2	Považská Bystrica Slovakia
109 C2	Povlen mt. Yugo.
106 B1	Póvoa de Varzim Port.
136 B2	Powell U.S.A.
135 D3	Powell, Lake resr U.S.A.
128 B3	Powell River Can.
154 B1	Poxoréu Brazil
	Poyang China see Boyang
71 B3	Poyang Hu l. China
109 D2	Požarevac Yugo.
145 C2	Poza Rica Mex.
109 C1	Požega Croatia
109 D2	Požega Yugo.
79 D2	Pozm Tīāb Iran
103 D1	Poznań Pol.
106 C2	Pozoblanco Spain
152 C2	Pozo Colorado Para.
109 B3	Pozzallo Sicily Italy
108 B2	Pozzuoli Italy
60 B2	Prabumulih Indon.
102 C2	Prachatice Czech Rep.
63 A2	Prachuap Khiri Khan Thai.
103 D1	Praděd mt. Czech Rep.
104 C3	Prades France
155 E1	Prado Brazil
102 C1	Prague Czech Rep.
	Praha Czech Rep. see Prague
139 C2	Prairie Dog Town Fork r. U.S.A.
140 A2	Prairie du Chien U.S.A.
60 A1	Prapat Indon.
154 C1	Prata Brazil
108 B2	Prato Italy
137 D3	Pratt U.S.A.
142 C2	Prattville U.S.A.
61 C2	Praya Indon.
63 B2	Preăh Vihear Cambodia
89 F2	Prechistoye Rus. Fed.
129 D2	Preeceville Can.
88 C2	Preiļi Latvia
53 C2	Premer Austr.
105 C2	Prémery France
101 F1	Premnitz Ger.
102 C1	Prenzlau Ger.
66 B2	Preobrazheniye Rus. Fed.
63 A2	Preparis Island Cocos Is
63 A2	Preparis North Channel Cocos Is
63 A2	Preparis South Channel Cocos Is
103 D2	Přerov Czech Rep.
138 A2	Prescott U.S.A.
138 A2	Prescott Valley U.S.A.
109 D2	Preševo Yugo.
152 B2	Presidencia Roque Sáenz Peña Arg.
151 E3	Presidente Dutra Brazil
154 B2	Presidente Epitácio Brazil
154 B1	Presidente Murtinho Brazil
155 C1	Presidente Olegário Brazil
154 B2	Presidente Prudente Brazil
138 C3	Presidio U.S.A.
103 E2	Prešov Slovakia
111 B3	Prespa, Lake Europe
141 F1	Presque Isle U.S.A.
	Pressburg Slovakia see Bratislava
101 F2	Pressel Ger.
98 B3	Preston U.K.
134 D2	Preston U.S.A.
96 B3	Prestwick U.K.
155 C1	Preto r. Brazil
123 C2	Pretoria S. Africa
	Pretoria-Witwatersrand-Vereeniging prov. S. Africa see Gauteng
111 B3	Preveza Greece
63 B2	Prey Vêng Cambodia
124 A4	Pribilof Islands U.S.A.
109 C2	Priboj Yugo.
135 D3	Price U.S.A.
142 C2	Prichard U.S.A.
106 C2	Priego de Córdoba Spain
88 B3	Prienai Lith.
122 B2	Prieska S. Africa
103 D2	Prievidza Slovakia
109 C2	Prijedor Bos.-Herz.
109 C2	Prijepolje Yugo.
76 A2	Prikaspiyskaya Nizmennost' lowland Kazakh./Rus. Fed.
111 B2	Prilep Macedonia
101 F3	Přimda Czech Rep.
91 D2	Primorsko-Akhtarsk Rus. Fed.
129 D2	Primrose Lake Can.
129 D2	Prince Albert Can.
122 B3	Prince Albert S. Africa
126 E2	Prince Albert Peninsula Can.
122 B3	Prince Albert Road S. Africa
126 D2	Prince Alfred, Cape Can.
122 A3	Prince Alfred Hamlet S. Africa
127 G2	Prince Charles Island Can.
55 H2	Prince Charles Mountains Antarctica
131 D3	Prince Edward Island prov. Can.
128 B2	Prince George Can.
51 D1	Prince of Wales Island Austr.
126 F2	Prince of Wales Island Can.
128 A2	Prince of Wales Island U.S.A.
126 E2	Prince of Wales Strait Can.
126 E1	Prince Patrick Island Can.
126 F2	Prince Regent Inlet sea chan. Can.
128 A2	Prince Rupert Can.
51 D1	Princess Charlotte Bay Austr.
55 H2	Princess Elizabeth Land reg. Antarctica
128 B2	Princess Royal Island Can.
128 B3	Princeton Can.
140 B3	Princeton IN U.S.A.
137 E2	Princeton MO U.S.A.
134 B2	Prineville U.S.A.
86 C2	Priozersk Rus. Fed.
	Pripet r. Belarus see Prypyats'
90 A1	Pripet Marshes Belarus/Ukr.
109 D2	Priština Yugo.
101 F1	Pritzwalk Ger.
105 C3	Privas France
109 C2	Privlaka Croatia
89 F2	Privolzhsk Rus. Fed.
109 D2	Prizren Yugo.
151 D2	Professor van Blommestein Meer resr Suriname
146 B3	Progreso Hond.
145 D2	Progreso Mex.
81 C1	Prokhladnyy Rus. Fed.
109 D2	Prokuplje Yugo.
	Prome Myanmar see Pyè
154 C2	Promissão Brazil
154 C2	Promissão, Represa resr Brazil
126 D3	Prophet r. Can.
128 B2	Prophet River Can.
51 D2	Proserpine Austr.
	Proskurov Ukr. see Khmel'nyts'kyy
103 D2	Prostějov Czech Rep.
89 E3	Protvino Rus. Fed.
110 C2	Provadiya Bulg.
105 D3	Provence reg. France
141 E2	Providence U.S.A.
146 B3	Providencia, Isla de i. Caribbean Sea
83 N2	Provideniya Rus. Fed.
105 C2	Provins France
135 D2	Provo U.S.A.
129 C2	Provost Can.
91 C2	Prubiynyy, Mys pt Ukr.
154 B3	Prudentópolis Brazil
126 C2	Prudhoe Bay U.S.A.
100 C2	Prüm Ger.
105 D3	Prunelli-di-Fiumorbo Corsica France
103 D1	Pruszcz Gdański Pol.
103 E1	Pruszków Pol.
110 C1	Prut r. Europe
88 B3	Pruzhany Belarus
91 D2	Pryazovs'ke Ukr.
91 C1	Pryluky Ukr.
91 D2	Prymors'k Ukr.
91 D2	Prymors'kyy Ukr.
139 D1	Pryor U.S.A.
90 B1	Prypyats' r. Belarus/Ukr.
103 E2	Przemyśl Pol.
103 E1	Przeworsk Pol.
	Przheval'sk Kyrg. see Karakol
111 C3	Psara i. Greece
81 C1	Psebay Rus. Fed.
91 D3	Pshekha r. Rus. Fed.
88 C2	Pskov Rus. Fed.
88 C2	Pskov, Lake Estonia/Rus. Fed.
111 B2	Ptolemaïda Greece
109 C1	Ptuj Slovenia
150 B3	Pucallpa Peru
71 B3	Pucheng China
65 B2	Puch'ŏn S. Korea
103 D1	Puck Pol.
92 I2	Pudasjärvi Fin.
86 C2	Pudozh Rus. Fed.
	Puduchcheri India see Pondicherry
145 C3	Puebla Mex.
136 C3	Pueblo U.S.A.
153 B3	Puelén Arg.
153 A3	Puente Alto Chile
106 C2	Puente-Genil Spain
153 A4	Puerto Aisén Chile
152 B1	Puerto Alegre Bol.
145 C3	Puerto Ángel Mex.
146 B4	Puerto Armuelles Panama
150 C2	Puerto Ayacucho Venez.
146 B3	Puerto Barrios Guat.
146 B3	Puerto Cabezas Nic.
153 A4	Puerto Cisnes Chile
144 A2	Puerto Cortés Mex.
145 C3	Puerto Escondido Mex.
152 B1	Puerto Frey Bol.
150 C2	Puerto Inírida Col.
152 C1	Puerto Isabel Bol.
150 B3	Puerto Leguízamo Col.
146 B3	Puerto Lempira Hond.
144 A2	Puerto Libertad Mex.
106 C2	Puertollano Spain
153 B4	Puerto Madryn Arg.
150 C4	Puerto Maldonado Peru
	Puerto México Mex. see Coatzacoalcos
147 D4	Puerto Miranda Venez.
153 A4	Puerto Montt Chile
153 A5	Puerto Natáles Chile
150 C2	Puerto Nuevo Col.
150 C2	Puerto Páez Venez.
144 A1	Puerto Peñasco Mex.
152 C2	Puerto Pinasco Para.
147 C3	Puerto Plata Dom. Rep.
150 B3	Puerto Portillo Peru
	Puerto Presidente Stroessner Para. see Ciudad del Este
64 A3	Puerto Princesa Phil.
154 A3	Puerto Rico Arg.
147 D3	Puerto Rico terr. West Indies
158 C3	Puerto Rico Trench sea feature Caribbean Sea
153 B5	Puerto Santa Cruz Arg.
152 C2	Puerto Sastre Para.
144 B2	Puerto Vallarta Mex.
87 D3	Pugachev Rus. Fed.
74 B2	Pugal India
54 B2	Pukaki, Lake N.Z.
49 K5	Pukapuka atoll Cook Is
129 D2	Pukatawagan Can.
65 B1	Pukchin N. Korea
65 B1	Pukch'ŏng N. Korea
109 C2	Pukë Albania
54 B1	Pukekohe N.Z.
65 B1	Puksubaek-san mt. N. Korea
	Pula China see Nyingchi
108 B2	Pula Croatia
108 A3	Pula Sardinia Italy
152 B2	Pulacayo Bol.
103 E1	Puławy Pol.
92 I3	Pulkkila Fin.
134 C1	Pullman U.S.A.
64 B3	Pulog, Mount Phil.
64 B3	Pulutan Indon.
150 A3	Puná, Isla i. Ecuador
152 B2	Puna de Atacama plat. Arg.
54 B2	Punakaiki N.Z.
123 D1	Punda Maria S. Africa

73 B3 Pune India
65 B1 P'ungsan N. Korea
121 C2 Púnguè r. Moz.
119 C3 Punia Dem. Rep. Congo
74 B1 Punjab state India
153 B3 Punta Alta Arg.
153 A5 Punta Arenas Chile
108 A2 Punta Balestrieri mt. Sardinia Italy
146 B3 Punta Gorda Belize
146 B3 Puntarenas Costa Rica
150 B1 Punto Fijo Venez.
92 I3 Puolanka Fin.
70 B3 Puqi China
82 G2 Pur r. Rus. Fed.
75 C3 Puri India
100 B1 Purmerend Neth.
Purnea India see Pūrnia
75 C2 Pūrnia India
75 C2 Puruliya India
150 C3 Purus r. Peru
61 B2 Purwakarta Indon.
61 C2 Purwodadi Indon.
65 B1 Puryŏng N. Korea
74 B3 Pusad India
65 B2 Pusan S. Korea
89 E3 Pushchino Rus. Fed.
Pushkino Azer. see Biläsuvar
89 E2 Pushkino Rus. Fed.
88 C2 Pushkinskiye Gory Rus. Fed.
88 C2 Pustoshka Rus. Fed.
62 A1 Putao Myanmar
71 B3 Putian China
Puting China see De'an
61 C2 Puting, Tanjung pt Indon.
101 F1 Putlitz Ger.
60 B1 Putrajaya Malaysia
122 B2 Putsonderwater S. Africa
102 C1 Puttgarden Ger.
150 B3 Putumayo r. Col.
61 C1 Putusibau Indon.
90 B2 Putyla Ukr.
91 C1 Putyvl' Ukr.
93 I3 Puula l. Fin.
130 C1 Puvurnituq Can.
70 B2 Puyang China
104 C3 Puylaurens France
119 C3 Pweto Dem. Rep. Congo
99 A3 Pwllheli U.K.
92 J2 Pyaozerskiy Rus. Fed.
63 A2 Pyapon Myanmar
83 G2 Pyasina r. Rus. Fed.
87 D4 Pyatigorsk Rus. Fed.
91 C2 P''yatykhatky Ukr.
62 A2 Pyè Myanmar
88 C3 Pyetrykaw Belarus
93 H3 Pyhäjärvi l. Fin.
92 H3 Pyhäjoki r. Fin.
92 I3 Pyhäsalmi Fin.
62 A1 Pyingaing Myanmar
62 A2 Pyinmana Myanmar
65 B2 Pyŏksŏng N. Korea
65 B2 P'yŏnggang N. Korea
65 B2 P'yŏngsong N. Korea
65 B2 P'yŏngt'aek S. Korea
65 B2 P'yŏngyang N. Korea
135 C2 Pyramid Lake U.S.A.
107 D1 Pyrenees mts Europe
Pyrénées mts Europe see Pyrenees
111 B3 Pyrgetos Greece
111 C3 Pyrgi Greece
111 B3 Pyrgos Greece
91 C1 Pyryatyn Ukr.
103 C1 Pyrzyce Pol.
88 C2 Pytalovo Rus. Fed.
62 A2 Pyu Myanmar
111 B3 Pyxaria mt. Greece

Q

127 H1 Qaanaaq Greenland
Qabqa China see Gonghe
123 C3 Qacha's Nek Lesotho
69 D2 Qagan Nur China
Qahremānshahr Iran see Kermānshāh
68 C2 Qaidam Pendi basin China
74 A1 Qaisar, Koh-i- mt. Afgh.
79 C2 Qalamat Abū Shafrah Saudi Arabia
77 C3 Qalāt Afgh.
78 A2 Qal'at al Azlam Saudi Arabia
78 A2 Qal'at al Mu'azzam Saudi Arabia

78 B2 Qal'at Bīshah Saudi Arabia
76 C3 Qal 'eh-ye Now Afgh.
129 E1 Qamanirjuaq Lake Can.
Qamanittuaq Can. see Baker Lake
79 C3 Qamar, Ghubbat al b. Yemen
68 C2 Qamdo China
78 B3 Qam Hadīl Saudi Arabia
127 I2 Qaqortoq Greenland
80 A3 Qara Egypt
Qarkilik China see Ruoqiang
Qarqan China see Qiemo
78 B2 Qaryat al Ulyā Saudi Arabia
127 I2 Qasigiannguit Greenland
79 D2 Qasr-e-Qand Iran
81 C2 Qasr-e Shīrīn Iran
116 A2 Qasr Farafra Egypt
127 I2 Qassimiut Greenland
78 B3 Qa'tabah Yemen
79 C2 Qatar country Asia
116 A2 Qattâra Depression Egypt
76 B3 Qāyen Iran
81 C1 Qazax Azer.
81 C1 Qazimämmäd Azer.
81 C2 Qazvin Iran
116 B2 Qena Egypt
127 I2 Qeqertarsuaq Greenland
127 I2 Qeqertarsuaq i. Greenland
127 I2 Qeqertarsuatsiaat Greenland
127 I2 Qeqertarsuup Tunua b. Greenland
79 C2 Qeshm Iran
70 A3 Qianjiang Chongqing China
70 B2 Qianjiang Hubei China
69 E1 Qianjin China
65 A1 Qian Shan mts China
71 A3 Qianxi China
70 C2 Qidong China
77 E3 Qiemo China
71 A3 Qijiang China
68 C2 Qijiaojing China
127 H2 Qikiqtarjuaq Can.
74 A2 Qila Ladgasht Pak.
68 C2 Qilian Shan mts China
127 J2 Qillak i. Greenland
70 B3 Qimen China
127 H1 Qimusseriarsuaq b. Greenland
Qincheng China see Nanfeng
70 C2 Qingdao China
68 C2 Qinghai Hu salt l. China
68 C2 Qinghai Nanshan mts China
Qingjiang China see Huaiyin
Qingjiang China see Zhangshu
70 B2 Qingshuihe China
70 A2 Qingtongxia China
70 A2 Qingyang China
71 B3 Qingyuan Guangdong China
Qingyuan China see Yizhou
65 A1 Qingyuan Liaoning China
68 B2 Qing Zang Gaoyuan plat. China
70 B2 Qingzhou China
70 B2 Qinhuangdao China
Qinjiang China see Shicheng
70 A2 Qin Ling mts China
Qinting China see Lianhua
70 B2 Qinyang China
71 A3 Qinzhou China
71 B4 Qionghai China
70 A2 Qionglai Shan mts China
71 B4 Qiongshan China
71 A4 Qiongzhong China
69 E1 Qiqihar China
81 D3 Qīr Iran
Qishan China see Qimen
79 C3 Qishn Yemen
66 B1 Qitaihe China
70 B2 Qixian Henan China
70 B2 Qixian Shanxi China
Qogir Feng mt. China/Jammu and Kashmir see K2
81 D2 Qom Iran
81 D2 Qomishēh Iran
Qomolangma Feng mt. China/Nepal see Everest, Mount

Qoqek China see Tacheng
80 B2 Qornet es Saouda mt. Lebanon
81 C2 Qorveh Iran
79 C2 Qoṭbābād Iran
101 C1 Quakenbrück Ger.
53 C2 Quambone Austr.
63 B2 Quang Ngai Vietnam
63 B2 Quang Tri Vietnam
Quan Long Vietnam see Ca Mau
Quan Phu Quoc i. Vietnam see Phu Quôc, Đao
71 B3 Quanzhou Fujian China
71 B3 Quanzhou Guangxi China
108 A3 Quartu Sant'Elena Sardinia Italy
138 A2 Quartzsite U.S.A.
81 C1 Quba Azer.
76 B3 Quchan Iran
53 C3 Queanbeyan Austr.
131 C3 Québec Can.
131 C2 Québec prov. Can.
101 E2 Quedlinburg Ger.
Queen Adelaide Islands Chile see La Reina Adelaida, Archipiélago de
128 A2 Queen Charlotte Can.
128 A2 Queen Charlotte Islands Can.
128 B2 Queen Charlotte Sound sea chan. Can.
128 B2 Queen Charlotte Strait Can.
126 E1 Queen Elizabeth Islands Can.
55 I2 Queen Mary Land reg. Antarctica
126 F2 Queen Maud Gulf Can.
55 E2 Queen Maud Land reg. Antarctica
55 P1 Queen Maud Mountains Antarctica
52 B3 Queenscliff Austr.
52 B1 Queensland state Austr.
51 D4 Queenstown Austr.
54 A3 Queenstown N.Z.
Queenstown Rep. of Ireland see Cóbh
123 C3 Queenstown S. Africa
121 C2 Quelimane Moz.
153 A4 Quellón Chile
Quelpart Island S. Korea see Cheju-do
138 B2 Quemado U.S.A.
Que Que Zimbabwe see Kwekwe
154 B2 Queréncia do Norte Brazil
145 B2 Querétaro Mex.
101 E2 Querfurt Ger.
128 B2 Quesnel Can.
128 B2 Quesnel Lake Can.
74 A1 Quetta Pak.
146 A3 Quezaltenango Guat.
64 A3 Quezon Phil.
64 B2 Quezon City Phil.
120 A2 Quibala Angola
150 B2 Quibdó Col.
104 B2 Quiberon France
120 A2 Quilengues Angola
104 C3 Quillan France
153 C3 Quilmes Arg.
73 B4 Quilon India
51 D2 Quilpie Austr.
153 A3 Quilpué Chile
120 A1 Quimbele Angola
152 B2 Quimili Arg.
104 B2 Quimper France
104 B2 Quimperlé France
135 B3 Quincy CA U.S.A.
143 D2 Quincy FL U.S.A.
137 E3 Quincy IL U.S.A.
141 E2 Quincy MA U.S.A.
63 B2 Qui Nhon Vietnam
107 C1 Quinto Spain
121 D2 Quionga Moz.
120 A2 Quirima Angola
53 D2 Quirindi Austr.
154 B1 Quirinópolis Brazil
131 D3 Quispamsis Can.
121 C3 Quissico Moz.
120 A2 Quitapa Angola
150 B2 Quito Ecuador
151 F3 Quixadá Brazil
71 A3 Qujing China
75 D1 Qumar He r. China
123 C3 Qumrha S. Africa
115 E1 Qunayyin, Sabkhat al salt marsh Libya

129 E1 Quoich r. Can.
52 A2 Quorn Austr.
79 C2 Qurayat Oman
77 C3 Qürghonteppa Tajik.
116 B2 Quseir Egypt
Quxar China see Lhazê
Quyang China see Jingzhou
71 B3 Quzhou China
Qyteti Stalin Albania see Kuçovë
Qyzyltū Kazakh. see Kishkenekol'

R

103 D2 Raab r. Austria
92 H3 Raahe Fin.
100 C1 Raalte Neth.
61 C2 Raas i. Indon.
61 B2 Raba Indon.
114 B1 Rabat Morocco
59 E3 Rabaul P.N.G.
50 C2 Rabbit Flat Austr.
78 A2 Rābigh Saudi Arabia
103 D2 Rabka Pol.
90 B2 Rābnița Moldova
Rabyānah, Ramlat des. Libya see Rebiana Sand Sea
131 E3 Race, Cape Can.
142 B3 Raceland U.S.A.
141 E2 Race Point U.S.A.
63 B3 Rach Gia Vietnam
103 D1 Racibórz Pol.
140 B2 Racine U.S.A.
78 B3 Radā' Yemen
110 C1 Rădăuți Romania
140 B3 Radcliff U.S.A.
74 B2 Radhanpur India
130 C2 Radisson Can.
103 E1 Radom Pol.
103 D1 Radomsko Pol.
90 B1 Radomyshl' Ukr.
111 B2 Radoviš Macedonia
88 B2 Radviliškis Lith.
78 A2 Radwá, Jabal mt. Saudi Arabia
90 B1 Radyvyliv Ukr.
75 C2 Rae Bareli India
128 C1 Rae-Edzo Can.
128 C1 Rae Lakes Can.
100 C2 Raeren Belgium
54 C1 Raetihi N.Z.
78 A2 Rāf hill Saudi Arabia
152 B3 Rafaela Arg.
118 C2 Rafaï C.A.R.
78 B2 Rafhā' Saudi Arabia
79 C1 Rafsanjān Iran
119 C2 Raga Sudan
64 B2 Ragang, Mount vol. Phil.
109 B3 Ragusa Sicily Italy
61 D2 Raha Indon.
88 D3 Rahachow Belarus
78 A3 Rahad r. Sudan
74 B2 Rahimyar Khan Pak.
73 B3 Raichur India
75 C2 Raigarh India
128 C2 Rainbow Lake Can.
134 B1 Rainier, Mount vol. U.S.A.
130 A3 Rainy Lake Can.
129 E3 Rainy River Can.
75 C2 Raipur India
93 H3 Raisio Fin.
88 C2 Raja Estonia
73 C3 Rajahmundry India
61 C1 Rajang r. Sarawak Malaysia
74 B2 Rajanpur Pak.
73 B4 Rajapalaiyam India
74 B2 Rajasthan state India
74 B2 Rajasthan Canal canal India
74 B2 Rajgarh India
60 B2 Rajik Indon.
74 B2 Rajkot India
75 C2 Raj Nandgaon India
74 B2 Rajpur India
75 C2 Rajshahi Bangl.
54 B2 Rakaia r. N.Z.
74 B1 Rakaposhi mt. Jammu and Kashmir
90 A2 Rakhiv Ukr.
91 D1 Rakitnoye Rus. Fed.
88 C2 Rakke Estonia
88 C2 Rakvere Estonia
143 E1 Raleigh U.S.A.
143 E2 Raleigh Bay U.S.A.
48 H3 Ralik Chain is Marshall Is
75 C2 Ramanuj Ganj India

123 C2 **Ramatlabama** S. Africa
104 C2 **Rambouillet** France
99 A4 **Rame Head** *hd* U.K.
97 C1 **Ramelton** Rep. of Ireland
89 E2 **Rameshki** Rus. Fed.
74 B2 **Ramgarh** India
81 C2 **Râmhormoz** Iran
78 B3 **Ramlat Dahm** *des.*
Saudi Arabia/Yemen
110 C1 **Râmnicu Sărat** Romania
110 B1 **Râmnicu Vâlcea** Romania
89 C3 **Ramon'** Rus. Fed.
135 C4 **Ramona** U.S.A.
123 C1 **Ramotswa** Botswana
75 B2 **Rampur** India
62 A2 **Ramree Island** Myanmar
98 A2 **Ramsey** Isle of Man
130 B3 **Ramsey Lake** Can.
99 D4 **Ramsgate** U.K.
81 C2 **Râmshir** Iran
62 A1 **Ramsing** India
75 C2 **Ranaghat** India
61 C1 **Ranau** *Sabah* Malaysia
153 A3 **Rancagua** Chile
154 B2 **Rancharia** Brazil
75 C2 **Ranchi** India
93 F4 **Randers** Denmark
63 B3 **Rangae** Thai.
75 D2 **Rangapara North** India
54 B2 **Rangiora** N.Z.
49 M5 **Rangiroa** *atoll*
Fr. Polynesia
54 C1 **Rangitaiki** *r.* N.Z.
60 B2 **Rangkasbitung** Indon.
Rangoon Myanmar *see*
Yangôn
75 C2 **Rangpur** Bangl.
129 E1 **Rankin Inlet** Can.
53 C2 **Rankin's Springs** Austr.
Rankovićevo Yugo. *see*
Kraljevo
96 B2 **Rannoch Moor** *moorland*
U.K.
74 B2 **Rann of Kachchh** *marsh*
India
63 A3 **Ranong** Thai.
59 C3 **Ransiki** Indon.
61 C2 **Rantaupanjang** Indon.
60 A1 **Rantauprapat** Indon.
61 C2 **Ranteppao** Indon.
92 I2 **Ranua** Fin.
93 E4 **Ranum** Denmark
78 B2 **Ranyah, Wādī**
watercourse Saudi Arabia
49 J6 **Raoul Island** Kermadec Is
49 M6 **Rapa** *i.* Fr. Polynesia
108 A2 **Rapallo** Italy
136 C2 **Rapid City** U.S.A.
88 B2 **Rapla** Estonia
74 A2 **Rapur** India
49 L6 **Rarotonga** *i.* Cook Is
153 B4 **Rasa, Punta** *pt* Arg.
Ras al Khaimah U.A.E. *see*
Ra's al Khaymah
79 C2 **Ra's al Khaymah** U.A.E.
116 B3 **Ras Dashen** *mt.* Eth.
88 B2 **Raseiniai** Lith.
116 B2 **Râs Ghârib** Egypt
81 C2 **Rasht** Iran
74 A2 **Ras Koh** *mt.* Pak.
110 C1 **Râşnov** Romania
88 C2 **Rasony** Belarus
79 C2 **Ra's Şirāb** Oman
108 B3 **Rass Jebel** Tunisia
87 D3 **Rasskazovo** Rus. Fed.
79 C2 **Ras Tannūrah**
Saudi Arabia
101 D1 **Rastede** Ger.
48 I2 **Ratak Chain** *is* Marshall Is
93 F3 **Rätan** Sweden
123 C2 **Ratanda** S. Africa
74 B2 **Ratangarh** India
63 A2 **Rat Buri** Thai.
62 A1 **Rathedaung** Myanmar
101 F1 **Rathenow** Ger.
97 C1 **Rathfriland** U.K.
97 C1 **Rathlin Island** U.K.
97 B2 **Rathluirc** Rep. of Ireland
100 C2 **Ratingen** Ger.
74 B2 **Ratlam** India
73 B3 **Ratnagiri** India
73 C4 **Ratnapura** Sri Lanka
90 A1 **Ratne** Ukr.
138 C1 **Raton** U.S.A.
96 D2 **Rattray Head** *hd* U.K.
93 G3 **Rättvik** Sweden
101 E1 **Ratzeburg** Ger.
78 B2 **Raudhatain** Kuwait
92 □B2 **Raufarhöfn** Iceland
54 C1 **Raukumara Range** *mts*
N.Z.

93 H3 **Rauma** Fin.
88 C2 **Rauna** Latvia
61 C2 **Raung, Gunung** *vol.*
Indon.
75 C2 **Raurkela** India
66 D2 **Rausu** Japan
90 B2 **Räut** *r.* Moldova
134 D1 **Ravalli** U.S.A.
81 C2 **Ravânsar** Iran
108 B2 **Ravenna** Italy
101 F1 **Ravensburg** Ger.
50 B3 **Ravensthorpe** Austr.
74 B1 **Ravi** *r.* Pak.
74 B1 **Rawalpindi** Pak.
103 D1 **Rawicz** Pol.
50 B3 **Rawlinna** Austr.
136 B2 **Rawlins** U.S.A.
153 B4 **Rawson** Arg.
75 C3 **Rāyagarha** India
69 E1 **Raychikhinsk** Rus. Fed.
78 B3 **Raydah** Yemen
87 E3 **Rayevskiy** Rus. Fed.
134 B1 **Raymond** U.S.A.
53 D2 **Raymond Terrace** Austr.
139 D3 **Raymondville** U.S.A.
129 C2 **Raymore** Can.
145 C2 **Rayón** Mex.
63 B2 **Rayong** Thai.
78 A2 **Rayyis** Saudi Arabia
104 B2 **Raz, Pointe du** *pt* France
81 C2 **Razāzah, Buḩayrat ar** *l.*
Iraq
110 C2 **Razgrad** Bulg.
110 C2 **Razim, Lacul** *lag.* Romania
111 B2 **Razlog** Bulg.
Raz"yezd 3km Rus. Fed.
see Novyy Urgal
104 B2 **Ré, Île de** *i.* France
99 C4 **Reading** U.K.
140 C3 **Reading** *OH* U.S.A.
141 D2 **Reading** *PA* U.S.A.
123 C2 **Reagile** S. Africa
115 E2 **Rebiana Sand Sea** *des.*
Libya
66 D1 **Rebun-tō** *i.* Japan
50 B3 **Recherche, Archipelago**
of the *is* Austr.
89 D3 **Rechytsa** Belarus
151 F3 **Recife** Brazil
123 C3 **Recife, Cape** S. Africa
100 C2 **Recklinghausen** Ger.
152 B3 **Reconquista** Arg.
137 D1 **Red** *r.* Can./U.S.A.
142 B3 **Red** *r.* U.S.A.
100 B3 **Redange** Lux.
143 C1 **Red Bank** U.S.A.
Red Basin China *see*
Sichuan Pendi
131 E2 **Red Bay** Can.
135 B2 **Red Bluff** U.S.A.
98 C2 **Redcar** U.K.
129 C2 **Redcliff** Can.
121 B2 **Redcliff** Zimbabwe
52 B2 **Red Cliffs** Austr.
128 C2 **Red Deer** Can.
126 E3 **Red Deer** *r.* Can.
129 D2 **Red Deer Lake** Can.
135 B2 **Redding** U.S.A.
99 C3 **Redditch** U.K.
137 D2 **Redfield** U.S.A.
137 D3 **Red Hills** U.S.A.
130 A2 **Red Lake** Can.
130 A2 **Red Lake** *l.* Can.
137 E1 **Red Lakes** U.S.A.
134 E1 **Red Lodge** U.S.A.
134 B2 **Redmond** U.S.A.
137 D2 **Red Oak** U.S.A.
104 B2 **Redon** France
106 B1 **Redondela** Spain
106 B2 **Redondo** Port.
78 A2 **Red Sea** Africa/Asia
128 B1 **Redstone** *r.* Can.
128 C2 **Redwater** Can.
137 E2 **Red Wing** U.S.A.
137 D2 **Redwood Falls** U.S.A.
97 C2 **Ree, Lough** *l.*
Rep. of Ireland
134 B2 **Reedsport** U.S.A.
54 B2 **Reefton** N.Z.
139 D3 **Refugio** U.S.A.
102 C2 **Regen** Ger.
155 E1 **Regência** Brazil
102 C2 **Regensburg** Ger.
126 G2 **Reggane** Alg.
109 C3 **Reggio di Calabria** Italy
108 B2 **Reggio nell'Emilia** Italy
110 B1 **Reghin** Romania
129 D2 **Regina** Can.
154 C1 **Registro** Brazil
122 A1 **Rehoboth** Namibia
80 B2 **Rehovot** Israel

101 F2 **Reichenbach** Ger.
143 E1 **Reidsville** U.S.A.
99 C4 **Reigate** U.K.
105 C2 **Reims** France
101 E1 **Reinbek** Ger.
129 D2 **Reindeer** *r.* Can.
129 D2 **Reindeer Island** Can.
129 D2 **Reindeer Lake** Can.
92 F2 **Reine** Norway
106 C1 **Reinosa** Spain
100 C3 **Reinsfeld** Ger.
123 C2 **Reitz** S. Africa
122 B2 **Reivilo** S. Africa
129 D1 **Reliance** Can.
107 D2 **Relizane** Alg.
52 A2 **Remarkable, Mount** *hill*
Austr.
79 C2 **Remeshk** Iran
105 D2 **Remiremont** France
100 C2 **Remscheid** Ger.
102 B1 **Rendsburg** Ger.
141 D1 **Renfrew** Can.
60 B2 **Rengat** Indon.
90 B2 **Reni** Ukr.
52 B2 **Renmark** Austr.
48 H5 **Rennell** *i.* Solomon Is
101 D2 **Rennerod** Ger.
104 B2 **Rennes** France
129 D1 **Rennie Lake** Can.
108 B2 **Reno** *r.* Italy
135 C3 **Reno** U.S.A.
70 A3 **Renshou** China
140 B2 **Rensselaer** U.S.A.
75 C2 **Renukut** India
54 B2 **Renwick** N.Z.
61 D2 **Reo** Indon.
136 D3 **Republican** *r.* U.S.A.
127 G2 **Repulse Bay** Can.
150 B3 **Requena** Peru
107 C2 **Requena** Spain
60 B2 **Resag, Gunung** *mt.* Indon.
111 B2 **Resen** Macedonia
154 B2 **Reserva** Brazil
91 C2 **Reshetylivka** Ukr.
152 C2 **Resistencia** Arg.
110 B1 **Reşiţa** Romania
126 F2 **Resolute** Bay Can.
127 H2 **Resolution Island** Can.
155 D1 **Resplendor** Brazil
145 C3 **Retalhuleu** Guat.
98 C3 **Retford** U.K.
105 C2 **Rethel** France
111 B3 **Rethymno** Greece
113 I8 **Réunion** *terr.* Indian Ocean
107 D1 **Reus** Spain
Reut *r.* Moldova *see* Răut
102 B2 **Reutlingen** Ger.
86 C2 **Revda** Rus. Fed.
128 C2 **Revelstoke** Can.
144 A3 **Revillagigedo, Islas** *is*
Mex.
128 A2 **Revillagigedo Island**
U.S.A.
75 C2 **Rewa** India
134 D2 **Rexburg** U.S.A.
135 B3 **Reyes, Point** U.S.A.
160 M4 **Reykjanes Ridge**
sea feature
N. Atlantic Ocean
92 □A3 **Reykjanestá** *pt* Iceland
92 □A3 **Reykjavík** Iceland
145 C2 **Reynosa** Mex.
Rezā'īyeh Iran *see*
Orūmīyeh
Rezā'īyeh, Daryācheh-ye
salt l. Iran *see*
Orūmīyeh, Daryācheh-ye
88 C2 **Rēzekne** Latvia
Rheims France *see* Reims
Rhein *r.* Ger. *see* Rhine
100 C1 **Rheine** Ger.
101 F1 **Rheinsberg** Ger.
Rhin *r.* France *see* Rhine
100 C2 **Rhine** *r.* Europe
140 B1 **Rhinelander** U.S.A.
101 F1 **Rhinluch** *marsh* Ger.
101 F1 **Rhinow** Ger.
108 A1 **Rho** Italy
141 E2 **Rhode Island** *state* U.S.A.
111 B3 **Rhodes** Greece
111 C3 **Rhodes** *i.* Greece
Rhodesia *country* Africa
see Zimbabwe
111 B2 **Rhodope Mountains**
Bulg./Greece
105 C3 **Rhône** *r.* France/Switz.
Rhum *i.* U.K. *see* Rum
Rhuthun U.K. *see* Ruthin
98 B3 **Rhyl** U.K.
155 D1 **Riacho dos Machados**
Brazil

154 C1 **Rialma** Brazil
154 C1 **Rianópolis** Brazil
60 B1 **Riau, Kepulauan** *is* Indon.
106 B1 **Ribadeo** Spain
106 B1 **Ribadesella** Spain
154 B2 **Ribas do Rio Pardo** Brazil
121 C2 **Ribáuè** Moz.
98 B3 **Ribble** *r.* U.K.
93 E4 **Ribe** Denmark
154 C2 **Ribeira** *r.* Brazil
154 C2 **Ribeirão Preto** Brazil
104 C2 **Ribérac** France
152 B1 **Riberalta** Bol.
Ribniţa Moldova *see*
Râbniţa
102 C1 **Ribnitz-Damgarten** Ger.
140 A1 **Rice Lake** U.S.A.
123 D2 **Richards Bay**
S. Africa
139 D2 **Richardson** U.S.A.
126 C2 **Richardson Mountains**
Can.
135 D3 **Richfield** U.S.A.
134 C1 **Richland** U.S.A.
140 A2 **Richland Center** U.S.A.
53 D2 **Richmond** *N.S.W.* Austr.
51 D2 **Richmond** *Qld* Austr.
134 B1 **Richmond** Can.
54 B2 **Richmond** N.Z.
122 B3 **Richmond** S. Africa
98 C2 **Richmond** U.K.
140 C3 **Richmond** *IN* U.S.A.
140 C3 **Richmond** *KY* U.S.A.
141 D3 **Richmond** *VA* U.S.A.
143 D2 **Richmond Hill** U.S.A.
53 D1 **Richmond Range** *hills*
Austr.
130 C3 **Rideau Lakes** Can.
135 C3 **Ridgecrest** U.S.A.
142 B2 **Ridgeland** U.S.A.
102 C1 **Riesa** Ger.
101 D1 **Rieste** Ger.
123 B2 **Riet** *r.* S. Africa
101 D2 **Rietberg** Ger.
122 B2 **Rietfontein** S. Africa
108 B2 **Rieti** Italy
136 B3 **Rifle** U.S.A.
88 B2 **Riga** Latvia
88 B2 **Riga, Gulf of**
Estonia/Latvia
79 C2 **Rīgān** Iran
134 D2 **Rigby** U.S.A.
131 E2 **Rigolet** Can.
93 H3 **Riihimäki** Fin.
55 D2 **Riiser-Larsen Ice Shelf**
Antarctica
108 B1 **Rijeka** Croatia
134 C2 **Riley** U.S.A.
105 C2 **Rillieux-la-Pape** France
78 B2 **Rimah, Wādī al**
watercourse Saudi Arabia
103 E2 **Rimavská Sobota**
Slovakia
128 C2 **Rimbey** Can.
108 B2 **Rimini** Italy
Rîmnicu Sărat Romania
see Râmnicu Sărat
Rîmnicu Vîlcea Romania
see Râmnicu Vâlcea
131 D3 **Rimouski** Can.
144 B2 **Rincón de Romos** Mex.
93 F3 **Ringebu** Norway
93 E4 **Ringkøbing** Denmark
92 G2 **Ringvassøy** *i.* Norway
99 C4 **Ringwood** U.K.
101 D1 **Rinteln** Ger.
154 B3 **Rio Azul** Brazil
150 B3 **Riobamba** Ecuador
155 D2 **Rio Bonito** Brazil
150 C4 **Rio Branco** Brazil
154 C3 **Rio Branco do Sul** Brazil
154 B2 **Rio Brilhante** Brazil
155 D2 **Rio Casca** Brazil
154 C2 **Rio Claro** Brazil
153 B3 **Rio Colorado** Arg.
153 B3 **Rio Cuarto** Arg.
155 D2 **Rio de Janeiro** Brazil
153 B5 **Rio Gallegos** Arg.
153 B5 **Rio Grande** Arg.
152 C4 **Rio Grande** Brazil
144 B2 **Rio Grande** Mex.
139 D3 **Rio Grande** *r.* Mex./U.S.A.
139 D3 **Rio Grande City** U.S.A.
150 B1 **Riohacha** Col.
150 B1 **Rioja** Peru
145 C2 **Río Lagartos** Mex.
151 F3 **Río Largo** Brazil
105 C2 **Riom** France
150 B1 **Rio Mulatos** Bol.
154 C3 **Rio Negro** Brazil
155 D1 **Rio Pardo de Minas** Brazil

154 C1 Rio Preto, Serra do hills Brazil
138 B1 Rio Rancho U.S.A.
150 B3 Rio Tigre Ecuador
64 A3 Rio Tuba Phil.
154 B1 Rio Verde Brazil
145 C2 Rio Verde Mex.
154 B1 Rio Verde de Mato Grosso Brazil
90 C1 Ripky Ukr.
99 C3 Ripley U.K.
107 D1 Ripoll Spain
98 C2 Ripon U.K.
66 D1 Rishiri-tō i. Japan
 Rişnov Romania see Râşnov
93 E4 Risør Norway
122 B2 Ritchie S. Africa
73 D3 Ritchie's Archipelago is India
134 C1 Ritzville U.S.A.
152 B2 Rivadavia Arg.
108 B1 Riva del Garda Italy
146 B3 Rivas Nic.
152 C3 Rivera Uru.
114 B4 River Cess Liberia
129 D2 Riverhurst Can.
52 C2 Riverina reg. Austr.
122 B3 Riversdale S. Africa
135 C4 Riverside U.S.A.
136 B2 Riverton U.S.A.
131 D3 Riverview Can.
105 C3 Rivesaltes France
131 D3 Rivière-au-Renard Can.
131 D3 Rivière-du-Loup Can.
141 F1 Rivière-Ouelle Can.
90 C1 Rivne Ukr.
108 A1 Rivoli Italy
120 B2 Rivungo Angola
54 B2 Riwaka N.Z.
78 B2 Riyadh Saudi Arabia
81 C1 Rize Turkey
70 B2 Rizhao China
105 C2 Roanne France
140 D3 Roanoke U.S.A.
143 E1 Roanoke r. U.S.A.
143 E1 Roanoke Rapids U.S.A.
135 E3 Roan Plateau U.S.A.
146 B3 Roatán Hond.
52 A3 Robe Austr.
52 B2 Robe, Mount hill Austr.
101 F1 Röbel Ger.
53 D1 Roberts, Mount Austr.
92 H3 Robertsfors Sweden
122 A3 Robertson S. Africa
114 A4 Robertsport Liberia
 Robert Williams Angola see Caála
130 C3 Roberval Can.
50 A2 Robinson Range hills Austr.
52 B2 Robinvale Austr.
129 D2 Roblin Can.
128 C2 Robson, Mount Can.
139 D3 Robstown U.S.A.
 Roçadas Angola see Xangongo
108 B3 Rocca Busambra mt. Sicily Italy
153 C3 Rocha Uru.
98 B3 Rochdale U.K.
154 B1 Rochedo Brazil
100 B2 Rochefort Belgium
104 B2 Rochefort France
52 B3 Rochester Austr.
137 E2 Rochester MN U.S.A.
141 E2 Rochester NH U.S.A.
141 D2 Rochester NY U.S.A.
94 A2 Rockall i. N. Atlantic Ocean
160 L4 Rockall Bank sea feature N. Atlantic Ocean
140 B2 Rockford U.S.A.
51 E2 Rockhampton Austr.
143 D2 Rock Hill U.S.A.
50 A3 Rockingham Austr.
140 A2 Rock Island U.S.A.
136 B1 Rock Springs MT U.S.A.
139 C3 Rocksprings U.S.A.
136 B2 Rock Springs WY U.S.A.
143 D1 Rockwood U.S.A.
136 C3 Rocky Ford U.S.A.
143 E1 Rocky Mount U.S.A.
128 C2 Rocky Mountain House Can.
124 F4 Rocky Mountains U.S.A.
100 B3 Rocroi France
102 C1 Rødbyhavn Denmark
131 E2 Roddickton Can.
104 C2 Rodez France
 Rodi i. Greece see Rhodes

89 F2 Rodniki Rus. Fed.
 Rodos Greece see Rhodes
 Rodos i. Greece see Rhodes
 Rodosto Turkey see Tekirdağ
50 A2 Roebourne Austr.
50 B1 Roebuck Bay Austr.
123 C1 Roedtan S. Africa
100 B2 Roermond Neth.
100 A2 Roeselare Belgium
127 G2 Roes Welcome Sound sea chan. Can.
128 C2 Rogers Can.
142 B1 Rogers U.S.A.
140 C3 Rogers, Mount U.S.A.
140 C1 Rogers City U.S.A.
157 G8 Roggeveen Basin sea feature S. Pacific Ocean
122 B3 Roggeveldberge esc. S. Africa
92 G2 Rognan Norway
134 B2 Rogue r. U.S.A.
74 B2 Rohtak India
49 M5 Roi Georges, Îles du is Fr. Polynesia
88 B2 Roja Latvia
60 B1 Rokan r. Indon.
88 C2 Rokiškis Lith.
90 B1 Rokytne Ukr.
154 B2 Rolândia Brazil
137 E3 Rolla U.S.A.
139 C2 Rolling Prairies reg. U.S.A.
51 D2 Roma Austr.
59 C3 Roma i. Indon.
 Roma Italy see Rome
123 C2 Roma Lesotho
139 D3 Roma U.S.A.
143 E2 Romain, Cape U.S.A.
110 C1 Roman Romania
158 E5 Romanche Gap sea feature S. Atlantic Ocean
110 B1 Romania country Europe
91 C3 Roman-Kosh mt. Ukr.
69 D1 Romanovka Rus. Fed.
105 D2 Romans-sur-Isère France
105 D2 Rombas France
64 B2 Romblon Phil.
108 B2 Rome Italy
143 C2 Rome GA U.S.A.
141 D2 Rome NY U.S.A.
99 D4 Romford U.K.
105 C2 Romilly-sur-Seine France
91 C1 Romny Ukr.
104 C2 Romorantin-Lanthenay France
99 C4 Romsey U.K.
134 D1 Ronan U.S.A.
96 □ Ronas Hill U.K.
151 D4 Roncador, Serra do hills Brazil
106 B2 Ronda Spain
154 B2 Rondon Brazil
154 B1 Rondonópolis Brazil
74 B1 Rondu Jammu and Kashmir
71 A3 Rong'an China
 Rongcheng China see Rongxian
 Rongcheng China see Jianli
71 A3 Rongjiang China
62 A1 Rongklang Range mts Myanmar
 Rongmei China see Hefeng
71 B3 Rønne Denmark
93 F4 Rønneby Sweden
55 A2 Ronne Ice Shelf Antarctica
101 D1 Ronnenberg Ger.
100 A2 Ronse Belgium
100 B1 Roordahuizum Neth.
74 B2 Roorkee India
100 B2 Roosendaal Neth.
135 E2 Roosevelt U.S.A.
128 B2 Roosevelt, Mount Can.
55 N2 Roosevelt Island Antarctica
140 B3 Roquefort France
150 C2 Roraima, Mount Guyana
93 F3 Røros Norway
90 C2 Ros' r. Ukr.
138 B3 Rosa, Punta pt Mex.

106 B2 Rosal de la Frontera Spain
153 B3 Rosario Arg.
144 A1 Rosario Mex.
144 B2 Rosario Mex.
144 B2 Rosario Mex.
147 C3 Rosario Venez.
152 B2 Rosario de la Frontera Arg.
151 D4 Rosário Oeste Brazil
144 A2 Rosarito Mex.
144 A1 Rosarito Mex.
138 A3 Rosarito Mex.
109 C3 Rosarno Italy
139 C2 Roscoe U.S.A.
104 B2 Roscoff France
97 B2 Roscommon Rep. of Ireland
97 C2 Roscrea Rep. of Ireland
147 D3 Roseau Dominica
137 D1 Roseau U.S.A.
134 B2 Roseburg U.S.A.
96 C2 Rosehearty U.K.
139 D3 Rosenberg U.S.A.
101 D1 Rosengarten Ger.
102 C2 Rosenheim Ger.
129 D2 Rosetown Can.
122 A2 Rosh Pinah Namibia
110 C2 Roşiori de Vede Romania
93 F4 Roskilde Denmark
89 D3 Roslavl' Rus. Fed.
134 B1 Roslyn U.S.A.
109 C3 Rossano Italy
97 B1 Rossan Point Rep. of Ireland
51 E1 Rossel Island P.N.G.
55 N1 Ross Ice Shelf Antarctica
131 D3 Rossignol, Lake Can.
128 C3 Rossland Can.
97 C2 Rosslare Rep. of Ireland
97 C2 Rosslare Harbour Rep. of Ireland
101 F2 Roßlau Ger.
101 E2 Roßleben Ger.
114 A3 Rosso Maur.
105 D3 Rosso, Capo c. Corsica France
99 B4 Ross-on-Wye U.K.
91 D1 Rossosh' Rus. Fed.
128 A1 Ross River Can.
55 N2 Ross Sea Antarctica
92 F2 Røssvatnet l. Norway
81 D2 Rostāq Iran
129 D2 Rosthern Can.
102 C1 Rostock Ger.
89 E2 Rostov Rus. Fed.
91 D2 Rostov-na-Donu Rus. Fed.
 Rostov-on-Don Rus. Fed. see Rostov-na-Donu
104 B2 Rostrenen France
92 G2 Røsvik Norway
92 H2 Rosvik Sweden
138 C2 Roswell U.S.A.
59 D2 Rota i. N. Mariana Is
59 C3 Rote i. Indon.
101 D1 Rotenburg (Wümme) Ger.
101 E3 Roth Ger.
98 C2 Rothbury U.K.
101 E3 Rothenburg ob der Tauber Ger.
98 C2 Rotherham U.K.
96 C2 Rothes U.K.
96 B3 Rothesay U.K.
53 C2 Roto Austr.
105 D3 Rotondo, Monte mt. Corsica France
54 C1 Rotorua N.Z.
54 C1 Rotorua, Lake N.Z.
101 E2 Rottenbach Ger.
102 C2 Rottenmann Austria
100 B2 Rotterdam Neth.
102 B2 Rottweil Ger.
49 I5 Rotuma i. Fiji
105 C1 Roubaix France
104 C2 Rouen France
 Roulers Belgium see Roeselare
53 D2 Round Mountain Austr.
131 E3 Round Pond l. Can.
139 D2 Round Rock U.S.A.
134 C1 Roundup U.S.A.
96 C1 Rousay i. U.K.
130 C3 Rouyn Can.
 Rouyuanchengzi China see Huachi
92 I2 Rovaniemi Fin.
91 D2 Roven'ki Rus. Fed.
91 D2 Roven'ky Ukr.
108 B1 Rovereto Italy
63 B2 Rôviĕng Tbong Cambodia
108 B1 Rovigo Italy

108 B1 Rovinj Croatia
53 C1 Rowena Austr.
 Równe Ukr. see Rivne
64 B3 Roxas Phil.
64 B2 Roxas Phil.
64 A2 Roxas Phil.
64 B2 Roxas Phil.
52 A2 Roxby Downs Austr.
138 C1 Roy NM U.S.A.
134 D2 Roy UT U.S.A.
140 B1 Royale, Isle i. U.S.A.
104 B2 Royan France
99 C3 Royston U.K.
90 C2 Rozdil'na Ukr.
91 C2 Rozdol'ne Ukr.
103 E2 Rožňava Slovakia
100 B3 Rozoy-sur-Serre France
87 D3 Rtishchevo Rus. Fed.
 Ruanda country Africa see Rwanda
54 C1 Ruapehu, Mount vol. N.Z.
54 A3 Ruapuke Island N.Z.
89 D2 Ruba Belarus
79 B3 Rub' al Khālī des. Saudi Arabia
119 D3 Rubeho Mountains Tanz.
91 D2 Rubizhne Ukr.
77 E1 Rubtsovsk Rus. Fed.
126 B2 Ruby U.S.A.
135 C2 Ruby Mountains U.S.A.
76 C3 Rudbar Afgh.
66 C2 Rudnaya Pristan' Rus. Fed.
89 D3 Rudnya Rus. Fed.
76 C1 Rudnyy Kazakh.
89 D2 Rudol'f, Lake salt l. Eth./Kenya see Turkana, Lake
82 E1 Rudol'fa, Ostrov i. Rus. Fed.
 Rudolph Island Rus. Fed. see Rudol'fa, Ostrov
101 E2 Rudolstadt Ger.
116 B3 Rufa'a Sudan
119 D3 Rufiji r. Tanz.
153 B3 Rufino Arg.
121 B2 Rufunsa Zambia
70 C2 Rugao China
99 C3 Rugby U.K.
136 C1 Rugby U.S.A.
102 C1 Rügen i. Ger.
119 C3 Ruhengeri Rwanda
101 E2 Ruhla Ger.
88 B2 Ruhnu i. Estonia
100 C2 Ruhr r. Ger.
71 C3 Rui'an China
138 B2 Ruidoso U.S.A.
119 D3 Rukwa, Lake Tanz.
96 A2 Rum i. U.K.
109 C1 Ruma Yugo.
78 B2 Rumāh Saudi Arabia
117 A4 Rumbek Sudan
147 C2 Rum Cay i. Bahamas
141 E2 Rumford U.S.A.
103 D1 Rumia Pol.
105 D2 Rumilly France
50 C1 Rum Jungle Austr.
66 D2 Rumoi Japan
121 C2 Rumphi Malawi
54 B2 Runanga N.Z.
98 B3 Runcorn U.K.
120 A2 Rundu Namibia
119 C2 Rungu Dem. Rep. Congo
119 D3 Rungwa Tanz.
68 B2 Ruoqiang China
130 C2 Rupert r. Can.
134 D2 Rupert U.S.A.
130 C2 Rupert Bay Can.
 Rusaddir N. Africa see Melilla
121 C2 Rusape Zimbabwe
110 C2 Ruse Bulg.
137 E1 Rush City U.S.A.
121 C2 Rushinga Zimbabwe
77 D3 Rushon Tajik.
136 C2 Rushville U.S.A.
53 C3 Rushworth Austr.
129 D2 Russell Can.
54 B1 Russell N.Z.
137 D3 Russell U.S.A.
142 C2 Russellville AL U.S.A.
142 B1 Russellville AR U.S.A.
140 B3 Russellville KY U.S.A.
101 D2 Rüsselsheim Ger.
82 G3 Russian Federation country Asia/Europe
81 C1 Rust'avi Georgia
123 C2 Rustenburg S. Africa
142 B2 Ruston U.S.A.
61 D2 Ruteng Indon.

Salem
221

98 B3 **Ruthin** U.K.
141 E2 **Rutland** U.S.A.
75 B1 **Rutog** China
119 C3 **Rutshuru** Dem. Rep. Congo
119 E4 **Ruvuma** *r.* Moz./Tanz.
79 C2 **Ruweis** U.A.E.
89 E2 **Ruza** Rus. Fed.
77 C1 **Ruzayevka** Kazakh.
87 D3 **Ruzayevka** Rus. Fed.
119 C3 **Rwanda** *country* Africa
89 E3 **Ryazan'** Rus. Fed.
89 F3 **Ryazhsk** Rus. Fed.
86 C2 **Rybachiy, Poluostrov** *pen.* Rus. Fed.
Rybach'ye Kyrg. *see* **Balykchy**
89 E2 **Rybinsk** Rus. Fed.
89 E2 **Rybinskoye Vodokhranilishche** *resr* Rus. Fed.
103 D1 **Rybnik** Pol.
Rybnitsa Moldova *see* **Râbniţa**
89 E3 **Rybnoye** Rus. Fed.
99 D4 **Rye** U.K.
Rykovo Ukr. *see* **Yenakiyeve**
89 D3 **Ryl'sk** Rus. Fed.
Ryojun China *see* **Lushunkou**
67 C3 **Ryōtsu** Japan
Ryukyu Islands Japan *see* **Nansei-shotō**
89 D3 **Ryzhikovo** Rus. Fed.
103 E1 **Rzeszów** Pol.
91 E1 **Rzhaksa** Rus. Fed.
89 D2 **Rzhev** Rus. Fed.

S

79 C2 **Sa'ādatābād** Iran
101 E2 **Saale** *r.* Ger.
101 E2 **Saalfeld** Ger.
134 B1 **Saanich** Can.
100 C3 **Saar** *r.* Ger.
102 B2 **Saarbrücken** Ger.
88 B2 **Sääre** Estonia
88 B2 **Saaremaa** *i.* Estonia
92 I2 **Saarenkylä** Fin.
93 I3 **Saarijärvi** Fin.
100 C3 **Saarlouis** Ger.
80 B2 **Sab' Ābār** Syria
107 D1 **Sabadell** Spain
67 C3 **Sabae** Japan
61 C1 **Sabah** *state* Malaysia
61 C2 **Sabalana** *i.* Indon.
146 B2 **Sabana, Archipiélago de** *is* Cuba
150 B1 **Sabanalarga** Col.
60 A1 **Sabang** Indon.
155 D1 **Sabará** Brazil
108 B2 **Sabaudia** Italy
122 B3 **Sabelo** S. Africa
119 D2 **Sabena Desert** Kenya
115 D2 **Sabhā** Libya
123 D2 **Sabie** *r.* Moz./S. Africa
123 D2 **Sabie** S. Africa
145 B2 **Sabinas** Mex.
145 B2 **Sabinas Hidalgo** Mex.
139 E3 **Sabine** *r.* U.S.A.
131 D3 **Sable, Cape** Can.
143 D3 **Sable, Cape** U.S.A.
131 E3 **Sable Island** Can.
106 B1 **Sabugal** Port.
78 B3 **Şabyā** Saudi Arabia
76 B3 **Sabzevār** Iran
107 D2 **Sa Cabaneta** Spain
137 D2 **Sac City** U.S.A.
120 A2 **Sachanga** Angola
130 A2 **Sachigo Lake** Can.
65 B3 **Sach'on** S. Korea
126 D2 **Sachs Harbour** Can.
154 C1 **Sacramento** Brazil
135 B3 **Sacramento** U.S.A.
135 B3 **Sacramento** *r.* U.S.A.
138 B2 **Sacramento Mountains** U.S.A.
135 B2 **Sacramento Valley** U.S.A.
110 B1 **Săcueni** Romania
123 C3 **Sada** S. Africa
107 C1 **Sádaba** Spain
Sá da Bandeira Angola *see* **Lubango**
78 B3 **Şa'dah** Yemen
63 B3 **Sadao** Thai.
79 B3 **Şadārah** Yemen
63 B2 **Sa Đec** Vietnam
74 B2 **Sadiqabad** Pak.
72 D2 **Sadiya** India
67 C3 **Sadoga-shima** *i.* Japan
107 D2 **Sa Dragonera** *i.* Spain
93 F4 **Säffle** Sweden
138 B2 **Safford** U.S.A.
99 D3 **Saffron Walden** U.K.
114 B1 **Safi** Morocco
155 D1 **Safiras, Serra das** *mts* Brazil
86 D2 **Safonovo** Rus. Fed.
89 D2 **Safonovo** Rus. Fed.
78 B2 **Safrā' as Sark** *esc.* Saudi Arabia
75 C2 **Saga** China
67 B4 **Saga** Japan
62 A1 **Sagaing** Myanmar
67 C3 **Sagamihara** Japan
74 B2 **Sagar** India
Sagarmatha *mt.* China/Nepal *see* **Everest, Mount**
140 C2 **Saginaw** U.S.A.
140 C2 **Saginaw Bay** U.S.A.
Saglouc Can. *see* **Salluit**
106 B2 **Sagres** Port.
146 B2 **Sagua la Grande** Cuba
141 F1 **Saguenay** *r.* Can.
107 C2 **Sagunto** Spain
76 B2 **Sagyndyk, Mys** *pt* Kazakh.
106 B1 **Sahagún** Spain
114 C3 **Sahara** *des.* Africa
Şahara el Gharbîya *des.* Egypt *see* **Western Desert**
Şahara el Sharqîya *des.* Egypt *see* **Eastern Desert**
Saharan Atlas *mts* Alg. *see* **Atlas Saharien**
74 B2 **Saharanpur** India
75 C2 **Saharsa** India
74 B1 **Sahiwal** Pak.
144 B2 **Sahuayo** Mex.
78 B2 **Şāḥūq** *reg.* Saudi Arabia
114 C1 **Saïda** Alg.
Saïda Lebanon *see* **Sidon**
75 C2 **Saidpur** Bangl.
67 B3 **Saigō** Japan
Saigon Vietnam *see* **Hô Chi Minh**
75 D2 **Saiha** India
70 B1 **Saihan Tal** China
67 B4 **Saiki** Japan
93 I3 **Saimaa** *l.* Fin.
144 B2 **Sain Alto** Mex.
96 C3 **St Abb's Head** *hd* U.K.
131 E3 **St Alban's** Can.
99 C4 **St Albans** U.K.
140 C3 **St Albans** U.S.A.
99 B4 **St Alban's Head** *hd* U.K.
St-André, Cap *pt* Madag. *see* **Vilanandro, Tanjona**
96 C2 **St Andrews** U.K.
131 E2 **St Anthony** Can.
134 D2 **St Anthony** U.S.A.
52 B3 **St Arnaud** Austr.
131 E2 **St-Augustin** Can.
131 E2 **St-Augustin** *r.* Can.
143 D3 **St Augustine** U.S.A.
99 A4 **St Austell** U.K.
104 C2 **St-Avertin** France
147 D3 **St-Barthélemy** *i.* West Indies
98 B2 **St Bees Head** *hd* U.K.
105 D3 **St-Bonnet-en-Champsaur** France
99 A4 **St Bride's Bay** U.K.
104 B2 **St-Brieuc** France
130 C3 **St Catharines** Can.
143 D2 **St Catherines Island** U.S.A.
99 C4 **St Catherine's Point** U.K.
137 E3 **St Charles** U.S.A.
140 C2 **St Clair, Lake** Can./U.S.A.
105 D2 **St-Claude** France
99 A4 **St Clears** U.K.
137 E1 **St Cloud** U.S.A.
140 A1 **St Croix** *r.* U.S.A.
147 D3 **St Croix Island** Virgin Is (U.S.A.)
99 A4 **St David's** U.K.
99 A4 **St David's Head** *hd* U.K.
113 I8 **St-Denis** Can.
104 C2 **St-Denis** France
St-Denis-du-Sig Alg. *see* **Sig**
105 D2 **St-Dié** France
105 C2 **St-Dizier** France
130 C3 **Ste-Adèle** Can.
131 D3 **Ste-Anne-des-Monts** Can.
141 E1 **Ste-Foy** Can.
105 D2 **St-Égrève** France
128 A1 **St Elias Mountains** Can.
131 D2 **Ste Marguerite** *r.* Can.
141 E1 **Ste-Marie** Can.
Ste-Marie, Cap *c.* Madag. *see* **Vohimena, Tanjona**
Sainte-Marie, Île *i.* Madag. *see* **Nosy Boraha**
Ste-Rose-du-Dégelé Can. *see* **Dégelis**
129 E2 **Ste Rose du Lac** Can.
104 B2 **Saintes** France
105 C2 **St-Étienne** France
104 C2 **St-Étienne-du-Rouvray** France
130 C3 **St-Félicien** Can.
97 D1 **Saintfield** U.K.
105 D3 **St-Florent** *Corsica* France
105 C2 **St-Flour** France
136 C3 **St Francis** U.S.A.
104 C3 **St-Gaudens** France
53 C1 **St George** Austr.
135 D3 **St George** U.S.A.
143 D3 **St George Island** U.S.A.
131 C3 **St-Georges** Can.
147 D3 **St George's** Grenada
131 E3 **St George's Bay** Can.
97 C3 **St George's Channel** Rep. of Ireland/U.K.
St Gotthard Pass *pass* Switz. *see* San Gottardo, Passo del
113 C7 **St Helena** *terr.* S. Atlantic Ocean
122 A3 **St Helena Bay** S. Africa
122 A3 **St Helena Bay** *b.* S. Africa
98 B3 **St Helens** U.K.
134 B1 **St Helens, Mount** *vol.* U.S.A.
95 C4 **St Helier** Channel Is
100 B2 **St-Hubert** Belgium
141 E1 **St-Hyacinthe** Can.
140 C1 **St Ignace** U.S.A.
130 B3 **St Ignace Island** Can.
99 A4 **St Ives** U.K.
St Jacques, Cap Vietnam *see* **Vung Tau**
128 A2 **St James, Cape** Can.
130 C3 **St-Jean, Lac** *l.* Can.
104 B2 **St-Jean-d'Angély** France
104 B3 **St-Jean-de-Luz** France
104 B2 **St-Jean-de-Monts** France
130 C3 **St-Jean-sur-Richelieu** Can.
141 E1 **St-Jérôme** Can.
134 C1 **St Joe** *r.* U.S.A.
131 D3 **Saint John** Can.
137 D3 **St John** U.S.A.
141 F1 **St John** *r.* U.S.A.
147 D3 **St John's** Antigua
131 E3 **St John's** Can.
138 B2 **St Johns** U.S.A.
143 D2 **St Johns** *r.* U.S.A.
141 E2 **St Johnsbury** U.S.A.
137 E3 **St Joseph** U.S.A.
130 A2 **St Joseph, Lake** Can.
St-Joseph-d'Alma Can. *see* **Alma**
130 B3 **St Joseph Island** Can.
141 E1 **St Jovité** Can.
104 C2 **St-Junien** France
94 B2 **St Kilda** *i.* U.K.
147 D3 **St Kitts and Nevis** *country* West Indies
151 D2 **St-Laurent-du-Maroni** Fr. Guiana
131 E3 **St Lawrence** Can.
131 D3 **St Lawrence** *inlet* Can.
131 D3 **St Lawrence, Gulf of** Can.
126 A2 **St Lawrence Island** U.S.A.
104 B2 **St-Lô** France
114 A3 **St Louis** Senegal
137 E3 **St Louis** U.S.A.
137 E1 **St Louis** *r.* U.S.A.
147 D3 **St Lucia** *country* West Indies
147 D3 **St Lucia Channel** Martinique/St Lucia
123 D2 **St Lucia Estuary** S. Africa
147 D3 **St Maarten** *i.* West Indies
96 □ **St Magnus Bay** U.K.
104 B2 **St-Malo** France
104 B2 **St-Malo, Golfe de** *g.* France
147 C3 **St Marc** Haiti
St Mark's S. Africa *see* **Cofimvaba**
147 D3 **St Martin** *i.* West Indies
122 A3 **St Martin, Cape** S. Africa
129 E2 **St Martin, Lake** Can.
141 D2 **St Marys** U.S.A.
124 A3 **St Matthew Island** U.S.A.
59 D3 **St Matthias Group** *is* P.N.G.
130 C3 **St Maurice** *r.* Can.
130 C3 **St-Michel-des-Saints** Can.
104 B2 **St-Nazaire** France
104 C1 **St-Omer** France
129 C2 **St Paul** Can.
137 E2 **St Paul** U.S.A.
156 A8 **St Paul, Île** *i.* Indian Ocean
137 E2 **St Peter** U.S.A.
95 C4 **St Peter Port** Channel Is
143 D3 **St Petersburg** U.S.A.
131 E3 **St-Pierre** St Pierre and Miquelon
141 E1 **St-Pierre, Lac** *l.* Can.
131 E3 **St Pierre and Miquelon** *terr.* N. America
104 B2 **St-Pierre-d'Oléron** France
105 C2 **St-Pourçain-sur-Sioule** France
131 D3 **St Quentin** Can.
105 C2 **St-Quentin** France
105 D3 **St-Raphaël** France
122 B3 **St Sebastian Bay** S. Africa
104 B2 **St-Sébastien-sur-Loire** France
131 D3 **St Siméon** Can.
129 E2 **St Theresa Point** Can.
130 B3 **St Thomas** Can.
105 D3 **St-Tropez** France
105 D3 **St-Tropez, Cap de** *c.* France
St Vincent, Cape Port. *see* São Vicente, Cabo de
52 A3 **St Vincent, Gulf** Austr.
147 D3 **St Vincent and the Grenadines** *i.* West Indies
147 D3 **St Vincent Passage** St Lucia/St Vincent
129 D2 **St Walburg** Can.
104 C2 **St-Yrieix-la-Perche** France
59 D1 **Saipan** *i.* N. Mariana Is
152 B1 **Sajama, Nevado** *mt.* Bol.
122 B2 **Sak** *watercourse* S. Africa
67 C4 **Sakai** Japan
67 B4 **Sakaide** Japan
78 B2 **Sakākah** Saudi Arabia
136 C1 **Sakakawea, Lake** U.S.A.
111 D2 **Sakarya** Turkey
111 D2 **Sakarya** *r.* Turkey
66 C3 **Sakata** Japan
65 B1 **Sakchu** N. Korea
66 D1 **Sakhalin** *i.* Rus. Fed.
123 C2 **Sakhile** S. Africa
81 C1 **Şäki** Azer.
114 C4 **Şaki** Nigeria
88 B3 **Šakiai** Lith.
69 E3 **Sakishima-shotō** *is* Japan
62 B2 **Sakon Nakhon** Thai.
74 A2 **Sakrand** Pak.
122 B3 **Sakrivier** S. Africa
67 D3 **Sakura** Japan
91 C2 **Saky** Ukr.
93 G4 **Sala** Sweden
130 C3 **Salaberry-de-Valleyfield** Can.
88 B2 **Salacgrīva** Latvia
109 C2 **Sala Consilina** Italy
135 C4 **Salada, Laguna** *salt l.* Mex.
152 C2 **Saladas** Arg.
152 B3 **Salado** *r.* Arg.
145 C2 **Salado** *r.* Mex.
114 B4 **Salaga** Ghana
122 B1 **Salajwe** Botswana
79 C2 **Salakh, Jabal** *mt.* Oman
115 D3 **Salal** Chad
78 A2 **Salâla** Sudan
79 C3 **Şalālah** Oman
145 B2 **Salamanca** Mex.
106 B1 **Salamanca** Spain
141 D2 **Salamanca** U.S.A.
106 B1 **Salas** Spain
59 C3 **Salawati** *i.* Indon.
61 D2 **Salayar** *i.* Indon.
157 G7 **Sala y Gómez, Isla** *i.* S. Pacific Ocean
Salazar Angola *see* **N'dalatando**
104 C2 **Salbris** France
88 C3 **Šalčininkai** Lith.
106 C1 **Saldaña** Spain
122 A3 **Saldanha** S. Africa
88 B2 **Saldus** Latvia
53 C3 **Sale** Austr.
86 F2 **Salekhard** Rus. Fed.
73 B3 **Salem** India
140 B3 **Salem** *IL* U.S.A.
137 E3 **Salem** *MO* U.S.A.

134 B2 Salem OR U.S.A.
137 D2 Salem SD U.S.A.
96 B2 Salen U.K.
109 B2 Salerno Italy
108 B2 Salerno, Golfo di g. Italy
98 B3 Salford U.K.
151 E2 Salgado r. Brazil
103 D2 Salgótarján Hungary
151 F3 Salgueiro Brazil
136 B3 Salida U.S.A.
111 C3 Salihli Turkey
88 C3 Salihorsk Belarus
121 C2 Salima Malawi
121 C2 Salimo Moz.
137 D3 Salina KS U.S.A.
135 D3 Salina UT U.S.A.
109 B3 Salina, Isola i. Italy
145 C3 Salina Cruz Mex.
155 D1 Salinas Brazil
144 B2 Salinas Mex.
135 B3 Salinas U.S.A.
135 B3 Salinas r. U.S.A.
151 E3 Salinópolis Brazil
99 C4 Salisbury U.K.
141 D3 Salisbury MD U.S.A.
143 D1 Salisbury NC U.S.A.
Salisbury Zimbabwe see Harare
99 B4 Salisbury Plain U.K.
151 E3 Salitre r. Brazil
92 I2 Salla Fin.
139 E1 Sallisaw U.S.A.
127 G2 Salluit Can.
75 C2 Sallyana Nepal
81 C2 Salmās Iran
128 C3 Salmo Can.
134 D1 Salmon U.S.A.
134 C1 Salmon r. U.S.A.
128 C2 Salmon Arm Can.
134 C2 Salmon River Mountains U.S.A.
100 C3 Salmtal Ger.
118 B2 Salo C.A.R.
93 H3 Salo Fin.
105 D3 Salon-de-Provence France
Salonica Greece see Thessaloniki
110 B1 Salonta Romania
87 D4 Sal'sk Rus. Fed.
122 B3 Salt watercourse S. Africa
107 D1 Salt Spain
138 A2 Salt r. U.S.A.
152 B2 Salta Arg.
99 A4 Saltash U.K.
96 B3 Saltcoats U.K.
145 B2 Saltillo Mex.
134 D2 Salt Lake City U.S.A.
154 C2 Salto Brazil
152 C3 Salto Uru.
155 E1 Salto da Divisa Brazil
154 B2 Salto del Guairá Para.
135 C4 Salton Sea salt l. U.S.A.
154 B3 Salto Osório, Represa resr Brazil
154 B3 Salto Santiago, Represa de resr Brazil
143 D2 Saluda U.S.A.
76 B3 Saluq, Kūh-e mt. Iran
108 A2 Saluzzo Italy
151 F4 Salvador Brazil
79 C2 Salwah Saudi Arabia
Salween r. China see Nu Jiang
62 A2 Salween r. Myanmar
81 C2 Salyan Azer.
140 C3 Salyersville U.S.A.
122 A1 Salzbrunn Namibia
102 C2 Salzburg Austria
101 E1 Salzgitter Ger.
101 D2 Salzkotten Ger.
101 E1 Salzwedel Ger.
144 B1 Samalayuca Mex.
66 D2 Samani Japan
64 B2 Samar i. Phil.
87 E3 Samara Rus. Fed.
Samarahan Malaysia see Sri Aman
59 E3 Samarai P.N.G.
61 C2 Samarinda Indon.
77 C3 Samarkand Uzbek.
81 C2 Sāmarrā' Iraq
81 C1 Şamaxı Azer.
119 C3 Samba Dem. Rep. Congo
61 C1 Sambaliung mts Indon.
75 C2 Sambalpur India
60 C2 Sambar, Tanjung pt Indon.
60 B1 Sambas Indon.
121 □E2 Sambava Madag.
74 B2 Sambhar India
90 A2 Sambir Ukr.

61 C2 Sambo Indon.
61 C2 Samboja Indon.
153 C3 Samborombón, Bahía b. Arg.
65 B2 Samch'ŏk S. Korea
Samch'ŏnp'o S. Korea see Sach'on
81 C2 Samdi Dag mt. Turkey
119 D3 Same Tanz.
121 B2 Samfya Zambia
78 B2 Samīrah Saudi Arabia
65 B1 Samjiyŏn N. Korea
Sam Neua Laos see Xam Hua
48 J5 Samoa country S. Pacific Ocean
156 E6 Samoa Basin sea feature S. Pacific Ocean
Samoa i Sisifo country S. Pacific Ocean see Samoa
109 C1 Samobor Croatia
110 B2 Samokov Bulg.
111 C3 Samos i. Greece
Samothrace i. Greece see Samothraki
111 C2 Samothraki Greece
111 C2 Samothraki i. Greece
61 C2 Sampit Indon.
119 C3 Sampwe Dem. Rep. Congo
139 E2 Sam Rayburn Reservoir U.S.A.
62 B2 Sầm Sơn Vietnam
80 B1 Samsun Turkey
81 C1 Samtredia Georgia
63 B3 Samui, Ko i. Thai.
63 B2 Samut Songkhram Thai.
114 B3 San Mali
78 B3 Şan'ā' Yemen
118 A2 Sanaga r. Cameroon
81 C2 Sanandaj Iran
146 B3 San Andrés, Isla de i. Caribbean Sea
106 B1 San Andrés del Rabanedo Spain
138 B2 San Andres Mountains U.S.A.
145 C3 San Andrés Tuxtla Mex.
139 C2 San Angelo U.S.A.
139 D3 San Antonio U.S.A.
135 C4 San Antonio, Mount U.S.A.
107 D2 San Antonio Abad Spain
152 B2 San Antonio de los Cobres Arg.
153 B4 San Antonio Oeste Arg.
108 B2 San Benedetto del Tronto Italy
144 A3 San Benedicto, Isla i. Mex.
135 C4 San Bernardino U.S.A.
135 C4 San Bernardino Mountains U.S.A.
138 B3 San Blas Mex.
143 C3 San Blas, Cape U.S.A.
146 C4 San Blas, Punta pt Panama
152 B1 San Borja Bol.
144 B2 San Buenaventura Mex.
64 B2 San Carlos Phil.
147 D4 San Carlos Venez.
153 A4 San Carlos de Bariloche Arg.
147 C4 San Carlos del Zulia Venez.
104 C2 Sancerrois, Collines du hills France
135 C4 San Clemente U.S.A.
135 C4 San Clemente Island U.S.A.
105 C2 Sancoins France
48 H5 San Cristobal i. Solomon Is
150 B2 San Cristóbal Venez.
145 C3 San Cristóbal de las Casas Mex.
123 D1 Sancti Spíritus Cuba
61 C1 Sandakan Sabah Malaysia
93 E3 Sandane Norway
111 B2 Sandanski Bulg.
114 A3 Sandaré Mali
96 C1 Sanday i. U.K.
139 C2 Sanderson U.S.A.
150 C4 Sandia Peru
135 C4 San Diego U.S.A.
111 D3 Sandıklı Turkey
93 E4 Sandnes Norway
92 F2 Sandnessjøen Norway
118 C3 Sandoa Dem. Rep. Congo
103 E1 Sandomierz Pol.

89 E2 Sandovo Rus. Fed.
62 A2 Sandoway Myanmar
94 B1 Sandoy i. Faroe Is
94 B1 Sandoy i. Faroe Is
134 C1 Sandpoint U.S.A.
71 B3 Sandu China
94 B1 Sandur Faroe Is
140 C2 Sandusky U.S.A.
122 A3 Sandveld mts S. Africa
122 A2 Sandverhaar Namibia
93 F4 Sandvika Norway
93 G3 Sandviken Sweden
131 E2 Sandwich Bay Can.
135 D2 Sandy U.S.A.
129 D2 Sandy Bay Can.
51 E2 Sandy Cape Austr.
130 A2 Sandy Lake Can.
130 A2 Sandy Lake l. Can.
143 D2 Sandy Springs U.S.A.
144 A1 San Felipe Mex.
145 B2 San Felipe Mex.
150 C1 San Felipe Venez.
144 A2 San Fernando Mex.
145 C2 San Fernando Phil.
64 B2 San Fernando Phil.
64 B2 San Fernando Phil.
106 B2 San Fernando Spain
147 D3 San Fernando Trin. and Tob.
150 C2 San Fernando de Apure Venez.
143 D3 Sanford FL U.S.A.
141 E2 Sanford ME U.S.A.
143 E1 Sanford NC U.S.A.
152 B3 San Francisco Arg.
135 B3 San Francisco U.S.A.
107 D2 San Francisco Javier Spain
74 B3 Sangamner India
83 J2 Sangar Rus. Fed.
108 A3 San Gavino Monreale Sardinia Italy
101 E2 Sangerhausen Ger.
61 C1 Sanggau Indon.
118 B3 Sangha r. Congo
109 C3 San Giovanni in Fiore Italy
59 C2 Sangir i. Indon.
59 C2 Sangir, Kepulauan is Indon.
65 B2 Sangju S. Korea
63 A2 Sangkulirang Indon.
73 B3 Sangli India
118 B2 Sangmélima Cameroon
121 C3 Sango Zimbabwe
105 D2 San Gottardo, Passo del pass Switz.
136 B3 Sangre de Cristo Range mts U.S.A.
75 C2 Sangsang China
144 A2 San Hipólito, Punta pt Mex.
145 D3 San Ignacio Belize
152 B1 San Ignacio Bol.
144 A2 San Ignacio Mex.
130 C2 Sanikiluaq Can.
71 A3 Sanjiang China
Sanjiang China see Jinping
67 C3 Sanjō Japan
135 B3 San Joaquin r. U.S.A.
153 B4 San Jorge, Golfo de g. Arg.
146 B3 San José Costa Rica
64 B2 San Jose Phil.
64 B2 San Jose Phil.
135 B3 San Jose U.S.A.
144 A2 San José, Isla i. Mex.
144 B2 San José de Bavicora Mex.
64 B2 San Jose de Buenavista Phil.
144 A2 San José de Comondú Mex.
144 B2 San José del Cabo Mex.
150 B2 San José del Guaviare Col.
152 B3 San Juan Arg.
146 B3 San Juan r. Costa Rica/Nic.
147 C3 San Juan Dom. Rep.
147 D3 San Juan Puerto Rico
135 D3 San Juan r. U.S.A.
152 C2 San Juan Bautista Para.
107 D2 San Juan Bautista Spain
145 C3 San Juan Bautista Tuxtepec Mex.
147 D4 San Juan de los Morros Venez.
145 C2 San Juan del Río Mex.

134 B1 San Juan Islands U.S.A.
144 B2 San Juanito Mex.
136 B3 San Juan Mountains U.S.A.
153 B4 San Julián Arg.
75 C2 Sankh r. India
100 C2 St Augustin Ger.
105 D2 St Gallen Switz.
105 D2 St Moritz Switz.
Sankt-Peterburg Rus. Fed. see St Petersburg
89 D2 St Petersburg Rus. Fed.
102 C2 St Veit an der Glan Austria
100 C3 St Wendel Ger.
80 B2 Şanlıurfa Turkey
138 B3 San Lorenzo Mex.
106 B2 Sanlúcar de Barrameda Spain
144 B2 San Lucas Mex.
153 B3 San Luis Arg.
145 B2 San Luis de la Paz Mex.
138 A2 San Luisito Mex.
135 B3 San Luis Obispo U.S.A.
135 B3 San Luis Obispo Bay U.S.A.
145 B2 San Luis Potosí Mex.
144 A1 San Luis Río Colorado Mex.
139 D3 San Marcos U.S.A.
108 B2 San Marino country Europe
108 B2 San Marino San Marino
144 B2 San Martín de Bolaños Mex.
153 A4 San Martín de los Andes Arg.
135 B3 San Mateo U.S.A.
153 B4 San Matías, Golfo g. Arg.
70 B2 Sanmenxia China
146 B3 San Miguel El Salvador
152 B2 San Miguel de Tucumán Arg.
135 B4 San Miguel Island U.S.A.
145 C3 San Miguel Sola de Vega Mex.
71 B3 Sanming China
153 B3 San Nicolás de los Arroyos Arg.
135 C4 San Nicolas Island U.S.A.
110 B1 Sânnicolau Mare Romania
123 C2 Sannieshof S. Africa
114 B4 Sanniquellie Liberia
103 E2 Sanok Pol.
64 B2 San Pablo Phil.
144 B2 San Pablo Balleza Mex.
152 B2 San Pedro Arg.
152 B1 San Pedro Bol.
114 B4 San-Pédro Côte d'Ivoire
144 A2 San Pedro Mex.
152 C2 San Pedro Bol.
138 A2 San Pedro watercourse U.S.A.
106 B2 San Pedro, Sierra de mts Spain
144 B2 San Pedro de las Colonias Mex.
138 A3 San Pedro el Saucito Mex.
146 B3 San Pedro Sula Hond.
108 A3 San Pietro, Isola di i. Sardinia Italy
96 C3 Sanquhar U.K.
144 A1 San Quintín, Cabo c. Mex.
153 B3 San Rafael Arg.
108 A3 San Remo Italy
139 D2 San Saba U.S.A.
147 C2 San Salvador i. Bahamas
146 B3 San Salvador El Salvador
152 B2 San Salvador de Jujuy Arg.
108 B2 Sansepolcro Italy
109 C2 San Severo Italy
109 C2 Sanski Most Bos.-Herz.
152 B1 Santa Ana Bol.
146 B3 Santa Ana El Salvador
144 A1 Santa Ana Mex.
135 C4 Santa Ana U.S.A.
152 B1 Santa Ana de Yacuma Bol.
144 B1 Santa Bárbara Mex.
135 C4 Santa Barbara U.S.A.
154 B2 Santa Bárbara, Serra de hills Brazil
152 B2 Santa Catalina Chile
135 C4 Santa Catalina Island U.S.A.
146 C2 Santa Clara Cuba
135 B3 Santa Clara U.S.A.

135 C4 Santa Clarita U.S.A.
107 D1 Santa Coloma de
Gramenet Spain
Santa Comba Angola see
Waku-Kungo
109 C3 Santa Croce, Capo c.
Sicily Italy
153 B5 Santa Cruz r. Arg.
152 B1 Santa Cruz Bol.
64 B2 Santa Cruz Phil.
135 B3 Santa Cruz U.S.A.
145 C3 Santa Cruz Barillas Guat.
155 E1 Santa Cruz Cabrália
Brazil
107 C2 Santa Cruz de Moya
Spain
114 A2 Santa Cruz de Tenerife
Canary Is
152 C2 Santa Cruz do Sul Brazil
135 C4 Santa Cruz Island U.S.A.
48 H5 Santa Cruz Islands
Solomon Is
106 B1 Santa Eugenia Spain
107 D2 Santa Eulalia del Río
Spain
152 B3 Santa Fé Arg.
138 B1 Santa Fe U.S.A.
154 B2 Santa Fé do Sul Brazil
154 B1 Santa Helena de Goiás
Brazil
153 B3 Santa Isabel Arg.
Santa Isabel
Equat. Guinea see Malabo
48 G4 Santa Isabel i. Solomon Is
154 B1 Santa Luisa, Serra de
hills Brazil
151 E3 Santa Luzia Brazil
144 A2 Santa Margarita, Isla i.
Mex.
152 C2 Santa Maria Brazil
144 B1 Santa Maria r. Mex.
135 B4 Santa Maria U.S.A.
123 D2 Santa Maria, Cabo de c.
Moz.
106 B2 Santa Maria, Cabo de c.
Port.
155 C1 Santa Maria, Chapadão
de hills Brazil
151 E3 Santa Maria das
Barreiras Brazil
109 C3 Santa Maria di Leuca,
Capo c. Italy
155 D1 Santa Maria do Suaçuí
Brazil
150 B1 Santa Marta Col.
135 C4 Santa Monica U.S.A.
151 E4 Santana Brazil
110 B1 Sântana Romania
106 C1 Santander Spain
108 A3 Sant'Antioco Sardinia Italy
108 A3 Sant'Antioco, Isola di i.
Sardinia Italy
151 D3 Santarém Brazil
106 B2 Santarém Port.
154 B1 Santa Rita do Araguaia
Brazil
153 B3 Santa Rosa Arg.
152 C2 Santa Rosa Brazil
135 B3 Santa Rosa CA U.S.A.
138 C2 Santa Rosa NM U.S.A.
146 B3 Santa Rosa de Copán
Hond.
135 B4 Santa Rosa Island CA
U.S.A.
142 C2 Santa Rosa Island FL
U.S.A.
144 A2 Santa Rosalía Mex.
134 C2 Santa Rosa Range mts
U.S.A.
154 B1 Santa Vitória Brazil
107 D1 Sant Carles de la Ràpita
Spain
135 C4 Santee U.S.A.
152 C2 Santiago Brazil
153 A3 Santiago Chile
147 C3 Santiago Dom. Rep.
144 B2 Santiago Mex.
146 B4 Santiago Panama
64 B2 Santiago Phil.
106 B1 Santiago de Compostela
Spain
146 C2 Santiago de Cuba Cuba
144 B2 Santiago Ixcuintla Mex.
144 B2 Santiago Papasquiaro
Mex.
106 C1 Santillana Spain
107 D1 Sant Jordi, Golf de g.
Spain
155 D2 Santo Amaro de Campos
Brazil
154 B2 Santo Anastácio Brazil

155 C2 Santo André Brazil
152 C2 Santo Angelo Brazil
154 B2 Santo Antônio da Platina
Brazil
151 F4 Santo Antônio de Jesus
Brazil
150 C3 Santo Antônio do Içá
Brazil
155 C2 Santo Antônio do Monte
Brazil
147 D3 Santo Domingo
Dom. Rep.
144 A2 Santo Domingo Mex.
138 B1 Santo Domingo Pueblo
U.S.A.
111 C3 Santorini i. Greece
155 D2 Santos Brazil
155 D2 Santos Dumont Brazil
157 I7 Santos Plateau
sea feature
S. Atlantic Ocean
152 C2 Santo Tomé Arg.
153 A4 San Valentín, Cerro mt.
Chile
146 B3 San Vicente El Salvador
144 A1 San Vicente Mex.
64 B2 San Vicente Phil.
150 B4 San Vicente de Cañete
Peru
108 B2 San Vincenzo Italy
108 B3 San Vito, Capo c. Sicily
Italy
71 A4 Sanya China
155 C2 São Bernardo do Campo
Brazil
152 C2 São Borja Brazil
154 C2 São Carlos Brazil
155 D1 São Felipe, Serra de hills
Brazil
151 D4 São Félix Brazil
151 D3 São Félix Brazil
155 D2 São Fidélis Brazil
155 D1 São Francisco Brazil
151 F4 São Francisco r. Brazil
154 C3 São Francisco, Ilha de i.
Brazil
154 C3 São Francisco do Sul
Brazil
152 C3 São Gabriel Brazil
155 D2 São Gonçalo Brazil
155 C1 São Gonçalo do Abaeté
Brazil
155 C1 São Gotardo Brazil
154 B1 São Jerônimo, Serra de
hills Brazil
155 D2 São João da Barra Brazil
155 C2 São João da Boa Vista
Brazil
106 B1 São João da Madeira
Port.
155 D1 São João da Ponte Brazil
155 D2 São João del Rei Brazil
155 D1 São João do Paraíso
Brazil
155 D1 São João Evangelista
Brazil
155 D2 São João Nepomuceno
Brazil
154 C2 São Joaquim da Barra
Brazil
152 D2 São José Brazil
154 C2 São José do Rio Preto
Brazil
155 C2 São José dos Campos
Brazil
154 C3 São José dos Pinhais
Brazil
154 A1 São Lourenço Brazil
155 C2 São Lourenço Brazil
151 E3 São Luís Brazil
154 C2 São Manuel Brazil
154 C1 São Marcos r. Brazil
151 E3 São Marcos, Baía de b.
Brazil
155 E1 São Mateus Brazil
154 B3 São Mateus do Sul
Brazil
105 C2 Saône r. France
155 C2 São Paulo Brazil
155 D2 São Pedro da Aldeia
Brazil
151 E3 São Raimundo Nonato
Brazil
155 C1 São Romão Brazil
São Salvador Angola see
M'banza Congo
São Salvador do Congo
Angola see
M'banza Congo
155 D2 São Sebastião, Ilha do i.
Brazil

154 C2 São Sebastião do
Paraíso Brazil
154 B1 São Simão Brazil
154 B1 São Simão, Barragem de
resr Brazil
59 C2 Sao-Siu Indon.
113 D5 São Tomé
São Tomé and Principe
113 D5 São Tomé i.
São Tomé and Principe
155 D2 São Tomé, Cabo de c.
Brazil
113 D5 São Tomé and Principe
country Africa
155 C2 São Vicente Brazil
106 B2 São Vicente, Cabo de c.
Port.
59 C3 Saparua Indon.
107 D2 Sa Pobla Spain
89 F3 Sapozhok Rus. Fed.
66 D2 Sapporo Japan
109 C2 Sapri Italy
139 D1 Sapulpa U.S.A.
81 C2 Saqqez Iran
81 C2 Sarāb Iran
63 B2 Sara Buri Thai.
Saragossa Spain see
Zaragoza
89 F3 Sarai Rus. Fed.
109 C2 Sarajevo Bos.-Herz.
87 E3 Saraktash Rus. Fed.
62 A1 Saramati mt.
India/Myanmar
141 E2 Saranac Lake U.S.A.
109 D3 Sarandë Albania
64 B3 Sarangani Islands Phil.
87 D3 Saransk Rus. Fed.
87 E3 Sarapul Rus. Fed.
143 D3 Sarasota U.S.A.
90 B2 Sarata Ukr.
136 B2 Saratoga U.S.A.
141 E2 Saratoga Springs U.S.A.
61 C1 Saratok Sarawak Malaysia
87 D3 Saratov Rus. Fed.
79 D2 Saravan Iran
63 B2 Saravan Laos
61 C1 Sarawak state Malaysia
111 C2 Saray Turkey
111 C3 Sarayköy Turkey
79 D2 Sarbāz Iran
76 B3 Sarbīsheh Iran
74 B2 Sardarshahr India
Sardegna i. Italy see
Sardinia
108 A2 Sardinia i. Italy
92 C2 Sarektjåkkå mt. Sweden
77 C3 Sar-e Pol Afgh.
158 C3 Sargasso Sea sea
Atlantic Ocean
74 B1 Sargodha Pak.
115 D4 Sarh Chad
79 D2 Sarhad reg. Iran
81 D2 Sārī Iran
111 C3 Sarıgöl Turkey
81 C1 Sarıkamış Turkey
61 C1 Sarikei Sarawak Malaysia
51 D2 Sarina Austr.
115 D2 Sarīr Tibesti des. Libya
65 B2 Sariwŏn N. Korea
111 C2 Sarıyer Turkey
77 D2 Sarkand Kazakh.
111 C2 Şarköy Turkey
104 C3 Sarlat-la-Canéda France
59 D3 Sarmi Indon.
153 B4 Sarmiento Arg.
140 C2 Sarnia Can.
90 B1 Sarny Ukr.
60 B2 Sarolangun Indon.
111 B3 Saronikos Kolpos g.
Greece
111 C2 Saros Körfezi b. Turkey
103 E2 Sárospatak Hungary
87 D3 Sarova Rus. Fed.
Sarpan i. N. Mariana Is see
Rota
105 D2 Sarrebourg France
106 B1 Sarria Spain
107 C1 Sarrión Spain
105 D3 Sartène Corsica France
Sartu China see Daqing
111 C3 Saruhanlı Turkey
103 D2 Sárvár Hungary
81 D3 Sarvestān Iran
76 B2 Sarykamyshkoye Ozero
salt l. Turkm./Uzbek.
77 D2 Saryozek Kazakh.
77 D2 Saryshagan Kazakh.
77 C2 Sarysu watercourse
Kazakh.
77 D3 Sary-Tash Kyrg.
75 C2 Sasaram India

67 A4 Sasebo Japan
129 D2 Saskatchewan prov. Can.
129 D2 Saskatchewan r. Can.
129 D2 Saskatoon Can.
83 I2 Saskylakh Rus. Fed.
123 C2 Sasolburg S. Africa
87 D3 Sasovo Rus. Fed.
114 B4 Sassandra Côte d'Ivoire
108 A2 Sassari Sardinia Italy
102 C1 Sassnitz Ger.
114 A3 Satadougou Mali
136 C3 Satanta U.S.A.
73 B3 Satara India
123 D1 Satara S. Africa
87 E3 Satka Rus. Fed.
75 C2 Satna India
77 C2 Satpayev Kazakh.
74 B2 Satpura Range mts India
63 B2 Sattahip Thai.
110 B1 Satu Mare Romania
63 B3 Satun Thai.
144 B2 Saucillo Mex.
93 E4 Sauda Norway
92 □B2 Sauðárkrókur Iceland
78 B2 Saudi Arabia country
Asia
105 C3 Saugues France
137 E1 Sauk Center U.S.A.
105 C2 Saulieu France
88 B2 Saulkrasti Latvia
130 B3 Sault Ste Marie Can.
140 C1 Sault Ste Marie U.S.A.
77 C1 Saumalkol' Kazakh.
59 C3 Saumlakki Indon.
104 B2 Saumur France
120 B1 Saurimo Angola
109 D2 Sava r. Europe
49 J5 Savai'i i. Samoa
91 E1 Savala r. Rus. Fed.
114 C4 Savalou Benin
143 D2 Savannah GA U.S.A.
142 C1 Savannah TN U.S.A.
143 D2 Savannah r. U.S.A.
63 B2 Savannakhét Laos
130 A2 Savant Lake Can.
111 C3 Savaştepe Turkey
114 C4 Savè Benin
105 D2 Saverne France
89 F2 Savino Rus. Fed.
86 D2 Savinskiy Rus. Fed.
105 D2 Savoie reg. France
108 A2 Savona Italy
93 I3 Savonlinna Fin.
Savoy reg. France see
Savoie
93 F4 Sävsjö Sweden
59 C3 Savu i. Indon.
92 I2 Savukoski Fin.
74 B2 Sawai Madhopur India
62 A1 Sawan Myanmar
62 A2 Sawankhalok Thai.
136 B3 Sawatch Range mts
U.S.A.
121 B2 Sawmills Zimbabwe
79 C3 Sawqirah, Dawḥat b.
Oman
Sawqirah Bay Oman see
Sawqirah, Dawḥat
53 D2 Sawtell Austr.
137 E1 Sawtooth Mountains hills
U.S.A.
134 C2 Sawtooth Range mts
U.S.A.
61 D2 Sawu Sea Indon.
68 C1 Sayano-Shushenskoye
Vodokhranilishche resr
Rus. Fed.
76 C3 Sayat Turkm.
79 C3 Sayhūt Yemen
93 I3 Säynätsalo Fin.
69 D2 Saynshand Mongolia
141 D2 Sayre U.S.A.
144 B3 Sayula Mex.
145 C3 Sayula Mex.
128 B2 Sayward Can.
Sayyod Turkm. see Sayat
89 E2 Sazonovo Rus. Fed.
114 B2 Sbaa Alg.
96 B2 Scafell Pike hill U.K.
109 C3 Scalea Italy
96 □ Scalloway U.K.
108 B2 Scandicci Italy
96 C1 Scapa Flow inlet U.K.
96 B2 Scarba i. U.K.
130 C3 Scarborough Can.
147 D3 Scarborough
Trin. and Tob.
98 C2 Scarborough U.K.
64 A2 Scarborough Shoal
sea feature Phil.
96 A2 Scarinish U.K.

Scarpanto i. Greece see Karpathos
100 B2 Schaerbeek Belgium
105 D2 Schaffhausen Switz.
100 B1 Schagen Neth.
102 C2 Schärding Austria
100 A2 Scharendijke Neth.
101 D1 Scharhörn sea feature Ger.
101 D1 Scheeßel Ger.
131 D2 Schefferville Can.
135 D3 Schell Creek Range mts U.S.A.
141 E2 Schenectady U.S.A.
139 D3 Schertz U.S.A.
101 E3 Scheßlitz Ger.
100 C1 Schiermonnikoog i. Neth.
100 B2 Schilde Belgium
108 B1 Schio Italy
101 F2 Schkeuditz Ger.
101 E1 Schladen Ger.
102 C2 Schladming Austria
101 E2 Schleiz Ger.
102 B1 Schleswig Ger.
101 D2 Schloß Holte-Stukenbrock Ger.
101 D2 Schlüchtern Ger.
101 E3 Schlüsselfeld Ger.
101 D2 Schmallenberg Ger.
Schmidt Island Rus. Fed. see Shmidta, Ostrov
101 F2 Schmölln Ger.
101 D1 Schneverdingen Ger.
101 E1 Schönebeck (Elbe) Ger.
101 E1 Schöningen Ger.
100 B2 Schoonhoven Neth.
59 D3 Schouten Islands P.N.G.
97 B3 Schull Rep. of Ireland
101 E3 Schwabach Ger.
102 B2 Schwäbische Alb mts Ger.
101 F3 Schwandorf Ger.
61 C2 Schwaner, Pegunungan mts Indon.
101 E1 Schwarzenbek Ger.
101 F2 Schwarzenberg Ger.
122 A2 Schwarzrand mts Namibia
102 B2 Schwarzwald mts Ger.
102 C2 Schwaz Austria
102 C1 Schwedt an der Oder Ger.
101 E2 Schweinfurt Ger.
101 E1 Schwerin Ger.
101 E1 Schweriner See l. Ger.
105 D2 Schwyz Switz.
108 B3 Sciacca Sicily Italy
95 B4 Scilly, Isles of U.K.
140 C3 Scioto r. U.S.A.
136 B1 Scobey U.S.A.
53 D2 Scone Austr.
110 B2 Scornicești Romania
55 C3 Scotia Ridge sea feature S. Atlantic Ocean
149 F8 Scotia Sea S. Atlantic Ocean
96 C2 Scotland admin. div. U.K.
128 B2 Scott, Cape Can.
123 D3 Scottburgh S. Africa
136 C3 Scott City U.S.A.
136 C2 Scottsbluff U.S.A.
142 C2 Scottsboro U.S.A.
96 B1 Scourie U.K.
141 D2 Scranton U.S.A.
98 C3 Scunthorpe U.K.
105 E2 Scuol Switz.
Scutari Albania see Shkodër
99 D4 Seaford U.K.
98 C2 Seaham U.K.
129 E2 Seal r. Can.
122 B3 Seal, Cape S. Africa
52 B3 Sea Lake Austr.
139 D3 Sealy U.S.A.
142 B1 Searcy U.S.A.
98 B2 Seascale U.K.
134 B1 Seattle U.S.A.
141 E2 Sebago Lake U.S.A.
144 A2 Sebastián Vizcaíno, Bahía b. Mex.
Sebastopol Ukr. see Sevastopol'
Sebenico Croatia see Šibenik
110 B2 Sebeș Romania
60 B2 Sebesi i. Indon.
88 C2 Sebezh Rus. Fed.
80 B1 Şebinkarahisar Turkey
143 D3 Sebring U.S.A.
61 C2 Sebuku i. Indon.
128 B3 Sechelt Can.
150 A3 Sechura Peru
73 B3 Secunderabad India
137 E3 Sedalia U.S.A.

105 C2 Sedan France
54 B2 Seddon N.Z.
114 A3 Sédhiou Senegal
138 A2 Sedona U.S.A.
101 E2 Seeburg Ger.
101 E1 Seehausen (Altmark) Ger.
122 A2 Seeheim Namibia
104 C2 Sées France
101 E2 Seesen Ger.
101 E1 Seevetal Ger.
114 A4 Sefadu Sierra Leone
123 C1 Sefare Botswana
93 F3 Segalstad Norway
60 B1 Segamat Malaysia
86 C2 Segezha Rus. Fed.
114 B3 Ségou Mali
106 C1 Segovia Spain
86 C2 Segozerskoye, Ozero resr Rus. Fed.
115 D2 Séguédine Niger
114 B4 Séguéla Côte d'Ivoire
139 D3 Seguin U.S.A.
107 C2 Segura r. Spain
106 C2 Segura, Sierra de mts Spain
120 B3 Sehithwa Botswana
93 H3 Seinäjoki Fin.
104 C2 Seine r. France
104 B2 Seine, Baie de b. France
105 C2 Seine, Val de val. France
103 E1 Sejny Pol.
60 B2 Sekayu Indon.
114 B4 Sekondi Ghana
134 B1 Selah U.S.A.
59 C3 Selaru i. Indon.
61 C2 Selatan, Tanjung pt Indon.
126 B2 Selawik U.S.A.
98 C3 Selby U.K.
136 C1 Selby U.S.A.
111 C3 Selçuk Turkey
120 B3 Selebi-Phikwe Botswana
Selebi-Pikwe Botswana see Selebi-Phikwe
105 D2 Sélestat France
Seletyteniz, Oz. salt l. Kazakh. see Siletiteniz, Ozero
92 □A3 Selfoss Iceland
114 A3 Sélibabi Maur.
138 A1 Seligman U.S.A.
116 A2 Selima Oasis Sudan
111 C3 Selimiye Turkey
114 B3 Sélingué, Lac de l. Mali
89 D2 Selizharovo Rus. Fed.
93 E4 Seljord Norway
129 E2 Selkirk Can.
96 C3 Selkirk U.K.
128 C2 Selkirk Mountains Can.
138 A2 Sells U.S.A.
142 C2 Selma AL U.S.A.
135 C3 Selma CA U.S.A.
99 C4 Selongey France
99 C4 Selsey Bill hd U.K.
89 D3 Sel'tso Rus. Fed.
Selukwe Zimbabwe see Shurugwi
150 B3 Selvas reg. Brazil
134 C1 Selway r. U.S.A.
129 D1 Selwyn Lake Can.
128 A1 Selwyn Mountains Can.
51 C2 Selwyn Range hills Austr.
60 B2 Semangka, Teluk b. Indon.
61 C2 Semarang Indon.
60 B1 Sematan Sarawak Malaysia
118 B2 Sembé Congo
81 C2 Semdinli Turkey
91 C1 Şemenivka Ukr.
87 D3 Semenov Rus. Fed.
61 C2 Semeru, Gunung vol. Indon.
91 E2 Semikarakorsk Rus. Fed.
89 E3 Semiluki Rus. Fed.
136 B2 Seminoe Reservoir U.S.A.
139 D2 Seminole U.S.A.
143 D2 Seminole, Lake U.S.A.
77 E1 Semipalatinsk Kazakh.
61 C1 Semitau Indon.
Sem Kolodezey Ukr. see Lenine
81 D2 Semnān Iran
61 C1 Semporna Sabah Malaysia
105 C2 Semur-en-Auxois France
Semyonovskoye Rus. Fed. see Bereznik
Semyonovskoye Rus. Fed. see Ostrovskoye
151 D2 Sena Madureira Brazil
120 B2 Senanga Zambia
67 B4 Sendai Japan

67 D3 Sendai Japan
143 D2 Seneca U.S.A.
114 A3 Senegal country Africa
114 A3 Sénégal r. Maur./Senegal
102 C1 Senftenberg Ger.
119 D3 Sengerema Tanz.
151 E4 Senhor do Bonfim Brazil
103 D2 Senica Slovakia
108 B2 Senigallia Italy
109 B2 Senj Croatia
92 G2 Senja i. Norway
122 B2 Senlac S. Africa
105 C2 Senlis France
63 B2 Senmonorom Cambodia
116 B3 Sennar Sudan
130 C3 Senneterre Can.
123 C3 Senqu r. Lesotho
105 C2 Sens France
109 D1 Senta Yugo.
128 B2 Sentinel Peak Can.
75 B2 Seoni India
65 B2 Seoul S. Korea
155 D2 Sepetiba, Baía de b. Brazil
59 D3 Sepik r. P.N.G.
61 C1 Sepinang Indon.
131 D2 Sept-Îles Can.
87 D4 Serafimovich Rus. Fed.
100 B2 Seraing Belgium
59 C3 Seram i. Indon.
59 C3 Seram Sea Indon.
60 B2 Serang Indon.
60 B1 Serasan, Selat sea chan. Indon.
109 D2 Serbia aut. rep. Yugo.
117 C3 Serdo Eth.
89 E3 Serebryanyye Prudy Rus. Fed.
60 B1 Seremban Malaysia
119 D3 Serengeti Plain Tanz.
121 C2 Serenje Zambia
90 B2 Seret r. Ukr.
87 D3 Sergach Rus. Fed.
86 F2 Sergino Rus. Fed.
89 E2 Sergiyev Posad Rus. Fed.
Sergo Ukr. see Stakhanov
61 C1 Seria Brunei
61 C1 Serian Sarawak Malaysia
111 B3 Serifos i. Greece
80 B2 Serik Turkey
59 C3 Sermata, Kepulauan is Indon.
Sernyy Zavod Turkm. see Kukurtli
86 F3 Serov Rus. Fed.
120 B3 Serowe Botswana
106 B2 Serpa Port.
Serpa Pinto Angola see Menongue
89 E3 Serpukhov Rus. Fed.
155 D2 Serra Brazil
155 C1 Serra das Araras Brazil
108 A3 Serramanna Sardinia Italy
154 B1 Serranópolis Brazil
100 A3 Serre r. France
111 B2 Serres Greece
151 F4 Serrinha Brazil
155 D1 Sêrro Brazil
154 C2 Sertãozinho Brazil
59 D3 Serui Indon.
120 B3 Serule Botswana
61 C2 Seruyan r. Indon.
68 C2 Sêrxü China
120 A2 Sesfontein Namibia
108 B2 Sessa Aurunca Italy
107 D2 Ses Salines, Cap de c. Spain
108 A2 Sestri Levante Italy
105 C3 Sète France
155 D1 Sete Lagoas Brazil
92 G2 Setermoen Norway
93 E4 Setesdal val. Norway
115 C1 Sétif Alg.
67 B4 Seto-naikai sea Japan
114 B1 Settat Morocco
98 B2 Settle U.K.
106 B2 Setúbal Port.
106 B2 Setúbal, Baía de b. Port.
130 A2 Seul, Lac l. Can.
81 C1 Sevan Armenia
76 A2 Sevan, Lake Armenia
Sevana Lich l. Armenia see Sevan, Lake
91 C3 Sevastopol' Ukr.
131 D2 Seven Islands Can. see Sept-Îles
99 D4 Sevenoaks U.K.
105 C3 Sévérac-le-Château France
130 B2 Severn r. Can.

122 B2 Severn S. Africa
99 B4 Severn r. U.K.
86 D2 Severnaya Dvina r. Rus. Fed.
83 H1 Severnaya Zemlya is Rus. Fed.
86 D2 Severnyy Rus. Fed.
86 F2 Severnyy Rus. Fed.
83 I3 Severobaykal'sk Rus. Fed.
86 C2 Severodvinsk Rus. Fed.
83 L3 Severo-Kuril'sk Rus. Fed.
92 J2 Severomorsk Rus. Fed.
86 C2 Severoonezhsk Rus. Fed.
83 H2 Severo-Yeniseyskiy Rus. Fed.
91 D3 Severskaya Rus. Fed.
135 D3 Sevier r. U.S.A.
135 D3 Sevier Lake U.S.A.
Sevilla Spain see Seville
106 B2 Seville Spain
Sevlyush Ukr. see Vynohradiv
89 D3 Sevsk Rus. Fed.
126 C2 Seward U.S.A.
126 B2 Seward Peninsula U.S.A.
128 A2 Sewell Inlet Can.
128 C2 Sexsmith Can.
144 B2 Sextin r. Mex.
86 G1 Seyakha Rus. Fed.
113 I6 Seychelles country Indian Ocean
92 □C2 Seyðisfjörður Iceland
80 B2 Seyhan r. Turkey
91 C1 Seym r. Rus. Fed./Ukr.
83 L2 Seymchan Rus. Fed.
53 C3 Seymour Austr.
123 C3 Seymour S. Africa
140 B3 Seymour IN U.S.A.
139 D2 Seymour TX U.S.A.
105 C2 Sézanne France
108 B2 Sezze Italy
111 B3 Sfakia Greece
110 C1 Sfântu Gheorghe Romania
115 D1 Sfax Tunisia
Sfintu Gheorghe Romania see Sfântu Gheorghe
's-Gravenhage Neth. see The Hague
96 A2 Sgurr Alasdair hill U.K.
70 A2 Shaanxi prov. China
Shabani Zimbabwe see Zvishavane
91 D2 Shabel'sk Rus. Fed.
77 D3 Shache China
55 C1 Shackleton Range mts Antarctica
74 A2 Shadadkot Pak.
86 F3 Shadrinsk Rus. Fed.
99 B4 Shaftesbury U.K.
126 B2 Shageluk U.S.A.
Shāhābād Iran see Eslāmābād-e Gharb
75 C2 Shahdol India
77 C3 Shah Fuladi mt. Afgh.
75 B2 Shahjahanpur India
76 B3 Shāh Kūh mt. Iran
81 D2 Shahr-e Bābak Iran
81 D2 Shahr-e Kord Iran
Shahrezā Iran see Qomisheh
Shāhrūd Iran see Emāmrūd
79 B2 Shaj'ah, Jabal hill Saudi Arabia
89 E2 Shakhovskaya Rus. Fed.
77 C3 Shakhrisabz Uzbek.
Shakhterskoye Ukr. see Pershotravens'k
91 E2 Shakhty Rus. Fed.
Shakhtyorskoye Ukr. see Pershotravens'k
86 D2 Shakhun'ya Rus. Fed.
66 D2 Shakotan-hantō pen. Japan
66 D2 Shakotan-misaki c. Japan
68 C2 Shaluli Shan mts China
129 E2 Shamattawa Can.
139 C1 Shamrock U.S.A.
70 A2 Shandan China
70 B2 Shandong prov. China
70 C2 Shandong Bandao pen. China
121 B2 Shangani Zimbabwe
121 B2 Shangani r. Zimbabwe
70 B1 Shangdu China
70 C2 Shanghai China

70 C2 **Shanghai** *mun.* China
71 B3 **Shanghang** China
70 B2 **Shangnan** China
70 B2 **Shangqiu** China
71 B3 **Shangrao** China
70 B2 **Shangshui** China
77 E2 **Shangyou Shuiku** *resr* China
70 C2 **Shangyu** China
69 E1 **Shangzhi** China
70 A2 **Shangzhou** China
134 B1 **Shaniko** U.S.A.
97 B2 **Shannon** *r.* Rep. of Ireland
97 B2 **Shannon, Mouth of the** Rep. of Ireland
62 A1 **Shan Plateau** Myanmar
Shansi *prov.* China *see* Shanxi
71 B3 **Shantou** China
Shantung *prov.* China *see* Shandong
70 B2 **Shanxi** *prov.* China
71 B3 **Shaoguan** China
71 B3 **Shaowu** China
70 C2 **Shaoxing** China
71 B3 **Shaoyang** China
96 C1 **Shapinsay** *i.* U.K.
116 C2 **Shaqrā'** Saudi Arabia
90 B2 **Sharhorod** Ukr.
79 C2 **Sharjah** U.A.E.
88 C2 **Sharkawshchyna** Belarus
50 A2 **Shark Bay** Austr.
78 A2 **Sharm el Sheikh** Egypt
140 C2 **Sharon** U.S.A.
86 D3 **Shar'ya** Rus. Fed.
121 B3 **Shashe** *r.* Botswana/Zimbabwe
117 B4 **Shashemenē** Eth.
Shashi China *see* Jingsha
134 B2 **Shasta, Mount** *vol.* U.S.A.
134 B2 **Shasta Lake** U.S.A.
115 D2 **Shāṭi', Wādi ash** *watercourse* Libya
Shatilki Belarus *see* Svyetlahorsk
89 E2 **Shatura** Rus. Fed.
129 D3 **Shaunavon** Can.
140 B2 **Shawano** U.S.A.
130 C3 **Shawinigan** Can.
139 D1 **Shawnee** U.S.A.
83 M2 **Shazhovyeyem** *r.* Rus. Fed.
50 B2 **Shay Gap** Austr.
89 E3 **Shchekino** Rus. Fed.
89 E2 **Shchelkovo** Rus. Fed.
Shcherbakov Rus. Fed. *see* Rybinsk
Shcherbinovka Ukr. *see* Dzerzhyns'k
89 E3 **Shchigry** Rus. Fed.
91 C1 **Shchors** Ukr.
88 B3 **Shchuchyn** Belarus
91 D1 **Shebekino** Rus. Fed.
77 C3 **Sheberghān** Afgh.
140 B2 **Sheboygan** U.S.A.
91 D3 **Shebsh** *r.* Rus. Fed.
97 C2 **Sheelin, Lough** *l.* Rep. of Ireland
136 B3 **Sheep Mountain** U.S.A.
99 D4 **Sheerness** U.K.
98 C3 **Sheffield** U.K.
139 C2 **Sheffield** U.S.A.
Sheikh Othman Yemen *see* Ash Shaykh 'Uthman
Shekhem West Bank *see* Nābluss
89 E2 **Sheksna** Rus. Fed.
89 E2 **Sheksninskoye Vodokhranilishche** *resr* Rus. Fed.
83 M2 **Shelagskiy, Mys** *pt* Rus. Fed.
131 D3 **Shelburne** Can.
140 B2 **Shelby** *MI* U.S.A.
134 D1 **Shelby** *MT* U.S.A.
143 D1 **Shelby** *NC* U.S.A.
140 B3 **Shelbyville** *IN* U.S.A.
142 C1 **Shelbyville** *TN* U.S.A.
83 L2 **Shelikhova, Zaliv** *g.* Rus. Fed.
126 B3 **Shelikof Strait** U.S.A.
129 D2 **Shellbrook** Can.
Shelter Bay Can. *see* Port-Cartier
134 B1 **Shelton** U.S.A.
137 D2 **Shenandoah** U.S.A.
141 D3 **Shenandoah** *r.* U.S.A.
141 D3 **Shenandoah Mountains** U.S.A.
118 A2 **Shendam** Nigeria

Shengli Feng *mt.* China/Kyrg. *see* Jengish Chokusu
86 D2 **Shenkursk** Rus. Fed.
70 B2 **Shenmu** China
Shensi *prov.* China *see* Shaanxi
70 C1 **Shenyang** China
71 B3 **Shenzhen** China
90 B1 **Shepetivka** Ukr.
53 C3 **Shepparton** Austr.
99 D4 **Sheppey, Isle of** *i.* U.K.
131 D3 **Sherbrooke** *N.S.* Can.
130 C3 **Sherbrooke** *Que.* Can.
97 C2 **Shercock** Rep. of Ireland
116 B3 **Shereiq** Sudan
136 B2 **Sheridan** U.S.A.
52 A2 **Sheringa** Austr.
86 F2 **Sherkaly** Rus. Fed.
139 D2 **Sherman** U.S.A.
87 E4 **'s-Hertogenbosch** Neth.
96 ☐ **Shetland Islands** U.K.
76 B2 **Shetpe** Kazakh.
Shevchenko Kazakh. *see* Aktau
91 D2 **Shevchenkove** Ukr.
137 D1 **Sheyenne** *r.* U.S.A.
79 B3 **Shibām** Yemen
67 C3 **Shibata** Japan
66 D2 **Shibetsu** Japan
Shibotsu-jima *i.* Rus. Fed. *see* Zelenyy, Ostrov
71 B3 **Shicheng** China
70 C2 **Shidao** China
96 B2 **Shiel, Loch** *l.* U.K.
Shigatse China *see* Xigazê
77 E2 **Shihezi** China
Shihkiachwang China *see* Shijiazhuang
Shijiao China *see* Fogang
70 B2 **Shijiazhuang** China
Shijiusuo China *see* Rizhao
74 A2 **Shikarpur** Pak.
67 B4 **Shikoku** *i.* Japan
66 D2 **Shikotsu-ko** *l.* Japan
86 D2 **Shilega** Rus. Fed.
75 C2 **Shiliguri** India
97 C2 **Shillelagh** Rep. of Ireland
75 D2 **Shillong** India
89 F3 **Shilovo** Rus. Fed.
69 E1 **Shimanovsk** Rus. Fed.
117 C3 **Shimbiris** *mt.* Somalia
67 C3 **Shimizu** Japan
74 B1 **Shimla** India
67 C4 **Shimoda** Japan
73 B3 **Shimoga** India
66 D2 **Shimokita-hantō** *pen.* Japan
67 B4 **Shimonoseki** Japan
89 D2 **Shimsk** Rus. Fed.
96 B1 **Shin, Loch** *l.* U.K.
62 A1 **Shingbwiyang** Myanmar
67 C4 **Shingū** Japan
123 D1 **Shingwedzi** S. Africa
123 D1 **Shingwedzi** *r.* S. Africa
66 D3 **Shinjō** Japan
119 D3 **Shinyanga** Tanz.
67 D3 **Shiogama** Japan
67 C3 **Shiono-misaki** *c.* Japan
71 A3 **Shiping** China
98 C3 **Shipley** U.K.
138 B1 **Shiprock** U.S.A.
71 A3 **Shiqian** China
Shiqizhen China *see* Zhongshan
70 A2 **Shiquan** China
78 B2 **Shi'r, Jabal** *hill* Saudi Arabia
67 C3 **Shirane-san** *mt.* Japan
67 C3 **Shirane-san** *vol.* Japan
81 D3 **Shīrāz** Iran
66 D2 **Shiretoko-misaki** *c.* Japan
66 D2 **Shiriya-zaki** *c.* Japan
76 B3 **Shirvān** Iran
74 B2 **Shiv** India
74 B2 **Shivpuri** India
70 B2 **Shiyan** China
70 A2 **Shizuishan** China
67 C4 **Shizuoka** Japan
89 D3 **Shklow** Belarus
109 C2 **Shkodër** Albania
83 H1 **Shmidta, Ostrov** *i.* Rus. Fed.
67 B4 **Shōbara** Japan
Sholapur India *see* Solāpur
158 F8 **Shona Ridge** *sea feature* S. Atlantic Ocean
76 B2 **Shor Barsa-Kel'mes** *salt marsh* Uzbek.

74 B1 **Shorkot** Pak.
135 C3 **Shoshone** *CA* U.S.A.
134 D2 **Shoshone** *ID* U.S.A.
135 C3 **Shoshone Mountains** U.S.A.
123 C1 **Shoshong** Botswana
91 C1 **Shostka** Ukr.
70 B2 **Shouxian** China
78 A3 **Showak** Sudan
138 A2 **Show Low** U.S.A.
91 C2 **Shpola** Ukr.
142 B2 **Shreveport** U.S.A.
99 B3 **Shrewsbury** U.K.
77 D2 **Shu** Kazakh.
Shuangjiang China *see* Tongdao
62 A1 **Shuangjiang** China
Shuangxi China *see* Shunchang
66 B1 **Shuangyashan** China
87 E4 **Shubarkuduk** Kazakh.
116 B1 **Shubrā el Kheima** Egypt
89 D2 **Shugozero** Rus. Fed.
Shuidong China *see* Dianbai
120 B2 **Shumba** Zimbabwe
110 C2 **Shumen** Bulg.
87 F3 **Shumikha** Rus. Fed.
88 C2 **Shumilina** Belarus
139 C3 **Shumla** U.S.A.
89 D3 **Shumyachi** Rus. Fed.
71 B3 **Shunchang** China
126 B2 **Shungnak** U.S.A.
78 B3 **Shuqrah** Yemen
77 C3 **Shurchi** Uzbek.
121 C2 **Shurugwi** Zimbabwe
89 F2 **Shushkodom** Rus. Fed.
81 C2 **Shushtar** Iran
128 C2 **Shuswap Lake** Can.
89 F2 **Shuya** Rus. Fed.
89 F2 **Shuyskoye** Rus. Fed.
62 A1 **Shwebo** Myanmar
62 A2 **Shwedwin** Myanmar
62 A2 **Shwegun** Myanmar
62 A2 **Shwegyin** Myanmar
62 A1 **Shweli** *r.* Myanmar
77 C2 **Shymkent** Kazakh.
74 B1 **Shyok** *r.* India
91 C2 **Shyroke** Ukr.
90 C2 **Shyryayeve** Ukr.
59 C3 **Sia** Indon.
74 A2 **Siahan Range** *mts* Pak.
74 B1 **Sialkot** Pak.
Siam *country* Asia *see* Thailand
Sian China *see* Xi'an
64 B3 **Siargao** *i.* Phil.
64 B3 **Siasi** Phil.
88 B2 **Šiauliai** Lith.
123 D1 **Sibasa** S. Africa
109 C2 **Šibenik** Croatia
83 G2 **Siberia** *reg.* Rus. Fed.
60 A2 **Siberut** *i.* Indon.
74 A2 **Sibi** Pak.
Sibir' *reg.* Rus. Fed. *see* Siberia
118 B3 **Sibiti** Congo
110 B1 **Sibiu** Romania
60 A1 **Sibolga** Indon.
62 A1 **Sibsagar** India
61 C1 **Sibu** *Sarawak* Malaysia
118 B2 **Sibut** C.A.R.
64 A3 **Sibutu** *i.* Phil.
64 B2 **Sibuyan** *i.* Phil.
64 B2 **Sibuyan Sea** Phil.
128 C2 **Sicamous** Can.
63 A3 **Sichon** Thai.
70 A2 **Sichuan** *prov.* China
70 A3 **Sichuan Pendi** *basin* China
105 D3 **Sicié, Cap** *c.* France
Sicilia *i.* Italy *see* Sicily
108 B3 **Sicilian Channel** Italy/Tunisia
108 B3 **Sicily** *i.* Italy
150 B4 **Sicuani** Peru
74 B2 **Siddhapur** India
111 C3 **Sideros, Akra** *pt* Greece
122 B3 **Sidesaviwa** S. Africa
75 C2 **Sidhi** India
107 D2 **Sidi Aïssa** Alg.
107 D2 **Sidi Ali** Alg.
114 B1 **Sidi Bel Abbès** Alg.
114 A2 **Sidi Ifni** Morocco
114 B1 **Sidi Kacem** Morocco
60 A1 **Sidikalang** Indon.
111 B2 **Sidirokastro** Greece
96 C2 **Sidlaw Hills** U.K.
99 B4 **Sidmouth** U.K.
134 B1 **Sidney** Can.
136 C1 **Sidney** *MT* U.S.A.

136 C2 **Sidney** *NE* U.S.A.
140 C2 **Sidney** *OH* U.S.A.
143 D2 **Sidney Lanier, Lake** U.S.A.
61 D1 **Sidoan** Indon.
80 B2 **Sidon** Lebanon
154 B2 **Sidrolândia** Brazil
103 E1 **Siedlce** Pol.
100 C2 **Sieg** *r.* Ger.
101 D2 **Siegen** Ger.
63 B2 **Siĕmréab** Cambodia
Siem Reap Cambodia *see* Siĕmréab
108 B2 **Siena** Italy
103 D1 **Sieradz** Pol.
138 B2 **Sierra Blanca** U.S.A.
153 B4 **Sierra Grande** Arg.
114 A4 **Sierra Leone** *country* Africa
158 E4 **Sierra Leone Basin** *sea feature* N. Atlantic Ocean
158 E4 **Sierra Leone Rise** *sea feature* N. Atlantic Ocean
144 B2 **Sierra Mojada** Mex.
138 A2 **Sierra Vista** U.S.A.
105 D2 **Sierre** Switz.
116 C3 **Sifenī** Eth.
111 B3 **Sifnos** *i.* Greece
107 C2 **Sig** Alg.
127 I2 **Sigguup Nunaa** *pen.* Greenland
110 B1 **Sighetu Marmaţiei** Romania
110 B1 **Sighişoara** Romania
60 A1 **Sigli** Indon.
92 ☐B2 **Siglufjörður** Iceland
102 B2 **Sigmaringen** Ger.
100 B3 **Signy-l'Abbaye** France
106 C1 **Sigüenza** Spain
114 B3 **Siguiri** Guinea
88 B2 **Sigulda** Latvia
63 B2 **Sihanoukville** Cambodia
92 I3 **Siilinjärvi** Fin.
81 C2 **Siirt** Turkey
60 B2 **Sijunjung** Indon.
74 B2 **Sikar** India
74 A1 **Sikaram** *mt.* Afgh.
114 B3 **Sikasso** Mali
111 B2 **Sikea** Greece
137 F3 **Sikeston** U.S.A.
66 B2 **Sikhote-Alin'** *mts* Rus. Fed.
111 C3 **Sikinos** *i.* Greece
103 D2 **Siklós** Hungary
88 B2 **Šilalė** Lith.
144 B2 **Silao** Mex.
101 D1 **Silberberg** *hill* Ger.
75 D2 **Silchar** India
77 D1 **Siletiteniz, Ozero** *salt l.* Kazakh.
75 C2 **Silgarhi** Nepal
80 B2 **Silifke** Turkey
75 C1 **Siling Co** *salt l.* China
110 C2 **Silistra** Bulg.
111 C2 **Silivri** Turkey
93 F3 **Siljan** *l.* Sweden
93 E4 **Silkeborg** Denmark
88 C2 **Sillamäe** Estonia
98 B2 **Silloth** U.K.
142 B1 **Siloam Springs** U.S.A.
123 D2 **Silobela** S. Africa
60 B1 **Siluas** Indon.
88 B2 **Šilutė** Lith.
81 C2 **Silvan** Turkey
154 C1 **Silvânia** Brazil
74 B2 **Silvassa** India
137 E1 **Silver Bay** U.S.A.
138 B2 **Silver City** U.S.A.
136 B3 **Silverton** U.S.A.
62 B1 **Simao** China
130 C3 **Simārd, Lac** *l.* Can.
111 C3 **Simav** Turkey
111 C3 **Simav Dağları** *mts* Turkey
118 C2 **Simba** Dem. Rep. Congo
140 C2 **Simcoe** Can.
141 D2 **Simcoe, Lake** Can.
78 A3 **Simēn Mountains** Eth.
60 A1 **Simeulu** *i.* Indon.
91 C3 **Simferopol'** Ukr.
75 C2 **Simikot** Nepal
135 C4 **Simi Valley** U.S.A.
Simla India *see* Shimla
110 B1 **Şimleu Silvaniei** Romania
100 C3 **Simmern (Hunsrück)** Ger.
92 I2 **Simo** Fin.
129 D2 **Simonhouse** Can.
60 B2 **Simpang** Indon.
51 C2 **Simpson Desert** Austr.
93 F4 **Simrishamn** Sweden

60 A1 **Sinabang** Indon.
116 B2 **Sinai** pen. Egypt
105 E3 **Sinalunga** Italy
71 A3 **Sinan** China
65 B2 **Sinanju** N. Korea
62 A1 **Sinbo** Myanmar
62 A1 **Sinbyugyun** Myanmar
150 B2 **Sincelejo** Col.
60 B2 **Sindangbarang** Indon.
111 C3 **Sındırgı** Turkey
86 E2 **Sindor** Rus. Fed.
111 C2 **Sinekçi** Turkey
106 B2 **Sines** Port.
106 B2 **Sines, Cabo de** c. Port.
116 B3 **Singa** Sudan
75 C2 **Singahi** India
60 B1 **Singapore** country Asia
61 C2 **Singaraja** Indon.
63 B2 **Sing Buri** Thai.
119 D3 **Singida** Tanz.
62 A1 **Singkaling Hkamti** Myanmar
61 D2 **Singkang** Indon.
60 B1 **Singkawang** Indon.
60 B2 **Singkep** i. Indon.
60 A1 **Singkil** Indon.
53 D2 **Singleton** Austr.
Sin'gosan N. Korea see Kosan
62 A1 **Singu** Myanmar
Sining China see Xining
108 A2 **Siniscola** Sardinia Italy
109 C2 **Sinj** Croatia
61 D2 **Sinjai** Indon.
116 B3 **Sinkat** Sudan
Sinkiang aut. reg. China see Xinjiang Uygur Zizhiqu
Sinkiang Uighur Autonomous Region aut. reg. China see Xinjiang Uygur Zizhiqu
151 D2 **Sinnamary** Fr. Guiana
Sînnicolau Mare Romania see Sânnicolau Mare
Sinoia Zimbabwe see Chinhoyi
80 B1 **Sinop** Turkey
65 B1 **Sinp'o** N. Korea
61 C1 **Sintang** Indon.
100 B2 **St Anthonis** Neth.
100 A2 **St-Laureins** Belgium
100 B2 **St-Niklaas** Belgium
139 D3 **Sinton** U.S.A.
100 C2 **St-Vith** Belgium
65 A1 **Sinŭiju** N. Korea
64 B3 **Siocon** Phil.
103 D2 **Siófok** Hungary
105 D2 **Sion** Switz.
137 D2 **Sioux Center** U.S.A.
137 D2 **Sioux City** U.S.A.
137 D2 **Sioux Falls** U.S.A.
130 A2 **Sioux Lookout** Can.
65 A1 **Siping** China
129 E2 **Sipiwesk Lake** Can.
55 P2 **Siple, Mount** Antarctica
55 P2 **Siple Island** Antarctica
Sipolilo Zimbabwe see Guruve
60 A2 **Sipura** i. Indon.
64 B3 **Siquijor** Phil.
93 E4 **Sira** r. Norway
Siracusa Italy see Syracuse
51 C1 **Sir Edward Pellew Group** is Austr.
110 C1 **Siret** Romania
110 C1 **Siret** r. Romania
79 C2 **Sīrīk** Iran
61 C1 **Sirik, Tanjong** pt Malaysia
62 B2 **Siri Kit Dam** Thai.
128 B1 **Sir James MacBrien, Mount** Can.
79 C2 **Sīrjān** Iran
81 C2 **Şırnak** Turkey
74 B2 **Širohi** India
60 A1 **Sirombu** Indon.
74 B2 **Sirsa** India
115 D1 **Sirte** Libya
115 D1 **Sirte, Gulf of** Libya
88 B2 **Širvintos** Lith.
109 C1 **Sisak** Croatia
63 B2 **Sisaket** Thai.
145 C2 **Sisal** Mex.
122 B2 **Sishen** S. Africa
81 C2 **Sisian** Armenia
127 I2 **Sisimiut** Greenland
129 D2 **Sisipuk Lake** Can.
63 B2 **Sisŏphŏn** Cambodia
105 D3 **Sisteron** France
Sitang China see Sinan
75 C2 **Sitapur** India

111 C3 **Siteia** Greece
123 D2 **Siteki** Swaziland
128 A2 **Sitka** U.S.A.
62 A2 **Sittang** r. Myanmar
100 B2 **Sittard** Neth.
62 A1 **Sittaung** Myanmar
62 A1 **Sittwe** Myanmar
61 C2 **Situbondo** Indon.
80 B2 **Sivas** Turkey
111 C3 **Sivaslı** Turkey
80 B2 **Siverek** Turkey
88 D2 **Siverskiy** Rus. Fed.
91 D2 **Sivers'kyy Donets'** r. Ukr.
80 B2 **Sivrihisar** Turkey
116 A2 **Siwa** Egypt
75 B1 **Siwalik Range** mts India/Nepal
116 A2 **Siwa Oasis** Egypt
105 D3 **Six-Fours-les-Plages** France
70 B2 **Sixian** China
123 C2 **Siyabuswa** S. Africa
Sjælland i. Denmark see Zealand
109 D2 **Sjenica** Yugo.
92 G2 **Sjøvegan** Norway
91 C2 **Skadovs'k** Ukr.
93 F4 **Skagen** Denmark
93 E4 **Skagerrak** str. Denmark/Norway
134 B1 **Skagit** r. U.S.A.
128 A2 **Skagway** U.S.A.
92 G3 **Skaland** Norway
93 F4 **Skara** Sweden
74 B1 **Skardu** Jammu and Kashmir
103 E1 **Skarżysko-Kamienna** Pol.
103 D2 **Skawina** Pol.
114 A2 **Skaymat** Western Sahara
128 B2 **Skeena** r. Can.
128 B2 **Skeena Mountains** Can.
98 D3 **Skegness** U.K.
92 H3 **Skellefteå** Sweden
92 H3 **Skellefteälven** r. Sweden
97 C2 **Skerries** Rep. of Ireland
93 F4 **Ski** Norway
111 B3 **Skiathos** i. Greece
97 B3 **Skibbereen** Rep. of Ireland
92 □B2 **Skíðadals-jökull** glacier Iceland
98 B2 **Skiddaw** hill U.K.
93 E4 **Skien** Norway
103 E1 **Skierniewice** Pol.
115 C1 **Skikda** Alg.
52 B3 **Skipton** Austr.
98 B3 **Skipton** U.K.
93 E4 **Skive** Denmark
92 H1 **Skjervøy** Norway
Skobelev Uzbek. see Fergana
111 B3 **Skopelos** i. Greece
89 E3 **Skopin** Rus. Fed.
111 B2 **Skopje** Macedonia
111 C3 **Skoutaros** Greece
93 F4 **Skövde** Sweden
83 J3 **Skovorodino** Rus. Fed.
141 F2 **Skowhegan** U.S.A.
92 H2 **Skröven** Sweden
88 B2 **Skrunda** Latvia
128 A1 **Skukum, Mount** Can.
123 D1 **Skukuza** S. Africa
88 B2 **Skuodas** Lith.
90 B2 **Skvyra** Ukr.
96 A2 **Skye** i. U.K.
111 B3 **Skyros** Greece
111 B3 **Skyros** i. Greece
93 F4 **Slagelse** Denmark
60 B2 **Slamet, Gunung** vol. Indon.
97 C2 **Slaney** r. Rep. of Ireland
88 C2 **Slantsy** Rus. Fed.
109 C1 **Slatina** Croatia
110 B2 **Slatina** Romania
139 C2 **Slaton** U.S.A.
129 C1 **Slave** r. Can.
114 C4 **Slave Coast** Africa
128 C2 **Slave Lake** Can.
77 D1 **Slavgorod** Rus. Fed.
88 C2 **Slavkovichi** Rus. Fed.
Slavonska Požega Croatia see Požega
109 C1 **Slavonski Brod** Croatia
90 B1 **Slavuta** Ukr.
90 C1 **Slavutych** Ukr.
66 B2 **Slavyanka** Rus. Fed.
Slavyanskaya Rus. Fed. see Slavyansk-na-Kubani
91 D2 **Slavyansk-na-Kubani** Rus. Fed.
89 D3 **Slawharad** Belarus
103 D1 **Sławno** Pol.

99 C3 **Sleaford** U.K.
97 A2 **Slea Head** hd Rep. of Ireland
130 C2 **Sleeper Islands** Can.
97 D1 **Slieve Donard** hill U.K.
97 B1 **Slieve Gamph** hills Rep. of Ireland
96 A2 **Sligachan** U.K.
80 D2 **Sligeach** Rep. of Ireland see Sligo
97 B1 **Sligo** Rep. of Ireland
97 B1 **Sligo Bay** Rep. of Ireland
93 G4 **Slite** Sweden
110 C2 **Sliven** Bulg.
Sloboda Rus. Fed. see Ezhva
110 C2 **Slobozia** Romania
128 C3 **Slocan** Can.
88 C3 **Slonim** Belarus
100 B1 **Sloten** Neth.
99 C4 **Slough** U.K.
103 D2 **Slovakia** country Europe
108 B1 **Slovenia** country Europe
91 D2 **Slov"yans'k** Ukr.
102 C1 **Słubice** Pol.
90 B1 **Sluch** r. Ukr.
100 A2 **Sluis** Neth.
103 D1 **Słupsk** Pol.
88 C3 **Slutsk** Belarus
97 A2 **Slyne Head** hd Rep. of Ireland
68 C1 **Slyudyanka** Rus. Fed.
131 D2 **Smallwood Reservoir** Can.
88 C3 **Smalyavichy** Belarus
88 C3 **Smarhon'** Belarus
129 D2 **Smeaton** Can.
109 D2 **Smederevo** Yugo.
109 D2 **Smederevska Palanka** Yugo.
91 C2 **Smila** Ukr.
88 C3 **Smilavichy** Belarus
88 C2 **Smiltene** Latvia
137 D3 **Smith Center** U.S.A.
128 B2 **Smithers** Can.
143 E1 **Smithfield** NC U.S.A.
134 D2 **Smithfield** UT U.S.A.
141 D3 **Smith Mountain Lake** U.S.A.
130 C3 **Smiths Falls** Can.
53 D2 **Smithtown** Austr.
53 D2 **Smoky Cape** Austr.
137 D3 **Smoky Hills** U.S.A.
92 E3 **Smøla** i. Norway
89 D3 **Smolensk** Rus. Fed.
89 D3 **Smolensko-Moskovskaya Vozvyshennost'** hills Rus. Fed.
111 B2 **Smolyan** Bulg.
66 B2 **Smolyoninovo** Rus. Fed.
130 B3 **Smooth Rock Falls** Can.
Smyrna Turkey see İzmir
91 D2 **Smyrnove** Ukr.
92 □B3 **Snæfell** mt. Iceland
98 A2 **Snaefell** hill Isle of Man
128 A1 **Snag** Can.
134 C1 **Snake** r. U.S.A.
134 D2 **Snake River Plain** U.S.A.
128 C1 **Snare Lake** Can.
Snare Lakes Can. see Snare Lake
92 F3 **Snåsvatn** l. Norway
100 B1 **Sneek** Neth.
97 B3 **Sneem** Rep. of Ireland
122 B3 **Sneeuberge** mts S. Africa
Snegurovka Ukr. see Tetiyiv
103 D1 **Sněžka** mt. Czech Rep.
108 B1 **Snežnik** mt. Slovenia
103 E1 **Śniardwy, Jezioro** l. Pol.
Sniečkus Lith. see Visaginas
91 C2 **Snihurivka** Ukr.
93 E3 **Snøhetta** mt. Norway
Snovsk Ukr. see Shchors
129 D1 **Snowbird Lake** Can.
99 A3 **Snowdon** mt. U.K.
Snowdrift Can. see Łutselk'e
129 C1 **Snowdrift** r. Can.
138 A2 **Snowflake** U.S.A.
129 D2 **Snow Lake** Can.
134 C1 **Snowshoe Peak** U.S.A.
52 A2 **Snowtown** Austr.
53 C3 **Snowy** r. Austr.
53 C3 **Snowy Mountains** Austr.
139 C2 **Snyder** U.S.A.
121 □D2 **Soalala** Madag.
121 □D2 **Soanierana-Ivongo** Madag.
90 B2 **Sob** r. Ukr.

65 B2 **Sobaek-sanmaek** mts S. Korea
117 B4 **Sobat** r. Sudan
100 C3 **Sobernheim** Ger.
89 F2 **Sobinka** Rus. Fed.
151 E4 **Sobradinho, Barragem de** resr Brazil
151 E3 **Sobral** Brazil
91 D3 **Sochi** Rus. Fed.
65 B2 **Sŏch'ŏn** S. Korea
49 L5 **Society Islands** Fr. Polynesia
150 B2 **Socorro** Col.
138 B2 **Socorro** NM U.S.A.
138 B2 **Socorro** TX U.S.A.
144 A3 **Socorro, Isla** i. Mex.
56 B4 **Socotra** i. Yemen
63 B3 **Soc Trăng** Vietnam
106 C2 **Socuéllamos** Spain
92 I2 **Sodankylä** Fin.
134 D2 **Soda Springs** U.S.A.
93 G3 **Söderhamn** Sweden
93 G4 **Södertälje** Sweden
116 A3 **Sodiri** Sudan
117 B4 **Sodo** Eth.
93 G3 **Södra Kvarken** str. Fin./Sweden
123 C1 **Soekmekaar** S. Africa
Soerabaia Indon. see Surabaya
101 D2 **Soest** Ger.
53 C2 **Sofala** Austr.
110 B2 **Sofia** Bulg.
Sofia Bulg. see Sofia
121 □D2 **Sofia** r. Madag.
Sofiyevka Ukr. see Vil'nyans'k
93 E3 **Sognefjorden** inlet Norway
111 D2 **Söğüt** Turkey
75 D1 **Sogxian** China
116 B2 **Sohâg** Egypt
Sohar Oman see Şuḩār
100 B2 **Soignies** Belgium
105 C2 **Soissons** France
90 A1 **Sokal'** Ukr.
65 B2 **Sokch'o** S. Korea
111 C3 **Söke** Turkey
81 C1 **Sokhumi** Georgia
114 C4 **Sokodé** Togo
89 F2 **Sokol** Rus. Fed.
101 F2 **Sokolov** Czech Rep.
115 C3 **Sokoto** Nigeria
115 C3 **Sokoto** r. Nigeria
90 B2 **Sokyryany** Ukr.
73 B3 **Solāpur** India
135 B3 **Soledad** U.S.A.
89 F2 **Soligalich** Rus. Fed.
99 C3 **Solihull** U.K.
86 E3 **Solikamsk** Rus. Fed.
87 E3 **Sol'-Iletsk** Rus. Fed.
100 C2 **Solingen** Ger.
122 A1 **Solitaire** Namibia
92 G3 **Sollefteå** Sweden
107 D2 **Sóller** Spain
101 D2 **Solling** hills Ger.
89 E2 **Solnechnogorsk** Rus. Fed.
60 B2 **Solok** Indon.
48 H4 **Solomon Islands** country S. Pacific Ocean
48 G4 **Solomon Sea** P.N.G./Solomon Is
61 D2 **Solor, Kepulauan** is Indon.
105 D2 **Solothurn** Switz.
81 D2 **Soltānābād** Iran
101 D1 **Soltau** Ger.
89 D1 **Sol'tsy** Rus. Fed.
96 C3 **Solway Firth** est. U.K.
120 B2 **Solwezi** Zambia
111 C4 **Soma** Turkey
117 C4 **Somalia** country Africa
120 B1 **Sombo** Angola
109 C1 **Sombor** Yugo.
144 B2 **Sombrerete** Mex.
140 C3 **Somerset** U.S.A.
123 C3 **Somerset East** S. Africa
126 F2 **Somerset Island** Can.
122 A3 **Somerset West** S. Africa
110 B1 **Someş** r. Romania
101 E2 **Sömmerda** Ger.
146 B3 **Somoto** Nic.
75 C2 **Son** r. India
93 E5 **Sønderborg** Denmark
101 E2 **Sondershausen** Ger.
Søndre Strømfjord inlet Greenland see Kangerlussuaq
108 A1 **Sondrio** Italy
63 B2 **Sông Cau** Vietnam
62 B1 **Sông Da, Hô** resr Vietnam
119 D4 **Songea** Tanz.

65 B1 Sŏnggan N. Korea
65 B1 Songhua Hu resr China
65 B1 Songjianghe China
Sŏngjin N. Korea see Kimch'aek
63 B3 Songkhla Thai.
69 E1 Songling China
65 B2 Sŏngnam S. Korea
65 B2 Songnim N. Korea
120 A1 Songo Angola
121 C2 Songo Moz.
Songololo Dem. Rep. Congo see Mbanza-Ngungu
69 E1 Songyuan China
Sonid Youqi China see Saihan Tal
74 B2 Sonipat India
89 E2 Sonkovo Rus. Fed.
62 B1 Son La Vietnam
74 A2 Sonmiani Pak.
74 A2 Sonmiani Bay Pak.
101 E2 Sonneberg Ger.
144 A2 Sonora r. Mex.
135 B3 Sonora CA U.S.A.
139 C2 Sonora TX U.S.A.
138 A2 Sonoyta Mex.
146 B3 Sonsonate El Salvador
Soochow China see Suzhou
117 A4 Sopo watercourse Sudan
103 D2 Sopron Hungary
74 B1 Sopur Jammu and Kashmir
108 B2 Sora Italy
130 C3 Sorel Can.
51 D4 Sorell Austr.
106 C1 Soria Spain
76 B2 Sor Mertvyy Kultuk dry lake Kazakh.
90 B2 Soroca Moldova
154 C2 Sorocaba Brazil
87 E3 Sorochinsk Rus. Fed.
Soroki Moldova see Soroca
59 D2 Sorol atoll Micronesia
59 C3 Sorong Indon.
119 D2 Soroti Uganda
92 H1 Sørøya i. Norway
108 B2 Sorrento Italy
92 G2 Sorsele Sweden
64 B2 Sorsogon Phil.
86 C2 Sortavala Rus. Fed.
92 G2 Sortland Norway
65 B2 Sŏsan S. Korea
123 C2 Soshanguve S. Africa
89 E3 Sosna r. Rus. Fed.
153 B3 Sosneado mt. Arg.
86 E2 Sosnogorsk Rus. Fed.
86 D2 Sosnovka Rus. Fed.
88 C2 Sosnovyy Bor Rus. Fed.
103 D1 Sosnowiec Pol.
91 C1 Sosnytsya Ukr.
86 F3 Sos'va Rus. Fed.
91 D2 Sosyka r. Rus. Fed.
145 C2 Soto la Marina Mex.
118 B2 Souanké Congo
111 B3 Souda Greece
104 C3 Souillac France
Sŏul S. Korea see Seoul
104 B2 Soulac-sur-Mer France
104 B3 Soulom France
80 B2 Soûr Lebanon
107 D2 Sour el Ghozlane Alg.
129 D3 Souris Man. Can.
131 D3 Souris P.E.I. Can.
129 E3 Souris r. Can.
151 F3 Sousa Brazil
115 D1 Sousse Tunisia
104 B3 Soustons France
122 B3 South Africa, Republic of country Africa
99 C4 Southampton U.K.
129 F1 Southampton, Cape Can.
129 F1 Southampton Island Can.
73 D3 South Andaman i. India
52 A1 South Australia state Austr.
142 B2 Southaven U.S.A.
138 B2 South Baldy mt. U.S.A.
130 B3 South Baymouth Can.
140 B2 South Bend U.S.A.
143 D2 South Carolina state U.S.A.
58 B2 South China Sea N. Pacific Ocean
South Coast Town Austr. see Gold Coast
136 C2 South Dakota state U.S.A.
99 C4 South Downs hills U.K.
159 E6 Southeast Indian Ridge sea feature Indian Ocean

55 O2 Southeast Pacific Basin sea feature S. Pacific Ocean
129 D2 Southend Can.
99 D4 Southend-on-Sea U.K.
54 B2 Southern Alps mts N.Z.
50 A3 Southern Cross Austr.
129 E2 Southern Indian Lake Can.
159 D7 Southern Ocean
143 E1 Southern Pines U.S.A.
Southern Rhodesia country Africa see Zimbabwe
96 B3 Southern Uplands hills U.K.
55 J2 South Geomagnetic Pole Antarctica
149 G8 South Georgia terr. S. Atlantic Ocean
149 G8 South Georgia and South Sandwich Islands terr. S. Atlantic Ocean
140 B2 South Haven U.S.A.
129 E1 South Henik Lake Can.
119 D2 South Horr Kenya
54 B2 South Island N.Z.
135 B3 South Lake Tahoe U.S.A.
55 K3 South Magnetic Pole Antarctica
128 B1 South Nahanni r. Can.
149 F9 South Orkney Islands S. Atlantic Ocean
136 C2 South Platte r. U.S.A.
98 B3 Southport U.K.
143 E2 Southport U.S.A.
130 C3 South River Can.
96 C1 South Ronaldsay i. U.K.
123 D3 South Sand Bluff pt S. Africa
149 H8 South Sandwich Islands S. Atlantic Ocean
55 C4 South Sandwich Trench sea feature S. Atlantic Ocean
129 D2 South Saskatchewan r. Can.
129 E2 South Seal r. Can.
149 E9 South Shetland Islands Antarctica
98 C2 South Shields U.K.
54 B1 South Taranaki Bight b. N.Z.
156 C8 South Tasman Rise sea feature Southern Ocean
130 C2 South Twin Island Can.
96 A2 South Uist i. U.K.
South-West Africa country Africa see Namibia
Southwest Peru Ridge sea feature S. Pacific Ocean see Nazca Ridge
53 D2 South West Rocks Austr.
99 D3 Southwold U.K.
109 C3 Soverato Italy
88 B2 Sovetsk Rus. Fed.
86 F2 Sovetskiy Rus. Fed.
91 C2 Sovyets'kyy Ukr.
123 C2 Soweto S. Africa
66 D1 Sōya-misaki c. Japan
65 B2 Soyang-ho l. S. Korea
104 C2 Soyaux France
90 C1 Sozh r. Europe
110 C2 Sozopol Bulg.
100 B2 Spa Belgium
106 C1 Spain country Europe
Spalato Croatia see Split
99 C3 Spalding U.K.
135 D2 Spanish Fork U.S.A.
Spanish Guinea country Africa see Equatorial Guinea
97 B2 Spanish Point Rep. of Ireland
Spanish Sahara terr. Africa see Western Sahara
146 C3 Spanish Town Jamaica
108 B3 Sparagio, Monte mt. Sicily Italy
135 C3 Sparks U.S.A.
140 A2 Sparta U.S.A.
111 B3 Sparti Greece
109 C3 Spartivento, Capo c. Italy
89 D3 Spas-Demensk Rus. Fed.
89 F2 Spas-Klepiki Rus. Fed.
66 D2 Spassk-Dal'niy Rus. Fed.
89 F3 Spassk-Ryazanskiy Rus. Fed.

111 B3 Spatha, Akra pt Greece
96 B2 Spean Bridge U.K.
136 C2 Spearfish U.S.A.
139 C1 Spearman U.S.A.
Spence Bay Can. see Taloyoak
137 D2 Spencer IA U.S.A.
134 D2 Spencer ID U.S.A.
52 A2 Spencer Gulf est. Austr.
98 C2 Spennymoor U.K.
54 B2 Spenser Mountains N.Z.
101 D3 Spessart reg. Ger.
96 C2 Spey r. U.K.
101 D3 Speyer Ger.
100 C1 Spiekeroog i. Ger.
100 B2 Spijkenisse Neth.
100 B3 Spincourt France
128 C2 Spirit River Can.
103 E2 Spišská Nová Ves Slovakia
82 C1 Spitsbergen i. Svalbard
102 C2 Spittal an der Drau Austria
93 E3 Spjelkavik Norway
109 C2 Split Croatia
129 E2 Split Lake Can.
129 E2 Split Lake l. Can.
134 C1 Spokane U.S.A.
140 A1 Spooner U.S.A.
102 C1 Spree r. Ger.
122 A2 Springbok S. Africa
131 E3 Springdale Can.
142 B1 Springdale U.S.A.
101 D1 Springe Ger.
138 C1 Springer U.S.A.
138 B2 Springerville U.S.A.
136 C3 Springfield CO U.S.A.
140 B3 Springfield IL U.S.A.
141 E2 Springfield MA U.S.A.
137 E3 Springfield MO U.S.A.
140 C3 Springfield OH U.S.A.
134 B2 Springfield OR U.S.A.
142 C1 Springfield TN U.S.A.
123 C3 Springfontein S. Africa
140 B3 Springhill U.S.A.
143 D3 Spring Hill U.S.A.
54 B2 Springs Junction N.Z.
51 D2 Springsure Austr.
135 D2 Springville U.S.A.
98 D3 Spurn Head hd U.K.
128 B3 Squamish Can.
109 C3 Squillace, Golfo di g. Italy
Srbija aut. rep. Yugo. see Serbia
110 C2 Sredets Bulg.
83 L3 Srednyy Khrebet mts Rus. Fed.
83 L2 Srednekolymsk Rus. Fed.
89 E3 Sredne-Russkaya Vozvyshennost' hills Rus. Fed.
83 I2 Sredne-Sibirskoye Ploskogor'ye plat. Rus. Fed.
110 B2 Srednogorie Bulg.
69 D1 Sretensk Rus. Fed.
61 C1 Sri Aman Sarawak Malaysia
73 B4 Sri Jayewardenepura Kotte Sri Lanka
73 C3 Srikakulam India
73 C4 Sri Lanka country Asia
74 B1 Srinagar Jammu and Kashmir
73 B3 Srivardhan India
101 D1 Stade Ger.
101 E1 Stadensen Ger.
100 C1 Stadskanaal Neth.
101 D2 Stadtallendorf Ger.
101 D1 Stadthagen Ger.
101 E2 Staffelstein Ger.
99 B3 Stafford U.K.
99 C4 Staines U.K.
91 D2 Stakhanov Ukr.
Stakhanov Rus. Fed. see Zhukovskiy
Stalin Bulg. see Varna
Stalinabad Tajik. see Dushanbe
Stalingrad Rus. Fed. see Volgograd
Staliniri Georgia see Ts'khinvali
Stalino Ukr. see Donets'k
Stalinogorsk Rus. Fed. see Novomoskovsk
Stalinogród Pol. see Katowice
Stalinsk Rus. Fed. see Novokuznetsk

103 E1 Stalowa Wola Pol.
140 B1 Stambaugh U.S.A.
99 C3 Stamford U.K.
141 E2 Stamford CT U.S.A.
139 D2 Stamford TX U.S.A.
Stampalia i. Greece see Astypalaia
122 A1 Stampriet Namibia
92 F2 Stamsund Norway
123 C2 Standerton S. Africa
140 C2 Standish U.S.A.
123 D2 Stanger S. Africa
Stanislav Ukr. see Ivano-Frankivs'k
Stanke Dimitrov Bulg. see Dupnitsa
153 C5 Stanley Falkland Is
136 C1 Stanley U.S.A.
Stanleyville Dem. Rep. Congo see Kisangani
Stann Creek Belize see Dangriga
111 B3 Stanos Greece
83 I3 Stanovoye Nagor'ye mts Rus. Fed.
83 J3 Stanovoy Khrebet mts Rus. Fed.
53 D1 Stanthorpe Austr.
137 E1 Staples U.S.A.
103 E1 Starachowice Pol.
Stara Planina mts Bulg./Yugo. see Balkan Mountains
89 D2 Staraya Rus. Fed.
89 D2 Staraya Toropa Rus. Fed.
110 C2 Stara Zagora Bulg.
49 L4 Starbuck Island Kiribati
103 D1 Stargard Szczeciński Pol.
89 D2 Staritsa Rus. Fed.
143 D3 Starke U.S.A.
142 C2 Starkville U.S.A.
102 C2 Sternberg Ger.
91 D2 Starobil's'k Ukr.
89 D3 Starodub Rus. Fed.
103 D1 Starogard Gdański Pol.
90 B2 Starokostyantyniv Ukr.
91 D2 Starominskaya Rus. Fed.
91 D2 Staroshcherbinovskaya Rus. Fed.
91 D2 Starotitarovskaya Rus. Fed.
89 F3 Staroyur'yevo Rus. Fed.
89 E3 Starozhilovo Rus. Fed.
99 B4 Start Point U.K.
88 C3 Staryya Darohi Belarus
86 G2 Staryy Nadym Rus. Fed.
89 E3 Staryy Oskol Rus. Fed.
101 E2 Staßfurt Ger.
103 E1 Staszów Pol.
141 D2 State College U.S.A.
143 D2 Statesboro U.S.A.
143 D1 Statesville U.S.A.
160 L1 Station Nord Greenland
141 D3 Staunton U.S.A.
93 E4 Stavanger Norway
87 D4 Stavropol' Rus. Fed.
Stavropol'-na-Volge Rus. Fed. see Tol'yatti
87 D4 Stavropol'skaya Vozvyshennost' hills Rus. Fed.
52 B3 Stawell Austr.
123 C2 Steadville S. Africa
136 B2 Steamboat Springs U.S.A.
101 E2 Stedten Ger.
128 C2 Steen River Can.
134 C2 Steens Mountain U.S.A.
100 C1 Steenwijk Neth.
126 E2 Stefansson Island Can.
Stegi Swaziland see Siteki
110 B1 Ştei Romania
101 E3 Steigerwald mts Ger.
100 B2 Stein Neth.
129 E3 Steinbach Can.
100 C1 Steinfurt Ger.
120 A3 Steinhausen Namibia
92 F3 Steinkjer Norway
122 A2 Steinkopf S. Africa
122 B2 Stella S. Africa
122 A3 Stellenbosch S. Africa
105 D3 Stello, Monte mt. Corsica France
105 D2 Stenay France
101 E1 Stendal Ger.
Steornabhagh U.K. see Stornoway
Stepanakert Azer. see Xankändi
52 B2 Stephens Creek Austr.
129 E2 Stephens Lake Can.

131 E3 **Stephenville** Can.
139 D2 **Stephenville** U.S.A.
Stepnoy Rus. Fed. *see* Elista
122 B3 **Sterling** S. Africa
136 C2 **Sterling** *CO* U.S.A.
140 B2 **Sterling** *IL* U.S.A.
136 C1 **Sterling** *ND* U.S.A.
140 C2 **Sterling Heights** U.S.A.
87 E3 **Sterlitamak** Rus. Fed.
101 E1 **Sternberg** Ger.
128 C2 **Stettler** Can.
140 C2 **Steubenville** U.S.A.
99 C4 **Stevenage** U.K.
129 E2 **Stevenson Lake** Can.
140 B2 **Stevens Point** U.S.A.
126 C2 **Stevens Village** U.S.A.
134 D1 **Stevensville** U.S.A.
128 B2 **Stewart** Can.
128 A1 **Stewart** *r.* Can.
54 A3 **Stewart Island** N.Z.
127 G2 **Stewart Lake** Can.
123 C3 **Steynsburg** S. Africa
102 C2 **Steyr** Austria
122 B3 **Steytlerville** S. Africa
128 A2 **Stikine** *r.* Can.
128 A2 **Stikine Plateau** Can.
122 B3 **Stilbaai** S. Africa
137 E1 **Stillwater** *MN* U.S.A.
139 D1 **Stillwater** *OK* U.S.A.
135 C3 **Stillwater Range** *mts* U.S.A.
109 D2 **Štip** Macedonia
96 C2 **Stirling** U.K.
52 A2 **Stirling North** Austr.
92 F3 **Stjørdalshalsen** Norway
103 D2 **Stockerau** Austria
93 G4 **Stockholm** Sweden
98 B3 **Stockport** U.K.
135 B3 **Stockton** U.S.A.
98 C2 **Stockton-on-Tees** U.K.
139 C2 **Stockton Plateau** U.S.A.
63 B2 **Stœng Trêng** Cambodia
96 B1 **Stoer, Point of** U.K.
99 B3 **Stoke-on-Trent** U.K.
98 C2 **Stokesley** U.K.
92 F2 **Stokmarknes** Norway
109 D2 **Stol** *mt.* Yugo.
109 C2 **Stolac** Bos.-Herz.
100 C2 **Stolberg (Rheinland)** Ger.
82 E2 **Stolbovoy** Rus. Fed.
88 C3 **Stolin** Belarus
101 F2 **Stollberg** Ger.
101 D1 **Stolzenau** Ger.
96 C2 **Stonehaven** U.K.
99 C4 **Stonehenge** *tourist site* U.K.
129 E2 **Stonewall** Can.
129 D2 **Stony Rapids** Can.
92 G2 **Storavan** *l.* Sweden
93 F4 **Store Bælt** *sea chan.* Denmark
92 F3 **Støren** Norway
92 I1 **Storfjordbotn** Norway
92 F2 **Storforshei** Norway
126 E2 **Storkerson Peninsula** Can.
137 D2 **Storm Lake** U.S.A.
93 E3 **Stornosa** *mt.* Norway
96 A1 **Stornoway** U.K.
86 E2 **Storozhevsk** Rus. Fed.
90 B2 **Storozhynets'** Ukr.
92 F3 **Storsjön** *l.* Sweden
92 H2 **Storslett** Norway
92 G2 **Storuman** Sweden
92 G2 **Storuman** *l.* Sweden
99 C4 **Stour** *r. England* U.K.
99 C3 **Stour** *r. England* U.K.
99 D4 **Stour** *r. England* U.K.
130 A2 **Stout Lake** Can.
88 C3 **Stowbtsy** Belarus
99 D3 **Stowmarket** U.K.
97 C1 **Strabane** U.K.
102 C2 **Strakonice** Czech Rep.
102 C1 **Stralsund** Ger.
122 A3 **Strand** S. Africa
93 E3 **Stranda** Norway
97 D1 **Strangford Lough** *inlet* U.K.
96 B3 **Stranraer** U.K.
105 D2 **Strasbourg** France
130 B3 **Stratford** Can.
54 B1 **Stratford** N.Z.
139 C1 **Stratford** U.S.A.
99 C3 **Stratford-upon-Avon** U.K.
128 C2 **Strathmore** Can.
96 C2 **Strathspey** *val.* U.K.
102 C2 **Straubing** Ger.
134 C2 **Strawberry Mountain** U.S.A.
51 C3 **Streaky Bay** Austr.

140 B2 **Streator** U.S.A.
99 B4 **Street** U.K.
110 B2 **Strehaia** Romania
94 B1 **Streymoy** *i.* Faroe Is
82 G2 **Strezhevoy** Rus. Fed.
101 F3 **Stříbro** Czech Rep.
111 B2 **Strimonas** *r.* Greece
153 B4 **Stroeder** Arg.
101 D1 **Ströhen** Ger.
109 C3 **Stromboli, Isola** *i.* Italy
96 B2 **Stromeferry** U.K.
96 C1 **Stromness** U.K.
92 G3 **Strömsund** Sweden
96 C1 **Stronsay** *i.* U.K.
53 D2 **Stroud** Austr.
99 B4 **Stroud** U.K.
100 C1 **Strücklingen (Saterland)** Ger.
111 B2 **Struga** Macedonia
88 C2 **Strugi-Krasnyye** Rus. Fed.
122 B3 **Struis Bay** S. Africa
111 B2 **Struma** *r.* Bulg.
99 A3 **Strumble Head** *hd* U.K.
111 B2 **Strumica** Macedonia
122 B2 **Strydenburg** S. Africa
93 E3 **Stryn** Norway
90 A2 **Stryy** Ukr.
90 A2 **Stryy** *r.* Ukr.
128 B2 **Stuart Lake** Can.
53 C2 **Stuart Town** Austr.
Stuchka Latvia *see* Aizkraukle
Stučka Latvia *see* Aizkraukle
130 A2 **Stull Lake** Can.
89 E3 **Stupino** Rus. Fed.
55 M3 **Sturge Island** Antarctica
140 B2 **Sturgeon Bay** U.S.A.
130 C3 **Sturgeon Falls** Can.
130 A3 **Sturgeon Lake** Can.
140 B2 **Sturgis** *MI* U.S.A.
136 C2 **Sturgis** *SD* U.S.A.
52 B1 **Sturt, Mount** *hill* Austr.
50 B1 **Sturt Creek** *watercourse* Austr.
50 C1 **Sturt Plain** Austr.
52 B1 **Sturt Stony Desert** Austr.
123 C3 **Stutterheim** S. Africa
102 B2 **Stuttgart** Ger.
142 B2 **Stuttgart** U.S.A.
92 □A2 **Stykkishólmur** Iceland
90 B1 **Styr** *r.* Belarus/Ukr.
155 D1 **Suaçuí Grande** *r.* Brazil
116 B3 **Suakin** Sudan
71 C3 **Suao** Taiwan
78 A3 **Suara, Mount** Eritrea
60 B1 **Subi Besar** *i.* Indon.
109 C1 **Subotica** Yugo.
110 C1 **Suceava** Romania
Suchan Rus. Fed. *see* Partizansk
97 B2 **Suck** *r.* Rep. of Ireland
152 B1 **Sucre** Bol.
154 B2 **Sucuriú** *r.* Brazil
Suczawa Romania *see* Suceava
89 E2 **Suda** Rus. Fed.
91 C3 **Sudak** Ukr.
116 A3 **Sudan** *country* Africa
130 B3 **Sudbury** Can.
99 D3 **Sudbury** U.K.
117 A4 **Sudd** *swamp* Sudan
89 F2 **Sudislavl'** Rus. Fed.
89 F2 **Sudogda** Rus. Fed.
94 B1 **Suðuroy** *i.* Faroe Is
89 E3 **Sudzha** Rus. Fed.
107 C2 **Sueca** Spain
116 B2 **Suez** Egypt
116 B2 **Suez, Gulf of** Egypt
80 B2 **Suez Canal** *canal* Egypt
141 D3 **Suffolk** U.S.A.
143 A2 **Sugar Land** U.S.A.
141 E1 **Sugarloaf Mountain** U.S.A.
53 D2 **Sugarloaf Point** Austr.
70 A2 **Suhait** China
79 C2 **Şuḩār** Oman
68 D1 **Sühbaatar** Mongolia
101 E2 **Suhl** Ger.
109 C1 **Suhopolje** Croatia
70 B2 **Suide** China
66 B2 **Suifenhe** China
69 E1 **Suihua** China
70 A2 **Suining** China
70 B2 **Suiping** China
97 C2 **Suir** *r.* Rep. of Ireland
Suixian China *see* Suizhou
70 B2 **Suizhou** China
74 B2 **Sujangarh** India
74 B1 **Sujanpur** India

74 A2 **Sujawal** Pak.
60 B2 **Sukabumi** Indon.
60 B2 **Sukadana** Indon.
67 D3 **Sukagawa** Japan
Sukarnapura Indon. *see* Jayapura
Sukarno, Puntjak *mt.* Indon. *see* Jaya, Puncak
89 E3 **Sukhinichi** Rus. Fed.
89 F2 **Sukhona** *r.* Rus. Fed.
62 A2 **Sukhothai** Thai.
74 A2 **Sukkur** Pak.
89 E2 **Sukromny** Rus. Fed.
59 C3 **Sula, Kepulauan** *is* Indon.
74 A1 **Sulaiman Ranges** *mts* Pak.
61 D2 **Sulawesi** *i.* Indon.
101 D1 **Sulingen** Ger.
150 A3 **Sullana** Peru
140 B3 **Sullivan** *IN* U.S.A.
137 E3 **Sullivan** *MO* U.S.A.
142 B2 **Sulphur** U.S.A.
139 D2 **Sulphur Springs** U.S.A.
140 C1 **Sultan** Can.
Sultanabad Iran *see* Arāk
64 B3 **Sulu Archipelago** *is* Phil.
64 A3 **Sulu Sea** N. Pacific Ocean
101 E3 **Sulzbach-Rosenberg** Ger.
79 C2 **Sumāil** Oman
60 A1 **Sumatera** *i.* Indon.
Sumatra *i.* Indon. *see* Sumatera
61 D2 **Sumba** *i.* Indon.
61 C2 **Sumba, Selat** *sea chan.* Indon.
61 C2 **Sumbawa** *i.* Indon.
61 C2 **Sumbawabesar** Indon.
119 D3 **Sumbawanga** Tanz.
120 A2 **Sumbe** Angola
96 □ **Sumburgh** U.K.
96 □ **Sumburgh Head** *hd* U.K.
119 C2 **Sumeih** Sudan
61 C2 **Sumenep** Indon.
67 D4 **Sumisu-jima** *i.* Japan
131 D3 **Summerside** Can.
140 C3 **Summersville** U.S.A.
143 D2 **Summerville** U.S.A.
137 D1 **Summit Lake** Can.
128 B2 **Summit Lake** Can.
103 D2 **Šumperk** Czech Rep.
81 C1 **Sumqayıt** Azer.
143 D2 **Sumter** U.S.A.
91 C1 **Sumy** Ukr.
75 C2 **Sunamganj** Bangl.
65 B2 **Sunan** N. Korea
79 C2 **Şunaynah** Oman
52 B3 **Sunbury** Austr.
141 D2 **Sunbury** U.S.A.
65 B2 **Sunch'ŏn** N. Korea
65 B3 **Sunch'ŏn** S. Korea
123 C2 **Sun City** S. Africa
93 H3 **Sund** Fin.
60 B2 **Sunda, Selat** *str.* Indon.
136 C2 **Sundance** U.S.A.
75 C2 **Sundarbans** *reg.* Bangl./India
74 B1 **Sundarnagar** India
Sunda Strait Indon. *see* Sunda, Selat
Sunda Trench *sea feature* Indian Ocean *see* Java Trench
98 C2 **Sunderland** U.K.
128 C2 **Sundre** Can.
93 G3 **Sundsvall** Sweden
123 D2 **Sundumbili** S. Africa
60 B2 **Sungailiat** Indon.
60 B2 **Sungaipenuh** Indon.
60 B1 **Sungai Petani** Malaysia
80 B1 **Sungurlu** Turkey
75 C2 **Sun Kosi** *r.* Nepal
93 E3 **Sunndalsøra** Norway
134 C1 **Sunnyside** U.S.A.
135 B3 **Sunnyvale** U.S.A.
143 D3 **Sunrise** U.S.A.
83 I2 **Suntar** Rus. Fed.
74 A2 **Suntsar** Pak.
114 B4 **Sunyani** Ghana
92 I3 **Suomussalmi** Fin.
67 B4 **Suō-nada** *b.* Japan
86 C2 **Suoyarvi** Rus. Fed.
138 A2 **Superior** *AZ* U.S.A.
137 D2 **Superior** *NE* U.S.A.
140 A1 **Superior** *WI* U.S.A.
140 B1 **Superior, Lake** Can./U.S.A.
63 B2 **Suphan Buri** Thai.
81 C2 **Suphan Dağı** *mt.* Turkey
89 D3 **Suponevo** Rus. Fed.
81 C2 **Sūq ash Shuyūkh** Iraq
70 B2 **Suqian** China

78 A2 **Sūq Suwayq** Saudi Arabia
Suquṭrā *i.* Yemen *see* Socotra
79 C2 **Şūr** Oman
74 A2 **Surab** Pak.
61 C2 **Surabaya** Indon.
61 C2 **Surakarta** Indon.
74 B2 **Surat** India
74 B2 **Suratgarh** India
63 A3 **Surat Thani** Thai.
89 D3 **Surazh** Rus. Fed.
109 D2 **Surdulica** Yugo.
100 C3 **Sûre** *r.* Lux.
74 B2 **Surendranagar** India
82 F2 **Surgut** Rus. Fed.
64 B3 **Surigao** Phil.
63 B2 **Surin** Thai.
151 D2 **Suriname** *country* S. America
75 C2 **Surkhet** Nepal
Surt Libya *see* Sirte
Surt, Khalīj *g.* Libya *see* Sirte, Gulf of
60 B2 **Surulangun** Indon.
81 C2 **Süsangerd** Iran
89 F2 **Susanino** Rus. Fed.
135 B2 **Susanville** U.S.A.
80 B1 **Suşehri** Turkey
141 D3 **Susquehanna** *r.* U.S.A.
131 D3 **Sussex** Can.
101 D1 **Süstedt** Ger.
100 C1 **Sustrum** Ger.
83 K2 **Susuman** Rus. Fed.
111 C3 **Susurluk** Turkey
74 B1 **Sutak** Jammu and Kashmir
53 D2 **Sutherland** Austr.
122 B3 **Sutherland** S. Africa
136 C2 **Sutherland** U.S.A.
134 B2 **Sutherlin** U.S.A.
74 B2 **Sutlej** *r.* India/Pak.
140 C3 **Sutton** U.S.A.
99 C3 **Sutton Coldfield** U.K.
98 C3 **Sutton in Ashfield** U.K.
66 D2 **Suttsu** Japan
49 I5 **Suva** Fiji
Suvalki Pol. *see* Suwałki
89 E3 **Suvorov** Rus. Fed.
90 B2 **Suvorove** Ukr.
103 E1 **Suwałki** Pol.
143 D3 **Suwanee Sound** *b.* U.S.A.
63 B2 **Suwannaphum** Thai.
143 D3 **Suwannee** *r.* U.S.A.
Suweis, Qanâ el *canal* Egypt *see* Suez Canal
65 B2 **Suwŏn** S. Korea
79 C2 **Sūzā** Iran
71 C2 **Suzdal'** Rus. Fed.
89 D3 **Suzemka** Rus. Fed.
70 C2 **Suzhou** *Anhui* China
70 C2 **Suzhou** *Jiangsu* China
67 C3 **Suzu** Japan
67 C3 **Suzu-misaki** *pt* Japan
82 B1 **Svalbard** *terr.* Arctic Ocean
90 A2 **Svalyava** Ukr.
92 H2 **Svappavaara** Sweden
91 D2 **Svatove** Ukr.
63 B2 **Svay Riêng** Cambodia
93 F3 **Sveg** Sweden
88 C2 **Švenčionys** Lith.
93 F4 **Svendborg** Denmark
Sverdlovsk Rus. Fed. *see* Yekaterinburg
111 B2 **Sveti Nikole** Macedonia
66 C1 **Svetlaya** Rus. Fed.
88 B3 **Svetlogorsk** Rus. Fed.
87 D4 **Svetlograd** Rus. Fed.
88 B3 **Svetlyy** Rus. Fed.
93 I3 **Svetogorsk** Rus. Fed.
103 E2 **Svidník** Slovakia
111 C2 **Svilengrad** Bulg.
110 B2 **Svinecea Mare, Vârful** *mt.* Romania
110 C2 **Svishtov** Bulg.
88 B3 **Svislach** Belarus
103 D2 **Svitavy** Czech Rep.
91 C2 **Svitlovods'k** Ukr.
69 E1 **Svobodnyy** Rus. Fed.
110 B2 **Svoge** Bulg.
92 F2 **Svolvær** Norway
88 C3 **Svyetlahorsk** Belarus
143 D2 **Swainsboro** U.S.A.
120 A3 **Swakopmund** Namibia
52 B3 **Swan Hill** Austr.
128 C2 **Swan Hills** Can.
128 C2 **Swan Lake** Can.
97 C1 **Swanlinbar** Rep. of Ireland
129 D2 **Swan River** Can.
53 D2 **Swansea** Austr.
99 B4 **Swansea** U.K.

122 B3 **Swartkolkvloer** *salt pan* S. Africa
123 C2 **Swartruggens** S. Africa
Swatow China *see* Shantou
123 D2 **Swaziland** *country* Africa
93 G3 **Sweden** *country* Europe
139 C2 **Sweetwater** U.S.A.
136 B2 **Sweetwater** *r.* U.S.A.
122 B3 **Swellendam** S. Africa
103 D1 **Świdnica** Pol.
103 D1 **Świdwin** Pol.
103 D1 **Świebodzin** Pol.
103 D1 **Świecie** Pol.
129 D2 **Swift Current** Can.
97 C1 **Swilly, Lough** *inlet* Rep. of Ireland
99 C4 **Swindon** U.K.
102 C1 **Świnoujście** Pol.
105 D2 **Switzerland** *country* Europe
97 C2 **Swords** Rep. of Ireland
88 C3 **Syanno** Belarus
89 C1 **Syas'troy** Rus. Fed.
89 D2 **Sychevka** Rus. Fed.
53 D2 **Sydney** Austr.
131 D3 **Sydney** Can.
131 D3 **Sydney Mines** Can.
91 D2 **Syeverodonets'k** Ukr.
86 E2 **Syktyvkar** Rus. Fed.
142 C2 **Sylacauga** U.S.A.
75 D2 **Sylhet** Bangl.
102 B1 **Sylt** *i.* Ger.
140 C2 **Sylvania** U.S.A.
51 C1 **Sylvester, Lake** *salt flat* Austr.
111 C3 **Symi** *i.* Greece
91 D2 **Synel'nykove** Ukr.
90 C2 **Synyukha** *r.* Ukr.
109 C3 **Syracuse** *Sicily* Italy
136 C3 **Syracuse** *KS* U.S.A.
141 D2 **Syracuse** *NY* U.S.A.
77 C2 **Syrdar'ya** *r.* Asia
80 B2 **Syria** *country* Asia
63 A2 **Syriam** Myanmar
80 B2 **Syrian Desert** Asia
111 B3 **Syros** *i.* Greece
91 D2 **Syvash, Zatoka** *lag.* Ukr.
91 C2 **Syvas'ke** Ukr.
87 D3 **Syzran'** Rus. Fed.
102 C1 **Szczecin** Pol.
103 D1 **Szczecinek** Pol.
103 E1 **Szczytno** Pol.
Szechwan *prov.* China *see* Sichuan
103 E2 **Szeged** Hungary
103 D2 **Székesfehérvár** Hungary
103 D2 **Szekszárd** Hungary
103 E2 **Szentes** Hungary
103 D2 **Szentgotthárd** Hungary
103 D2 **Szerencs** Hungary
103 E2 **Szolnok** Hungary
103 D2 **Szombathely** Hungary
Sztálinváros Hungary *see* Dunaújváros

T

117 C4 **Taagga Duudka** *reg.* Somalia
64 B2 **Tabaco** Phil.
78 B2 **Tābah** Saudi Arabia
108 A3 **Tabarka** Tunisia
76 B3 **Tabas** Iran
79 C1 **Tabāsīn** Iran
81 D3 **Tābask, Kūh-e** *mt.* Iran
150 C3 **Tabatinga** Brazil
154 C2 **Tabatinga** Brazil
114 B2 **Tabelbala** Alg.
128 C3 **Taber** Can.
64 B2 **Tablas** *i.* Phil.
102 C2 **Tábor** Czech Rep.
119 D3 **Tabora** Tanz.
114 B4 **Tabou** Côte d'Ivoire
81 C2 **Tabriz** Iran
48 L3 **Tabuaeran** *i.* Kiribati
78 A2 **Tabūk** Saudi Arabia
93 G4 **Täby** Sweden
77 E2 **Tacheng** China
102 C2 **Tachov** Czech Rep.
64 B2 **Tacloban** Phil.
150 B4 **Tacna** Peru
134 B1 **Tacoma** U.S.A.
152 C4 **Tacuarembó** Uru.
138 B3 **Tacupeto** Mex.
114 C2 **Tademaït, Plateau du** Alg.
114 C2 **Tadjikistan** *country* Asia *see* Tajikistan

117 C3 **Tadjoura** Djibouti
80 B2 **Tadmur** Syria
129 E2 **Tadoule Lake** Can.
Tädzhikskaya S.S.R. *country* Asia *see* Tajikistan
65 B2 **T'aebaek-sanmaek** *mts* N. Korea/S. Korea
Taech'ŏn S. Korea *see* Poryŏng
65 B2 **Taegu** S. Korea
65 B2 **Taejŏn** S. Korea
65 B3 **Taejŏng** S. Korea
65 B2 **T'aepaek** S. Korea
107 C1 **Tafalla** Spain
152 B2 **Tafí Viejo** Arg.
79 D2 **Taftān, Kūh-e** *mt.* Iran
91 D2 **Taganrog** Rus. Fed.
91 D2 **Taganrog, Gulf of** Rus. Fed./Ukr.
62 A1 **Tagaung** Myanmar
64 B2 **Tagaytay City** Phil.
64 B3 **Tagbilaran** Phil.
64 B2 **Tagudin** Phil.
51 E1 **Tagula Island** P.N.G.
64 B3 **Tagum** Phil.
106 B2 **Tagus** *r.* Port./Spain
60 B1 **Tahan, Gunung** *mt.* Malaysia
115 C2 **Tahat, Mont** *mt.* Alg.
69 E1 **Tahe** China
49 M5 **Tahiti** *i.* Fr. Polynesia
139 E1 **Tahlequah** U.S.A.
135 B3 **Tahoe, Lake** U.S.A.
135 B3 **Tahoe City** U.S.A.
126 E2 **Tahoe Lake** Can.
115 C3 **Tahoua** Niger
79 C2 **Tahrūd** Iran
128 B3 **Tahsis** Can.
116 B2 **Tahta** Egypt
64 B3 **Tahuna** Indon.
70 B2 **Tai'an** China
70 A2 **Taibai Shan** *mt.* China
Taibus Qi China *see* Baochang
71 C3 **T'aichung** Taiwan
70 B2 **Taihang Shan** *mts* China
54 C1 **Taihape** N.Z.
71 B3 **Taihe** China
70 C2 **Tai Hu** *l.* China
52 A3 **Tailem Bend** Austr.
71 C3 **T'ainan** Taiwan
111 B3 **Tainaro, Akra** *pt* Greece
155 D1 **Taiobeiras** Brazil
71 C3 **T'aipei** Taiwan
Taiping China *see* Chongzuo
60 B1 **Taiping** Malaysia
Tairbeart U.K. *see* Tarbert
71 B3 **Taishan** China
153 A4 **Tai Shan** *hills* China
Taitao, Península de *pen.* Chile
71 C3 **T'aitung** Taiwan
92 I2 **Taivalkoski** Fin.
92 H2 **Taivaskero** *hill* Fin.
71 C3 **Taiwan** Asia
Taiwan Shan *mts* Taiwan *see* Chungyang Shanmo
71 B3 **Taiwan Strait** China/Taiwan
70 B2 **Taiyuan** China
70 B2 **Taizhou** *Jiangsu* China
71 C3 **Taizhou** *Zhejiang* China
78 B3 **Ta'izz** Yemen
145 C3 **Tajamulco, Volcán de** *vol.* Guat.
77 D3 **Tajikistan** *country* Asia
74 B2 **Taj Mahal** *tourist site* India
Tajo *r.* Spain *see* Tagus
63 A2 **Tak** Thai.
54 B2 **Takaka** N.Z.
115 C2 **Takalous, Oued** *watercourse* Alg.
67 B4 **Takamatsu** Japan
67 C3 **Takaoka** Japan
54 B1 **Takapuna** N.Z.
67 C3 **Takasaki** Japan
122 B1 **Takatokwane** Botswana
122 B1 **Takatshwaane** Botswana
67 C3 **Takayama** Japan
67 C3 **Takefu** Japan
60 A1 **Takengon** Indon.
67 C4 **Takēv** Cambodia
Takhiatash Uzbek. *see* Gulabie
63 B2 **Ta Khmau** Cambodia
74 B1 **Takht-i-Sulaiman** *mt.* Pak.
66 D2 **Takikawa** Japan
128 B2 **Takla Lake** Can.
128 B2 **Takla Landing** Can.

Takla Makan *des.* China *see* Taklimakan Shamo
Taklimakan Desert China *see* Taklimakan Shamo
77 E3 **Taklimakan Shamo** *des.* China
128 A2 **Taku** *r.* Can./U.S.A.
63 A3 **Takua Pa** Thai.
115 C4 **Takum** Nigeria
88 C3 **Talachyn** Belarus
74 B1 **Talagang** Pak.
146 B4 **Talamanca, Cordillera de** *mts* Costa Rica
150 A3 **Talara** Peru
74 A2 **Talar-i-Band** *mts* Pak.
59 C2 **Talaud, Kepulauan** *is* Indon.
106 C2 **Talavera de la Reina** Spain
153 A3 **Talca** Chile
153 A3 **Talcahuano** Chile
89 E2 **Taldom** Rus. Fed.
77 D2 **Taldykorgan** Kazakh.
Taldy-Kurgan Kazakh. *see* Taldykorgan
59 C3 **Taliabu** *i.* Indon.
64 B2 **Talisay** Phil.
61 C2 **Taliwang** Indon.
81 C2 **Tall 'Afar** Iraq
143 D2 **Tallahassee** U.S.A.
53 C3 **Tallangatta** Austr.
88 B2 **Tallinn** Estonia
142 B2 **Tallulah** U.S.A.
104 B2 **Talmont-St-Hilaire** France
90 C2 **Tal'ne** Ukr.
117 B3 **Talodi** Sudan
74 A1 **Tāloqān** Afgh.
91 E1 **Talovaya** Rus. Fed.
126 F2 **Taloyoak** Can.
88 B2 **Talsi** Latvia
152 A2 **Taltal** Chile
129 C1 **Taltson** *r.* Can.
60 A1 **Talu** Indon.
53 C1 **Talwood** Austr.
114 B4 **Tamale** Ghana
115 C2 **Tamanrasset** Alg.
99 A4 **Tamar** *r.* U.K.
Tamatave Madag. *see* Toamasina
144 B2 **Tamazula** Mex.
145 C2 **Tamazunchale** Mex.
114 A3 **Tambacounda** Senegal
60 B1 **Tambelan, Kepulauan** *is* Indon.
86 G1 **Tambey** Rus. Fed.
61 C1 **Tambisan** *Sabah* Malaysia
61 C2 **Tambora, Gunung** *vol.* Indon.
91 E1 **Tambov** Rus. Fed.
119 C2 **Tambura** Sudan
62 A1 **Tamenglong** India
145 C2 **Tamiahua, Laguna de** *lag.* Mex.
Tammerfors Fin. *see* Tampere
143 D3 **Tampa** U.S.A.
143 D3 **Tampa Bay** U.S.A.
93 H3 **Tampere** Fin.
145 C2 **Tampico** Mex.
69 D1 **Tamsagbulag** Mongolia
102 C2 **Tamsweg** Austria
53 D2 **Tamworth** Austr.
99 C3 **Tamworth** U.K.
119 E3 **Tana** *r.* Kenya
Tana, Lake Eth. *see* T'ana Hāyk'
67 C4 **Tanabe** Japan
92 I1 **Tana Bru** Norway
117 B3 **T'ana Hāyk'** *l.* Eth.
60 A2 **Tanahbala** *i.* Indon.
61 C2 **Tanahgrogot** Indon.
61 D2 **Tanahjampea** *i.* Indon.
60 A2 **Tanahmasa** *i.* Indon.
50 C1 **Tanami Desert** Austr.
63 B2 **Tân An** Vietnam
126 B2 **Tanana** U.S.A.
Tananarive Madag. *see* Antananarivo
108 A1 **Tanaro** *r.* Italy
65 B1 **Tanch'ŏn** N. Korea
64 B3 **Tandag** Phil.
110 C2 **Tāndārei** Romania
153 C3 **Tandil** Arg.
74 A2 **Tando Adam** Pak.
74 A2 **Tando Muhammmad Khan** Pak.
52 B2 **Tandou Lake** *imp. l.* Austr.
67 B4 **Tanega-shima** *i.* Japan
114 B2 **Tanezrouft** *reg.* Alg./Mali
119 D3 **Tanga** Tanz.
75 C2 **Tangail** Bangl.

Tanganyika *country* Africa *see* Tanzania
119 C3 **Tanganyika, Lake** Africa
55 F3 **Tange Promontory** *hd* Antarctica
Tanger Morocco *see* Tangier
75 D1 **Tanggula Shan** *mt.* China
75 C1 **Tanggula Shan** *mts* China
114 B1 **Tangier** Morocco
75 C1 **Tangra Yumco** *salt l.* China
70 B2 **Tangshan** China
68 C2 **Taniantaweng Shan** *mts* China
59 C3 **Tanimbar, Kepulauan** *is* Indon.
64 B3 **Tanjay** Phil.
61 C2 **Tanjung** Indon.
60 A1 **Tanjungbalai** Indon.
60 B2 **Tanjungkarang-Telukbetung** Indon.
60 B2 **Tanjungpandan** Indon.
60 B1 **Tanjungpinang** Indon.
61 C1 **Tanjungredeb** Indon.
61 C1 **Tanjungselor** Indon.
74 B1 **Tank** Pak.
48 H5 **Tanna** *i.* Vanuatu
115 C3 **Tanout** Niger
75 C2 **Tansen** Nepal
116 B1 **Tanta** Egypt
114 A2 **Tan-Tan** Morocco
145 C2 **Tantoyuca** Mex.
119 D3 **Tanzania** *country* Africa
Tao'an China *see* Taonan
Taocheng China *see* Yongchun
Taolanaro Madag. *see* Tôlañaro
69 E1 **Taonan** China
109 C3 **Taormina** *Sicily* Italy
138 B1 **Taos** U.S.A.
114 B2 **Taoudenni** Mali
114 B1 **Taounate** Morocco
114 B1 **Taourirt** Morocco
88 C2 **Tapa** Estonia
145 C3 **Tapachula** Mex.
151 D3 **Tapajós** *r.* Brazil
60 A1 **Tapaktuan** Indon.
145 C3 **Tapanatepec** Mex.
150 C3 **Tapauá** Brazil
114 B4 **Tapeta** Liberia
74 B2 **Tāpi** *r.* India
141 D3 **Tappahannock** U.S.A.
54 B2 **Tapuaenuku** *mt.* N.Z.
150 C3 **Tapurucuara** Brazil
154 B1 **Taquaral, Serra do** *hills* Brazil
154 B1 **Taquari** Brazil
154 A1 **Taquari** *r.* Brazil
154 B1 **Taquari, Serra do** *hills* Brazil
154 C2 **Taquaritinga** Brazil
53 D1 **Tara** Austr.
115 D4 **Taraba** *r.* Nigeria
Țarābulus Libya *see* Tripoli
54 C1 **Taradale** N.Z.
61 C1 **Tarakan** Indon.
111 D2 **Tarakli** Turkey
88 A3 **Taran, Mys** *pt* Rus. Fed.
Taranaki, Mount *vol.* N.Z. *see* Egmont, Mount
106 C2 **Tarancón** Spain
109 C2 **Taranto** Italy
109 C2 **Taranto, Golfo di** *g.* Italy
150 B3 **Tarapoto** Peru
90 C2 **Tarashcha** Ukr.
91 E2 **Tarasovskiy** Rus. Fed.
150 B3 **Tarauacá** Brazil
150 C3 **Tarauacá** *r.* Brazil
48 I3 **Tarawa** *atoll* Kiribati
54 B1 **Tarawera** N.Z.
77 D2 **Taraz** Kazakh.
107 C1 **Tarazona** Spain
77 E2 **Tarbagatay, Khrebet** *mts* Kazakh.
96 C2 **Tarbat Ness** *pt* U.K.
97 B2 **Tarbert** Rep. of Ireland
96 A2 **Tarbert** *Scotland* U.K.
96 B3 **Tarbert** *Scotland* U.K.
104 C3 **Tarbes** France
96 B2 **Tarbet** U.K.
143 E1 **Tarboro** U.S.A.
52 A2 **Tarcoola** Austr.
53 D2 **Taree** Austr.
110 C1 **Târgoviște** Romania
110 C1 **Târgu Frumos** Romania
110 B1 **Târgu Jiu** Romania
110 B1 **Târgu Lăpuş** Romania
110 B1 **Târgu Mureş** Romania

110 C1 Târgu Neamţ Romania
110 C1 Târgu Ocna Romania
79 C2 Tarif U.A.E.
152 B2 Tarija Bol.
79 B3 Tarīm Yemen
Tarim Basin China see
Tarim Pendi
119 D3 Tarime Tanz.
77 E2 Tarim He r. China
77 E3 Tarim Pendi basin China
77 C3 Tarīn Kowt Afgh.
59 D3 Taritatu r. Indon.
123 C3 Tarkastad S. Africa
82 G2 Tarko-Sale Rus. Fed.
114 B4 Tarkwa Ghana
64 B2 Tarlac Phil.
105 C3 Tarn r. France
92 G2 Tärnaby Sweden
77 C3 Tarnak r. Afgh.
110 B1 Târnăveni Romania
103 E1 Tarnobrzeg Pol.
Tarnopol Ukr. see Ternopil'
103 E1 Tarnów Pol.
51 D2 Taroom Austr.
114 B1 Taroudannt Morocco
143 D3 Tarpon Springs U.S.A.
108 B2 Tarquinia Italy
107 D1 Tarragona Spain
107 D1 Tàrrega Spain
80 B2 Tarsus Turkey
152 B2 Tartagal Arg.
104 B3 Tartas France
88 C2 Tartu Estonia
80 B2 Tarţūs Syria
155 D1 Tarumirim Brazil
89 E3 Tarusa Rus. Fed.
90 B2 Tarutyne Ukr.
108 B1 Tarvisio Italy
Tashauz Turkm. see
Dashkhovuz
Tashi Chho Bhutan see
Thimphu
81 D3 Tashk, Daryācheh-ye l.
Iran
77 C2 Tashkent Uzbek.
130 C2 Tasiat, Lac l. Can.
131 D2 Tasiujaq Can.
77 E2 Taskesken Kazakh.
54 B2 Tasman Bay N.Z.
51 D4 Tasmania state Austr.
54 B2 Tasman Mountains N.Z.
156 D8 Tasman Sea
S. Pacific Ocean
130 C2 Tassialujjuaq, Lac l. Can.
115 C2 Tassili du Hoggar plat.
Alg.
115 C2 Tassili n'Ajjer plat. Alg.
61 D2 Tataba Indon.
103 D2 Tatabánya Hungary
90 B2 Tatarbunary Ukr.
83 K3 Tatarskiy Proliv str.
Rus. Fed.
Tatar Strait Rus. Fed. see
Tatarskiy Proliv
67 C4 Tateyama Japan
128 C1 Tathlina Lake Can.
78 B3 Tathlīth Saudi Arabia
78 B2 Tathlīth, Wādī
watercourse Saudi Arabia
53 C3 Tathra Austr.
62 A1 Tatkon Myanmar
128 B2 Tatla Lake Can.
103 D2 Tatra Mountains
Pol./Slovakia
Tatry mts Pol./Slovakia see
Tatra Mountains
74 A2 Tatta Pak.
154 C2 Tatuí Brazil
139 C2 Tatum U.S.A.
81 C2 Tatvan Turkey
151 E3 Taua Brazil
155 C2 Taubaté Brazil
101 D3 Tauberbischofsheim Ger.
54 C1 Taumarunui N.Z.
122 B2 Taung S. Africa
62 A1 Taunggyi Myanmar
62 A2 Taunqup Myanmar
74 B1 Taunsa Pak.
99 B3 Taunton U.K.
101 C2 Taunus hills Ger.
54 C1 Taupo N.Z.
54 C1 Taupo, Lake N.Z.
88 B2 Tauragė Lith.
54 C1 Tauranga N.Z.
141 E1 Taureau, Réservoir resr
Can.
Taurus Mountains Turkey
see Toros Dağları
111 C3 Tavas Turkey
86 F3 Tavda Rus. Fed.
106 B2 Tavira Port.

99 A4 Tavistock U.K.
63 A2 Tavoy Myanmar
111 C3 Tavşanlı Turkey
99 A4 Taw r. U.K.
140 C2 Tawas City U.S.A.
61 C1 Tawau Sabah Malaysia
64 A3 Tawitawi i. Phil.
71 C3 Tawu Taiwan
145 C3 Taxco Mex.
77 D3 Taxkorgan China
96 C2 Tay r. U.K.
96 C2 Tay, Firth of est. U.K.
96 B2 Tay, Loch l. U.K.
128 B2 Taylor Can.
140 C2 Taylor MI U.S.A.
139 D2 Taylor TX U.S.A.
140 B3 Taylorville U.S.A.
78 A2 Taymā' Saudi Arabia
83 H2 Taymura r. Rus. Fed.
83 H2 Taymyr, Ozero l. Rus. Fed.
83 G2 Taymyr, Poluostrov pen.
Rus. Fed.
Taymyr Peninsula
Rus. Fed. see
Taymyr, Poluostrov
63 B2 Tây Ninh Vietnam
96 C2 Tayport U.K.
64 A2 Taytay Phil.
76 C3 Tayyebād Iran
77 C1 Tayynsha Kazakh.
82 G2 Taz r. Rus. Fed.
114 B1 Taza Morocco
129 D2 Tazin Lake Can.
86 G2 Tazovskaya Guba
sea chan. Rus. Fed.
81 C1 T'bilisi Georgia
91 E2 Tbilisskaya Rus. Fed.
118 B3 Tchibanga Gabon
115 C3 Tchin-Tabaradene Niger
118 B2 Tcholliré Cameroon
103 D1 Tczew Pol.
144 B2 Teacapán Mex.
54 A3 Te Anau N.Z.
54 A3 Te Anau, Lake N.Z.
145 C3 Teapa Mex.
54 C1 Te Awamutu N.Z.
115 C1 Tébessa Alg.
60 B2 Tebingtinggi Indon.
60 A1 Tebingtinggi Indon.
144 A1 Tecate Mex.
114 B4 Techiman Ghana
144 B3 Tecomán Mex.
144 B2 Tecoripa Mex.
145 B3 Técpan Mex.
144 B2 Tecuala Mex.
110 C1 Tecuci Romania
76 C3 Tedzhen Turkm.
76 C3 Tedzhen r. Turkm.
68 C1 Teeli Rus. Fed.
98 C2 Tees r. U.K.
111 C3 Tefenni Turkey
60 B2 Tegal Indon.
146 B3 Tegucigalpa Hond.
115 C3 Teguidda-n-Tessoumt
Niger
129 E1 Tehek Lake Can.
114 B4 Téhini Côte d'Ivoire
81 D2 Tehrān Iran
145 C3 Tehuacán Mex.
145 C3 Tehuantepec, Golfo de g.
Mex.
Tehuantepec, Gulf of
Mex. see
145 C3 Tehuantepec, Golfo de
Tehuantepec, Istmo de
isth. Mex.
114 A2 Teide, Pico del vol.
Canary Is
99 A3 Teifi r. U.K.
119 D3 Teita Hills Kenya
Teixeira de Sousa Angola
see Luau
Tejo r. Port. see Tagus
145 B3 Tejupilco Mex.
54 B2 Tekapo, Lake N.Z.
145 D2 Tekax Mex.
116 B3 Tekezē Wenz r.
Eritrea/Eth.
111 C2 Tekirdağ Turkey
54 C1 Te Kuiti N.Z.
75 C2 Tel r. India
81 C1 T'elavi Georgia
80 B2 Tel Aviv-Yafo Israel
145 D2 Telchac Puerto Mex.
128 A2 Telegraph Creek Can.
154 B2 Telêmaco Borba Brazil
61 C1 Telen r. Indon.
50 B2 Telfer Mining Centre
Austr.
99 B3 Telford U.K.

128 B2 Telkwa Can.
60 A2 Telo Indon.
86 E2 Tel'pos-Iz, Gora mt.
Rus. Fed.
88 B2 Telšiai Lith.
60 B1 Teluk Anson Malaysia
60 B2 Telukbatang Indon.
60 A1 Telukdalam Indon.
114 C4 Tema Ghana
130 C3 Temagami Lake Can.
60 C2 Temanggung Indon.
123 C2 Temba S. Africa
83 H2 Tembenchi r. Rus. Fed.
60 B2 Tembilahan Indon.
123 C2 Tembisa S. Africa
120 A1 Tembo Aluma Angola
Tembué Moz. see
Chifunde
99 B3 Teme r. U.K.
135 C4 Temecula U.S.A.
63 B3 Temengor, Tasik resr
Malaysia
60 B1 Temerluh Malaysia
77 D1 Temirtau Kazakh.
141 D1 Témiscamingue, Lac l.
Can.
53 C2 Temora Austr.
138 A2 Tempe U.S.A.
139 D2 Temple U.S.A.
97 C2 Templemore
Rep. of Ireland
102 C1 Templin Ger.
145 C2 Tempoal Mex.
120 A2 Tempué Angola
91 D2 Temryuk Rus. Fed.
91 D2 Temryukskiy Zaliv b.
Rus. Fed.
153 A3 Temuco Chile
54 B2 Temuka N.Z.
145 C2 Tenabo Mex.
139 E2 Tenali India
73 C3 Tenali India
63 A2 Tenasserim Myanmar
99 A4 Tenby U.K.
117 C3 Tendaho Eth.
105 D3 Tende France
105 D3 Tende, Col de pass
France/Italy
73 D4 Ten Degree Channel India
114 A3 Te-n-Dghâmcha, Sebkhet
salt marsh Maur.
67 D3 Tendo Japan
114 B3 Ténenkou Mali
115 C2 Ténéré reg. Niger
115 D2 Ténéré du Tafassâsset
des. Niger
114 A2 Tenerife i. Canary Is
107 D2 Ténès Alg.
61 C2 Tengah, Kepulauan is
Indon.
Tengcheng China see
Tengxian
62 A1 Tengchong China
61 C2 Tenggarong Indon.
70 A2 Tengger Shamo des.
China
Tengiz, Ozero salt l.
71 B3 Tengxian China
119 C4 Tenke Dem. Rep. Congo
114 B3 Tenkodogo Burkina
51 C1 Tennant Creek Austr.
142 C1 Tennessee r. U.S.A.
142 C1 Tennessee state U.S.A.
61 C1 Tenom Sabah Malaysia
145 C3 Tenosique Mex.
61 D2 Tenteno Indon.
53 D1 Tenterfield Austr.
143 D3 Ten Thousand Islands
U.S.A.
154 B1 Teodoro Sampaio Brazil
155 D1 Teófilo Otôni Brazil
145 C3 Teopisca Mex.
59 C3 Tepa Indon.
144 B3 Tepache Mex.
54 B1 Te Paki N.Z.
144 B3 Tepalcatepec Mex.
144 B2 Tepatitlán Mex.
144 B2 Tepehuanes Mex.
109 D2 Tepelenë Albania
144 B2 Tepic Mex.
102 C1 Teplice Czech Rep.
89 E3 Teploye Rus. Fed.
90 B2 Teplyk Ukr.
54 C1 Te Puke N.Z.
144 B2 Tequila Mex.
49 K3 Teraina i. Kiribati
108 B2 Teramo Italy
52 B3 Terang Austr.
89 E3 Terbuny Rus. Fed.
90 B2 Terebovlya Ukr.

87 D4 Terek r. Rus. Fed.
154 B2 Terenos Brazil
151 E3 Teresina Brazil
155 D2 Teresópolis Brazil
63 A3 Teressa Island India
100 A3 Tergnier France
80 B1 Terme Turkey
77 C3 Termez Uzbek.
108 B3 Termini Imerese Sicily
Italy
145 C3 Términos, Laguna de lag.
Mex.
59 C2 Termoli Italy
59 C2 Ternate Indon.
100 A2 Terneuzen Neth.
66 C1 Terney Rus. Fed.
108 B2 Terni Italy
90 B2 Ternopil' Ukr.
52 A2 Terowie Austr.
69 F1 Terpeniya, Mys c.
Rus. Fed.
69 F1 Terpeniya, Zaliv g.
Rus. Fed.
128 B2 Terrace Can.
130 B3 Terrace Bay Can.
122 B2 Terra Firma S. Africa
142 B3 Terrebonne Bay U.S.A.
140 B3 Terre Haute U.S.A.
131 E3 Terrenceville Can.
100 B1 Terschelling i. Neth.
108 A3 Tertenia Sardinia Italy
107 C1 Teruel Spain
92 H2 Tervola Fin.
109 C2 Tešanj Bos.-Herz.
116 B3 Teseney Eritrea
66 D2 Teshio Japan
66 D2 Teshio-gawa r. Japan
128 A1 Teslin Can.
128 A1 Teslin Lake Can.
154 B1 Tesouro Brazil
115 C3 Tessaoua Niger
99 C4 Test r. U.K.
121 C2 Tete Moz.
90 C1 Teteriv r. Ukr.
101 F1 Teterow Ger.
90 B2 Tetiyiv Ukr.
114 B1 Tétouan Morocco
110 B2 Tetovo Macedonia
Tetyukhe Rus. Fed. see
Dal'negorsk
Teuchezhsk Rus. Fed. see
Adygeysk
152 B2 Teuco r. Arg.
144 B2 Teul de González Ortega
Mex.
101 D1 Teutoburger Wald hills
Ger.
108 B2 Tevere r. Italy
54 A3 Teviot N.Z.
96 C3 Teviot r. U.K.
96 C3 Teviothead U.K.
61 C2 Tewah Indon.
51 E2 Tewantin Austr.
99 B4 Tewkesbury U.K.
139 E2 Texarkana U.S.A.
53 D1 Texas Austr.
139 D2 Texas state U.S.A.
139 E3 Texas City U.S.A.
145 C3 Texcoco Mex.
100 B1 Texel i. Neth.
139 D2 Texoma, Lake U.S.A.
123 C2 Teyateyaneng Lesotho
89 F2 Teykovo Rus. Fed.
89 F2 Teza r. Rus. Fed.
75 D2 Tezpur India
72 D2 Tezu India
129 E1 Tha-anne r. Can.
123 C2 Thabana-Ntlenyana mt.
Lesotho
123 C2 Thaba Nchu S. Africa
123 C2 Thaba Putsoa mt.
Lesotho
123 C2 Thaba-Tseka Lesotho
123 C1 Thabazimbi S. Africa
123 C2 Thabong S. Africa
63 A2 Thagyettaw Myanmar
62 B1 Thai Binh Vietnam
63 B2 Thailand country Asia
63 B2 Thailand, Gulf of Asia
62 B1 Thai Nguyên Vietnam
74 B1 Thal Pak.
63 A3 Thalang Thai.
74 B1 Thal Desert Pak.
101 E2 Thale (Harz) Ger.
63 B2 Thale Luang lag. Thai.
62 B2 Tha Li Thai.
53 C1 Thallon Austr.
123 C1 Thamaga Botswana
78 B3 Thamar, Jabal mt. Yemen
79 C3 Thamarīt Oman

130 B3 Thames r. Can.
54 C1 Thames N.Z.
99 D4 Thames est. U.K.
99 D4 Thames r. U.K.
79 B3 Thamūd Yemen
Thana India see Thāne
63 A2 Thanbyuzayat Myanmar
74 B3 Thāne India
62 B2 Thanh Hoa Vietnam
73 B3 Thanjavur India
74 A2 Thano Bula Khan Pak.
62 B1 Than Uyen Vietnam
74 A2 Thar Desert India/Pak.
52 B1 Thargomindah Austr.
62 A2 Tharrawaddy Myanmar
81 C2 Tharthār, Buḥayrat ath l. Iraq
111 B2 Thasos Greece
111 B2 Thasos i. Greece
62 B1 Thất Khê Vietnam
62 A2 Thaton Myanmar
62 A1 Thaungdut Myanmar
63 A2 Thayetchaung Myanmar
62 A2 Thayetmyo Myanmar
62 A1 Thazi Myanmar
146 C2 The Bahamas country West Indies
98 B2 The Cheviot hill U.K.
134 B1 The Dalles U.S.A.
136 C2 Thedford U.S.A.
53 D2 The Entrance Austr.
99 C3 The Fens reg. U.K.
114 A3 The Gambia country Africa
116 B2 The Great Oasis Egypt
79 C2 The Gulf Asia
100 B1 The Hague Neth.
129 E1 Thelon r. Can.
101 E2 Themar Ger.
123 C2 Thembalihle S. Africa
96 A1 The Minch sea chan. U.K.
97 A1 The Mullet b. Rep. of Ireland
99 C4 The Needles stack U.K.
150 C3 Theodore Roosevelt r. Brazil
129 D2 The Pas Can.
111 B2 Thermaïkos Kolpos g. Greece
136 B2 Thermopolis U.S.A.
53 C3 The Rock Austr.
The Skaw spit Denmark see Grenen
99 C4 The Solent str. U.K.
130 B3 Thessalon Can.
111 B2 Thessaloniki Greece
99 D3 Thetford U.K.
131 C3 Thetford Mines Can.
62 A1 The Triangle mts Myanmar
147 D3 The Valley Anguilla
131 D2 Thévenet, Lac l. Can.
99 D3 The Wash b. U.K.
99 D4 The Weald reg. U.K.
139 D2 The Woodlands U.S.A.
142 B3 Thibodaux U.S.A.
129 E2 Thicket Portage Can.
137 D1 Thief River Falls U.S.A.
Thiel Neth. see Tiel
105 C2 Thiers France
114 A3 Thiès Senegal
119 D3 Thika Kenya
73 B4 Thiladhunmathee Atoll Maldives
75 C2 Thimphu Bhutan
105 D2 Thionville France
111 C3 Thira Greece
Thira i. Greece see Santorini
98 C2 Thirsk U.K.
Thiruvananthapuram India see Trivandrum
93 E4 Thisted Denmark
129 E1 Thlewiaza r. Can.
62 A2 Thoen Thai.
123 D1 Thohoyandou S. Africa
101 E1 Thomasburg Ger.
97 C2 Thomastown Rep. of Ireland
142 C2 Thomasville AL U.S.A.
143 D2 Thomasville GA U.S.A.
100 C2 Thommen Belgium
129 E2 Thompson Can.
128 E3 Thompson r. U.S.A.
134 C1 Thompson Falls U.S.A.
128 B2 Thompson Sound Can.
51 D2 Thomson watercourse Austr.
143 D2 Thomson U.S.A.
63 B2 Thon Buri Thai.
63 A2 Thongwa Myanmar

138 B1 Thoreau U.S.A.
96 C3 Thornhill U.K.
136 C3 Thornton U.S.A.
55 F2 Thorshavnheiane reg. Antarctica
123 C2 Thota-ea-Moli Lesotho
104 B2 Thouars France
62 A1 Thoubal India
134 D1 Three Forks U.S.A.
128 C2 Three Hills Can.
63 A2 Three Pagodas Pass Myanmar/Thai.
114 B4 Three Points, Cape Ghana
140 B2 Three Rivers MI U.S.A.
139 D3 Three Rivers TX U.S.A.
Thrissur India see Trichur
63 B2 Thu Dầu Một Vietnam
100 B2 Thuin Belgium
Thule Greenland see Qaanaaq
121 B3 Thuli Zimbabwe
102 B2 Thun Switz.
130 B3 Thunder Bay Can.
130 B3 Thunder Bay b. Can.
63 A3 Thung Song Thai.
101 E2 Thüringer Becken reg. Ger.
101 E2 Thüringer Wald mts Ger.
Thuringian Forest mts Ger. see Thüringer Wald
97 C2 Thurles Rep. of Ireland
59 D3 Thursday Island Austr.
96 C1 Thurso U.K.
96 C1 Thurso r. U.K.
55 R2 Thurston Island Antarctica
101 D1 Thüster Berg hill Ger.
121 C2 Thyolo Malawi
Thysville Dem. Rep. Congo see Mbanza-Ngungu
79 C2 Tiāb Iran
151 E3 Tianguá Brazil
70 B2 Tianjin China
70 B2 Tianjin mun. China
71 A3 Tianlin China
70 B2 Tianmen China
69 E2 Tianshan China
70 A2 Tianshui China
70 A2 Tianzhu China
107 D2 Tiaret Alg.
114 B4 Tiassalé Côte d'Ivoire
154 B3 Tibagi Brazil
154 B3 Tibagi r. Brazil
118 B2 Tibati Cameroon
Tiber r. Italy see Tevere
Tiberias, Lake Israel see Galilee, Sea of
115 D2 Tibesti mts Chad
Tibet aut. reg. China see Xizang Zizhiqu
Tibet, Plateau of China see Qing Zang Gaoyuan
52 B1 Tibooburra Austr.
144 A2 Tiburón, Isla i. Mex.
114 B3 Tichît Maur.
114 A2 Tichla Western Sahara
105 D2 Ticino r. Italy/Switz.
141 E2 Ticonderoga U.S.A.
145 C2 Ticul Mex.
114 A3 Tidjikja Maur.
100 B2 Tiel Neth.
70 C1 Tieling China
75 B1 Tielongtan Aksai Chin
100 A2 Tielt Belgium
100 B2 Tienen Belgium
68 B2 Tien Shan mts China/Kyrg.
Tientsin China see Tianjin
Tientsin mun. China see Tianjin
93 G3 Tierp Sweden
145 C3 Tierra Blanca Mex.
145 C3 Tierra Colorada Mex.
153 B5 Tierra del Fuego, Isla Grande de i. Arg./Chile
106 B1 Tiétar, Valle de val. Spain
154 C2 Tietê Brazil
154 B2 Tietê r. Brazil
140 C2 Tiffin U.S.A.
Tiflis Georgia see T'bilisi
143 D2 Tifton U.S.A.
90 B2 Tighina Moldova
75 C2 Tigiria India
118 B2 Tignère Cameroon
131 D3 Tignish Can.
150 B3 Tigre r. Ecuador/Peru
81 C2 Tigris r. Asia
114 B2 Tiguent Maur.
114 B3 Tiguesmat hills Maur.

115 D3 Tigui Chad
145 C2 Tihuatlán Mex.
144 A1 Tijuana Mex.
91 E2 Tikhoretsk Rus. Fed.
89 D2 Tikhvin Rus. Fed.
89 D2 Tikhvinskaya Gryada ridge Rus. Fed.
157 F7 Tiki Basin sea feature S. Pacific Ocean
54 C1 Tikokino N.Z.
81 C2 Tikrīt Iraq
83 J2 Tiksi Rus. Fed.
100 B2 Tilburg Neth.
152 B2 Tilcara Arg.
52 B1 Tilcha Austr.
114 C3 Tilemsi, Vallée du watercourse Mali
Tilimsen Alg. see Tlemcen
114 C3 Tillabéri Niger
134 B1 Tillamook U.S.A.
63 A3 Tillanchong Island India
111 C3 Tilos i. Greece
52 B2 Tilpa Austr.
86 F2 Til'tim Rus. Fed.
89 E3 Tim Rus. Fed.
86 D2 Timanskiy Kryazh ridge Rus. Fed.
54 B2 Timaru N.Z.
91 D2 Timashevsk Rus. Fed.
Timashevskaya Rus. Fed. see Timashevsk
114 B3 Timbedgha Maur.
50 C1 Timber Creek Austr.
Timbuktu Mali see Tombouctou
115 C3 Timia Niger
114 C2 Timimoun Alg.
110 B1 Timiş r. Romania
110 B1 Timişoara Romania
130 B3 Timmins Can.
89 E2 Timokhino Rus. Fed.
151 E3 Timon Brazil
59 C3 Timor i. Indon.
59 C3 Timor Sea Austr./Indon.
Timor Timur terr. Asia see East Timor
93 G3 Timrå Sweden
78 B2 Tin, Jabal hill Saudi Arabia
114 B2 Tindouf Alg.
53 D1 Tingha Austr.
75 C2 Tingri China
93 F4 Tingsryd Sweden
92 E3 Tingvoll Norway
Tingzhou China see Changting
59 D2 Tinian i. N. Mariana Is
Tinnelvelly India see Tirunelveli
152 B2 Tinogasta Arg.
111 C3 Tinos Greece
111 C3 Tinos i. Greece
100 A3 Tinqueux France
115 C2 Tinrhert, Plateau du Alg.
62 A1 Tinsukia India
52 B3 Tintinara Austr.
136 C1 Tioga U.S.A.
107 D2 Tipasa Alg.
97 B2 Tipperary Rep. of Ireland
151 E3 Tiracambu, Serra do hills Brazil
109 C2 Tirana Albania
Tiranë Albania see Tirana
108 B1 Tirano Italy
52 A1 Tirari Desert Austr.
90 B2 Tiraspol Moldova
122 A2 Tiraz Mountains Namibia
111 C3 Tire Turkey
96 A2 Tiree i. U.K.
Tîrgovişte Romania see Târgovişte
Tîrgu Frumos Romania see Târgu Frumos
Tîrgu Jiu Romania see Târgu Jiu
Tîrgu Lăpuş Romania see Târgu Lăpuş
Tîrgu Mureş Romania see Târgu Mureş
Tîrgu Neamţ Romania see Târgu Neamţ
Tîrgu Ocna Romania see Târgu Ocna
74 B1 Tirich Mir mt. Pak.
Tîrnăveni Romania see Târnăveni
155 C3 Tiros Brazil
118 C2 Tiroungoulou C.A.R.
73 B3 Tiruchchirāppalli India
73 B4 Tirunelveli India
73 B3 Tirupati India
73 B3 Tiruppattur India

73 B3 Tiruppur India
109 D1 Tisa r. Europe
109 D2 Tisa r. Yugo.
129 D2 Tisdale Can.
107 D2 Tissemsilt Alg.
75 C2 Tista r. India
103 E2 Tisza r. Hungary
55 L1 Titan Dome ice feature Antarctica
152 B1 Titicaca, Lago l. Bol./Peru
Titicaca, Lake Bol./Peru see Titicaca, Lago
75 C2 Titlagarh India
Titograd Yugo. see Podgorica
Titova Mitrovica Yugo. see Kosovska Mitrovica
Titovo Užice Yugo. see Užice
Titovo Velenje Slovenia see Velenje
Titov Veles Macedonia see Veles
Titov Vrbas Yugo. see Vrbas
110 C2 Titu Romania
143 D3 Titusville U.S.A.
99 B4 Tiverton U.K.
108 B2 Tivoli Italy
79 C2 Tiwi Oman
63 A2 Ti-ywa Myanmar
145 D2 Tizimín Mex.
107 D2 Tizi Ouzou Alg.
114 B2 Tiznit Morocco
92 G2 Tjaktjajaure l. Sweden
Tjirebon Indon. see Cirebon
145 C3 Tlacotalpán Mex.
144 B2 Tlahualilo Mex.
145 C3 Tlalnepantla Mex.
145 C3 Tlapa Mex.
145 C3 Tlaxcala Mex.
145 C3 Tlaxiaco Mex.
114 B1 Tlemcen Alg.
123 C1 Tlokweng Botswana
128 B2 Toad River Can.
121 □D2 Toamasina Madag.
60 A1 Toba, Danau l. Indon.
Toba, Lake Indon. see Toba, Danau
74 A1 Toba and Kakar Ranges mts Pak.
147 D3 Tobago i. Trin. and Tob.
59 C2 Tobelo Indon.
130 B3 Tobermory Can.
96 A2 Tobermory U.K.
129 D2 Tobin Lake Can.
60 B2 Toboali Indon.
76 C1 Tobol r. Kazakh./Rus. Fed.
86 F3 Tobol'sk Rus. Fed.
Tobruk Libya see Tubruq
151 E3 Tocantinópolis Brazil
151 E3 Tocantins r. Brazil
143 D2 Toccoa U.S.A.
108 A1 Toce r. Italy
152 A2 Tocopilla Chile
53 C3 Tocumwal Austr.
59 C3 Todeli Indon.
108 B2 Todi Italy
144 A2 Todos Santos Mex.
128 B3 Tofino Can.
96 □ Toft U.K.
61 D2 Togian i. Indon.
61 D2 Togian, Kepulauan is Indon.
Togliatti Rus. Fed. see Tol'yatti
114 C4 Togo country Africa
74 B2 Tohana India
143 D3 Tohopekaliga, Lake U.S.A.
126 C2 Tok U.S.A.
116 B3 Tokar Sudan
69 E3 Tokara-rettō is Japan
91 E1 Tokarevka Rus. Fed.
80 B1 Tokat Turkey
49 J4 Tokelau terr. S. Pacific Ocean
77 D2 Tokmak Kyrg.
91 D2 Tokmak Ukr.
54 C1 Tokoroa N.Z.
68 B2 Toksun China
67 B4 Tokushima Japan
67 C3 Tōkyō Japan
121 □D3 Tôlañaro Madag.
Tolbukhin Bulg. see Dobrich
154 B2 Toledo Brazil
106 C2 Toledo Spain
140 C2 Toledo U.S.A.

106 C2 Toledo, Montes de mts Spain
142 B2 Toledo Bend Reservoir U.S.A.
121 □D3 Toliara Madag.
Toling China see Zanda
61 D1 Tolitoli Indon.
108 B1 Tolmezzo Italy
108 B1 Tolmin Slovenia
103 D2 Tolna Hungary
104 B3 Tolosa Spain
145 C3 Toluca Mex.
87 D3 Tol'yatti Rus. Fed.
140 A2 Tomah U.S.A.
140 B1 Tomahawk U.S.A.
66 D2 Tomakomai Japan
61 D2 Tomali Indon.
61 C1 Tomani Sabah Malaysia
106 B2 Tomar Port.
103 E1 Tomaszów Lubelski Pol.
103 E1 Tomaszów Mazowiecki Pol.
144 B3 Tomatlán Mex.
154 C2 Tomazina Brazil
142 C2 Tombigbee r. U.S.A.
120 A1 Tomboco Angola
155 D2 Tombos Brazil
114 B3 Tombouctou Mali
138 A2 Tombstone U.S.A.
120 A2 Tombua Angola
123 C1 Tom Burke S. Africa
106 C2 Tomelloso Spain
53 C2 Tomingley Austr.
61 D2 Tomini, Teluk g. Indon.
109 C2 Tomislavgrad Bos.-Herz.
103 D2 Tompa Hungary
50 A2 Tom Price Austr.
82 G3 Tomsk Rus. Fed.
93 F4 Tomtabacken hill Sweden
83 K2 Tomtor Rus. Fed.
145 C3 Tonalá Mex.
150 C3 Tonantins Brazil
99 D4 Tonbridge U.K.
59 C2 Tondano Indon.
49 J5 Tonga country S. Pacific Ocean
123 D2 Tongaat S. Africa
49 J6 Tongatapu Group is Tonga
71 B3 Tongcheng China
70 A2 Tongchuan China
71 A3 Tongdao China
65 B2 Tongduch'ŏn S. Korea
100 B2 Tongeren Belgium
65 B2 Tonghae S. Korea
71 A3 Tonghai China
65 B1 Tonghua China
65 B2 Tongjosŏn-man b. N. Korea
62 B1 Tongking, Gulf of China/Vietnam
69 E2 Tongliao China
70 B2 Tongling China
52 B2 Tongo Austr.
Tongquan China see Malong
71 A3 Tongren China
70 B2 Tongshan China see Xuzhou
71 A4 Tongshi China
Tongtian He r. China see Yangtze
96 B1 Tongue U.K.
70 B2 Tongxian China
65 B3 T'ongyŏng S. Korea
69 E2 Tongyu China
65 A1 Tongyuanpu China
Tongzhou China see Tongxian
71 A3 Tongzi China
119 C2 Tonj Sudan
74 B2 Tonk India
81 D2 Tonkābon Iran
63 B2 Tônlé Sab l. Cambodia
Tonle Sap l. Cambodia see Tônlé Sab
135 C3 Tonopah U.S.A.
93 F4 Tønsberg Norway
135 D2 Tooele U.S.A.
52 B3 Tooleybuc Austr.
53 D1 Toowoomba Austr.
137 D3 Topeka U.S.A.
144 B2 Topia Mex.
144 B2 Topolobampo Mex.
86 C2 Topozero, Ozero l. Rus. Fed.
134 B1 Toppenish U.S.A.
111 C3 Torbalı Turkey
76 B3 Torbat-e Heydariyeh Iran
76 C3 Torbat-e Jām Iran
131 E3 Torbay Can.
106 C1 Tordesillas Spain

107 C1 Tordesilos Spain
92 H2 Töre Sweden
107 D1 Torelló Spain
100 B1 Torenberg hill Neth.
Toretam Kazakh. see Baykonur
101 F2 Torgau Ger.
100 A2 Torhout Belgium
67 D4 Tori-shima i. Japan
117 B4 Torit Sudan
154 B1 Torixoreu Brazil
89 D2 Torkovichi Rus. Fed.
106 B1 Tormes r. Spain
92 H2 Torneälven r. Sweden
131 D2 Torngat Mountains Can.
92 H2 Tornio Fin.
106 B1 Toro Spain
130 C3 Toronto Can.
89 D2 Toropets Rus. Fed.
119 D2 Tororo Uganda
80 B2 Toros Dağları mts Turkey
52 B3 Torquay Austr.
99 B4 Torquay U.K.
135 C4 Torrance U.S.A.
106 B2 Torrão Port.
106 B1 Torre mt. Port.
107 D1 Torreblanca Spain
106 B1 Torre de Moncorvo Port.
106 C1 Torrelavega Spain
106 C2 Torremolinos Spain
52 A2 Torrens, Lake salt flat Austr.
107 C2 Torrent Spain
144 B2 Torreón Mex.
106 B2 Torres Novas Port.
156 C6 Torres Strait Austr.
106 B2 Torres Vedras Port.
107 C2 Torrevieja Spain
96 B2 Torridon U.K.
96 B2 Torridon, Loch b. U.K.
106 C2 Torrijos Spain
141 E2 Torrington CT U.S.A.
136 C2 Torrington WY U.S.A.
107 D1 Torroella de Montgrí Spain
94 B1 Tórshavn Faroe Is
108 A3 Tortolì Sardinia Italy
108 A2 Tortona Italy
107 D1 Tortosa Spain
81 D2 Torūd Iran
103 D1 Toruń Pol.
97 B1 Tory Island Rep. of Ireland
97 B1 Tory Sound sea chan. Rep. of Ireland
89 D2 Torzhok Rus. Fed.
67 B4 Tosashimizu Japan
122 B2 Tosca S. Africa
108 A2 Toscano, Arcipelago is Italy
89 D2 Tosno Rus. Fed.
68 C1 Tosontsengel Mongolia
152 B2 Tostado Arg.
101 D1 Tostedt Ger.
80 B1 Tosya Turkey
86 D3 Tot'ma Rus. Fed.
151 D2 Totness Suriname
67 B3 Tottori Japan
114 B4 Touba Côte d'Ivoire
114 B1 Toubkal, Jbel mt. Morocco
118 B2 Touboro Cameroon
114 B3 Tougan Burkina
115 C1 Touggourt Alg.
105 D2 Toul France
71 C3 Touliu Taiwan
105 D3 Toulon France
104 C3 Toulouse France
62 A2 Toungoo Myanmar
Tourane Vietnam see Đa Nẵng
104 B2 Tourlaville France
100 A2 Tournai Belgium
115 D2 Tourndo, Oued watercourse Alg./Niger
105 C2 Tournus France
151 F3 Touros Brazil
104 C2 Tours France
115 D2 Tousside, Pic mt. Chad
122 B3 Touwsrivier S. Africa
150 B2 Tovar Venez.
66 D2 Towada Japan
134 D1 Townsend U.S.A.
51 D1 Townsville Austr.
61 C2 Towori, Teluk b. Indon.
77 E2 Toxkan He r. China
66 D2 Tōya-ko l. Japan
67 C3 Toyama Japan
67 C3 Toyohashi Japan
67 C3 Toyota Japan

115 C1 Tozeur Tunisia
81 C1 Tqvarch'eli Georgia
80 B2 Trâblous Lebanon
80 B1 Trabzon Turkey
106 B2 Trafalgar, Cabo c. Spain
128 C3 Trail Can.
88 B3 Trakai Lith.
97 B2 Tralee Rep. of Ireland
Trá Li Rep. of Ireland see Tralee
97 C2 Tramore Rep. of Ireland
93 F4 Tranås Sweden
63 A3 Trang Thai.
59 C3 Trangan i. Indon.
55 L2 Transantarctic Mountains Antarctica
Transylvanian Alps mts Romania see Carpaţii Meridionali
108 B3 Trapani Sicily Italy
53 C3 Traralgon Austr.
75 D2 Trashigang Bhutan
63 B2 Trat Thai.
102 C2 Traunstein Ger.
54 B2 Travers, Mount N.Z.
140 B2 Traverse City U.S.A.
63 B3 Tra Vinh Vietnam
103 D2 Třebíč Czech Rep.
109 C2 Trebinje Bos.-Herz.
103 E2 Trebišov Slovakia
Trebizond Turkey see Trabzon
109 C1 Trebnje Slovenia
Trefynwy U.K. see Monmouth
153 C3 Treinta-y-Tres Uru.
153 B4 Trelew Arg.
93 F4 Trelleborg Sweden
130 C3 Tremblant, Mont hill Can.
109 C2 Tremiti, Isole is Italy
134 D2 Tremonton U.S.A.
107 D1 Tremp Spain
103 D2 Trenčín Slovakia
153 B3 Trenque Lauquén Arg.
98 C3 Trent r. U.K.
108 B1 Trento Italy
141 D2 Trenton MO U.S.A.
141 E2 Trenton NJ U.S.A.
131 E3 Trepassey Can.
153 B3 Tres Arroyos Arg.
155 D2 Três Corações Brazil
154 B2 Três Irmãos, Represa resr Brazil
154 B2 Três Lagoas Brazil
153 A4 Tres Lagos Arg.
155 C1 Três Marias, Represa resr Brazil
155 C2 Três Pontas Brazil
153 B4 Tres Puntas, Cabo c. Arg.
155 D2 Três Rios Brazil
101 F1 Treuenbrietzen Ger.
Treves Ger. see Trier
108 A1 Treviglio Italy
108 B1 Treviso Italy
99 A4 Trevose Head hd U.K.
109 C3 Tricase Italy
Trichinopoly India see Tiruchchirāppalli
73 B3 Trichur India
53 C2 Trida Austr.
100 C3 Trier Ger.
108 B1 Trieste Italy
108 B1 Triglav mt. Slovenia
111 B3 Trikala Greece
59 D3 Trikora, Puncak mt. Indon.
97 C2 Trim Rep. of Ireland
73 C4 Trincomalee Sri Lanka
154 C1 Trindade Brazil
152 B1 Trinidad Bol.
147 D3 Trinidad i. Trin. and Tob.
136 C3 Trinidad U.S.A.
147 D3 Trinidad and Tobago country West Indies
139 E3 Trinity r. U.S.A.
131 E3 Trinity Bay Can.
111 B3 Tripoli Greece
Tripoli Lebanon see Trâblous
115 D1 Tripoli Libya
75 D2 Tripura state India
113 B9 Tristan da Cunha i. S. Atlantic Ocean
73 B4 Trivandrum India
108 B2 Trivento Italy
103 D2 Trnava Slovakia
59 E3 Trobriand Islands P.N.G.
92 F2 Trofors Norway
109 C2 Trogir Croatia

109 C2 Troia Italy
100 C2 Troisdorf Ger.
106 C2 Trois Fourches, Cap des c. Morocco
130 C3 Trois-Rivières Can.
87 F3 Troitsk Rus. Fed.
86 E2 Troitsko-Pechorsk Rus. Fed.
151 D3 Trombetas r. Brazil
Tromelin Island Micronesia see Fais
123 C3 Trompsburg S. Africa
92 G2 Tromsø Norway
92 F3 Trondheim Norway
75 D2 Trongsa Bhutan
96 B3 Troon U.K.
89 E3 Trosna Rus. Fed.
97 C1 Trostan hill U.K.
128 C2 Trout Lake Alta Can.
128 B1 Trout Lake l. N.W.T. Can.
130 A2 Trout Lake l. Ont. Can.
99 B3 Trowbridge U.K.
142 C2 Troy AL U.S.A.
141 E2 Troy NY U.S.A.
105 C2 Troyes France
135 C3 Troy Peak U.S.A.
109 D2 Trstenik Yugo.
89 D3 Trubchevsk Rus. Fed.
Truc Giang Vietnam see Bên Tre
106 B1 Truchas Spain
Trucial Coast country Asia see United Arab Emirates
79 C2 Trucial Coast U.A.E.
Trucial States country Asia see United Arab Emirates
146 B3 Trujillo Hond.
150 B3 Trujillo Peru
106 B2 Trujillo Spain
147 C4 Trujillo Venez.
Trujillo, Monte mt. Dom. Rep. see Duarte, Pico
142 B1 Trumann U.S.A.
131 D3 Truro Can.
99 A4 Truro U.K.
61 C1 Trus Madi, Gunung mt. Malaysia
138 B2 Truth or Consequences U.S.A.
103 D1 Trutnov Czech Rep.
93 F3 Trysil Norway
103 D1 Trzebiatów Pol.
103 D1 Trzebnica Pol.
68 B1 Tsagaannuur Mongolia
Tsaidam Basin China see Qaidam Pendi
121 □D2 Tsaratanana, Massif du mts Madag.
110 C2 Tsarevo Bulg.
122 A2 Tsaukaib Namibia
Tselinograd Kazakh. see Astana
Tsementnyy Rus. Fed. see Fokino
122 A2 Tses Namibia
122 B1 Tsetseng Botswana
68 C1 Tsetserleg Mongolia
Tsetserleg Mongolia see Halban
122 B2 Tshabong Botswana
122 B1 Tshane Botswana
91 D2 Tschikskoye Vodokhranilishche resr Rus. Fed.
118 B3 Tshela Dem. Rep. Congo
118 C3 Tshikapa Dem. Rep. Congo
118 C3 Tshikapa r. Dem. Rep. Congo
123 C2 Tshing S. Africa
123 D1 Tshipise S. Africa
118 C3 Tshitanzu Dem. Rep. Congo
120 B3 Tshootsha Botswana
118 C3 Tshuapa r. Dem. Rep. Congo
87 D4 Tsimlyanskoye Vodokhranilishche resr Rus. Fed.
Tsinan China see Jinan
Tsingtao China see Qingdao
Tsining China see Jining
121 □D2 Tsiroanomandidy Madag.
76 A2 Ts'khinvali Georgia
123 C3 Tsomo S. Africa
67 C4 Tsu Japan
67 D3 Tsuchiura Japan

66 D2	Tsugarū-kaikyō str. Japan
	Tsugaru Strait Japan see
	Tsugarū-kaikyō
120 A2	Tsumeb Namibia
122 A1	Tsumis Park Namibia
120 B2	Tsumkwe Namibia
67 C3	Tsuruga Japan
66 C3	Tsuruoka Japan
67 A4	Tsushima is Japan
67 B3	Tsuyama Japan
123 C2	Tswelelang S. Africa
88 C3	Tsyelyakhany Belarus
91 C2	Tsyurupyns'k Ukr.
	Tthenaagoo Can. see
	Nahanni Butte
59 C3	Tual Indon.
97 B2	Tuam Rep. of Ireland
49 M5	Tuamotu Archipelago is
	Fr. Polynesia
54 A3	Tuapeka Mouth N.Z.
91 D3	Tuapse Rus. Fed.
54 A3	Tuatapere N.Z.
138 A1	Tuba City U.S.A.
61 C2	Tuban Indon.
152 D2	Tubarão Brazil
102 B2	Tübingen Ger.
115 E1	Tubruq Libya
144 A1	Tubutama Mex.
152 C1	Tucacuca Bol.
128 B1	Tuchitua Can.
138 A2	Tucson U.S.A.
139 C1	Tucumcari U.S.A.
150 C2	Tucupita Venez.
151 E3	Tucuruí Brazil
151 E3	Tucuruí, Represa resr
	Brazil
107 C1	Tudela Spain
106 B1	Tuela r. Port.
62 A1	Tuensang India
157 F2	Tufts Abyssal Plain
	sea feature
	N. Pacific Ocean
123 D2	Tugela r. S. Africa
64 B2	Tuguegarao Phil.
106 B1	Tui Spain
59 C3	Tukangbesi, Kepulauan is
	Indon.
126 D2	Tuktoyaktuk Can.
88 B2	Tukums Latvia
119 D3	Tukuyu Tanz.
145 C2	Tula Mex.
89 E3	Tula Rus. Fed.
	Tulach Mhór
	Rep. of Ireland see
	Tullamore
145 C2	Tulancingo Mex.
135 C3	Tulare U.S.A.
138 B2	Tularosa U.S.A.
110 C1	Tulcea Romania
90 B2	Tul'chyn Ukr.
	Tuléar Madag. see Toliara
129 E1	Tulemalu Lake Can.
139 C2	Tulia U.S.A.
128 B1	Tulit'a Can.
142 C1	Tullahoma U.S.A.
53 C2	Tullamore Austr.
97 C2	Tullamore Rep. of Ireland
104 C2	Tulle France
97 C2	Tullow Rep. of Ireland
51 D1	Tully Austr.
139 D1	Tulsa U.S.A.
126 B2	Tuluksak U.S.A.
83 H3	Tulun Rus. Fed.
150 B2	Tumaco Col.
123 C2	Tumahole S. Africa
93 G4	Tumba Sweden
118 B3	Tumba, Lac l.
	Dem. Rep. Congo
61 C2	Tumbangtiti Indon.
53 C3	Tumbarumba Austr.
150 A3	Tumbes Peru
128 B2	Tumbler Ridge Can.
52 A2	Tumby Bay Austr.
65 B1	Tumen China
150 C2	Tumereng Guyana
64 A3	Tumindao i. Phil.
74 A2	Tump Pak.
151 D2	Tumucumaque, Serra hills
	Brazil
53 C3	Tumut Austr.
99 D4	Tunbridge Wells, Royal
	U.K.
80 B2	Tunceli Turkey
53 D2	Tuncurry Austr.
118 A1	Tundun-Wada Nigeria
119 D4	Tunduru Tanz.
110 C2	Tundzha r. Bulg.
128 B1	Tungsten Can.
115 D1	Tunis Tunisia
108 B3	Tunis, Golfe de g. Tunisia
115 C1	Tunisia country Africa
150 B2	Tunja Col.
92 F3	Tunnsjøen l. Norway
	Tunxi China see
	Huangshan
75 D1	Tuotuoheyan China
154 B2	Tupã Brazil
154 C1	Tupaciguara Brazil
142 C2	Tupelo U.S.A.
152 B2	Tupiza Bol.
83 H2	Tura Rus. Fed.
86 F3	Tura r. Rus. Fed.
78 B2	Turabah Saudi Arabia
83 J3	Turana, Khrebet mts
	Rus. Fed.
54 C1	Turangi N.Z.
76 B2	Turan Lowland Asia
77 D2	Tura-Ryskulova Kazakh.
78 A1	Turayf Saudi Arabia
88 B2	Turba Estonia
74 A2	Turbat Pak.
150 B2	Turbo Col.
110 B1	Turda Romania
	Turfan China see Turpan
76 C2	Turgay Kazakh.
76 C1	Turgayskaya Stolovaya
	Strana reg. Kazakh.
110 C2	Türgovishte Bulg.
111 C3	Turgutlu Turkey
80 B1	Turhal Turkey
107 C2	Turia r. Spain
108 A1	Turin Italy
86 F3	Turinsk Rus. Fed.
90 A1	Turiya r. Ukr.
90 A1	Turiys'k Ukr.
90 A2	Turka Ukr.
119 D2	Turkana, Lake salt l.
	Eth./Kenya
77 C2	Turkestan Kazakh.
103 E2	Türkeve Hungary
80 B2	Turkey country
	Asia/Europe
50 B1	Turkey Creek Austr.
76 B2	Turkmenbashi Turkm.
76 B2	Turkmenistan country
	Asia
	Turkmeniya country Asia
	see Turkmenistan
	Turkmenskaya S.S.R.
	country Asia see
	Turkmenistan
147 C2	Turks and Caicos Islands
	terr. West Indies
147 C2	Turks Islands
	Turks and Caicos Is
93 H3	Turku Fin.
119 D2	Turkwel watercourse
	Kenya
135 B3	Turlock U.S.A.
155 D1	Turmalina Brazil
54 C2	Turnagain, Cape N.Z.
146 B3	Turneffe Islands Belize
100 B2	Turnhout Belgium
129 D2	Turnor Lake Can.
	Türnovo Bulg. see
	Veliko Türnovo
110 B2	Turnu Măgurele Romania
68 B2	Turpan China
76 C2	Turriff U.K.
76 C2	Turtkul' Uzbek.
64 A3	Turtle Islands Phil.
77 D2	Turugart Pass China/Kyrg.
82 G2	Turukhansk Rus. Fed.
142 C2	Tuscaloosa U.S.A.
142 C2	Tuskegee U.S.A.
81 C2	Tutak Turkey
89 E2	Tutayev Rus. Fed.
73 B4	Tuticorin India
121 C1	Tutubu Tanz.
49 J5	Tutuila i. American Samoa
120 B3	Tutume Botswana
93 H3	Tuusula Fin.
49 I4	Tuvalu country
	S. Pacific Ocean
78 B2	Tuwayq, Jabal hills
	Saudi Arabia
78 B2	Tuwayq, Jabal mts
	Saudi Arabia
78 A2	Tuwwal Saudi Arabia
144 B2	Tuxpan Mex.
145 C2	Tuxpan Mex.
145 C3	Tuxtla Gutiérrez Mex.
62 B1	Tuyên Quang Vietnam
63 B2	Tuy Hoa Vietnam
	Tuz, Jabal at Turkey see
	Tuz Gölü
80 B2	Tuz Gölü salt l. Turkey
81 C2	Tuz Khurmātū Iraq
109 C2	Tuzla Bos.-Herz.
91 E2	Tuzlov r. Rus. Fed.
89 E2	Tver' Rus. Fed.
98 B1	Tweed r. U.K.
53 D1	Tweed Heads Austr.
122 A2	Twee Rivier Namibia
135 C4	Twentynine Palms U.S.A.
131 E3	Twillingate Can.
134 D2	Twin Falls U.S.A.
137 E1	Two Harbors U.S.A.
128 C2	Two Hills Can.
	Tyddewi U.K. see
	St David's
139 D2	Tyler U.S.A.
83 J3	Tynda Rus. Fed.
	Tyndinskiy Rus. Fed. see
	Tynda
96 B2	Tyndrum U.K.
98 C2	Tyne r. England U.K.
95 C2	Tyne r. Scotland U.K.
93 F3	Tynset Norway
	Tyre Lebanon see Soûr
69 E1	Tyrma Rus. Fed.
111 B3	Tyrnavos Greece
52 B3	Tyrrell, Lake dry lake
	Austr.
108 B2	Tyrrhenian Sea
	France/Italy
76 B2	Tyub-Karagan, Mys pt
	Kazakh.
87 E3	Tyul'gan Rus. Fed.
86 F3	Tyumen' Rus. Fed.
83 J2	Tyung r. Rus. Fed.
	Tyuratam Kazakh. see
	Baykonur
99 A4	Tywi r. U.K.
123 D1	Tzaneen S. Africa

U

	Uaco Congo Angola see
	Waku-Kungo
120 B2	Uamanda Angola
150 C3	Uarini Brazil
150 C3	Uaupés Brazil
155 D2	Ubá Brazil
155 D1	Ubaí Brazil
151 F4	Ubaitaba Brazil
81 D1	Ubal Karabaur hills
	Uzbek.
118 B3	Ubangi r.
	C.A.R./Dem. Rep. Congo
	Ubangi-Shari country
	Africa see
	Central African Republic
67 B4	Ube Japan
106 C2	Úbeda Spain
154 C1	Uberaba Brazil
154 C1	Uberlândia Brazil
123 D2	Ubombo S. Africa
63 B2	Ubon Ratchathani Thai.
119 C3	Ubundu Dem. Rep.
	Congo
150 B3	Ucayali r. Peru
100 B2	Uccle Belgium
74 B2	Uch Pak.
77 E2	Ucharal Kazakh.
66 D2	Uchiura-wan b. Japan
76 C2	Uchkuduk Uzbek.
83 J3	Uchur r. Rus. Fed.
99 D4	Uckfield U.K.
128 B3	Ucluelet Can.
83 I2	Udachnyy Rus. Fed.
74 B2	Udaipur India
91 C1	Uday r. Ukr.
93 F4	Uddevalla Sweden
92 G2	Uddjaure l. Sweden
100 B2	Uden Neth.
74 B1	Udhampur
	Jammu and Kashmir
108 B1	Udine Italy
89 E2	Udomlya Rus. Fed.
62 B2	Udon Thani Thai.
73 B3	Udupi India
83 K3	Udyl', Ozero l. Rus. Fed.
67 C3	Ueda Japan
61 D2	Uekuli Indon.
118 C2	Uele r. Dem. Rep. Congo
83 N2	Uelen Rus. Fed.
101 E1	Uelzen Ger.
119 C2	Uere r. Dem. Rep. Congo
87 E3	Ufa Rus. Fed.
119 D3	Ugalla r. Tanz.
119 D2	Uganda country Africa
89 F1	Uglegorsk Rus. Fed.
89 E2	Uglich Rus. Fed.
89 D2	Uglovoye Rus. Fed.
89 D3	Ugra Rus. Fed.
103 D2	Uherské Hradiště
	Czech Rep.
	Uibhist a' Deas i. U.K. see
	South Uist
	Uibhist a' Tuath i. U.K. see
	North Uist
101 E2	Uichteritz Ger.
96 A2	Uig U.K.
120 A1	Uíge Angola
65 B2	Ŭijŏngbu S. Korea
65 A1	Ŭiju N. Korea
135 D2	Uinta Mountains U.S.A.
120 A3	Uis Mine Namibia
65 B2	Ŭisŏng S. Korea
123 C3	Uitenhage S. Africa
100 C1	Uithuizen Neth.
131 D2	Uivak, Cape Can.
	Ujiyamada Japan see Ise
74 B2	Ujjain India
61 C2	Ujung Pandang Indon.
89 F3	Ukholovo Rus. Fed.
62 A1	Ukhrul India
	Ukhta Rus. Fed. see
	Kalevala
86 E2	Ukhta Rus. Fed.
135 B3	Ukiah U.S.A.
127 I2	Ukkusissat Greenland
88 B2	Ukmergė Lith.
90 C2	Ukraine country Europe
	Ukrainskaya S.S.R.
	country Europe see
	Ukraine
69 D1	Ulaanbaatar Mongolia
68 C1	Ulaangom Mongolia
59 E3	Ulamona P.N.G.
70 A2	Ulan China
	Ulan Bator Mongolia see
	Ulaanbaatar
	Ulanhad China see
	Chifeng
69 E1	Ulanhot China
87 D4	Ulan-Khol Rus. Fed.
69 D1	Ulan-Ude Rus. Fed.
75 D1	Ulan Ul Hu l. China
65 B2	Ulchin S. Korea
	Uleåborg Fin. see Oulu
88 C2	Ulenurme Estonia
74 B3	Ulhasnagar India
69 D1	Uliastai China
68 C1	Uliastay Mongolia
59 D2	Ulithi atoll Micronesia
53 D3	Ulladulla Austr.
96 B2	Ullapool U.K.
98 B2	Ullswater l. U.K.
65 C2	Ullŭng-do i. S. Korea
102 B2	Ulm Ger.
65 B2	Ulsan S. Korea
96 □	Ulsta U.K.
97 C1	Ulster reg.
	Rep. of Ireland/U.K.
52 B3	Ultima Austr.
145 D3	Ulúa r. Hond.
111 C3	Ulubey Turkey
111 D3	Uluborlu Turkey
111 C2	Uludağ mt. Turkey
123 D2	Ulundi S. Africa
77 E2	Ulungur Hu l. China
	Uluqsaqtuuq Can. see
	Holman
50 C2	Uluru hill Austr.
98 B2	Ulverston U.K.
90 C2	Ul'yanovka Ukr.
87 D3	Ul'yanovsk Rus. Fed.
136 C3	Ulysses U.S.A.
90 C2	Uman' Ukr.
86 C2	Umba Rus. Fed.
59 D3	Umboi i. P.N.G.
59 D3	Umbukul P.N.G.
92 H3	Umeå Sweden
92 H3	Umeälven r. Sweden
123 D2	Umhlanga S. Africa
127 J2	Umiiviip Kangertiva inlet
	Greenland
126 E2	Umiimmaktok Can.
123 D2	Umlazi S. Africa
78 A2	Umm al Birak
	Saudi Arabia
79 C2	Umm as Samīm salt flat
	Oman
116 A3	Umm Keddada Sudan
78 A2	Umm Lajj Saudi Arabia
78 A2	Umm Mukhbār, Jabal hill
	Saudi Arabia
116 B3	Umm Ruwaba Sudan
115 E1	Umm Sa'ad Libya
134 B2	Umpqua r. U.S.A.
120 A2	Umpulo Angola
123 D3	Umtata S. Africa
123 C3	Umtentweni S. Africa
154 B2	Umuarama Brazil
123 D2	Umzimkulu S. Africa
109 C1	Una r. Bos.-Herz./Croatia
155 E1	Una Brazil

154 C1 Unaí Brazil
126 B2 Unalakleet U.S.A.
78 B2 'Unayzah Saudi Arabia
136 B3 Uncompahgre Peak U.S.A.
52 B3 Underbool Austr.
136 C1 Underwood U.S.A.
89 D3 Unecha Rus. Fed.
53 C2 Ungarie Austr.
52 A2 Ungarra Austr.
127 H2 Ungava, Péninsule d' pen. Can.
131 D2 Ungava Bay Can.
Ungeny Moldova see Ungheni
65 C1 Unggi N. Korea
90 B2 Ungheni Moldova
Unguja i. Tanz. see Zanzibar Island
119 E3 Ungwana Bay Kenya
154 B3 União da Vitória Brazil
150 C3 Unini r. Brazil
134 C1 Union U.S.A.
142 C1 Union City U.S.A.
122 B3 Uniondale S. Africa
141 D3 Uniontown U.S.A.
79 C2 United Arab Emirates country Asia
United Arab Republic country Africa see Egypt
95 C3 United Kingdom country Europe
United Provinces state India see Uttar Pradesh
133 B3 United States of America country N. America
129 D2 Unity Can.
100 C2 Unna Ger.
96 ☐ Unst i. U.K.
101 E2 Unstrut r. Ger.
89 E3 Upa r. Rus. Fed.
119 C3 Upemba, Lac l. Dem. Rep. Congo
122 B2 Upington S. Africa
74 B2 Upleta India
49 J5 Upolu i. Samoa
134 B2 Upper Alkali Lake U.S.A.
128 C2 Upper Arrow Lake Can.
54 C2 Upper Hutt N.Z.
134 B2 Upper Klamath Lake U.S.A.
128 B1 Upper Liard Can.
97 C1 Upper Lough Erne l. U.K.
137 E1 Upper Red Lake U.S.A.
Upper Tunguska r. Rus. Fed. see Angara
Upper Volta country Africa see Burkina
93 G4 Uppsala Sweden
78 B2 'Uqlat aş Şuqūr Saudi Arabia
Urad Qianqi China see Xishanzui
76 B2 Ural r. Kazakh./Rus. Fed.
53 D2 Uralla Austr.
87 E3 Ural Mountains Rus. Fed.
76 B1 Ural'sk Kazakh.
Ural'skiy Khrebet mts Rus. Fed. see Ural Mountains
119 D3 Urambo Tanz.
53 C3 Urana Austr.
129 D2 Uranium City Can.
86 F2 Uray Rus. Fed.
98 C2 Ure r. U.K.
86 D3 Uren' Rus. Fed.
82 G2 Urengoy Rus. Fed.
144 A2 Ures Mex.
Urfa Turkey see Şanlıurfa
76 C2 Urgench Uzbek.
100 B1 Urk Neth.
111 C3 Urla Turkey
110 C2 Urlaţi Romania
Urmia Iran see Orūmīyeh
Urmia, Lake salt l. Iran see Orūmīyeh, Daryācheh-ye
109 D2 Uroševac Yugo.
144 B2 Uruáchic Mex.
151 E4 Uruaçu Brazil
144 B3 Uruapan Mex.
150 B4 Urubamba r. Peru
151 D3 Urucara Brazil
151 E3 Uruçuí Brazil
151 E3 Uruçuí, Serra do hills Brazil
151 D3 Urucurituba Brazil
152 C2 Uruguaiana Brazil
153 C3 Uruguay country S. America
Urumchi China see Ürümqi
68 B2 Ürümqi China

Urundi country Africa see Burundi
53 D2 Urunga Austr.
78 B3 'Urūq al Awārik des. Saudi Arabia
119 D3 Uruwira Tanz.
110 C2 Urziceni Romania
67 B4 Usa Japan
86 E2 Usa r. Rus. Fed.
111 C3 Uşak Turkey
120 A3 Usakos Namibia
88 C2 Ushachy Belarus
82 G1 Ushakova, Ostrov i. Rus. Fed.
77 D2 Ushtobe Kazakh.
Ush-Tyube Kazakh. see Ushtobe
153 B5 Ushuaia Arg.
86 E2 Usinsk Rus. Fed.
99 B4 Usk r. U.K.
88 C3 Uskhodni Belarus
89 E3 Usman' Rus. Fed.
86 D2 Usogorsk Rus. Fed.
104 C2 Ussel France
66 C1 Ussuri r. China/Rus. Fed.
66 B2 Ussuriysk Rus. Fed.
Ust'-Abakanskoye Rus. Fed. see Abakan
Ust'-Balyk Rus. Fed. see Nefteyugansk
91 E2 Ust'-Donetskiy Rus. Fed.
108 B3 Ustica, Isola di i. Sicily Italy
83 H3 Ust'-Ilimsk Rus. Fed.
86 E2 Ust'-Ilych Rus. Fed.
102 C1 Ústí nad Labem Czech Rep.
Ustinov Rus. Fed. see Izhevsk
103 D1 Ustka Pol.
83 L3 Ust'-Kamchatsk Rus. Fed.
77 E2 Ust'-Kamenogorsk Kazakh.
86 F2 Ust'-Kara Rus. Fed.
86 E2 Ust'-Kulom Rus. Fed.
83 I3 Ust'-Kut Rus. Fed.
91 D2 Ust'-Labinsk Rus. Fed.
Ust'-Labinskaya Rus. Fed. see Ust'-Labinsk
88 C2 Ust'-Luga Rus. Fed.
86 E2 Ust'-Nem Rus. Fed.
83 K2 Ust'-Nera Rus. Fed.
83 I2 Ust'-Olenek Rus. Fed.
83 K2 Ust'-Omchug Rus. Fed.
83 H3 Ust'-Ordynskiy Rus. Fed.
103 E2 Ustrzyki Dolne Pol.
86 E2 Ust'-Tsil'ma Rus. Fed.
86 D2 Ust'-Ura Rus. Fed.
76 B2 Ustyurt Plateau Kazakh./Uzbek.
89 E2 Ustyuzhna Rus. Fed.
146 B3 Usulután El Salvador
Usumbura Burundi see Bujumbura
89 D2 Usvyaty Rus. Fed.
135 D3 Utah state U.S.A.
135 D2 Utah Lake U.S.A.
118 D3 Utena Lith.
119 D3 Utete Tanz.
63 B2 Uthai Thani Thai.
74 A2 Uthal Pak.
141 D2 Utica U.S.A.
107 C2 Utiel Spain
128 C2 Utikuma Lake Can.
93 G4 Utlängan i. Sweden
100 B1 Utrecht Neth.
123 D2 Utrecht S. Africa
106 B2 Utrera Spain
92 I2 Utsjoki Fin.
67 C3 Utsunomiya Japan
87 D4 Utta Rus. Fed.
62 B2 Uttaradit Thai.
75 B2 Uttar Pradesh state India
127 H1 Uummannaq Greenland
127 I2 Uummannaq Greenland
127 I2 Uummannaq Fjord inlet Greenland
93 H3 Uusikaupunki Fin.
120 A2 Uutapi Namibia
139 D3 Uvalde U.S.A.
119 D3 Uvinza Tanz.
119 D3 Uvongo S. Africa
68 C1 Uvs Nuur salt l. Mongolia
78 A2 Uwajima Japan
'Uwayrid, Ḥarrat al lava field Saudi Arabia
116 A2 Uweinat, Jebel mt.
83 H3 Uyar Rus. Fed.
115 C4 Uyo Nigeria
79 B2 Uyun Saudi Arabia

152 B2 Uyuni, Salar de salt flat Bol.
76 C2 Uzbekistan country Asia
Uzbekskaya S.S.R. country Asia see Uzbekistan
Uzbek S.S.R. country Asia see Uzbekistan
104 C2 Uzerche France
105 C3 Uzès France
90 C1 Uzh r. Ukr.
90 A2 Uzhhorod Ukr.
Uzhgorod Ukr. see Uzhhorod
109 C2 Užice Yugo.
89 E3 Uzlovaya Rus. Fed.
111 C3 Üzümlü Turkey
111 C2 Uzunköprü Turkey

V

123 B2 Vaal r. S. Africa
92 I3 Vaala Fin.
123 C2 Vaal Dam S. Africa
123 C1 Vaalwater S. Africa
92 H3 Vaasa Fin.
103 D2 Vác Hungary
152 C2 Vacaria Brazil
154 B2 Vacaria, Serra hills Brazil
135 B3 Vacaville U.S.A.
74 B2 Vadodara India
92 I1 Vadsø Norway
105 D2 Vaduz Liechtenstein
94 B1 Vágar i. Faroe Is
94 B1 Vágur Faroe Is
103 D2 Váh r. Slovakia
49 I4 Vaiaku Tuvalu
88 B2 Vaida Estonia
136 B3 Vail U.S.A.
77 C3 Vakhsh Tajik.
Vakhstroy Tajik. see Vakhsh
79 C2 Vakīlābād Iran
108 B1 Valdagno Italy
Valdai Hills Rus. Fed. see Valdayskaya Vozvyshennost'
89 D2 Valday Rus. Fed.
89 D2 Valdayskaya Vozvyshennost' hills Rus. Fed.
106 B2 Valdecañas, Embalse de resr Spain
93 G4 Valdemarsvik Sweden
105 D2 Val-de-Meuse France
106 C2 Valdepeñas Spain
153 B4 Valdés, Península pen. Arg.
126 C2 Valdez U.S.A.
153 A3 Valdivia Chile
130 C3 Val-d'Or Can.
143 D2 Valdosta U.S.A.
128 C2 Valemount Can.
152 E1 Valença Brazil
105 C3 Valence France
107 C2 Valencia Spain
107 C2 Valencia reg. Spain
150 C1 Valencia Venez.
107 D2 Valencia, Golfo de g. Spain
106 B1 Valencia de Don Juan Spain
97 A3 Valencia Island Rep. of Ireland
105 C1 Valenciennes France
136 C2 Valentine U.S.A.
64 B2 Valenzuela Phil.
150 B2 Valera Venez.
88 C2 Valga Estonia
109 C2 Valjevo Yugo.
88 C2 Valka Latvia
93 H3 Valkeakoski Fin.
100 B2 Valkenswaard Neth.
91 D2 Valky Ukr.
55 G2 Valkyrie Dome ice feature Antarctica
145 D2 Valladolid Mex.
106 C1 Valladolid Spain
107 C2 Val de Uxó Spain
93 E4 Valle Norway
145 C2 Vallecillos Mex.
150 C2 Valle de la Pascua Venez.
150 B1 Valledupar Col.
145 C2 Valle Hermoso Mex.
135 B3 Vallejo U.S.A.
152 A2 Vallenar Chile
84 F5 Valletta Malta
137 D1 Valley City U.S.A.

134 B2 Valley Falls U.S.A.
128 C2 Valleyview Can.
107 D1 Valls Spain
129 D3 Val Marie Can.
88 C2 Valmiera Latvia
104 B2 Valognes France
88 C3 Valozhyn Belarus
154 B2 Valparaíso Brazil
153 A3 Valparaíso Chile
105 C3 Valréas France
59 D3 Vals, Tanjung c. Indon.
74 B2 Valsād India
122 B2 Valspan S. Africa
91 D1 Valuyki Rus. Fed.
106 B2 Valverde del Camino Spain
81 C2 Van Turkey
Van, Lake salt l. Turkey see Van Gölü
81 C1 Vanadzor Armenia
83 H2 Vanavara Rus. Fed.
142 B1 Van Buren AR U.S.A.
141 F1 Van Buren ME U.S.A.
Van Buren U.S.A. see Kettering
128 B3 Vancouver Can.
134 B1 Vancouver U.S.A.
128 B3 Vancouver Island Can.
140 B3 Vandalia IL U.S.A.
140 C3 Vandalia OH U.S.A.
123 C2 Vanderbijlpark S. Africa
128 B2 Vanderhoof Can.
122 B3 Vanderkloof Dam resr S. Africa
50 C1 Van Diemen Gulf Austr.
88 C2 Vändra Estonia
Väner, Lake Sweden see Vänern
93 F4 Vänern l. Sweden
93 F4 Vänersborg Sweden
121 ☐D3 Vangaindrano Madag.
81 C2 Van Gölü salt l. Turkey
138 C2 Van Horn U.S.A.
59 D3 Vanimo P.N.G.
83 K3 Vanino Rus. Fed.
104 B2 Vannes France
Vannovka Kazakh. see Tura-Ryskulova
59 D3 Van Rees, Pegunungan mts Indon.
122 A3 Vanrhynsdorp S. Africa
93 H3 Vantaa Fin.
49 I5 Vanua Levu i. Fiji
48 H5 Vanuatu country S. Pacific Ocean
140 C2 Van Wert U.S.A.
122 B3 Vanwyksvlei S. Africa
122 B2 Van Zylsrus S. Africa
75 C2 Varanasi India
92 I1 Varangerfjorden sea chan. Norway
92 I1 Varanger Halvøya pen. Norway
88 C2 Varapayeva Belarus
109 C1 Varaždin Croatia
93 F4 Varberg Sweden
111 B3 Varda Greece
111 B2 Vardar r. Macedonia
93 E4 Varde Denmark
92 J1 Vardø Norway
101 D1 Varel Ger.
88 B3 Varėna Lith.
141 E1 Varennes Can.
108 A1 Varese Italy
155 C2 Varginha Brazil
93 I3 Varkaus Fin.
110 C2 Varna Bulg.
93 F4 Värnamo Sweden
155 D1 Várzea da Palma Brazil
86 C2 Varzino Rus. Fed.
88 C3 Vasilyevichy Belarus
88 C2 Vasknarva Estonia
110 C1 Vaslui Romania
93 G4 Västerås Sweden
93 G3 Västerdalälven r. Sweden
88 A2 Västerhaninge Sweden
93 G4 Västervik Sweden
108 B2 Vasto Italy
91 D2 Vasylivka Ukr.
90 C1 Vasyl'kiv Ukr.
91 D2 Vasyl'kivka Ukr.
104 C2 Vatan France
111 B3 Vathia Greece
92 ☐B3 Vatican City Europe
92 ☐B3 Vatnajökull ice cap Iceland
110 C1 Vatra Dornei Romania
Vätter, Lake Sweden see Vättern
93 F4 Vättern l. Sweden

138 B2 Vaughn U.S.A.
105 C3 Vauvert France
121 □D2 Vavatenina Madag.
49 J5 Vava'u Group is Tonga
88 B3 Vawkavysk Belarus
93 F4 Växjö Sweden
Vayenga Rus. Fed. see Severomorsk
86 E1 Vaygach, Ostrov i. Rus. Fed.
154 C1 Vazante Brazil
101 D1 Vechta Ger.
110 C2 Vedea r. Romania
100 C1 Veendam Neth.
100 B1 Veenendaal Neth.
92 F2 Vega i. Norway
128 C2 Vegreville Can.
106 B2 Vejer de la Frontera Spain
93 E4 Vejle Denmark
110 B2 Velbŭzhdki Prokhod pass Macedonia
122 A3 Velddrif S. Africa
100 B1 Veldhoven Neth.
109 B2 Velebit mts Croatia
100 C2 Velen Ger.
109 C1 Velenje Slovenia
109 D2 Veles Macedonia
106 C2 Vélez-Málaga Spain
155 D1 Velhas r. Brazil
109 D2 Velika Plana Yugo.
88 C2 Velikaya r. Rus. Fed.
89 D2 Velikiye Luki Rus. Fed.
89 D2 Velikiy Novgorod Rus. Fed.
86 D2 Velikiy Ustyug Rus. Fed.
110 C2 Veliko Tŭrnovo Bulg.
108 B2 Veli Lošinj Croatia
89 D2 Velizh Rus. Fed.
108 B2 Velletri Italy
73 B3 Vellore India
86 D2 Vel'sk Rus. Fed.
101 F1 Velten Ger.
91 D1 Velykyy Burluk Ukr.
Velykyy Tokmak Ukr. see Tokmak
159 E4 Vema Trench sea feature Indian Ocean
108 B2 Venafro Italy
154 C2 Venceslau Bráz Brazil
104 C2 Vendôme France
108 B1 Veneta, Laguna lag. Italy
89 E3 Venev Rus. Fed.
Venezia Italy see Venice
150 C2 Venezuela country S. America
150 B1 Venezuela, Golfo de g. Venez.
108 B1 Venice Italy
143 D3 Venice U.S.A.
108 B1 Venice, Gulf of Europe
100 C2 Venlo Neth.
93 E4 Vennesla Norway
100 B2 Venray Neth.
88 B2 Venta r. Latvia/Lith.
88 B2 Venta Lith.
123 C2 Ventersburg S. Africa
123 C3 Venterstad S. Africa
108 A2 Ventimiglia Italy
99 C4 Ventnor U.K.
88 B2 Ventspils Latvia
135 C4 Ventura U.S.A.
139 C3 Venustiano Carranza, Presa resr Mex.
107 C2 Vera Spain
154 C2 Vera Cruz Brazil
145 C3 Veracruz Mex.
74 B2 Veraval India
108 A1 Verbania Italy
108 A1 Vercelli Italy
105 D3 Vercors reg. France
92 F3 Verdalsøra Norway
154 B1 Verde r. Brazil
154 B2 Verde r. Brazil
144 B2 Verde r. Mex.
138 A2 Verde r.
155 D1 Verde Grande r. Brazil
101 D1 Verden (Aller) Ger.
154 B1 Verdinho, Serra do mts Brazil
105 D3 Verdon r. France
105 D2 Verdun France
123 C2 Vereeniging S. Africa
106 B1 Verín Spain
91 D3 Verkhnebakanskiy Rus. Fed.
89 D3 Verkhnedneprovskiy Rus. Fed.
92 J2 Verkhnetulomskiy Rus. Fed.

92 J2 Verkhnetulomskoye Vodokhranilishche resr Rus. Fed.
87 D4 Verkhniy Baskunchak Rus. Fed.
91 E1 Verkhniy Mamon Rus. Fed.
86 D2 Verkhnyaya Toyma Rus. Fed.
89 E3 Verkhov'ye Rus. Fed.
90 A2 Verkhovyna Ukr.
83 J2 Verkhoyanskiy Khrebet mts Rus. Fed.
129 C2 Vermilion Can.
137 D2 Vermillion U.S.A.
130 A3 Vermillion Bay Can.
141 E2 Vermont state U.S.A.
135 E2 Vernal U.S.A.
122 B2 Verneuk Pan salt pan S. Africa
128 C2 Vernon Can.
139 D2 Vernon U.S.A.
143 D3 Vero Beach U.S.A.
111 B2 Veroia Greece
108 B1 Verona Italy
140 B2 Verona U.S.A.
104 C2 Versailles France
104 B2 Vertou France
123 D2 Verulam S. Africa
100 B2 Verviers Belgium
105 C2 Vervins France
105 D3 Vescovato Corsica France
87 E3 Veselaya, Gora mt. Rus. Fed.
91 C2 Vesele Ukr.
91 E2 Veselyy Rus. Fed.
105 D2 Vesoul France
142 C2 Vestavia Hills U.S.A.
92 F2 Vesterålen is Norway
92 F2 Vestfjorden sea chan. Norway
94 B1 Vestmanna Faroe Is
92 □A3 Vestmannaeyjar Iceland
92 □A3 Vestmannaeyjar is Iceland
93 E3 Vestnes Norway
108 B2 Vesuvio vol. Italy
Vesuvius vol. Italy see Vesuvio
89 E2 Ves'yegonsk Rus. Fed.
103 D2 Veszprém Hungary
93 G4 Vetlanda Sweden
86 D3 Vetluga Rus. Fed.
86 D3 Vetluzhskiy Rus. Fed.
100 A2 Veurne Belgium
119 D2 Veveno r. Sudan
105 D2 Vevey Switz.
91 D1 Veydelevka Rus. Fed.
80 B1 Vezirköprü Turkey
Vialar Alg. see Tissemsilt
152 C3 Viamao Brazil
151 E3 Viana Brazil
106 B1 Viana do Castelo Port.
Viangchan Laos see Vientiane
62 B1 Viangphoukha Laos
154 C1 Vianópolis Brazil
108 B2 Viareggio Italy
93 E4 Viborg Denmark
Viborg Rus. Fed. see Vyborg
109 C3 Vibo Valentia Italy
107 D1 Vic Spain
144 A1 Vicente Guerrero Mex.
108 B1 Vicenza Italy
89 F2 Vichuga Rus. Fed.
105 C2 Vichy France
142 B2 Vicksburg U.S.A.
155 D2 Viçosa Brazil
52 A3 Victor Harbor Austr.
50 C1 Victoria r. Austr.
52 B3 Victoria state Austr.
Victoria Cameroon see Limbe
128 B3 Victoria Can.
153 A3 Victoria Chile
Victoria Malaysia see Labuan
113 I6 Victoria Seychelles
139 D3 Victoria U.S.A.
119 D3 Victoria, Lake Africa
52 B2 Victoria, Lake Austr.
62 A1 Victoria, Mount Myanmar
59 D3 Victoria, Mount P.N.G.
120 B2 Victoria Falls waterfall Zambia/Zimbabwe
120 B2 Victoria Falls Zimbabwe
126 E2 Victoria Island Can.
55 M2 Victoria Land coastal area Antarctica
145 D3 Victoria Peak Belize

50 C1 Victoria River Downs Austr.
141 E1 Victoriaville Can.
122 B3 Victoria West S. Africa
135 C4 Victorville U.S.A.
143 D2 Vidalia U.S.A.
110 C2 Videle Romania
92 □A2 Viðidalsá Iceland
110 B2 Vidin Bulg.
74 B2 Vidisha India
102 B2 Vidor U.S.A.
153 B4 Viedma Arg.
153 A4 Viedma, Lago l. Arg.
102 C2 Viehberg mt. Austria
110 B2 Vielha Spain
100 B2 Vielsalm Belgium
101 E2 Vienenburg Ger.
103 D2 Vienna Austria
140 C3 Vienna U.S.A.
105 C2 Vienne France
104 C2 Vienne r. France
62 B2 Vientiane Laos
100 C2 Viersen Ger.
104 C2 Vierzon France
144 B2 Viesca Mex.
109 C2 Vieste Italy
62 B2 Vietnam country Asia
62 B1 Viêt Tri Vietnam
64 B2 Vigan Phil.
108 A1 Vigevano Italy
106 B1 Vigo Spain
Viipuri Rus. Fed. see Vyborg
73 C3 Vijayawada India
92 □B3 Vík Iceland
111 B2 Vikhren mt. Bulg.
128 C2 Viking Can.
92 F3 Vikna i. Norway
Vila Alferes Chamusca Moz. see Guija
Vila Arriaga Angola see Bibala
Vila Bugaço Angola see Camanongue
Vila Cabral Moz. see Lichinga
Vila da Ponte Angola see Kuvango
Vila de Aljustrel Angola see Cangamba
Vila de Almoster Angola see Chiange
Vila de João Belo Moz. see Xai-Xai
Vila de Trego Morais Moz. see Chókwé
Vila Fontes Moz. see Caia
106 B2 Vila Franca de Xira Port.
106 B1 Vilagarcía de Arousa Spain
123 D1 Vila Gomes da Costa Moz.
106 B1 Vilalba Spain
Vila Luísa Moz. see Marracuene
Vila Marechal Carmona Angola see Uíge
Vila Miranda Moz. see Macaloge
121 □D2 Vilanandro, Tanjona pt Madag.
88 C2 Viļāni Latvia
106 B1 Vila Nova de Gaia Port.
107 D1 Vilanova i la Geltrú Spain
Vila Paiva de Andrada Moz. see Gorongosa
Vila Pery Moz. see Chimoio
106 B1 Vila Real Port.
106 B1 Vilar Formoso Port.
Vila Salazar Angola see N'dalatando
Vila Salazar Zimbabwe see Sango
Vila Teixeira de Sousa Angola see Luau
155 D2 Vila Velha Brazil
150 B4 Vilcabamba, Cordillera mts Peru
92 G3 Vilhelmina Sweden
150 C4 Vilhena Brazil
88 C2 Viljandi Estonia
123 C2 Viljoenskroon S. Africa
88 B3 Vilkaviškis Lith.
83 H1 Vil'kitskogo, Proliv str. Rus. Fed.
144 B1 Villa Ahumada Mex.
106 B1 Villablino Spain
102 C2 Villach Austria

Villa Cisneros Western Sahara see Ad Dakhla
144 A2 Villa Constitución Mex.
144 B2 Villa de Cos Mex.
152 B3 Villa Dolores Arg.
145 C3 Villa Flores Mex.
153 C3 Villa Gesell Arg.
145 C2 Villagrán Mex.
145 C3 Villahermosa Mex.
144 A2 Villa Insurgentes Mex.
107 C2 Villajoyosa Spain
152 B3 Villa María Arg.
152 B3 Villa Montes Bol.
144 B2 Villanueva Mex.
106 B2 Villanueva de la Serena Spain
106 C2 Villanueva de los Infantes Spain
152 C2 Villa Ocampo Arg.
138 B3 Villa Ocampo Mex.
108 A3 Villaputzu Sardinia Italy
152 C2 Villarrica Para.
106 C2 Villarrobledo Spain
Villasalazar Zimbabwe see Sango
152 B2 Villa Unión Arg.
144 B2 Villa Unión Mex.
144 B2 Villa Unión Mex.
150 B2 Villavicencio Col.
152 B2 Villazon Bol.
104 C3 Villefranche-de-Rouergue France
105 C2 Villefranche-sur-Saône France
107 C2 Villena Spain
100 A2 Villeneuve-d'Ascq France
104 C3 Villeneuve-sur-Lot France
142 B2 Ville Platte U.S.A.
100 A3 Villers-Cotterêts France
105 C2 Villeurbanne France
123 C2 Villiers S. Africa
102 B2 Villingen Ger.
137 E2 Villisca U.S.A.
88 C3 Vilnius Lith.
91 C2 Vil'nohirs'k Ukr.
91 D2 Vil'nyans'k Ukr.
100 B2 Vilvoorde Belgium
88 C3 Vilyeyka Belarus
83 J2 Vilyuy r. Rus. Fed.
93 G4 Vimmerby Sweden
153 A3 Vina del Mar Chile
107 D1 Vinaròs Spain
140 B3 Vincennes U.S.A.
55 J3 Vincennes Bay Antarctica
141 D3 Vineland U.S.A.
62 B2 Vinh Vietnam
63 B2 Vinh Long Vietnam
139 D1 Vinita U.S.A.
90 B2 Vinnytsya Ukr.
55 R2 Vinson Massif mt. Antarctica
93 E3 Vinstra Norway
108 B1 Vipiteno Italy
64 B2 Virac Phil.
74 B2 Viramgam India
80 B2 Viranşehir Turkey
129 D3 Virden Can.
104 B2 Vire France
120 A2 Virei Angola
155 D1 Virgem da Lapa Brazil
138 A1 Virgin r. U.S.A.
123 C2 Virginia S. Africa
137 E1 Virginia U.S.A.
141 D3 Virginia state U.S.A.
141 D3 Virginia Beach U.S.A.
135 C3 Virginia City U.S.A.
147 D3 Virgin Islands (U.K.) terr. West Indies
147 D3 Virgin Islands (U.S.A.) terr. West Indies
63 B2 Virôchey Cambodia
109 C1 Virovitica Croatia
100 B3 Virton Belgium
88 B2 Virtsu Estonia
73 B4 Virudunagar India
109 C2 Vis i. Croatia
88 C2 Visaginas Lith.
135 C3 Visalia U.S.A.
74 B2 Visavadar India
64 B2 Visayan Sea Phil.
93 G4 Visby Sweden
126 E2 Viscount Melville Sound sea chan. Can.
151 E3 Viseu Brazil
106 B1 Viseu Port.
110 B1 Vişeu de Sus Romania
73 C3 Visakhapatnam India
88 C2 Viški Latvia
109 C2 Visoko Bos.-Herz.
Vistula r. Pol. see Wisła

Vitebsk Belarus see Vitsyebsk
108 B2 Viterbo Italy
49 I5 Viti Levu i. Fiji
83 I3 Vitim r. Rus. Fed.
155 D2 Vitória Brazil
151 E4 Vitória da Conquista Brazil
106 C1 Vitoria-Gasteiz Spain
104 B2 Vitré France
105 C2 Vitry-le-François France
89 D2 Vitsyebsk Belarus
105 D2 Vittel France
108 B3 Vittoria Sicily Italy
108 B1 Vittorio Veneto Italy
106 B1 Viveiro Spain
136 C2 Vivian U.S.A.
Vizagapatam India see Vishakhapatnam
138 A3 Vizcaíno, Desierto de des. Mex.
144 A2 Vizcaíno, Sierra mts Mex.
111 C2 Vize Turkey
73 C3 Vizianagaram India
100 B2 Vlaardingen Neth.
87 D4 Vladikavkaz Rus. Fed.
89 F2 Vladimir Rus. Fed.
66 B2 Vladivostok Rus. Fed.
109 D2 Vlasotince Yugo.
100 B1 Vlieland i. Neth.
100 A2 Vlissingen Neth.
109 C2 Vlorë Albania
102 C1 Vltava r. Czech Rep.
102 C2 Vöcklabruck Austria
109 C2 Vodice Croatia
Vogelkop Peninsula Indon. see Doberai, Jazirah
101 D2 Vogelsberg hills Ger.
Vohémar Madag. see Iharaña
Vohibinany Madag. see Ampasimanolotra
Vohimarina Madag. see Iharaña
121 □D3 Vohimena, Tanjona c. Madag.
121 □D3 Vohipeno Madag.
119 D3 Voi Kenya
105 D2 Voiron France
131 D2 Voisey Bay Can.
109 C1 Vojvodina prov. Yugo.
92 J3 Voknavolok Rus. Fed.
Volcano Bay Japan see Uchiura-wan
Volcano Islands Japan see Kazan-rettō
Volchansk Ukr. see Vovchans'k
89 E2 Volga Rus. Fed.
89 F2 Volga r. Rus. Fed.
87 D4 Volgodonsk Rus. Fed.
87 D4 Volgograd Rus. Fed.
87 D4 Volgogradskoye Vodokhranilishche resr Rus. Fed.
89 D2 Volkhov Rus. Fed.
89 D1 Volkhov r. Rus. Fed.
101 E2 Volkstedt Ger.
91 D2 Volnovakha Ukr.
90 B2 Volochys'k Ukr.
91 D2 Volodars'ke Ukr.
Volodarskoye Kazakh. see Saumalkol'
90 B1 Volodars'k-Volyns'kyy Ukr.
90 B1 Volodymyrets' Ukr.
90 A1 Volodymyr-Volyns'kyy Ukr.
89 E2 Vologda Rus. Fed.
89 E2 Volokolamsk Rus. Fed.
91 D1 Volokonovka Rus. Fed.
111 B3 Volos Greece
88 C2 Volosovo Rus. Fed.
89 D2 Volot Rus. Fed.
89 E3 Volovo Rus. Fed.
87 D3 Vol'sk Rus. Fed.
114 C4 Volta r. Ghana
114 C4 Volta, Lake resr Ghana
155 D2 Volta Redonda Brazil
110 C2 Voluntari Romania
87 D4 Volzhskiy Rus. Fed.
92 □C2 Vopnafjörður Iceland
88 C3 Voranava Belarus
160 K3 Voring Plateau sea feature N. Atlantic Ocean
86 F2 Vorkuta Rus. Fed.
88 B2 Vormsi i. Estonia
83 G2 Vorogovo Rus. Fed.
89 E3 Voronezh Rus. Fed.
89 E3 Voronezh r. Rus. Fed.
91 E1 Vorontsovka Rus. Fed.

Voroshilov Rus. Fed. see Ussuriysk
Voroshilovgrad Ukr. see Luhans'k
Voroshilovsk Rus. Fed. see Stavropol'
Voroshilovsk Ukr. see Alchevs'k
91 C2 Vorskla r. Rus. Fed.
88 C2 Võrtsjärv l. Estonia
88 C2 Võru Estonia
122 B3 Vosburg S. Africa
105 D2 Vosges mts France
89 E2 Voskresensk Rus. Fed.
93 E3 Voss Norway
86 C2 Vostochnaya Litsa Rus. Fed.
Vostochno-Sibirskoye More sea Rus. Fed. see East Siberian Sea
83 H3 Vostochnyy Sayan mts Rus. Fed.
66 C1 Vostok Rus. Fed.
49 L5 Vostok Island Kiribati
86 E3 Votkinsk Rus. Fed.
86 E3 Votkinskoye Vodokhranilishche resr Rus. Fed.
154 C2 Votuporanga Brazil
105 C2 Vouziers France
91 D1 Vovchans'k Ukr.
92 J2 Voynitsa Rus. Fed.
86 E2 Voyvozh Rus. Fed.
91 C2 Voznesens'k Ukr.
76 B2 Vozrozhdeniya, Ostrov i. Uzbek.
93 E4 Vrådal Norway
90 C2 Vradiyivka Ukr.
66 B2 Vrangel' Rus. Fed.
83 N2 Vrangelya, Ostrov i. Rus. Fed.
109 D2 Vranje Yugo.
110 C2 Vratnik pass Bulg.
110 B2 Vratsa Bulg.
109 C1 Vrbas r. Bos.-Herz.
109 C1 Vrbas Yugo.
122 A3 Vredenburg S. Africa
122 A3 Vredendal S. Africa
100 B3 Vresse Belgium
100 C1 Vriezenveen Neth.
109 D1 Vršac Yugo.
122 B2 Vryburg S. Africa
123 D2 Vryheid S. Africa
89 D1 Vsevolozhsk Rus. Fed.
109 D2 Vučitrn Yugo.
109 C1 Vukovar Croatia
86 E2 Vuktyl' Rus. Fed.
123 C2 Vukuzakhe S. Africa
90 B2 Vulcănești Moldova
109 B3 Vulcano, Isola i. Italy
Vulkaneshty Moldova see Vulcănești
63 B2 Vung Tau Vietnam
92 H2 Vuollerim Sweden
92 I2 Vuotso Fin.
74 B2 Vyara India
Vyarkhowye Belarus see Ruba
Vyatka Rus. Fed. see Kirov
89 D2 Vyaz'ma Rus. Fed.
88 C1 Vyborg Rus. Fed.
88 C1 Vyborgskiy Zaliv b. Rus. Fed.
86 D2 Vychegda r. Rus. Fed.
88 C2 Vyerkhnyadzvinsk Belarus
89 D3 Vyetka Belarus
89 D3 Vygonichi Rus. Fed.
86 C2 Vygozero, Ozero l. Rus. Fed.
87 D3 Vyksa Rus. Fed.
90 B2 Vylkove Ukr.
90 A2 Vynohradiv Ukr.
89 D2 Vypolzovo Rus. Fed.
89 D2 Vyritsa Rus. Fed.
91 D2 Vyselki Rus. Fed.
90 C1 Vyshhorod Ukr.
89 D2 Vyshnevolotskaya Gryada ridge Rus. Fed.
Vyshniy-Volochek Rus. Fed.
103 D2 Vyškov Czech Rep.
89 E2 Vysokovsk Rus. Fed.
86 C2 Vytegra Rus. Fed.

W

114 B3 Wa Ghana
100 B2 Waal r. Neth.
100 B2 Waalwijk Neth.

119 D2 Waat Sudan
128 C2 Wabasca r. Can.
128 C2 Wabasca-Desmarais Can.
140 B3 Wabash r. U.S.A.
117 C4 Wabē Gestro r. Eth.
117 C4 Wabē Shebelē Wenz r. Eth.
129 E2 Wabowden Can.
103 D1 Wąbrzeźno Pol.
143 D3 Waccasassa Bay U.S.A.
101 D2 Wächtersbach Ger.
139 D2 Waco U.S.A.
74 A2 Wad Pak.
115 D2 Waddān Libya
100 B1 Waddeneilanden is Neth.
Wadden Islands Neth. see Waddeneilanden
100 B1 Waddenzee sea chan. Neth.
128 B2 Waddington, Mount Can.
100 B1 Waddinxveen Neth.
129 D2 Wadena U.S.A.
137 D1 Wadena U.S.A.
50 B1 Wadeye Austr.
Wadhwan India see Surendranagar
116 B2 Wadi Halfa Sudan
116 B3 Wad Medani Sudan
122 B3 Waenhuiskrans S. Africa
70 C2 Wafangdian China
100 B2 Wageningen Neth.
127 G2 Wager Bay Can.
53 C3 Wagga Wagga Austr.
137 D2 Wagner U.S.A.
74 B1 Wah Pak.
137 D2 Wahoo U.S.A.
137 D1 Wahpeton U.S.A.
54 B2 Waiau r. N.Z.
59 C3 Waigeo i. Indon.
61 C2 Waikabubak Indon.
54 C1 Waikaremoana, Lake N.Z.
52 A2 Waikerie Austr.
54 B2 Waimate N.Z.
75 B3 Wainganga r. India
61 D2 Waingapu Indon.
129 C2 Wainwright Can.
126 B2 Wainwright U.S.A.
54 C1 Waiouru N.Z.
54 B2 Waipara N.Z.
54 C1 Waipawa N.Z.
54 B2 Wairau r. N.Z.
54 C1 Wairoa N.Z.
54 B2 Waitaki r. N.Z.
54 B2 Waitara N.Z.
54 B1 Waiuku N.Z.
67 C3 Wajima Japan
119 E2 Wajir Kenya
67 C3 Wakasa-wan b. Japan
54 A3 Wakatipu, Lake N.Z.
129 D2 Wakaw Can.
67 C4 Wakayama Japan
48 H2 Wake Atoll terr. N. Pacific Ocean
136 D3 WaKeeney U.S.A.
54 B2 Wakefield N.Z.
98 C3 Wakefield U.K.
Wakeham Can. see Kangiqsujuaq
66 D1 Wakkanai Japan
123 D2 Wakkerstroom S. Africa
120 A2 Waku-Kungo Angola
103 D1 Wałbrzych Pol.
53 D2 Walcha Austr.
100 C1 Walchum Ger.
103 D1 Wałcz Pol.
99 B3 Wales admin. div. U.K.
53 C2 Walgett Austr.
119 C3 Walikale Dem. Rep. Congo
135 C3 Walker Lake U.S.A.
134 C1 Wallace ID U.S.A.
143 E2 Wallace NC U.S.A.
52 A2 Wallaroo Austr.
98 B3 Wallasey U.K.
134 C1 Walla Walla U.S.A.
101 D3 Walldürn Ger.
122 A3 Wallekraal S. Africa
53 C2 Wallendbeen Austr.
49 J5 Wallis, Îles is Wallis and Futuna Is
49 J5 Wallis and Futuna terr. S. Pacific Ocean
96 □ Walls U.K.
98 B2 Walney, Isle of i. U.K.
99 C3 Walsall U.K.
136 C3 Walsenburg U.S.A.
101 D1 Walsrode Ger.
143 D2 Walterboro U.S.A.
120 A3 Walvis Bay Namibia
158 F6 Walvis Ridge sea feature S. Atlantic Ocean

119 C2 Wamba Dem. Rep. Congo
52 B1 Wanaaring Austr.
54 A2 Wanaka N.Z.
54 A2 Wanaka, Lake N.Z.
71 B3 Wan'an China
130 B3 Wanapitei Lake Can.
154 B3 Wanda Arg.
66 B1 Wanda Shan mts China
62 A1 Wanding China
Wandingzhen China see Wanding
54 C1 Wanganui N.Z.
54 B1 Wanganui r. N.Z.
53 C3 Wangaratta Austr.
65 B1 Wangqing China
62 A1 Wan Hsa-la Myanmar
Wankie Zimbabwe see Hwange
71 B4 Wanning China
100 B2 Wanroij Neth.
99 C4 Wantage U.K.
70 A2 Wanxian China
70 A2 Wanyuan China
117 A4 Warab Sudan
73 B3 Warangal India
101 D2 Warburg Ger.
50 B2 Warburton Austr.
52 A1 Warburton watercourse Austr.
74 B2 Wardha India
96 C1 Ward Hill U.K.
128 B2 Ware Can.
101 F1 Waren Ger.
101 C2 Warendorf Ger.
53 D1 Warialda Austr.
122 A2 Warmbad Namibia
135 C3 Warm Springs U.S.A.
134 C2 Warner Lakes U.S.A.
134 B2 Warner Mountains U.S.A.
143 D2 Warner Robins U.S.A.
152 B3 Warnes Bol.
52 B3 Warracknabeal Austr.
53 C3 Warrandyte Austr.
53 C2 Warrego r. Austr.
53 C2 Warren Austr.
142 B2 Warren AR U.S.A.
140 C2 Warren OH U.S.A.
141 D2 Warren PA U.S.A.
97 C1 Warrenpoint U.K.
122 B2 Warrenton S. Africa
115 C4 Warri Nigeria
98 B3 Warrington U.K.
52 B3 Warrnambool Austr.
103 E1 Warsaw Pol.
140 B2 Warsaw U.S.A.
Warszawa Pol. see Warsaw
103 C1 Warta r. Pol.
53 D1 Warwick Austr.
99 C3 Warwick U.K.
141 E2 Warwick U.S.A.
134 D3 Wasatch Range mts U.S.A.
135 C3 Wasco U.S.A.
136 C1 Washburn U.S.A.
137 E2 Washington IA U.S.A.
140 B2 Washington IL U.S.A.
140 B3 Washington IN U.S.A.
137 E3 Washington MO U.S.A.
143 E1 Washington NC U.S.A.
140 C2 Washington PA U.S.A.
135 D3 Washington UT U.S.A.
134 B1 Washington state U.S.A.
141 D3 Washington D.C. U.S.A.
141 E2 Washington, Mount U.S.A.
140 C3 Washington Court House U.S.A.
74 A2 Washuk Pak.
130 C2 Waskaganish Can.
129 E2 Waskaiowaka Lake Can.
122 A2 Wasser Namibia
101 D2 Wasserkuppe hill Ger.
130 C3 Waswanipi, Lac l. Can.
61 D2 Watampone Indon.
Watenstedt-Salzgitter Ger. see Salzgitter
141 E2 Waterbury U.S.A.
129 D2 Waterbury Lake Can.
97 C2 Waterford Rep. of Ireland
97 C2 Waterford Harbour Rep. of Ireland
100 B2 Waterloo Belgium
137 E2 Waterloo U.S.A.
99 C4 Waterlooville U.K.
123 C2 Waterpoort S. Africa
141 E2 Watertown NY U.S.A.
137 D2 Watertown SD U.S.A.
140 B2 Watertown WI U.S.A.
97 A3 Waterville Rep. of Ireland

141 F2 Waterville U.S.A.
99 C4 Watford U.K.
136 C1 Watford City U.S.A.
129 D2 Wathaman r. Can.
Watling Island Bahamas see San Salvador
139 D1 Watonga U.S.A.
129 D2 Watrous Can.
119 C2 Watsa Dem. Rep. Congo
140 B2 Watseka U.S.A.
118 C3 Watsi Kengo Dem. Rep. Congo
128 B1 Watson Lake Can.
135 B3 Watsonville U.S.A.
59 C3 Watubela, Kepulauan is Indon.
59 D3 Wau P.N.G.
117 A4 Wau Sudan
53 D2 Wauchope Austr.
140 B2 Waukegan U.S.A.
140 B2 Waukesha U.S.A.
139 D2 Waurika U.S.A.
140 B2 Wausau U.S.A.
99 D3 Waveney r. U.K.
137 E2 Waverly U.S.A.
130 B3 Wawa Can.
143 D2 Waycross U.S.A.
137 D2 Wayne U.S.A.
143 D2 Waynesboro GA U.S.A.
141 D3 Waynesboro VA U.S.A.
137 E3 Waynesville MO U.S.A.
143 D1 Waynesville NC U.S.A.
74 B1 Wazirabad Pak.
60 A1 We, Pulau i. Indon.
98 C2 Wear r. U.K.
139 D1 Weatherford OK U.S.A.
139 D2 Weatherford TX U.S.A.
134 B2 Weaverville U.S.A.
139 D3 Webb U.S.A.
130 B2 Webequie Can.
117 C4 Webi Shabeelle r. Somalia
137 D1 Webster U.S.A.
137 E2 Webster City U.S.A.
55 C3 Weddell Abyssal Plain sea feature Southern Ocean
55 B3 Weddell Sea Antarctica
123 D2 Weenen S. Africa
100 B2 Weert Neth.
53 C2 Weethalie Austr.
53 C2 Wee Waa Austr.
100 C2 Wegberg Ger.
103 E1 Wegorzewo Pol.
103 E1 Węgrów Pol.
70 B2 Wei r. China
70 B1 Weichang China
101 F3 Weiden in der Oberpfalz Ger.
Weidongmen China see Qianjin
70 B2 Weifang China
70 C2 Weihai China
53 C1 Weilmoringle Austr.
101 E2 Weimar Ger.
139 D3 Weimar U.S.A.
70 A2 Weinan China
71 A3 Weining China
51 D1 Weipa Austr.
53 C1 Weir r. Austr.
140 C2 Weirton U.S.A.
62 B1 Weishan China
101 E2 Weiße Elster r. Ger.
101 E2 Weißenfels Ger.
102 C2 Weißkugel mt. Austria/Italy
71 A3 Weixin China
Weizhou China see Wenchuan
103 D1 Wejherowo Pol.
140 C3 Welch U.S.A.
117 B3 Weldiya Eth.
123 C2 Welkom S. Africa
99 C3 Welland r. U.K.
51 C1 Wellesley Islands Austr.
99 C3 Wellingborough U.K.
53 C2 Wellington Austr.
54 B2 Wellington N.Z.
122 A3 Wellington S. Africa
136 B2 Wellington CO U.S.A.
137 D3 Wellington KS U.S.A.
135 D3 Wellington UT U.S.A.
153 A4 Wellington, Isla i. Chile
53 C3 Wellington, Lake Austr.
128 B2 Wells Can.
99 B4 Wells U.K.
134 D2 Wells U.S.A.
50 B2 Wells, Lake salt flat Austr.
54 B1 Wellsford N.Z.
99 D3 Wells-next-the-Sea U.K.
138 A2 Wellton U.S.A.
102 C2 Wels Austria
99 B3 Welshpool U.K.

Welwitschia Namibia see Khorixas
123 C2 Wembesi S. Africa
130 C2 Wemindji Can.
134 B1 Wenatchee U.S.A.
71 B4 Wenchang China
114 B4 Wenchi Ghana
Wenchow China see Wenzhou
70 A2 Wenchuan China
70 C2 Wendeng China
101 E1 Wendisch Evern Ger.
117 B4 Wendo Eth.
135 D2 Wendover U.S.A.
71 B3 Wengyuan China
Wenhua China see Weishan
97 C2 Wenlan China see Mengzi
Wenlin China see Renshou
71 C3 Wenling China
Wenquan China see Yingshan
71 A3 Wenshan China
52 B2 Wentworth Austr.
71 C3 Wenzhou China
123 C2 Wepener S. Africa
122 B2 Werda Botswana
101 F2 Werdau Ger.
101 F1 Werder Ger.
101 F3 Wernberg-Köblitz Ger.
101 E2 Wernigerode Ger.
101 D2 Werra r. Ger.
52 B2 Werrimull Austr.
53 D2 Werris Creek Austr.
101 D3 Wertheim Ger.
100 C2 Wesel Ger.
101 E1 Wesendorf Ger.
101 D1 Weser r. Ger.
101 D1 Weser sea chan. Ger.
51 C1 Wessel, Cape Austr.
51 C1 Wessel Islands Austr.
123 C2 Wesselton S. Africa
55 P2 West Antarctica reg. Antarctica
156 B7 West Australian Basin sea feature Indian Ocean
80 B2 West Bank terr. Asia
140 B2 West Bend U.S.A.
75 C2 West Bengal state India
99 C3 West Bromwich U.K.
141 E2 Westbrook U.S.A.
137 E2 West Des Moines U.S.A.
100 C2 Westerburg Ger.
100 C1 Westerholt Ger.
141 E2 Westerly U.S.A.
50 B2 Western Australia state Austr.
122 B3 Western Cape prov. S. Africa
116 A2 Western Desert Egypt Western Dvina r. Europe see Zapadnaya Dvina
73 B3 Western Ghats mts India
114 A2 Western Sahara terr. Africa
Western Samoa country S. Pacific Ocean see Samoa
Western Sayan Mountains reg. Rus. Fed. see Zapadnyy Sayan
100 A2 Westerschelde est. Neth.
100 C1 Westerstede Ger.
100 C2 Westerwald hills Ger.
153 B5 West Falkland i. Falkland Is
140 B3 West Frankfort U.S.A.
West Frisian Islands Neth. see Waddeneilanden
96 C2 Westhill U.K.
55 I3 West Ice Shelf Antarctica
147 D2 West Indies N. America
100 A2 Westkapelle Neth.
96 A1 West Loch Roag b. U.K.
128 C2 Westlock Can.
100 B2 Westmalle Belgium
Westman Islands Iceland see Vestmannaeyjar
53 C1 Westmar Austr.
156 C4 West Mariana Basin sea feature N. Pacific Ocean
142 B1 West Memphis U.S.A.
140 C3 Weston U.S.A.
99 B4 Weston-super-Mare U.K.
143 D3 West Palm Beach U.S.A.
137 E3 West Plains U.S.A.
54 B2 West Point N.Z.
97 B2 Westport Rep. of Ireland
129 D2 Westray Can.

96 C1 Westray i. U.K.
West Siberian Plain Rus. Fed. see Zapadno-Sibirskaya Ravnina
100 B1 West-Terschelling Neth.
136 A2 West Thumb U.S.A.
97 B1 West Town Rep. of Ireland
135 D2 West Valley City U.S.A.
140 C3 West Virginia state U.S.A.
53 C2 West Wyalong Austr.
134 D2 West Yellowstone U.S.A.
59 C3 Wetar i. Indon.
128 C2 Wetaskiwin Can.
119 D3 Wete Tanz.
101 D2 Wetzlar Ger.
59 D3 Wewak P.N.G.
97 C2 Wexford Rep. of Ireland
97 C2 Wexford Harbour b. Rep. of Ireland
129 D2 Weyakwin Can.
129 D3 Weyburn Can.
101 D1 Weyhe Ger.
99 B4 Weymouth U.K.
54 C1 Whakatane N.Z.
129 E1 Whale Cove Can.
96 □ Whalsay i. U.K.
54 B1 Whangamomona N.Z.
54 B1 Whangaparaoa N.Z.
54 B1 Whangarei N.Z.
98 C3 Wharfe r. U.K.
139 D3 Wharton U.S.A.
128 C1 Wha Ti Can.
136 B2 Wheatland U.S.A.
140 B2 Wheaton U.S.A.
142 C2 Wheeler Lake resr U.S.A.
138 B1 Wheeler Peak NM U.S.A.
135 D3 Wheeler Peak NV U.S.A.
140 C2 Wheeling U.S.A.
98 B2 Whernside hill U.K.
128 B2 Whistler Can.
98 C2 Whitby U.K.
128 A1 White r. Can./U.S.A.
142 B2 White r. AR U.S.A.
140 B3 White r. IN U.S.A.
50 B2 White, Lake salt flat Austr.
131 E3 White Bay Can.
136 C1 White Butte mt. U.S.A.
52 B2 White Cliffs Austr.
128 C2 Whitecourt Can.
134 D1 Whitefish U.S.A.
98 B2 Whitehaven U.K.
97 D1 Whitehead U.K.
128 A1 Whitehorse Can.
142 B3 White Lake U.S.A.
51 D4 Whitemark Austr.
135 C3 White Mountain Peak U.S.A.
116 B3 White Nile r. Sudan/Uganda
White Russia country Europe see Belarus
36 C2 White Sea Rus. Fed.
134 D1 White Sulphur Springs U.S.A.
143 E2 Whiteville U.S.A.
114 B3 White Volta watercourse Burkina/Ghana
136 B3 Whitewater U.S.A.
138 B2 Whitewater Baldy mt. U.S.A.
130 B2 Whitewater Lake Can.
129 D2 Whitewood Can.
96 B3 Whithorn U.K.
54 C1 Whitianga N.Z.
135 C3 Whitney, Mount U.S.A.
99 D4 Whitstable U.K.
51 D2 Whitsunday Island Austr.
53 C3 Whittlesea Austr.
52 A2 Whyalla Austr.
62 A2 Wiang Pa Pao Thai.
62 A1 Wiang Phran Thai.
100 A2 Wichelen Belgium
137 D3 Wichita U.S.A.
139 D2 Wichita Falls U.S.A.
139 D2 Wichita Mountains U.S.A.
96 C1 Wick U.K.
138 A2 Wickenburg U.S.A.
97 C2 Wicklow Rep. of Ireland
97 D2 Wicklow Head hd Rep. of Ireland
97 C2 Wicklow Mountains Rep. of Ireland
98 B3 Widnes U.K.
101 D2 Wiehengebirge hills Ger.
100 C2 Wiehl Ger.
103 D1 Wieluń Pol.
Wien Austria see Vienna
103 D2 Wiener Neustadt Austria
100 B1 Wieringerwerf Neth.
101 D2 Wiesbaden Ger.
100 C1 Wiesmoor Ger.

103 D1 Wieżyca hill Pol.
98 B3 Wigan U.K.
99 C3 Wight, Isle of i. U.K.
96 B3 Wigtown U.K.
100 B2 Wijchen Neth.
130 B3 Wikwemikong Can.
52 B2 Wilcannia Austr.
Wilczek Land i. Rus. Fed. see Zemlya Vil'cheka
123 C3 Wild Coast S. Africa
101 D1 Wildeshausen Ger.
136 C2 Wild Horse Hill mt. U.S.A.
123 C2 Wilge r. S. Africa
48 F4 Wilhelm, Mount P.N.G.
101 D1 Wilhelmshaven Ger.
141 D2 Wilkes-Barre U.S.A.
55 K3 Wilkes Land reg. Antarctica
129 D1 Wilkie Can.
134 B1 Willamette r. U.S.A.
134 B1 Willapa Bay U.S.A.
138 B2 Willcox U.S.A.
100 B2 Willebroek Belgium
147 D3 Willemstad Neth. Antilles
52 B3 William, Mount Austr.
52 A1 William Creek Austr.
138 A1 Williams U.S.A.
140 C3 Williamsburg KY U.S.A.
141 D3 Williamsburg VA U.S.A.
128 B2 Williams Lake Can.
140 C3 Williamson U.S.A.
141 D2 Williamsport U.S.A.
143 E1 Williamston U.S.A.
122 B3 Williston S. Africa
136 C1 Williston U.S.A.
128 B2 Williston Lake Can.
135 B3 Willits U.S.A.
137 D1 Willmar U.S.A.
122 B3 Willowmore S. Africa
135 B3 Willows U.S.A.
123 C3 Willowvale S. Africa
50 B2 Wills, Lake salt flat Austr.
52 A3 Willunga Austr.
52 A2 Wilmington Austr.
141 D3 Wilmington DE U.S.A.
143 E2 Wilmington NC U.S.A.
140 C3 Wilmington OH U.S.A.
143 D2 Wilmington Island U.S.A.
Wilno Lith. see Vilnius
101 D2 Wilnsdorf Ger.
101 D1 Wilseder Berg hill Ger.
143 E1 Wilson U.S.A.
53 C3 Wilson's Promontory pen. Austr.
100 B3 Wiltz Lux.
50 B2 Wiluna Austr.
99 D4 Wimereux France
123 C2 Winburg S. Africa
99 B4 Wincanton U.K.
99 C4 Winchester U.K.
140 C3 Winchester KY U.S.A.
141 D3 Winchester VA U.S.A.
98 B2 Windermere l. U.K.
122 A1 Windhoek Namibia
137 D2 Windom U.S.A.
51 D2 Windorah Austr.
136 B2 Wind River Range mts U.S.A.
53 D2 Windsor Austr.
130 B3 Windsor Can.
147 D3 Windward Islands Caribbean Sea
147 C3 Windward Passage Cuba/Haiti
137 D3 Winfield U.S.A.
100 A2 Wingene Belgium
53 D2 Wingham Austr.
130 B2 Winisk r. Can.
130 B2 Winisk Lake Can.
63 A2 Winkana Myanmar
129 E3 Winkler Can.
114 B4 Winneba Ghana
140 B2 Winnebago, Lake U.S.A.
134 C2 Winnemucca U.S.A.
136 C2 Winner U.S.A.
142 B2 Winnfield U.S.A.
137 E1 Winnibigoshish, Lake U.S.A.
129 E2 Winnipeg Can.
129 E2 Winnipeg r. Can.
129 E2 Winnipeg, Lake Can.
129 E2 Winnipegosis, Lake Can.
141 E2 Winnipesaukee, Lake U.S.A.
142 B2 Winnsboro U.S.A.
137 E2 Winona MN U.S.A.
142 C2 Winona MS U.S.A.
100 C1 Winschoten Neth.
101 D1 Winsen (Aller) Ger.
101 E1 Winsen (Luhe) Ger.

138 A1 Winslow U.S.A.
143 D1 Winston-Salem U.S.A.
101 D2 Winston Ger.
143 D3 Winter Haven U.S.A.
100 C2 Winterswijk Neth.
105 D2 Winterthur Switz.
51 D2 Winton Austr.
54 A3 Winton N.Z.
52 A2 Wirrabara Austr.
52 A2 Wirraminna Austr.
99 D3 Wisbech U.K.
140 A2 Wisconsin r. U.S.A.
140 B2 Wisconsin state U.S.A.
140 B2 Wisconsin Rapids U.S.A.
103 D1 Wisła r. Pol.
101 E1 Wismar Ger.
123 C2 Witbank S. Africa
122 A2 Witbooisvlei Namibia
98 D3 Witham r. U.K.
98 D3 Withernsea U.K.
100 B1 Witmarsum Neth.
99 C4 Witney U.K.
123 D2 Witrivier S. Africa
123 C3 Witteberg mts S. Africa
101 E1 Wittenberge Ger.
101 E1 Wittenburg Ger.
50 A2 Wittenoom Austr.
101 E1 Wittingen Ger.
100 C3 Wittlich Ger.
100 C1 Wittmund Ger.
101 F1 Wittstock Ger.
122 A1 Witvlei Namibia
101 D2 Witzenhausen Ger.
103 D1 Władysławowo Pol.
103 D1 Włocławek Pol.
53 C3 Wodonga Austr.
59 C3 Wokam i. Indon.
62 A1 Wokha India
99 C4 Woking U.K.
101 F2 Wolfen Ger.
101 E1 Wolfenbüttel Ger.
101 D2 Wolfhagen Ger.
136 B1 Wolf Point U.S.A.
101 E1 Wolfsburg Ger.
100 C3 Wolfstein Ger.
131 D3 Wolfville Can.
102 C1 Wolgast Ger.
102 C1 Wolin Pol.
129 C2 Wollaston Lake Can.
129 D2 Wollaston Lake l. Can.
126 E2 Wollaston Peninsula Can.
53 D2 Wollongong Austr.
101 E2 Wolmirsleben Ger.
101 E1 Wolmirstedt Ger.
100 C1 Wolvega Neth.
99 B3 Wolverhampton U.K.
65 B2 Wŏnju S. Korea
128 B2 Wonowon Can.
65 B2 Wŏnsan N. Korea
53 C3 Wonthaggi Austr.
52 A2 Woocalla Austr.
51 C1 Woodah, Isle i. Austr.
99 D3 Woodbridge U.K.
134 B1 Woodburn U.S.A.
136 B3 Woodland Park U.S.A.
140 A3 Wood River U.S.A.
50 C2 Woodroffe, Mount Austr.
51 C1 Woods, Lake salt flat Austr.
129 E3 Woods, Lake of the Can./U.S.A.
53 C3 Woods Point Austr.
131 D3 Woodstock N.B. Can.
140 C2 Woodstock Ont. Can.
54 C2 Woodville N.Z.
139 D1 Woodward U.S.A.
98 B2 Wooler U.K.
53 D2 Woolgoolga Austr.
52 A2 Woomera Austr.
140 C2 Wooster U.S.A.
122 A3 Worcester S. Africa
99 B3 Worcester U.K.
141 E2 Worcester U.S.A.
102 C2 Wörgl Austria
98 B2 Workington U.K.
98 C3 Worksop U.K.
136 B2 Worland U.S.A.
101 D3 Worms Ger.
99 A4 Worms Head hd U.K.
122 A1 Wortel Namibia
99 C4 Worthing U.K.
137 D2 Worthington U.S.A.
61 D2 Wotu Indon.
61 D2 Wowoni i. Indon.
Wrangel Island Rus. Fed. see Vrangelya, Ostrov
128 A2 Wrangell U.S.A.
96 B1 Wrath, Cape U.K.
136 C2 Wray U.S.A.
122 A2 Wreck Point S. Africa

Wrecsam U.K. see Wrexham
99 B3 Wrexham U.K.
136 B2 Wright U.S.A.
63 A2 Wrightmyo India
138 A2 Wrightson, Mount U.S.A.
128 B1 Wrigley Can.
103 D1 Wrocław Pol.
103 D1 Września Pol.
70 B2 Wu'an China
Wuchow China see Wuzhou
70 A2 Wudu China
70 A2 Wuhai China
70 B2 Wuhan China
70 B2 Wuhu China
71 A3 Wu Jiang r. China
Wujin China see Changzhou
115 C4 Wukari Nigeria
62 B1 Wuliang Shan mts China
59 C3 Wuliaru i. Indon.
118 B2 Wum Cameroon
71 A3 Wumeng Shan mts China
101 D1 Wümme r. Ger.
130 B2 Wunnummin Lake Can.
101 F2 Wunsiedel Ger.
101 D1 Wunstorf Ger.
62 A1 Wuntho Myanmar
100 C2 Wuppertal Ger.
122 A3 Wuppertal S. Africa
101 E2 Wurzbach Ger.
101 D3 Würzburg Ger.
101 F2 Wurzen Ger.
101 D2 Wüstegarten hill Ger.
59 D3 Wuvulu Island P.N.G.
70 A2 Wuwei China
70 A2 Wuxi Chongqing China
70 C2 Wuxi Jiangsu China
Wuxing China see Huzhou
71 A3 Wuxuan China
Wuyang China see Zhenyuan
69 E1 Wuyiling China
71 B3 Wuyishan China
71 B3 Wuyi Shan mts China
70 A1 Wuyuan China
70 A2 Wuzhong China
71 B3 Wuzhou China
51 D2 Wyandra Austr.
53 C2 Wyangala Reservoir Austr.
52 B2 Wycheproof Austr.
99 B4 Wye r. U.K.
50 B1 Wyndham Austr.
52 B3 Wyndham-Werribee Austr.
142 B1 Wynne U.S.A.
129 D2 Wynyard Can.
140 B2 Wyoming U.S.A.
136 B2 Wyoming state U.S.A.
53 D2 Wyong Austr.
103 E1 Wyszków Pol.
140 C3 Wytheville U.S.A.

X

117 D3 Xaafuun Somalia
121 C3 Xai-Xai Moz.
70 A1 Xamba China
62 B1 Xam Hua Laos
120 A1 Xá-Muteba Angola
120 A2 Xangongo Angola
81 C2 Xankändi Azer.
111 B2 Xanthi Greece
154 B3 Xanxerê Brazil
150 C4 Xapuri Brazil
107 C2 Xàtiva Spain
120 B3 Xhumo Botswana
Xiaguan China see Dali
71 B3 Xiamen China
70 A2 Xi'an China
70 A3 Xianfeng China
62 A1 Xiangcheng China
70 B2 Xiangfan China
Xianghuang Qi China see Xin Bulag
Xiangjiang China see Huichang
71 B3 Xiang Jiang r. China
62 B2 Xiangkhoang Laos
71 B3 Xiangtan China
Xiangyang China see Xiangfan
71 B3 Xiangyin China
70 B2 Xianning China
70 B2 Xiantao China
70 A2 Xianyang China
70 B2 Xiaogan China

69 E1 Xiao Hinggan Ling mts China
70 C2 Xiaoshan China
70 B2 Xiaowutai Shan mt. China
Xiayingpan China see Luzhi
Xibu China see Dongshan
71 A3 Xichang China
145 C2 Xicohténcatl Mex.
70 A2 Xifeng Gansu China
71 A3 Xifeng Guizhou China
Xifengzhen China see Xifeng
75 C2 Xigazê China
71 A3 Xilin China
69 D2 Xilinhot China
68 C2 Xímiao China
70 B3 Xin'anjiang Shuiku resr China
70 B1 Xin Bulag China
70 B2 Xincun China see Dongchuan
Xindi China see Honghu
71 B3 Xing'an China
Xingba China see Lhünzê
67 B3 Xinghai China
67 B4 Xinghua China
86 B3 Xinping China
70 A2 Xinping China
70 B2 Xingtai China
151 D3 Xingu r. Brazil
151 D3 Xinguara Brazil
71 A3 Xingyi China
71 B3 Xinhua China
70 A2 Xining China
75 C1 Xinjiang Uygur Zizhiqu aut. reg. China
Xinjing China see Jingxi
65 A1 Xinmin China
71 B3 Xinning China
71 A3 Xinping China
Xinshiba China see Ganluo
70 B2 Xintai China
Xinxian China see Xinzhou
70 B2 Xinxiang China
70 B2 Xinyang China
71 A4 Xinying China
71 B3 Xinyu China
77 E2 Xinyuan China
70 B2 Xinzhou Shanxi China
106 B1 Xinzo de Limia Spain
Xiongshan China see Zhenghe
Xiongzhou China see Nanxiong
70 A2 Xiqing Shan mts China
151 E4 Xique Xique Brazil
70 A1 Xishanzui China
71 A3 Xiushan China
Xiushan China see Tonghai
71 B3 Xiushui China
71 B3 Xiuying China
70 B2 Xixia China
75 C1 Xizang Zizhiqu aut. reg. China
63 B2 Xom Duc Hanh Vietnam
Xuancheng China see Xuanzhou
70 B1 Xuanhua China
71 A3 Xuanwei China
70 B2 Xuanzhou China
70 B2 Xuchang China
Xucheng China see Xuwen
117 C4 Xuddur Somalia
Xuefeng Shan see Mingxi
Xujiang China see Guangchang
71 B3 Xun Jiang r. China
71 B3 Xunwu China
71 B3 Xuwen China
71 A3 Xuyong China
70 B2 Xuzhou China
111 B3 Xylokastro Greece

Y

71 B3 Ya'an China
117 B4 Yabēlo Eth.
69 D1 Yablonovyy Khrebet mts Rus. Fed.
143 D1 Yadkin r. U.S.A.
75 C2 Yadong China
55 A4 Yaghan Basin sea feature S. Atlantic Ocean
89 E2 Yagnitsa Rus. Fed.
83 K2 Yagodnoye Rus. Fed.

118 B1 Yagoua Cameroon
128 C3 Yahk Can.
91 C1 Yahotyn Ukr.
144 B2 Yahualica Mex.
80 B2 Yahyalı Turkey
67 C4 Yaizu Japan
134 B1 Yakima U.S.A.
134 C1 Yakima r. U.S.A.
74 A2 Yakmach Pak.
114 B3 Yako Burkina
66 D2 Yakumo Japan
67 B4 Yaku-shima i. Japan
126 C3 Yakutat U.S.A.
128 A2 Yakutat Bay U.S.A.
83 J2 Yakutsk Rus. Fed.
91 D2 Yakymivka Ukr.
63 B3 Yala Thai.
118 C2 Yalinga C.A.R.
53 C3 Yallourn Austr.
111 C2 Yalova Turkey
90 B2 Yalpuh, Ozero l. Ukr.
91 C3 Yalta Ukr.
65 A1 Yalu Jiang r. China/N. Korea
86 F3 Yalutorovsk Rus. Fed.
67 D3 Yamagata Japan
67 B4 Yamaguchi Japan
86 F1 Yamal, Poluostrov pen. Rus. Fed.
Yamal Peninsula Rus. Fed. see Yamal, Poluostrov
Yamankhalinka Kazakh. see Makhambet
53 D1 Yamba Austr.
150 B2 Yambi, Mesa de hills Col.
117 A4 Yambio Sudan
110 C2 Yambol Bulg.
86 G2 Yamburg Rus. Fed.
62 A1 Yamethin Myanmar
88 C2 Yamm Rus. Fed.
51 D2 Yamma Yamma, Lake salt flat Austr.
114 B4 Yamoussoukro Côte d'Ivoire
91 C1 Yampil' Ukr.
90 B2 Yampil' Ukr.
75 C2 Yamuna r. India
62 A1 Yamzho Yumco l. China
83 K2 Yana r. Rus. Fed.
70 A2 Yan'an China
78 A2 Yanbu' al Baḥr Saudi Arabia
70 C2 Yancheng China
50 A3 Yanchep Austr.
114 B3 Yanfolila Mali
118 C2 Yangambi Dem. Rep. Congo
70 B2 Yangcheng China
71 B3 Yangchun China
65 B2 Yangdok N. Korea
71 B3 Yangjiang China
63 A2 Yangōn Myanmar
70 B2 Yangquan China
71 B3 Yangshuo China
62 B1 Yangtouyan China
70 C23 Yangtze r. China
70 C2 Yangtze, Mouth of the China
Yangtze Kiang r. China see Yangtze
70 A2 Yangxian China
70 B2 Yangzhou China
65 B1 Yanji China
137 D2 Yankton U.S.A.
83 K2 Yano-Indigirskaya Nizmennost' lowland Rus. Fed.
70 B1 Yanqing China
71 A3 Yanshan China
83 K2 Yanskiy Zaliv g. Rus. Fed.
53 C1 Yantabulla Austr.
70 C2 Yantai China
118 B2 Yaoundé Cameroon
59 D2 Yap i. Micronesia
59 D3 Yapen i. Indon.
59 D3 Yapen, Selat sea chan. Indon.
144 A2 Yaqui r. Mex.
51 D2 Yaraka Austr.
86 D3 Yaransk Rus. Fed.
48 H4 Yaren Nauru
78 B3 Yarīm Yemen
Yarkand China see Shache
Yarkant China see Shache
77 D3 Yarkant He r. China
Yarlung Zangbo r. China see Brahmaputra
131 D3 Yarmouth Can.
138 A2 Yarnell U.S.A.

86 F2 Yarongo Rus. Fed.
89 E2 Yaroslavl' Rus. Fed.
66 B2 Yaroslavskiy Rus. Fed.
53 C3 Yarra Junction Austr.
53 C3 Yarram Austr.
89 D2 Yartsevo Rus. Fed.
89 E3 Yasnogorsk Rus. Fed.
63 B2 Yasothon Thai.
53 C2 Yass Austr.
81 D2 Yāsūj Iran
111 C3 Yatağan Turkey
119 D3 Yata Plateau Kenya
129 E1 Yathkyed Lake Can.
67 B4 Yatsushiro Japan
150 C3 Yavari r. Brazil/Peru
73 B2 Yavatmāl India
90 A2 Yavoriv Ukr.
67 B4 Yawatahama Japan
62 A1 Yawng-hwe Myanmar
Yaxian China see Sanya
81 D2 Yazd Iran
142 B2 Yazoo r. U.S.A.
142 B2 Yazoo City U.S.A.
111 B3 Ydra Greece
111 B3 Ydra i. Greece
63 A2 Ye Myanmar
77 D3 Yecheng China
107 C2 Yecla Spain
144 B2 Yécora Mex.
Yedintsy Moldova see Edineţ
89 E3 Yefremov Rus. Fed.
91 E2 Yegoryksaya Rus. Fed.
89 E2 Yegor'yevsk Rus. Fed.
117 B4 Yei Sudan
86 F3 Yekaterinburg Rus. Fed.
Yekaterinodar Rus. Fed. see Krasnodar
Yekaterinoslav Ukr. see Dnipropetrovs'k
Yekaterinovskaya Rus. Fed. see Krylovskaya
Yelenovskiye Kar'yery Ukr. see Dokuchayevs'k
89 E3 Yelets Rus. Fed.
89 D2 Yeligovo Rus. Fed.
114 A3 Yélimané Mali
Yelizavetgrad Ukr. see Kirovohrad
96 □ Yell i. U.K.
128 C1 Yellowknife Can.
53 C2 Yellow Mountain hill Austr.
Yellow River r. China see Huang He
69 E2 Yellow Sea N. Pacific Ocean
136 C1 Yellowstone r. U.S.A.
136 A2 Yellowstone Lake U.S.A.
88 C3 Yel'sk Belarus
78 B3 Yemen country Asia
90 B1 Yemil'chyne Ukr.
86 E2 Yemva Rus. Fed.
91 D2 Yenakiyeve Ukr.
62 A1 Yenangyaung Myanmar
62 B1 Yên Bai Vietnam
114 B4 Yendi Ghana
111 C3 Yenice Turkey
111 C3 Yenifoça Turkey
68 C1 Yenisey r. Rus. Fed.
Yeotmal India see Yavatmāl
53 C2 Yeoval Austr.
99 B4 Yeovil U.K.
51 E2 Yeppoon Austr.
Yeraliyev Kazakh. see Kuryk
83 I2 Yerbogachen Rus. Fed.
81 C1 Yerevan Armenia
77 D1 Yereymentau Kazakh.
Yermentau Kazakh. see Yereymentau
139 C3 Yermo Mex.
135 C4 Yermo U.S.A.
89 D3 Yershichi Rus. Fed.
87 D3 Yershov Rus. Fed.
150 B4 Yerupaja mt. Peru
Yerushalayim Israel/West Bank see Jerusalem
65 B2 Yesan S. Korea
77 C1 Yesil' Kazakh.
111 C3 Yeşilova Turkey
83 H2 Yessey Rus. Fed.
99 A4 Yes Tor hill U.K.
62 A1 Yetman Austr.
62 A1 Yeu Myanmar
104 B2 Yeu, Île d' i. France
87 D4 Yevlax Azer.
91 C2 Yevpatoriya Ukr.
Yexian China see Laizhou
91 D2 Yeysk Rus. Fed.

88 C2 Yezyaryshcha Belarus
Y Fenni U.K. see Abergavenny
71 A3 Yibin China
70 B2 Yichang China
69 E1 Yichun Heilong. China
71 B3 Yichun Jiangxi China
Yidu China see Qingzhou
66 A1 Yilan China
110 C2 Yıldız Dağları mts Turkey
80 B2 Yıldızeli Turkey
Yilong China see Shiping
70 A2 Yinchuan China
65 B1 Yingchengzi China
71 B3 Yingde China
70 C1 Yingkou China
70 B2 Yingshan Hubei China
70 A2 Yingshan Sichuan China
71 B3 Yingtan China
Yining China see Xiushui
77 E2 Yining China
62 A1 Yinmabin Myanmar
70 A1 Yin Shan mts China
117 B4 Yirga Alem Eth.
119 D2 Yirga Ch'efê Eth.
119 D2 Yirol Sudan
Yishan China see Yizhou
70 B2 Yishui China
62 A1 Yi Tu, Nam r. Myanmar
68 C2 Yiwu China
70 C1 Yixian China
71 B3 Yiyang China
71 B3 Yizhang China
71 A3 Yizhou China
Yizhou China see Yixian
92 I2 Yli-Kitka l. Fin.
92 H2 Ylitornio Fin.
92 H3 Ylivieska Fin.
93 H3 Ylöjärvi Fin.
83 K2 Ynykchanskiy Rus. Fed.
Ynys Môn i. U.K. see Anglesey
61 C2 Yogyakarta Indon.
118 B2 Yokadouma Cameroon
118 B2 Yoko Cameroon
67 C3 Yokohama Japan
66 D3 Yokote Japan
115 D4 Yola Nigeria
67 D3 Yonezawa Japan
71 B3 Yong'an China
Yongbei China see Yongsheng
71 B3 Yongchun China
70 A2 Yongdeng China
65 B3 Yŏngdŏk S. Korea
65 B2 Yŏnghŭng N. Korea
Yongjing China see Xifeng
65 B2 Yŏngju S. Korea
71 C3 Yongkang China
Yongning China see Zhen'an
62 B1 Yongren China
62 B1 Yongsheng China
71 B3 Yongzhou China
141 E2 Yonkers U.S.A.
105 C2 Yonne r. France
150 B2 Yopal Col.
50 A3 York Austr.
98 C3 York U.K.
142 C3 York AL U.S.A.
137 D2 York NE U.S.A.
141 D3 York PA U.S.A.
51 D1 York, Cape Austr.
52 A3 Yorke Peninsula Austr.
52 A3 Yorketown Austr.
98 C3 Yorkshire Wolds hills U.K.
129 D2 Yorkton Can.
87 D3 Yoshkar-Ola Rus. Fed.
97 C3 Youghal Rep. of Ireland
53 C2 Young Austr.
52 A3 Younghusband Peninsula Austr.
140 C2 Youngstown U.S.A.
114 B3 Youvarou Mali
71 A3 Youyang China
77 E2 Yuyi Feng mt. China/Rus. Fed.
80 B2 Yozgat Turkey
154 A2 Ypé-Jhú Para.
134 B2 Yreka U.S.A.
Yr Wyddfa mt. U.K. see Snowdon
59 D3 Ysabel Channel P.N.G.
105 C2 Yssingeaux France
93 F4 Ystad Sweden
Ysyk-Köl Kyrg. see Balykchy
77 D2 Ysyk-Köl salt l. Kyrg.
Y Trallwng U.K. see Welshpool
92 □A3 Ytri-Rangá r. Iceland
83 J2 Ytyk-Kyuyel' Rus. Fed.

71 A3 Yuanbao Shan mt. China
71 A3 Yuanjiang China
62 B1 Yuan Jiang r. China
71 B3 Yuanling China
71 A3 Yuanmou China
70 B2 Yuanping China
135 B3 Yuba City U.S.A.
66 D2 Yūbari Japan
145 C3 Yucatán pen. Mex.
146 B2 Yucatan Channel Cuba/Mex.
70 B2 Yuci China
50 C2 Yuendumu Austr.
71 C3 Yueqing China
71 B3 Yueyang China
86 F2 Yugorsk Rus. Fed.
109 D2 Yugoslavia country Europe
71 B3 Yujiang China
83 L2 Yukagirskoye Ploskogor'ye plat. Rus. Fed.
89 E3 Yukhnov Rus. Fed.
126 B2 Yukon r. Can./U.S.A.
139 D1 Yukon r. U.S.A.
128 A1 Yukon Territory admin. div. Can.
50 C2 Yulara Austr.
71 B3 Yulin Guangxi China
70 A2 Yulin Shaanxi China
62 B1 Yulongxue Shan mt. China
138 A2 Yuma AZ U.S.A.
136 C2 Yuma CO U.S.A.
135 D4 Yuma Desert U.S.A.
70 B2 Yumen China
80 B2 Yunak Turkey
70 B2 Yuncheng China
70 B2 Yunfu China
71 A3 Yun Gui Gaoyuan plat. China
Yunjinghong China see Jinghong
Yunling China see Yunxiao
71 A3 Yunnan prov. China
52 A2 Yunta Austr.
71 B3 Yunxiao China
70 B2 Yunyang China
Yuping China see Libo
71 A3 Yuping China
82 G3 Yurga Rus. Fed.
150 B3 Yurimaguas Peru
75 C1 Yurungkax He r. China
Yuryev Estonia see Tartu
71 C3 Yü Shan mt. Taiwan
70 B2 Yushe China
68 C2 Yushu China
Yushuwan China see Huaihua
81 C1 Yusufeli Turkey
75 C1 Yutian China
71 A3 Yuxi China
89 F2 Yuzha Rus. Fed.
66 D2 Yuzhno-Kuril'sk Rus. Fed.
83 K3 Yuzhno-Sakhalinsk Rus. Fed.
91 C2 Yuzhnoukrayinsk Ukr.
Yuzovka Ukr. see Donets'k
105 D2 Yverdon Switz.
104 C2 Yvetot France

Z

100 B1 Zaandam Neth.
69 D1 Zabaykal'sk Rus. Fed.
119 C2 Zabia Dem. Rep. Congo
78 B3 Zabīd Yemen
79 D1 Zābol Iran
79 D2 Zāboli Iran
145 D3 Zacapa Guat.
144 B2 Zacapu Mex.
144 B2 Zacatecas Mex.
145 C3 Zacatepec Mex.
145 C3 Zacatlán Mex.
111 B3 Zacharo Greece
91 C2 Zachepylivka Ukr.
144 B2 Zacoalco Mex.
145 C3 Zacualtipán Mex.
109 C2 Zadar Croatia
63 A3 Zadetkyi Kyun i. Myanmar
89 E3 Zadonsk Rus. Fed.
80 B3 Za'farâna Egypt
106 B2 Zafra Spain
103 C1 Zagań Pol.
114 B1 Zagora Morocco
109 C1 Zagreb Croatia
81 C2 Zagros, Kūhhā-ye mts Iran

Zagros Mountains Iran see Zagros, Kūhhā-ye
79 D2 Zāhedān Iran
80 B2 Zahlé Lebanon
78 B3 Zahrān Saudi Arabia
Zaïre country Africa see Congo, Democratic Republic of
Zaječar Yugo.
121 C3 Zaka Zimbabwe
89 E3 Zakharovo Rus. Fed.
81 C2 Zākhō Iraq
86 C2 Zakhrebetnoye Rus. Fed.
111 B3 Zakynthos Greece
Zakynthos i. Greece see Zante
103 D2 Zalaegerszeg Hungary
110 B1 Zalău Romania
78 B2 Zalim Saudi Arabia
116 A3 Zalingei Sudan
90 B2 Zalishchyky Ukr.
78 A2 Zalmā, Jabal az mt. Saudi Arabia
128 C2 Zama City Can.
121 C2 Zambeze r. Moz.
120 C2 Zambezi r. Africa
120 B2 Zambezi Zambia
120 C2 Zambezi Escarpment Zambia/Zimbabwe
120 B2 Zambia country Africa
64 B3 Zamboanga Phil.
64 B3 Zamboanga Peninsula Phil.
103 E1 Zambrów Pol.
106 B1 Zamora Spain
144 B3 Zamora de Hidalgo Mex.
103 E1 Zamość Pol.
Zamost'ye Pol. see Zamość
75 B1 Zanda China
100 B2 Zandvliet Belgium
100 B1 Zandvoort Neth.
140 C3 Zanesville U.S.A.
77 D3 Zangguy China
75 C1 Zangsêr Kangri mt. China
81 C2 Zanjān Iran
111 B3 Zante i. Greece
119 D3 Zanzibar Tanz.
119 D3 Zanzibar Island Tanz.
89 E3 Zaokskiy Rus. Fed.
115 C2 Zaouatallaz Alg.
Zaouet el Kahla Alg. see Bordj Omer Driss
70 B2 Zaoyang China
83 H3 Zaozernyy Rus. Fed.
70 B2 Zaozhuang China
89 D2 Zapadnaya Dvina r. Europe
89 D2 Zapadnaya Dvina Rus. Fed.
82 G2 Zapadno-Sibirskaya Ravnina plain Rus. Fed.
68 B1 Zapadnyy Sayan reg. Rus. Fed.
139 D3 Zapata U.S.A.
92 J2 Zapolyarnyy Rus. Fed.
91 D2 Zaporizhzhya Ukr.
101 E2 Zappendorf Ger.
81 C1 Zaqatala Azer.
Zara Croatia see Zadar
80 B2 Zara Turkey
145 B2 Zaragoza Mex.
107 C1 Zaragoza Spain
79 C1 Zarand Iran
76 C3 Zaranj Afgh.
88 C2 Zarasai Lith.
89 E3 Zaraysk Rus. Fed.
150 C2 Zaraza Venez.
115 C3 Zaria Nigeria
90 B1 Zarichne Ukr.
81 D3 Zarqān Iran
66 B2 Zarubino Rus. Fed.
103 D1 Żary Pol.
115 D1 Zarzis Tunisia
74 B1 Zaskar Mountains India
88 C3 Zaslawye Belarus
123 C3 Zastron S. Africa
Zavitaya Rus. Fed. see Zavitinsk
69 E1 Zavitinsk Rus. Fed.
89 F2 Zavolzhsk Rus. Fed.
Zavolzh'ye Rus. Fed. see Zavolzhsk
103 D1 Zawiercie Pol.
115 E1 Zāwiyat Masūs Libya
77 E2 Zaysan Kazakh.
77 E2 Zaysan, Lake Kazakh. see Zaysan, Ozero
77 E2 Zaysan, Ozero l. Kazakh.
62 A1 Zayü China
90 B2 Zbarazh Ukr.

90 B1 **Zdolbuniv** Ukr.
93 F4 **Zealand** i. Denmark
100 A2 **Zedelgem** Belgium
100 A2 **Zeebrugge** Belgium
123 C2 **Zeerust** S. Africa
101 F1 **Zehdenick** Ger.
50 C2 **Zeil, Mount** Austr.
101 F2 **Zeitz** Ger.
109 C2 **Zelena Gora** mt. Bos.-Herz.
87 D3 **Zelenodol'sk** Rus. Fed.
88 C1 **Zelenogorsk** Rus. Fed.
89 E2 **Zelenograd** Rus. Fed.
88 B3 **Zelenogradsk** Rus. Fed.
66 D2 **Zelenyy, Ostrov** i. Rus. Fed.
88 B3 **Zel'va** Belarus
119 C2 **Zémio** C.A.R.
82 E1 **Zemlya Aleksandry** i. Rus. Fed.
82 E1 **Zemlya Frantsa-Iosifa** is Rus. Fed.
82 F1 **Zemlya Vil'cheka** i. Rus. Fed.
107 D2 **Zemmora** Alg.
145 C3 **Zempoaltépetl, Nudo de** mt. Mex.
109 D2 **Zemun** Yugo.
65 B1 **Zengfeng Shan** mt. China
109 C2 **Zenica** Bos.-Herz.
107 D2 **Zenzach** Alg.
101 F2 **Zerbst** Ger.
105 D2 **Zermatt** Switz.
91 E2 **Zernograd** Rus. Fed.
Zernovoy Rus. Fed. see Zernograd
101 E2 **Zeulenroda** Ger.
101 D1 **Zeven** Ger.
100 C2 **Zevenaar** Neth.
100 B2 **Zevenbergen** Neth.
83 J3 **Zeya** Rus. Fed.
79 C2 **Zeydābād** Iran
79 C2 **Zeynalābād** Iran
83 J3 **Zeyskoye Vodokhranilishche** resr Rus. Fed.
103 D1 **Zgierz** Pol.
75 C2 **Zhabdün** China
88 B3 **Zhabinka** Belarus
Zhabye Ukr. see Verkhovyna
Zhaksy Sarysu watercourse Kazakh. see Sarysu
76 A2 **Zhalpaktal** Kazakh.
77 C1 **Zhaltyr** Kazakh.
Zhambyl Kazakh. see Taraz
76 B2 **Zhanaozen** Kazakh.
Zhangaqazaly Kazakh. see Ayteke Bi

Zhangde China see Anyang
Zhangdian China see Zibo
66 A1 **Zhangguangcai Ling** mts China
Zhangjiajie China see Dayong
70 B1 **Zhangjiakou** China
71 B3 **Zhangping** China
71 B3 **Zhangshu** China
65 A1 **Zhangwu** China
70 A2 **Zhangxian** China
68 C2 **Zhangye** China
71 B3 **Zhangzhou** China
71 B3 **Zhanjiang** China
71 B3 **Zhao'an** China
69 E1 **Zhaodong** China
Zhaoge China see Qixian
71 B3 **Zhaoqing** China
71 A3 **Zhaotong** China
75 C1 **Zhari Namco** salt l. China
77 E2 **Zharkent** Kazakh.
89 D2 **Zharkovskiy** Rus. Fed.
77 E2 **Zharma** Kazakh.
90 C2 **Zhashkiv** Ukr.
Zhaxi China see Weixin
77 D2 **Zhayrem** Kazakh.
Zhdanov Ukr. see Mariupol'
71 C3 **Zhejiang** prov. China
82 F1 **Zhelaniya, Mys** c. Rus. Fed.
Zheleznodorozhnyy Rus. Fed. see Yemva
Zheleznodorozhnyy Uzbek. see Kungrad
89 E3 **Zheleznogorsk** Rus. Fed.
Zheltyye Vody Ukr. see Zhovti Vody
70 A2 **Zhen'an** China
70 A2 **Zhenba** China
71 A3 **Zheng'an** China
71 B3 **Zhenghe** China
70 B2 **Zhengzhou** China
70 B2 **Zhenjiang** China
71 A3 **Zhenyuan** China
91 E1 **Zherdevka** Rus. Fed.
86 D2 **Zheshart** Rus. Fed.
77 C2 **Zhezkazgan** Kazakh.
77 C2 **Zhezkazgan** Kazakh.
83 J2 **Zhigansk** Rus. Fed.
70 B2 **Zhijiang** China
76 C1 **Zhitikara** Kazakh.
89 D3 **Zhizdra** Rus. Fed.
88 D3 **Zhlobin** Belarus
90 B2 **Zhmerynka** Ukr.
74 A1 **Zhob** Pak.
88 C3 **Zhodzina** Belarus
83 L1 **Zhokhova, Ostrov** i. Rus. Fed.

Zholkva Ukr. see Zhovkva
Zhongba China see Jiangyou
62 A1 **Zhongdian** China
Zhongduo China see Youyang
70 A2 **Zhongning** China
Zhongping China see Huize
71 B3 **Zhongshan** China
Zhongshan China see Lupanshui
70 A2 **Zhongwei** China
Zhongxin China see Zhongdian
70 B2 **Zhoukou** China
70 C2 **Zhoushan** China
90 A1 **Zhovkva** Ukr.
91 C2 **Zhovti Vody** Ukr.
65 A2 **Zhuanghe** China
70 B2 **Zhucheng** China
89 D3 **Zhukovka** Rus. Fed.
89 E2 **Zhukovskiy** Rus. Fed.
70 B2 **Zhumadian** China
Zhuoyang China see Suiping
71 B3 **Zhuzhou** Hunan China
71 B3 **Zhuzhou** Hunan China
90 A2 **Zhydachiv** Ukr.
88 C3 **Zhytkavichy** Belarus
90 B1 **Zhytomyr** Ukr.
103 D2 **Žiar nad Hronom** Slovakia
70 B2 **Zibo** China
Ziel, Mount Austr. see Zeil, Mount
103 D1 **Zielona Góra** Pol.
100 A2 **Zierikzee** Neth.
62 A1 **Zigaing** Myanmar
115 E2 **Zighan** Libya
71 A3 **Zigong** China
70 B2 **Zigui** China
114 A3 **Ziguinchor** Senegal
144 B3 **Zihuatanejo** Mex.
103 D2 **Žilina** Slovakia
115 D2 **Zillah** Libya
83 H3 **Zima** Rus. Fed.
145 C2 **Zimapán** Mex.
121 C3 **Zimbabwe** country Africa
114 A4 **Zimmi** Sierra Leone
110 C2 **Zimnicea** Romania
86 C2 **Zimniy Bereg** coastal area Rus. Fed.
115 C3 **Zinder** Niger
78 B3 **Zinjibār** Yemen
91 C1 **Zin'kiv** Ukr.
Zinoyevsk Ukr. see Kirovohrad
150 B2 **Zipaquirá** Col.
103 D2 **Zirc** Hungary

75 D2 **Ziro** India
79 C2 **Zir Rūd** Iran
103 D2 **Zistersdorf** Austria
145 B3 **Zitácuaro** Mex.
103 C1 **Zittau** Ger.
87 E3 **Zlatoust** Rus. Fed.
103 D2 **Zlín** Czech Rep.
115 D1 **Zlītan** Libya
103 D1 **Złotów** Pol.
89 D3 **Zlynka** Rus. Fed.
89 E3 **Zmiyevka** Rus. Fed.
91 D2 **Zmiyiv** Ukr.
89 E3 **Znamenka** Rus. Fed.
91 E1 **Znamenka** Rus. Fed.
91 C2 **Znam"yanka** Ukr.
103 D2 **Znojmo** Czech Rep.
122 B3 **Zoar** S. Africa
70 A2 **Zoigê** China
91 D1 **Zolochiv** Ukr.
90 A2 **Zolochiv** Ukr.
91 C2 **Zolotonosha** Ukr.
89 E3 **Zolotukhino** Rus. Fed.
121 C2 **Zomba** Malawi
118 B2 **Zongo** Dem. Rep. Congo
80 B1 **Zonguldak** Turkey
105 D3 **Zonza** Corsica France
114 B4 **Zorzor** Liberia
115 D2 **Zouar** Chad
114 A2 **Zouérat** Maur.
109 D1 **Zrenjanin** Yugo.
89 D2 **Zubtsov** Rus. Fed.
105 D2 **Zug** Switz.
81 C1 **Zugdidi** Georgia
Zuider Zee l. Neth. see IJsselmeer
106 B2 **Zújar** r. Spain
100 C2 **Zülpich** Ger.
100 A2 **Zulte** Belgium
121 C2 **Zumbo** Moz.
145 C3 **Zumpango** Mex.
138 B1 **Zuni Mountains** U.S.A.
71 A3 **Zunyi** China
109 C1 **Županja** Croatia
105 D2 **Zürich** Switz.
105 D2 **Zürichsee** l. Switz.
100 C1 **Zutphen** Neth.
115 D1 **Zuwārah** Libya
90 C2 **Zvenyhorodka** Ukr.
121 C3 **Zvishavane** Zimbabwe
103 D2 **Zvolen** Slovakia
109 C2 **Zvornik** Bos.-Herz.
114 B4 **Zwedru** Liberia
123 C3 **Zwelitsha** S. Africa
103 D2 **Zwettl** Austria
101 F2 **Zwickau** Ger.
100 C1 **Zwolle** Neth.
83 L2 **Zyryanka** Rus. Fed.
77 E2 **Zyryanovsk** Kazakh.

KEY TO MAP PAGES
AFRICA, NORTH AMERICA, SOUTH AMERICA
(see front endpapers for Oceania, Asia and Europe)

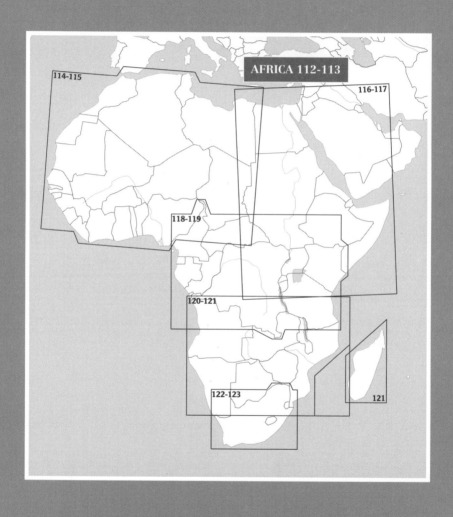

114-115

AFRICA 112-113

116-117

118-119

120-121

122-123

121